...nental Laws.

...he Institution shall be

...Baptist Church ; and

...essorships in this Semina...

...uch acceptance, as enga...

...nce with, and not con...

...Principles hereinafter

...from which principles

...nsidered ground for

...oval by the Trustees —

...tures.

...Old and New Testaments

...God, and are the only

...thoritative rule of all

...nd obedience.

...the Nuther Possesses a...

ABSTRACT
OF
SYSTEMATIC THEOLOGY

REV. JAMES PETIGRU BOYCE, D. D., LL. D.

*Joseph Emerson Brown Professor of Systematic Theology
in The Southern Baptist Theological Seminary*

THE
SOUTHERN BAPTIST
THEOLOGICAL SEMINARY

First published in 1887 by James Petigru Boyce
Copyright © 2013 by SBTS Press
All Rights Reserved.

SBTS Press c/o Communications
2825 Lexington Road
Louisville, KY 40280
press@sbts.edu
http://www.sbts.edu/press

Original manuscript of *Abstract of Systematic Theology* provided by The James P. Boyce Centennial Library at Southern Seminary. Digital manuscript of *Abstract of Systematic Theology* provided by Founders Press, Cape Coral, FL 33915. Manuscript copyedited by Kevin D. Shell.

ISBN: 978-0-615-89164-4

Printed in the United States of America.

ORIGINAL DEDICATION AFFIXED
TO THE 1887 EDITION

To the HON. JOSEPH E. BROWN, President of the Board of Trustees of The Southern Baptist Theological Seminary, this book is respectfully dedicated, as a token of high personal esteem, and in recognition of his deep interest in the cause of education, and especially of the theological education of the Christian ministry; as evinced, among other generous gifts, by his endowment in The Southern Baptist Theological Seminary of the Chair of Systematic Theology, with which the author is officially connected.

CONTENTS

FOREWORD

JAMES PETIGRU BOYCE AND THEOLOGICAL EDUCATION
By R. Albert Mohler Jr.

THE book now in your hands is a theological classic. The *Abstract of Systematic Theology* by James Petigru Boyce represents the most important book written by one of the most important evangelical leaders of the nineteenth century. To read this book is to enter Boyce's classroom and hear him lecture. The very fact that it is now republished in this special edition, more than 125 years after its first release, underlines both the importance of this volume and the greatness of the man who wrote it.

James Petigru Boyce is rightly seen, not only as the founder of The Southern Baptist Theological Seminary and its first president, but also as the leading founder of the vision for organized theological education within the Southern Baptist Convention. This is an audacious but sustainable claim made from the vantage point of well more than a century after Boyce's famous manifesto, "Three Changes in Theological Institutions," which articulated with consummate clarity his vision for theological education. This vision was founded within the Baptist tradition and upon the impregnable rock of Christian truth.

By the sovereign providence of God, James Boyce was superbly equipped and endowed with gifts for ministry, incredible leadership ability, and the full measure of theological conviction. These attributes placed Boyce in the singular position as the Southern Baptist leader best equipped to articulate a founding vision and to draw together the necessary constituencies and resources in order to establish the institution which became known as The Southern Baptist Theological Seminary.

Born and raised in Charleston, South Carolina as the son of one of the South's most illustrious citizens, James Boyce was in a privileged position to receive an enviable education. But Boyce's father wisely prescribed a term of toil in his businesses working as a common laborer. Boyce, though equipped physically for physical labor, found that the experience increased his discipline as applied to classical studies.

Boyce's background in education was matched by the unparalleled experience of growing up among the membership of the First Baptist Church of Charleston, South Carolina under the tutelage of its gifted pastors. Among these, Basil

vii

Manly Sr. exerted a tremendous influence upon Boyce, framing his theological convictions as well as offering a stellar example of Christian ministry.

The Charleston congregation was the first Baptist church in the South. It was a stalwart Baptist congregation founded on clear Baptist principles and confessing the faith in a constant line of Baptist conviction as articulated in the Philadelphia Confession. That confession was formally adopted by the Charleston association as its own and was even commonly referred to as both the "Charleston Confession" and the "Century Confession."

Basil Manly Sr. was one of the most able exponents of Baptist theology and conviction as well as an able expositor of scripture. He well represented the classical type identified by historian E. Brooks Holifield as "the gentleman theologian."[1] As John A. Broadus stated of Basil Manly Sr.:

> His preaching was always marked by deep thought and strong argument, expressed in a very clear style, and by an extraordinary earnestness and tender pathos, curiously combined with positiveness of opinion and a masterful nature. People were borne down by his passion, convinced by his arguments, melted by tenderness, swayed by the force of will.[2]

Basil Manly Sr. provided not only a stellar ministry and example for young James Boyce, but he also provided his own son, Basil Manly Jr., as Boyce's boyhood comrade and Sunday school classmate and, later, as his founding colleague at The Southern Baptist Theological Seminary.

Boyce experienced a happy and privileged childhood in Charleston, a city of great refinement and prosperity. He attended Charleston College from 1843 to 1845 and there studied under Dr. W. T. Brantly, another significant gentleman theologian of strong Baptist conviction who served as both pastor of the First Baptist Church and president of the college.

BROWN UNIVERSITY AND FRANCIS WAYLAND

A significant turning point in Boyce's life came in 1845 when he moved to Brown University, which had been founded as a Baptist college at Warren, Rhode Island in 1765 and moved to Providence five years later. At Brown, Boyce came into sustained contact with Baptists from the North, and in

---

[1] E. Brooks Holifield, *The Gentleman Theologians: American Theology in Southern Culture 1795-1860* (Durham, North Carolina: Duke University Press, 1978).

[2] John A. Broadus, *Memoir of James Petigru Boyce* (New York: A. C. Armstrong and Son, 1893), 16.

particular with one significant individual who was greatly to mold his vision of higher education. That individual was Francis Wayland who had been president of Brown University for eighteen years when Boyce arrived as a student. Broadus commented that Wayland "made a more potent impression upon the character, opinions, and usefulness of James Boyce than any other person with whom he came in contact."[3] Wayland was one of the most significant educators in antebellum America, a man of tremendous gifts and very definite convictions concerning the educational enterprise.

So far as Wayland was concerned, education was primarily a matter of fine-tuning the intellectual endowments of his students and increasing their moral vision. Nevertheless, Wayland was not a Baptist figure who was greatly marked by definite theological convictions. It is at least fair to say that Wayland advocated a fluid notion of doctrinal development and was opposed to the very form of confessionalism Boyce himself would later represent.

It was perhaps Wayland's view concerning ministerial education that was most formative on James Boyce as a student at Brown University. He was greatly stirred by Wayland's lectures on morality, but he seems to have been much more impressed with Francis Wayland as a leader and administrator who understood both the need for quality institutions of higher education the limitations represented by an institution which required classical preparation prior to entry into formal courses of study.

Wayland, who had been pastor of the First Baptist Church in Boston prior to his election as president at Brown, is in many ways best described as a pragmatist in terms of ministerial education. Many of his students at Brown had been called into the ministry and would leave the university in order to study at one of the existing seminaries in the North. Wayland was not opposed to this. Indeed he felt that men who had received the benefit of a classical education and university could and should extend their study through the formal academic programs of a theological seminary. Nevertheless, Wayland was insistent that based upon Baptist conviction the ministry should be seen as open to all those whom God called into the service of his church, regardless of their academic preparation.

Wayland was an exemplar of the democratic impulse in antebellum America. He was fully convinced that the genius of Baptist expansion would be found in the reluctance of Baptists to place artificial requirements, educational or otherwise, upon those whom God called into the ministry and leadership of his church.

---

[3] Broadus, 34.

Put plainly, Wayland placed high confidence in the Baptist understanding
of the Christian ministry. He was an ardent congregationalist, and he insisted
that each congregation was fully capable of calling out one of its own number
to serve as pastor and minister. These ministers who would be called out by
churches on the frontier or rural settings were unlikely to have the benefit of
classical secondary education or formal programs of higher education. Wayland
insisted that theological education based on the model of Andover Seminary
should not become the expectation of Baptists as their movement spread across
the growing nation.

But Wayland's concerns regarding theological education went beyond this
congregational impulse. Wayland was convinced that theological seminaries
were inclined to produce sterile, passionless, and overly intellectual graduates
who had little power in the pulpit.

As Wayland reflected in a letter to James W. Alexander, son of Archibald
Alexander and himself a former professor of Princeton Seminary:

> The tendency of seminaries is to become schools for theological and philo-
> logical learning and elegant literature, rather than schools to make preachers
> of the Gospel. With every year the general tendency is in this direction as I
> think I have observed.[4]

Interestingly, Wayland seemed to exempt Princeton Theological Seminary from
this critique, at least in this correspondence with one of its former professors,
who was also the son of Princeton Seminary's founding figure.

Near the close of his life, Wayland reflected upon his reputation as a critic of
theological education. His intention, as he understood himself, was not at all to
oppose theological seminaries, but rather to protect the congregational convictions held among Baptists and to argue for increased attention to developing
a passionate ministry as well as a cultured ministry of refinement. As Wayland
stated near the close of his life:

> I was said to be opposed to ministerial education because I held that a man
> with the proper moral qualifications might be called to the ministry by any
> church and be a useful minister of Christ and that we had no right to exclude
> such a man because he had not gone through a nine or ten years' course
> of study. God calls men to the ministry by bestowing upon them suitable
> endowments, and an earnest desire to use them for His service. Of these thus

---

[4] James O. Murray, *Francis Wayland*, "American Religious Leaders", (Boston: Houghton
Mifflin and Company, 1891), 181-182.

called, some may not be by nature adapted to the prosecution of a particular course of study. Many others are too old. Some are men with families. Only a portion are of an age and under conditions which will allow them to undertake what is called a regular training for the ministry, that is, two or three years in an academy, four years in college, and three years in a seminary. But does not every man require the improvement of his mind in order to preach the Gospel? I think he does.[5]

Through a review of Wayland's *Memoir*, one gains an understanding of the formative influence Wayland exerted upon young James Boyce. This was part of Boyce's preparation for his great task and calling.

Though Boyce received the benefit of a privileged formal education, he was well aware that many of his Baptist brethren were bereft of such preparation and would have no opportunity to pursue such courses of study. In a passage that would be echoed in Boyce's famous address at Furman University, Wayland wrote:

A theological seminary should be so constructed as to give the greatest assistance to each of these various classes of candidates. Some may be able to take a smaller, others a greater amount of study. Let each be at liberty to take what he can, and then the seminary is at rest. It has done what it could. The rest is left to Providence.[6]

While Wayland had a remarkable influence on James Petigru Boyce in terms of academic vision and understanding of the Christian ministry, it is important also to realize that the influence of Francis Wayland extended to Boyce's own conversion. The Second Great Awakening spread from Yale College to Brown University while Boyce was enrolled there. Boyce, though raised within the fellowship of the First Baptist Church in Charleston, had not yet been converted. This, he held in common with several other members of his junior class at Brown University—a fact that caused no little distress to the university's president.

Upon his arrival at Brown, Boyce found himself the concern of many of his fellow classmates who prayed for his conversion. Furthermore, Dr. Wayland himself was anxious concerning the salvation of Boyce and several of his classmates. The college held its usual fast on the last Thursday in February of 1846.

---

[5] Murray, *Francis Wayland*, 183-184.

[6] Francis Wayland, *A Memoir of the Life and Labors of Francis Wayland*, Volume 2, pp. 163-164. See also Francis Wayland, *Notes on the Principles and Practices of Baptist Churches*, (New York: Sheldon, Blakeman and Company, 1857), esp. 72-79.

Dr. Wayland himself led in morning worship and delivered a powerful sermon in the afternoon addressed to those who had not yet been converted. Shortly thereafter Boyce returned by steamer from New York to Charleston, and during that voyage he struggled greatly with the state of his own soul. By the time Boyce arrived in Charleston he was, as Broadus later described him, "deeply under conviction of sin."[7]

Boyce's conversion came under the preaching of Dr. Richard Fuller, who had come from Beaufort to preach in Charleston. The gracious mercy of God as demonstrated in his loving providence was made clear in the life of James Petigru Boyce. As Broadus later reflected, "let us pause to notice that young James Boyce had thus, by the age of nineteen, been brought under the special influence of six of the most notable Baptist ministers in America, Manly and Brantly, Tucker, Wayland, Crawford, and Fuller."[8]

PRINCETON THEOLOGICAL SEMINARY

After completing his course of study at Brown, Boyce became editor of *The Southern Baptist*, located in Charleston. The paper had been established in May of 1846 by parties related to the First Baptist Church. Boyce became editor on November 22, 1848. He was introduced by a notice which stated: "Mr. Boyce is a graduate of Brown University, a licentiate of the First Baptist Church in Charleston, and possesses qualities of mind and heart which give promise of distinction and usefulness in the new field of labor he has entered."[9]

The pages of *The Southern Baptist* were filled with news of interest related to Baptist life in the larger Christian community. More importantly, the mark of Boyce's editorship was found in the serious attention given to doctrinal and theological concerns. In particular, an extensive series of articles entitled "On Imputation" appeared in successive issues of the journal. This was later found remarkable by no less than John A. Broadus.

An unusual article appeared on March 28, 1849 that advocated the establishment of a "central theological institution" for all Baptists in the South. This issue was not entirely new to Baptist discussion, but it reflects without question the thoughts of the editor as he prepared to leave Charleston to attend Princeton Theological Seminary.

James Boyce enrolled at Princeton in September 1849. By God's providence, he arrived at a critical moment in the life of that institution. The faculty of

---

[7] Broadus, 44.

[8] Broadus, 45.

[9] Broadus, 60.

Princeton at that time included its first professor, Archibald Alexander, and his two sons, James and Addison. Dr. Samuel Miller, the second professor named to the institution, had been elevated as emeritus professor in 1849—the very year of Boyce's arrival—though he continued to teach.

In 1840, Archibald Alexander relinquished the chair of didactic theology to Dr. Charles Hodge. Thus, Boyce entered the life of Princeton Theological Seminary just as it was reaching the very height of its elevation as the center for convictional theological education in the Reformed tradition.

Without doubt, the influence of Charles Hodge is most notable in the theological lectures later offered by James Boyce. He learned the Princeton Theology from its very fountain. He imbibed from Charles Hodge and other faculty colleagues an intense hunger and thirst for theological substance based solidly within the exposition of Scripture. The Princetonians were ardent systematicians. They were unwilling to leave theological truths as unrelated or marginal issues in relation to the marrow of the church. To the contrary, they exhibited in themselves and inculcated in their students an understanding of the unity of truth.

Though Professor Samuel Miller was to live for only a brief time after Boyce's arrival at Princeton, his influence on Boyce's later thought can scarcely be exaggerated; and yet it has been neglected. Miller was a sturdy and committed Presbyterian and an ardent confessionalist. He was also a prophet vindicated by later events within the Presbyterian denomination. By the middle of the nineteenth century, Miller was already convinced that American Protestants were in the process of abdicating their theological heritage and diluting the convictions that established the bedrock unity of the true Church. In 1824, Miller published his most important book, *The Utility and Importance of Creeds and Confessions*. The book, later published under the title *Doctrinal Integrity*, is one of the most forceful and significant arguments put forth by any American theologian concerning the importance of confessional statements and their application as regulative creeds binding members of a church or Christian fellowship together on the basis of truth. Many of the passages from Miller's *Doctrinal Integrity* were reflected in Boyce's address, «Three Changes in Theological Institutions.»

As Miller argued, "The necessity and importance of creeds and confessions appear from the consideration, that one great design of establishing a Church in our world was that she might be, in all ages, a depository, a guardian, and a witness of the truth."[10] Miller sought to answer the opponents of creeds and

---

[10] Samuel Miller, *Doctrinal Integrity: The Utility and Importance of Creeds and Confessions and Adherence to Our Doctrinal Standards*, (Philadelphia: Presbyterian Board of Publication, 1824, 1839, 1841, republished Dallas: Presbyterian Heritage Publication, 1989), 11.

confessions by suggesting that any opposition was inherently linked to a desire, conscious or unconscious, to compromise and dilute the truth. The arguments against creeds and confessions most often voiced within contemporary Protestantism, and in particular within the Southern Baptist Convention in recent years, were hardly new to Samuel Miller in the nineteenth century. His arguments stand irrefutable:

> It will surely not be said, by any considerate person, that the Church, or any of her individual members, can sufficiently fulfill the duty in question, by simply proclaiming from time to time, in the midst of surrounding error, her adherence and attachment to the Bible. Everyone must see that this would be, in fact, doing nothing as 'witnesses of the truth': because it would be doing nothing peculiar, nothing distinguishing, nothing which every heretic in Christendom is not ready to do, or rather is not daily doing, as loudly, and as frequently as the most orthodox church.[11]

Miller's arguments for the usefulness and critical importance of creeds and confessions are argued throughout Boyce's call for what became the Abstract of Principles, which is the confessional basis for all teaching at The Southern Baptist Theological Seminary.

Upon Boyce's return from Princeton, he became pastor of the First Baptist Church in Columbia, South Carolina. During his ordination examination, Boyce was asked if he had committed himself to the pastorate for the remainder of his life. Boyce answered in the affirmative but added, "provided I do not become a professor of theology."[12]

Boyce enjoyed a happy pastorate in Columbia where he was able to see his young, small congregation grow consistently. In Columbia, he was in close proximity to the Presbyterian Theological Seminary and had opportunity to come to know James H. Thornwell, George Howe, and Benjamin Morgan Palmer, who were all leading figures in the Presbyterian church of that day. They represented continuity with the Princeton tradition, to which they added the genteel approach common to the South.

Boyce's caveat uttered during his ordination council was brought to the fore when he was elected professor of theology at Furman University in July 1855. At Furman, Boyce quickly distinguished himself as a professor. As his student John G. Williams once reflected: "Dr. Boyce taught us systematic theology (using Dick's Theology as a textbook), church history, Greek New Testament

---

[11] Miller, 13.
[12] Broadus, 88.

exegesis, and Hebrew. It was easy to see then that theology was his strong point and had already taken a strong hold on him."[13]

THE BIRTH OF THE SOUTHERN BAPTIST THEOLOGICAL SEMINARY

The *Magna Carta* of The Southern Baptist Theological Seminary was set forth in July 1856 when Boyce delivered his inaugural address as a professor at Furman University. The address, entitled "Three Changes in Theological Institutions," set forth a bold, innovative, and thoroughly comprehensive vision for a central theological institution to serve the needs of Baptists in the South.

The address was perhaps the most important single contribution toward an understanding of theological education in the history of the Southern Baptist Convention. Boyce laid out a vision that incorporated the democratic impulse of Francis Wayland, the academic and scholarly commitments of the most ambitious educational cultures, and a clear mechanism for ensuring convictional fidelity. The address must have stirred those who heard the young theology professor speak both from the clarity of his mind and the passion of his heart. In any event, his message set in motion and accelerated the move toward a centralized theological institution for the Southern Baptist Convention.

Hopes for a denominational theological institution had been voiced even during the organizing sessions of the Southern Baptist Convention in 1845. Nevertheless, the young denomination turned first to the tasks of home and foreign missions, and it was not until fourteen years after the organization of the convention that its first institution was established.

Events led to the 1858 report of the Committee on the Plan of Organization. The committee brought forth a draft of the Fundamental Laws of the institution and stipulated that an Abstract of Principles was to be set in place as a safeguard. As described in the report, the Abstract of Principles was to be "selected as the fundamental principles of the Gospel, shall be subscribed to by every professor elect as indicative of his concurrence in its correctness as an epitome of Biblical truth; and it shall be the imperative duty of the Board to remove any professor of whose violation of the pledge they feel satisfied."[14]

Boyce's vigorous vision for theological education was set forth by the three changes he suggested in relation to theological institutions. The changes reveal the depth and breadth of Boyce's visionary hopes.

---

[13] Broadus, 105.

[14] Report of the Committee on Organization, *The Southern Baptist*, May 11, 1858, 1.

The first of these changes was reflective of the influence of Francis Wayland. Boyce was concerned that most theological institutions had become elitist and removed from the life and work of local Baptist congregations. Though Boyce made clear from the onset his insistence upon the vital importance of education and the dignity and utility of graduate education, he nonetheless feared that Baptists would be sidetracked into a false sense of educational aspiration. Should this aspiration be transformed into standards for ministry in the churches, Boyce felt that both biblical imperatives and denominational advance would be compromised. As Boyce stated:

> The Scriptural qualifications of the ministry do, indeed, involve the idea of knowledge, but that knowledge is not of the sciences nor of philosophy nor of the languages, but of God and His plan of salvation. He who has not this knowledge, though he be learned in all the learning of the schools, is incapable of preaching the Word of God. But he who knows it, not superficially, not merely in those plain and simple declarations known to every believing reader, but in the power as revealed in its precious and sanctifying doctrines, is fitted to bring forth out of his treasure things new and old, and is a workman that needeth not to be ashamed, although he may speak to his hearer in uncouth words or in manifest ignorance of all the sciences, the one belongs to the class of educated ministers, the other to the ministry of educated men, and the two things are essentially different.[15]

In this regard, Boyce compared John Bunyan with Theodore Parker. Better to be a preacher unlearned in the worldly sciences than a well-educated minister who distorts and manipulates the Word of God. Boyce's point here is easily misunderstood. This was hardly a call for lowering educational standards or for minimizing the importance of theological education. To the contrary, the issue was not the value of theological education but access to theological education.

In this respect, Boyce significantly advanced beyond the argument of Francis Wayland. Boyce called for a change in theological institutions that would open them to those who were without benefit of a classical education in order that such students might better understand the Word of God and prepare themselves for ministry. As Boyce argued:

> Let such a change be made in the theological department as shall provide an English course of study for those who have only been able to obtain a

---

[15] James Petigru Boyce, "Three Changes in Theological Institutions," in *James Petigru Boyce: Selected Writings*, edited by Timothy George (Nashville: Broadman Press, 1989), 35-36.

plain English education. Let that course comprise the evidences of Christianity, systematic and polemic theology, the rules of interpretation applied to the English version; some knowledge of the principles of rhetoric, extensive practice in the development from texts of subjects and skeletons of sermons, whatever amount of composition may be expedient, and full instruction in the nature of pastoral duties—let the studies of this course be so pursued as to train the mind to habits of reflection and analysis, to awaken it to conceptions of the truths of Scripture, to fill it with arguments from the Word of God in support of its doctrines, and to give it facility in constructing and presenting such arguments—and the work will be accomplished.[16]

Thus, the theological seminary would train those who came with the benefit of a classical education and study in Greek and Latin, but would train as well those who came with a basic education in English.

This would constitute a virtual revolution in theological education. Boyce's vision transformed the concerns of Francis Wayland into the glory of an institution that would train both the academic elite and those who had no background in classical scholarly aspirations. Focused upon the former, Boyce's full sympathy rested with the latter.

Boyce's second change can be seen as the complementary parallel to the democratic impulse reflected in his first concern. Boyce's concern in this regard was the class of educated men who had no access to theological education designed specifically to train the preacher and minister of the Word of God. If his concern related to the first change was access to theological education for those who had no classical training, his second change called for the development of a quality theological institution that would call forth and train the most highly qualified minister of the gospel.

Boyce was concerned that churches were calling educated men who were not educated ministers. Or, as Boyce argued, though these ministers are "familiar with all the sciences which form parts of the college curriculum, they are ignorant for the most part of that very science which lies at the foundation of all their ministerial labors."[17]

Boyce was greatly concerned that these "educated men" who were not yet "educated ministers" would do great damage to the church. He listed concerns that ranged from "unsettled" doctrines and theological error to ill-fed congregations. Boyce prescribed a comprehensive course of theological education based upon the finest and most faithful scholarship, which would include study of the

---

[16] Boyce, 39.
[17] Boyce, 41.

biblical languages, including Greek, Hebrew, and Chaldee. These individuals would be expected to study theology and church history from Greek and Latin primary sources. The benefit of classical education would be put to direct use in their study of the whole counsel of God.

Beyond this, Boyce called for the development of a superior theological library within such a seminary that could rival the great theological libraries of Europe. To this Boyce added a call for the scholars who would emerge from such a seminary to take on German scholarship and other continental scholars through writing, research, and teaching.

The third change for which Boyce contended in his famous address reflected his sincere concern that doctrinal compromise would in fact threaten both the theological seminary and its denomination. As he stated, "The change which I would in the last place propose is not intended to meet an evil existing in our theological institutions so much as one which is found in the denomination at large, and which may at some future time injuriously affect this educational interest."[18] In order to meet this concern, Boyce called for a "declaration of doctrine" that would be required of all those who would teach within the institution. Boyce quickly reviewed the legacy of heresy that had called forth this imperative. Even in his own day, Campbellism and Arminianism had already infected many Baptist churches, "and even some of our ministry have not hesitated publicly to avow them."

Southern Baptists should hear with proper rebuke and reproof the words with which Boyce stated his theological concern:

> That sentiment, the invariable precursor, or accompaniment of all heresy—that the doctrines of theology are matters of mere speculation, and its distinctions only logomachines and technicalities, has obtained at least a limited prevalence. And the doctrinal sentiments of a large portion of the ministry and membership of the churches are seen to be either very much unsettled or radically wrong.[19]

Boyce warned of a "crisis in Baptist doctrine" which he saw close on the horizon. Those who would stand for historic Baptist convictions and essential evangelical doctrines would have to do so against the tide of modern critical scholarship, which was even by that time beginning to erode conviction among the churches.

Boyce made clear that his concern was for the integrity of the theological seminary in the midst of doctrinal decline. The one who would teach the ministry,

---

[18] Boyce, 49.
[19] Boyce, 49.

"who is to be the medium through which the fountain of Scripture truth is to flow," stands before God with a much higher responsibility and accountability than any other teacher. Boyce argued that it is only proper that such a teacher should be held to a formal and explicit confession of faith that would set forth without compromise, and without forsaking clarity, precisely what would be taught within the institution.

This Abstract of Principles constitutes an unbreakable bond and covenant between the seminary and its churches through the denomination. This covenant would in no way compromise the appropriate freedom of the theological professor. To the contrary, that freedom is located within the liberty of the confession itself. That is, the theological professor is fully free to teach within the boundaries and parameters of that doctrinal covenant. The professor is not free to violate that covenant either through implicit or explicit disavowal. As Boyce argued:

> The theological professor is to teach ministers, to place the truth, and all the errors connected with it in such a manner before his pupils, that they shall arrive at the truth without danger of any mixture of error therewith. He cannot do this if he has any erroneous tendencies, and hence his opinions must be expressly affirmed to be upon every point in accordance with the truth we believe to be taught in the Scriptures.[20]

Particular obligations lie upon those who would teach the ministry. Such an individual is entrusted with great responsibility, for a theological professor would affect and influence not just one congregation but multitudes of churches through the generations of ministers who would sit in the classroom.

Theological error was pervasive even in the mid-nineteenth century, and Boyce put forth the historical argument that doctrinal error begins in most cases with one individual who had been entrusted with influence and authority. Such an individual would be dangerous in the extreme, as was Alexander Campbell, Boyce's chief illustration in this regard.

The doctrinal integrity of the seminary surpassed all other institutional concerns. Doctrinal integrity was more important than finances, facilities, and all other related factors. The theological institution, no matter how healthy by all other organizational barometers, would be only injurious to the church if it did not stand under this covenant and confession of conviction.

Boyce was neither embarrassed nor hesitant to identify the Abstract of Principles as a creed. Though he rejected the authority of any secular power to

---

[20] Boyce, 51.

infringe upon the Christian conscience, he asserted that the imposition of a creed upon the one who voluntarily taught within a theological institution was in no way a compromise of the Baptist understanding of liberty. His statement is of such importance that it deserves citation in full:

> It is, therefore, gentlemen, in perfect consistency with the position of Baptists, as well as Bible Christians, that the test of doctrine I have suggested to you should be adopted. It is based upon principles and practices sanctioned by the authority of Scripture and by the usage of our people. In so doing you will be acting simply in accordance with propriety and righteousness. You will infringe the rights of no man, and you will secure the rights of those who have established here an instrumentality for the production of a sound ministry. It is no hardship to those who teach here to be called upon to sign the declaration of their principles, for there are fields of usefulness open elsewhere to every man, and none need accept your call who cannot conscientiously sign your formulary. And while all this is true, you will receive by this an assurance that the trust committed to you by the founders is fulfilling in accordance with their wishes, that the ministers that go forth have here learned to distinguish truth from error, and to embrace the former, and that the same precious truths of the Bible which were so dear to the hearts of its founders, and which I trust are equally dear to yours, will be propagated in our churches, giving to them vigor and strength and causing them to flourish by the Godly sentiments and emotions they will awaken within them. May God impress you deeply with the responsibility under which you must act in reference to it![21]

Thus would the theological integrity of the institution be established.

The Abstract of Principles came primarily from the editorial pen of Basil Manly Jr., who had been assigned the task of drafting the confession. Manly drew from the very finest and most faithful Baptist tradition by turning to the Charleston confession and its Reformed Baptist orthodoxy. The Abstract of Principles stands as a brilliant summary of biblical and Baptist conviction. It is solidly based within the confessional tradition of the Baptists and was, as acknowledged by those who set it in place, a faithful repetition of the central truths found within the Westminster Confession.

Thus the great truths of the sovereignty of God and the doctrines of grace were incorporated within the heart of Southern Baptists' first theological institution. Here was to be found no lack of doctrinal clarity and no ambiguity on the great doctrines that had united Baptists to this date.

---

[21] Boyce, 56.

Sincere and earnest Southern Baptists who wish to understand the true substance of our theological heritage need look no further than the Abstract of Principles for a clear outline of the doctrines once most certainly held among us. Let there be no doubt that in the years to come Southern Seminary will be unashamedly and unhesitantly committed to these same doctrinal convictions as set forth in this incomparable document.

THE LEGACY OF JAMES PETIGRU BOYCE

It is most fitting that we draw attention and honor to this giant of Southern Baptist heritage, who gave birth by heart and calling to The Southern Baptist Theological Seminary. By the sovereign providence of God, James Petigru Boyce was used to awaken the hearts of Southern Baptists to the need for a theological seminary and, of even greater importance, to understand the requirements that should be made of such an institution in order to guard its integrity for the benefit of the churches. The Southern Baptist Theological Seminary stands in tribute to those founding fathers who brought this institution into being, shared those convictions which shaped its substance, and gave of their lives, their fortunes, and their affections in order that this institution might serve the churches.

The first change called for in Boyce's famous address was realized most fully in the openness of Southern Seminary to persons of all educational backgrounds. Southern Seminary was the first theological institution to offer formal course work in the English Bible. This was a revolution in theological education which was fiercely criticized by sister seminaries at the time. Nevertheless, within twenty years almost all theological seminaries in the country had followed Southern Seminary's example. A further development of this concern was reflected in the establishment twenty years ago of the Boyce Bible School in 1994, and its elevation to a four-year, bachelor's degree-granting program in 1998. That school stands to meet the contemporary needs of God-called ministers who have not yet been able to attain an undergraduate education and thus be qualified to enter the graduate programs of the Seminary.

Boyce's second change, his concern for scholarship, was realized in Southern Seminary's doctoral program. The institution awarded its first doctor of philosophy degree in 1894, the very first non-university based institution in the United States to offer such a degree. Southern Seminary must represent unquestioned and unparalleled theological and biblical scholarship.

But, as Boyce recognized, that scholarship must ever be in defense of the Word of God and never at the expense of the Word of God. Thus the Abstract of Principles stands. In our present generation, which has experienced moral and doctrinal decline beyond James Boyce›s most dreadful imagination, it is absolutely and undeniably vital that these doctrinal commitments be restated clearly, loudly, and consistently. For we now live in the midst of a generation suffering from theological and historical amnesia concerning the Baptist heritage. Ours is the task to train, educate, and prepare a generation of God-called ministers of the gospel who will stand for these convictions without compromise, give their testimony to the glorious gospel of the Lord Jesus Christ by their faithful exercise of the Christian calling, and see the conversion of souls as God adds to his kingdom.

In the original preface that Dr. Boyce prepared for this volume, he described *Abstract of Systematic Theology* as a "practical text book, for the study of the system of doctrine taught in the Word of God." In that sense, Boyce was a practical theologian. But his real passion was the affirmation of the Christian faith and the defense of biblical truth. "The author has aimed to make the discussions in this volume especially Scriptural," Boyce wrote. "He believes in the perfect inspiration and absolute authority of the divine revelation, and is convinced that the best proof of any truth is that it is there taught."

Those sentences reveal the deep theological commitments held by James Petigru Boyce; and they explain why this book is so worthy of republication in the twenty-first century. We all owe an immense debt to this great scholar, educator, preacher, and theologian.

R. Albert Mohler Jr. is the president of
The Southern Baptist Theological Seminary
and Joseph Emerson Brown Professor of Christian Theology.

INTRODUCTION

JAMES Petigru Boyce published the *Abstract of Systematic Theology* in 1887, just one year before his death. This book is deeply important because of what is in it—the carefully developed explanations of the Bible's teaching from the pen of one of the nineteenth century's great evangelical leaders. Boyce designed it as a textbook for his classes in systematic theology at The Southern Baptist Theological Seminary, and it is a model of concise, cogent, and clear theological statement—the culmination of a lifetime of careful study and painstaking teaching of the doctrines of the Bible.[1]

This book is deeply important also because it represents the basis of the spiritual and moral power of an extraordinary man of God whose sacrifices and accomplishments extend their powerful influence down to the present day. Boyce accomplished what no other man had been able to accomplish, though many others tried: he led Southern Baptists to support the establishment of a theological seminary designed to serve the whole denomination. And he did what no other man could have done: he kept the seminary from dying when there was no realistic hope of its survival. His vision, his courage, and his relentless determination to preserve the seminary derived from his conviction of the truth and power of the teachings of the Bible collected and explained in this volume. Boyce's commitment to orthodox theological education—making the seminary accountable to the seminary's confession of faith, the Abstract of Principles, and leading the seminary and the denomination to reject liberalism's errors—deepened Southern Baptists' commitment to orthodoxy and provided a heroic example that continues to inspire faithfulness to the revealed truth of scripture.

Boyce was born in Charleston, South Carolina on January 11, 1827, the son of one of the South's wealthiest merchants, Ker Boyce. He grew up faithfully attending the Charleston First Baptist Church, where his mother was a

---

[1] James P. Boyce, *Abstract of Systematic Theology* (Baltimore: H. M. Wharton, 1887). This introduction is adapted in part from Gregory A. Wills, *Southern Baptist Theological Seminary, 1859–2009* (New York: Oxford University Press, 2009), 3–188. For more extensive discussion of Boyce, The Southern Baptist Theological Seminary, and the *Abstract of Systematic Theology*, see also: Thomas J. Nettles, *James Petigru Boyce: A Southern Baptist Statesman* (Phillipsburg, NJ: P&R Publishing, 2009), and John A. Broadus, *Memoir of James Petigru Boyce* (New York: A. C. Armstrong and Son, 1893).

member. In 1846, at the age of nineteen, he came under the conviction that he was a sinner in need of the grace that could be found in Jesus Christ alone. He experienced conversion and was baptized shortly after.[2]

Boyce immediately applied himself with great earnestness to prayer, Bible reading, and evangelistic work among his friends at Brown University, where he was a student. After graduation in 1847, he resolved to apply himself to the ministry of the gospel. In 1848, he and his wife, Elizabeth Ficklin Boyce, moved to New Jersey, where Boyce took the full theological course at Princeton Theological Seminary in two years by taking the second and third year courses simultaneously. In 1851, the Columbia First Baptist Church ordained Boyce and he was its pastor for four years. When his father died in 1854, he became executor of his father's estate, a position that demanded considerable attention for the rest of his life.[3]

When Boyce was ordained to the gospel ministry in 1851, Thomas Curtis asked him if he planned to make preaching his life's work. Boyce replied, "Yes, provided I do not become a professor of theology."[4] Boyce soon concluded that it was his duty under God to do all in his power to establish a Southern Baptist seminary. His friend, J. P. Tustin, reported that Boyce refused his election to the presidency of Mercer University in Georgia in 1857 because it seemed "to him, at present, to militate against cherished plans, long since formed—labored during many years—and apparently now within his reach."[5] Boyce felt deeply his duty before Christ to lead Southern Baptists to establish a theological seminary to promote the soundness and effectiveness of the Baptist ministry in the South.

The Long Struggle for the Seminary

In 1856, Southern Baptist educational leaders asked the state conventions to determine whether their endowments for theological education could be donated to a new theological seminary. The South Carolina Baptist Convention appointed a committee consisting of Boyce, the president of Furman

---

[2] Broadus, *Memoir of Boyce*, 34–35, 43–45.

[3] Broadus, *Memoir of Boyce*, 46–47, 53–88, 93–95, 336. The terms of his father's will required that the estate remain in executorship until the youngest of his grandchildren entered majority, which did not occur until one month after James Boyce's death. The estate was reputed to be worth $17,000,000 in 1854 ("Notes from the Life of a Southern Millionaire," newspaper clipping from Chattanooga paper, in box 16, Broadus Papers).

[4] Broadus, *Memoirs of Boyce*, 88.

[5] J. P. Tustin, "Southern Baptist Theological Seminary," *Southern Baptist*, 22 Sept. 1857, 2; "Report of the Board of Trustees of Mercer University," in Georgia Baptist Convention, *Minutes*, 1858, 15.

University, and the convention's leading layman to prepare the convention's response. Boyce judged that if one state took up the burden in a bold and generous initiative, Baptists in the other states would support the plan. He was certain that if South Carolina Baptists pledged to raise one-half of the total endowment needed, the plan would succeed and the seminary would be established. Anything less would mean failure. Boyce failed to persuade the other two committee members of the wisdom of his plan. As it turned out, they could have saved themselves time and trouble if they yielded from the start.

When the committee offered its report proposing to do nothing, Boyce moved the substitution of his minority report with his daring proposal. The convention debated the issues posed by the alternative reports for all of Tuesday afternoon and much of Wednesday morning, and Boyce ultimately persuaded the convention to adopt his proposal.[6] The delegates agreed to donate Furman University's theological education endowment, worth about $26,000, and to raise an additional $74,000 in South Carolina, for a total of $100,000 toward the new seminary's endowment, provided that it be located in Greenville, South Carolina, and that the other southern states raised jointly an additional $100,000.[7]

The South Carolina Baptist Convention adopted Boyce's proposal at the end of the morning session on July 30, 1856. That evening, Boyce gave his inaugural address as professor of theology at Furman University, titled "Three Changes in Theological Institutions," in which he explained the three fundamental principles that should frame the new seminary's organization. That morning, he had placed the seminary movement on a solid financial and denominational footing; that evening, he presented the blueprint of its essential principles.[8]

In the address, Boyce argued that a theological seminary needed to secure three things. The first was a curriculum that permitted students at every level of educational preparation to study there. Few Southern Baptist pastors attended college. Boyce proposed to admit students without regard to previous college work, and to combine them in the same classes. This meant that all theology students should take instruction based on the English version of the Bible and English-language texts. College graduates and other able students could take advanced courses, studying the Bible in Hebrew and Greek, and studying theology using Latin-language texts. But for most courses necessary for theological

---

[6] J. P. Tustin, "South Carolina Baptist State Convention," *Southern Baptist*, 12 Aug. 1856, 2; South Carolina Baptist Convention, *Minutes*, 1856, 9.

[7] South Carolina Baptist Convention, *Minutes*, 1856, 18–19.

[8] James P. Boyce, *Three Changes in Theological Institutions* (Greenville, SC: C. J. Elford, 1856).

training, all students, from the least educated to the most advanced, would take the same courses. "Let us abandon," Boyce urged, "the false principle" of requiring a "classical education" of Greek and Latin, and establish an "English course of study for those who have only been able to attain a plain English education." The proposed curriculum relied first on studying the Bible in English.[9]

The second change was a curriculum that permitted the ablest students to pursue advanced studies. In areas of biblical studies and church history, Baptists depended on German scholarship, much of it based on a "defective standpoint." To answer this need, Boyce proposed two remedies. First, the theological school needed an extensive library that collected not only rare books from the past but also the most advanced scholarship of the present. Second, the school should provide for advanced study of one or two years after graduation for the study of such languages as Arabic and Syriac, or for original scholarship. If Baptists made such provisions in a theology school, Boyce predicted, "a band of scholars would go forth" to make valuable contributions to theological study and to the defense of distinctive Baptist principles.[10]

The third change was the adoption of a confession of faith that determined the boundaries of acceptable belief among the faculty. He proposed the third change because he believed that a "crisis in Baptist doctrine" was approaching. Years before, while visiting the Baptists of Culpepper and Rapahannock counties in Virginia, he judged that the "current of the people" was strongly toward Arminianism, and that Baptist preachers, though at the time still sound, "may become Arminians." The beliefs of a "large portion of the ministry and membership" of Baptist churches were "either very much unsettled or radically wrong."[11] The errors of Campbellism, of Arminianism, and of the idea that all doctrine is mere opinion, prevailed increasingly. To protect the theological school from such errors, Boyce suggested adopting a confession of faith such as that of the Charleston Baptist Association, which was the Philadelphia Confession of Faith and was essentially the same as the Second London Confession, publish by London Baptists in 1677 and 1689.[12]

Boyce explained that the Bible effectively commanded the churches to adopt creeds, for scripture taught in many places that churches must reject false doctrine and false teachers. A seminary had even greater obligation to require agreement with a creed. Its professors shaped the "conceptions of the doctrines of the Bible" for ministers of the gospel. If a seminary's professors were sound and

---

[9] Boyce, *Three Changes*, 17–18.

[10] Boyce, *Three Changes*, 25, 28–29, 31.

[11] James P. Boyce, untitled, *Southern Baptist*, 18 Sept. 1850, 2.

[12] Boyce, *Three Changes*, 34, 38.

orthodox, it would be a powerful instrument for the "production of a sound ministry."[13] The confession was necessary to safeguard the orthodoxy of the faculty.

It was also a matter of trust with donors. Trustees had a solemn duty to donors to assure that "the ministers that go forth have here learned to distinguish truth from error" and to propagate in the churches "the same precious truths of the Bible" that they held.[14] Those who founded the school by their exertions and donations expected that the school would maintain the principles on which they established it.

A. M. Poindexter, secretary of the Southern Baptist Convention's Foreign Mission Board, called Boyce's two-hour address "the ablest thing of the kind he had ever heard." Brown University president Francis Wayland called it the "first common sense discourse on theological education I have yet seen."[15] J. P. Tustin, editor of South Carolina's *Southern Baptist*, thought it outstanding. It made a "marked impression" on the audience and Furman's trustees took immediate steps to secure its publication.[16]

The remarkable victory that Boyce achieved, and the clear vision that he expressed at the 1856 South Carolina Baptist Convention meeting, earned him the responsibility to lead the effort to establish a Southern Baptist seminary to a successful conclusion. Boyce did succeed. The state conventions throughout the South affirmed the South Carolina plan and Boyce raised the needed endowment funds from South Carolina and the other states. Baptist leaders adopted the plan for the organization and curriculum of the seminary in accordance with Boyce's grand vision. The Southern Baptist Theological Seminary opened in Greenville, South Carolina, on October 1, 1859, under the brightest prospects, with a modest but encouraging student enrollment and with a remarkable faculty that included Boyce, John A. Broadus, Basil Manly Jr., and William Williams.

The seminary's bright prospects, however, withered before the ravages of war. When the Civil War ended in 1865, the seminary counted no students, possessed no remaining endowment to pay faculty salaries, and had little prospect of raising sufficient funds for years to come. The war also severely diminished the vast estate left by Boyce's father, and what remained was at risk of total loss.

[13] Boyce, *Three Changes*, 35, 44.

[14] Boyce, *Three Changes*, 44. See also, Boyce, "The Two Objections to the Seminary, V," *Christian Index*, 25 June 1874, 2.

[15] Poindexter and Wayland quoted in Timothy George, "Preface," in George, ed., *James Petigru Boyce: Selected Writings* (Nashville: Broadman Press, 1989).

[16] J. P. Tustin, "Prof. Boyce's Address," *Southern Baptist*, 12 Aug. 1856, 3.

Boyce was a partner or shareholder in various businesses, and under the laws of the time, creditors could hold him liable for the entire debt of any partnership.[17] Boyce feared that he would be compelled to leave the seminary, for at least a year or two, to earn enough money to pay his debts and care for his family. The faculty recognized that if the seminary was to survive, it would have to rely on his leadership and his ability to loan funds to the seminary in the lean times ahead. "We ought to make the future of the seminary a matter of special daily prayer," Broadus urged Manly in May, 1865. "We can't yet see what is to be feasible for the seminary. If Boyce's private fortune is spared, he will probably work it along. But all is uncertain."[18]

In Greenville, at the end of August, 1865, Boyce insisted that "the seminary must not fall below three professors." If William Williams refused to return, Boyce would feel it his duty to stay in Greenville and teach in order to preserve the seminary, though his inability to attend to his business affairs would involve him in "enormous losses." Boyce asked Williams to return as a "favor to him personally." When the four professors met for a decision, Broadus convinced them to venture their all to sustain the seminary: "Suppose we quietly agree that the seminary may die, but we'll die first." In early September, they announced that the school would reopen on November 1, 1865.[19]

Those on the faculty gave their lives to sustaining the seminary, for the purpose of teaching and equipping pastors for Southern Baptist churches, because it was their duty under Christ. They did so at great sacrifice. In an 1867 appeal for funds, Boyce pleaded that "our professors have had scarcely any of their salary paid since the close of the war. Although offered other positions at much larger salaries and salaries that will be paid punctually, they prefer to stay at their present posts, if they can only get necessary food and clothing for their families."[20] In 1868, the South Carolina Railroad asked Boyce to be the company's president at an annual salary of $10,000. Similar offers came to Boyce across the years. Louisville's Walnut Street Baptist Church pressed Boyce to be their pastor in 1875.[21] Manly received offers of the presidency of the Richmond

---

[17] G. G. Wells to John A. Broadus, 9 Nov. 1892, box 14, Broadus Papers; Broadus, *Memoir of Boyce*, 202–203.

[18] John A. Broadus to Basil Manly Jr., 22 May 1865, Manly Collection of Manuscripts, microfilm, reel 2, SBTS.

[19] John A. Broadus to Basil Manly Jr., 25 Aug. 1865, quoted in Robertson, *Life of Broadus*, 214; Broadus, *Memoir of Boyce*, 200; Basil Manly Jr. to John A. Broadus, 9 Sept. 1865, box 2, Broadus Papers.

[20] James P. Boyce to Sister _____ [form letter], 1 July 1867, box 1, Boyce Papers.

[21] Broadus, *Memoir of Boyce*, 208–209. James P. Boyce to John A. Broadus, 9 Mar. 1875, box 6, Broadus Papers.

Female Institute, the University of Alabama, Union University in Tennessee, and Georgetown College in Kentucky, as well as the Home Mission Board.[22] Missouri's William Jewell College wanted Williams as its president.[23] Even when the professors received no salary for twelve months and had to buy their necessities on credit, doing "the work of two or three men on half the salary of one man, with that salary in arrears and no certainty of ever receiving it," they, however, stood by Boyce and the seminary for the cause of an orthodox and effective ministry.[24]

By 1870, it was clear that, unless the seminary took extraordinary action, it would die. Strenuous efforts to raise a new endowment failed. Boyce borrowed heavily on his personal credit to meet expenses and could borrow no more. Even if the seminary sold its Greenville property, the proceeds would scarcely cover the debt. Its only asset, it seemed to Manly, was Boyce's "earnest determination, the echo of his confidence and zeal." Remaining in Greenville would likely mean the seminary's failure, he thought, but they would not despair, for "the seminary must live somewhere."[25]

The best hope was to move. Other cities wanted the seminary and were prepared to raise money for a new endowment. When the board of trustees met in May 1872, they appointed a committee of seven trustees to visit Atlanta, Chattanooga, Nashville, and Louisville and to choose the new location for the board. They chose Louisville, and the seminary moved there in 1877.[26]

The seminary's move, however, proved ineffectual as the nation's economy collapsed. They needed an extraordinary gift—a providential sign that would reignite support. Boyce began praying that God would move someone to give $50,000 to "stimulate others" to give and "awaken a new interest" in the endowment movement in order to attract other donations to raise at least $200,000 in new endowment funds. He asked his colleagues to pray likewise. On the seminary's missionary day, when all students gathered for prayer, he explained

---

[22] Basil Manly Jr. to J. B. Taylor, 28 Aug. 1865, Manly Collection of Manuscripts, reel 2, SBTS; Basil Manly Jr. to John A. Broadus, 13 July 1871, box 3, Broadus Papers; Manly to Broadus, 27 Dec. 1872, box 4, Broadus Papers; Manly to Broadus, 13 May 1875, box 6, Broadus Papers.

[23] Lottie Broadus to John A. Broadus, 4 June 1871, box 3, Broadus Papers.

[24] Broadus, *Memoir of Boyce*, 207, 205–206.

[25] Basil Manly Jr. to Crawford H. Toy, 7 Feb. 1873, Letterbook II, Southern Historical Collection, microfilm, University of North Carolina, Chapel Hill.

[26] "Southern Baptist Convention," *Christian Index*, 23 May 1872, 82; Broadus, *Memoir of Boyce*, 202–203; Board of Trustees, Southern Baptist Theological Seminary, Minutes, May 1872.

the seminary's financial crisis and asked them to pray that God would raise up such a donor.[27]

In a desperate appeal for funds, Boyce added a line expressing his hope that God would raise up a donor to give $50,000. When Joseph E. Brown, former governor of Georgia, railroad president, and finally a United States Senator, read Boyce's notice, he felt immediately that he was the individual. He wrote Boyce at once and told him that "if he could be satisfied as to the financial condition and prospects of the seminary," he would give the money. Boyce visited Brown in Atlanta and satisfied him of the soundness of the seminary's stewards and of the worthiness of the enterprise—he gave Boyce $50,000.[28] With the money, trustees endowed the Joseph Emerson Brown Professorship of Systematic Theology.[29]

Brown's gift saved the seminary. It bore no conditions, but Boyce astutely determined to make it part of a campaign to raise $200,000 in invested endowment. Boyce persuaded donors to give their donations for the campaign on the condition of raising a total of $200,000.[30] To assure donors of the safety of their gifts, Boyce persuaded trustees to amend the seminary charter to prohibit inviolably the spending of endowment principal and to establish a financial board to oversee the management of the endowment. Boyce solicited $50,000 from the seminary's Louisville benefactors.[31] Broadus raised more than $40,000 in New York City. With help from various others, Boyce succeeded in raising the additional $150,000, making $200,000 in new endowment funds deriving from Brown's initial gift.[32] "The seminary is now safe—humanly speaking," Boyce exulted.[33]

Brown's gift marked a turning point in the seminary's history. The seminary's survival was no longer in doubt. For Boyce, the faculty, and the friends of the seminary, it stood as an instance of God's extraordinary providence. Some years later, Boyce reflected on this: "With all our anxiety and hopes and fears how true it is that in our agony of trouble as to what will occur we find that God has found us ways of which we have never dreamed. Witness the gift of Governor Brown. We were praying for help and crying out in our despair and without

---

[27] John A. Broadus, "Hon. Joseph Emerson Brown," *Seminary Magazine* 7 (1894): 206.

[28] Broadus, "Hon. Joseph Brown," 206–207; William Whitsitt, "The Ordering of Providence," *Seminary Magazine* 5 (1892): 472–474.

[29] Minutes, Board of Trustees, Southern Baptist Theological Seminary, May 1880.

[30] James P. Boyce to John A. Broadus, 8 Feb. 1881, box 9, Broadus Papers; Minutes, Board of Trustees, Southern Baptist Theological Seminary, May 1881.

[31] John A. Broadus to William Rockefeller, 22 Feb. 1881, box 9, Broadus Papers.

[32] Broadus, *Memoir of Boyce*, 273–274.

[33] James P. Boyce to M. T. Yates, 13 July 1881, Letterpress Book 7, June-Nov. 1881, 434, SBTS.

our lifting a single finger almost it came from a quarter to which we had never looked for such a sum."[34] God had crowned their labors, sacrifices, and sufferings with success at last.

During those long years of struggle for the seminary's life, Broadus was confident that as long as Boyce survived, the seminary would also. "By living for the seminary you will, I am right confident, save it; by dying for it you inevitably kill it—buried in your grave."[35] The seminary, Broadus said, "would have perished a dozen times" had it not been for Boyce's "exertions and sacrifices."[36] Its existence and survival rested to an unusual degree in the person of James P. Boyce. As a result, the denomination identified the seminary with his name above all others.

Boyce did not own or control the seminary, but in every other way, it was his seminary:

> If to have longed for the existence of such an institution from before the time of my ordination to the ministry, if to have prayed and labored for it, for the past nineteen years, if to have urged it upon unwilling hearts, and to have argued for it with those who found objections to it in other theological seminaries which had no application here, if to have succeeded in developing a plan which had never before been adopted of combining all classes of our ministry in one institution without detriment to any, if to have sacrificed for it the ease and comfort which might otherwise easily have been mine, if to have spent days and years of humiliation in begging for it, stooping to do for this institution what I would not do for bread to eat if I were starving, if to have foregone numberless opportunities of bettering my pecuniary condition, and to have oftentimes incurred embarrassments that its credit might be sustained and its faculty paid, if to have subjected my family to deprivations which have caused my nearest friends to accuse me of injustice to them, if to have spent sleepless nights and to have more than once endangered my health and even my life, if to have done these things makes the seminary mine—and in what other sense is it so?—I accept it as such to make all that it is and all its glorious possibilities a free gift to the Baptist denomination of the South.[37]

Boyce especially symbolized the seminary, for the institution owed its existence to him to a peculiar degree, and he had stamped it with his vision from

---

[34] James P. Boyce to John A. Broadus, 31 Oct. 1888, box 12, Broadus Papers.

[35] John A. Broadus to James P. Boyce, 19 Mar. 1874, box 11, Boyce Papers.

[36] John A. Broadus to James P. Boyce, 11 Oct. 1873, box 5, 1873.

[37] James P. Boyce, "The Two Objections to the Seminary, I," *Christian Index*, 16 Apr. 1874, 2.

the beginning. And he won the confidence and support of the churches. The Southern Baptist Convention acknowledged Boyce's leadership and accomplishments, and elected Boyce president of its annual meetings nine times, 1872–1879 and 1888.

Defending the Bible

The seminary faced a new kind of challenge in the late 1870s, when Old Testament professor Crawford H. Toy began teaching the new modernist view of inspiration and the new historical-critical views of the Bible. Science, Toy concluded, had established the great antiquity of the earth and he could no longer harmonize the Genesis account of creation with the fact of the earth's extended age. He concluded also that the order of creation in Genesis contradicted both reason and the geological strata of the fossil record.[38] Around the same time, Toy adopted evolutionary views after studying Herbert Spencer and Charles Darwin. In 1874, he told his students that they should "not deny evolution on Christian grounds," for Christianity and evolution were compatible.[39] If evolutionary views of geology and biology were correct, then the Genesis history of the origin of the earth and of living things was false. He could not repudiate the new science, but he was loathe to give up the Bible.

Around 1875 Toy solved the problem by adopting a new view of inspiration: the Bible's spiritual meaning was inspired but its historical and scientific meaning was not inspired. This view, however, had wide interpretive ramifications. It required a reconstruction and reinterpretation of the Bible. Toy adopted the reconstruction of the history of Israel advanced by modern historical criticism.[40] Toy saw the Old Testament in terms of the gradual development of spiritual religion, which consisted centrally in monotheism and an ethic of love and justice. The religious value of Old Testament texts inhered in their promotion of such spiritual truths.[41]

He accepted the theory that Genesis was not written by Moses but derived from a Jehovist source and an Elohist source.[42] Leviticus, Toy said in 1874, was not written by Moses, but was written later by someone in the spirit of Moses:

---

[38] Toy, "A Bit of Personal Experience," *Religious Herald*, 1 Apr. 1880, 1. See also C. H. Toy, quoted in A. J. Holt, "Student Notebook of C. H. Toy's O.T. Class, 28 Sept. 1874 ("The word day then can not mean a geological period").

[39] C. H. Toy, in quoted in A. J. Holt, "Student Notebook of C. H. Toy's O.T. Class, 9 Oct. 1874, 155.

[40] Broadus, *Memoir of Boyce*, 260.

[41] See Toy, "Kuenen's Life and Work," *Christian Register*, 21 Jan. 1892, 4.

[42] Holt, Lecture Notes, 168.

"The genius given by Moses was elaborated in the after history of Israel." In this sense, it could be called "the teachings of Moses."[43] He now regarded the Pentateuch as the work of the priests and of Ezra during the time of the exile, though Moses provided the germ.[44] The Law, Toy told students, represented declension from the pure religion of the prophets—the Law "imprisoned" spiritual religion and produced formalism.[45] In 1874, he defended the unity of Isaiah, but in 1877 he assigned portions to three different authors.[46]

In 1877, Toy taught students that the traditional Messianic prophecies in the Psalms, Isaiah, Micah, Joel did not refer to Christ, but that Christ was the fulfillment of all truly spiritual longings, and in this sense only the passages were messianic.[47] Over and over Toy told students that specific prophecies were not fulfilled and "never came to pass," but they were fulfilled in a general way by Christ, because he represented spiritual redemption.[48]

Also in 1877, Toy also began to publish some of his conclusions based on the historical-critical reconstruction of the history of Israel. He reinterpreted the Bible's miracle accounts as natural events. He interpreted Isaiah 42:1–10 and 53:1–11 as references to Israel, although New Testament writers understood them to refer to Christ. The New Testament authors misinterpreted the texts, Toy believed, but they still taught truth about Christ, for "Christ was by divine appointment the consummation of all God's revelation of truth in ancient Israel."[49] Indeed, for Toy, the entire history of Israel was the "anticipatory, predictive picture of the Messiah."[50] Only in this general sense did these prophecies refer to Jesus. It did not matter that they got the history or interpretation wrong, Toy assured, but through this error they taught spiritual truth. In a broad sense, Toy made every passage in the Old Testament messianic. The New Testament writers thus often quoted Old Testament passages in ways false to their original meaning.

---

[43] Holt, Lecture Notes, 182. In 1874, Toy held that it was "morally certain" that Moses wrote Exodus, though Moses could not have written all of it (Holt, Lecture Notes, 168, 194).

[44] Hugh C. Smith, Lectures in Old Testament English by C. H. Toy, 130–132, Archives and Special Collections, SBTS.

[45] Holt, Lecture Notes, 148–246; Hugh C. Smith, Lectures in Old Testament English by C. H. Toy, 1–139, 132 (quote), Archives and Special Collections, SBTS.

[46] Holt, Lecture Notes, 239; Smith, Lectures, 68.

[47] Smith, Lectures, 44, 49–51, 58–60, 67–69, 118–124.

[48] Smith, Lectures, 48, 56–57, 65–68, 108.

[49] Toy, "Critical Notes," *Sunday School Times*, 12 Apr. 1879, 231.

[50] Toy, "Critical Notes," *Sunday School Times*, 19 Apr. 1879, 247.

Boyce and Broadus apparently told Toy that it was his duty to resign. At the trustee meeting on May 7, 1879, in Atlanta, Toy resigned. Toy did not, however, believe that his resignation would be accepted. Toy's resignation letter, therefore, was an essay consisting of an extended defense of his views on inspiration. Boyce, Broadus, and most trustees held the traditional Protestant theory of inspiration, the plenary verbal view, which was concerned chiefly with the results of inspiration, not the manner of it. It held that God inspired the Bible with the result that its every part and its every word, though written by human authors, was precisely what the Holy Spirit intended. The Bible was therefore God's very word, not in a general or spiritual sense only, but also in its historical and scientific statements.

Toy claimed that his view was in full accord with the *Abstract of Principles*, and that it established divine truth more firmly than the old view. His teaching was "not only lawful for me to teach as professor in the seminary, but one that will bring aid and firm standing-ground to many a perplexed mind and establish the truth of God on a surer foundation."[51] The trustees appointed a committee of five, who discussed the matter with Toy and learned his views in greater detail. They recommended that the board accept Toy's resignation because his views diverged significantly from those commonly held among Southern Baptists. "After a full discussion" the board voted sixteen to two in favor of Toy's dismissal.[52]

Boyce and Broadus grieved at Toy's tragic departure from orthodoxy. They felt the pain of this breach keenly, but they were unmoved from their duty to Christ and to the church to dismiss him. When Toy went to catch the train for his final departure from Louisville, Boyce and Broadus accompanied him to the station. While they waited, Boyce threw his left arm around Toy's neck, and "lifted the right arm before him and said, in a passion of grief, 'Oh, Toy, I would freely give that arm to be cut off if you could be where you were five years ago, and stay there.'"[53] Toy would not go back.

In the years following Toy's dismissal, many Southern Baptists defended Toy's progressive views. Boyce led the seminary faculty to defend the traditional

---

[51] Toy, "Full Text," *Baptist Courier*, 27 Nov. 1879, 2.

[52] Minutes, Board of Trustees, Southern Baptist Theological Seminary, 7–13 May 1879; James C. Furman, chmn., "Report of Dr. Toy's Committee of Resignation," Archives and Special Collections, SBTS. The two who voted against dismissal, John A. Chambliss and D. W. Gwin, submitted a formal statement of protest against the board's action, which the board received. The statement apparently did not survive, as the trustee books of reports, with all such exhibits, were evidently lost for the period through 1888.

[53] Boyce, quoted in Broadus, *Memoir of Boyce*, 263–264.

view of inspiration. At the 1883 meeting of the Southern Baptist Convention, for example, Broadus defended the orthodox view in the convention sermon, "Three Questions as to the Bible." He argued that through the agency of men, the Bible says precisely what God intended it to say. God's use of human authors did not render the Bible liable to error any more than the incarnation rendered Jesus liable to error.[54] The inspired writers were "moved by the Holy Ghost" so that they "will not only say what He wishes, but say it as He wishes."[55] Broadus was convinced that the Bible's authors "were preserved by the Holy Spirit from error" and that "there is no proof that the inspired writers made any mistake of any kind."[56]

Basil Manly Jr., who returned to his position at the seminary to replace Toy, taught the traditional view of inspiration and began preparing a book on the subject.[57] In 1888 he published *The Bible Doctrine of Inspiration*, an able defense of plenary verbal inspiration. It was a fallacy, Manly said, to hold "that God can not inspire and so use a human being as to keep his message free from error."[58]

Boyce held the same view. God so inspired the Bible authors that they wrote "exactly" what God wished—"as if he had written every word himself."[59] He believed in the "verbal inspiration" of the Bible's writers, that they "were guided in their very language by Him to whom are 'known all His works from the beginning of the world.'"[60]

Boyce and Broadus took additional precautions to make sure that unsound views of inspiration did not intrude again on the faculty or spread further among the churches. In 1881, Boyce was in the forefront of an important episode in the inspiration controversy when he interfered in the appointment of two missionaries who agreed with Toy's views of inspiration. In April 1881

---

[54] John A. Broadus, *Three Questions as to the Bible* (Philadelphia: American Baptist Publication Society, 1883), 26–27.

[55] John A. Broadus, "Quotations in Matthew," ms. notebook, 23, Archives and Special Collections, SBTS.

[56] John A. Broadus, *Catechism of Bible Teaching* (Philadelphia: American Baptist Publication Society, 1892).

[57] Manly taught inspiration that year in Biblical Introduction, a class he took over when Whitsitt became too ill to teach. See. Jerome R. Baer, Notebook for Biblical Introduction 1879–80, Archives and Special Collections, SBTS.

[58] Basil Manly Jr., *The Bible Doctrine of Inspiration Explained and Vindicated* (New York: A. C. Armstrong and Son, 1888), 29, 90, 30.

[59] James P. Boyce, *A Brief Catechism of Bible Doctrine* (Greenville, SC: Sunday School Board of the Southern Baptist Convention, 1864), 1.

[60] James P. Boyce, *Three Changes in Theological Institutions* (Greenville, SC: C. J. Elford's Press, 1856), 27.

the Southern Baptist Foreign Mission Board appointed two seminary gradu-ates, John Stout and T. P. Bell, as missionaries to China. Each aligned himself with Toy's view. Boyce had discovered the fact and felt that it was his duty to advise the board against their appointments. The board rescinded their appoint-ments.[61] Boyce and the faculty kept up their insistence on orthodoxy and their opposition to the new liberal theology while they lived.

Boyce's Legacy

Boyce's health deteriorated in 1887. He traveled to the West that summer to seek to recover his health.[62] For the same purpose he traveled with his family to Europe in 1888. His physician told him that it was imperative for him to give up all responsibilities, and he announced to Broadus his determination to resign effective May 1889.[63] Boyce did not recover. He died in Pau in southern France on December 28, 1888.[64]

Students loved and admired Boyce. Boyce was a master of public ceremony and a delightful companion. Students valued his prayers before each lecture. One student, who was not expected to return for a second year, nevertheless returned. When some students asked him why he returned, he said: "I came back to hear Dr. Boyce pray."[65] Some mistook his natural reserve for distance. Broadus attributed this to his dislike of small talk and thought him remarkably genial and open. Many students experienced his remarkable generosity of spirit as he aided and advised students in numerous ways. Alumnus John Adams testified that "most of you professors in the seminary seemed to me like fathers but Dr. Boyce was my friend, not only in my marriage, but also in my time of need."[66] Another student remembered vividly Boyce's "ever thoughtful tender-ness. The Dr. did me several favors while in China. One of which was to lend me more than a hundred dollars for several months, for which he would have no compensation. I greatly love Dr. Boyce."[67] G. W. Samson represented the

---

[61] John Stout, "Appointment of Rev. John Stout and Rev. T. P. Bell Withdrawn," *Baptist Courier*, 7 July 1881, 2–3; H. A. Tupper to John Stout, 21 May 1881, Lide-Coker-Stout Family Papers, South Caroliniana Library, University of South Carolina; T. P. Bell to H. A. Tupper, ca. 21 May 1881, ibid.; T. P. Bell, "Statement of Brother Bell," *Baptist Courier*, 14 July 1881, 2.

[62] See e.g. James P. Boyce to John A. Broadus, 28 Aug. 1887, box 11, Broadus Papers.

[63] James P. Boyce to John A. Broadus, 5 Oct. 1888, box 12, Broadus Papers; Boyce to Broadus, 19 Oct. 1888, ibid.

[64] See Broadus, *Memoir of Boyce*, 341–342.

[65] Quoted by H. H. Tucker, "Memoir of Dr. Boyce," *Christian Index*, 7 Feb. 1889, 9.

[66] John Adams to John A. Broadus, 26 Jan. 1889, box 12, Broadus Papers.

[67] J. M. Joiner to John A. Broadus, 6 June 1889, box 12, Broadus Papers.

feelings of many who knew him: "Boyce was in every respect the noblest spirit I ever met."[68]

Broadus provided the most thorough description of Boyce's character:

> If I were to talk to you for hours and tell you of all he went through you could but half conceive it. I do not think the strongest type of character is the man who stands unmoved amid difficuties and trials, but he who does feel, and feels keenly and deeply, feels depressed and at times almost overwhelmed, and still does not give up. And such was the history in this case. Many times it seemed impossible to go on, and but for his heroic efforts the seminary would have been closed. That was what wore out this life ten years too soon, that long, sore, terrible struggle. He had lost by the war the greater part of his fortune. He had many opportunities to recover it with his wonderful business talents, and they were often pressed upon his acceptance, but he had made up his mind that, God helping him, this enterprise to which he had given his life should not fail; and blessed be God, before he died he knew that although it was not yet fully established and its wants met, yet it had before it a glorious future. Friends, you do not know the future he dreamed for it, and the future I believe is coming, if those to whom he looked rally around it as I trust they will do now. It will have a future compared with which anything you have seen will seem little. I speak not of the plans of an idle dreamer, but of a great projecting mind who knew whereof he thought and hoped. . . .
>
> James P. Boyce was a genuine man, . . . made out of good timber all the way through. Who ever found a flaw in his make-up? That is a very strong statement. That is surely the very highest character a man can have in this world, to be thoroughly genuine all the way through. And I bear that testimony personally as one who knew him better than I knew my own brother. . . .
>
> What an adviser he was. Ah, there were so many occasions when no counsel but his would do, and that cannot be had anymore. He had great knowledge of character, great insight. I thought he was prejudiced sometimes, as everyone is likely to be, but oftener than otherwise, it would turn out that he was right, for good or ill.
>
> He was a man of very strong convictions, and very decided opinions, and immense tenacity of purpose, a man who knew why he thought a thing was right and knew why he was determined to do something; and yet it was never impossible to convince him that he was wrong. It was not easy, but it was never impossible. There was no pride of pertinacity, no reluctance at all to listen to opposing opinions and weigh the argument; but strong in conviction, decided in opinion and tenacious of purpose because he saw good reason for it, and as long as he saw no sufficient reason to the contrary. . . .

---

[68] G. W. Samson to John A. Broadus, 5 Feb. 1889, box 12, Broadus Papers.

He was a man utterly regardless of personal considerations, where he was sure he was doing right, and ever willing to wait for a better judgment if he be misjudged. And yet he was surpassingly considerate of other people's wishes and opinions.

In the highest and broadest sense of that term our friend was a generous man. His whole view of mankind had something generous about it. He liked to think well of people if he could. He was always glad to give other people with whom he was associated the amplest meed of commendation for their joint work. If he was ever extravagant in language it was when he praised his friends. In the ordinary sense of generosity, nobody can ever tell, as has been already said, in how many beautifully delicate ways he manifested it. . . .

He was a man of honor. . . . He was a Christian gentleman. That ought to be the highest style of man. I never saw him impatient about anything except where someone had been ungentlemanly in speech or action; he could not bear it.

He was a very deep and strong thinker. People who knew him in business and saw what a knowledge of business he possessed could hardly be persuaded that he was a great student or thinker; and yet I never knew a man who combined those two each in so high a degree. . . .

He was a man of remarkable general attainments. His reading in politics was very wide, and his ideas of political questions came out in conversation sometimes in a way to startle men who had devoted their lives to such subjects. I never knew a man who had read so much of recent poetry as he had, and it was a mark of his talent that a man so engrossed in other things should take so much delight in poetry. He was rich in his make-up, exhibiting a love of art in every way. He would stand entranced before a beautiful picture.[69]

A man's character does not prove the truth of his religious convictions, but it necessarily reflects them. The testimony of Boyce's character and deeds lends credibility and attractiveness to his theological commitments and to his *Abstract of Systematic Theology*.

Boyce's Theology

Boyce's theological convictions were of the evangelical Protestant variety and were decidedly in the traditionally orthodox category. His theology, Broadus explained, was also distinctly Calvinist: "James P. Boyce from profound conviction and life-long study was led to believe that the Bible teaches that which

---

[69] John A. Broadus, "Address of Dr. John A. Broadus at the Funeral of James P. Boyce," *Seminary Magazine* 2 (1889): 51–52.

men call for praise or blame by the name of Calvinism. If you want to see old fashioned straight-forward Calvinism drawn right out of the Bible with full sincerity of conviction and with infinite painstaking, you will read it in his *Abstract of Systematic Theology*."[70]

Calvinism was the prevailing theology of Baptists in the nineteenth-century South and was expressed clearly in the creeds of the churches and associations, but commitment to it was not uniform or universal.[71] A significant number rejected the doctrine of "limited atonement" and the rest did not make belief in it a condition of fellowship. But the churches and associations generally refused fellowship with pastors or churches who rejected other aspects of Calvinism.[72]

The non-Landmark leaders of the southeastern states drew on a well established Calvinist tradition. Jeremiah B. Jeter, president of the Foreign Mission Board and a seminary trustee, explained to his readers that Baptists believed in predestination. God "elects or predestinates some to be saved," and others "are destined to be lost."[73] Samuel Boykin, editor of *Kinds Words* and other Sunday school publications, explained that since Christ's death was vicarious, it was "necessary to limit the extent of his atonement to the number of those for whom he died."[74] Henry H. Tucker, editor of Georgia's *Christian Index* and president of Mercer University, taught in striking terms the doctrines of total depravity, predestination, and particular redemption.[75] David Shaver, another editor of Georgia's *Christian Index*, wrote that the rejection of the distinctive teachings of Calvinism was a passage "to grievous forms of error—an avenue in which Henry Ward Beecher stands but midway."[76] C. T. Bailey, editor of North Carolina's *Biblical Recorder*, reassured his readers of his orthodoxy by affirming

---

[70] Broadus, "Address" *Seminary Magazine* 2 (1889): 51–52.

[71] See E. Brooks Holifield, *Theology in America: Christian Thought from the Age of the Puritans to the Civil War* (New Haven, CT: Yale University Press, 2003), 273–290; Thomas J. Nettles, *By His Grace and for His Glory: A Historical, Theological, and Practical Study of the Doctrines of Grace in Baptist Life* (Grand Rapids, MI: Baker, 1986); Anthony L. Chute, A *Piety above a Common Standard: Jesse Mercer and the Defense of Evangelistic Calvinism* (Macon, GA: Mercer University Press, 2004).

[72] See e.g. Minutes, Chattahoochee Baptist Association, 1871, in manuscript minute book, 76.

[73] Jeremiah B. Jeter, "Queries," *Religious Herald*, 16 May 1878, 2.

[74] Samuel Boykin, "Extent of the Atonement," *Christian Index*, 6 Mar. 1861, 2.

[75] See e.g. H. H. Tucker, "The Doctrine of Election," *Christian Index*, 29 Jan. 1880, 4; Tucker, "Election—Fatalism," ibid., 4 Mar. 1880, 4; Tucker, "The Divine Particularity in the Salvation of Sinners," ibid., 25 Mar. 1880, 4; Tucker, "Total Depravity," ibid., 15 Feb. 1883, 8.

[76] David Shaver, "Calvinism," *Christian Index*, 26 Oct. 1871, 166.

that he believed "in the doctrine of predestination and personal election."[77] The creeds adopted by the churches and associations reflected these commitments.

The Baptist leaders of the southwest, many of whom embraced the distinctive views of Landmark Baptist leader James R. Graves, were also keen to advance Calvinism in the nineteenth century. Graves himself disavowed the label of Calvinism but nonetheless advocated traditional five-point Calvinism. When Graves was preparing to debate Methodist preacher Jacob Ditzler on baptism, communion, and perseverance in 1875, he asked Broadus's advice on defending "limited atonement" from objections based on 1 John 2:2 and 2 Corinthians 5:19. His argument, he told Broadus was "wholly based on the covenant of redemption. Christ undertook to save those his Father gave him—for these he died. These he ransomed by his death."[78] Graves did indeed establish the doctrine of perseverance on the covenant of redemption, including total depravity, unconditional election, limited atonement, and irresistible grace.[79] Jesus was the "surety, mediator, only for 'the seed of Abraham'—the elect of mankind." Their names "were put in the eternal contract" and none for whom Christ died would be lost. There was "no universal atonement."[80]

Landmark leader James B. Gambrell, editor of Mississippi's *Baptist Record* and later editor of Texas's *Baptist Standard* and executive secretary of the Texas Baptist Convention, assured Mississippi Baptists that he believed "most fully and firmly in predestination" and that "all the saved will owe their salvation to predestination."[81] He held that although men were "free agents," acting as they chose, their free agency "does not prevent God's governing men as he chooses." God "can cause men to do freely what he wishes them to do." Gambrell also taught particular redemption: "Those for whom Christ atoned must be pardoned . . . If justice is satisfied, who shall lay any charge against God's elect, for whom Christ died? The sacrifice of the Lamb of God . . . makes the salvation of all for whom it is offered certain."[82] Jesus bore the sins of the elect only, Gambrell wrote, for "Christ pays with his blood . . . and gets all he pays for."[83]

---

[77] C. T. Bailey, "Personal and Other Items," *Biblical Recorder*, 13 July 1881, 2.

[78] James R. Graves to John A. Broadus, 1 Nov. 1875, box 6, Broadus Papers.

[79] James R. Graves, *The Graves-Ditzler, or, Great Carrollton Debate: Final Perseverance*, vol. VI (Memphis, TN: Southern Baptist Publication Society, 1876), 1126–1142.

[80] Graves, *Graves-Ditzler*, 1136, 1138.

[81] James B. Gambrell, "Free Agency," *Baptist Record*, 8 Nov. 1877, 2; ibid., "Note," *Baptist Record*, 23 May 1878, 2.

[82] James B. Gambrell, "Bro. Everett on the Atonement," *Baptist Record*, 9 Jan. 1879, 2.

[83] James B. Gambrell, "Eld. J. P. Everett on the Atonement," *Biblical Recorder*, 30 Jan. 1879, 2.

Joseph Creath, a career missionary in Texas and president of the Texas Baptist Convention, "thrilled" delegates at the 1867 meeting of the Southern Baptist Convention by his "rugged eloquence," and assured them that he was sound, being an "old-fashioned predestinarian Baptist."[84] R. M. Dudley, editor of Kentucky's *Western Recorder* and afterward president of Georgetown College, explained that the "old Pauline doctrine of predestination" taught that "God determined before the foundation of the world that certain individuals should become the heirs of salvation."[85] Landmark leader Thomas T. Eaton, editor of the *Western Recorder* from 1887 to 1907 and a seminary trustee, took it for granted that Baptists were Calvinists: "The essence of Baptist doctrine, called usually the great Calvinistic faith, is that it makes God great."[86]

The number of Southern Baptists who opposed Calvinism or were indifferent to it was sufficient to alarm many Baptist preachers. Few Southern Baptists were Arminians—probably none among the clergy—but many held "lax views" of the doctrine of election, most commonly by teaching that God elected persons because he foresaw that they would repent and believe.[87] G. T. Wilburn worried in 1874 that many Texas Baptists rejected the doctrine of election or made election dependent on God's foreknowledge, but assured readers that many others were "faithful contenders of the truth" and preferred "to please God rather than men."[88]

The trend strengthened in the early twentieth century. A few Baptist leaders of the era, William O. Carver perhaps above all, opposed Calvinism openly, but when they opposed it, they usually did not argue against its doctrines directly. They instead argued that the old statements of theology were not adequate for the needs of the modern church. They suggested not that the Calvinism was wrong but that it was passé. And so it seemed to be.

Fears of defection from Calvinist doctrine led Baptist leaders to urge the importance of defending and promoting it. Rufus C. Burleson, president of Baylor University in Texas and a seminary trustee, urged his fellow pastors in

---

[84] Joseph W. D. Creath, quoted in Richard Furman (II), "The Convention at Memphis," *South Carolina Baptist*, 14 June 1867, 2.

[85] R. M. Dudley, "Predestination and Free Salvation," *Western Recorder*, 5 Nov. 1870, 2.

[86] T. T. Eaton, quoted in A. J. S. Thomas, "Brag Will Out," *Baptist Courier*, 16 Mar. 1893, 2.

[87] B. W. Whilden, "Baptist Confession of Faith and the Doctrine of Election," *Baptist Sentinel* 2 (1871): 409. See also David Shaver, "Calvinism," *Christian Index*, 26 Oct. 1871, 166.

[88] G. T. Wilburn, "Texas Baptists," *Christian Index*, 2 Apr. 1874, 2. See similarly, E. F. T., "The Texas Baptist State Convention," *South Carolina Baptist*, 30 Oct. 1868, 2.

1849 to preach such doctrines as "total depravity" and "election," even if "contending for our doctrines will diminish our popularity."[89] David Shaver agreed that the Calvinist doctrines were unpopular in general society, but reminded his fellow Baptist ministers that "we must faithfully proclaim them."[90] James B. Gambrell repeatedly urged the importance of preaching such doctrines as election and depravity.[91]

Boyce and the seminary faculty taught Calvinism because they discovered it in the Bible. It was, they said, the doctrine of Jesus and Paul. The system of doctrine "commonly called Calvinism," Broadus wrote, "is believed by many of us to be really the teaching of the apostle Paul."[92] Boyce taught a traditional five-point Calvinism. It was the doctrine of the founders of the Philadelphia and Charleston Baptist associations, and of such preachers as Richard Furman and Jesse Mercer, who initiated the great missionary and educational organizations of Baptists in the South. These facts made the doctrine more dear to Boyce, but they did not make it true. Above all, he held the doctrine because he found it in the Bible. This was the theology that sustained and guided him.

The Abstract of Systematic Theology

Boyce assigned a variety of textbooks for his systematic theology courses over the years: John L. Dagg's *Manual of Theology*, John Dick's *Lectures on Theology*, Charles Hodge's *Systematic Theology*, J.J. Van Oosterzee's *Christian Dogmatics*, Alvah Hovey's *Manual of Systematic Theology*, A. A. Hodge's *Outlines of Theology*, and finally his own condensed *Abstract of Systematic Theology*. In his Latin theology course he assigned Francis Turretin's classic statement of Calvinist doctrine, *Institutio Theologiae Elencticae*.[93] Boyce required students

---

[89] Rufus C. Burleson, "The Importance of Sound Doctrine," in Union Baptist Association (Texas), *Minutes*, 1849, 6–7.

[90] David Shaver, "Calvinism and Policy," *Christian Index*, 10 Sept. 1868, 142.

[91] James B. Gambrell, "Free Agency," *Baptist Record*, 8 Nov. 1877, 2; Gambrell, "Calvinism and Arminianism, or Predestination and Free Agency," ibid., 20 June 1878, 2; Gambrell, "Anti-ism," ibid., 1 Sept. 1881, 2; Gambrell, note concerning Isaiah Watson, "Bible Election vs. Arminian Election," *Baptist Standard*, 21 Sept. 1911, 22; Gambrell, "Predestination in a Storm," ibid., 3 Oct. 1912, 1; Gambrell, "Editorial Notes and Comment," ibid., 28 Aug. 1913, 8.

[92] John A. Broadus, *Memoir of Boyce*, 310; see also ibid., 73.

[93] James P. Boyce to John A. Broadus, 10 Oct. 1860, box 1, Broadus Papers; John Stout to Fanny Coker, 18 Sept. 1869, Lide-Coker-Stout Family Papers, South Caroliniana Library, University of South Carolina; James P. Boyce to John A. Broadus, 30 Aug. 1878, box 8, Broadus Papers; Broadus, *Memoir of Boyce*, 268, 304–307.

to memorize the outline of the analysis of each doctrine, but wanted them to be able to explain each idea or argument in their own language. Boyce entered into discussions with classes on the various topics and gave his own ideas throughout the course.

None of the textbooks, however, had the combination of readability, comprehensiveness, compactness, and suitability that he wanted. Over the years he developed more and more lectures of his own, and finally, in 1882, printed a small edition of his lectures to serve as his textbook. He revised and rewrote the lectures to produce the printed edition in 1887.

Boyce omitted discussion of canon, inspiration, ecclesiology, and polemics because these topics received careful treatment in other courses in the seminary curriculum. Although Boyce designed the book for use in his course in systematic theology, the book is well suited to the needs of the ordinary reader who is seeking to understand the Bible's teaching.

Boyce's *Abstract of Systematic Theology* remained the textbook of the seminary's systematic theology courses for thirty years after its publication. Boyce's successor as professor of systematic theology, Franklin H. Kerfoot, published a revised edition of Boyce's *Abstract of Systematic Theology* in 1899. Kerfoot's successor in systematic theology, seminary president Edgar Y. Mullins, continued to assign Boyce's *Abstract of Systematic Theology* until 1917, when he published his own textbook, *The Christian Religion in Its Doctrinal Expression*.

In the early twentieth century, Southern Baptists viewed the *Abstract of Systematic Theology* as an exemplary expression of Baptist orthodoxy. When, for example, Mullins received letters questioning the soundness of the seminary's doctrine in 1908, he certified the seminary's soundness by appealing to the fact that Boyce's *Abstract of Systematic Theology* was the textbook in systematic theology courses.[94] When a correspondent asked Mullins about how to know what Baptists believed, he replied that if he wanted to learn the doctrines of Baptists, he "could not do better than get a copy of Dr. J. P. Boyce's *Abstract of Systematic Theology*."[95] When W. O. Carver came under intense criticism for his views on the virgin birth of Christ in 1914, he satisfied his critics by professing his agreement with Boyce's statements concerning the matter in the *Abstract of Systematic Theology*.[96]

---

[94] See e.g. Mullins to H. G. Garrett, 14 Sept. 1908, Letterpress Book 34, Jan. 20, 1908-Jan. 2, 1909, Archives and Special Collections, SBTS, 501.

[95] Mullins to Robert Strange, 15 Oct. 1908, Letterpress Book 34, Jan. 20, 1908-Jan. 2, 1909, Archives and Special Collections, SBTS, 638.

[96] W. O. Carver to J. W. Porter, 2 July 1914, William O. Carver Papers, box 23, folder 49, Southern Baptist Historical Library and Archives, Nashville, TN.

The direct influence of Boyce's *Abstract of Systematic Theology* waned after 1917, but the memory of Boyce's judicious leadership, grand vision, and heroic sacrifices endured through the twentieth century and ensured that his influence on Southern Baptists and especially on Southern Seminary endured. And as a result, interest in his *Abstract of Systematic Theology* revived in the late twentieth century.

Let us study Boyce's theology. And let us sustain John Broadus's wish concerning Boyce's legacy: "May the men who teach and the men who learn in the seminary which he beyond all other persons put together built up, feel still the impress of that high character, that noble simplicity, that genuineness, that love of God, that faith in prayer, that simple, humble hope of heaven, that willingness to turn from the highest earthly inducements and live a life of sacrifice to accomplish something for the good of man and the glory of God."[97]

Gregory A. Wills is dean of the School of Theology and professor of church history at The Southern Baptist Theological Seminary. He is the author of *Southern Baptist Theological Seminary, 1859–2009* (Oxford University Press, 2009).

---

[97] Broadus, "Address of Dr. John A. Broadus at the Funeral of James P. Boyce," *Seminary Magazine* 2 (1889): 53.

PREFACE

by James P. Boyce
to the first edition of
Abstract of Systematic Theology

THIS volume is published the rather as a practical text book, for the study of the system of doctrine taught in the Word of God, than as a contribution to theological science. It was originally prepared for the use of the classes taught by its author, and is indeed but a reprint with numerous and extensive alterations and additions of a book privately printed in 1882, exclusively for his students. He hopes that other teachers may find it useful as a text book for class instruction. It may also be of value to the large number of pastors who have had no advantages of seminary study, or to others who may choose to take up again the subject of which it treats, after the method which is herewith suggested. The experience such pastors have already had, and the knowledge, though only partial, heretofore acquired, will make this very practicable, even without the aid of an instructor. In writing the book for his pupils, the author found it necessary, while attempting a comprehensive exhibit of Systematic Theology to make it so brief as to be within the compass of about one hundred recitations. This was made possible by omitting extensive exegetical discussions, and by presenting theology with as little reference as possible to its polemical aspects. The separate existence of schools of Exegesis and of Polemic Theology, in the institution in which he was teaching, made this not only practicable but advisable. For a like reason there are not here discussed such matters as belong to what is commonly known as Church Government. These have been taught by the author in a school separate from that of Systematic Theology. The material appropriate to these other schools of instruction will therefore only be found in this book when necessary for the proper presentation of some topic belonging to Systematic Theology.

It ought to be added that the study of the text book has been accompanied by familiar talks by the professor, by free discussions with his pupils, which are always encouraged, and has been supplemented by extensive reading in the Latin Systematic Theology class of the works of Turretine and Aquinas and other writers in the Latin language.

The author deems it appropriate to state the method of instruction which he has always pursued. Thus will not only be exhibited the reason why this science is presented in this abbreviated form, but also suggested to private students, as well as teachers, what seems to him the most effective method of study for the mastery of any subject. There are special reasons why such thorough work should be applied to Systematic Theology.

In the use of this method the student is taught to prepare a brief but accurate analysis of each lesson. With this thoroughly memorized, every paragraph is then studied so as to fix in the mind the thoughts presented in it. It is possible to do this with great minuteness. With this preparation the recitation is made without the use of questions, not in the very words of the book, but in such as naturally proceed from the attempt to state all the thoughts of the lesson. This will be found to be quite difficult at first, and will make it necessary that the earlier lessons be very short—of only three or four pages. But the student will very soon acquire great facility, not only in preparing these analyses, but also in reciting from them. The Advance lesson of one day is repeated as an Immediate Review on the next. After five or six lessons in connection with the Advance and Immediate Review, a Back Review is made comprising the equivalent of two Advance lessons. This soon goes over the ground already covered in the Advance, and permits the beginning of another Back Review. This is followed by another Back Review, and yet again by others until the book is finished; each series of the Back Reviews being an increase in length of the one which had preceded it. The student will thus be constantly advancing, and at the same time reviewing, until, on the completion of the book, he will have so fully mastered all its contents as to be perfectly familiar with every portion of it, and to be able to recall any part of it at will.

The usefulness of this method of study is not urged upon the single experience of the author of this work. It had been for some time in use when he was a student in Brown University, over forty years ago, and has not only been continued there ever since, but has been adopted by numerous other teachers, who there learned its great value. It not only accomplishes the mastery of any study, but it trains the mind in analyzing and remembering readily any book that may be read, or discourse that may be heard. It cultivates the memory to a marvelous degree. It especially begets logical accuracy and arrangement of thought. It is also one of the best means of cultivating readiness of extemporaneous speech. Could the writer illustrate these points from his experience, both as a pupil and instructor, he is sure that many would be led to undergo the great labour in the beginning for the greater profit in the end of pursuing this plan of study.

The author has aimed to make the discussions in this volume especially Scriptural. He believes in the perfect inspiration and absolute authority of the divine revelation, and is convinced that the best proof of any truth is that it is there taught. He questions, indeed, whether man can know with absolute certainty any truth which is not thus uttered by God. Into all else must enter the liability to error which arises from human imperfection. So far, therefore, as the Scriptures speak, and so far only does man have certainty of knowledge. This has led, therefore, in the proofs presented, to the constant quotation of the language of Holy Writ. In this reprint these have been all taken from the Canterbury Revision as furnishing the most accurate translation into English of the inspired originals. Such proofs should always be most satisfactory to pastors for their own use, and most efficacious in the proclamation of the truth to their hearers.

The presentation of truth in the Scriptures, however, is not made by mere statement only, but also by emphasis of statement. Its true aspects are like those of a country or continent, not to be measured only by lines and angles, but by elevations and depressions; or like the execution of a piece of music which is not sufficiently accomplished by the striking of the correct notes, but by giving each its due length of time, its due emphasis of touch, with that expression which is only possible for one whose soul enters into the harmony of sound, and to whom the music speaks thought as distinctly as would written or spoken words. The possession of such soul-sympathy with the Divine Word and the power to feel and express, with delicate exactness, the true measure and weight of its emphasis of statement would give the system of theology in all the perfection which Revelation affords. The lack of this is the great cause of difference of doctrinal sentiment among those who really revere and gladly receive the Scriptures as God's Word. The tendency of Calvinists, for example, is to emphasize, perhaps too strongly, the sovereignty of God, and to receive only in a guarded manner the statements as to the freedom of the human will. That of Arminians is exactly the reverse. The differences between these are due not to any contrariety of teaching in the Word of God, but to human failure to emphasize correctly. It is not probable that this can ever be wholly avoided. But it is unquestioned wisdom and duty to approach so far as possible unto perfection. In order to secure unity Christians are often urged to ignore their differences and unite upon the great points of general agreement. But the better plan is to recognize these differences as starting-points for such investigations as shall result in greater nearness to the truth, and therefore in greater nearness to each other. To this end it is necessary that a system of theology should be mapped out before the human mind. The more correct the system the better will it be. But one had better have an incorrect system than none at all. To this every reading of the Word of God, and indeed all study of divine truth will contribute; to verify it, to correct it, to add to it, to take away from it, and to test and adjust its emphasis of statement. It is necessary only to remember always that the system in the mind is a survey of the truth, and not the truth itself. The worst map a surveyor can obtain is better than none at all, though it gives him only a starting-point. If any of the metes and bounds can be established there will be great gain. As the land becomes more familiar the map can be made more perfect. The lines and angles having been fixed, the measurements of the elevations and depressions can be added, and the survey finally made as exact as the instruments will allow.

The map of theological science has already, in great part, been agreed upon. But it is necessary that such accepted facts be received in their exact statement and their proper emphasis, and not be magnified nor emasculated because of any special theories or any unwillingness to believe what God has taught.

Hence the value of this method of study, which, by a thorough mastery of it, maps out theology in the mind and furnishes the basis for future corrections or additions. This book is published from a desire to lead many others to such study, and to furnish a practical means of pursuing it. The author fervently prays God to bless it to this end, as well as to all other useful purposes for which it may be a fit instrument.

Chapter 1

The Science of Theology

THE word Theology means literally a discourse concerning God, but in analogy with other words, as geology, chronology and biology, it means the science which treats of God.

It naturally concerns itself with such questions as these: Is there a God; can he be known; what is his nature, and character; what are the relations he sustains to the universe, particularly to intelligent beings possessed of spiritual natures, and above all, as most important to us, to men; in what ways has he made himself known; and especially in what aspect does he reveal himself to them as sinner. This is Theology proper.

In connection with this last relation it treats, particularly, of man as a creature of God placed under the government of his moral law. It inquires into his original condition of innocence, and happiness; the manner in which he fell therefrom; and his present state of sinfulness, and condemnation and inability for self-rescue. This is Anthropology.

It is thus led, also, to discuss the nature of the salvation which God has provided as seen in the person and character of Jesus Christ, through whom it has come, and in the works of active and passive obedience, by which he has wrought out reconciliation to God. This is Soteriology.

In like manner, also, does it consider the nature and work of the Holy Spirit, through whom man is led to accept the provisions of God's grace, and to attain through penitence and faith unto a salvation in Christ, which consists in freedom, not from condemnation only, but also from the dominion and defilement of sin, and in attainment of the holiness and happiness of children of the Heavenly Father. This is Pneumatology.

It follows man also beyond the death of the body, and makes known the future state of both the righteous and the wicked, as we before as after the resurrection of the body, together with the final judgment of both these classes, and the heaven and hell which shall be their respective abodes forever. This is Eschatology.

Finally it teaches the great end which God is accomplishing through all his works, in the manifestation to all his creatures of his own glory, as seen in its twofold aspect of mercy and justice in his dealings with this fallen race of man. This is Teleology.

1

The term "theology" is applied, not only to the science itself, but to any treatise on that science. This is true, not only of a discourse upon the one true God, but even of one upon the many false gods of the heathen. It is also true, though the treatise be not a scientific discussion, but simply an imaginative narrative or poem. Thus "Orpheus and Homer were called theologians among the Greeks, because their poems treated of the nature of the gods." (Charles Hodge Sys. Theol. Vol. 1, p. 19.) Even the poems of Ossian, though probably written in England within the past century, is a book of theology. Mythology is not less theology because it treats of false gods, and in works of the imagination.

The term "theology" is, however, especially applicable to learned and scientific works upon God, or the gods. Of these, many are to be found connected with Heathenism. Such are the Vedas, the most ancient of the sacred books of the Hindoos. Such is the Zendavesta of the ancient Persians. The Edda, which sets forth the Scandinavian mythology, consists of poetic songs, and also of dialogues on the origin of the gods, on the creation of the world, and other like topics. [See Gardner's Faiths of the World, Vol. 1, p. 795.]

The most valuable discussions among the heathen, however, are to be found in the works of the Greek philosophers, the greater part of which, when not directly upon the nature of the gods, involved questions as to the origin, of the world, and the presence therein of a divine controlling Spirit, as well as upon the nature of the soul, and its duties, and its immortality. Of their works many have come down to us in fragments only, while a large portion of what they taught is found only in the records and reports made by others; but there are also many complete works which profess to have been written by the authors of these speculations. Confessedly the most important of these Greek writings are Xenophon's Memorabilia of Socrates, and the works of Plato, and Aristotle. But from the beginning of Grecian philosophy in Thales and Pythagoras to its culmination in Socrates, Plato, and Aristotle, was not quite two hundred years, while its whole history covers a period of six centuries and a half before, and five centuries after the coming of Christ. No human mind can estimate the value of these contributions, nor the influence they have exerted even over those possessed of the Christian Revelation.

The Latin writers also produced several works of a theological character, pre-eminent among which is that of Cicero "Concerning the nature of the Gods."

Theology is, also, frequently used for the set of opinions exhibited by a writer, or class of writers, in any one or more productions. Thus we have the theology of Calvin, or of Arminius, or of Baxter, that of the Reformation, Princeton theology, and New England theology. Men also speak of the theology of the Old, or of the New Testament, the theology of the Psalms, of the various Evangelists, especially of John, and Petrine, and Pauline theology.

Theology is defined as a science. It is eminently worthy of that name. It lacks nothing that constitutes a science. It is concerned in the investigation of facts. It inquires into their existence, their relations to each other, their systematic arrangement, the laws which govern them, and the great principles which are the basis of this existence, and these relations.

As in other sciences, there is much that is absolutely known, much beyond this that is little questioned, much that is still matter of speculation, and much as to which there is decided difference of opinion. New facts are constantly developing in this science, as in others, which enable us to verify the facts and principles heretofore accepted, when true, and to modify them when erroneous. New theories present themselves for the better explanation of facts already known, and are tested by these, and by others subsequently discovered, and are received or rejected, according to their ascertained correctness. The knowledge of the past is built upon for progression towards the future.

The discovery of the facts is conducted, as in all other sciences, by study of what the field affords. Geology examines the earth, and derives its facts from the structure of that earth. Astronomy investigates the stars. Theology, likewise, studies the sources of its knowledge. Each science seeks to arrive at the truth. The votaries of each are certain that it is to be found in their fields, either partially, or completely. The perfect attainment of all facts prepares for the exactness of scientific knowledge. The absence of any must make the knowledge incomplete. The proper generalization of all is essential in this, as in all other kinds of science. A full knowledge of all the facts, and a perfect generalization of them, will constitute theology an exact science.

Theology is also as sensitive to the absence of facts as is any other science. The astronomer finds that his calculations, based upon correct theories, are not exactly verified, and at once suspects the presence of some disturbing body as the cause of this variation. So, also, in theology. The omission of a single fact, however small, must affect the whole universe of doctrine. The common mind does not perceive this, and hence is not prepared to value the discovery of the new fact. But the theologian finds in the new and more exact adjustment, thus made possible, the proof of the truth of his whole system, and therefore prizes it, even sometimes beyond what he ought.

Regarded as a science, theology may be classified in various forms.

1. According to the method of revelation, into natural and supernatural theology.

Natural theology embraces what man may attain by the study of God in Nature. This extends not only to what is beheld of him in the Heavens and the Earth, but also in the intellectual and spiritual nature of man himself.

Supernatural theology is that derived from such special information as God has given by what we commonly call Revelation.

2. According to the purpose which it contemplates, into Systematic Theology, also called Didactic, or Dogmatic; Polemic or Controversial Theology; and Practical or Experimental Theology.

3. According to the main religious idea associated with it, as Pantheistic Theology; Deistic Theology; Rationalistic Theology, etc.

4. According to the name of its founder, or the race in which it originated, or flourishes, as Christian Theology; Judaistic Theology; Mohammedan Theology, etc.

5. According to the sources from which it is derived, into Biblical Theology; Christian Dogmatic Theology; and Ecclesiastical Dogmatics.

Biblical Theology consists in the facts of the Bible, harmonized by scriptural comparison, generalized by scriptural theories, crystalized into scriptural doctrines, and so systematized as to show the system of truth taught, to the full extent that it is a system, and no farther. As in Botany, one gathers all the plants of the world, and arranges them without attempting to introduce new plants, even to fill up manifest gaps, so Biblical Theology, duly presented, shows scriptural truth in all the perfection, and in all the imperfection with which God has given it.

True Biblical Theology should recognize the inspired source whence come its teachings. But, as now technically used, Biblical Theology refers to the statement and development of doctrine by the various Biblical writers, or in other words to the development of Jewish religious thought without assuming or denying the inspiration of the Bible.

Christian Dogmatics is not confined, as is Biblical, to the facts and theories and statements of doctrine expressly and formally set forth in the Scriptures. It comprises in addition such philosophical explanations as seem necessary to make a complete and harmonious system. These additions are not necessarily non-scriptural, for they are often the embodiment of the very essence of Bible truth, though not of its formal utterances. They may be as much a part of Scripture as the theory of gravitation is of the revelation of nature. They should never be so far unscriptural as not to be either probable inferences from the Word of God or natural explanations of its statements. The more perfectly they accord with that word, and the greater the proportion of its facts which they explain, the more clearly do they establish their own truth, and the more forcibly do they demand universal acceptance. Failure to explain all difficulties or to harmonize all facts does not deprive them of confidence, but only teaches the need of further investigation. Direct opposition, however, to any one scriptural truth is enough to prove the existence of error in any Christian Dogmatic statement.

Ecclesiastical Dogmatics consists of authoritative statements of doctrine put forth by some body of Christians claiming to be a church of Christ. These are to be found in creeds, symbols, decrees, apologies and resolutions. They may also appear in the form of authoritative discussions of the creed or system of doctrine of any church.

It thus appears that a perfect system of theology will combine all of these classes. It must be based upon Biblical Dogmatics which shall have so collected and systematized all the teachings of a full revelation as to be concurrent with the facts and doctrines of Christian Dogmatics.

The Ecclesiastical Dogmatics will have gone no farther than fully authorized by the Word of God, and therefore will concur with Biblical Dogmatics, while the fullness of revelation will have left to Christian Dogmatics no speculative questions; but in all its discussions it will have been able to attain unto full knowledge of the facts, and ascertainment of all the doctrines.

But this concurrence can only be when Theology has been reduced to an exact science. This can never be looked for in this life.

The causes of doctrinal variation will therefore be apparent.

If men came to the study of Biblical Theology with minds entirely unprejudiced, capable of examining its truths with the same mental powers, and with the same amount of study, all would agree as to its facts and doctrines. But this cannot be done. Mental capacities vary. All men have their prejudices. All have not equal time for study, and all use not equally the time that they have. Thus variety is certain even in studying Biblical Theology.

The same causes increase this in Christian Dogmatics, because here the human element enters more largely than in Biblical Theology; while reverence for antiquity, opposition to change, and the influence of the learned of the past and the present, prevent the alteration of Ecclesiastical creeds which embody Ecclesiastical Dogmatics, and thus lead men constantly to continuance in error, and refusal to accept truth.

These facts show with what spirit we should study Theology:

1. With reverence for truth, and especially for the truth taught in the Word of God.

2. With earnest prayer for Divine help.

3. With careful searching of heart against prejudice.

4. With timidity, as to the reception and propagation of new doctrine.

5. But with a spirit willing and anxious to examine, and to accept whatever we may be convinced is true.

6. With teachable humility, which, knowing that God has not taught us in his Word all the truth that exists, not even all the truth on many a single point, accepts with implicit faith all that he has taught, and awaits his own time for that more full revelation which shall remove all our present perplexities.

The advantages of studying theology systematically are several.

1. We thus ascertain all that nature and the Scriptures teach on each point.

2. We compare all these teachings one with another and are enabled to define their mutual limitations.

3. We are brought face to face with the fact that our knowledge is bounded by God's Revelation, and are led to acknowledge it as its source.

4. We are consequently warned not to omit any of the truth ascertained from any source, nor to add to it anything not properly embraced therein. A departure from this rule will lead into inevitable error.

5. The harmony, and consistency, which will be found in all God's teachings, from whatever source we may draw them, will become conclusive proof of the divine origin of revelation. This will result, not only from a comparison of what Reason and Nature teach, with the revelations of God's Word, but of each of the several books of the Bible with the others, and especially of the body of the Old Testament as one book, with that of the New Testament as another.

6. We are thus led to value each of the doctrines of the Word of God. Each is true. Each has been revealed that it might be believed. We cannot therefore omit any one, because of its forbidding aspect, or its seeming unimportance, or its mysterious nature, or its demand for great personal sacrifice, or its humiliating assertions, or requirements, or the free terms upon which it assures of life and salvation.

CHAPTER 2

THE BEING OF GOD

THE fundamental doctrine of Theology is that there is a God; for if this is not true, there can be no science of God.

The first duty of Theology, therefore, is to set forth the reasons men have for believing that such a being exists, and is a true object of dependence and worship.

I. GOD CAN BE SUFFICIENTLY KNOWN

1. It is objected, however, to any science of God, that, if there is a God, he cannot be so known and comprehended as to be a true object of worship.

(1.) If by this is meant that we cannot know the essential nature of God, it proceeds upon a principle upon which we can know nothing, for we do not know the essential nature of anything. We know not even the nature of our own essence. We cannot know that of any existent being or substance, not indeed of the smallest atom of matter. We can only judge what it must be from the qualities it is perceived to possess, or from its outward manifestations. In like manner we can discover something of the nature of God from the different ways in which he has manifested himself in ourselves and in the universe.

(2.) If it is claimed that we cannot know him because his nature may be or must be wholly different from ours, the natural answer is that we do know many things which differ greatly from the mind which takes cognizance of them. Thus our own bodies, though purely material, are known through our mental faculties, and yet we believe mind and matter to be essentially diverse. We comprehend also our modes of existence, and those of other objects in time and space, though these modes are essentially different from the things which exist in them.

Besides, until we know what God is, we cannot be sure that he is in all respects different from ourselves. If there are any points of similarity, we can know him so far as these exist; and, if it is true that we have been made, in any respect, in the likeness and image of God, our knowledge of God may approach at least to such completeness as to enable us to recognize his more manifest perfections, and to perceive that because of these he ought to be reverenced and worshipped.

Guided by the analogy of our own natures we expect to find in him a personal, conscious, intelligent, and moral being, and this expectation is confirmed by the manifestations of his presence, and operations in the universe. This teaching of analogy is not worthless because it has also led some to believe that God has a material body, as has man. Analogy does not furnish proof, but only probability; in some instances only possibilities. It does not show what God is, but what he may be. That which it suggests is confirmed or denied by other sources of knowledge. But we are so far taught through its aid that we learn that God must either be a Spirit, such as we are, or that he must have a higher nature to which belong all those attributes of spirit which constitute conscious personality and intelligent purpose.

(3.) Does the objection mean that we cannot know God because we cannot come in contact with him through the senses as we do with our fellow-men, and cannot learn his nature through his conduct and personal action as we do theirs? But it is not only through personal contact with men that we know that they are and what they are; we both know and judge of them by their works, though we have never seen nor known them personally. In like manner through our senses are we brought into contact with God, who, though not material, is an artificer in material things, and has displayed before us, in the universe around, the evidences of his wisdom, power and goodness. Surely so great a structure as this, which manifests a grasp of thought, and a power of performance so wonderfully beyond that of any human being, and a minuteness of detail and execution and finish, the limitations of which defy discovery through the most powerful microscope that man can ever make, shows that it has been fashioned, if not created, by some being of personal purposing skill and power immeasurably beyond anything that we can possibly conceive.

(4.) Is it asserted that the outward phenomena of the universe cannot give such mental and spiritual knowledge of God as is essential to our apprehension and worship of him? Even were this true, we get that knowledge through our own spiritual and mental operations. We find in ourselves consciousness of existence, of thought and of purpose, and thus learn not only what these are in other intelligent beings, but that they must exist in every being whose nature is as high as, or higher than, that of man. We perceive that the mind is governed by laws no less binding and effective, no less regular and permanent, than those of matter. In the study of these we learn the nature of mind and spirit, not by direct apprehension of their essences, but, as in matter, by indirectly apprehending them through their phenomena. That nature we ascribe to the Divine Mind and Spirit. The differences of mental and spiritual capacities in men convince us that there are degrees of greater or less in mental and spiritual natures. Hence we assign to God mind and spirit in the highest degree, because as their author he must himself be greater than all his mental and spiritual creations.

But, in addition to this, we have a peculiar source of information. We find our minds capable of intuitive knowledge. Some abstract principles need only to be understood, and the conviction that they are true immediately follows. That "the whole is greater than any one of its parts" is perceived as soon as understood, as is likewise that "a thing cannot be, and not be, at the same time." Whence is this knowledge? We say that the mind is so constituted that it cannot believe otherwise. Who has so constituted it? It must proceed from some one upon whose veracity we rely, when we accept what our nature teaches. But, if from any one, then there is a creating mind, and that mind operates directly upon mind without the intervention of matter, and thus teaches us truth. When, then, we find other convictions of like nature relative to our dependent upon a higher being, our obligations of duty to him, our sense of right, and wrong, and the duty to do the right, and not to do the wrong, we cannot avoid believing that these intuitions come from the same source, and are his instructions to us as to our moral relations, and duties to him.

2. But it is further objected that, if there is a God we cannot know him because he must be the Absolute, the Infinite, the Unconditioned, and, therefore, cannot be an object of comprehension to us, whose nature is finite, and whose mode of existence is only relative, finite and conditioned.

But the objection itself presents its own refutation. How do we know that God must be such, if there is a God? In whatever way we know this, we know at least that much of God that he must be the Absolute, the Infinite, the Unconditioned. Even before we are supposed to know that he exists, therefore, we know this much of the nature which must be his, and upon the first evidence of his existence have the right to attribute to him all that is therein contained. The characteristics thus ascribed to him, reveal him, therefore, to us, as an infinite existence, without other limitations than are found in his own nature, or essence, who, as Absolute, cannot be dependent, but must be the source and Sovereign of all else; and, as the Unconditioned, cannot be subject to time, and space, and matter, and must therefore exist without possibility of growth, or increase, and without that succession of periods, such as yesterday, today, and tomorrow, and those measures of space, and location, which belong to matter. The God, therefore, who is thus proclaimed to be unknowable is at least known as a self-existent spirit, infinite, eternal and unchangeable in all the perfections that belong to his nature. Let but the least evidence appear that there is a God, and at once this nature may be ascribed to him.

The recognition and contemplation of such a being, though his other perfections are unknown, awaken the reverence and fear, and conviction of the littleness and dependence of man which enter so largely into the sense of the supernatural and lead men everywhere, when in danger or distress, to call upon God, though not moved to prayer by any promise of answers thereto.

3. Again, it is objected that though we should learn something of God, we can only attain partial knowledge of him. This is readily admitted. But partial knowledge is actual knowledge as far as it goes. We have complete knowledge of nothing. All our knowledge is partial. The child only partially knows its parent. The subject only partially knows his sovereign. Yet enough is known for the recognition of dependence, and of the duties of obedience and love. So, also, with the Heavenly Father, the King of Kings; although we can only know him in part, we know enough to lead us to revere his sovereign power, and gratefully adore his Fatherly affection. The Scripture teaching upon this subject is twofold.

(1.) It agrees with Agnosticism in asserting that God cannot be fully known. The questions of Zophar have been, with full reverence for God, and earnest worship for such an one as it is believed that he must be, the language of the pious of all ages. "Canst thou by searching find out God? Canst thou find out the Almighty unto perfection? It is as high as Heaven; what canst thou do? deeper than Hell; what canst thou know?" Job 11:7–8. Elizur is represented as saying, "Behold, God is great and we know him not." Job 36:26. And Job, after his description of God's acts of power, declared, "Lo, these are but the outskirts of his ways; and how small a whisper do we hear of him! But the thunder of his power who can understand?" Job 26:14. The Psalmist, referring to the omniscience and omnipresence of God, cried out, "Such knowledge is too wonderful for me; it is high, I cannot attain unto it." Ps. 139:6.

(2.) On the other hand, in opposition to Agnostics, the Bible declares that the partial knowledge of God attained by men is actual knowledge and not some inferior conception. God said through Jeremiah, "I will give them an heart to know me that I am the Lord" (Jer. 24:7), and again "they shall all know me from the least of them unto the greatest of them." Jer. 25:34. Our Lord himself, in his prayer to the Father, referring to those given to him that to them he should give eternal life declares "This is life eternal that they should know thee the only true God and him whom thou didst send, even Jesus Christ." John 17:3. The apostle who recorded this prayer uses this language, "He that knoweth God heareth us" (1 John 4:6), and also "He that loveth not, knoweth not God." 1 John 4:8.

The Bible, therefore, plainly teaches that God may be known, and so known as to be truly worshipped.

II. ALMOST UNIVERSAL BELIEF IN GOD; ITS SOURCES

Belief in the existence of God has been almost universal among men. The same ideal of perfection has not everywhere been found. Some have gone no farther than to be moved by the sense of the supernatural, and to believe in a power to which they are subject, and upon which they depend. But at least this much is to be found in the lowest forms of fetish worshippers. Others have multiplied the numbers and forms of those towards whom they have felt this sense of dependence, and have accepted the existence of many gods. Yet, among these polytheists, the traces of the One God have not entirely disappeared, for they have referred the gods themselves to one originating source. Some, following too closely the analogy of man's nature, have believed God to be the animating soul of the world. The highest spiritual conception of God has been found only in those nations which have been recipients of his revelation. But the most ancient records show that, in the earliest times, the knowledge possessed by all was comparatively simple and pure.

So universal has been this belief, that but very few of the millions of the race in all its ages have denied the existence of God. It has been questioned whether these few have been deceived as to their actual convictions, or have been insincere in their avowal of Atheism; because it has seemed so impossible for man not to believe in a God. A greater number still have been skeptical; sometimes led by wishes born of depravity and sin, but, also, sometimes misled by philosophical speculations, and apparently earnestly desirous to know the truth.

But the firm conviction of mankind in general that this belief is unavoidable in any man in his normal condition, and that its absence is due to some crushing out or erasure of his necessary moral capabilities, is seen, not only in the general horror which men have for those who profess Atheism, but in the denial to such men of the right to testify in the courts of justice.

1. This almost universal concurrence of men ought to be ascribe primarily to tradition.

Belief in God has been handed down from parent to child through out all past generations. Some theologians are unwilling to recognize this fact or to accept it as a cause of the universal belief in God. Some have sought that cause in the idea of God as innate in the mind. Others have simply rested upon other arguments for God's existence, and taken the universal consent of mankind as evidence that this is not an idea unnatural to them, since they have yielded ready assent to the proofs of it commonly given. But a recognition of the traditional teaching will not weaken the argument. Even if it does, it is a fact which must be acknowledged.

In favour of this as the primary source of this general belief it may be said,

(1.) That this is the natural manner in which every child among us learns about God. Its own questionings, or its parent's convictions of the importance of this knowledge cause it to be imparted at an early period, and by direct teaching of the fact alone without proof.

(2.) Information obtained by travellers, and especially by Christian missionaries, teaches that our own customs agree with those of heathen nations, as they also do with those of Christendom in general.

(3.) This accounts for the fact, that, while the belief has varied at different times and places, it is held in the same form by almost every one within a single nation at a single period.

(4.) The uniformity, too, in which it has continued among any one people for many generations, is also proof of traditional origin.

(5.) The general existence of it in a purer form the nearer we approach the origin of the race, shows that belief in a God was the primeval belief of man, and has thence been handed down from father to son, until it has reached our own age and ourselves.

(6.) This accounts also for the fact that, when that faith has been corrupted, it has continued in the corrupted form until some new mental or spiritual force has arisen to introduce change, and to give new shape to the belief for some time to come.

2. The belief thus dependent on this traditional teaching is of great value as proof of the truth of this doctrine.

(1.) Its general prevalence shows that this doctrine is suitable to all mankind. It is one that, though worthy of the wisest thought, is not dependent upon philosophical conceptions, or abstract, or logical reasoning for its acceptance. The most ignorant of men have been able to grasp it. It is like that teaching of the Great Master, whom "the common people heard gladly." There has been something, in it, or connected with it, that has made all men believe it. What this is will be hereafter shown. But the fact that this simple teaching, from father to son, throughout all the ages, has been enough to make it dwell as a powerful and controlling influence in the hearts of the masses of mankind, is a strong proof not only of its truth, but also that it has come from God, whose universal gifts are of this simple nature, suitable to all.

(2.) That it has come down through all the ages, shows that it has come in contact with all the best thoughts of the wisest of mankind. That, in its study, the wisest and best, even among the heathen, have approached, in their noblest conceptions of it, to what we believe we have received through the revelation of God, affords a convincing argument, not only in favour of this noblest conception, but of the Divine Word which reveals it. The least that can be said is, that, after being subjected to every variety of thought, and philosophical speculation, this traditional belief has maintained itself as truth, and convincingly withstood every objection that has been brought against it.

(3.) The variety of forms in which it has appeared shows some universal cognition of some one or more fundamental truths which has led all men to believe in the existence of some kind of Divinity. It also teaches that, through the knowledge of no additional truth than such as is afforded by the light of nature only, some have attained more correct ideas approximating, though in very different degrees, that true knowledge which is attainable only through the revelations of Holy Scripture.

(4.) These simplest truths are seen to be a common possession of the higher heathen ideal, and of Divine revelation.

(5.) There is thus manifested, also, the existence of that knowledge of God in all men, which enforces the duty of worship and reverence, and causes account-ability to him.

(6.) The continuance of this belief among those whose self-interest, because of sin, would naturally have led them to reject it, is a strong proof of the sincer-ity with which it has been held.

III. IS THE KNOWLEDGE OF GOD INNATE?

The knowledge of the insufficiency of mere tradition to prove the truth of any doctrine leads us to seek some other ground of this universal belief of man-kind. Tradition has been pointed out as the primary source of this faith. But it is primary, in point of time only, not as the real cause of the general acceptance of the doctrine. Neither does the belief in a God arise from any of the various arguments which have been devised for its support. All men reach conviction on this subject before they ever hear any discussion about it. To the mass of men the arguments have been utterly unknown. While these arguments are, there-fore, to be presented as confirmatory proof, we must seek some other cause for this continued general belief of man.

The true reason of it is that such is the constitution of the human mind that it naturally accepts as true the idea it has attained of God, and rests upon belief in his existence, as a fact that ought not to be doubted.

1. This is generally expressed by the statement that the idea of God is "innate." But the expression seems to be unfortunate.

(1.) There are no innate truths in the ordinary acceptation of the word innate. The mind possesses no ideas independent of all suggestion, or inward contem-plation. No truth becomes truth to the mind, until it is perceived to be truth.

(2.) If the idea of God were innate in the mind, as this word is commonly understood, that idea would be as perfect in one man as in another. But there are evidently various degrees of that perfection. These, therefore, must arise from the different measures of cultivation and thought, as well as from the different circumstances by which the elements which compose that idea in its perfection are suggested.

(3.) Inasmuch as the idea of God, possessed by most men in Christian lands, is the result of the teachings of the Scriptures, or at least of the philosophical studies of men of thought, and is therefore one of the loftier conceptions of God, when the innateness of such an idea is urged as a reason for belief in God, we are naturally met by the avowal, on the part of many, if not all, that they have no such innate idea.

(4.) Any idea of God which we have is not an idea of himself, but of certain relations existing between him, and man, or the universe, or of his relation to certain facts which we perceive in connection with these.

2. A better statement, therefore, is that the belief in God is based upon the intuitive perception by the mind of certain truths, which necessarily involve the existence of God, and of the verity of which it attains absolute conviction.

It has been already stated that man attains intuitive conceptions. He is not confined to a single method of obtaining knowledge. He arrives at truth through sensation. He is taught it by experience. He believes testimony. He is conscious of himself. But he is also so constituted as to certain truths, that they are self-evident upon an intelligent conception of what is meant by them. No reasoning about them can make them more convincing. No study of them, except as to the nature of the things affirmed, gives deeper conviction of their truth. No personal experience, nor testimony of others, gives stronger witness to their reliability. In each individual mind, according to its comprehension of what is meant by the things spoken of, there arises personal conviction of their indubitable truth. This is really what is meant, when it is affirmed that these ideas an innate in man.

All that is necessary, prior to such intuitive conception, is a knowledge of the meaning of the truth which is to be intuitively perceived. Take, for example, the mathematical axiom before quoted, "the whole is greater than any one of its parts." Before the truth of this is perceived, it is necessary to know what is meant by "whole," and "part," and "greater." As soon as these are known, the truth of the affirmation at once appears. It is on this account that the term "God," or the expression "the true idea of God," cannot be a part of an intuitive conception. We cannot know "God." We may know certain things about God. We have not "the true idea of God." We only have some true idea of God. Hence our statement was limited to the assertion, that "such is the constitution of the human mind that it naturally accepts the idea it has attained of God as true."

These intuitive conceptions are originally single. Sir William Hamilton makes simplicity a characteristic of intuitive truth. In opposition to this statement which he quotes, Dr. Charles Hodge contends that "all of the propositions of the First Book of Euclid were as plain at first sight to Newton as the axioms, and the same is true in our moral and religious nature. The more that nature is purified, and exalted, the clearer is its vision, and the wider the scope of its intuitions. . . . If a proposition be capable of resolution into simpler factors, it may still, to a powerful intellect, be seen as self-evidently true. What is seen immediately, without the intervention of proof, to be true, is, according to the common mode of expression, said to be seen intuitively." Sys. Theol. Vol. 1, p. 193. Both of these writers appear to be right, and both wrong. Hamilton is correct in stating that simplicity is a characteristic of intuitive truth, but incorrect in maintaining, as a consequence, that no complex truth can be intuitively perceived. For the mind, in perceiving separately the correctness of two intuitive truths, may, at the same time, combine them into a single conception, if they are homogeneous, just as we unite the different qualities of any object, as a table, or chair, and express them by a single term. But the mind apprehends these separately before it thus connects them. Indeed, it never so unites them as not still to preserve their separable character, and to cognize them as such. "The clearer is its vision," and "the wider the slope of its intuitions," to use the figurative language of Hodge, the more distinctly separate and the more plainly plural do these intuitions appear.

3. In seeking, therefore, for the intuitive conceptions which enter into the idea of God, we ought not to be surprised that they are simple, and yet that two or more of them may unite in the proof of his existence. Thus is it, that, so far as God is known, his existence is intuitively known, however few or many may be the intuitions involved; for the mind, while originally perceiving them separately, still combines them together, and, as the result of all, as of each, believes that God exists. But the meaning of what is thus affirmed, in relation to a single intuition only, is far less than in relation to two, or three, or all.

Of these intuitive conceptions we shall find that only the simplest are universally accepted. Greater intelligence, cultivation and thoughtfulness lead to the knowledge of others by some. Were these so stated to all as to be comprehended, they would be as fully acceptable to all as to any. They are limited as to their reception, not because they are less true, nor because the nature of one man accepts, while that of another rejects them, but because they have either not been suggested to the intellect, or, if suggested, their meaning has not been understood. The more of these that we know, and the higher the nature of the thought conveyed by them, the purer and the greater will be the meaning to us of the being of God.

4. Some of the more manifest of these may be taken as examples of their nature, and of their manner in which men arrive, through them, at the knowledge of God's existence.

(1.) That which is dependent must have its final support in something purely independent.

(2.) Derived existence must have its ultimate origin in that which is self-existent.

(3.) Every effect must have its cause, either within, or without itself.

The truth of the above affirmations must be admitted as soon as their meaning is perceived. But, if the first be true, there is some being upon whom men depend, and to whom, therefore, they are under obligations of duty and obedience, whom they must fear, and whose protection they must seek. This is the most general idea of God. If the second be true, the being upon whom men depend is, also, the one through whom they exist; or there are two beings, the one the source of life, the other the cause of its preservation and support. One of these will be independent, and the other self-existent. That the uncultivated should not perceive that these two are necessarily one, is not a matter of surprise. The possibility of this has allowed the existence of polytheism. But when they are thus united, the idea of God has been that of an independent, self-existent being, which is a complex idea, and is consciously based upon, not one, but two intuitive conceptions, though they are now united together. In like manner the third of these is accepted as soon as comprehended. It is only necessary to know what is meant by the terms "effect," and "cause within or without itself." This is attained through observation and experience. The idea of cause and effect is found even in very young children, who cannot be persuaded that anything has happened without a cause. Nor is it difficult to teach what is meant by "having the cause within or without itself." It may be illustrated by the difference between a clock moving its own hands because of its own mechanism, and the hands of the same clock moved by some person; or by that between a horse which has the power of self-motion, and the cart which moves only because he draws it. The meaning of the terms of this intuitive suggestion has not been difficult to comprehend, consequently the existence of God, as based upon it, has been generally accepted. To the common mind, especially, it has commended itself as teaching that God is the creator of the world, and thus accounting for the existence of all things that have been made. In this case, also, men have not always associated the things which we see with the one God. In some forms of belief, they have divided the universe among more gods than one. In others, they have conceived of it as made by a god inferior to the Great Supreme, whom they recognized. But, in these varied ways, they have shown a universal acceptance of the idea of causality, and of the intuitive conception which arises upon its comprehension. The only objection made to it, is that of Hume and Kant, who have thought that the knowledge of causation must be limited by our experience. But this is an objection to the amount of evidence we have of the effects of causation, which truly is measured by experience only, but our knowledge of the universal nature of the law comes not from experience, but from intuitive conceptions based upon the knowledge of its meaning.

5. Other intuitive conceptions might be added which are not so simple, but which are as truly believed by those who comprehend them. Take for example some of those which enter into the idea of God as the perfect Being.

(1.) The distinctions of right and wrong must have some absolute standard, which is personal, conscious, unchangeable, and without limitations of time or space. But this is God.

(2.) Moral perfection cannot be merely ideal, but must have some real embodiment; else there could be no imperfection, and, especially, no degrees of imperfection, since degrees imply the existence of that to which imperfection approaches, or from which it recedes, and this can only be absolute perfection. But absolute perfection is itself God.

IV. THE ARGUMENTS WHICH CONFIRM THIS BELIEF

The theistic proofs have been divided into arguments *a priori* and *a posteriori*. This is a convenient division, although some of those *a priori* have in them some elements of *a posteriori* nature, and some of those *a posteriori* depend upon *a priori* principles. As to some of them, also, it is difficult to draw an exact line, and assign them to the one class or to the other.

An argument *a priori* is one to prove the existence of some effect, or fact, from the knowledge we have of an antecedent cause, or of some reason, or principle, in the nature of things, which necessarily involves the existence of a certain consequence.

1. Some of the arguments *a priori* in proof of God's existence.

An argument *a priori*, for the Being of God, is one based upon some reason in the nature of things, or some principle cognized by the human mind, by which, independent of any examination of the works of God, we are led to infer his existence.

(1.) The most celebrated of all of these is that which argues the being of God from the idea we have of him in the mind. It is supposed to have been first presented by Anselm, Archbishop of Canterbury, England, in his work called "Proslogium seu Allogium de Dei natura." His form of the argument may be

briefly stated thus. By definition God is a being such as that no greater can be
conceived of. But we can conceive of a being whose non-existence is impossible.
If God, then, does not necessarily exist, we can conceive of a greater than God,
which is contrary to the definition. Therefore, God must exist. [See chapters
2, 3, 4.]

This argument, from the idea of God in the mind, was a favorite with the
Schoolmen. It appears in various forms in the works of many of them. It has,
however, been commonly called the Cartesian argument, having been set forth
with signal ability by Descartes. One form in which he gives it is based upon
the idea in the mind of supreme perfection. To this we attain, though ourselves
only creatures of imperfection. Whence is it? It must come from the All Perfect,
who has stamped it on our being, as the artificer sets his trade-mark on the work
of his intelligence.

Descartes also presents, in the following syllogism, an argument more closely
resembling that of Anselm.

"To affirm that any attribute is contained in the nature or conception of a
thing, is to affirm that such a attribute is true of the thing, and that it is surely
contained in it;

"But, necessary existence is contained in the nature and conception of the
Deity;

"Therefore, necessary existence is a true attribute of the Deity; or God of
necessity exists."

[See Blunt's Theological Dictionary, Art. Theism: in which are also more full
statements of all the above mentioned forms of this argument.]

But the clearest and most complete presentation of this argument is given
by Bishop Stillingfleet. Origines Sacræ, vol. 1, pp. 484–492. The following is
a mere statement of the syllogistic form presented, without the arguments that
support it.

That, which we do clearly and distinctly perceive to belong to the nature and
essence of a thing, may be with truth affirmed of the thing; a clear and distinct
perception in the mind being the greatest evidence we can have of its truth.

But we do have a clear and distinct perception that necessity of existence
doth belong to the nature of God.

Therefore, he must exist.

This argument, from the idea of God, has been strenuously objected to. Kant
opposed it on the ground that "the mere supposableness or logical possibility of
a perfect being, is no proof of the objective or real possibility of such a being,
and existence cannot be inferred from a mere idea." Knapp's Theology, p. 86.

But, in reply to this objection it may be said that the argument against
which it is presented, does not prove the mere logical possibility, but the logical

certainty, or necessity, for such a being. Moreover, it is not contended that every subjective conception must have an objective reality; but only that certain ones may have such a reality, and that this one, the idea of God, which itself involves the idea of necessary existence, must, in consequence of the idea thus involved, possess that reality.

Hodge objects that if it "has any validity it is unimportant. It is only saying that what must be, actually is." But this is not merely such an abstract statement. It is a proof that something, namely, the being of God, actually is, because of the proof of the correctness of our conception that necessary existence belongs to his nature.

It has also been objected to it that "it confounds ideal existence with real existence" [A. H. Strong's Sys. Theol. p. 49.] But certainly there is no confounding of ideal existence and real existence, abstractedly, nor of forms of ideal and real existence, generally, but the arguments only show the actuality of a single form of ideal existence, because the very nature of the idea involves its correspondent reality.

(2.) A second *a priori* argument for the existence of God was devised by Moses Lowman, and is from the nature of existence, and the relation between necessary and contingent existence. The following is a still more brief statement than the points of the argument, given by Dr. J. Pye Smith, in his First Lines of Christian Theology, pp. 99–101.

1. Positive existence is possible, for it involves no contradiction.

2. All possible existence is either necessary, which must be, and in its own nature cannot but be, or contingent, which may be, or may not be.

3. Soul existence is necessary, for if all existence were contingent, all existence might not be, as well as might be; and that thing which might not be, never could be without some other thing as the prior cause of its existence, since every effect must have a cause. If, therefore, all possible existence were contingent, all existence would be impossible; because the idea or conception of it would be that of an effect without a cause, which involves a contradiction.

4. Necessary existence must be actual existence.

5. Necessary existence must be always.

6. Necessary existence must be wherever any existence is possible.

7. There can be but one necessarily existent being, for two could in no respect differ from each other; that is, they would be one and the same being.

8. The one necessarily existent being must have all possible perfections.

9. The one necessarily existent being must be a free agent.

10. Therefore, there is one necessarily existent being, the cause of all contingent existence, that is, of all other existences besides himself; and this being is eternal, infinite, possessed of all possible perfections, and is an intelligent free agent—that is, this being is God.

(3.) A third argument *a priori* is that of Dr. Samuel Clarke, in the Boyle Lectures which he delivered. It may be briefly presented thus.

Something must have existed from all eternity, for since something now exists, it is evident that something always was; otherwise the things which now are must have been produced out of nothing, absolutely, and without cause, which is absurd, for nothing can be produced, and yet be without cause.

But, now, if something has existed from all eternity, either there must always have been some unchangeable and infinite being, or else an infinite succession of changeable and dependent beings, without any original cause, which is absurd.

Dr. Clarke does not discuss the absurdity of an infinite series in the past.

The impossibility of such a series appears, however, from its very nature. There can be no past infinite series, because an infinite series is one, the last term of which can never be attained, or completed. But, in an infinite series going backward, the term now present is the first of the series, and not the last. The last term of the series is really the first in existence. But that first was completed before the second. It has already existed. The series, therefore, as now before us is one, all of whose terms have already appeared, and the series, therefore, however indefinite in the numbers of its terms, is still a completed, and, therefore, a finite series. [See this matter ably discussed by Rev. Joseph Tracy, in the Bibliotheca Sacra, Vol. 7, pp. 613–626. Also Turretine, Theol., Vol. I, Book 3, Ques. 1, par. 6, p. 154.]

The value of the arguments *a priori* has been questioned. But on the other hand they have seemed to some eminently satisfactory. To these, they have appeared to be clothed with the authority of God himself speaking through the constitution he has given to the mind, and its capacity for the intuitive conception of underlying principles. To those who perceive these principles, the proofs are as conclusive as the consciousness of their own existence, and as authoritative as the dictates of conscience. These principles are accepted, and arguments are formed upon them in the same way as in mathematical demonstrations, and afford those who perceive the truth of them actual demonstrations of the fact that God exists.

But many have thought them fallacious, and have denied the possibility of demonstrative proof that there is a God. To such the arguments *a posteriori* have alone seemed to be valuable. Whether or not this be true, they are certainly of much greater value in general, because much more simple, and better adapted to force conviction upon the minds of the masses of mankind.

2. The arguments *a posteriori*.

The value of these arguments has not been duly appreciated. Men have looked for that kind of demonstration of God's existence, called mathematical, which can only arise from arguments based upon admitted axioms, and which proceed thence to their conclusions by invincible logical processes. Such arguments, if they exist, can only be of the nature of those *a priori* already considered.

But while no such demonstration is afforded by them, the arguments for God *a posteriori* are as conclusive as similar ones on any other subject. Their nature is precisely like that of those upon which all physical science is based, and upon which men act in all the affairs of life.

Physical science pursues the inductive method. It gathers all the facts in any matter. It recognizes that there are general laws which unite these facts in some one principle, and those who study them devise a theory to explain them. Such a theory must account for all the facts, and not be opposed by any one of them. If the series of facts can be traced very generally, and any theory universally accounts for them, while no other can, that theory which at first in the presence of a few facts, was only probable, becomes more and more certain, and finally unquestionable.

Thus, the theory of gravitation has been accepted as a great law of the universe, binding it together, keeping all its parts in all their courses, and everywhere equally effective according to a fixed proportion of numbers, and yet seen only in its effects.

In like manner we arrive, according to the strictest scientific method of induction, at the existence of God. The only theory which accounts for the universe with all its phenomena is that which asserts that it has proceeded from him. This alone has been satisfactory in the eyes of most men, from the beginning of all historic records. Mankind have been incredulous as to the sanity or sincerity of those who have denied it. No scientific theory has ever been held about facts so universally existent and so generally known. None has dealt with matters of more vital importance or absorbing interest. None has been, as has this, an object of thought to every intelligent human being. None has so commended itself at once to practical men and philosophers. None, after having been so far forgotten, because of sin and ignorance, as to be remembered only in its name and its simplest facts, has risen to a beauty of conception which beyond all else constitutes the glory of Grecian philosophy; while at the same time its belief has been preserved in another race in its purity by a literature which, despite all tendencies to corrupt the theory, has maintained it in its purest form for generation after generation.

(1.) The first argument *a posteriori* to be considered is commonly called the cosmological, because it argues the existence of God, as a First Cause, from the effects seen in the world. It should, however, be named the argument from causation, to distinguish it from the teleological argument and others which are equally cosmological.

A very striking form of it was put forth by Bishop Berkeley and is quoted in Dwight's Theology, Vol. 1, pp. 79 and 80:

"We acknowledge the existence of each other to be unquestionable. We say that we know this from our senses. Yet, after all, it is intuitively certain that what we see is not the living, thinking being which we call man. On the contrary, they are merely effects of which that living, acting thing is the cause. We conclude the existence of the cause from the effects.

"So in the universe around us we perceive a great variety of effects produced by some cause adequate to their production.

"This cause is God, or a being possessed of sufficient intelligence and power to contrive and bring them to pass.

"If it be said that these are only the effect of certain inherent powers of matter, and mind, and, therefore, demand no extrinsic agency, the answer is that this affects the conclusion only by removing it one step farther back in the course of reasoning."

By this is meant that these inherent powers are only effects which themselves demand an adequate cause.

It will be seen that this argument is based upon the law of causality. Hence it should be called the argument from causation.

I proceed now to give this argument in another form, simpler indeed, but yet more complete.

It may be stated syllogistically thus:

A. Every fact or effect must have its adequate cause, either within or without itself.

B. There are effects in the universe which have no adequate cause, either in themselves or in the universe.

C. Therefore, there must be an adequate cause for their existence in some being without, which is the Supreme Being, the cause of all things.

We consider first the proof of the major premise of the syllogism namely, A., that every effect must have its adequate cause, either within or without itself.

Objection 1. It has been objected to this that there is no such thing as causation, and that all of which we have any experience is mere antecedence and consequence.

But it may be replied that experience teaches us that there are effects in some consequents which are the result of relation to, and power in certain antecedents.

We admit the existence of many antecedents and consequents between which there is no relation of cause and effect, but experience plainly teaches that relation in others.

This has been so far admitted that Hume and Kant have simply attempted to confine the law of causation to our experience. But

(i.) It is evident that causes must exist independently of our experience, and that when we see an effect (namely, something evidently requiring some power for its production), we know that it has had its adequate cause, even though we have never had experience of its special cause. Indeed one of the most important branches of scientific inquiry is into the unknown causes of existing phenomena, which, without experience, we know must be effects of adequate causes. Thus Geology leads to inquiries into the cause of the original stratifications in the rocks, the existence of fossil remains, and the phenomena connected with the upheavals of rocks. So Astronomy presents its problems about the perturbations of the planets, the movements of stars and their dissappearances, the spots upon the sun, and the rugged volcanic condition of the moon. So also Medicine forces investigation into the origin of disease, as of yellow fever. Even Social Science seeks adequate physical causes for matters in which the human will or accident seems to have been most free from external influence, so as to establish that the number of marriages and murders, or railway accidents or suicides is governed by controlling law.

(ii.) It might also he justly added that this point needs no proof, because the idea that every effect must have its cause is an intuitive conception of the human mind. It arises upon the first perception of what is meant by power. The conviction of its truth is seen in the very earliest stages of infancy.

Objection 2. It is again objected that we ought to carry this idea of causation farther back and apply it to the great First Cause. If subsequent effects, or facts, or existences must have had a cause, why should not this being, whom we call God, and who is more wonderful in his nature than all others, be himself an effect and himself have a cause?

The reply to this is, that experience does not teach us that every thing has a cause without itself, but only every thing which has not its cause in itself.

Wherever there is the principle of life, there is, to a limited extent at least, self-causation in its development.

(i.) Thus the tree puts forth its own leaves, and flowers, and fruits. It is true that it needs to have had its seed planted in a favourable position and to be surrounded by favourable circumstances. Yet, despite this, even here, though in a very limited way, there is self-causation.

So with the motion in a watch, the cause of which is in its own mechanism.

(ii.) This is more distinctly seen as we reach higher forms of life. Here the movement is self-caused. Such is the movement of a bird as it shoots into the air, or of a beast as it springs upon its prey. The higher form of this is apparent. The watch needed some action upon it from without, before its springs within would act, but in these living forms no outward impelling cause originates the power. This may be illustrated by the difference between a steamboat, moved by its machinery under the guidance of men, and the movement of a fish which by its own powers swims through the seas.

(iii.) In a still higher degree is this seen in man. Here is found a self-determining will which puts forth effects which may be more confidently spoken of as self-originated. We have not here the mere instinct which perhaps blindly prompts the mere animal to act, but a will which acts as it pleases through liberty of choice, and is governed only by motives to which it yields of its own self-choice.

We do not presume to say that this explains to us God's self-existence and independence, nor how he is self-caused, having the cause of causes in himself, but we simply assert that our experience of causes does not force us to find an outside cause for every effect, and, therefore, a cause for what we call the first or final cause, but simply a cause for every thing which has not its cause of existence and action in itself.

We may also claim from this that, if, between the lifeless clod and the man made from it, such difference exists, that the one is no cause at all in itself, and the other capable of such self-causation, then, when we rise to the Great Being, who has made the Universe, we have the right to expect such infinite superiority to man, that he should be, not only the cause of all things, but, being self-existent, should have within himself the cause or ground of his own existence.

The existence of such a Great First Cause is beyond the denial of any. That which satisfies our minds of that existence is, that we are so constituted that we cannot rest under this conviction of causation, until the idea is presented of a Great First Cause having self-existence or the cause of his own existence in himself.

If there is not such a self-existent and self-contained cause we are driven to adopt the idea of an infinite series of finite causes from Eternity, or an infinite succession of such series, each of which is both impossible and absurd.

B. There are effects in the Universe which have no adequate cause in themselves, nor in the Universe as a whole.

This may be argued from the Universe as a whole, as an existing substance (an entity), or from its component parts as existing substances (entities).

We have the phenomena of the material world about us.

As presented to our eyes, it is a wonderful mechanism, more so than the most perfect machinery man can devise, and presents an effect in itself, and in its parts, which demands a cause of more power and skill than we can conceive.

Was it made as it is? If so, how great the cause which will account for its phenomena!

But it is asserted that it was not thus made, but is a growth which has been reached by long ages of gradual development, accompanied by destruction, and renewal, and modification until it has attained its present form.

We shall not deny this, but admit the force of all the evidence which suggests it.

But, after all, this growth is also an effect. It has proceeded either from some inherent power of self-development, or has been produced by the power and will of some outward cause.

It is claimed by anti-theists that it is a self-development of matter which has taken upon itself form after form until this result has been attained.

This theory involves the idea that all growth, and life, and mind, are the outcome of original inorganic matter. It claims that in the ultimate analysis we reach simple molecules of matter, and that, from the development of these, we have this whole universal structure.

Admit now all that is thus claimed as a fact by anti-theists, even go so far as to suppose that there has been a time when nothing existed but molecules, even a few, even two only, even one, if it should be desired; reduce the whole material universe to a speck the one millionth part of a grain of sand, and still we have in that molecule an effect entirely unaccounted for, except as it with all its vast possibilities was made by some creative energy. There is, therefore, even here a demand for the self-existent cause.

Yet, to admit all of the above, is to admit more than we ought, more than there is the slightest reason to suppose to be true; for there no evidence that any matter has been added to the universe since its creation. Matter is seen to expand and contract, to take on one form and then another, but there is evidence neither of diminution on the one hand, nor of increase on the other. But there must have been such increase of matter unless the world had in its molecule period as many molecules containing in themselves as much material as is now existent. Whatever growth or development, therefore, may be ascribed to the world, the whole of it has existed from the beginning, whether in an organized form or in simple molecules. It is, however, as difficult, without admitting a producing cause, to account for the world-mass of molecules, even for a single molecule, as for the universe created in the forms in which it appears today.

Let us now consider certain actual effects seen in the universe as farther proof of an external cause.

(i.) Motion. The principle of motion in the universe is beautifully developed. The universe is regular. It is governed by fixed laws. There is harmony in its movements. The principles of centripetal and centrifugal action governed by the law of gravitation, not only regulate this motion, but cause the universe to be self-balanced; so that we have a kind of mechanism not only impossible for man to imitate, but the principle of which he cannot comprehend, though he sees and acknowledges it as a fact.

Now whence this motion? Inert matter has no motion. A piece of rock, or a clod of soil, even a tree, remains always where it is unless moved by some outward power.

Our knowledge of this inertness in matter is such that we know that an infant's ball will remain forever where it has been put, unless disturbed from without.

Whence, then, this motion of the universe which is not a simple movement, such as is given to a ball by striking it, but a complex motion, involving the description of circles and ellipses and parabolas, and so involving them as to keep each in its sphere without confusion or distraction?

Can any one persuade himself that ten thousand balls laid upon a plain surface will have any more power of motion than one, or that a universe of them created without motion, would not, unless influenced from without, remain utterly and forever at rest?

Something, therefore, must account for the motion.

Now our experience is that all motion primarily proceeds from mind or will. Thus I move a ball as the result of will influenced by my mind. Even if I accidentally kick it, not intending to do so, and even ignorant that I have done so, this is still true. I had willed to move my body and that body by its contact when in motion with the ball, has moved it.

Before motion then we have mind; before the motion of these atoms a directing mind; so that not only for the creation, but for the motion of molecules we must recognize God.

If it be said that this motion was caused by wind, we inquire whence came that wind? Was it not itself produced by motion? If so, it cannot have been the primary cause of motion. We are still forced to the supposition that motion has proceeded from God.

If it be claimed that it came from heat, whence was the heat? Heat is also the result of motion. What caused the movement which led to its existence?

If it be said that the motion was a matter of chance, we ask what is chance? Is there any such reality? We apply the name variously, but in all cases the thoughtful mind knows that there is no "chance" in the sense of uncaused, unwilled forces present.

Thus I place dice in a box and throw them. I say that the resultant numbers come by chance. But I know that that result has followed unerringly under law from the forces present. But law supposes the mind of the law-giver, and the results of his law are from purpose, not from chance. Hence the proverb: "The lot is cast into the lap; but the whole disposing thereof is of the Lord." Prov. 16:33.

So also when I meet in New York an acquaintance from Texas, I say, "We met by chance." By this I mean that the meeting was not because of the purpose of either of us. But I do not deny the laws which have governed each of us, through which, guided by a higher power, we have met as he had purposed we should.

In no usage of the word chance, therefore, do we mean to assert absence of mental purpose. There is no such kind of chance, and by none such can we account for the existence of motion in the universe.

(ii.) Form and life also appear among the effects of the universe.

Matter is not simply inorganic with the form and shape which might have been bestowed upon it by motion; but it takes special forms of life.

Between the inorganic and this organic life there is a wide interval. Even in the very lowest forms of vegetable life there is movement and growth and capacity to absorb and increase and give forth which shows a new kingdom in nature.

It is admitted that here the whole substance is material, and that the growth of vegetables is nothing more than the absorption into life of what has been already in inorganic nature.

But this power of taking on form and life is very striking. If the change could be made into a single form only, it would be still surprising. But the forms are innumerable. Not only this, but the specific form, having been once assumed, attains not only fixedness in the original, but power continuously in the species to reproduce its like. Yet, nevertheless, there is a certain power of adaptation by which, within fixed limits, there is variation.

This is the law of plants. In a still higher degree is it true of animals.

Now whence this change from inorganic to such organic matter?

Is it inherent in matter? Then matter would be constantly engaged in thus developing the organic from the inorganic. This is evident from what we see in crystallization. Here there is power in matter to assume special forms. The law under which this is done in each kind is known, and, in accordance with such law, and not otherwise, are the shapes in crystallization assumed. We can place the proper substances in their appropriate relations and produce the result. Why? Because here certain matter has inherent power to assume certain forms. But this matter cannot assume other forms. Other matter cannot assume these forms. And thus is it seen that matter, as such, has not the inherent power to assume form, but that such power has been bestowed only on certain kinds of matter under the action of specific law and not of its own prompting.

Yet from this power of crystallization has been argued the power of matter to produce both vegetable and animal life. The most that could be concluded is that some kinds of matter (such as we now see to do so), under circumstances (under which they now so act), are capable of producing vegetable and animal life. But we see this done only by propagation and generation from like to like. Therefore, only thus are we authorized to infer that such life and form has been heretofore produced from matter alone. This still leaves necessary the creation of the first forms through which matter has this power.

Various attempts have been made to produce animals and plants by spontaneous generation. But these attempts have thus far utterly failed.

Because of this inability to produce by any means the organic directly from the inorganic, anti-theists have been driven to adopt the idea (a mere idea without proof), that there is a substance which they call protoplasm, which common substance underlies all life-forms, vegetable or animal, and that, in its varied changes, ordinary inorganic matter finally attains to this protoplasm.

As to this we should remember:

(a.) That protoplasm is not the name of a substance which has been found developed from inorganic matter. No such substance has as yet been discovered. This is only the name that would be given to it if it should be.

(b.) That the name is applied to the earliest forms of organic life, as being what protoplasm would be if thus developed from inorganic matter. But the substance here found is really a part of organic life, produced by the process of propagation or generation through which matter of this kind becomes life and form.

The whole idea of protoplasm, therefore, is a figment, except within the limits of organic life.

But, admit this to be true, and that the first forms (the protoplasm) that we see, are the results, directly, of inorganic matter and not of organic, it must still be acknowledged that in all the protoplasm yet examined there is no variation, that all of it is exactly alike, there being but one kind of protoplastic germs so far as investigation can perceive or material elements indicate. Yet, from a number of specimens of this protoplasm, come several different kinds of life. It is as though from seed, precisely the same, should come wheat and barley, and rice, and rye, and maize. Now, what is here the directing power which, from the same substance, apparently, produces different forms of life, some vegetable and some animal, and various vegetables, as well as various animals, and which so produces them without variation that the protoplasm of one species of animals always produces that species and not another? This can be understood, if this be organic life which is acting, and acting under the laws which propagate species; but how explain it of mere matter which has become mere protoplasm, a substance whose forms and material have no difference in themselves, and which therefore must be indebted to some other directing power for the difference seen in its results.

It is evident, therefore, that in protoplasm we have matter not in a process of self-development, but matter already organized in organic forms, under a law for reproducing species; a law which can in no respect account for the origin of the species, and, therefore, forces us back to the idea of its direct creation.

But if this be true, the principle of form and life in the Universe speaks to us distinctly of a God.

(iii.) Mind also appears among the effects in the Universe which can only be accounted for upon the supposition of a God.

The whole history of man teaches that the powers of the human mind are wonderful. Of this we are conscious in ourselves, and we are taught it by experience about others.

Instinct in plants and animals is itself incomprehensible. We cannot tell why the vine should put forth entwining tendrils, or the root of a plant seek a piece of bone, or push forward to a well of water, nor why the birds should fly southward, or a horse or dog should dread danger which man cannot perceive, or an ox should utter cries of distress at the smell of blood, or a bee construct its cells of the most economical shape. We account for it by saying, that God has so constituted irrational creatures for their protection and happiness. But an anti-theist would say, these are qualities inherent in matter, so that it is the matter that acts in the animal as it does in the vine.

But we have in mind something of which this cannot be said. Mind is not mere instinct. Indeed it differs widely from instinct. Thus:

(a.) Mind is individual will or purpose; instinct is common to the whole species.

(b.) The will or purpose is not a blind tendency, but is the result of mental perceptions, comprehensions of facts, logical reasoning, personal fancy, and other like causes.

(c.) Its governing principle, being its prevailing motive, is the desire of the individual himself, not of another, not even of God, not even the dictate of conscience, nor of wisdom, but merely of self-choice.

(d.) It often acts contrary to appetite, and desire, and passion. The will refuses to do that to which these prompt. This is a peculiar mark of excellence, not merely in the wise use of the power, but in the possession of the power itself. Its value in such exercise may be illustrated by the proverb of Solomon: "He that is slow to anger is better than the mighty, and he that ruleth his spirit than he that taketh a city." Prov. 16:32.

These are some of the most important particulars in which mind is seen to be far superior to instinct. They have been presented as though admitting that instinct is a quality of matter.

But there is no reason for such admission. Instinct is a governing power over animals. But whence comes it? Is it a growth in them, or is it something bestowed on them by God for their control, just as he gives man conscience; or for their guidance, as he gives man intuitive conceptions? It is doubtless not a growth; but, admit that it is, whence the power for such growth in some matter and not in all? If it is a property of some of these united molecules, or of these particles of protoplasm, and these are only matter self-developed, why has all matter not attained this growth? And why does not the growth develop itself alike in all?

No reason can be given for the phenomena of instinct which does not reject the idea of mere matter alone thus developing. Either

1. The power was first bestowed on some molecules to germinate this instinct, or

2. It was more directly given in connection with the development of the animal life, or

3. The animal was originally created with these functions, and they have continued by propagation to appear throughout the species.

If originating in either of these ways, the existence of the instinct proves that of a regulating, and originating, or creating mind.

But, as we have seen, mind is still higher than instinct, and, if instinct cannot be accounted for as a material growth, very much less so can mind. Even the most persistent advocates for the development of life from matter, admit that between the mind and the body which it inhabits there is a wide interval, and while they contend for the development of the latter through protoplasm as the work of unaided matter, they admit that they have never been able to discover anything which can account for the existence of mind.

But if mind has no cause for its existence in the material universe, it must be the direct product of the infinite mind, the intelligent, personal God. There is an old book of Jewish origin, called "Genesis" in which, long before the days of scientific inquiry into the origin of man, was given the only account which has ever satisfied or will ever satisfy the inquirer into that origin. "The Lord God formed man of the dust of the ground, and breathed into his nostrils the breath of life, and man became a living soul." Gen. 2:7. This was in fulfillment of the divine counsels, "Let us make man it our image after our likeness," Gen. 1:26. Strange that any writer of that day should have known that the body of man is of the same material as the inorganic matter of the earth, and stranger still that he should ascribe such origin to his mind and soul as fully accounts for the soul's existence and its union with matter; and, strangest of all, that he should have put forth a theory such as the world, with all the wisdom of the intervening ages to this day, has not bettered, but which has forced acceptance of its truth on all. Is not this God telling us what God did, and informing us through his servant of the true origin of mind?

(iv.) Among the many other phenomena of the world which might be selected, one other only, namely, conscience, need be mentioned.

Of what is this an effect? Is it the result of matter or of mind? What is it but a controlling power, located in each man, and made a part of his nature, which commands him to do the right and avoid the wrong, and reproves, rebukes, and punishes him for disobedience to its dictates?

Upon the theory that it is God-given, its presence and its phenomena may be explained, but upon no other.

If there is a God,

(a.) There must be eternal principles of right and wrong which may form a foundation for conscience.

(b.) There must be obligation to act in accordance with these principles, the non-fulfillment of which would involve punishment by God, and a reason for the apprehensions of conscience.

(c.) If there is a God who has created man with his fellows, that God would seek the happiness of the race as such, which cannot be attained if moral obligations be ignored, and hence would place conscience in each man to enforce these obligations.

(d.) If there is a God, he must love the right and hate the wrong. How naturally would he seek through conscience to have man do right and avoid wrong.

If, on the other hand, there is no God, then

(a.) Is there any right and wrong as conscience teaches that there is?

(b.) Are we under any obligation to our fellow-men? Have they any rights we should respect? Is our right to possess, to have any other limit than our power to attain?

(c.) How can we account for the terror which strikes men for crimes which have been committed, terror not of punishment here, but hereafter?

Conscience, therefore, argues the existence of God perhaps even more wonderfully than mind; for conscience is the exponent of the law which keeps the moral universe in being and fixes the limits of its wanderings, as much and as truly as the law of gravitation does the material. Even the defeats of it in our race, caused by sin, only prove the more conclusively the power of its law and its necessity to human existence. While the understanding is the guide to what is right and wrong, conscience is the authority which enforces the right and forbids the wrong, and the avenging judge inflicting punishment on those who disobey. In the state of innocence it was perfect in its guidance, effective in its authority, and peaceful in its approval. In our present state, it is imperfect in its guidance and has only partial authority and limited punitive power. In the future it must be like the worm that dieth not, and the fire that is not quenched.

Now whence this conscience, if it be not the messenger God sets in the heart, teaching man more plainly than the starry heavens show God's glory that there is a God, that he rules over man and governs him by laws of right and wrong and punishes the sinful and disobedient, and rewards the righteous and obedient.

The four effects in the universe which have been mentioned, motion, form and life, mind, and conscience, prove this second point [B] of our syllogism, namely, that there are effects in the universe which have no adequate cause either in themselves or in the universe; and from A and B follows the conclusion C, that there must be an adequate cause for the existence of these effects in some being without, who must be the supreme being and the first cause of all things.

It can only be objected to this conclusion that the being who has made our universe may himself have been created by some other, and that he is not the supreme mind. But if this be so, then there must be some being who created him, and thus we are led to look one step further back until we reach an infinite being not created, but having self-existence, himself the cause of all other beings and things.

We are shut up by the argument from causation to this result, or to the adoption of the idea of an infinite succession of finite beings, which is absurd and impossible.

The remaining *a posteriori* arguments may be more briefly presented than this first one from causation, for the principles involved in this to some extent underlie all the rest.

(2.) The second *a posteriori* argument is that from design, commonly called the teleological argument.

It may be expressed as a syllogism, thus:

A. Whatever gives proof of design must have had a designer.

B. The Universe gives proof of design.

C. Therefore, it must have had a designer.

Design may be seen either in arrangement or adaptation. In both these respects the Universe gives proof of design.

1. In its arrangement the specific purpose may not be evident as it is in special adaptation. But evidence is given in that arrangement of the unity and universality which mark design throughout the whole universe.

The syllogism of Principal Tulloch presents the argument in a convenient form. [Burnett Prize Essay on Theism, p. 147.]

I.   Order universally proves mind.

II. The works of nature discover order.

III. The works of nature prove mind.

The point here to be proved is the major premise. There can be no question about the existence of order and arrangement throughout the universe. This is a matter of universal experience. It is also the testimony of all science.

But does order universally prove mind?

(i.) We shall ascertain that it does by noticing that order always proceeds from law by which arrangement occurs, or from direct arrangement. In either event mind is the cause of the order, and, therefore, is proved by it. That the origin of order is in one of these ways, is a matter of universal experience, and we may from experience argue, at least, that such is everywhere true. There is no exception to the rule.

(ii.) But, again, we may argue this to be true from the fact that such is the constitution of the human mind that "we cannot help apprehending everywhere in phenomena of order the operation of a rational will or mind, . . . the laws of our rational nature compel us to do so. These will not permit us to rest short of mind as an ultimate explanation of such phenomena." Tulloch, Prize Essay, p. 50.

(iii.) Having proved the existence of causation in the preceding argument we have also the right here to apply its principles. The order is an effect, and since every effect must have its adequate cause, so, because this is an effect of mind, we argue from it the existence of the supreme mind, which is alone sufficient to account for such harmony and arrangement.

(iv.) Finally we may argue this from the very meaning of the word order. If order means arrangement, then it involves the existence of one who arranges. If order means plan, this demands mind to devise such plan. If order means laws or regulation, the word involves the idea of a lawgiver.

Thus is it that simply considering design as order or arrangement we prove from it the existence of mind.

2. But the proof is much stronger when we look at design as adaptation to the object in view.

The same arguments here as in the syllogism by Tulloch prove the major premise—whatever shows marks of design must have had a designer.

The illustrations of the minor premise are numerous and convincing:

(i.) In the vegetable world; in the structure and arrangement of plants, in their connection with soil, climate and atmosphere; is their relations to the necessities of surrounding animal life; and in their material structure, fitting them to receive and assimilate food, and to breathe the atmosphere and absorb its gases, and to reproduce themselves.

(ii.) In the animal world; in adaptation to climate, vegetable productions for food, and all the circumstances which make life possible at various places for some animals and not for all, especially in the peculiarity that man is fitted for all climates, and that the animals necessary to be present with him are capable of equal variety of climate.

(iii.) It is also seen in the formation of the various parts of the body, especially of the eye, which presents signal evidences of design, in its structure for seeing, in its capacity for motion, in its instinct against danger, and in its protective apparatus.

So also in the hand and foot, especially the thumb in man, which gives him such superiority over all other animals, in felling trees, chopping wood, sewing clothes, use of mechanic's tools and numberless other respects, intimately and essentially connected with a condition of high civilization, as well as of mere physical capacity to prevail over brute force.

So with a thousand times a thousand marks of special design in the forms of life in this world. All prove a designer, and that designer to be the Creator of the world and its forms of life.

It is vain to say that all these members of the body have been developed from inferior forms.

There is no evidence of any different structure in these particulars in the individuals of today than in those which earliest appear. Whatever changes have occurred in animal life have been within fixed limits and under the regulation of law. They have always been such as have preserved those characteristics of the animals upon which difference in species is based. There is in each individual a wonderful capacity to enlarge, by exercise, the powers both of mind and body. But this goes not beyond what, according to some law of its nature, is a common property of humanity.

(3.) Another argument *a posteriori* may be drawn from the evidences of God's providential care and control of the world.

It may be thus stated:

Man perceives in his own life and in the lives of others, and in the history of nations and of the race, evidence of a superintending power, governing, guiding and protecting, and by means sometimes most insignificant or minute, accomplishing ends of greater or less magnitude. In the workings of this power there are traceable evidences of designing purpose which are so marked as to show it to be not mere blind force or established law, but an intelligent agent exercising such oversight as is rendered necessary by the presence of free will in man, which, but for such oversight, would prevent the accomplishment of ends, which would certainly be attained through mere laws alone, were the universe, with its inhabitants, a mere machine governed only by purely mechanical laws—and such oversight also as supplies to man the information and resources needed at particular stages in the world's progress, and as preserves from excess or deficiency the equilibrium of food and work in the world and its various parts.

As none but the supreme mind, which is omniscient, omnipresent and omnipotent, can exercise such care, the proof that this care is exercised is a proof of the existence of God.

It will be seen from this that all the proof which can be presented of providential care becomes a proof of a God. This is very strong and conclusive, and is to be found in the historical accounts of mankind, as well as in the constant testimony of individual men.

(4.) The fourth argument *a posteriori* is from the miracles wrought by messengers from God.

A miracle is an extraordinary act performed, or event brought to pass by God, not through the established laws of nature, nor mere providential control, but by direct action without the use of efficient means.

The working of a miracle, therefore, shows the presence and act of a power superior to nature which can be no other than its creator and lawgiver.

A miracle is, therefore, evidence of the existence of God.

This argument rests upon the proof that miracles have been wrought. Of this fact it is universally acknowledged that we have abundant testimony. But the credibility of the testimony, as for example of the New Testament miracles, has been questioned. If it be credible then the fact has been proved.

1. It is charged that the witnesses are not credible, because they were not disinterested.

(a.) But disinterestedness is not necessary in a witness. Formerly courts required this, but now, in the more civilized communities, all evidence is heard' and due weight is given to each part of it in connection with all the other circumstances and facts testified to.

(b.) None of the witnesses for miracles were interested except upon the supposition that the facts which they attested were true. They could have no purpose, therefore, in testifying falsely.

(c.) They published their testimony at a time when multitudes were alive who had been present at the times and places when the miracles were said to have been wrought. Had the facts not been believed by all present on such occasions they would have been disputed and the witnesses exposed. This was especially true of the miracles wrought by Christ and his apostles.

(d.) To the above may be added that the statements made about these miracles were such as to affect the character and position of men in public authority, and in some cases appealed to acts of the rulers in council, by whom the miracles were admitted. None could have dared to make such statements, unless they knew they spoke the truth.

2. It is charged that the witnesses were themselves deceived.

But it was impossible that deception could take place in many of the miracles.

Could Israel be deceived about the plagues in Egypt, or the passage through the Red Sea, or that of the Jordan, or the fall of the walls of Jericho, or the guidance of the pillar of cloud and fire, etc., etc.?

But the rationalist will say that the history of these events was not written at the same time with the events themselves, and that the people in the wilderness never saw nor heard the record.

While this is not admitted of the Old Testament it cannot be justly said of the New Testament histories. The statements are by eyewitnesses. Could they have been deceived about the stilling of the waves, the feeding of the five thousand on one occasion, and of the four thousand on another, about the raising from the dead of the daughter of Jairus, of the son of the widow of Nain, of Lazarus, and especially the self-resurrection of Christ himself? One who looks at these facts is obliged to deny that these witnesses were deceived. They have either knowingly stated what is false, or their testimony is true.

3. But it is maintained by Hume and others, that even if a miracle had been wrought it would be proof only to those who saw it. No testimony could convince others of the fact.

The argument is, that the uniformity of the laws of nature is a matter of universal experience, and that such is our knowledge of that uniformity that no testimony can convince us of the existence of a fact which is not consistent with it.

But the history of the world shows the contrary. Hume is actually presenting his argument, that no such proof could or would be accepted, to men who have already actually accepted it.

There are many events in the world which seem contrary to the uniformity of nature; as much so to the ignorant mind as the most wonderful miracle to the educated. Are such not accepted? What is more apparently opposed to the uniformity of nature, as perceived by ignorant men, than eclipses of the sun or moon, or, to those who have never seen the sea, the phenomenon of water running or swelling upwards in the tides.

Yet testimony of the facts is readily taken as evidence.

The truth is that men almost universally believe, when there is no apparent reason to the contrary, in the truthfulness of their fellows and their capacity to perceive what has happened. Even strangers are trusted to this extent. But when men of known probity, having no motive to deceive and who cannot be self-deceived, testify to any fact, however incredible, conviction of the truthfulness of such persons is stronger than belief in the uniformity of nature.

What would appear more wonderful than that a world, the greater part of the surface of which is water, should be burned up with fire? Yet a whole audience, to nine-tenths of whom previously such a thing would have seemed incredible, has been known to accept it as a fact upon the mere statement of a single scientific man.

In this argument the statements of the Bible have been used not as inspired truth, but merely as containing human testimony. In like manner in the succeeding argument the Bible is treated merely upon its own apparent merits as a book, without reference to its divine character.

(5.) The fifth argument *a posteriori* is from the contents of a book we call the Bible, which claims to have come from God. If these contents show a supernatural origin they prove the existence of a mind supreme above nature

This proof may be presented:

1. With respect to the prophecies of the Bible. Events were predicted and recorded by its writers long periods, even centuries, before they took place. Many of them were minutely described, as to their nature, locality, persons, times, circumstances and causes. Such descriptions show such knowledge as belongs only to one who uses no conjectural knowledge, but knows certainly what will come to pass. But such knowledge of the far future can arise not otherwise than from full knowledge of the eternal purpose of God.

2. It may be presented with reference to the great central figure of the Bible, our Lord Jesus Christ.

The Scriptures taken as a whole is his biography. The causes of his existence as seen in the original and fallen state of man and in God's mercy to our sinful race, the preparation for his coming, the gradual development of the doctrine of his person and work, the prophecy of his kingdom, his appearance, life, death, resurrection, the establishment of his throne in heaven upon his ascension from earth, the gift of the Holy Ghost, the power and progress of his religion and its suitableness to our sinful race, all present a life of developed growth as plainly the result of a creative mind as the most wonderful creation of fiction. The unity of purpose is seen throughout. In the beginning we see but dimly what is taught and catch but feebly the outlines of the plot; but as we progress it grows upon us as a genuine creation. Whatever was at first dim is cleared up by the final record, and as we begin to read it over once more, its perfect unity, its exactness of detail without superfluity, its development in the far future of the importance of facts which at first were only casually stated, as though of no special importance, its skillful interweaving of the minor characters and events, and its use of them in all their fullness to bring on the final catastrophe and its results, the great power with which the theme is handled, the majestic simplicity which everywhere pervades it, all show a master artist creating a character and work, through the instrumentality of writers so numerous, of such different capacities, under such various circumstances, with such manifest unity, as proclaims the mind of God which alone could conceive of such a character and work, and alone could thus reveal it to man, as he alone could create the real persons and events which embody the idea presented.

3. A further proof from the Bible is suggested by Nitzsch: namely, the revelation which it makes of God in Christ.

He says, "The proof which is peculiar to Christianity, independent and historical, is not indeed, as some designate it, miracle, but the accomplishment of the passage in Isaiah 40:9. 'Behold your God.' It is revelation in an eminent sense, the existence of God in Christ, John 14:9." [Nitzsch: System of Christian Doctrine, p. 140.]

This is not the same argument as the last. That was an argument from a development extending over so many thousand years, and proving the existence of one, who was contemporaneous with all those years, working out the character of Christ as the Saviour of mankind.

This is based upon the evidence of divine perfection seen in Christ while here on earth. "He that hath seen me, hath seen the Father." John 14:9.

The revelation of the nature of God seen in the universe commends to us the fact that he exists, for the nature indicated is one worthy of such a being. Hence the force of Paul's language in Rom. 1:20. "For the invisible things of him since the creation of the world are clearly seen, being perceived through the things that are made, even his Everlasting power and Divinity."

So also with equal self-recommendation comes the character of God set forth in the words of the Bible in which he tells us what he is, and commends his spiritual nature with its unspeakable holiness, justice, goodness, and truth, with its infinite power and wisdom, as the character alone worthy of a God, and which makes us say a once: This is the true character of God. If he exists he must be such as is thus described.

But in his incarnate Son we see the embodiment of that which before had appeared as but an ideal. Although appearing here on earth most obviously as a man, yet the divine attributes and character were so exhibited in him that we perceive the truthfulness with which Christ said to Philip: "He that hath seen me, hath seen the Father." John 14:9.

(6.) The sixth argument *a posteriori* is the historical, based upon the fact that the records of history cover so brief a period of time. If man has lived forever, where is the record of that life? It is strange that we find no historical monuments which go beyond few thousand years.

(7.) Finally, an argument *a posteriori* may be drawn from geology. This science teaches:

(a.) That there was a time when life, both vegetable and animal, began upon this globe.

(b.) That the remoteness of the period of that beginning, even according to the wildest hypothesis, is capable of calculation.

(c.) That, in both the vegetable and animal life, of which we have fossil remains, there have been distinct successive genera which began with small numbers, gradually increased to their culminating points and then as gradually decreased.

History and geology, therefore, furnish us conclusive proof against the eternity of form and life in the universe, and especially oppose the absurd idea of endless succession of finite objects or beings, in the past. Geology, indeed, seems also to give proof of an actual direct creation of the first beginnings of each of these genera.

Thus, through the proofs of the existence of God, derived from many sources, do we arrive at that certainty of the fact which confirms the teaching of tradition. In the *a priori* arguments we proceed from admitted first principles to the existence of God, through demonstration, and acknowledge that the arguments are inconclusive if they fail to secure such absolute conviction as do the problems of mathematics. But the arguments *a posteriori* do not belong to this class of proof, but to that which is the only one found in the accepted theories of science. Scientific proof is only inductive proof, and no induction of science is more certainly true than that God exists. No theory of science more fully answers all of the demands for the explanation of facts than does the theory that God exists respond to all the explanations required. None has been so universally, and so variously, and so successfully, tested. The theory of gravitation has been constantly becoming more acceptable until now it is held as scientifically certain, because of its success in accounting for all facts connected with it. In like manner has the theory that God exists been confirmed to almost universal satisfaction, by the fact that without it there is no explanation of the innumerable facts around us, while with it there is nothing lacking to account for the cause and origin of all things.

CHAPTER 3

REASON AND REVELATION

HAVING considered the proofs of the existence of God, we should discuss the ways in which he has made himself known, before we study his nature, and attributes, and relations to us. These constitute the sources of our knowledge of Theology, which are two, Reason and Revelation.

Reason is that power in man, which enables him to have mental perceptions, to exercise thought, and reflection, to know facts, to inquire into their mutual relations, and to deduce, logically, the conclusions which may be drawn from them.

Reason may be used either with reference to the natural or supernatural means of knowledge conferred by God.

When we refer to reason as a source of knowledge distinct from revelation, we mean the information attained, by the use of this faculty, in connection only with the natural, as distinguished from the supernatural.

By revelation, we mean the knowledge which God conveys by direct supernatural instruction, pre-eminently that given in the book known as the Bible.

Reason involves all the cognitive powers of man, which are the faculties through which the mind attains knowledge. These faculties are not separate, and independent, but are merely the instruments of the mind.

The mind is not itself an original source of knowledge, like the Scriptures, but is merely an instrument by which the man attains knowledge through the exercise of its appropriate faculties. There are no such things as innate ideas. These arrive only through the exercise of proper thought and reflection, in connection with some perceived facts.

The means by which the mind attains knowledge in the exercise of its faculties, are five.

1. Consciousness, by which we learn our own existence, and the fact that we think, and are personal beings, possessing personal identity during the term of our natural life.

2. Observation, and experience of the world about us, through the senses.

3. Through intuitive conceptions, by which, upon the suggestion, through some external object, of some principle, we find ourselves at once convinced of its correctness.

4. The dispositions, instincts and tendencies of our natures.

41

5. The course of events in nature, as tending to good or evil, to what is desirable or disastrous.

It is manifest that the knowledge obtained from these various sources must be abundant to teach man the simple facts upon which rests his duty to God; namely, that there is a God to whom he owes existence, and consequent reverence, service and love, and whose greatness and goodness enforce this obligation; also to show him that that duty has not been discharged, and that he has not the disposition to discharge it; and consequently to render him uneasy in his relations to God, and anxious to appease him, and secure some assurance of his pardon and approval. It has also been thought by many, that through reason alone man attains the conviction of immortality and of a future state of rewards and punishments.

However abundant may be the information thus conveyed to man, it is nevertheless clear that his knowledge in these directions must still remain very imperfect.

This must have been true of man even in a state of innocence. His finite nature and the finite conditions which surrounded him must still have left him ignorant upon many desirable matters. It is natural, therefore, to believe that, in that condition, he received direct communications from God, which are properly esteemed revelations.

But this imperfection must have been greatly increased by any subsequent fall from innocence. By this the perceptions of right and wrong would be dimmed, the power of conscience to enforce the right would be impaired, the desire to do the right would be diminished, prejudices against the right would be created, and affection for God would be greatly decreased, if not entirely obliterated.

Upon these grounds we may infer the necessity of some further source of knowledge of God, and of his will with respect to man.

We may also argue *a priori* as to the nature of this revelation.

1. It must come from God, the source of all our other knowledge. No other could give it, and it is fit that no other should do so.

2. It must be suited to our present condition, confirming the truth already known, and teaching what is practically useful to man as a sinner before God.

3. It must be secured from all possibility of error, so that its teachings may be relied on with equal, if not greater, confidence than those of reason.

4. It must come with authority, claiming and proving its claim to be the Word of God, who has the right to command, and to punish those who disobey his commands; with authority also, that man may with confidence believe and trust the promises and hopes pardon and peace it may hold out.

5. That it will be accompanied by difficulties and mysteries is what may be expected, since these are found frequently attending the knowledge derived from reason.

The gift of such a revelation must of course depend absolutely upon the will of God. It is not for man to say, before it is given, whether it certainly will, or will not, be bestowed.

That it is not improbable may be inferred from the fact that God has already made himself known to us in various ways in ourselves and in nature. If we need further revelation we may hope for it.

The only reason to the contrary is that we have sinned against God, and he may have chosen to abandon us to our fate. But this is not so truly understood until revelation has confirmed our conviction of our sinful estate. On the other hand, the favors which God still bestows, and the means of continued knowledge of him which he affords, indicate that he has not yet consigned us to our deserved fate, and that he may have purposes of mercy towards us.

That which renders it highly probable is the expectation seen in man, in the conceptions he has formed of God, as one to be propitiated by sacrifices and approached with prayer.

If the expectations thus formed are to be verified, the important question arises, in what way can God make known to us the new truth he wills to teach.

They manifestly speak unadvisedly who assert that this can in nowise be done.

If he should so choose, he could impress it on each one in like manner as we attain intuitive conceptions. He might reveal it to individuals in dreams and visions, so as to make each one feel and know that the vision is from God. Those through whom he has revealed himself have in some such way attained absolute conviction that God has spoken to and through them, and with God there is neither impossibility nor difficulty in producing like certainty in the mind of each individual of the race.

But as God usually acts through means, so he has revealed himself to a few, and through them to mankind in general.

The only question then is, how can he give evidence to the race at large that the men he has inspired are indeed his messengers?

This also might be done in various ways, but he has chosen to do it by attesting their mission by miracles wrought through them.

As to the measure of authority to be ascribed to these miracles, men differ in opinion.

Some teach that any miracle wrought is of itself sufficient attestation of the messenger and of the truth which he teaches.

Others, that miracles are only proofs to those who behold them, and dubious proofs even then, and that the true purpose of them is not to set the seal of God's authority, but simply to awaken attention and excite awe, and thus prepare the way for a proper hearing of the divine message. These assert that the revelation comes to us with the authority only of the self-convincing nature of the truth made known.

It is necessary, in this difference of opinions, to seek carefully after the true theory. From no source can we better obtain it than from the revelation itself, the teaching of which will be seen to be fully corroborated otherwise.

The Scripture theory seems to be this, that in any new revelation the prophet of God must present a doctrine perfectly consistent with every past revelation and with the knowledge conveyed by nature, and must, at the same time, confirm by miracles his authority as a teacher from God. Without the miracle the new truth has no evidence that it is not simply the product of human reason or imagination. The coincidence in doctrine is necessary to protect against pretended miracles and the tricks of unprincipled men. Besides, the new truth can have no higher authority than the old, and therefore cannot supersede it, for the old also has come from God. No truth ever taught by God can be opposed by any new truth from him. What with God is truth is eternal truth. Like himself, it is the same "yesterday, to-day and forever." It may be more abundantly or clearly revealed. We may learn to comprehend it better and to correct our own misapprehensions of it, but whatever God has once given as truth must so remain forever, as changeless as his own life.

1. The Scriptural authority for this theory is conclusive.

Moses announced the law, which shows the miracle alone not to be conclusive. See Deut. 13:1, 2, 3. "If there arise in the midst of thee a prophet, or a dreamer of dreams, and he give thee a sign or a wonder, and the sign or the wonder come to pass, whereof he spake unto thee, saying, let us go after other gods which thou hast not known, and let us serve them; thou shalt not hearken unto the words of that prophet, or unto that dreamer of dreams: for the Lord your God proveth you to know whether ye love the Lord your God with all your heart and with all your soul." This passage shows that even a miracle, wrought by one teaching doctrine not in accordance with that already received, should not tempt to belief in the divine authority of him who should work it.

The Apostle Paul gives similar instruction to the Galatians, Gal. 1:8: "Though we, or an angel from heaven, should preach unto you any gospel other than that which we preached unto you, let him be anathema." Whatever might be the accredited authority of the messenger, his teachings were not to be received.

Yet, with all this, the Scriptures do not disparage the miracle. The miracles of Mosaic times are constantly referred to as indubitably marking it as divine. Nicodemus recognized the high position assigned to miracles by the Jews, John 3:2: "No man can do these signs that thou doest, except God be with him." Christ himself says, John 10:25: "The works that I do in my Father's name, these bear witness of me."

This theory of the Scriptures is not necessarily based upon the idea that real miracles can be wrought otherwise than by divine power. Still the language sometimes used is liable to this construction. And much depends upon the definition of a miracle. If a miracle be a suspension of the fixed laws which God has established for the world, that suspension can only occur through his special permission. Taking this as the true meaning of the word, we can understand why such stress is laid in the Scriptures upon the Mosaic miracles and those of Christ, since many of them are such as nothing but divine power could accomplish. But the word miracle in the Scriptures has not this restricted meaning, but is applied likewise to any marked supernatural event. Because men are apt to put these upon a level with the miracles which God alone can work, they are warned not to follow after what is thus supernaturally done, if it be accompanied by such teaching as is contrary to truth already received.

See the apparent reality of such miracles in connection with the magicians of Egypt, Ex. 7:11; chap. 8:7, and compare with it the conviction expressed by the magicians, Ex. 8:19, when they failed to produce lice from the dust, "This is the finger of God."

Notice also what Christ says, Mark 13:22: "For there shall arise false Christs and false prophets, and shall shew signs and wonders, that they may lead astray, if possible, the elect."

See also Rev. 16:13, 14: "And I saw coming out of the mouth of the dragon, and out of the mouth of the beast, and out of the mouth of the false prophet, three unclean spirits, as it were frogs, for they are spirits of devils, working signs; which go forth unto the kings of the whole world, to gather them together unto the war of the great day of God the Almighty."

It is because of this liability to be deceived, that the Scriptures require the miracle and the concurrent doctrine as both essential to the reception of a new revelation.

2. This theory alone concurs with the course to which nature necessarily impels us.

To the extent that we are fully convinced of the truth of a doctrine, no subsequent revelation could change our belief. It is true that this does not apply when we have doubts; but when our knowledge is fixed, we cannot be moved. No amount of miracle could convince a Christian that the nature of God is otherwise than pure and holy, or that he delights in worship not of the heart, or that he is not infinite in justice and holiness, in goodness, mercy and truth, or that be will pardon sin without due satisfaction to his law.

3. This theory accords with the progressive character of divine revelation.

The earliest revelation came to those who had heretofore been guided only by reason. This was true even down to the beginnings of the Old Testament Scriptures, and, in that economy, only preparation was made for the future glory of the New Testament revelation. Hence the truths taught were, for the most part, only those which come within the compass of discovery by reason, or acceptance by it upon due suggestion, namely—the existence of one God, the fact of creation, the law of moral obligation to God and man, the punishment of sinners, the duty of repentance, the pardoning mercy of God, and the law of sacrifices, with substitution and satisfaction.

The new economy goes further in its clear instructions: it teaches the vicarious atonement of Christ, involving representation in him and also in Adam, the doctrine of the Trinity in the Godhead, the mysterious union in the person of Christ, and many other truths heretofore only very indistinctly revealed.

These could not have been presented to those only taught heretofore by reason. But the revelation which stood between foreshadowed them in different ways. From it alone originally they would not have been discovered. But now that they are made known, that former revelation is seen to concur with the new statements, and the conformity of the clearly expressed doctrines to the mere outlines of them in the past sustains the fact that they have a common author, and that the divine revealer is the same. It is like the presence in animals of the same genus in earlier days of germs which find their development in species which come later.

4. This accords with our means of judging what course of action infinite wisdom would have devised.

The conviction we have of past truth renders it impossible that we should throw it aside. We must, therefore, still hold it fast. That conviction has come from God, and we can have no higher evidence.

Yet, other statements and doctrines very probably or even certainly true, may be taught by men, as revealed to them, when they are either self-deceived, or attempting to deceive others. Hence, we must have the attesting miracle.

On the other hand, we are liable to be deceived as to what is supernatural, and especially, in the supernatural, as to what is within the limits of created power. Hence, we may be misled by the craft of men, or by the superhuman power of wicked spirits. Therefore, no doctrine must be accepted contrary to a truth already received.

A revelation, such as we have described, having been given and proved, another question arises: what is the relation which reason bears towards it?

We may lay down the following facts:

1. That reason is the first revelation, and is consequently presupposed in any other.

2. That the facts of reason cannot be denied by any subsequent revelation. No truth can destroy other truth.

A limitation must, however, be put on the province of reason. The doctrines of which it may judge, are those only which come within its sphere. Upon the presentation of a new doctrine reason may decide whether it agrees with former knowledge. If agreeable thereto, it must be accepted, if opposed, it must be rejected. But, if it be above reason, it must stand or fall with the rest of the revelation. God may, in his mercy, refrain from trying faith by a revelation of supernatural doctrine, but, if he reveals it, it must be no barrier to the reception of that doctrine itself, or of the revelation which accompanies it. In an able article in the *Southern Presbyterian Review*, Vol. I, pp. 1–34, on "Reason and Revelation," Dr. Thornwell puts this limitation upon reason, that it is sole arbiter within its own bounds, but no judge beyond them. He thinks that in this way only can it be applied as a test of doctrine.

The theory is undoubtedly correct. It fails only in not recognizing the precise manner in which Scripture brings it in as an arbiter, not as the judge of truth as disconnected from the past, but as related to the various times and forms in which God has taught it. Reason should judge a new revelation, not by the truths taught by reason alone, but also by those which have been made known in any previous revelation.

The office of reason with respect to revelation, is therefore seen to be:

1. To examine the evidence of the miracles upon which it rests.

2. To compare its doctrines with the teaching of the past, and recognize their correspondence with or opposition to that teaching.

3. To adopt or reject the revelation according to the evidence afforded that it is God's truth.

4. To interpret its contents, according to the best light which learning affords.

CHAPTER 4

THE UNITY OF GOD

THE arguments by which we have proved the existence of God have shown us:

1. From that of causation; that he is self-existent, having the cause of his existence in himself.

2. From the proof of design and from his creation of spirit; that he is an intelligent personal and spiritual being.

3. From the non-eternity of matter; that he alone is eternal.

4. From providence and miracles; that he continues to rule and govern the world which he has created.

In them all have been the foundations upon which proofs of his wisdom, power, and goodness, as well as many other attributes are based.

The information thus received is however insufficient, and is capable of being greatly increased by further examination. Having proved that God is, we naturally desire to know more of what he is and who he is.

This leads to an inquiry into his nature or essence, and, since the nature and essence of all being, even of ourselves, can be known only by considering its mode of existence, its qualities and its manner of manifestation, we are led to inquire into the mode of God's existence and into the attributes and works by which he has made himself known to us.

Preliminary to this, however, are two subjects which demand attention, viz.: The Unity and the Spirituality of God.

THE UNITY OF GOD

1. The proof thus far attained, to say the least of it, is not inconsistent with that unity. Indeed one God is all that is demanded by or involved in that proof.

But one first cause is needed; but one designer is suggested; one being alone meets all the conditions arising from our sense of dependence on another; but one is required to account for the evidences of providential care over the world; but one for the wonders in miracles; but one for the Scriptures with their prophesies and their revelation of Christ and God; and but one for the common consent of mankind.

48

This last point is the only apparent exception.

But (1.) Universal consent only goes so far as to admit the existence of one God. Many have in one way or another assumed that there are more, but the belief in more than one is not universal.

(2.) The belief of more than one God was not the earliest type, but has been the result of corruption of the truth. This may be accounted for either from reverence for objects as representations of the divinity, as of the heavenly lights or for animals or statues representing deified attributes of God; or from veneration for men after death regarded as exponents of such attributes.

(3.) The belief of one God thus found in the earliest records of all nations was maintained among most men of intelligence even in the days of Heathenism. See Cudworth's Intellectual System of the Universe, Vol. I., pp. 293–638, for ancient Latin, Greek, Persian and Egyptian opinions.

As to Brahminism, see Maurice's Religions of the World, p. 59.

As to Buddhism, see Maurice, p. 102–3.

As to the classic writers, see also the testimony of Cicero de Natura deorum, pp. 11–13 of translation in Bohn's library.

As to the mass of Heathenism we have this testimony from Tertullian, quoted by Tholuck on Heathenism, p. 23.

"In the deepest emotions of their minds they never directed their exclamations to their false gods, but employed the words 'By God,' 'As truly as God lives,' 'God help me.' Moreover they do not have their eyes directed to the capitol, but to heaven."

This belief in one God is true, even of that dualism which arose among the Persians because of their knowledge of the struggle between good and evil connected with the presence of sin in the world. They believed in a God superior to the two contestants in this struggle and thus they may be claimed as accepting the idea of the unit of God. See Cudworth, Vol. I., p. 411, etc.

The argument for universal consent therefore does not demand more than one God.

2. But the proof of God's existence is not only not inconsistent with the unity of God, but renders that unity highly probable and indeed almost certain.

The unity of the first cause, and of the designer is naturally if not necessarily involved in the unity of will or purpose or design, seen in the effects produced in Creation and Providence.

These show at least such perfect harmony and agreement between the wills of all gods, if there be more than one, as can result only from one Being, or from several as fully agreeing together as though they were but one.

But the very idea of will involves choice, and choice involves such right and possibility to select between two or more things as forbids universal original agreement in choice between two different beings. Either, therefore, there must be difference of choice, which would destroy the uniformity, or there must be a subordination of will one to another, which gives supremacy to one of the beings. This result would be to make that one a first cause of will or action to the others, and therefore to make him alone God.

If, therefore, there is uniformity in the designs and works of nature, that is almost if not quite certain proof that there is but one God.

That uniformity is seen,

(1.) In the materials which compose it.

(2.) In the qualities possessed by these materials.

(3.) In the nature of the forces which they evolve.

(4.) In the unity of design between all living forms, fishes, reptiles, birds, and mammalia in all parts of the world whether adapted for air, water or earth, whether in fossils of the past or living organisms of the present; and in like unity seen in one species only as germs and developed into perfected organs in another separated from it by a wide interval of time.

3. The only objection to the unity of God which can be drawn from the world arises from the presence of pain and ill, of sorrow and suffering, of guilt and sin, together with the violent and destructive forces of nature.

(1.) But these are not inconsistent with the unity of God.

(a.) If they ought not to be and God could prevent them, they would prove lack of goodness, not of unity.

(b.) If they ought not to be and God cannot prevent them, then they would prove some other being to exist greater than he, and then that other being would be God.

(c.) The evils referred to are as apparently under uniform general laws as any other facts or events of nature.

(2.) But there is no evidence that these evils ought not to be, and are not perfectly consistent with God's goodness.

(a.) They may be part of a system which best exists in connection with them. We see this in part so far as the destructive forces of the world are concerned.

(b.) We find among them traces of a working together for final and intermediate good ends, and hence they may safely be said neither to militate against goodness nor unity.

4. But while some of the arguments for God are only consistent with his unity and highly suggestive of the same, and others make it so highly probable as to be almost certain, there are others which establish it with absolute certainty.

(1.) The idea of God in the mind, to which is attached that of necessary existence, is the idea of one God, and one only. The notion of two or more gods is self-contradictory, for neither of them can be the absolute and perfect and independent being which is our idea of God. All the evidence for God therefore contained in the first of the *a priori* arguments is for one God and one only.

(2.) In the argument from the nature of necessary existence (the second *a priori*), the 7th point was: "There can be but one necessarily existent being, for two necessarily existent beings could in no respect whatever differ from each other; that is, they would be one and the same being."

The nature of necessary existence therefore proves the unity of God.

5. The proofs we have thus far presented from nature for the unity of God are abundantly confirmed by the statements of Scripture.

(1.) The passages which declare explicitly that God is one: Deut. 6:4; Mal. 2:10: "Hath not one God created us?" Mark 12:29, 32; 1 Tim. 2:5; Eph. 4:5, 6; James 2:19.

(2.) Those that assert that there is none else or none beside him: Deut. 4:35, 39; 1 Sam. 2:2; 2 Sam. 7:22; 1 Kings 8:60; Isa. 44:6, 8; Isa. 45:5, 6, 21, 22; Isa. 46:9; Joel 2:27.

(3.) That there is none like him nor to be compared with him: Ex. 8:10; 9:14; 15:11; 2 Sam. 7:22; 1 Kings 8:23; 2 Chron. 6:14; Isa. 40:25; Isa. 46:5; Jer. 10:6.

(4.) That he alone is God: 2 Sam. 22:32; Neh. 9:6; Ps. 18:31; 86:10; Isa. 37:16; 43:10, 12; 46:9; John 17:3; 1 Cor. 8:4–6.

(5.) That he alone is to be worshipped: Ex. 20:5; 34:14; 1 Sam. 7:3; 2 Kings 17:36; Matt. 4:10; Rom. 1:25; Rev. 19:10.

(6.) Those which forbid any one else to be accepted as God: Ex. 20:3; Deut. 5:7; Isa. 42:8; Hosea 13:4.

(7.) Which proclaim him as supreme over all so-called gods: Deut. 10:17; Josh. 22:22; Ps. 96:4, 5; Jer. 14:22; 1 Cor. 8:4–6.

(8.) Which declare him to be the true God: Jer. 10:10; 1 Thess. 1:9.

This Scripture doctrine of the unity of God is not affected by some expressions which at first sight appear to contradict it.

(a.) The Bible does not deny that unity where the gods of the heathen are spoken of as their gods: Deut. 10:17, "The Lord your God, he is God of gods and Lord of lords;" Josh. 22:22, "The Lord the God of gods, the Lord the God of gods, he knoweth and Israel he shall know;" Judges 8:33; 9:27; 11:24; 16:23, 24; 1 Sam. 5:7; 1 Kings 11:33; 2 Kings 1:2, 16, and many other passages. Psalm 96:4, 5: "For great is the Lord and highly to be praised; he is to be feared above all gods. For all the gods of the peoples are idols; but the Lord made the heavens."

Jeremiah 14:22: "Are there any among the vanities of the heathen that can cause rain? or can the heavens give showers? art not thou he, O Lord our God?"

1 Cor. 8:4, 5, 6: "Concerning therefore the eating of things sacrificed to idols, we know that no idol is any thing in the world, and that there is no god but one. For though there be that are called gods, whether in heaven or on earth; as there are gods many, and lords many; yet to us there is one God, the Father, of whom are all things, and we unto him."

1. Such gods are only so-called gods and exalted to such places by the false conceptions of men.

2. Many of them have solely imaginary existence.

3. Where there is any corresponding existence, they are but creatures of God, dependent upon him for existence and even permission to exercise power and influence.

4. Many of these gods are identified in the New Testament with the devils which Christ cast out, and which were subject to him and his disciples, and who are only the angels or messengers of Satan, and therefore fallen created angels.

Acts 17:18. Some of the philosophers who met Paul at Athens said of him, "He seemeth to be a setter forth of strange gods," (demons). This passage shows that the word which is constantly used in the New Testament for the devils cast out, was a word properly used by these Greeks as applicable to their gods.

But we have places in which the word is applied by the sacred writers themselves to these gods.

1 Cor. 10:20, 21. "The things which the Gentiles sacrifice, they sacrifice to devils, and not to God: and I would not that ye should have communion with devils. Ye cannot drink the cup of the Lord, and the cup of devils: ye cannot partake of the table of the Lord, and of the table of devils."

Rev. 9:20. "And the rest of mankind which were not killed with these plagues, repented not of the works of their hands, that they should not worship devils, and the idols of gold, and of silver, and of brass, and of stone, and of wood which can neither see, nor hear nor walk."

(b.) The word god is also applied to Moses and others.

Ex. 4:16. "And he (Aaron) shall be thy spokesman unto the people: and it shall come to pass, that he shall be to thee a mouth, and thou shalt be to him as God."

Ex. 7:1. "And the Lord said, unto Moses, See, I have made thee a god to Pharaoh."

John 10:34, 35. "Jesus answered them, Is it not written in your law, I said, ye are gods? If he called them gods, unto whom the word of God came [and the Scripture cannot be broken]."

The reference is to Ps. 82:6, 7, "I said ye are gods, (Elohim,) and all of you sons of the Most High. Nevertheless ye shall die like men, and fall like one of the princes."

As to these passages referring to Moses, the idea manifestly is that he stood before Aaron and Pharaoh as the representative of God, clothed with his authority and having the right to demand confidence in his utterances and obedience to his commands. But all of this, not because of any partaking of divine nature, but because he was God's ambassador.

As to the passage in the Psalms, quoted by Christ, it is equally manifest that this was a metaphorical use of the words to denote the recognition of exalted dignity and mighty power. In the psalm, from which the words are taken, it is said in the 1st verse, "God standeth in the congregation of God; he judgeth among the gods." This language and the threat that they "shall die like men" in the 6th verse, show that it was applied to men who are only metaphorically spoken of as gods.

The doctrine of the Trinity is not opposed to the unity of God, but only enables us to form just conceptions as to that unity.

It presents to us three Persons who are not three gods, but one God, and, as will hereafter be seen, shows us that the unity of God is to be found in his nature or essence and not in the personal relations in that essence, so that there is but one divine nature or essence, one being, one god, although there are three persons subsisting therein, who, by virtue of that subsistence, are each God.

We are not led by this doctrine of the unity of God, therefore, to adopt the Arian notion that the Father is Supreme God and the Son only a divine being in a subordinate sense. Nor is it proper to accept the Sabellian notion, that God is one person, manifesting himself sometimes as Father, sometimes as Son, and sometimes as Holy Ghost. "Neither does it at all teach tritheistic unity by which these are really three gods, but considered one because they have the same nature, just as three men may be said to be one because of the same human nature." See Gill, vol. 1, pp. 183, 184 from which this is condensed.

Chapter 5

Spirituality of God

HAVING in the last chapter discussed the unity of God, we proceed in this to the consideration of his spirituality. This is the second subject preliminary to that of his attributes. The attempt will be made to prove, not only that God has a spiritual nature, but that he is a pure spirit without outward form or material organization.

I. The one God has undoubtedly a spiritual nature.

1. He is the creator of spirits. But spirit is the highest order of existence and its creator must himself have the nature which belongs to that order.

2. The creation and government of the world give evidence of wisdom, skill, knowledge and purpose, but there are attributes of spirit. God therefore must have a spiritual nature.

3. We arrive at the idea of the perfect being by the exclusion of all imperfection and the ascription of all perfection. But spiritual nature is in every respect a perfection. Therefore we ascribe it to God.

4. The Scriptures ascribe a spiritual nature to God.

It is involved in the abundant language about the spirit of God, in which, however, reference is had distinctively to the third person in the Trinity.

It is also presupposed in all the intellectual, moral, and emotional thoughts and acts ascribed to him.

But it is directly asserted in two places: John 4:24, the language of our Lord to the woman of Sychar: "God is a spirit, and they that worship him must worship in spirit and truth."

Again in Heb. 12:9, where fathers of the flesh and of the spirit are contrasted. "Furthermore, we have had the fathers of our flesh to chasten us, and we gave them reverence: shall we not much rather be in subjection unto the Father of spirits and live?"

Compare also Acts 17:24, 25. "The God that made the world and all things therein, he, being Lord of heaven and earth, dwelleth not in temples made with hands; neither is he served by men's hands, as though he needed anything," etc.

II. But when we ascribe spirituality to God, we do not intend simply to assert that he possesses a spiritual nature, but that his nature is exclusively spiritual. By this we mean that he has no material organization, that he has neither body nor members of the body such as we have, neither shape nor form, neither passions nor limitations, but only a spiritual nature.

1. This is evident from his immensity and eternity (infinity in time and space).

To have an omnipresent and eternal mode of existence is possible for a spiritual nature, because spirit has not of necessity succession of time and specific limitation of location. But these of necessity belong to matter. It is of necessity that it has a here, and not an everywhere; spirit alone can combine the two, the here and the everywhere. It is also of necessity that matter exists in time; we know that it exists now, that it existed yesterday, that it may exist tomorrow. We know that it necessarily has this succession and difference of time. But with the eternal God there can be no succession of time, and consequently he can have no material nature but must be purely spiritual.

2. It also follows from his independence and immutability.

If God have body, he is capable of being influenced from without, for all matter is thus capable of being influenced, of being moved, divided, added to and diminished. But if thus capable of influence from without he is not independent. Therefore the independent God cannot be material.

Again, if he is body, he is mutable, for all matter is capable of change. Therefore the immutable God cannot be material.

3. This may be proved from his absolute perfection.

(a.) Negatively. From the idea of absolute perfection we exclude all that admits of limitation or change. But body is both limited and changeable. Therefore the absolute perfection of God excludes a bodily organism.

(b.) Positively. To absolute perfection we ascribe the possession of intelligence, will and moral perception. But these do not belong to body. Therefore body cannot be either in part or whole the absolutely perfect one.

4. We realize in ourselves, the defects of a material organization, how it confines us, how it causes pain and suffering, how it imposes on us joy in sensual pleasures, how incapable it is of knowledge and power in itself. Hence we naturally disbelieve that in God is to be found an organism so necessarily imperfect. On the other hand we find our spiritual natures to be of wondrous power and capacity, endowed with intelligence, skill and wisdom, capable of knowing right and wrong, and the true and the false, and possessed of liberty of choice, and we therefore ascribe to God the possession of such a nature to an infinite extent, with infinite intelligence, skill and wisdom, and a will absolutely untrammeled from without.

In apparent opposition to this doctrine of the pure spirituality of God is a large number of passages, which represent God in or with bodily form. This language is partly figurative, and partly used as an accommodation to human thought, and to the incapacity of human language to express exclusively divine things. Such language is called anthropomorphic, and is generally so obviously such, as to make no false impression, even upon the most ignorant.

The following is a corrected list of the passages as collected in West's *Analysis*, pp. 17–19.

Those which speak of him *as having location:* Gen. 4:16; Ex. 19:17–21; 20:21; 33:14, 15.

As having motion: Gen. 17:22; 18:33; Ex. 19:20; Num. 12:5; 23:4; Deut. 33:2; Judg. 5:4; 1 Sam. 4:7; Ps. 47:5; 68:7, 8; Ezek. 11:23; Micah 1:3; Hab. 3:3; Zech. 2:13.

As using vehicles: 2 Sam. 22:11; Ps. 18:10; 104:3; Hab. 3:8, 15; Zech. 9:14.

He is said to dwell on the earth: Ex. 25:8; 29:43, 44; 1 Kings 6:13; 8:12, 13; 2 Chron. 6:1, 2; Ps. 132:14; Mic. 1:2, 3; Hab. 2:20.

He dwells with man: Ex. 29:45; Lev. 26:11, 12; 2 Chron. 6:18; Zech. 2:10; Rev. 21:3.

He dwells in men: 1 Cor. 3:16, 17; 6:19.

He has face: Gen. 32:30; Ex. 33:11, 20; Deut. 5:4; 34:10; Rev. 20:11; *eyes:* 2 Chron. 16:9; Prov. 22:12; *nostrils:* 2 Sam. 22:9, 16; Ps. 18:15; *mouth:* Num. 12:8; Ps. 18:8; *lips and tongue:* Isa. 30:27; *breath:* Isa. 30:28; *shoulders:* Deut. 33:12; *hand and arms:* Ex. 33:22, 23; Ps. 21:8; 74:11; 89:13; 118:16; Isa. 52:10; Hab. 3:4; *fingers:* Ps. 8:3; *back:* Ex. 33:23; *feet:* Ps. 18:9; *voice:* Ex. 19:19; 20:22; Lev. 1:1; Num. 7:89; 12:4; 22:9; Deut. 4:12, 36; 1 Kings 19:12, 13; Ps. 29:3–9; 68:33; Jer. 25:30, 31; Ezek. 43:6.

His voice is spoken of as dreaded: Ex. 20:19; Deut. 4:33; 5:24–26; Joel 2:11; 3:16; Amos 1:2; Heb. 12:19, 26.

He is said to exercise laughter: Ps. 2:4.

He appears to men: Gen. 35:9; 48:3; Ex. 3:2–6; 19:9; 1 Kings 9:2; Job 42:5, 6; Amos 9:1.

His appearance is described: Ex. 24:10; Deut. 31:15; Isa. 6:1; Ezek. 8:1, 2, 4; 43:2; Dan. 7:9, 10; Rev. 4:5.

He is in human form: Gen. 18:1; Ezek. 1:26, 27; Rev. 4:2, 3.

III. The value of true ideas as to the spirituality of God may be seen from the important consequences which follow from this characteristic of God.

1. It involves concerning the nature of God:

(1.) That he is invisible and intangible, or incapable of apprehension by the bodily senses.

(2.) That he is unchangeable, incorruptible and indestructible.

(3.) That he is simple and uncompounded.

(4.) That he is a living personal being, intelligent, moral, free and active.

(5.) That he is infinite and eternal.

2. Upon it depends in the relation of God to creation:

(1.) His knowledge of all events, and especially of his spiritual creatures.

(2.) His control of all events.

(3.) His purposing all things that shall come to pass.

3. Because of it, he must receive spiritual worship:

(1.) Not that of the body only.

(2.) Nor of the outward form.

(3.) Nor of pretended service.

(4.) But of genuine emotion.

(5.) Because of it, he cannot be represented in that worship by outward forms or images. He is to be approached, not with the bodily senses, but with the communings of the heart. Hence the second commandment, "Thou shalt not make unto thee any graven image, or any likeness of anything that is in heaven above, or that is in the earth beneath, or that is in the water under the earth; thou shalt not bow down thyself to them, nor serve them." Ex. 20:4, 5.

IV. Spirituality has been by some classified as one of the attributes of God. This has possibly arisen from the twofold sense which the word spirituality has. It is used among men as a description of character, when it means that that character is exalted to an extraordinary sense above the fleshly appetites and passions, and devoted to spiritual affairs. In this sense spirituality would be an attribute of character, and therefore of the person possessing that character. But when spirituality is spoken of with reference to God, it is used in the sense in which man is spoken of as a spiritual as well as material being. It is declarative of God as possessing a spiritual nature in the sense that his nature is that of a spirit. It is, therefore, a simple declaration of what his nature is, and not a statement of an attribute of that nature. It is, consequently, no more to be classed among the attributes of God than is his unity. These two subjects have, therefore, been treated separately and as preliminary questions to the consideration of his attributes.

Chapter 6

Divine Attributes

THE Attributes of God are those peculiarities which mark or define the mode of his existence, or which constitute his character.

They are not separate nor separable from his essence or nature, and yet are not that essence, but simply have the ground or cause of their existence in it, and are at the same time the peculiarities which constitute the mode and character of his being.

As they are not separable from his essence, so they are not to be regarded as so many different powers and peculiarities or faculties, which so belong to God that he is "composed of different elements." Hodge, 1:369. This would take away the simplicity of the divine nature and make it compound and therefore divisible and changeable.

But, on the other hand, they are not simply our different conceptions of God. They have existence independently of his creatures. There is some true foundation in God himself for the distinctions between them, so that, when we speak of God as wise, we do not only say that we conceive of him differently than when we call him just, but we mean that there is that in God which makes it proper that we should conceive of him under the different aspects of wisdom and justice.

CLASSIFICATIONS

Various divisions have been made of the attributes of God.

1. One is into communicable and incommunicable.

The communicable attributes are those which, to a limited degree, he can also bestow upon his creatures. Such are power, knowledge, wisdom, love, holiness, etc.

The incommunicable are those which cannot thus be bestowed, but which, of necessity, exist only in God. Such are self-existence, immutability, and infinity including immensity and eternity.

2. Another division is into relative and absolute. The relative are those which may be exercised towards objects which are without, the absolute, which exist only in connection with God.

3. Still another division is into transient attributes, or such as pass over to his creatures, and immanent, or such as ever remain in God alone.

4. A fourth division is into positive and negative attributes, the positive being those which ascribe perfections to God, and the negative those which deny imperfections.

These four divisions are however identical. The attributes ranked under the communicable are also placed among the relative, and the transient, and the positive, and those defined as incommunicable are classified as absolute, and immanent, and negative.

5. A further division has been made into the natural and moral attributes.

By the natural attributes are meant those which describe the mode of his existence without respect to personal character; by the moral, those which describe his character.

Dr. Charles Hodge justly objects to this division because the "word natural is ambiguous. Taking it in the sense of what constitutes or pertains to the nature, the holiness and justice of God are as much natural as his power or knowledge. And on the other hand God is infinite and eternal in his moral perfections, although infinity and eternity are not distinctively moral perfections. In the common and familiar sense of the word natural, the terms natural and moral express a real distinction."—Sys. Theol., Vol. I., pp. 375, 376.

In the discussion of the divine attributes, those which belong to the incommunicable, or absolute, or immanent, or negative class will first be considered. These are simplicity, which denies composition; infinity, which, either as eternity denies limitation as to time, or as immensity denies it as to space; and immutability, which rejects all possibility of change in God. After that will be taken up, in the order named, the communicable, relative, transient, or positive attributes of power, knowledge, wisdom, holiness, goodness, love, truth and justice. The remainder of this chapter will be devoted to the simplicity and infinity of God.

THE SIMPLICITY OF GOD

By this we mean, that the nature of God, comprising his essence and his attributes, is simple or uncompounded pure spirit.

It means more than his unity, for the latter expresses only the fact that there is but one being, that is, God. Were God both matter and spirit, or compounded in any other way, his unity would not be affected.

Were there but one man in the world, we should ascribe to him unity, and if there could be but one we should ascribe *essential unity*.

It means more than the spirituality of God, for that includes only that he must be spiritual, and, also, as we have seen, that he should be purely spiritual.

But there is nothing contradictory in the idea, that created spirits might have a composite spiritual nature, composed, for example, of mind, soul and spirit, as three distinct essences, or that a spiritual nature should have a spiritual body, as well as a spiritual soul.

But in God there can be no composition, and therefore his spiritual nature must be uncompounded. Even his attributes and his nature must be in such a manner one, that his attributes essentially inhere in that nature and are not capable of separation from it, which really makes them one with that nature.

The reasons for this are:

1. Because composition (or a putting together) involves possibility of separation. But this would involve destructibility, and changeableness, each of which is inconsistent with absolute perfection and necessary existence.

2. Composition involves a time of separate existence of the parts compounded. If so, then there was a time when God did not exist, because the parts of his nature had not been united, or, when he existed imperfectly, not having yet received to his essential nature the additions subsequently made; all of which is inconsistent with absolute perfection and necessary existence.

3. If the parts have been compounded, it has been done by some force from without, or has been a growth in his nature. They have not been added from without, because God is independent, and therefore cannot be affected from without. Besides all outward form and all else than God had its origin in him, and he existed as God before it. They have not been a growth in him, for, if so, he is not unchangeable. Any such addition to God or growth in him is also inconsistent with absolute perfection and necessary existence.

In ascribing simplicity to God, therefore, we declare that his nature is so purely or simply one as not to be compounded of separate substances, as matter and spirit, or even of the same substance, in different forms, or of a substance with separable attributes; and we assert that even his attributes are one with his essence, and that he is not only essentially spiritual, but also essentially wise, and good, and holy, and just, and true, and almighty, and omnipotent.

INFINITY OF GOD

When we say that God is infinite, we deny to him all limitation in his nature or essence. We are conscious of the finite nature of our soul as well as of our body; it has limitations as to place, time and capabilities. In arriving at the idea of the perfect being by way of negation, we deny all such limitation in him, and therefore ascribe to him infinity as to time and space, as well as infinite perfection in his mode of existence, in his power, wisdom, goodness, justice, holiness and truth.

The infinity of God as to time is called

HIS ETERNITY

By this we mean:

(1.) That he has no beginning nor end.

(2.) That with him there is no succession of moments.

It is difficult to attain any conception of the mode of existence which is thus ascribed to him. It is so different from our own. Yet a brief consideration of what is involved in the nature of God must convince us that the idea which we express by these statements is just and true.

1. As to the statement that he has no beginning nor end.

When we say that we shall live forever, we can understand how a life once begun may never be completed.

But it is difficult to conceive of a life which goes back equally forever as one may go forward. The past is always completed, and as completed, must be measurable. That which has been by succession of moments or days must have had some first day or moment with which it began. We can form no other conception of it.

That division of eternity, therefore, which is called eternity *a parte post* we can comprehend; but the complement of it, the eternity *a parte ante,* which is united with it to express infinite duration, is felt at once to be an attempted conception of the mind to express the eternity which we know must be true, and yet which we perceive is inadequately conceived as well as incorrectly expressed.

While, therefore, we know that God has had no beginning, we see that his mode of existence cannot have been one in which he has had in the past that ever continuing indefinite duration which corresponds to what may be ours in the future.

2. When we say that during some period a certain being has always existed and will always exist, we mean that there has not only been no moment in that period when he has not existed and will be none in which he will not exist, but that during that period he has been and will be existent in a constant succession of moments. There is at all times, after the beginning, a past and present, and will be, until the end, a future. One moment passes away, and another succeeds. But with God there can be no succession of moments.

(1.) Because then he would have had a beginning, which is opposed to his infinity.

(2.) Because then he would not be unchangeable, for that would be true of him today which was not yesterday and will not be tomorrow.

(3.) He would not be perfect because something could be added to him from day to day. He would become older. He would have new experiences. Indeed there would be either increase or diminution of his power, wisdom, etc.

The schoolmen attempted to express the eternity of God by saying that it is "punctum stans" or "nunc semper stans."

This is the conception of eternity which we strive to attain. Our difficulty in doing so is that we can no more conceive of duration without succession than we can of an eternity *a parte ante.* But we see that in this conception we are not arriving at a thought in itself erroneous, as in the other case, but are simply recognizing the fact that God's mode of existence, as to time, is different from ours. Ours has succession of moments, increase in the length of the period, is not all of it possessed at the same time, has had beginning and might have an end, and has a past and future as well as present. God has no succession, no increase of life, is possessed of the whole of his existence at once, and eternally possessed, has had no beginning, can have no end, and lives in the present only, having no past or future.

This accords with the statements of Scripture. God is always spoken of in the present.

He calls himself I AM. His name Jehovah has been supposed mystically to express this.

The psalmist says: "Before the mountains were brought forth, or ever thou hadst formed the earth and the world, even from everlasting to everlasting, thou art God." Ps. 90:2.

Thus our Lord, when he would declare his equality with the Father, uses the present tense for each. "My Father worketh even until now, and I work." John 5:17.

So also in like manner he declared his divinity by saying, "Before Abraham was, I am." John 8:58.

A question arises, what then is the relation of time and eternity to each other?

Time is not a part of eternity, for if it were, eternity must have succession, viz.: *before* time, *during* time, *after* time.

They are in reality different modes of existence which are unlike each other, time being suited to the measurement of creation periods and creature life. True eternity belongs only to the life of God.

While time, however, is not a part of eternity, it co-exists with it.

Through the divine purpose all its events have been eternally present with God, and as well known and realized by him as though actually existent. And, in the actual existence of time, it has been present actually with God and with eternity, although not constituting a part of eternity.

The nature of these relations we cannot understand. Our ideas are vague, and the language in which we would convey them is incapable of expressing even what we perceive and know. But while this is true, we have no question as to the possibility of better knowledge in the future on this point. The difficulty is in reality no greater than in the connection between the immensity and omnipresence of God. Yet from the knowledge of the presence of our spirits as compared with that of our bodies, we comprehend the fact of the omnipresence of God with all created things, while the space in which they exist is no more a part of his immensity than is time a part of his eternity.

Corresponding to the infinity of God in respect to time, is his infinity in respect to space, which is called

HIS IMMENSITY

God is not confined to space any more than he is measured by time.

Space must have its limitations because its existence is commensurate only with the universe. Where there is no creation, there can be no space nor time. But creation cannot be infinite, but must have its bounds, impossible as it may be for us to imagine the nonexistence of space. In our mode of existence, space and time are so necessary that we cannot even deny their existence without using words which involve that existence. Thus if we say, "Where there is no universe, there is no space," the very words "where" and "there" involve the notion of space.

But notwithstanding this, we know that, just as time is the period, so is space the location, in which creation exists.

When, therefore, we speak of God's immensity, we mean more than his filling all space, just as when we speak of his eternity, we mean more than his existing throughout all time.

We can only express the idea by the fiction of infinite space, as in the other, we have done by that of infinite time.

Immensity is the absolute attribute of God to which corresponds the relative one

HIS OMNIPRESENCE

By this word we express the relation of God as present with creation.

He is present everywhere. He is present at one and the same time everywhere. His presence is not merely contact, but energy and power.

It is not merely through his knowledge of it, or the exertion of his power upon it, but he fills it with his essence.

He fills it, not as part to part, but the whole infinite deity is entirely, undividedly present, at each point of creation, in each moment of time.

The following valuable questions and answers are taken from the Outlines of Theology, by Dr. A. A. Hodge, p. 141, of the new edition.

"What are the different modes of the divine presence?

"God may be conceived of as present in any place, or with any creature, in several modes; first, as to his essence; second, as to his knowledge; third, as manifesting that presence to any intelligent creature; fourth, as exercising his power in or upon his creatures. As to essence and knowledge his presence is the same everywhere and always. As to his self-manifestation and the exercise of his power, his presence differs endlessly in different cases, in degree and mode. Thus God is present to the church as he is not to the world. Thus he is present in hell in the manifestation and execution of righteous wrath, while he is present in heaven in the manifestation and communication of gracious love and glory.

"How may it be proved that he is everywhere present as to his essence?

"That God is everywhere present as to his essence is proved *from Scripture*. 1 Kings 8:27; Ps. 139:7–10; Isaiah 66:1; Acts 17:27, 28. *And from reason.* (1.) It follows necessarily from his infinitude. (2.) From the fact that his knowledge is his essence knowing, and his actions are his essence acting, yet his knowledge and his power reach to all things.

"State the different relations that bodies, created spirits and God sustain to space.

"Turretine says: 'Bodies are conceived of as existing in space *circumscriptively*, because, occupying a certain portion of space, they are bounded by space upon every side. Created spirits do not occupy any portion of space, nor are they embraced by any; they are, however, in space *definitely* as here and not there. God on the other hand is in space *repletively*, because in a transcendent manner his essence fills all space. He is included in no space; he is excluded from none. Wholly present to each point he comprehends all space at once.'"

CHAPTER 7

THE IMMUTABILITY OF GOD

BY the immutability of God is meant that he is incapable of change, either in duration of life, or in nature, character, will or happiness. In none of these, nor in any other respect is there any possibility of change.

1. This is implied in his absolute perfection. Perfection permits neither increase as though he lacks, nor decrease as though he can lose. Change must be for the worse or for the better, but God cannot become worse or better.

2. It arises in like manner from the pure simplicity of his nature. That which is not and cannot be compounded cannot be changed.

3. It is expressly taught by the Scriptures in the following as well as in other particulars. A few passages out of many are referred to in support of each.

(a.) They declare him to be unchangeable in *duration and life:* Gen. 21:33; Deut. 32:39, 40; Ps. 9:7; 55:19; 90:2; 102:12; Hab. 1:12; Rom. 16:26; 1 Tim. 1:17; 6:16.

(b.) They affirm the unchangeableness of his *nature:* Ps. 104:31; Mal. 3:6; Rom. 1:23; James 1:17.

(c.) They also assert that his *will* is without change: Job 23:13; Ps. 33:11; Prov. 19:21.

(d.) His *character* is also said to be immutable, as for example his *justice:* Gen. 18:25; Job 8:3; Rom. 2:2; his *mercy:* Ex. 34:7; Deut. 4:31; Ps. 107:1; Lam. 3:22, 23; Mal. 3:6; his *truth:* Num. 23:19; 1 Sam. 15:29; Mic. 7:20; Rom. 3:3; 11:2, 29; 2 Tim. 2:13; Titus 1:2; his *holiness:* Job 34:10; Hab. 1:13; James 1:13; and his *knowledge:* Isa. 40:13, 14, 27, 28.

The immutability thus set forth in the Scriptures and implied in the simplicity and absolute perfection of God is not, however, to be so understood as to deny in him some real ground for the Scripture statements of emotional feeling in the exercise of love, pity, longsuffering and mercy, or of anger, wrath and avenging justice. We could as well deny some real ground for the attributes of love, justice and truth which are at the basis of these emotions. We must never forget that we know but little, if anything, of the mode of operation of the divine mind. We are sure that we have to think and speak of it erroneously when our thoughts or words involve successive emotions in God or such as have beginning or end. And yet the only way in which change in him in such emotional acts could occur would involve both beginning, and end, and succession. Wherefore, we know that whatever possibility of change in God appears is due only to our own imperfection of knowledge and incapacity to form true conceptions.

It is also true that the unchangeableness of God is not incompatible with such outward activity and relations as exist in connection with Creation, Providence and Redemption. But as this has not been so readily admitted, it may be well to consider more particularly the objections which have been made.

I. It is objected that a change must have taken place in God in the creation of the universe. It is claimed that he must then have formed a new purpose, and must have passed from a state of rest to one of activity.

(a.) But this objection is based upon a forgetfulness of the fact, that in him there is no succession, and no change of time from one moment to another. The creation of the universe is no less an outward act than is the time in which it has existence. It appears in time and with time. But with God there is no time and no relation of time, exclusive of time itself. There was not before its creation. There will not be when there shall be no more time in creation. We may not be able to understand how this is, but we know that the fact must be so.

It is on this account that the purpose of God to create was not a new one, formed at one time and not at another. On the contrary, that purpose, and, indeed, his whole will is eternal. Whatever may have given rise to that purpose, does not exclude this fact.

(b.) There was nothing outside to influence him. He was moved entirely by his own will. Whether that will was altogether voluntary, or arose from some necessity in his nature, we need not now consider. If it was either the one or the other, in either event it was eternal, for if his nature be eternal, then any necessity of his nature is an eternal necessity, and any purpose he forms, whether of necessity, or voluntarily, must be eternal volition. So much for the objection, based upon a supposed new purpose.

That from a transition from rest to labour is equally baseless. It supposes labour and toil in God. But the Scripture account of creation, as well as the dictates of reason, forbid this. There was no laborious work of God. There never is; there never can be. His infinite power compasses his infinite will, in the mere wishing. Neither in the creation nor in the sustentation of the universe is there in God any of that busy, careful thought, and protracted weary effort by which man maintains government or sustains the lives of those dependent on him.

This view of God's creation accords with reason. It alone is worthy of an all-wise, all-powerful, independent and self-existent God.

It is established by Scripture. Heb. 11:3. "By faith we understand that the worlds have been framed by the word of God, so that what is seen hath not been made out of things which do appear."

The whole account of the creation in Genesis, chap. 1:1 to chap. 2:3, is full of this truth. In every case it is simply, "And God said," etc.

Psalm 33:9. "For he spake, and it was done; he commanded and it stood fast."

When it is said that he rested on the seventh day, no more is implied than that he ceased as to further creation; for the sustentation of the universe requires constantly the same exercise of power and will as its creation.

II. It is again objected, that the Scriptures represent change in God, when they speak of him as "repenting" of the acts which he had done.

Gen. 6:6. "And it repented the Lord that he had made man on the earth, and it grieved him at his heart."

1 Sam. 15:35. "And the Lord repented that he had made Saul king over Israel."

Ps. 106:45. "And he remembered for them his covenant, and repented according to the multitudes of his mercies."

Amos 7:3. "The Lord repented concerning this: It shall not be saith the Lord."

Jonah 3:10. "And God repented of the evil which he said he would do unto them."

In reply to this objection, it may be stated that these are merely anthropopathic expressions, intended simply to impress upon men his great anger at sin, and his warm approval of the repentance of those who had sinned against him. The change of conduct, in men, not in God, had changed the relation between them and God. Sin had made them liable to his just displeasure. Repentance had brought them within the possibilities of his mercy. Had he not treated them differently then there would have been change in him. His very unchangeableness makes it necessary that he shall treat differently those who are innocent and those who are guilty, those who harden themselves against him and those who turn toward him for mercy, with repentant hearts. So far as the first of these passages is concerned, it is simply a protest against the great wickedness into which the race of man has fallen. The Scriptures show that God has had a purpose with reference to such sin, which, from the beginning, contemplated the fall of man and the different stages of wickedness by which in various ages that fall has been accompanied. These statements differ widely from those which declare love, pity, or anger, for there is no emotion in God correspondent with the outward declaration.

III. Again it has been objected that God must be changeable or he could not answer prayer. It is said if his purposes stand forever and he changes not his will, then there is no place for prayer.

It is unquestionably true that God promises to answer prayer. It is also true that prayers have been answered, and that the course of human events has thus been different from what it would have been had there been no prayer and no answer to it.

But the mistake arises from supposing that there has been change in God's purpose or action from what he always contemplated.

The difficulty is not one that affects prayer only; it arises as well in connection with labour, or with any other act, by which, through man, a new force is introduced into the universe.

It proceeds from the fact that man, being a voluntary agent, may act according to choice at any moment of his life. That choice puts his action outside of the mere mechanical movements of the universe. Over these it is admitted that God has absolute control, and that his purpose relative to them has no change. But it is thought, that if man can choose one thing, or another, or can do, or not do, any special act he pleases, then so much of the future being dependent upon and resultant from his act or volition, God must change his purpose to correspond with that act or volition.

To this it may be replied that, even without explanation, we know that such cannot be the case, for this would take away the independence of God. It would make his volitions dependent upon those of man. If it be therefore true, that man cannot be a free agent, without such mechanical action, on his part, as would leave God free, we know that free agency does not belong to him. But we are so fully conscious of our free agency, that that consciousness becomes to us the highest revelation from God that it has real existence. If prayer then be offered, the only doubt about it, as a power and force, the effect of which does not change, is whether God answers it. And, in his word he has so plainly taught this, as to leave no room for doubt.

In what aspect, then, are we to regard prayer? Evidently in this simple way; that it is a secondary cause, which has a place, like all other secondary causes, which, like other such, is necessary to produce the result, to which God has given means of efficient entrance into the working of the universe, the existence of which has been as fully known and purposed as any other secondary cause, and the presence of which can in no way take God by surprise, nor render any new purpose or action on his part necessary. So far then from changing his purpose when he answers prayer, God is in reality only carrying out that purpose. But even if we be not able to explain how any will or act of ours can be at the same time as fixed and certain with God, as if it were a decree about some mechanical action of the universe, or were his own personal purpose, and at the same time be perfectly voluntary with man, so that man can either will or not will, do or not do, as he may himself choose, we are perfectly sure that it must be so, from our consciousness of ourselves, and our certainty of what is the nature of God.

IV. It is further objected, that there was change in God, in the act of the incarnation of the second person of the Trinity.

The objection is met here, because this is the most suitable place in our course to do so, though the explanation may not be fully comprehended, until we have discussed the Trinity, and the relations of the persons of the Godhead in it.

It is based upon a misconception of the Scripture doctrine of the incarnation.

1. It was not the divine nature, which became incarnate, but simply one of the persons subsisting in it.

2. No change took place in the divine nature. The human and divine natures of the Son of God were so related to his person and to each other, that while he was truly God and truly man, possessing every characteristic of each, the two natures remained entirely distinct, each with its own peculiarities and properties. The divine nature was in no degree affected. The Son of God, therefore, was as truly divine after, as before the incarnation.

3. So distinct were these natures, that in becoming man, the Son took not simply a human body, but also a human soul. These were united with the personality with which he subsists in the divine nature, but not with the divine nature itself. Christ lacked nothing to make him as separate from God in his human nature as any other man, except separate human personality. He united his human nature to himself by subsisting in it in the same personality with which he subsists in the divine nature.

4. The Son has not divine nature separate from the Father and the Spirit, so that we can say *his* divine nature in the exclusive sense, in which we speak of the human nature of Paul and Peter. Human nature is distributed among individual men, so that each one has his own, and in nowise partakes with another. But the one divine nature is common to the three persons.

These statements will show why God has not been changed in the act of incarnation.

(1.) There would have been change, had the human nature been so united to the divine, as to add to it such qualities, properties and conditions as do not belong to God. These may be possessed by a divine person in the human nature he has assumed, for thus is there no change in his nature as God, but they cannot be transferred to the divine nature without making it finite as well as infinite, material as well as spiritual, fallible as well as infallible, mortal as well as immortal. These contradictory states may exist in the one person, but cannot in any such compounded nature.

(2.) There would have been change, had the divine nature become the soul of the human nature. This would have made that nature subject to human passions and appetites, to human frailties and imperfections, and liable to pain, suffering, and temptation, and to limitation in goodness, knowledge, power and wisdom.

The knowledge therefore of the true doctrine of the incarnation shows conclusively, that in it there has been no change in God.

V. It is alleged that God cannot be without change, because he suffered during the incarnation of Christ.

The argument is that the declarations about Christ's suffering are made, not simply of the human nature, but of both natures combined, and that thus we are taught, that it was not merely man, but God also that suffered. This position is assumed by some who maintain that Christ had a complete human, as well as divine nature, not a mere human body, but also a rational soul. It is necessarily also the position of those who claim that he had no human soul, but that his divine nature took the place of a rational soul.

The reply to this argument is that the Scripture statements do not teach that the divine nature suffered. This is nowhere said. They teach that the second person of the Trinity, who became man, suffered. But they plainly refer that suffering to his human nature only. They teach us, that in the relations of his natures to his person, he preserved unchanged the properties and qualities which belonged to them separately, and that this was especially true of the divine nature. There were, indeed, some communications from the divine nature to the human, but none from the human to the divine. But while thus distinct, they were united together in a single personality, and by such a union, that whatever might be said to be true of or to be done or to be suffered by either of the natures, might in like manner be affirmed of the person in whom they were united. It is because of this that Christ, the Son of God, is said to have suffered. He did this in his human, though not in his divine nature. The Scripture declarations that Christ suffered, are no proof that God suffered, or that God can change in this respect.

But there are those who do not receive the above statements as an exposition of the teachings of Scripture on this point. They claim, as necessary, an interpretation which asserts suffering of the divine nature. Those, indeed, who hold that the divine nature is in the place of the human soul, are forced to maintain such an interpretation. It is in reply to both of these that the unchangeableness of the divine nature is presented as conclusive against any such interpretation. Against their position are adduced the numerous statements of Scripture asserting that God does not change, and that he is immutable in his nature, and in his various perfections. There are also arguments from reason, by which the same error may be refuted. So incontestable are these statements and reasonings that the objectors readily admit that there is no power or being who can change God contrary to his will, and that the idea of enforced suffering is revolting. The possibility of change and suffering in God, they conceive, therefore, to result from his own will and his own voluntary choice.

This raises the question of the possibility of voluntary suffering on the part of God.

If this be possible, it must arise in one of two ways; either the nature of God is essentially such as to admit suffering, or the will of God is capable of so changing his nature for a time, as to enable it to suffer. In the first instance the essence of God itself is supposed to remain unchanged, but to be capable of existing in different states at the dictation of his will. In the other, the essence itself is changed by the will, and made capable of that, which otherwise it could not have.

In the first case God could suffer, because of the contingent conditions of his life liable to the action of his will, just as we can inflict suffering upon ourselves.

In the last case, the nature of God would be so dependent on his will that be could change it at pleasure.

This last view, however, is based upon an erroneous conception of the relation of the will of God to his nature. That relation is not causal. The will does not create the nature nor confer upon it its powers nor exercise a controlling influence upon it. It is the nature that influences the will. It is because he is holy, just, and good, that he wills holiness, justice, and goodness, and wills these in himself, because he alone is the infinitely holy, just, and good. His will, therefore, so far from causative, is only approbative and complacent, and his essence can in no degree be affected by it. If this were not so, the nature of God must be the effect of the will of God as a cause, and must be dependent upon that will. The foundation of all excellence, righteousness and holiness would be, not what God is, but what he happens to will at any one time, and would make him differ again and again should he so will. And such will would be capricious; for in making the will superior to the nature, there is taken away all reason for choice in God to good or ill, or in one direction or another, and he is left, without motive, to accidental or capricious volition only. Moreover, if God is capable of this kind of change in any respect, he is so in all others, for the power of the will to effect one modification in the divine nature, necessarily involves the power to effect any or all other such.

As the will, therefore, cannot change the essence of God, but is itself controlled by that essence, it is not possible that it can confer the power to suffer, which otherwise God would not have. If, therefore, this power of suffering be not inherent in the divine nature, it can have no existence.

But if this be inherent in the divine nature, it must be a quality necessarily and constantly belonging to the nature of God, and must, therefore, be destructive of the blessedness so fully and eminently ascribed to God in the Scriptures, or it must exist there after the manner of the contingent conditions of our life, because of which we can pass from a state of happiness into one of suffering, and back to happiness again; and its passage from one of these states to the other, must be the result of the exercise of a divine volition.

But with God there can be no such contingent conditions.

1. The very nature of his necessary existence forbids this.

2. The language of Scripture "I, the Lord, change not," Mal. 3:6, and "with whom can be no variation, neither shadow that is cast by turning," James 1:17, is expressly contrary to such a supposition.

3. The contrast drawn in the Bible between God and men in respect to change, is distinctly based upon that contingency in man, to which there is no similarity in God.

4. The truth and faithfulness of God are magnified in the Scriptures by the fact of their exercise where man would thus change, but where God does not, because he is fixed and constant. The passage, "I change not" is presented in a context, where the will of God might be presumed to induce change, and the assertion that this is his nature is made to show why that will would not so affect him.

5. In addition to all of this, such contingent conditions or states are incompatible with the nature of his eternity, which, as being without succession, excludes change; as well as with his simplicity which denies separation between his essence and his attributes, and therefore gives no room for change; while they are absolutely excluded by the perfection of God, which cannot be always asserted of him if the states or conditions of his being can be changed, unless in all these states he could be equally perfect in all respects, which surely cannot be affirmed of the two states of happiness and suffering.

CHAPTER 8

THE POWER OF GOD

WE derive our knowledge of power from the consciousness of our will or purpose to effect an end, and from our experience that we have accomplished that end.

Over our own bodies our will acts directly, without the intervention of any means known to us. Thus, when we will to move the arm, the arm is moved, but whatever necessity there may be of nervous influence or muscular action, we know of no such connection between these and our will, save the fact that the will puts these into operation.

Over other material objects we can only act through our bodies and other necessary means of contact.

Experience teaches us, however, that mind can act upon mind without such contact, though the mode in which this is done is still mysterious.

The action of our minds upon our material structure and over other minds also suggests that mind, by some subtle connection, may act upon outward matter, as we see, that our minds act upon our bodies.

In this way many of the curious phenomena which have been falsely used for the proof of the spiritualistic theories of the present day will probably be accounted for.

But, whatever may be the power of man, it is evident that it is marked by limitations, not only as to what can be done, but also as to the way in which it may be done.

In ascribing power to God, however, we must exclude all such limitation. Not only is he all powerful (almighty), but he needs not instrumental contact.

But, although this is true, God accomplishes much that he does through secondary means which partake of the nature of instrumental contact. Such action, however, is with him not a matter of necessity, but simply his economic way of doing what he could as perfectly and as easily do by direct action.

Power in God, therefore, may be defined to be the effective energy inherent in his nature by which he is able to do all things. The exercise of that power is dependent upon his will or purpose, and is limited not by what he can do, but by what he chooses to do.

We ascribe power to God.

1. Because we perceive that its possession is a perfection in us, and is therefore to be attributed to the all-perfect being.

2. Because we cannot account for the existence and phenomena of the universe without ascribing to God the power which has produced them.

3. Because our own sense of dependence assures us that there must be power to create, preserve, and protect us, in him in whom we live and move and have our being.

4. The Scriptures also teach us to ascribe power to God.

(a.) In such passages as directly ascribe power to him: Jer. 32:17; Ps. 115:3; Eph. 1:19; 3:20.

(b.) By reference to his unlimited works: Jer. 10:12; John 1:3; Acts 17:24.

(c.) By declaring that what he does is done by mere will without labour, by his word; as in the whole account of creation in the beginning of Genesis and in Ps. 33:9.

(d.) By denying the necessity of great means and asserting that what he does can be done with the many or the few: 1 Sam. 14:6; 2 Chron. 14:11.

(e.) By figurative or anthropomorphic expressions, as "the hand," "the right hand of God," "the strong hand," "the arm," "the arm not shortened." Ex. 15:6; Num. 11:23; Joshua 4:24; Neh. 1:10; Job 40:9; Ps. 98:1; Isa. 50:2; 59:1.

God's power may be described as:

I. *Absolute*, which is equivalent to what he can do, and is measured by his nature.

II. *Actual*, which is what he exercises, and is measured by his will. It is what is put in action by him.

Knapp makes a division of absolute and ordinate, making the absolute that by which he created the world out of nothing, and the ordinate that by which he continues to create or produce according to the laws he has established, as by secondary causes, as in the production of plants, animals, etc. But these are different kinds of exercise of power, but not different kinds of power.

Our power differs from that of God in three particulars:

1. We cannot do whatever we choose, even if it be right.

2. We cannot do it without intermediate means.

3. We cannot do it at any moment we please, but only when the circumstances favour.

But, while God is not subject to the limitations which thus affect us, he also is limited in his power. These limitations, however, are such as arise, not from without, but from the excellence and perfection of his own nature. Hence the limitations are concurrent with his will, which can never desire to do what his nature does not permit.

1. God cannot create a being or world to which his essential incommunicable attributes can be given, viz.: infinity, embracing eternity and immensity, and self-existence.

2. He cannot create a being whose nature is sinful. The nature he bestows on any creature becomes the law of that creature, so that for any nature to be sinful, it must have been changed from conformity to the law of its creation.

3. He cannot impose laws which are not accordant with righteousness and holiness.

4. He cannot deal with any of his creatures unjustly.

5. He cannot commit sin.

6. He cannot change his own nature.

7. He cannot change his decrees or purpose.

8. He cannot do impossibilities.

If it be asked why he can do none of these things, the answer is, because his own nature is to him the law of what he does, as well as of what he wills and of what he is. He is not just and holy because he wills to be so, but he wills to be just and holy because he is so. His will does not make his nature, but his nature controls his will.

An apparent objection to the infinite power of God is the presence of sin in the universe.

The holiness, justice, and even goodness of God render it impossible that sin can be either created or permitted as something indifferent to God. He must hate it, and punish it wherever it appears.

Its presence therefore is due either to the fact that he could not prevent it, or that he has permitted it for some wise purpose.

What that wise purpose is, ought properly to be shown in proof that the existence of evil is consistent with God's goodness.

That its presence is due to such purpose, rather than to lack of power of God, appears from the fact that he could have prevented it. This he could have done

1. By not creating beings capable of sinning.

2. By not allowing them to be placed in circumstances which would lead to sin.

3. By sustaining and fortifying them in those circumstances, so as to counteract the temptation and keep them from sinning.

4. And, (as the objection is the rather to the continued existence of sin than its origin,) by the immediate destruction of those who have sinned.

But so far from the presence of sin showing lack of power in God, it has served the more signally to display that power.

1. Over sin itself, in its destruction and punishment.

2. Over its final victims, by causing them to feel and acknowledge the terrible power of his wrath.

3. Over others, by their signal deliverance through his power, not only from the penalty, but from the presence of sin.

4. In the sin itself, by exhibiting that restraining and conquering power, by which God makes evil itself to work out his purposes of good and glory.

CHAPTER 9

THE KNOWLEDGE OF GOD

GOD is an intelligent being possessed of knowledge.

This may be proved:

1. From his spirituality; for intelligence is an essential element of spiritual existence.

2. From his perfection; for the perfect one must have intelligence as one of his perfections.

3. From his causal relations to other beings and things.

(1.) As the cause of mental power and action in others, he must himself be possessed of mind. As the Scriptures aptly inquire, "He that planted the ear, shall he not hear? he that formed the eye, shall he not see?" Ps. 94:9; so may we ask, he that made the mind, and gave the power of thought and knowledge, shall he be without intelligence?

(2.) The effects he has produced show that they are the result of conscious action in the fulfillment of purpose, which he has formed. His causation is not like that of mechanical or chemical forces, which operate with blind productiveness or effective operation towards ends unknown to them, and not predetermined. This is possible to secondary causes, because they are the instruments of some other cause, itself intelligent and purposing. But intelligence and purpose are necessarily present in him, who is the great first cause, the prime mover and designer of all else that exists. All the evidences of design in creation, therefore, prove the intelligence of him who bears to it the relation of its first cause.

(3.) It is sometimes argued from his omnipresence, but omnipresence alone would not prove intelligence. His intelligence, however, having been established, his omnipresence enables us to determine the extent of his knowledge.

How does God know? Or in what way does he possess knowledge?

1. Not as we gain it, by using faculties fitted to acquire it. There is in him nothing corresponding to observation, comparison, generalization, deduction, processes of reasoning, by which we pass from one step to another, or the contemplation or conjecture of suppositions or theories by which we account for facts.

2. It is even improper to speak of his knowing by intuition, as is frequently done.

3. All that we can say is that his knowledge is his essence or nature knowing. It is not something acquired, but something belonging to that nature itself and identical with it, in like manner as are his love, and truth, and justice. It is something so inherent in his nature that it exists exclusively of any means of attaining or perceiving it, which we call action.

4. The knowledge of God, therefore, not being acquired, cannot be increased. Time does not add to it. Succession of events does not bring it before God. All the objects of his knowledge are to him eternally present and known.

What then are the objects of his knowledge?

1. Himself, his nature, or essence; the personal relations subsisting in that essence; all that that nature is, and all that it can appear to be in its manifestations; all that the purposes of God include, and all that might be purposed by him, whether to be done or to be permitted.

2. His creation in all its fullness; in its whole extent, whether marked by magnitude, or minuteness, or variety. The whole universe, with its innumerable worlds, is ever before him, while not an atom of dust, nor the most microscopic of sensitive existencies is unperceived thoroughly.

3. Not merely inanimate matter, nor simple animal natures, but all spiritual beings; he knowing their essences which to them remain unknown, and having perfect perception of the intents and thoughts of their hearts. "When Thales was asked if some of the actions of men were not unknown to God, he replied, 'not even their thoughts.'" [Knapp's Theology.] An inspired writer has taught us that God knows us even better than we know ourselves. "Hereby shall we know that we are of the truth, and shall assure our heart before him, whereinsoever our heart condemn us; because God is greater than our heart, and knoweth all things." 1 John 3:19, 20. His knowledge is not limited to the manifestations and operations of spiritual beings, but extends to their essences, and includes not only what they are, but also those tendencies which indicate what they may be.

4. He knows all the past, present, and future of all things, knowing the future with the same certainty and accuracy with which he knows the present and past; for that future is already as present to him as though actually existing with the creatures and time belonging to it, and is as distinctly perceived as it shall be then.

But more specifically as to his knowledge of future events it may be said:

1. That he knows all events that are certain or fixed. The certainty that they will come to pass is based upon his decree. He therefore knows all things that shall come to pass.

2. He knows all events that could possibly come to pass. This is based upon his infinite knowledge of himself and of all his creatures, by which all things or

events, which could at any time or under any circumstances occur, are known to him.

In these two classes are necessarily included all objects of knowledge.

Knapp lays down a third kind of knowledge, namely, the knowledge of contingent events, or events which might take place under certain circumstances; for example, that God foresees that if James lives until he is grown, he will commit murder; he therefore determines to prevent this by removing him from life. The knowledge of the murder is here claimed to be that of a contingent event. And hence it is claimed to be another kind of knowledge.

But to examine this. It is readily admitted that the murder does not come under the classification of things certain or decreed, because it will not take place. But it does come under the head of things possible, and between it and all other possible things no distinction can be made. All possible things are contingent until made certain by a decree. Every possible thing is only possible in connection with the circumstances under which it can happen. There is therefore no distinction between possible things and contingent things, and consequently no third class is to be added.

The kind of knowledge which he thus speaks of as contingent is stated by Knapp to be what is called Scientia Media. It is one form only, in which Scientia Media is presented by those who maintain it.

Another form of Scientia Media is, however held by some. According to this, the future event to which it refers is known to God as an event that will take place, but his knowledge of that fact is attained, not through his decree, but through his foreknowledge that, under certain circumstances, a man will pursue one course of action rather than another.

This kind of Scientia Media teaches:

(1.) The future event as certain.

(2.) That God knows it as such.

(3.) That this knowledge does not arise from his decree.

(4.) But, from his knowledge of the nature of the man, together with that of the circumstances that will surround him, he knows that he will act in a particular way.

The only question here is as to the 3rd and 4th, for it agrees with the usual orthodox statement in saying, 1st, that it is certain, and 2nd, that God knows it as such.

But the 3rd and 4th assert that this knowledge is the result of a foreknowledge of God as to how a man will act under certain circumstances. It is evident, however, that this foreknowledge is necessarily accompanied by a determination to allow him so to act.

Now the question arises, is this universally the method of God's action? If it be so, then God has left the world entirely to itself, without any influence from him. Everything has come to pass, not because of his will and action, but because he has left the general laws, under which he has placed the world, to work out their results without any action or influence on his part.

But this is so manifestly untrue and unscriptural, that it never has been maintained by any Christian men, and it is by Christian writers only that the idea of Scientia Media referred to above has been presented.

It is therefore denied that this is what is meant, and they say that while God does operate in and interfere with the world, and carry on his own purposes in certain matters, he does not choose in other events to exercise any influence, but simply refrains and leaves the events to work out their own effects; and that the knowledge which he has of these events is based upon the fact that they will take place if he does not thus interfere.

The theory thus presented, as will be seen, admits the continued preservation of all things, with all their powers. This can only result from God's providential action, and involves all that concurrence with events on the part of God through which alone they preserve and exercise effectively the powers he has given them.

This being admitted, then the views held by these parties, stated in any form in which they could hold them, would involve no additional fact beyond the distinction, recognized by all orthodox divines, between the absolute and permissive decrees of God.

But in any event there is a decree, determination, intention, purpose, or whatever else men may call it—in the broadest language, a will, or volition—to leave these things so to operate. And upon this will or decree is based his knowledge that these things will be; for without the knowledge of such a purpose, how could he know that he will not at some time choose to change the circumstances or prevent their accomplishment of the event?

It will be seen that in neither of the forms of Scientia Media thus far referred to is there any serious disagreement from the truth. The objection to them is more the lack of accuracy and the mistaken notion that some new idea is involved; or rather the great objection has been the purpose by which men have been led, viz., a desire to lay down the distinction of conditional decrees in salvation. According to these decrees:

(1.) God offers salvation to every man.

(2.) But does not decree his salvation or damnation.

(3.) Yet only decrees his salvation if he believes.

(4.) Or his damnation if he does not believe.

(5.) The knowledge which God is admitted to have had of the event from the beginning arises from foresight that, under the circumstances in which the man is placed, he will exercise, or will not exercise belief.

The Scientia Media is, therefore, introduced to show how an event can be known as something that will actually take place, and yet as something not fixed by a decree of God, and consequently known upon some other ground than because decreed. This we have shown to be a mistaken conception in the forms already examined.

But a third kind of Scientia Media is by no means as harmless as the two already presented, although its absurdity is readily seen. It is given in Dr. J. Pye Smith's first lines of Christian Theology, p. 145, as follows:

"That God foresees all future events, depending upon the will of His voluntary agents, (i.e., all possible beings and all possible actions of all possible beings), under a position of antecedents endlessly varied; and that, then, in every case certain consequents will follow. The Deity does not certainly know which, in the endless number of possible antecedents, a voluntary creature will choose and practice; but he knows what will be the result under every possible variation of these antecedents. When, therefore, the creature has made his election and fulfilled his course of action, the Deity may say that he foreknew the whole."

The objections to this scheme are manifest.

(1.) It makes the God, whose purposes we see constantly manifested to us, a God of no purpose at all. He can have no end; he can only know that at any time given in the universe, some one end of many myriads may be the one attained.

(2.) It is contrary to the power to prophesy the actual events which shall happen at a given time, which God has exercised through his prophets.

(3.) It is opposed to his independence, for it makes him dependent upon the will of his creatures, and not their actions dependent upon him.

(4.) It is opposed to his perfection, for that perfection forbids the idea of increase or addition from without; yet, according to this view, his knowledge is constantly increasing as to what is done by his creatures. Every moment, that which heretofore has been only one of many possibilities, becomes a certain event.

(5.) As there can be no reason for God's will not being effective at least in some respects in man, this Scientia Media, which rests upon the idea that God ought not thus to operate on the mind, even by a purpose, must be a misconception. Else how could God bestow influences upon intelligent creatures which are fitted to affect their minds, as in the gift of Christ, or of the Spirit. Even the conscience within ought not to exercise its powers, nor even to exist in man. If it be said that these would only operate with the free consent of the party, it may be replied that such is the case with all the influences arising in connection with God's decrees. Is it said that these are influences for good only? So also is it in connection with his decrees. The effective decrees of God, by which he changes in any respect the will of his creatures, are altogether connected with influences for good. In all other respects men are left to act as they please. But their action is known, and known because of God's decree to leave them thus to act.

(6.) That God should exert no influence over his intelligent creatures also involves that he be excluded from the physical universe.

The very circumstances under which men are supposed to act in Scientia Media are circumstances arising from things around as well as within. Neither can he who can control these circumstances be shut out from the control of those physical events which he knows will affect the will of a voluntary agent. If it be necessary to responsible freedom of the will that man shall not be influenced at all, God must be excluded from the universe; yea, every other being and thing except man. Every man also must be completely isolated from all others, even so far that he shall suppose that he owes no obligations of obedience, and that none shall know his action. These absurd conclusions might even be further extended.

The passages in Scripture supposed to support Scientia Media do not sustain it. These are Genesis 3:22; Ex. 4:8; 1 Sam. 23:5–14; Jeremiah 38:17–20; Matt. 11:21, 23; Acts, 27:22, 31.

THE WISDOM OF GOD

Wisdom is that power which enables one to put to practical use the knowledge and skill which he possesses, to choose wise ends of action, and to attain these ends by wise means. It is that guidance of the understanding under which the will determines wisely its pleasure, and puts forth power to accomplish it.

Wisdom in God is infinite and unerring, choosing always the best end and the best means of attaining it. It is seen in creation, and in providence, but is most signally manifested in redemption.

CHAPTER 10

HOLINESS, GOODNESS, LOVE AND TRUTH

AFTER the consideration of the wisdom and knowledge of God, which correspond to the characteristics of our mental organism, we take up that of those attributes sometimes called moral, because they correspond to those which form our moral character. These are holiness, goodness, truth and justice.

HOLINESS

Holiness is, however, not a distinctive attribute, but rather the combination of all these attributes. We may suppose a being in whom there may be love without justice, or truth, or any one of these to the exclusion of the other two; but no being can be holy, who does not combine in himself all of these, and all other moral perfections. Nor, when we have such a combination, is there anything to be added to constitute holy character. It is evident, therefore, that holiness is the sum of all excellence and the combination of all the attributes which constitute perfection of character.

In the study of these constituents, we first consider

GOODNESS

In one aspect of this word, it is merely equivalent to holiness. If we look at it as marking the excellence of God's nature, as we often use it with reference to man, we mean by it simply holiness. Thus, when we say of anyone, he is a good man, we mean to assert the combination of traits of character, such as have just been pointed out as constituting holiness. This is the goodness which terminates in God himself.

On the other hand, the goodness of God may be spoken of as kindness, benevolence, or beneficence towards others, in which it is seen to terminate outside of himself. Thus we speak of him, as being very good to us. Thus the Psalmist says: "Surely goodness and mercy shall follow me all the days of my life." Ps. 23:6.

It is on account of this ambiguity in this word, that it is best to consider it, in its first aspect, as merely holiness, and, therefore, as disposed of in what we have said of that, and to refer it in this second respect to one of the divisions into which the love of God naturally falls.

We therefore take up next

LOVE

Of this there are five kinds, which vary according to the object upon which love is exercised. The attribute in God is the same; but it is in its exit, or in its termination, that it assumes these different forms.

1. There is the love of complacency or approbation. This is exercised towards a worthy object in which excellencies are perceived. It is of the nature of the love of the beautiful, or the good, or the useful in us. It complacently or approvingly regards, because there is in the object something worthy of such regard.

This is exercised by God, in its highest degree, in the love of himself, of his own nature and character, because the infinitely excellent must be to God the highest object of complacent love.

Were God but one person, in this way only could such love be exercised. But in the Trinity of the Godhead, there is found, in the love of the separate persons towards each other, another mode in which this love of complacency may in this highest sense be exercised.

Such love is also felt by God for his purposes. As he perceives them to be just, wise and gracious, he approves and regards them with complacent love.

But this love extends itself also to the creations, which result from this purpose.

This is true of inanimate creation. It is perfect, as far as conformed to his will, and fitted to accomplish his end, and as such God can regard it and pronounce it good. Thus we find that he did in the creation, Genesis, chap. 1:10, 12.

The same record is made, in verse 25, as to the animal creation, before that of man; and after the creation, and investiture of man with the dominion over the earth, with its plants and animals, we are told, verse 31, "And God saw everything that he had made, and, behold, it was very good."

The complacent love of God, therefore, extends not only to himself and his will, but to all his innocent creation and even to inanimate nature.

This love of complacency, however, as it is exercised in its highest degree towards himself, so also is it exhibited, in the nearest approach to that, towards those beings who are most like himself, having been made in his nature and likeness. An innocent angel, or an innocent man is therefore by nature a joy to God, as is the child to the father who sees in it a peculiar likeness to himself.

But the guilty cannot thus be loved. Sinful man cannot receive such love, so long as sinful. Even the penitent believer in Jesus, until the time of his perfect sanctification in the life to come, and doubtless even then, has access to God only through Christ, and, of himself, can in no respect secure the approbation of God.

2. The second kind of love, is the love of benevolence, which corresponds to the idea of God's goodness towards his creatures.

This is the product of his wishes for their happiness. It is not dependent on their character, as is the love of complacency, but is exercised towards both innocent and guilty.

It is general in its nature, not special, and exists towards all, even towards devils, and wicked men, because God's nature is benevolent, and, therefore, he must wish for the happiness of his creatures.

That that happiness is not attained, nor attainable, is due, not to him, but to their own sin.

When the benevolence of God is exercised actively in the bestowment of good things upon his creatures, it is called his beneficence. By the former, he wishes them happiness, by the latter, he confers blessings to make them so.

This is done to the wicked also, as well as to the righteous. It is to this that Christ refers, Matt. 5:45, "He maketh his sun to rise on the evil and the good, and sendeth rain on the just and the unjust."

3. The third form of love is the love of compassion.

This corresponds to our idea of pity. It is benevolent disposition to those who are suffering or in distress.

This also may be exercised towards the guilty or the innocent, if it be possible to suppose that guilt and suffering are separable.

It has been very commonly held that they are inseparable. Pain, suffering and distress have been believed to be the result of sin, and consequently inseparable from guilt.

But this is a mistaken notion. Man in a state of innocence was made capable of physical suffering. That capacity was necessary to the protection of his physical organism.

The lower animals also suffer.

Whatever addition to the capacity of suffering has, therefore, been made by the fall, and is the consequence of sin, we are not, on that account, forced to the conclusion that there can be no suffering where there has been no sin.

The capacity to suffer may so belong to a higher organism, that we would naturally choose that organism, with that capacity, rather than a lower one without it. If so God can justly so create us.

If misery, then, may be the lot of the innocent, God's love of compassion can be exercised toward such.

It can be and is also exercised toward the guilty. We see this in the forbearance with which he delays their punishment, in his constant offers of mercy, in his yearnings after their salvation, and most signally, in the gift of his only begotten Son, "that whosoever believeth on him should not perish, but have eternal life." John 3:16.

4. A fourth form of the love of God corresponds to what we call mercy.

This can be exercised only toward sinners.

Its very nature contemplates guilt in its objects.

It consists, not only in the desire not to inflict the punishment due to sin, and the neglect and refusal to do so, but in the actual pardon of the offender.

It cannot be exercised towards a righteous being, because in him is no sin or guilt to be pardoned.

It is, however, no new attribute in God, which has arisen because of the existence of sin, and which is, therefore, an addition to his attributes.

It is a virtue inherent in his nature, and is especially only one form in which his love exhibits itself, the same love as that benevolence which innocent creatures call forth, and the same love which in another form of complacency has been eternally exercised in the Godhead.

When we say that this mercy must be exercised in accordance with the truth and justice of God, we say no more than is true of every attribute of God. No one can be exercised in such a way as to destroy another. Every one must be in harmony with the others. Or, remembering what we have before stated, that these attributes are not separate faculties, all that is meant in this case, as in all others, is that God must act in harmony with his nature.

The objects of the exercise of this attribute are all those to whom God pardons offenses of any kind.

They are not to be confined to redeemed sinners, although this is the most signal exhibition.

Under the ancient economy, God ruled as theocratic ruler over Israel. Sins of the nation and sins of individuals in their capacity of citizens of the nation, were pardoned.

Under that dispensation God occupied to that people the position of an earthly ruler, and consequently could pardon sins against his government at will, upon repentance, and upon merely governmental principles—that is, such as would secure obedience to the law, and peace and order, and the welfare of the nation. These were offences against the mere person of the king or the laws of his state, and not against the fundamental principles of holiness and righteousness; hence sovereignty and expediency could decide in each case what might be done, and mercy was exercised and justice dispensed accordingly.

But this is very different from the case of God, the righteous judge, the dispenser, not of arbitrary law, but of a law based upon his own nature and that of man, essential obedience to which is necessary, not for maintaining government, but for preserving and maintaining the right and preventing the violation with impunity of eternal law.

In both cases God must act in harmony with his whole nature.

But in that of Israel no obstacle was presented by that nature to the pardon of individual and national sins against the theocratic king.

Hence mercy was extended, apparently at least, without compensation to justice.

Yet amid it all, there was, in the sacrificial offerings with which the people were required to approach God, seeking pardon for both individual and national political sins, such a typical relation to the atonement made by Christ as shows that in some way in that atonement, may, after all, be found the reason why God, even in those cases, could be just and yet justify the offenders.

5. The fifth form of love is that of affection.

This differs from that of complacency inasmuch as it does not always demand a worthy object. This is exhibited in the parable of the "Prodigal Son."

It differs from that of benevolence, inasmuch as its object is not viewed in general with all others, but is one of special interest.

It differs from that of compassion and that of mercy, because the object may neither be in distress, nor sinful.

It arises from,

(1.) Mutual relationship; as of the Father to the Son, and of all the persons in the Trinity toward each other; of God to Israel, of Christ to his apostles, his disciples and his church, and of the adopted sons to God the Father.

(2.) From dependence; as of creatures on the creator, and of the redeemed upon the redeemer.

(3.) From ownership; as of God over man of God over Israel, and of Christ over the redeemed. This is illustrated in the lost coin in Luke 15:8, 9.

This kind of love originates in each of these ways in man, and, as the Scriptures show, is also found in God.

It is from this aspect of God's love that proceeds grace, which is to be distinguished from love, and pity, and mercy.

Love, as we have seen, is the general characteristic, exhibiting itself in these five different forms.

Mercy is one of these, but is given to the guilty only.

Pity is given to guilty or innocent, who may be in distress, pain or suffering.

Grace is also given to guilty, or innocent, and does not necessarily suppose distress in the object, but involves an affectionate interest in it, arising either from peculiar relation to it, or ownership of it, or compassion for its dependence.

Grace is undeserved favour to innocent or guilty arising from affection.

Mercy is undeserved compassion to the guilty only.

THE TRUTH OF GOD

The expression, "truth of God," is ambiguous, and must be considered under the specific terms which set forth its various meanings.

I. His Verity. He is True God. By this is meant, the exact correspondence of the nature of God with the ideal of absolute perfection. The foundation of that ideal may be indeterminable. But, whether it is in the nature of God himself, or in his will proceeding from his nature, or in eternal principles of the fit and the necessary and the right, which exactly coincide with that nature, God and that ideal must be perfect counterparts. That ideal can only be partially comprehended by any of his creatures, because of their imperfections; but it is known by God in all its supreme excellence, and his nature must fully correspond to it as thus known. Otherwise he would not be God.

It is in this aspect of God's truth, that the Scriptures call him the true God. See 2 Chron. 15:3; Jer. 10:10; John 17:3; 1 Thess. 1:9; 1 John 5:20; Rev. 3:7.

II. His Veracity. By this is meant, God's truthfulness or incapacity to deceive. It is an attribute of his nature, which, like his power, exists, and makes him what he is, even though there be no outward relation to it. By virtue of it, he is the source of all truth, not moral only, but even mathematical.

In its relation to God's creatures, it is the foundation of their confidence in the knowledge obtained through the use of their own faculties, whether by intuition, observation or reason. Whatever imperfection there is in such knowledge, is perceived to be due to the creature, and not to God the creator. Upon it is also based belief in the revelations God makes to man of facts beyond the attainment of merely human power.

The Scriptures affirm the veracity of God in the strongest terms. In addition to its assertion in numerous passages, we are told, Ps. 108:4, that his "truth reacheth unto the skies." In Titus 1:2, he is called "God, who cannot lie."

III. His Faithfulness. This consists in the truth of God viewed in its relation to his purposes whether secret, or revealed. When revealed, these become either promises, or threats. But as promises, the ground upon which these purposes must be fulfilled is, not any obligation to the creature, for God can come under none, but simply because of his own faithfulness to his purposes. Hence his faithfulness demands equally the performance of his threatenings, as of his promises.

This faithfulness is based upon the veracity of his nature considered above. It is by virtue of that veracity, that God must be faithful; yet the faithfulness is a new aspect, in which God's truthfulness appears.

This faithfulness is the ground both of hope and of fear. In the Scriptures it is more frequently presented as a reason for hope and trust. But it is also the foundation of belief in future judgement and punishment. The faithful God has been true to his threatenings, as well as his promises. His faithfulness assures us that he will so continue.

CHAPTER 11

JUSTICE OF GOD

BY justice is meant that rectitude of character which leads to the treatment of others in strict accordance with their deserts.

The justice of God differs in no respect from this attribute as seen among his rational creatures; except that his justice must be perfect while theirs is imperfect, and his must be impartial, while theirs is partial. These differences, however, exist in the exercise of justice, and not in the thing itself. They arise from the limited knowledge, reason, and perception of right and wrong among men, and from the extent to which they naturally yield to their prejudices and passions. In the all-perfect being, however, justice has none of these deficiencies, and must be exercised according to its strictest nature, and in every conceivable form of perfection. To all, therefore, he must deal out the most absolute justice, whatever they deserve, only what they deserve, and the full measure of their deserts.

Inasmuch as the justice of God may be considered as it exists in himself, or as it is manifested towards his creatures, a distinction has been made in it as viewed in these aspects, into the absolute and relative justice of God.

By absolute justice is meant that rectitude of the divine nature, in consequence of which God is infinitely righteous in himself. This rectitude is essential to him, and existed before there was a creation in which to exhibit it.

By the relative justice of God is meant that justice, as exhibited towards, and exercised upon, his creatures in the dispensation of the universe. It is seen in the nature of the laws he gives, in his impartiality in dealing with those subjected to them, and in his maintenance of right and virtue, by the threats and promises he attaches to them, and his punishment of those who violate them. To this form of justice is often applied the name of rectoral justice, inasmuch as it is justice exercised by a ruler, in the form of government, and by means of laws.

There is a form of justice, known among men as commutative justice, which consists in giving to each one his due in the barter and exchange of commerce, or in any other of the mutual relations of life. As it is based upon the ground of mutual obligation, and, therefore, is not suited to a being entirely independent of others, it cannot properly be ascribed to God. The blessings given in consequence of his promises to man, are not matters of obligation, but of grace. The

90

only aspect, in which this could be connected with God, would be as between the Father and the Son, in conferring upon his people those blessings which the Son had purchased through his sufferings. It is in this sense that the Scripture says, that God is "faithful and righteous to forgive us our sins, and to cleanse us from all unrighteousness." 1 John 1:9.

In the administration of the affairs of his creatures, God exercises distributive justice. By this is meant, the rewarding and punishing his subjects, according to the sanctions of his law. His justice is here evinced in the maintenance of punishment, if the law be broken, but not in the bestowment of rewards, since these are given graciously as further inducements to duty. While, therefore, God gives all the rewards promised, they are given because promised, and not because due. These punishments further show forth the justice of God as they are impartially inflicted.

The ground upon which the offenders against God's law are punished, is not simply the fact that a law of God has been broken, but, that, in the breaking of that law, essential right has been violated and wrong committed. It would be sufficient to authorize punishment, that the law of the ruler is broken. Still it might appear that the will of the ruler might remit a punishment due to a mere violation of his will. But the law of God is based upon the immutable distinctions between right and wrong, and sin and holiness, as they exist in the nature of God. Its violation, therefore, is sin. It is a destruction of the right. Hence, that which impels God to punish, is not his rectoral character, but his holy nature. It is when justice is regarded in this respect, that it is called punitive or vindicatory.

But punitive justice is not admitted by all, nor that God punishes sin in any other respect, than as a violation of his will; nay, it is even disputed whether he even punishes the violations of his will.

Three questions, therefore, arise here.

1. Does God punish the violations of his will?

2. Does he punish them, because they are mere violations, or because they are sin?

3. Is this done because of anything essential in his nature, or because it is expedient for governmental or other purposes?

Upon these questions there have been several opinions expressed.

1. The Universalists and some of the Socinians deny that God punishes even the violations of his law. They regard the precepts of morality and duty set forth in his Word as merely intended to guide us in this life. When this life is ended,

there may be no dealing with man for such violation. They are only for a temporary purpose, and having accomplished that purpose, will have no further effect. God looks now only to the good of his creatures, and if the same method of dealing be extended beyond this life, it will be only for a time, and only for the good of those who suffer. According to this, these are not punishments, but chastisements, and God is moved by goodness and not by justice.

2. A second theory is, that the laws given by God are merely exponents of his will; that the ground upon which he commands is simply his sovereignty; that, looking at the universe as a world to be created and to be occupied by his moral creatures, he selected such a system of laws as seemed to him best to secure the welfare of those creatures, and that these laws while seeking the happiness, not of the individuals, but of the mass, are such as are really best fitted to that end; and that the justice of God is seen in so administering these laws, by rewarding those who obey, and punishing those who disobey, as to maintain his government, and thus secure the welfare of the whole. God punishes sin, therefore, under this system, but he punishes it, not because of its heinous nature, but because it is best that men should not sin, and thus the best interest of all is secured by preventing by punishment the commission of sin. The end he has in view, therefore, is rather to furnish a spectacle which shall restrain sin, than to perform an act demanded by the inherent nature of sin. It is his rectoral justice, therefore, rather than his vindicatory justice, that is thus shown.

This theory embraces four points.

(1.) God punishes offences or sins.

(2.) The object is thus the better to secure the welfare of his moral creatures.

(3.) The laws of his government are based entirely upon his mere will.

(4.) Consequently he punishes sin, not because of its inherent desert, but because the general happiness of his creatures, and not his own holiness demands it.

3. The third theory is different in all respects, except the first of these points.

(1.) It agrees, that God punishes sin.

(2.) But it makes his object the maintenance of the right.

(3.) His laws and actions are based upon the immutable principles of right.

(4.) He punishes sin, because, from its nature, it demands punishment from him.

The great difficulty in attaining a correct result in this matter, is that whatever might have been the origin of these laws, they would have been the same. Hence, no conclusion can be drawn from the nature of the laws themselves. It is manifest, that God, in the establishment of the government of the world for any purpose, will not give to it laws contrary to his nature.

It does not follow, however, that because the same effect may be produced by either of these causes, it is, therefore, unimportant to which of them it is assigned. There may be, and in the present case it is believed that there are important reasons, why only one cause should be assigned, and that it should be ascertained to exist in the nature of God. Matters of great moment, in connection with the atonement especially, but also with other parts of the plan of salvation, demand the true answer.

But this fact is not to be allowed to warp our judgement or lead us away from the truth. It is only mentioned to show the importance of the subject now under consideration.

As to the first of these theories, it need only be said, that the objections to it are partly involved in those to the second and that those peculiar to it, are too plain to need presentation here. They will more properly be considered in connection with the subject of future punishment.

As to the second, it may be objected:

(1.) "That it makes happiness, and not holiness and virtue, the great end of God. The dictates of nature teach us all plainly, that happiness does not occupy this place." Dr. Charles Hodge: manuscript lecture.

(2.) "It destroys the essential difference between right and wrong, which conscience teaches us." Dr. Charles Hodge: manuscript lecture.

(3.) It supposes, that God might have made a world, in which precisely opposite moral laws might have prevailed by his command; and that thus it would by his duty, in this world to reward, in that world to punish, his creatures for the same action.

(4.) It is opposed to the relation of the true will of God to his nature. It ascribes the laws of God to that will. It recognizes those laws as flowing from it alone. They are as God pleased. Now, it is not denied that they come from the free will of God, and are such as please him. But they have a higher basis even than his will. That will is influenced by his nature, and is its exponent. Now, whether that nature is itself the basis of good and right, or whether good and right considered as distinct from it in the nature of things simply accord perfectly with that nature, the result is the same; the will is influenced by the nature to establish the moral laws for the government of his creatures according to the immutable principles of right and wrong.

(5.) This theory is also opposed to the independence of God, who is thus forced to punish sin, not by any law of his own nature, which would still maintain that independence, but from a regard to the government of his creatures, which could not be otherwise maintained. (Altered from Dr. A. A. Hodge's Outlines.)

(6.) The instinctive sense of justice in man testifies to the ill desert of sin. This is the universal testimony of conscience. But conscience speaks for God, and, therefore, testifies to the fact that, independent of the evil to society, the wrongdoer deserves punishment proportioned to his offence.

(7.) Dr. A. A. Hodge, in his Outlines, thus argues this from the love of holiness and hatred of sin in God: "If the reason for God's punishing was founded only in God's arbitrary will, then he could not be said to hate sin, but only to love his own will, or, if his reason for punishing sin rested upon governmental considerations, then he could not be strictly said to hate sin, but only its consequences." But both conscience and Scripture teach that God does hate sin, and love holiness.

Leaving these considerations as to the second theory, with the statement of these objections, we proceed to establish the third theory by the teachings of Scripture. It will be seen that the Scriptures represent God as a just God, thus ascribing that character to him; that they do it in such a way as shows that his justice is not simply in his will, but is a part of his nature; that they challenge denial of the position that the acts of God are in accordance with right and justice, and that not of his sovereignty, but because of the absolute justice of his nature; that they present him as actually claiming vindicatory or avenging justice, speaking of his justice as hatred of sin, and not as a desire to maintain government; nay, that they are constantly showing us instance after instance in which God has exercised that avenging justice, commencing with the ejection of Adam from Paradise, and culminating in its highest and most signal example in the sacrificial work of Christ.

It is remarkable that all of this can be established from the Scriptures in favour of vindicatory justice, and not a passage can be given in proof that God is only active for the maintenance of his government, or the mere happiness of his creatures. Indeed, in the Scriptures everywhere, it is God's glory and dishonor, his holiness and sin, his love and his justice, that are placed in fearful contrast.

1. Passages in which God is spoken of as having a just character, and in which this is held forth as an excellence in him. How can these be accounted for, if justice and will are the same, or even if justice is no more than the administration of human affairs according to his plan? While this is done there are no passages in which he asserts his power, or choice, or justice in changing the essential laws laid down for our rule. Deut. 32:4; Job 8:3; 34:10–12; 36:2, 3; Ps. 9:4; 11:7; 33:4, 5; 71:19; 89:14; 92:15; 97:2; 99:4; 119:137, 138; Zeph. 3:5; Rom. 2:2.

2. Passages in which God's claim to this character is vindicated by asserting his justice and his impartiality toward all men. Gen. 18:16–33; Deut. 10:17;

Job 37:24; Eccl. 3:17; 12:14; Ezek. 18:29; Acts 10:34, 35; 17:31; Rom. 2:3–6, 11; 14:12; Gal. 2:6; Eph. 6:8; Col. 3:25; 1 Pet. 1:17; Jude 15.

3. In those passages in which God's justice is spoken of, it is never based upon his will, nor his economy, but,

(a.) Judgement is always based upon his righteousness. Ps. 9:8; 50:4, 6; 96:10, 13; 98:9.

(b.) His economy among the Jews is commended, not because of its setting forth his will, but because of its justice or righteousness. Deut. 4:8; Ps. 19:7–9; Ps. 119:138.

4. Passages in which God speaks of his justice as being a hatred of sin. Ps. 5:4, 5; Hab. 1:13.

5. Passages in which God is spoken of as a jealous God, exercising avenging justice. Ex. 20:5; Deut. 32:34, 35, 39, 41–43; Ps. 94:1, 2; Is. 34:8; 66:6; Heb. 10:26–31.

6. Passages in which the dealings of God with his enemies are spoken of, in connection with such words as anger, wrath, fury, etc. Num. 12:9; Deut. 32:22; Judges 10:7; 2 Sam. 22:8; Job 19:11; Ps. 2:5; 7:11; 21:9; 90:11; Is. 28:21; 30:30; Jer. 30:24; Lam. 2:3; 3:43; Ezek. 5:13; 38:18; Hos. 12:14; Nahum 1:6.

7. Passages in which angels are spoken of as ministers of such vengeance. These are not introduced as proof of the justice of God, but simply as parts of transactions, by which that justice is manifested. Num. 22:22–31; 2 Sam. 24:16; 1 Chron. 21:14–16, 27; Ps. 35:5, 6; Rev. 7:1–3; 9:15; 15:1; 16:17.

8. The instances given of the actual exercise of God's wrath are associated, not merely with the idea of producing effect in his moral government, nor with the exercise of his mere will, but as results produced by his emotions against sin, or, in other words, his avenging justice.

Some of these are (1.) The fallen angels, (2.) our first parents, (3.) Sodom and Gomorrah, (4.) the flood, (5.) the plagues of Egypt, (6.) the punishments of the children of Israel in the wilderness, (7.) the captivity of the Jews, (8.) God's punishment of heathen nations, because of their wicked instrumentality in the exercise of his wrath against the delinquent Israelites, and (9.) the threatened eternal punishment of the wicked.

9. Passages which point out something in the work of Christ as essential before God could pardon sin. Matt. 26:39; Rom. 3:26; 2 Cor. 5:21.

CHAPTER 12

THE WILL OF GOD

BY the will of God is meant that power inherent in his nature, by which he purposes and chooses any end or object, or determines its existence.

I. That God must have this power is evident.

1. Because it is an attribute of personality. A conscious personal being cannot be without will. Every proof that we have, therefore, that God has personal existence, is evidence that he must have will.

2. Will is also a perfection, and must be found in the being of all perfection.

3. The absolutely independent God, who is controlled by, and dependent upon no person nor thing, must have will, which determines his own acts.

4. It cannot be separated from the possession of the power and wisdom seen in the creation of the universe and in all God's outward acts, for, without it, the things which wisdom devises and power executes could neither be devised nor executed.

5. It is essential to the sovereignty by which he rules the universe, for will is the element in which sovereignty consists.

6. Without it there could be no existence whatever, not even of God himself.

II. The objects of that will are all beings that exist, and all events that take place.

1. God must will his own existence and nature. These are objects of supreme desire. The infinite excellence of that nature, which furnishes a completely worthy object of his complacent love, cannot be contemplated without a correspondingly infinite desire that it should exist, and should be what it is. The will thus exercised, however, is not causal, as it is towards all other objects. It does not give existence to God, nor make his nature what it is, but on the contrary, it is because God exists and has such a nature, that he must so will.

2. The will of God is also exercised in establishing and maintaining the personal relations revealed to us as existing in the Godhead. It is by the will of the Father that he begets the Son, and by the will of the Father and the Son that the Spirit proceeds. The action of the will here is causal, although these relations are eternal, and are characteristic of the Godhead. They are the results of the divine activity, and, as effects, must find their ultimate cause in the will which moves

to action. The fact that because this is divine will and action, there can be no priority of time in the will to the act, does not forbid the causal relation which, because of the eternity of God, must make cause and effect in him co-eternal.

3. Another exhibition of will in the divine being is connected with the mutual love of the divine persons toward each other. This love proceeds from these persons as one form of eternal activity, and is willed by each to the full extent of its infinite exercise.

4. The will of God is more plainly made known, however, to his creatures, in his outward activity in creation. This was called into existence by the word of his power. He willed, and it was done. But for that will, it had not been. Viewed as a whole, or in its minutest part, the universe presents everywhere the impress of its maker's will. To that will is due not only all material, but also all spiritual existence.

5. The will of God is also manifested in his providential care and government of the universe. In creating it, he has established laws, both mechanical and spiritual, by which it is regulated. Yet he has not withdrawn his own presence and power in its continued guidance and preservation; but is constantly developing, through it and in it, his eternal purpose.

6. In human affairs, however, the will of God is most distinctively exhibited in the work of redemption. Let this be admitted as a true work of God, and, at once, appear the proofs of a far-reaching end, accomplished by frequent acts of interposition and guidance, in which concenters and culminates the entire scope of God's outward activity. The will of God is seen to be the propelling force of his devising wisdom and executing power in the accomplishment of one great purpose to which is indissolubly linked all his other acts and volitions.

III. A question arises as to this will of God, whether, in its exercise, he acts necessarily or freely.

It has been answered, that his will is exercised both necessarily and freely, according to the object of that will.

1. He is said to will necessarily, himself, his holy nature, and character, and the personal relations in the Godhead. This language may be admitted, if it be borne in mind, that the necessity here declared, is not one of fate, nor of outward compulsion. Whatever is meant by it must be fully consistent with God's free agency. It is a necessity that arises from his nature, because of which, such must be the will of God, that he wills himself, his existence, and the relations of the persons of the Godhead. Such being the nature of the necessity, it would be better to express it in some way which would indicate its source and prevent misapprehension. The word "naturally" would suffice, were it not for its ambiguity in common use; consequently "essentially" is suggested as expressive of all

the necessity, and at the same time of all the freedom which must accompany an act of the will proceeding from the very essence or nature of God.

2. As to all else than himself, God wills freely, whether his will has regard to their existence, or mode of existence, or their actions, or the events which influence or control them. He does his own will, not that of another. He chooses what, and whom he will create, and the times, places and circumstances in which he will place those he creates. He marks out to all his intelligent creatures the paths of their lives. He uses them for his purposes. Though he gives to them, also, like freedom of will, yet is their will subordinate to his, and, with their actions, is controlled by it. Yet is this so wisely done, and so truly in accordance with their own natures, as fully to preserve in them consciousness and conviction of the power of contrary choice, and of full responsibility for what they choose and do.

When it is said, however, that God wills freely, it is not meant that no influence is exerted upon his will. It is only intended to deny that his will is influenced from without. In all his outward acts, as well as in those within, he is governed by his own nature. That nature, and that will, must always be in unison. As he is infinitely wise, so must his will and action be directed towards wise ends in the use of wise means. His infinite justice forbids that he should will or do anything contrary to the strictest justice. The God of truth must also purpose in accordance with truth and faithfulness. His love, too, which is so gracious a characteristic of God, forbids that he shall will otherwise than benevolently towards all; securing the happiness of the innocent, and desiring that even of the guilty, when it can be made consistent with his justice. The holiness of his nature makes it essential that, as all perfection, in perfect harmony, is involved in that holiness, so also must it be found in every purpose which he forms, as well as in every action by which his purposes are accomplished. When, therefore, God is said to will freely in all matters which are without, it is not meant to deny that he is governed by his nature in all respects, in which that nature ought to affect his will.

But, even in the volition thus formed, God does not will freely, in the sense of willing arbitrarily. He is not indifferent as to what he will do. There is choice, and not arbitrary choice. There are reasons perceived by him, which induce him to choose one end, rather than another, and one set of means to that end, in preference to others. There is in each case a prevailing motive, not necessarily dependent upon its own force or power, but upon the simple fact, that, in the midst of the numerous ends and means known to him through his infinite knowledge, this motive makes this end, and these means best pleasing to him. The very nature of choice in any being of intelligence and free agency makes this the method by which the will forms its decision. There is nothing in the nature of the omniscient and all-purposing God, which forbids that this also should be the method of his volitions. Our conception of God in this respect cannot be incorrect, although, as in all instances in which we attempt to arrive at the perfections of God through those recognized as such in man, this conception may be very inadequate.

IV. The discussion of the preceding question shows how truly man, so far as his will is concerned, had been made in the image of God. It suggests the propriety, therefore, of setting forth more particularly the points of similarity and dissimilarity between the will of man and that of God.

1. Some points of similarity may be mentioned.

(1.) In man, will is the element in which sovereignty exists; so also in God.

(2.) In man, will depends upon the understanding, that is, it is exercised, all other things being equal, in accordance with its dictates; so also in God.

(3.) In man, the will is essentially influenced by his nature; so also in God.

(4.) In man, the will is controlled by the prevailing motive, which is made the strongest, because it is that most pleasing to him; so also in God.

2. But there are also points of dissimilarity between these wills.

(1.) God never wills what he cannot do; man often does.

(2.) In God, the will is never influenced from without; in man this is frequently done.

By the outward control in man is not here meant that physical compulsion by which a man is sometimes said to act against his will; but those legitimate outward influences from persons, circumstances, and events, which lead men freely to choose, in accordance with the laws of the mind.

(3.) In God, the prevailing motive is not only the most pleasing, but, presumably, the best; in man, it is only the most pleasing, not the most reasonable and right, nor the most conducive to happiness; but often the very contrary of these.

(4.) In God there is but one will, or purpose, which comprehends all his ends and means; he does not will, by successive acts, nor in successive moments, but simultaneously, and eternally; man wills successively, one will follows another, and the volition of one man often succeeds the acts, as well as the volitions, of others.

(5.) The will of God is always accomplished; that of man is often defeated.

(6.) God never changes his will, nor perceives any reason for such change; man changes his frequently, from caprice, or because of new information, or because he sees the importance of a better life, or is carried off by passion to one that is worse.

V. Various distinctions as to the will of God have been pointed out, some of which are correct, or at least admissible, and others incorrect, and objectionable.

The following list is given by Turretine in the fifteenth and sixteenth questions of his third book. The statements made are in the main taken from his discussion.

1. The correct distinctions.

(1.) The first distinction is between the decretive and preceptive will of God.

By the decretive will is meant that will of God by which he purposes or decrees, whatever shall come to pass, whether he wills to accomplish it himself effectively, or causatively, or to permit it to occur through the unrestrained agency or will of his creatures. In either case, however, he has determined, purposed, or decreed, either to bring it to pass, or to cause, or to permit it to be brought to pass.

By the preceptive will is meant that which he has prescribed to be done by others. Such are the laws under which he places his creatures, or the duties which he enjoins upon them. It is the rule of duty.

The decretive will must always be fulfilled; the preceptive may be disobeyed, and therefore remain unfulfilled.

(2.) Nearly corresponding to this first distinction is another into the will of eudokia, and that of euarestia. As the former was taken from two Latin, so this is from two Greek words, and these Greek words are scriptural. The former division was made in connection with purpose to do; this in connection with pleasure in doing, or desire to do, or to see done. But the two correspond in the fact that the will of eudokia, like that of decree, comprises what shall certainly be accomplished, and that of euarestia like that of precept embraces simply what it pleases God that his creatures shall do.

It must not be supposed, however, that, because of the meaning eudokia (well pleasing), the decretive will, expressed by this word, is confined to those volitions of God, in which the happiness and blessing of man are involved. It was with reference both to evil to some, and blessing to others, that Christ used it when he said, "Yea Father for so it was well pleasing in thy sight." Matt. 11:26. The decretive will of God, whatever its effect upon his creatures, is "well pleasing" to God.

(3.) A third distinction is between the will of the signum and that of the beneplacitum.

By the beneplacitum is intended, a will of God which is confined to himself, until he makes it known by some revelation, or by the event itself. Any will thus made known becomes the signum. Manifestly these may differ in several respects.

If the will of the beneplacitum be confined, as it should be, to the decretive will of God, it will be broader, and narrower, than that of the signum; broader, because at no time has the whole decretive will of God been revealed; and narrower, because the will of the signum must extend, also, to the preceptive will of God, which God prescribes as duty, and yet does not determine shall be performed. In some cases, God even gives commands, which are, for the time, a rule of duty, and, therefore, a part of his preceptive will, and thus also of this will of signum, obedience to which he actually intends to prevent. Thus he ordered Abraham by the will of signum to sacrifice Isaac, which was thus made to his servant a rule of duty, yet, by the will of the beneplacitum, he not only did not purpose the sacrifice, but intended to interpose to prevent it.

(4.) A fourth distinction is between the secret and the revealed will of God. Turretine says, "The former of these is commonly referred to the will of decree, which for the most part is hidden in God; the latter to the will of the precept, which is revealed, and disclosed in the Law and the Gospel. Its basis is sought in Deut. 29:29: 'The secret things belong unto the Lord our God: but the things that are revealed belong unto us and to our children forever, that we may do all the words of this law.' The former is called a great deep and an unsearchable abyss. Ps. 36:6; Rom. 11:33, 34. The latter is accessible to all, nor is it far from us. Deut. 30:14; Rom. 10:8. That has for its object all those things which God will either to effect, or permit, and which, especially, he wishes to do concerning each man, and which are, therefore, absolute and fixed without exception. The latter refers to those things which belong to our duty, and which are conditionally set forth. The former is always done, the latter is often violated."

2. The incorrect distinctions:

(1.) That of antecedent and consequent volitions.

By this is not meant one will, or decree, which precedes another in its logical order in the divine mind, or in its execution by God, as that of the creation of man, before that of his redemption; nor one will of the precept, which consists in the prescribed duty, followed by another which sets forth the consequent rewards and punishments. Were this so, the distinction would be objectionable only because of its inaccuracy in transferring to God such methods of our action, or logical conception, as belong to that succession in our acts and will which cannot exist in God. It would be only the same kind of misstatement, of which orthodox theologians are guilty, when under the form of sublapsarianism, or supralapsarianism, they attempt to set forth the order of God's decrees. In one form, in which this distinction is incorrectly made, it is claimed that a consequent will in God arises after he sees the results of one which is previous, or antecedent; another that he forms a particular volition, especially affecting an individual man, following upon a general volition, or disposition, to seek the happiness of his creatures, or to prescribe a course by which that happiness may be secured.

To the distinction of antecedent, and consequent volitions, in these forms, there are many objections.

(a.) It admits succession in the decrees of God, and makes them many, when they are but one.

(b.) It makes them temporal, when they are eternal.

(c.) Turretine ably argues, that thus contrary wills would exist in God, who would thus be at one and the same time willing, and not willing, the same event.

(d.) He also justly states, that the antecedent will thus spoken of, could be only a mere wishing (velleitas), and not a will (voluntas.)

(e.) He suggests that thus the independence of God would be taken away, since he must wait upon man to will, and act, before he could will.

(2.) A second incorrect distinction is between the efficacious and inefficacious will of God.

This distinction would also be admissible, if by the efficacious will were meant that of the decree, and by the inefficacious, that of the precept. But, as introduced, both terms are applied to the will of the decree. Turretine objects to the application, in the first place, "because the scripture testifies, that the purpose of God is immutable, and his will cannot be resisted. Isa. 46:10; Rom. 9:19; but, if it cannot be resisted, he will surely perfect that which he intends; secondly, inefficacious will cannot be attributed to God, unless he is accused either of ignorance, because he knew not that the event would not occur, or of impotence, because he could not accomplish the result he purposed; finally, the same reasons which prove that antecedent and consequent will are not allowable, are also proofs against efficacious and inefficacious."

(3.) The third of the incorrect distinctions is that of absolute and conditional.

If, by the conditional will, were meant the conditions appended to the preceptive will of God, in the promises and threats given as inducements to duty, it would not be objected to. But the object of those who present it, is to apply it to the decretive will, and to suppose that God, in his purposes, determines, on certain conditions, that he will do a certain act, which he will not do if those conditions fail. Whether these conditions shall fail, or not, is supposed to be unknown to God, or, if known, yet at least so far undetermined, that he has formed no purpose whether or not to permit, or to accomplish them. The purposes of God, thus formed, are not, therefore, absolute decrees, as are all those concerning what shall actually and absolutely take place, but are only conditional ones, based upon some antecedent condition, which must first occur.

This distinction is introduced, chiefly, to show how God can make an absolute decree about the salvation of mankind in general, and, yet, not about that of any one man in particular. Absolutely he decrees the salvation in general of all who believe. But the salvation of each one is decreed, only upon the condition that he believes. Whether that faith will be exercised by any one, is not determined by God. Nor so far as involved in any purpose made by him is it even known to God.

Such is the theory and purpose of this distinction. The objections presented against the other two of these incorrect distinctions are also justly made against it.

CHAPTER 13

THE DECREES OF GOD

THE decrees of God may be defined as that just, wise, and holy purpose or plan by which eternally, and within himself, he determines all things whatsoever that come to pass.

I. This purpose or plan is just, wise, and holy. Since it is formed by God it must have this character. His nature forbids that anything otherwise shall proceed from him. Though what he permits may be unrighteous, or foolish, or sinful, these characteristics belong to it because of others; while his will, purpose, or plan continues just, wise, and holy.

It is needful that this fact be always remembered.

1. Since, on account of the ignorance of man, there must be much in connection with this subject, which cannot be comprehended; because (1.) man's finite knowledge cannot compass the nature, and mode, and reasons of the will, and action of the infinite God, (2.) because of the difficulty of reconciling the free agency and responsibility of man, with the pre-existent knowledge and purposes of God, and (3.) because of the perplexities which arise from the existence of sin in a world planned, created and governed by a holy, all-wise, and almighty God.

2. The same fact should also not be forgotten, because of the natural corruption of the human heart, which makes it (1.) revolt against the sovereignty of God, (2.) seek refuge from the condemnation justly due to sin, and (3.) endeavor to find excuses for continuance therein.

It is our duty, therefore, (1.) to seek to learn all the facts made known by reason and revelation, (2.) to accept them, (3.) to recognize them as the testimony of God, (4.) to admit that our knowledge is still imperfect, (5.) to believe that further information will still further remove the difficulties, (6.) to refuse on account of the difficulties to reject what God has actually taught, and (7.) amid all, to believe that whatever that teaching is, it must accord with justice, wisdom and holy perfection, because it is God of whom these things are affirmed.

II. These decrees are properly defined to be God's purpose or plan.

The term "decree" is liable to some misapprehension and objection, because it conveys the idea of an edict, or of some compulsory determination. "Purpose" has been suggested as a better word. "Plan" will sometimes be still more suitable. The mere use of these words will remove from many some difficulties and prejudices which make them unwilling to accept this doctrine. They perceive that, in the creation, preservation, and government of the world, God must have had a plan, and that that plan must have been just, wise and holy, tending both to his own glory and the happiness of his creatures. They recognize that a man who has no purpose, nor aim, especially in important matters, and who cannot, or does not, devise the means by which to carry out his purpose, is without wisdom and capacity, and unworthy of his nature. Consequently, they readily believe and admit that the more comprehensive, and, at the same time, the more definite is the plan of God, the more worthy is it of infinite wisdom. Indeed they are compelled to the conclusion that God cannot be what he is, without forming such a purpose or plan.

III. Any such plan or purpose of God must have been formed eternally, and within himself.

1. It must have been eternally purposed, because God's only mode of existence, as has been heretofore proved, is eternal, and therefore his thoughts, and purpose, and plan must be eternal. The fact also that his knowledge is infinite, and cannot be increased, forbids the forming of plans in time, which, as they become known to him, would add to that knowledge. It is also to be remembered that the plan must precede its execution, but as time began with that execution, the plan could not have been formed in time, and must be eternal.

2. In like manner, also, was it formed within himself. He needed not to go without himself, either for the impulse which led to it, or the knowledge in which it was conceived. He had all knowledge, both of the actual and the possible, all wisdom as to the best end and means, all power to execute what he devised in the use, or without the use of appropriate secondary means, and free will to select, of all possible plans and means, whatever he himself should please, and the impulse which moved him existed alone in that knowledge and will.

IV. By this plan or purpose God determined all things which it included.

This is manifestly true, even if all things whatsoever were not thus embraced.

To say the least, all the parts of it, as well as the whole, were known to him. But this knowledge, apart from any decree, determines, marks out, and fixes the nature, limits, time, sequence and relation to each other of the whole, and of all the parts. Things which are known by God as future, must certainly be future. A determination, or decree to bring them to pass, and even their actual existence, does not make them more certain.

But whence is God's knowledge of the futurity of any events, except from the knowledge of his purpose, to cause or permit them to come to pass? The knowledge of the futurity of any event, over which any one has absolute control, is the result of his purpose, not its cause. And, as God has such absolute control over all things, his knowledge that they will be, must proceed from his purpose that they shall be. It cannot be from mere perception of their nature, for he gives that nature, and in determining to give it, determines what it shall be, and thus determines the effects which that nature will cause. Nor is it from mere knowledge of the mutual relations which will be sustained by outward events or beings, for it is he that establishes these relations for the accomplishment of his own purposes. To say that this nature and these relations are from God, and are not from his purpose, is in the highest degree fatalistic, for it would involve that they originate in some necessity of the nature of God, because of which he must give them existence without so willing, and even against his will. In this way alone could God be said to know, and yet not to purpose them. His knowledge would arise from knowledge of his nature, and of what that nature compels him to do, and not from knowledge of his purpose and of his will involved in that purpose. This, and this alone, would make equally certain and known what will come to pass, without basing that knowledge upon his purpose; but it would not only be destructive of his free agency and will, but, from the nature of necessity, would make the outward events eternal and prevent the existence of time, and the relation to it of all things whatsoever.

V. This plan, or purpose, includes all things whatsoever that come to pass; not some things, but all things; not all things in general, but each thing in particular.

So interwoven are all these things, that the lack of purpose, as to any one, would involve that same lack as to multitudes of others, indeed as to every other connected in the slightest degree with the one not purposed.

This is evidently true as to all subsequent events; but it is equally so as to those that are antecedent, for these thus connected antecedent events have been established with efficient causative power, relative to all their effects. God knows the existence of this power; he has in fact ordained and bestowed it. He knows also what will be its effects. With this knowledge, God must, therefore, either allow them to act, because he purposes that the result shall follow, or he must hinder, or restrain, or accelerate their action because he would change the effect. In each case he purposes, in the one to effect, in the other to permit, and his purpose thus extends to all things. Any limitation of his purpose involves limitation of his knowledge, and this cannot be true of the omniscient God.

To such an extent is the force of this realized, that it is admitted by all, that, in the mechanical universe, and even in the control of the lower animals, this is true. But the free agency of man, and of other rational and moral agents, is supposed to prevent God's purposing, or willing, all things with reference to them. It is said that such purposing would take away that free agency, and consequent responsibility.

The Scriptures recognize both the sovereignty of God, and the free agency, and accountability of man. Consciousness assures us of the latter. The nature of God, as has just been shown, proves the former. The Bible makes no attempt to reconcile the two. Paul even declines to discuss the subject, saying, "Nay but, oh man, who art thou that repliest against God?" Rom. 9:20. The two facts are plainly revealed. They cannot be contradictory, they must be reconcilable. That we cannot point out the harmony between them is a proof, only of our ignorance, and limited capacity, and not that both are not true. It is certain, however, that, whatever may be the influences which God exercises, or permits, to secure the fulfillment of his purposes, he always acts in accordance with the nature, and especially with the laws of mind he has bestowed upon man. It is equally true, that his action is in full accord with that justice, and benevolence, which are such essential attributes of God himself.

Acting, however, upon the belief that the purpose of God, accomplishing his will in his rational creatures, is inconsistent with their free agency, several classes of theologians have presented theories in opposition to the scriptural doctrine of decrees above set forth.

1. The most objectionable theory is that of the Socinians, who deny that God can know what a free agent will choose, or do, before he acts, or wills. They maintain that the will is, at the moment of its choice, in such perfect equilibrium, that there are no tendencies in any direction which prevent an absolute freedom of choice. No knowledge, therefore, of the will itself, nor of the circumstances which surround its action, will enable any one to say, before it is exercised, what will be its choice. Its act, therefore, is entirely undetermined and indeterminable, until the free agent wills. It cannot even be known beforehand by God himself.

The objections to this theory are obvious.

(1.) It is based upon a wrong conception of the nature of free agency; for it supposes each act of the will to be an arbitrary choice. But such arbitrary choice is not found even in God. As regards man, we know, from consciousness and experience, that his will is influenced by motives. Indeed, so truly is it governed by the nature of the man, and the attendant influences, that even we can predict his will and action in many cases, and only fail to do so perfectly in all because of our limited knowledge. The omniscient God cannot fail to know everything that affects the decision, and, therefore, what the decision will be.

(2.) This theory is also opposed to the independence of God. It supposes him to have made beings of such a nature, that his own actions and will must depend upon theirs, and that he must await their decision, wherever it will have any influential bearings on anything future, before he can know or purpose what he himself will do.

(3.) It is also manifest, from what has been said under the first objection, that this theory is opposed to the omniscience of God. It expressly puts a limitation, upon that omniscience, by declaring that he is limited in his knowledge, at least, so far as not to know beforehand the decision of the will of his creatures. But ignorance of this would also involve ignorance of all things in the future, with which it may be connected. This would, in a world inhabited by free agents, constitute no small part of all that will occur.

(4.) It is opposed to the instances mentioned in Scripture of the prediction beforehand by God, even of the bad actions of certain men. See as to Pharaoh, Ex. 7:3, 4; Hazael, 2 Kings 8:13; Judas, Matt. 26:21; Peter, Matt. 26:34, etc., etc.

(5.) It is opposed to the power of forming habits, which is a matter of universal experience. Such habits, when known, constitute a source of information, upon which, to some degree, reliance can be placed in foretelling what any man will do. A perfect knowledge of his habits, as well as of all else that influences, would secure infallible prediction of the choice. God has this perfect knowledge, and if he cannot foreknow the decision, it must be because it is not true that habits can be formed which according to the law of habit will influence and control.

2. Another theory has been advanced by some Arminians, who maintain that God does not know the free actions of men, not because he cannot know them, but because he chooses not to do so.

(1.) The first objection to this theory is, that, were it true, it would not give greater freedom to the will, than does the orthodox statement.

Though this theory honours God more than the former, it is inferior to it with respect to the object for which it is introduced. If it could be true as the first theory claims, that so indeterminate is the future will of a free agent, that even God cannot know it, then that future will would certainly be entirely under the control of the free agent, and he would to the utmost extreme be free. His will would be in absolute equilibrium in the act of choosing. Neither would any motive exist to influence that choice. It would be thoroughly arbitrary.

But the second theory has not this advantage, for it does not suppose this condition of equilibrium. In claiming, that God does not choose to know, what he might know if he should so choose, it admits that there are the same surrounding circumstances and conditions, and the same prevailing motive, through foresight of which God could know if he should so will. But, if this be true, there can be no state of equilibrium. The certainty of what will occur is as much fixed as though known to God. It is not his knowledge of these things, and of their certain result in the act of the will, that makes it certain what it will be. It is the fact, that these things are such as they are, which makes it possible for him to know them. If he barely determines to permit what his knowledge perceives will surely take place, the event is not made any more certain by that knowledge, than it was before. Unquestionably, therefore, so far as the permissive decrees of God are involved, this theory has no advantage over that of the Scriptures.

The same fact is true as to God's effective decrees, for the fact that God does not choose to know the result, does not prevent his introduction of active influences towards that result. Because a man does not know the decision which a judge will make in a case in court, and does not choose, because of the impropriety of so doing, to ascertain from the judge what will be his decision, he does not, therefore, refrain from using all proper arguments to influence the judge. There can be no reason why God, in ignorance of what will be the decision, could not exert every influence which would be possible if that decision were known to him. He could only exert such influences as, under the circumstances, would be just and right. He could do this only in accordance with the nature of his creatures, in strict conformity to the laws of the human mind. Therefore, it may be affirmed as true, that, even under his efficient decrees, when he knows the result, his creatures are left as free as they could be, were that result unknown to him.

(2.) The chief objection, to this theory is, that it is based upon a wrong conception of the relation of the will of God to his nature. That will does not confer the attributes of his nature, nor does it control them, but is itself influenced by them. God knows all things, not because he wills to know them, but, because, from his nature, he has infinite knowledge—knowledge of all things possible, and knowledge of all things certain. If, by his will, he could refrain from knowing, he would change his nature. As well speak of a man not choosing to see, with his eyes open, the objects presented to his sight, as of God not choosing to know anything, whether that be only something which is possible, or something which in any way has been made certain.

3. There is, beside the theories already referred to, the ordinary Arminian theory. This is, that God knows all things that will come to pass, but does not decree all, but only some of them. The decisions of free agents are among those things which he is supposed not to decree.

(1.) The manifest objection to this theory is, that it does not accord with the statements of the Bible. This will be subsequently shown, by the passages of Scripture which will be advanced, in proof of the various points involved in the ordinary Calvinistic theory.

(2.) But a second objection will be found in the fact that this theory does not thus secure that freedom from certainty in the decisions of free agents, which is the great reason of the objections to the decrees of God concerning them.

If by decreeing such decisions, is meant effectively causing them, it is true that God does not decree all things; for, while he effectually causes some, he only permissively decrees others. Hence the objection to the word "decree," and the previous suggestion of the words "purpose" or "plan."

But, if God knows that any event will occur, and can prevent it, and does not, it is evident that he purposes that it shall exist, and makes it a part of his plan.

His knowledge of the futurity of any event makes it as certain as any purpose he could form effectively to cause it. That knowledge is perfect and infallible. What he knows will come to pass, must necessarily take place. Otherwise, he would know a thing as future which will not be future. His knowledge of it would be false. He would be himself deceived. To suppose, then, that he knows it as certain, when it is not certain, is to deny his infinite knowledge, and to reduce this theory to the plane of one or the other of those previously mentioned.

(3.) Neither does this theory accomplish another object for which it is introduced, namely, to secure such a relation of God to any free act of man as shall take away the influence upon it exerted by his decree.

His decree to permit it, is as hidden from his creatures as his knowledge that they will so act, and can have no other influence upon them than that knowledge.

The only apparent advantage is that God is supposed thus not to interfere with their free agency, so as to destroy their accountability. But we have seen that, so far as the permissive decree is concerned, the knowledge of the event is as effective in making it certain, and in influencing the free agent, as would be any decree, purpose or plan of God. It is only when the decree is effective, and introduces the means for its accomplishment, that the free agency is affected. In this case, God does not destroy the free agency, although he exerts an influence towards the result. But that God is thus active, sometimes, as in his gracious influences upon men, is held as firmly by Arminians as Calvinists. In all such gracious acts, both parties claim that he is both merciful and just. Calvinists extend these no further than do Arminians, for they deny as strenuously as others, that God acts effectively to lead men to wicked decisions and deeds. So far as the nature of God's actions upon free agents is concerned, both parties agree. But the Arminian theory, in asserting foreknowledge without purpose, and in alleging that the foreknowledge is all that there is in God, is contrary to the relations of God's will to his knowledge, as well as to the statements of Scripture about the decrees of God; and while it leaves the event equally certain, supposes fully as much influence over the will of the creature, and has equal difficulty in reconciling the free agency, and consequent responsibility, with the inevitable certainty of the event.

The chief difficulty connected with the doctrine of decrees arises from the existence of sin. According to that doctrine, sin has not accidentally occurred, nor was it simply foreknown, but it was a part of the plan and purpose of God, that it should exist. The difficulty is freely admitted. In this respect the dispensation of God is surrounded with "clouds and darkness."

The following statements, however, may be made:

(1.) That its being a part of the purpose or plan of God, renders its presence no more difficult of explanation than that he should have foreknown its appearance, and not exerted his unquestioned power to prevent it.

(2.) That, amid all the darkness, we can yet see that God is so overruling sin as to cause it greatly to redound to his glory and the happiness of his creatures.

(3.) That even without any explanation of it, we can rest in our knowledge of the justice, wisdom, and goodness of God.

(4.) That we cannot see how its possible entrance into the world could have been prevented, consistently with the creation and putting upon probation of beings with moral natures, endowed with free will, and necessarily fallible because mere creatures; while the right thus to put on probation, without such influence as would make his creatures certainly persevere in holiness, is one which none could justly deny to God. But that which God could possibly (under any contingency) permit, cannot, if it has actual existence, militate against his pure and holy character.

The Scriptural authority for the doctrine of decrees will appear from the following statements and references, gathered with slight modifications from Hodge's Outlines, pp, 205–213:

1. God's decrees are eternal. Acts 15:18; Eph. 1:4; 3:11; 1 Pet. 1:20; 2 Thess. 2:13; 2 Tim. 1:9; 1 Cor. 2:7.

2. They are immutable. Ps. 33:11; Isa. 46:9.

3. They comprehend all events.

(1.) The Scriptures assert this of the whole system in general embraced in the divine decrees. Dan. 4:34, 35; Acts 17:26; Eph 1:11.

(2.) They affirm the same of fortuitous events. Prov. 16:33; Matt. 10:29, 30.

(3.) Also of the free actions of men. Eph. 2:10, 11; Phil. 2:13.

(4.) Even the wicked actions of men. Acts 2:23; 4:27, 28; 13:29; 1 Pet. 2:8; Jude 4; Rev. 17:17. As to the history of Joseph, compare Gen. 37:28, with Gen. 45:7, 8, and Gen. 50:20. See also Ps. 17:13, 14; Isa. 10:5, 15.

4. The decrees of God are not conditional. Ps. 33:11; Prov. 19:21; Isa. 14:24, 27; 46:10; Rom. 9:11.

5. They are sovereign. Isa. 40:13, 14; Dan. 4:35; Matt. 11:25, 26; Rom. 9:11, 15–18; Eph. 1:5, 11.

6. They include the means. Eph. 1:4; 2 Thess. 2:13; 1 Pet. 1:2.

7. They determine the free actions of men. Acts 4:27, 28; Eph. 2:10.

8. God himself works in his people that faith and obedience which are called the conditions of salvation. Eph. 2:8; Phil. 2:13; 2 Tim. 2:25.

9. The decree renders the event certain. Matt. 16:21; Luke 18:31–33; 24:46; Acts 2:23; 13:29; 1 Cor. 11:19.

10. While God has decreed the free acts of men, the actors have been none the less responsible. Gen. 50:20; Acts 2:23; 3:18; 4:27, 28.

CHAPTER 14

THE TRINITY

THE Scripture doctrine of the Trinity is set forth in the Abstract of Principles of the Southern Baptist Theological Seminary in these words (Art. III.): "God is revealed to us as Father, Son and Holy Spirit, each with distinct personal attributes, but without division of nature, essence or being."

The peculiarity of this definition is that it is a mere statement of the Scriptural facts revealed, while, at the same time, it includes every point involved in the doctrine of the Trinity as held by orthodox Christians of all ages. There is no addition to the Scripture facts, but the complete exhibition which these words make of the doctrine, shows that it has been correctly formulated from what God has himself revealed. As he alone can know and reveal what he is, so we must accept his statements, however mysterious and incomprehensible may be his revelation.

This definition suggests to us a method of treatment by which, in the utmost simplicity and Scripturalness, the whole truth on this important subject may be attained.

I. THE RELATION OF FATHER AND SON

God is revealed to us as the Father; not merely in the general way in which he is called the Father of all created beings, and they his sons; nor in that in which he is the Father of those who are his sons, in virtue of the adoption, which is in Christ Jesus; but the Father as indicative of a special relation between him and another person whom the Scriptures call his only begotten Son. There are several classes of Scripture passages which reveal this.

1. That class in which, in recognition of this relation, Christ addresses God as "Father." Matt. 11:25, 26; Mark 14:36; Luke 10:21; 22:42; 23:34, 46; John 12:26, 27, 28; 17:1, 5, 11, 24, 25.

2. That class in which Christ speaks of him as peculiarly his Father. The expression "our Father" is never used by him, except in the Lord's prayer when he is teaching the disciples how to pray. Matt. 10:32, 33; 15:13; 16:17; 18:10, 19; 20:23; 24:36; 25:34; 26:29, 39, 42, 53; Luke 2:49; 22:29; 24:49; John 5:17, 43; 6:32; 8:19, 38, 49, 54; 10:18, 25, 29, 30, 32, 37; 12:26; 14:7, 20, 21, 23; 15:1, 8, 10, 15, 23; 20:17; Rev. 2:27; 3:5.

3. That class in which the Father is spoken of as sending and as giving the Son.

This does not include many passages in which Christ is said to be sent, but only those in which he is referred to as sent by the Father. John 3:16, 17; 5:37; 6:37–40, 57; 8:16–19; 10:36; John 12:45, 49; 14:24; 17:18; 20:21.

4. A fourth class represents the Father as knowing and loving the Son. Matt. 11:27; Luke 10:22; John 3:35; 5:20.

5. There is, also, a class in which Christ and the Father are said to be co-workers, or in which the works of Christ are claimed to be the Father's witness to him. John 5:17; 10:25, 32, 36, 37, 38.

6. That class in which the Father is said to put special honour on the Son. John 3:35; 5:23, 25, 26, 27.

7. There is yet another class in which peculiarity of relation is shown by such terms, as

(1.) "My beloved Son;" the language is very strong and emphatic, "my Son, the beloved." Matt. 3:17; 17:5; Mark 1:11; Luke 3:22; 2 Pet. 1:17.

(2.) "Only begotten Son." John 1:14, 18; 3:16, 18; 1 John 4:9.

(3.) "His own Son." Rom. 8:32. In connection with this, it should be remembered that, in John 5:18, the charge made against Christ by the Jews was that he "called God his own Father making himself equal with God."

8. The statements that the Son alone has seen, and known, and revealed the Father, also show peculiarity of this relationship. John 1:18; 14:6–11; 17:25, 26.

9. The same peculiarity is shown by the manner in which Christ speaks of the works he does by virtue of it. See his Sabbath day discourse after curing the man at the pool of Bethesda. John 5:19–31, 36, 37; also, John 14:10, 11.

II. THIS FATHER IS GOD

The relation pointed out above, is one borne by Christ to the supreme God. It is he, whom the Scriptures call God in the true sense of that word, to whom Christ is said by them to be Son to the Father.

1. There are the passages which expressly call Christ "Son of God." All are here omitted where the name is given by devils, or by the Centurion, or in any other way in which the authority of inspired teaching may not be claimed for its use. Mark 1:1; Luke 1:35; John 5:25; 10:36; 11:27; Acts 9:20; Gal. 4:4; 1 John 4:15; 5:5, 20, 21.

2. There are other passages in which the epithet "God" is ascribed to the Father in this relationship.

John 1:18; 3:16, 17; 5:18; Rom. 1:1–4; 8:31, 32; 2 Pet. 1:17; 1 John 4:9, 10; 2 John 3.

III. THIS SON IS GOD

1. He is expressly called God. It is not denied that this epithet, like that of Lord, is applied in an inferior sense to others. The mere use of these titles would not prove that the one to whom they are attributed has the divine nature. But the manner in which they are applied to Christ, and the frequency of that application, become, along with the other evidences presented, an incontestable proof, that he, as well as the Father, is true God. If they were not ascribed to Christ in the Scriptures, their absence would be conspicuous and well-fitted to cast doubt on the other evidence. Matt. 1:23; John 1:1; 20:28; Rom. 9:5; Titus 1:3; Heb. 1:8.

In the above are omitted, as, on various grounds, doubtful. Acts 20:28; 1 Tim. 3:16; and 1 John 5:20. An exegetical study of these passages will show, even with the text of the recent critics, that they strongly corroborate the doctrine that Christ is God.

2. Christ is also called Lord. This title is used in both the Old and New Testaments still more generally than is that of God. An examination of the texts here quoted, will show that, in a peculiar sense, only suited to Christ as God, is it applied to him. Matt. 12:8; 22:41–45; Mark 2:28; Luke 6:46; 20:41–44; John 13:13, 14; Acts 10:36; Rom. 14:9; 1 Cor. 2:8; Gal. 1:3; 6:18; Phil. 2:11; 2 Thess. 2:16; Jude 4; Rev. 17:14; 19:13, 16.

3. He is a peculiar object of worship. The worship paid to him is not merely that reverential respect offered to kings and others in authority, but such worship as was refused by the apostles with horror, because they were mere men (Acts 14:13–15), and against which, when offered to him by John, even the mighty angel (Revelation 19:10; 22:9) earnestly protested. All doubtful cases of worship are here omitted, even that of the wise men (Matt. 2:2, 11) in which perhaps divine worship was paid. Matt. 14:33; Luke 24:52; Acts 7:59, 60; 2 Cor. 12:8, 9; Phil. 2:10; Heb. 1:6; Rev. 5:8–14; 7:9–12.

4. He is to be honoured equally with the Father. John 5:23.

5. His relations to the Father are those of identity and unity. John 1:18; 5:17–19; 8:16, 19; 10:30; 12:44, 45; 14:7–11; 15:24; Heb. 1:3; Col. 1:15, 19; 2:9; 1 John 2:23, 24.

6. They are equally known to each other, and unknown to all others. Matt. 11:27; Luke 10:22; John 1:18; 6:46; 10:15.

7. He is the creator of all things. John 1:3, 10; 1 Cor. 8:6; Col. 1:16; Heb. 1:10.

8. He upholds and preserves all things. Col. 1:17; Heb. 1:3.

9. He is the manifestation of the Divine Being in this world. John 1:10, 14, 18; 14:8–11; 16:28–30; Col. 1:15; 1 Tim. 3:16; 1 John 1:2.

10. He is greater than all others; greater than Moses, and David, and Solomon, and Jonah, and the Baptist; and not greater than man only, but than all the spiritual intelligences of the universe. Matt. 3:11; 12:41, 42; Mark 12:37; Luke 11:31, 32; John 1:17; Eph. 1:21; Phil. 2:9; Heb. 1:4, 5; 3:3; 1 Pet. 3:22.

11. He is the source of all spiritual blessing.

(a.) He gives the Holy Spirit. Luke 24:49; John 16:7; 20:22; Acts 2:33.

(b.) He forgives sins. Mark 2:5–10; Luke 5:20–24; 7:47–49; Acts 5:31.

(c.) He gives peculiar peace. John 14:27; 16:33. Is not he the one who is called "God of Peace?" Rom. 15:33; 16:20; 2 Cor. 13:11; Phil. 4:9; 1 Thess. 5:23; Heb. 13:20.

(d.) He gives light. John 1:4, 7, 8, 9; 8:12; 9:5; 12:35, 46; 1 John 1:5–7; Rev. 21:23.

(e.) He gives faith. Luke 17:5; Heb. 12:2.

(f.) He gives eternal life. John 17:2.

(g.) He confers all the spiritual gifts bestowed upon his churches. Eph. 4:8–13.

12. All the incommunicable attributes of God are ascribed to him.

(a.) Self-existence. He has power over his own life. John 2:19; 10:17, 18. He has life in himself, as has the Father. John 5:26.

(b.) Eternity of existence. John 1:1, 2; 17:5, 24; Heb. 1:8, 10–12; 1 John 1:2.

(c.) Omniscience. Matt. 9:4; 12:25; Mark 2:8; Luke 6:8; 9:47; 10:22; John 1:48; 2:24, 25; 10:15; 16:30; 21:17; Col. 2:3; Rev. 2:23.

(d.) Omnipresence. Matt. 18:20; 28:20; John 3:13; Eph. 1:23.

(e.) Omnipotence. Matt. 28:18; Luke 21:15; John 1:3; 10:18; 1 Cor. 1:24; Eph. 1:22; Phil. 3:21; Col. 2:10; Rev. 1:18.

(f.) Immutability. Heb. 1:11, 12; 13:8.

13. The judgement of the world is entrusted to him. Matt. 16:27; 24:30; 25:31; John 5:22, 27; Acts 10:42; 17:31; Rom. 2:16; 14:10; 2 Cor. 5:10; 2 Tim. 4:1.

14. Absolute equality with the Father is ascribed to Him. This shows that the unity and identity, before referred to, is not of will, but of nature; and that the names, and worship, and attributes of God are not bestowed on any other ground than that he is true God.

(a.) Equality in works. John 5:17–23.

(b.) Equality in knowledge. Luke 10:22; John 10:15.

(c.) Equality in nature. John 5:18; 10:33; Phil. 2:6; Col. 2:9; Heb. 1:3.

It will be seen by the foregoing statements that the Scriptures distinctly teach the existence of God in the personal relations of Father and Son, and that each of them is God. No reference has been made to the Old Testament, in proof of the divinity of Christ. The New Testament is the most natural source of such instruction, because it reveals to us the fulfillment of God's purpose in sending his Son into the world, and teaches us clearly his nature and relation to the Father. What the nature of this relation of Son and Father is, will be hereafter examined in the discussion of the eternal Sonship of Christ. What the Old Testament says of Christ will also be presented hereafter.

There remains, however, to be shown that

IV. THE FATHER AND SON HAVE DISTINCT PERSONAL ATTRIBUTES

This fact is so manifest, from the manner in which the Scripture speaks of each, as to need but brief discussion.

The mere use of the names Father and Son points out a relation between two persons. That to each of them is ascribed the attributes of character, such as love, hate, goodness, mercy, truth, and justice, which can only exist in, and be exercised by persons, shows separate personality. Neither, except through distinct personal relation, can mutual love be said to be exercised, as by Christ to the Father, John 14:31; and by the Father to Christ, John 3:35; 5:20; 10:17; 17:24. Manifestly, also, there must be two persons, when one is said to send, and another to be sent; one to give, and another to be given; one to teach, and another to be taught; one to show, and another to perceive what is shown; one to receive power, and another to bestow it; and one to be declared, with respect to another, to be "the effulgence of his glory and the very image of his substance," Heb. 1:2; and, because in the form of that other, to have "counted it not a prize to be on an equality with God." Phil. 2:6.

We have here, therefore, not the one God, manifesting himself sometimes as Father, and sometimes as Son; but a distinction of persons in the Godhead, in which we are taught that in that Godhead there exists a personal relation of Father to Son, and Son to Father, with a distinct individuality and personality of each.

V. THE HOLY SPIRIT A PERSON

The Scriptures designate, by several very similar terms, the third personality revealed in the Godhead. He is called "the Spirit," "the Spirit of God," "the Holy Spirit," "my Spirit," "the Spirit of the Lord," "the Spirit of Christ," "thy good Spirit," "the Spirit of glory, "the Spirit of grace," "the Spirit of knowledge and understanding, the Spirit of counsel and might, the Spirit of knowledge and of the fear of the Lord," "the Holy Spirit of promise," "the Spirit of truth," and "the Spirit of wisdom." Christ also called him "the Comforter," and "another Comforter."

The divine Spirit, thus denominated, must either be some power or influence exerted by God, or a distinct person in the Godhead. It cannot be simply the spiritual part of God, as is the spirit in man, for God is not compounded of spirit and body. This is manifest from his immateriality. Neither can it be in any way a part of his spiritual nature, as sometimes a distinction is made in man, between his mind and spirit, or his soul and spirit. The perfect simplicity of God, which forbids all composition, makes this impossible. It is, therefore, either God himself exercising some power or influence, or a person in the Godhead. An examination of the Scripture shows that it is the latter.

1. The evidences of personal action show that the Spirit is not merely a power or influence from God, but is either God himself or a divine person.

(1.) The Scriptures speak of the Spirit as in a state of activity. Gen. 1:2; Matt. 3:16; Acts 8:39. The language in these passages may be anthropomorphic, but the state of activity taught is undoubtedly real.

(2.) They declare that the Spirit teaches and gives instruction. Luke 12:12; John 14:26; 16:8, 13, 14; Acts 10:19; 1 Cor. 12:3.

(3.) The Spirit is also spoken of by them, as a witness of Christ to his people. John 15:26.

(4.) They also assert that he witnesses to believers that they are the children of God, and becomes the earnest of their inheritance. Rom. 8:16; 2 Cor. 1:22; 5:5; Eph. 1:13, 14; 4:30.

(5.) He is spoken of as leading the sons of God. Rom. 8:14.

(6.) He is also said to dwell within them in such a way that his presence is that of God. John 14:16, 17; Rom. 8:9, 11; 1 Cor. 3:16, 17; 6:19.

(7.) We are taught that he is grieved. Eph. 4:30.

(8.) Ananias is charged with having lied to him. Acts 5:3.

(9.) Blasphemy against him is the unpardonable sin. Matt. 12:31, 32.

(10.) He is spoken of as resisted by men. Acts 7:51.

(11.) Also as vexed by them. Isa. 63:10.

(12.) As striving with them. Gen. 6:3.

(13.) As inspiring men. Acts 2:4; 8:29; 13:2; 15:28; 2 Pet. 1:21.

(14.) As interceding for them. Rom. 8:26, 27.

(15.) As bestowing diversities of gifts. 1 Cor. 12:4–11.

In all these cases there is personal activity, thought, and feeling. What is thus declared, cannot be true of a mere power, or influence. The only question can be, whether this person is God, distinct from any plurality of personal relations, or whether he is another personality in the divine nature.

2. The Scriptures show that he is a separate person from the Father and the Son.

(1.) It is stated that he proceeds from the Father. John 15:26. A personal being, proceeding from a person, cannot be that person himself. The proofs above given, therefore, of his personal action and emotion, show that this Spirit is another person.

(2.) He is given, or sent by the Father. John 14:16, 26; Acts 5:32, and by the Son, John 15:26; 16:7; Acts 2:33. He that is sent cannot be identical with him that sends.

(3.) He is called the Spirit of the Father. Eph. 3:16; and also the Spirit of Christ, and of the Son. Rom. 8:9; Gal. 4:6; perhaps also 2 Thess. 2:8.

(4.) The Son is said to send the Spirit from the Father. John 15:26; and God is said to send the Spirit of the Son. Gal. 4:6.

(5.) The Spirit is distinguished from the Father, and the Son, in passages which directly connect them with each other. Matt. 3:16, 17; 28:19; John 14:26; 15:26; 16:13; Acts 2:33; Eph. 2:18; 1 Cor. 12:4–6; 2 Cor. 13:14; 1 Pet. 1:2.

(6.) The personality of the Spirit is also ably argued from "the use of the personal pronouns in relation to him," by Dr. Charles Hodge, Sys. Theol., Vol. I, p. 524. Not only are personal pronouns used by the Spirit, and of the Spirit, but there is a departure from grammatical rule, in the use of a masculine pronoun in connection with a neuter noun, unless the masculine is warranted by the fact, that a person is referred to who may be called "he."

VI. THE HOLY SPIRIT IS GOD

So completely do the Scriptures identify the Spirit with the Supreme God, that the fact of his personality having been established, his essential divinity will at once be admitted. In the discussion of the Trinity, therefore, the point of necessary proof as to the Spirit is his personality, while that as to the Son is his divinity. The abundant proof of the divinity of the Spirit is found:

1. In the passages which call him "the Spirit of God" and "the Spirit of the Lord," as well as those in which God calls him "my Spirit." These are conclusive, in like manner, as is the divinity of Christ from those which call him the Son of God. The titles "Spirit of God," and "Spirit of the Lord," are each used about twenty-five times in the Bible. "My Spirit" is used in reference to God's Spirit in Gen. 6:3; Prov. 1:23; Isa. 44:3; 59:21; Ezek. 36:27; 39:29; Joel 2:28; Haggai 2:5; Zech. 4:6.; Matt. 12:18; Acts 2:17, 18.

2. The writers of the New Testament declare that certain things, which in the Old Testament are ascribed to Jehovah, were said by the Spirit. Compare Acts 28:25–27, and Hebrews 3:7–9, with Isaiah 6:9, and also Heb. 9:8, with Ex. 25:1, and 30:10.

3. The sacred writers of the Old Testament were the messengers of God, and spake for him, yet the influence by which they became such is called in the New Testament the Holy Ghost. Compare Luke 1:70 with 2 Peter 1:21; 2 Tim. 3:16, and Heb. 1:1 with 1 Peter 1:11; also Jer. 31:31, 33, 34, with Heb. 10:15–17.

4. The creation of the world is ascribed to the Spirit. Gen. 1:2; Job 26:13; Ps. 104:30.

5. He is said to search, and know even the deep things of God. 1 Cor. 2:10.

6. He is spoken of as omnipresent. Ps. 139:7–10, and omniscient. Ps. 139:11; 1 Cor. 2:10.

7. The divinity of the Spirit is peculiarly proved by his influences over Christ. It having been shown that Christ the Son is God, the connection of the Spirit of God with Christ, though it were only in his human nature, is a convincing proof that the Spirit, which is not a mere power of God, but a person, as we have seen above, must be also God.

(1.) In his birth. Matt. 1:18, 20; Luke 1:31–35.

(2.) Mental and spiritual influences from the Spirit were predicted. Isa. 11:2, and Isaiah 61:1.

(a.) And these were fulfilled at his baptism. Matt. 3:16; John 1:33.

(b.) At the time of the temptation in the wilderness. Matt. 4:1; Mark 1:12.

(c.) In his preaching. Luke 4:14, 18–21.

(d.) In his casting out devils. Matt. 12:28.

(3.) This spiritual influence was without measure. John 3:34.

8. The indwelling of the Spirit in the people of God is said to make them the temple of God. Compare 1 Cor. 3:16, and 6:19 with 2 Cor. 6:16, and Eph. 2:22.

9. The Spirit is expressly called God in connection with the falsehood of Ananias and Sapphira. Acts 5:3, 4, 9.

VII. THE THREE REVEALED DISTINCTLY

The scriptural proofs of the personality and divinity of the Father, Son and Holy Spirit having now been considered, it is proper to notice a few passages of Scripture in which the Three are revealed distinctly, by being mentioned, or manifested together. [See others under V. 2. (5.), pp. 118–19.]

1. At the baptism of Christ are seen the Son, who has just been baptized, and the "Spirit of God descending as a dove," while, from Heaven above, [and therefore from the Father and not from the Spirit, who is thus manifested distinctly from the Father,] is heard "a voice," "saying, this is my beloved Son, in whom I am well pleased." Matt. 3:17.

2. An equally plain distinction is set forth in the language of Christ, Matt. 28:19, in which he commanded baptism to be performed "into the name of the Father and of the Son and of the Holy Ghost." This act of baptism is such as to involve the divinity as well as the personality of the Three, for it is an act of worship such as can be paid to God only; it is a profession of faith in God and his righteousness, which can be due to God only; and it is a pledge of fealty, such as God has plainly taught he will share with no other.

3. In our Lord's last discourse he promises to send "the Comforter," "even the Holy Spirit," "from the Father, even the Spirit of truth, which proceedeth from the Father." Here the Son sends, the Spirit is sent, and the Spirit proceeds from the Father. He is also referred to as one "whom the Father will send in my name." See John 14:26, and 15:26.

4. The apostle Paul evidently refers to this same Three, when he writes the Corinthians of "the same Spirit," "the same Lord," and "the same God." 1 Cor. 12:4–6.

5. The benediction, with which Paul closes his second epistle to the Corinthians, also presents unitedly, yet separately, the same Three; certain blessings are invoked, but with no apparent distinction of rank among those of whom they are asked. If there be any prominence, it is given the rather to the Son than to the Father.

VIII. THESE THREE ARE ONE GOD

Our definition states that these Three are revealed as without division of nature, essence, or being. It is not intended to indicate, by the use of these three words, any wide distinction between them. They are nearly alike. Yet some distinction exists. By nature is meant that peculiar character of being which makes one kind of being to differ from another. Thus we speak of the divine nature, or the angelic nature, or the human nature, or the brute nature; meaning that peculiarity of life, and character, and personal condition, which makes a God, or an angel, or a man, or a brute. By essence is meant, that peculiarity, in the nature itself, which constitutes what is necessary to its existence, so that we cannot say, in the absence of that essence, that such a nature exists. Take away from human nature that which is its essential quality, and it must cease to be human nature. Being is the essence of any nature becoming actually existent in that nature. In God nature and essence must be identical, because everything in the nature of God is necessary to his existence, and consequently the nature can neither be greater nor less than the essence; indeed they must be the same. Neither can being be separated from the nature and essence of God, though it is not identical with them. The necessity of his actual existence is something inherent in his nature. There could be no such nature without necessarily involving the existence of some person or persons in it.

When it is affirmed, therefore, that there is no "division of nature, essence, or being," all that is meant is simply that there is but one God; that such is the divine nature that it cannot be multiplied, or divided, or distributed, any more than God can be thus divided in his omnipresence with all things. The divine nature is so possessed, by each of the persons in the Trinity, that neither has his own separate divine nature, but each subsists in one divine nature, common to the three. Otherwise the three persons would be three Gods. So also, in that divine nature, its essential quality is not divided in its relation through the nature to the persons. Were this so, there would be three separate parts of the divine nature. But that this cannot be, is manifest from the identity in God of nature and essence. That it is not so, is declared by the Scriptures, when they teach that there is but one God. In God there is also but one divine being, because there is but one divine essence and nature. There is but one that can have actuality of existence. The being of person, not being identical with that of nature, a fact which is true of all natures, created or uncreated, the unity of the nature, and of the essence does not forbid plurality of persons. The threeness of the persons, therefore, does not destroy the unity of the nature or essence, and consequently, not that of the being of God.

The Scriptures teach everywhere the unity of God explicitly and emphatically. There can be no doubt that they reveal a God that is exclusively one. But their other statements, which we have been examining, should assure us that they also teach that there are three divine persons. It is this peculiar twofold teaching, which is expressed by the word "trinity." The revelation to us, is not that of tritheism or three Gods; nor of triplicity, which is threefoldness, and would involve composition, and be contrary to the simplicity of God; nor of mere manifestation of one person in three forms, which is opposed to the revealed individuality of the persons; but it is well expressed by the word trinity, which is declarative, not simply of threeness, but of three-oneness. That this word is not found in Scripture is no objection to it, when the doctrine, expressed by it, is so clearly set forth.

CHAPTER 15

PERSONAL RELATIONS IN TRINITY

THE Scripture doctrine of the Trinity, as we have seen, presents three persons occupying mutual relations to each other. There consequently arise certain questions as to these relations. What is their nature? What has originated them? When did they begin? In what respects do the persons differ from each other? Is there perfect equality between them? If there is any kind of subordination, in what does it consist?

These questions will be best answered, first by some general statements applicable to all the relations; next by special consideration of the Sonship of Christ, and of the Procession of the Spirit; followed by an examination of the equality, and subordination of the Son and Spirit.

I. GENERAL STATEMENTS

1. The nature of these relations can be indicated in no other forms than those set forth in Scripture. They are matters of pure revelation. The fact of their existence is beyond the attainment of reason. Nor, after the revelation of the doctrine, has that fact been strengthened by any philosophical speculations, or its difficulties removed by any arguments, or illustrations from analogy. [See statements of some of these in Hodge's Systematic Theology, Vol. 1, pp. 478–482.] We are constrained to fall back upon the simple Scripture statements. The only explanations of these, which are justifiable, are such as arise from recognizing that, as the persons, transactions, and relations are divine, there must be separated from them all that belongs to human conditions, and imperfections. But this must not lead us so far as to deny the reality of these things, or the existence, in the highest degree, of relations of the nature indicated, of which our best conception is gained from the terms which are used. Thus no physical generation, nor any that could begin, or end, or be measured by succession, can be ascribed to the divine Father. No dependent existence, nor previous lack, and subsequent attainment of being, can be true of a Son who is himself God. No communication, nor reception, of a portion of the divine essence, or nature, is possible between two divine persons. If the term "begotten" is intended to teach a communication of the divine essence to the Son by the Father, it must be one of the whole essence, otherwise there would no longer be only one God,

one divine nature, or essence. So also, when the Spirit proceeds from the Father, there can be no breathing out of a part of the divine nature, nor can that breathing begin, or end, or exist in successive moments of time. These internal acts in God necessarily conform to that eternity, and unity, of the nature of God, which exist even in his purposes towards things which are without. All human imperfections must be removed. But, this being done, the Scripture teachings must be accepted with unquestioning belief that relations, corresponding to these titles, exist in God, and that they, and the causes assigned for them, are duly expressed by the language of his word.

2. These relations exist in the nature of God. They are not revelations to us of what God is not; but of what he is. It is because God is one in three persons, and because the three persons are one God, that he thus makes himself known to us. Though it is true that the Father wills to beget the Son, and the Father and Son will to send forth the Spirit; yet the will thus exercised, is not at mere good pleasure, but it results necessarily from the nature of God, that the Father should thus will the begetting, and the Father and the Son the sending forth. The will, thus exercised, is not like that of his purposes, in which God acts of free pleasure, choosing between various purposes which he might form; but, like that by which he necessarily wills his own existence. Otherwise, these relations might, or might not, have existed. But, if this were possible, the Son, and the Spirit, would only have been creatures of God, however exalted might have been their nature, or extraordinary their faculties. Theirs would only have been contingent existence, until made certain by the will of God. None of the incommunicable attributes of God could have been ascribed to them. In no sense could they have had self-existence, or eternity of existence, or independent existence, or immutability of nature. When, therefore, we find the Scriptures assigning such attributes to any other persons than the Father, we have conclusive evidence that the divine nature of these persons is perfectly equal to that of the Father; and when it is also asserted, that God is but one, and yet that each of the three is God, we are plainly taught, that all have the same undivided divine essence, or nature. That of the Son, or of the Spirit, is identical with that of the Father. It is not simply a similar nature, but even numerically the same. Were it otherwise, there would be three Gods. If, however, this be true, the relations belong to the nature of God, and are not something superadded to that nature. The simplicity of God is a proof of this. It could only be in a God compounded of nature, and relations, that the relations would not be in, and of, that nature itself.

3. These relations must also be eternal. The nature being eternal, so also must be the relations which are in, and of that nature. Moreover, if not eternal, they must have had a beginning, and there must have been a time when they did not exist. But this argues changeableness in God, in virtue of which he,

who once was one person only, has now become three. It is no reply to this, that the expressions "begotten," and "proceedeth from," involve the idea of the antecedent existence of him who begets, and from whom there is procession. For these are terms of human language, applied to divine actions, and must be understood suitably to God. There is no greater difficulty here than in other cases in which this principle is readily recognized. We cannot speak of the eternity of the life of God, without using language which implies beginning, and succession. Neither can we think of his eternal purpose, except as numerous determinations formed and thought out in successive moments, and following upon God's infinite knowledge; which, by placing before him all things possible, has presented various objects and plans from which he has chosen. Nor yet can we talk of his presence divested of the ideas and language that belong to space, nor conceive of his immensity without the fiction of infinite space. This has not been done even by the inspired authors of the Scriptures. Dealing, therefore, with the terms expressive of the divine relations, it is natural, and right, that we treat them after the same fashion, and divest them of those ideas of time, and succession, which are known to have no place in God. When this is done, nothing forbids the belief that, as these relations are in and of the nature of God, they are eternal.

4. So far as true divinity is involved, the persons must be absolutely equal, As each possesses the undivided divine essence, so neither can, as God, be superior, or inferior to the others. No difference in the mode, or order of subsistence in that essence, can make an inequality in the divinity of either of them, inasmuch as that subsistence makes each of them partakers of the same essence, and undividedly of all of it. Even if there be inequality relative to each other as persons, because of the respective relations, this would no more require one to be an inferior God to the others, than the three separate persons make necessary such a threefold distinction in the divine nature, as to constitute them three Gods.

These general statements will shorten and simplify the separate discussions as to the Sonship of Christ, and the Procession of the Spirit. So far as these have elements in common, a statement and explanation of these points in each case is rendered unnecessary. They are also more plainly exhibited, as to both the relations, than they could be separately. Moreover, we have in them answers to most of the questions suggested at the beginning. The nature of the relations is perceived to be properly indicated by the Scripture language which expresses them and to be such as belongs to the essence and nature of God. They have originated in that essence, acting through the person of the Father, and the persons of the Son and the Father. The perfect equality in that divine nature has been seen. It remains simply to inquire in what respects they differ from each other, and whether with the equality, relative to the divine essence, there co-exists any inequality of person, or any kind of subordination. These points will be appropriately presented in the separate discussions of the Sonship of Christ, and of the Procession of the Spirit, which discussions will, also, throw still further light upon the questions already answered.

II. THE ETERNAL SONSHIP OF CHRIST

In the previous lecture it was shown that Christ is Son of God in a sense peculiar to himself. The Father called him, at his baptism, "My beloved Son;" and he is spoken of by the sacred writers as God's "only begotten Son," and "his own Son."

The Scripture proofs were also presented, that this Son is not only called "God;" but possesses all the incommunicable attributes of God, together with such unity and identity with the Father, as make him truly God; that he is equal with the Father in his works, and knowledge, and nature; and, that not only to him are all the acts of creation, providence, and judgement to be ascribed, but that he is to be honoured, and worshipped equally with the Father, he being indeed the manifestation in the world, of the divine Father, "the image of the invisible God" (Col. 1:15), in whom "dwelleth all the fulness of the Godhead bodily," (Col. 2:9) "being the effulgence of his glory, and the very image of his substance." Heb. 1:3.

These proofs of this eternal Sonship may be strengthened by further reference to the Scripture teaching both as to the nature and eternity of the relation.

1. That the relation is one of nature, is additionally shown.

(a.) By passages, which declare that the Son is so "from God," and "in God," as to have perfect knowledge of him. John 1:18; 7:29; 16:27–30; 17:25. He is here spoken of as proceeding from God, not merely being sent as a messenger. The claim asserted, is one of intimate fellowship in and participation of the divine nature. It is made of him in the capacity of God's Son. Consequently it betokens a sonship of nature, not one of mere office, or name.

(b.) By such passages as contrast the divine and human natures, ascribing the divine nature to the Son. Rom. 1:3, 4; Phil. 2:5–11.

(c.) The divine nature of the Sonship is plainly taught by John in the 1st chapter of his gospel. "The only begotten Son," which "is in the bosom of the Father," who alone has "seen God" and "declared him," v. 18, is "the Word" that "became flesh, and dwelt among men," v. 14, and yet, which was not only "in the beginning," but "was with God," and "was God." If the Word and the Son are identical, the divine nature ascribed to the Word is truly the divine nature of the Son.

2. Of the eternity of this relation, we may also find further proof.

(1.) Christ's existence before birth in this world is taught

(a.) In such passages as show that Christ, of his own will, assumed this life. John 6:38; Phil. 2:7; Heb. 2:14, 16; 10:5, 9.

(b.) Such as show peculiar coming into the world. John 3:13; 6:33, 38, 62.

(c.) Where it is said, that he had seen and known the Father; which implies a previous state of existence. John 6:46.

(d.) Such passages as declare, that he, the Son, was sent into the world by the Father. See p. 114, I.3.

(2.) His existence when creation occurred, is announced in John 1:3, 10; Col. 1:16; Heb. 1:10.

(3.) The Scriptures also declare that he was in the beginning, before all things, when time began, which was, therefore, eternal existence. John 1:1; 17:5, 24; Col. 1:17; Heb. 1:10.

(4.) They expressly state that it was eternal. 1 John 1:1–3.

In the general statements above, it has been argued that the relations, borne by these two persons, are to be learned only from the Scripture revelations, and that these are to be modified in no respect, except by removing from them whatever is necessary to make them conform to divine transactions. It was also urged that all the divine relations being in and of God, who, with all his plurality of person, is but one God, these relations are in the same undivided divine essence, and, consequently, belong to the nature of God, and must be eternal.

In applying these statements and the Scripture proofs to the relation of Father and Son in God, we arrive at the doctrine commonly called the Eternal Sonship of Christ.

By this is meant, that paternity, and filiation in God are, not mere names for something which does not exist, nor for some relation, different from that of father and son, to which these titles were first applied in connection with Christ's creation, or birth, or resurrection, or exaltation; but are realities which exist eternally in his nature, and are as properly described by the names which express them are his attributes by the various terms of wisdom, power, truth, justice and love.

No attempt is made by those who accept this doctrine to state the nature of this generation. Some are even content to suppose that nothing more may be meant than to express by sonship what would be the result of such a relation. As human sonship is accompanied by earnest love between father and son, and implies likeness of character, and similarity of nature; so they have been willing to rest at this point, and accept the divine sonship, as meaning no more than the existence of perfect likeness, and infinite mutual love. But, manifestly, if nothing more than this be meant, the Father might equally be called Son, and the Son Father. The Scriptures, on the contrary, indicate that the likeness is the result of the relation, and not that the terms of the relation are given because of the likeness. It is not the resemblance of Christ to the Father, which is set forth as the reason he is called the Son, but it is because he is the Son that this resemblance exists.

But, even if these titles could be ascribed because of the likeness, we still have to account for the use of the peculiar word "begotten." This is evidently intended to tell us something of a great mystery. It proclaims some kind of activity in the divine Father, and passivity in the Son. We cannot tell what it is, but it at least resembles, in some way, that impartation of nature which occurs in the act of human begetting, and conveys to us the idea of the communication of the essence of God by the Father, through this act, to the Son. The continued unity of God shows that it is a communication of the whole essence, in which, however, the Father still continues to subsist, while imparting to the Son subsistence also in the same. Such impartation must partake of the nature of the "Eternal Now" in God. It never began and will never end, it has no succession, no past, and no future. It is the ever present, having no reference even to a past, or to a future. It is such a generation as constitutes eternal Sonship, and Fatherhood.

Many have rejected this doctrine because of misconceptions as to the nature of an Eternal Divine Sonship.

1. They have objected to the idea of Sonship itself.

(1.) They have urged that Sonship implies inferiority, and, therefore, that the Son cannot be truly God equal with the Father.

But how can we know what is and what is not possible in this matter with God? If the Scriptures assert the Divine generation, and the equality of the Son and the Father, why should any deny their consistency with each other?

After all, however, does sonship imply inferiority of nature? There may be subordination of rank, or office. But surely there is none of nature. Even human sonship results from the impartation of the same nature by the father; not the same numerically, but the same in kind, and degree, the same partitively. The son of any man partakes alike, and equally, with his father, in human nature. The divine communication differs from the human in not so dividing the nature that two gods result, as in human generation do two men.

That sonship may imply inferiority of official rank and personal relation, is readily admitted. But it does not always do this. Such subordination of person, indeed, seems to be taught of the Son of God to his Father. But it is equality and sameness of nature, not of office, which makes the Son truly God. He is such, because he is a true subsistence in the Divine essence. He does not cease to be such because the Father is officially greater than he, nor even because the Father bestows, and the Son receives the communication of the divine essence.

(2.) It has also been objected that Fatherhood implies priority of existence, and that this is impossible towards another divine person. But this is based upon a forgetfulness of the nature of eternal acts. Though we may not be able to explain how they are so, we nevertheless know that, in such acts, there is no beginning nor end, no first nor second, no antecedent nor consequent, indeed, no succession of any kind. Were it otherwise, God would exist in successive moments. He would have had a beginning. He would form new purposes, and would increase in knowledge from day to day.

Arguing from the nature of eternal acts in God, we, therefore, judge that the eternal generation of the Son is not a single act, which was accomplished at a definite moment in the divine nature; but one ever continuing. With God there may be such definitely completed acts, when they are performed outside of himself, as in creation; but, not when they are purely within. Such an act must be ever continuing, and completed only in the sense of its being always perfect, though not ended. Even the expression "continuing" is imperfect so far as it involves the idea of successive moments in God. It is only "ever continuing" as viewed by man. Sonship in God, therefore, does not imply priority of existence. Even in man paternity and filiation are co-existent. One becomes a father, only, when another becomes his son. Priority of existence is necessary, as a mere accident of human birth, because of the necessity of growth, and maturity in a man before he can become a father. But, even here, the sonship and fatherhood exist at the same moment. In God, however, priority, even of the existence of one person before another, can have no place, since he is self-existent, and eternal, who never began to be, and whose perfect maturity is not attained by growth or increase.

(3.) Again it is said, "If Christ is Son, if he is God of God, he is not self-existent and independent. But self-existence, independence, etc., are attributes of the divine essence, and not of one person in distinction from the others. It is the triune God, who is self-existent, and independent. Subordination, as to the mode of subsistence, and operation, is a scriptural fact; and so also is the perfect and equal godhead of the Father, and the Son, and, therefore, these facts must be consistent. In the consubstantial identity of the human soul, there is a subordination of one faculty to another, and so, however incomprehensible to us, there may be a subordination in the trinity consistent with the identity of essence in the godhead." Charles Hodge, Systematic Theology, 1, 474.

2. There are objections also made to the eternity of this relation. They are based upon Scripture statements, and are, on that account, even more worthy of consideration.

It is well to remember, however, that Christ is revealed to us, in the Scriptures, as one person in two natures, by virtue of which he is frequently called the Theanthropos, or Godman. The doctrine of his person will be hereafter discussed. It is sufficient here to state that, while the two natures are distinct, and preserve their respective attributes and qualities, yet, because of the one personality in both natures, whatever belongs to the person as person may be attributed to either nature. Thus the Spirit is not only called the Spirit of Christ, "but also the Spirit of Jesus." Acts 16:7. Inasmuch, then, as the sonship expresses a mere personal relation in the Godhead, the title Son of God may be applied to Christ in mere human relations. That this is sometimes done, does not then destroy the force of its much more frequent application to him in his divine nature, and especially of such an application, when it is accompanied by the ascription to him of divine titles, attributes, acts, and worship, together with assertions of equality, identity, and unity with the Father.

"Bishop Pearson, one of the most strenuous defenders of eternal generation, and of all the peculiarities of the Nicene doctrine of the Trinity, gives four reasons why the Theanthropos, or Godman is called the Son of God. (1.) His miraculous conception. (2.) The high office to which he was designated. John 10:34, 35, 36. (3.) His resurrection according to one interpretation of Acts 13:33. 'The grave,' he says, 'is as the womb of the earth; Christ, who is raised from thence, is as it were begotten to another life, and God, who raised him, is his Father.' (4.) Because after his resurrection, he was made the heir of all things. Heb. 1:2–5. Having assigned these reasons why the Godman is called Son, he goes on to show why the Logos is called Son. There is nothing, therefore, in the passages cited inconsistent with the church doctrine of the eternal sonship of our Lord." Charles Hodge, Systematic Theology, 1, 476.

1. The first objection to the eternity of the sonship, is that the title "Son" is given because of his birth.

This is based upon Luke 1:35. "And the angel answered and said unto her, The Holy Ghost shall come upon thee, and the power of the Most High shall overshadow thee: wherefore also that which is to be born shall be called holy, the Son of God."

Upon this passage it may be remarked, as the foundation of all just interpretation, that no relation to the Holy Ghost, which constitutes a personal relation in the Godhead, can refer to the Sonship, because this relation is one of Christ to the Father, and not to the Holy Ghost. Some other reason, then, than the act of the Spirit in his conception, must be found for the ascription here of the title "Son of God."

Again, it must be recognized, that the title "Son" is not here prophesied of in connection with the divine nature of our Lord, but is declared of that "which is to be born," which was undoubtedly his human nature, or himself in his human nature.

One interpretation of the passage affixes to the term "Power of the Highest" a personal sense, explaining it as a title of the Divine Logos. According to this, it is the overshadowing and permanent abiding of the divine Son, in union with the human nature conceived under the influence of the Holy Ghost, which will cause that "holy thing" to be "called the Son of God." Instances are quoted of the use of "Power" in a divine sense from Philo, and other Jewish writers. The early Christian fathers are stated to have applied generally the word "power" to the divine nature of Christ, and many of them are quoted as maintaining this interpretation of this passage. Acts 8:10, and 1 Cor. 1:24 are referred to as illustrating this use of the word power. [See Treffry, on the Doctrine of the Eternal Sonship, 3rd edition, pp. 120–133, and 142–144.]

If this be the interpretation, then, it is the coming of the Eternal Son upon this human nature, and his presence with it, that causes it to be called the Son of God.

This is, therefore, perfectly consistent with both the requirements before mentioned as necessary to the true interpretation. The Spirit is not associated with the ascription of the title Son of God, and that title is appropriately given to the human nature, and yet the eternity of the divine Sonship is not affected. If this use of the word "Power" can be fully verified, no valid objection can be made to the interpretation. Treffry gives very strong proof that it is so used.

If, however, we should adopt the more generally received interpretation, which supposes that "the power of the Highest" is either descriptive of the Holy Ghost, or of the divine power which accompanied his coming upon Mary, there will still be no difficulty in ascribing the title Son of God to the presence of the Eternal Son, who in his divine personality "became flesh, and dwelt among us." John 1:14. Such an explanation of the title would still be consistent with his relation, both to the Father and the Holy Ghost. The text would then still teach that the title Son of God is to be given to Christ as man, in like manner as that of Lord, because we have not here a mere human person, but simply a human nature, in which the divine Person, the Son, subsists without ceasing also to subsist in the divine nature. As that divine Person, and not the divine nature, is the Son, so also the divine Person in his human nature, and not that human nature, or a mere man is called Son of God. The title, therefore, though given to him as man, arises not from his birth, but from his eternal Sonship.

The Holy Ghost is, therefore, set forth here merely as the originator of the human nature of Christ. That nature is from God, not acting through the divine essence, which is never affirmed of God in any of his acts, but through a person in the Godhead, according to the usual mode as revealed to us, and as exhibited in creation, providence and redemption, and even in the eternal acts within the Godhead. The Scriptures make known no influence, nor action of the Spirit on the Son in his divine relations. On the contrary, the Son acts through the Spirit, but not the Spirit through the Son. But the instances of the influence of the Spirit on the human nature are abundant. At his birth, Luke 1:35, at his baptism, Matt. 3:16, in leading him to be tempted, Matt. 4:1, in the working of his miracles, Matt. 12:28, in his return from temptation "in the power of the Spirit into Galilee," Luke 4:14, and in his giving commandments through the Holy Spirit to the Apostles, Acts 1:2, we have express mention of this influence. Was it not to this that the author of Hebrews referred, "A body didst thou prepare for me?" Heb. 10:5.

2. Again it is objected, that Christ did not become Son of God until the day of his resurrection.

Two passages are quoted in favour of this objection.

(1.) That in Rom. 1:4. "Who was declared to be the Son of God with power, according to the Spirit of holiness, by the resurrection of the dead."

The word translated "declared" in this passage means "determined," "marked out as." It has no reference to a new ascription of title. All that is taught is that the resurrection of Christ plainly and distinctly evinced that "Jesus Christ, our Lord" (v. 5) is "Son of God." Of this fact, the resurrection from the dead of him who had constantly claimed to be the Son of God, is an unquestionable proof.

(2.) The other passage is Acts 13:32, 33. This reads in the King James Version, "And we declare unto you glad tidings, how that the promise that was made unto the fathers, God hath fulfilled the same unto us their children, in that he hath raised up Jesus again;" as it is also written in the second psalm, "Thou art my Son, this day have I begotten thee."

Upon this objection, Dr. Charles Hodge justly says: "Here there is no reference to the resurrection. The glad tidings, which the Apostle announced, was not the resurrection, but the advent of the Messiah. That was the promise made to the fathers, which God had fulfilled by raising up, i.e., bringing into the world the promised deliverer. Compare Acts 2:30; 3:22, 26; 7:37; in all which passages where the same word is used, the 'raising up' refers to the advent of Christ; as when it is said, 'A prophet shall the Lord God raise up unto you from among your brethren, like unto me.' The word is never used absolutely in reference to the resurrection, unless, as in Acts 2:32, where the resurrection is spoken of in the context. Our translators have obscured the meaning by rendering it, 'having raised up again,' instead of simply 'having raised up,' as they render it elsewhere." Sys. Theo. 1, 475.

The Canterbury Revision has simply "raised up," omitting the word "again."

We might, then, rest the reply to this objection upon the denial that the Sonship is spoken of as given in connection with the resurrection. But, on the other hand, we might admit it to be thus given, and yet the doctrine of the Eternal Sonship would not be affected. For, so long as we may justly confine any such declaration to the Theanthropos, it might still be true that to the God-man the name could thus be given, and yet, all the teachings of Scripture relative to the eternity and nature of the divine sonship remain true. The truth is, that it would be more difficult to establish positively that the title Son of God ever was bestowed upon Christ, in consequence of any event connected with his humanity, than that it is confined to him in his human relations. At least, it is manifest from the Scriptures that, if ever applied to this divine person because of his birth, or resurrection, that was not the first period of such application; for the title is given to him in connection with the acts of creation, and he is said to have been before all things, their creator, in whom they consist, as the one who laid the foundations of the world, the existence of which is perishable, while his is eternal.

(3.) A further objection is made by Arians, and others who deny the proper divinity of Christ, and claim that he is but a creature. These assert that the title Son of God was given to Christ by virtue of his creation. The obvious reply to this objection, is to produce the Scripture teachings which prove the true deity of the Son, especially such as assert that he is God and Lord, and to be honoured, and worshipped, and that he performs all the divine acts of creation, providence and redemption, and has all the incommunicable attributes of God, together with perfect equality, exact resemblance, absolute unity, and sameness of nature with the Father.

The passage in Col. 1:15, has been claimed in support of this objection; Christ being there called, according to the King James Version, "the first born of every creature." But the true rendering is "the first born of all creation," and it is so translated in the Canterbury Revision. There is a similar passage in Rev. 3:14, where Christ calls himself "the beginning of the creation of God." The word translated "beginning" in this passage, means also "the origin." It is also used for "the first place, or power, the sovereignty." The "first born" in the former passage, is the same word used in Heb. 1:6, and there translated "first begotten." The "first created" would have been differently expressed in the Greek. The fact that this is a begotten Son, and not a created being, and that he is not said to be born at the time of Creation, but before it, actually shows that the eternal generation of the eternal Son, which took place before all things, is here spoken of. Such pre-existence is plainly taught in the context of Hebrews, but it is directly asserted in that of Colossians.

III. THE PROCESSION OF THE SPIRIT

The relation of the Spirit, in the Godhead, differs from that of the Son in several respects. What is the ground, or reason of this, it is impossible to state. The Scriptures give no information upon this point. We must be content, therefore, simply to point out what they reveal upon this subject.

1. An obvious distinction is made between the names given to the two persons. While the one is called the Son, the other is called "the Spirit," and other names of like import, as stated p. 117, V. That these names are indicative of some specific difference, may be argued from the fact that they are never interchanged. The Spirit is never called the Son, nor is the Son ever called the Spirit. When it is remembered, that these names describe persons subsisting in the same divine essence, this fact becomes very significant of some peculiar distinction between them in the mode of such subsistence. The word "*pneuma*," which is the designation in the Greek original, means spirit, breath, or wind, and seems to indicate some influence, or power which proceeds from God, not impersonally, but with a personal relation in the Godhead. The work of the Spirit, in the creation and government of the world, in the inspiration of the sacred writers, in the miraculous conception of, and gracious influences upon the human nature of Christ, and in the regeneration and sanctification of the people of God, points him out as the outwardly operating power of the Godhead in this world.

2. A distinction is also revealed, between these persons, as to the mode of action by which they proceed from the Father. The Son is said to be generated, the Spirit is simply said to proceed. The relation of the Spirit to the divine Father has been generally expressed by the term "Procession." This is admissible, if it be recognized as a term merely declarative of such a procession from the Father as is not exclusive of a procession also of the Son. This expression is applied to the Spirit upon the authority of Christ, who calls him in John 15:26, "the Spirit of truth, which proceedeth from the Father." But our Lord uses a similar word as to himself, though not the same, in John 16:28, "I came out from the Father, and am come into the world." The disciples use this last word in John 16:30. The verb in these two passages means sometimes "came out," and sometimes "went out," and, in the latter signification, is precisely equivalent to the other verb, which in a different tense appears in John 15:26. From the "proceeding from" of the Spirit, therefore, cannot be argued a difference in his mode of procedure from that of the Son. The terms applied to both are general, and cannot express a difference. Procession, therefore, may be asserted of both the Son and the Spirit. The mode of the procession of the Son is specifically designated by

the generation which is asserted of him. That of the Spirit appears likewise to be pointed out by the name given to him. He is the breath of God, which fact, already expressed in his name, was taught by our Lord when, on the evening of his resurrection, he breathed upon his apostles, saying unto them: "Receive ye the Holy Ghost." John 20:22. It is not unlikely, however, that the human breath of the Theanthropos was, on that occasion, used as a symbol of the divine out-breathing of the Spirit by the divine Son. This may be well assumed as true, if, indeed, the Spirit proceeds from the Son, as well as from the Father.

This outbreathing of God is even more difficult to interpret, and the nature of the relation thus indicated even more incomprehensible than that of the generation of the Son. In this, therefore, as in that, we must be content to accept the statement, just as it is revealed, being only careful to separate from it all ideas inconsistent with acts of God. This would exclude everything like a physical breathing, or several acts of breathing, at various times, which may be successive. The procession of the Spirit, must, therefore, be regarded as eternal action, completed, only because perfect, and continuing, only in the sense of not ended.

It seems therefore proper, that we should regard the peculiarity of the mode of the procedure of both these persons, to be indicated by the names given respectively to each. The term "procession" may be especially appropriated to the Spirit only, because, in his case, "Spirit" does not as distinctly point out the mode of procedure, as does Sonship, in that of the Son.

The preposition, with which the verbs are compounded in each of these three passages of John, is the same, and shows a procession from within God. Wherever the terms "Spirit of God" and "Spirit of Christ" appear, the simple genitive is used without a preposition, but this same preposition is found with the genitive of God, in 1 Cor. 2:12 and Rev. 11:11. In this latter passage, how-ever, the Holy Spirit is probably not meant. The procedure is, therefore, taught as being from within God, which shows that the coming from, and the going forth from, are both in and of the Divine nature, and are not to be limited to such action as occurs when an ambassador is sent from a king, or one man simply proceeds from the presence of another.

3. Western Christendom, in opposition to Eastern, has maintained that there is also a distinction between the relations of Son and Spirit, as to the source. The procession of the Spirit is said, by the East, to be from the Father only, as is the generation of the Son; but by the West, to be from both the Father and the Son.

Eastern Christians have urged that the Scriptures only actually declare pro-cession from the Father. It must be acknowledged that this is true, inasmuch as there is but one passage of Scripture which speaks of his Procession (John 15:26), the language of which is "which proceedeth from the Father." But in 1 Cor. 2:12 the Spirit of said to be "of God," which may mean of the Father alone, or, as of God, so of the Son also. The Spirit is also spoken of as the Spirit of Jesus (Acts 16:7) and of Christ, and of the Lord, and of the Son (Gal. 4:6), as well as the Spirit of the Father, and the Spirit of God. Our Lord also declared, that he would send the Spirit. More than this, the action of Christ, when he breathed upon the disciples, and said, "Receive ye the Holy Ghost," (John 20:22) is very significant, and strongly indicates the procession of the Spirit from him. See also Acts 16:7. This act of Christ, however, may have been no more than giving the Spirit to his disciples, without intending to teach any procession from himself. The breathing, which in any event was symbolical, may have been so only of the divine act of the Father, from whom alone the Spirit may truly proceed. In this event, may we not also believe that the relation to the procession of the Son differs from that of the Father? Would it not be a more exact statement of the Scripture teaching to say, that the Son, or Christ, sends the Spirit, and gives the Spirit, which is his, because the right to bestow it is his, either essentially, or as given him in his office as Messiah, and that the Spirit thus sent proceeds from the Father? In this event the Father would be the source of the procedure, and the Son the agent in sending it forth. Is not this bestowment on the Messiah, of this right to send the Spirit, suggested by Christ's declaration, "If I go not away, the Comforter will not come unto you," (John 16:7) as well as by the language, "The Spirit was not yet given, because Jesus was not yet glorified." John 7:39. These points are presented for consideration, while it is admitted that the assertion, that the Spirit proceeds also from the Son, is less objectionable than the denial. The Scriptures seem to leave it so doubtful, as to forbid any positive statement about it. But the preponderance of evidence is in favour of a procession from both Father and Son.

IV. SUBORDINATION BETWEEN THE PERSONS

The absolute equality of each of these persons, as God, has already been pointed out; and the possibility of inferiority, in other respects, was then intimated. There are some scriptural statements which seem to indicate this. Christ said expressly of himself, "The Father is greater than I." John 14:28. He also not only taught that the Father had sent him, but compared with that his own sending of his disciples, (John 17:18) and declared that he came, not to do his own will but that of him that sent him, (John 6:38); that he came not of himself, (John 7:28); that he spoke not of himself, but that the Father had given him a commandment, what he should say, and speak, (John 12:49); that his teaching was not his own, (John 7:16); that the word they heard was not his, but his Father's, (John 14:24); that he had given and spoken the words given him by the Father, (John 8:26; 17:8); that the Father had given him to do the work he had accomplished, (John 17:4); that he could do nothing of himself, but what he saw the Father doing, (John 5:19); that the Father was with him, and had not left him alone, (John 8:29); and that the Father had sanctified (consecrated) him, (John 10:36). Peter also preached to Cornelius "Jesus of Nazareth, how that God anointed him with the Holy Ghost, and with power," and that he performed beneficent and miraculous acts because "God was with him." (Acts 10:38). Christ also denied the goodness of any but God, (Matt. 19:17; Mark 10:38; Luke 18:19), and as to the day of judgement, asserted that "of that day or that hour knoweth no one, not even the angels in heaven, neither the Son, but the Father," (Mark 13:32, ["but the Father only," Matt. 24:36]); and, that to sit on his right hand, and on his left, was not his to give, but that these positions shall be given to those for whom it is prepared of his Father, (Matt. 20:23; Mark 10:40). We are told also of his prayers to God, of which the remarkable statement is made, that "in the days of his flesh," he "offered up prayers and supplications with strong crying and tears unto him that was able to save him from death, and having been heard for his godly fear." (Heb. 5:7). Christ also speaks of the power he had over all flesh, as given him by the Father, (John 17:2), and Paul in Eph. 1:17, 20, assigns his exaltation over all things, and as head of the church, described in vv. 19–22, to "the Father of glory." While it is said that the Father "put all things in subjection under his feet," we are told that "he is excepted, who did subject all things unto him," (1 Cor. 15:27), that "then cometh the end, when he shall deliver up the kingdom to God, even the Father," (v. 24); and "when all things have been subjected unto him, then shall the Son also himself be subjected unto him that did subject all things unto him, that God may be all in all," v. 28. The climax of these statements is reached, when we find that not only did Paul say that "the head of Christ is God," (1 Cor. 11:3) and call the Father "the God of our Lord Jesus Christ, the Father of glory," (Eph. 1:17); but our Lord himself spoke of him to Mary Magdalene as "my Father and your Father," and "my God and your God." John 20:17.

An examination of these, and all similar statements in the Scriptures, shows they are in no respect inconsistent with the perfect equality of the persons as to the divine nature.

1. Almost all of them have reference to Christ as man; or as the Son in his relations to his human nature; or as Messiah, securing for his people eternal life, and bestowing it upon them, or ruling over the universe, and the church.

2. This explanation may be thought by some insufficient to account fully for the subjection of the Son referred to in 1 Cor. 15:28, or for the superior

greatness ascribed to the Father in John 14:28. But, if so, we are only taught an
inferiority of one person in the Trinity to another, as a person. Nothing indicates that it is of one of them as God, to another as God, or of the Godhead of
one to the Godhead of another. It is only of the Son to the Father, and not of
God the Son to God the Father. The subsistence of each of the persons in the
same divine nature may still remain true, as well as that partaking of all of it by
each, which makes all equally God.

3. The personal inferiority which is thus made possible, so far as it is natural, is due doubtless to the difference in the modes of subsistence in the divine
essence. The Father thus subsists independently of the will, or the action of
any other person. He is thus simply God; not originated, not begotten, not
proceeding from. The Son is originated, his filiation is willed, though necessarily, by the Father, and he is begotten, and is, as the Athanasian creed asserts,
"very God" of "very God." The Holy Spirit is also originated; he is not however
begotten, but proceeds from the Father, or from the Father and the Son. His
procession is also willed, though necessarily, and he, likewise, is "very God" of
"very God." In this mode of subsistence, therefore, inferiority of the person of
the Son to the Father, and of the Spirit to the Father and Son, may be said to
exist. Without any superiority as God, therefore, the Father may be said to be
greater than the Son, because of the personal relations in the Trinity.

4. But there is also a subordination of office or rank still more plainly taught.
By virtue of this, the Father sends the Son, and the Father and Son send the
Spirit. This could exist between persons in all respects equal to each other, both
in nature and relation. In God, however, it is probable that the official subordination is based upon that of the personal relations. It corresponds exactly with
the relations of the persons, from which has probably resulted their official subordination in works without, and especially in the work of redemption.

The order of this subordination is plainly apparent from the scriptural names
and statements about the relations. The Father is unquestionably first, the Son
second, and the Holy Spirit third. This is their rank, as well because of the mode
of subsistence, as of its order. Hence they are commonly spoken of in this order,
as the First, Second and Third Persons of the Trinity.

V. "THE INHABITATION OF THE PERSONS"

"As the essence of the Godhead is common to the several persons, they have
a common intelligence, will, and power. There are not in God three intelligences, three wills, three efficiencies. The Three are one God, and, therefore,
have one mind and will. This intimate union was expressed in the Greek church
by the word *'perichoresis,'* which the Latin words inexistentia, inhabitatio, and

intercommunio were used to explain. These terms were intended to express the scriptural facts that the Son is in the Father, and the Father in the Son; that where the Father is, there the Son and Spirit are; that what the one does, the others do.". . .

"This fact—of the intimate union, communion, and inhabitation of the persons of the Trinity—is the reason why everywhere in Scripture and instinctively by all Christians, God as God is addressed as a person, in perfect consistency with the Tri-personality of the Godhead. We can, and do pray to each of the Persons separately; and we pray to God as God; for the three persons are one God; one not only in substance, but in knowledge, will, and power. To expect that we, who cannot understand anything, not even ourselves, should understand these mysteries of the Godhead, is to the last degree unreasonable. But as in every other sphere, we must believe what we cannot understand; so we may believe all that God has revealed in his word concerning himself, although we cannot understand the Almighty unto perfection." Charles Hodge, Sys. Theol., vol. 1, pp. 461–462.

CHAPTER 16

OUTWARD RELATIONS OF THE TRINITY

THE universe, with all it is, and all it contains, is the result of the outward working of the triune God. It exists, not because of any necessity in God's nature to create it, but as the result purely of his will. It is the form in which the voluntary activity of God manifests itself outwardly.

Activity, in some form, is essential to a personal, intelligent being. God must therefore be eternally active. But this necessity for eternal activity finds ample scope for its exercise, within the Godhead, in the acts involved in the mutual relations of the persons, and in the purposes which he forms relative to things without. His outward workings are the results of those purposes alone, and therefore proceed purely from his will. The universe consequently hears no other relation to God than that of a mere creation of his wisdom and power. It is not eternal, but has those peculiarities of beginning, and succession, which belong to time, as well as the dependence, change and imperfection, which are naturally found in that which is neither divine nor self-existent.

There are three kinds of divine acts.

1. Immanent, and intrinsic acts. These are within God, and have no reference to things without. Such are the generation of the Son, and the spiration of the Spirit.

2. Immanent, and extrinsic acts. These, also, are within God, but have reference to things without. Such are his decrees.

3. Extrinsic, and transitive acts. These are outside of himself, having no existence within him, but nevertheless proceed efficiently from him, and terminate upon his creatures. Such are creation, providence and redemption. [See Turretine's Institutes, Book 4, Ques. 1, Sec. 4.]

The first kind of divine acts is revealed to us in what the Scriptures teach of the personal relations within the Godhead. The second, and especially the third, are made known to us in what we are told of the creation of the world, of God's Providential care over it, and of his redemption of man. As might have been anticipated, we find the activity of God in the second and third kinds of acts manifested in accordance with the personal relations revealed in the first. Each of the persons performs such divine acts as show that he is God. Each demands and accepts equal honour and worship from man. Each has his own especial relation to every work. In it the same subordination, revealed in the personal

140

relations, is preserved. Yet, along with this, we find that same intercommunion, by which what one does is also spoken of as done by each of the others. The evidence of this last point needs especially and constantly to be borne in mind, lest we emphasize too much the distinct acts of the persons, and forget that essential union, and intercommunion, which, as well as subsistence in the same undivided essence, or nature, makes the three persons only one God.

The method of this action, and the distinct subordination in it, will not in all cases appear equally plain. We must, therefore, observe with caution what is exactly revealed. Whatever, from other circumstances, may appear probable, must be taken only as such. This is more especially necessary as this method will be seen somewhat to vary, although, so far as exhibited, the same order of subordination will be perceived.

I. IN CREATION

Creation, as the first outward manifestation of God, demands the first place in this treatment.

1. Whatever distinction may sometimes appear, it is generally attributed to the one God. This does not forbid that each person has performed his distinctive part, for it is also referred to the Father, and to the Son, and to the Spirit. We have here only the evidence of that intercommunion which, even through the distinct action of each, still makes any divine act performed by any one of the persons to be the act of the whole Godhead. The passages which teach this are the numerous ones in which "God" is spoken of as the creator. These must refer either to the triune God, or to the Father alone. But whatever may be the relation of the Father to this act, the Scriptures, by revealing that the Son and the Spirit were also associated with him, show that creation was the act of the whole Godhead.

2. The method of this act is revealed in a few passages. These teach that creation came from the Father, as the source, that it was accomplished by, or through the Son, as the efficient instrumental creating agent, and by, or through the Spirit, as the transforming power. The first two of these facts is taught in 1 Cor. 8:6, "Yet to us there is one God, the Father, of whom are all things, and we unto him; and one Lord, Jesus Christ, through whom are all things, and we through him." Here the Father is declared to be the source of all things, and Jesus Christ, the divine Son, the instrument through whom they exist. We have the same truth in Heb. 1:2, "Through whom also he made the worlds."

The creation is also attributed separately to the Father in Acts 4:24. He is indeed there called "Lord," but is shown to be the Father by the quotation from the second psalm as well as by the reference to his "holy child Jesus," which marks a distinction between two persons. In Rev. 4:11 it is manifestly the Father, to whom the four and twenty elders ascribe creation; for he is distinguished from the Lamb that redeemed us. See chap. 5:8, 9. In Eph. 3:9, God is said to have created all things and the context shows that it is God the Father who is spoken of.

That the creation was by, or through the Son, is also separately declared. John says of the divine Word, "All things were made by him, and without him was not anything made that hath been made.". . . "He was in the world, and the world was made by him." John 1:3, 10. Paul says, that "in him were all things created, in the heavens and upon the earth, things visible and things invisible, . . . all things have been created through him, and unto him." Col. 1:16. See also Ps. 33:6.

The transforming power of the Spirit is shown in Gen. 1:2. Here the Hebrew verb is in the Piel form, and means "to brood over," and, Gesenius in his lexicon says, is used "tropically of the Spirit of God as thus brooding over and vivifying the chaotic mass of the earth." This work of the Spirit seems to have been known to Job and his friends. Job himself says: "By his Spirit the heavens are garnished," Job 26:13, and Elihu declares, "The Spirit of God hath made me, and the breath (Spirit) of the Almighty giveth me life." Job 33:4. In Psalm 33:6 it is also stated, that "By the word of the Lord were the heavens made; and all the host of them by the breath (Spirit) of his mouth." In Psalm 104:30, God is addressed thus: "Thou sendest forth thy Spirit, they are created; and thou renewest the face of the ground." The creation here referred to is simply transformation.

The above statements show that the creation of the world is ascribed to God as One, yet that all things are of the Father, who is thus the source; that they were created by, or through the Son; and that the Spirit has been their transforming and life-giving power. We find then in this outward action of the persons the same relations and subordination exhibited personally in the Trinity. The Father acts through the Son (Eph. 3:14–19; Heb. 1:2) and sends forth the Spirit, Ps. 104:30.

II. IN PROVIDENCE

In the statements made as to the acts of Providence, the subordination of the Son and Spirit is not distinctly taught. It is not denied, however, and there is no reason for supposing that it does not exist. Still, in the absence of specific revelation, we dare not positively affirm that it does. Throughout the Scriptures, however, all the acts of providence are ascribed to God. Whether by this is meant the Father alone, or the Triune God, does not appear. There is no revelation as to the method by which this is done. But each of the persons is revealed as performing acts of providence. Christ declared this of the Father, Matt. 6:25–32, especially verse 32, and 10:29–31. The upholding of the world is asserted of the Son, Heb. 1:3, and it is said that "in him all things consist." Col. 1:17. The providential care of the Spirit is abundantly exercised in connection with the life of believers in Christ, who may well be said spiritually to "live, and move, and have their being" in him. That this is done in the sphere of redemption makes it no less providential than if it were in that of creation. In this latter, however, the Spirit is also spoken of as engaged in providential acts. Isaiah 59:19; 63:14.

III. IN REDEMPTION

The distinctive action of the three persons is more plainly exhibited in connection with redemption. This is due, probably, to the fact that upon this subject we have more full information than upon the acts of creation or providence. God is also brought nearer to us, and thus is more clearly revealed. It is in connection with this that the revelation has been made of the relations within the Trinity, together with the equality of the persons in the divine nature, and their subordination within and in the work without. The whole work of redemption is ascribed to the Triune God, but each of the persons is revealed as sustaining distinct official relation to it.

1. All of this appears even in the manner in which it has been revealed.

(a.) The Scriptures are explicitly declared to be from God, John 3:34; 10:35; 1 Cor. 2:9, 10; 1 Thess. 2:13; 2 Tim. 3:16; Heb. 1:1.

(b.) Christ attributes to the Father his own power and authority to speak, and declares him to be the source of what was revealed by himself. John 3:34; 7:16; 12:49; 15:15. The same truth is taught in Rev. 1:1, where the distinction between the persons shows that "the Revelation of Jesus Christ, which God gave him," was given by the Father. It is from the Father also as a source, that the Spirit derives the truth which he reveals. It is as the Spirit of truth that Christ declared that he proceeds from the Father. John 15:26. The cause he assigned for his subsequent promise that the Spirit should guide into all truth was "he shall not speak from himself; but what things soever he shall hear, these shall he speak." John 16:13. That the truth, thus spoken, should be from the Father, through the Son, appears from vv. 14 and 15. The same is also taught in 1 Cor. 2:7–11, in which it is said that "God revealed through the Spirit" the "deep things of God," which "the Spirit searcheth," "even the wisdom that hath been hidden, which God foreordained before the worlds unto our glory." The whole context shows that it is the Father from whom these things are learned.

(c.) But while the Father is thus declared to be the source of the revelation
of redemption, it is the Son by whom he has made it known. He is, in his
divine relation, especially called the Word of God. Him we are commanded
by the Father to hear as his "beloved Son." Matt. 17:5. In his own person he
so manifested the Father that he could say, "He that hath seen me, hath seen
the Father." John 14:9. During his incarnation he spoke personally, as did the
prophets of old. Heb. 1:1, 2. He was that prophet whom Moses foretold, Deut.
18:15–19; and is so proclaimed in Acts 3:20–22. He declared himself to be the
light of the world. John 8:12. He foretold the future as to himself, his disciples,
Jerusalem, and the world. He began the preaching of the great salvation. Heb.
2:3. He gave especial instruction to his apostles, both before his death and after
his resurrection, not only as to the gospel of the kingdom, but as to all things
which were to be observed by them, and by those whom they should teach.
Especially, during this latter period, did he instruct them as to the relation of
his sufferings and death to the prophecies of the Old Testament.

(d.) In this work of revelation, however, the Holy Spirit is made known to us
as the operating agent. Everywhere it is the Spirit to whom the word sent by God
is referred. "Men spake from God, being moved by the Holy Ghost." 2 Pet. 1:21.
This is spoken of the Old Testament writers in general. It is specifically declared
of David, Matt. 22:43; Acts 1:16; and of Isaiah, Acts 28:25, and of the author of
the 96th Psalm, in Heb. 3:7. These Old Testament writers constantly attribute
their instructions to the Spirit of God, as, for example, David in 2 Sam. 23:2.
Nehemiah asserts it of the prophets, by whom God had warned his people. Neh.
9:30. Isaiah (48:16) proclaims "the Lord God hath sent me and his Spirit."

The same is pre-eminently true of the inspired revelations of New Testament
days. Even the ministry of our Lord was subjected to the Spirit. While, as the
Divine Son, he works through the Spirit in this, as in other divine acts, yet, as
the God-man, he was fostered in his human nature by its influences, and was
anointed by it for his work. Our Lord declared this in the first act of his ministry, Luke 4:16–21. The immeasurable extent of this influence was taught by
John the Baptist. John 3:34. In like manner, also, were the Apostles of Christ
prepared for their work. Eph. 3:5. The teaching of the Lord had not sufficed. In
recalling and revealing that teaching they must need be made infallible. Other
truths were also to be made known. Therefore the Spirit was promised, which
promise was signally fulfilled on the day of Pentecost; nor then only, nor upon
those there alone, but during all the period of New Testament revelation, and
upon multitudes who spake, as well as upon those who wrote. The effect of this
influence is distinctly asserted. At Pentecost they "began to speak with other
tongues, as the Spirit gave them utterance." Acts 2:4. The boldness with which
such men as those could speak of Christ, is attributed to their being filled with

the Spirit. Acts 4:31. Paul claimed that his preaching was in "demonstration of the Spirit and of power," 1 Cor. 2:4, and that he spake "not in words which man's wisdom teacheth, but which the Spirit teacheth." 1 Cor. 2:13.

2. If we turn now to the work of redemption itself, we shall still find those mutual relations sustained. Salvation or redemption is ascribed everywhere to the Triune God. Examples of this are to be found in Luke 1:68–71; 3:6; Acts 28:28; Rom. 1:16; 2 Thess. 2:13; Tit. 2:11.

(1.) But it is specifically assigned as to its source to the Father. Its sphere is within the creation which is from him, and under the providential influences which originate in him. He is the lawgiver, whose law has been broken, and who exacts the penalty; as the administrator of that law. The redemption is the effect of his purpose. 1 Cor. 2:7; Eph. 3:11; 2 Tim. 1:9. That purpose flows from his benevolent love for mankind. John 3:16. He has even sent his own Son "that the world should be saved through him." John 3:17. It was his will that the Son came to fulfill. Heb. 10:7; John 6:38–40; Gal. 1:3, 4. For this he delivered him up (Rom. 8:32), according to his "determinate counsel" (Acts 2:23), thus saving men "according to his own purpose and grace" (2 Tim. 1:9), and thus "gave unto us eternal life, and this life is in his Son." 1 John 5:11. It is he, also, who "chose us" in Christ "before the foundation of the world," and "freely bestowed on us in the beloved his grace," Eph. 1:4, 6, and hath given us to Christ, John 17:6–11, to whom, says Christ himself, "no man can come" "except the Father, which sent me draw him," John 6:44, "having foreordained us unto adoption as sons through Jesus Christ unto himself, according to the good pleasure of his will." Eph. 1:5. That men may thus be drawn, he promised and gave his Spirit to Christ (Acts 2:33) and through him unto men, that they might be regenerated (John 3:5) and "quickened," while "dead through trespasses and sins" (Eph. 2:1), that they might have faithfulness (Gal. 5:22) and the spirit of sonship (Gal. 4:6) and may be sealed with the Holy Spirit of promise (Eph. 1:13), which witnesses to believers that they are "children of God; and, if children, then heirs; heirs of God, and joint-heirs with Christ" Rom. 8:16, 17. It is thus, also, that God, having predestinated that they shall "be conformed to the image of his Son," sanctifies them, in the sense of consecrating them, "in the truth" (John 17:17), and, also, in that of cleansing and purifying them from sin, Eph. 5:26; 1 Thess. 4:7, and causes them "to be transformed into the same image from glory to glory." 2 Cor. 3:18. Throughout all of this work the Father is also the person who is especially addressed in prayer in the name of Jesus, Eph. 2:18; 3:14, through the moving of the Spirit, Eph. 6:18; Rom. 8:26, and from whom comes "Every good gift and every perfect boon," James 1:17, as well as the justification, pardon, adoption and sanctification of believers, and also the heavenly kingdom he has prepared for them.

These are some particulars which show how completely the Father is identified with the redemption of man. They are not exhaustive of what we are
taught. Indeed the whole is from him as its source, and not merely in a general
way in the gift of his Son and Spirit, but as working by and through them in
each particular. In redemption, as in creation and providence, he is ever present,
constantly willing, and continually working; though not directly by himself,
but through the Son and the Spirit.

Some portions of this work of the Father will need hereafter more full discussion; though not so much as some of that of the Son, and of that of the Spirit,
all of the acts of whom must be more particularly and minutely examined.

A short statement is, however, necessary here as a summary of what will be
discussed as to each hereafter, and also that the official subordination may be
shown.

(2.) The action of the Son in redemption is briefly, yet almost fully described
in Phil. 2:5–11. We are there taught of that official subordination to the Father
which he willingly assumed for the discharge of this work, which corresponds
with the statement, elsewhere, that he was sent by the Father. We are also told
of that act of condescension, by which he assumed our nature, and became man
in his incarnation; of his voluntary humiliation to the death of the cross; and of
that honour, bestowed upon him, in that nature, by which in his exaltation he
has been made an object of universal worship, "to the glory of God the Father."

We learn, elsewhere, that in the period of his earthly residence he became
our example as man, as he likewise in it set forth in his own person the image
of his Father. By his active obedience to the law he fulfilled for his people the
righteousness due by them. By his sufferings, and death, he paid the penalty of
their sin. As the reward of his work, he received the promised Spirit which he
sends forth for the salvation of those whom God has given him. All power has
also been bestowed upon him, that his gospel may be preached with success,
and he is now made king in Zion, and invested with mediatorial dominion
over all things. Sitting at the right hand of God, he exercises the dominion thus
conferred, and at the same time makes intercession for his people. Thence shall
he come to judge the world, and to assign to the righteous and the wicked their
everlasting portions.

The subordination of office, in all the positions thus occupied, is plainly
revealed. Speaking prophetically, when the hour had come for his betrayal and
crucifixion, as though already the work were over, Christ himself declared of all
that he had done, thus contemplated as finished, that it was the work the Father
gave him to do, John 17:4. So also, had he said, that he came to do the Father's
will (John 6:38) and to "work the works of him that sent him." John 9:4. It

was the Father whose law he honoured in the fulfillment of all its demands, and unto whom, he, "though he was a Son, yet learned obedience by the things which he suffered." Heb. 5:8. The rewards he received were all given by the Father; namely, the Spirit (Acts 2:33), his people (John 17:9), and his exaltation, Acts 2:33, 36. Even the future judgement of the world is to be his office, because of the ordination of God (Acts 10:42; 17:31; Rom. 2:16), and has been committed to him by the Father. John 5:22.

(3.) The works of the Spirit in redemption are even more numerous than those of the Son, and bring him into the most intimate relations to the people of God.

It was by him that the human body of Christ was prepared for the indwelling of the divine person (Luke 1:35), and by his gracious influences, that the mind and heart of Christ were fitted for his work. Isa. 11:1–5; John 3:34; Luke 4:14. Likewise he prepares the Church which is the spiritual body of Christ "for a habitation of God." Eph. 2:22. It is he, in whom they are so baptized as to be thoroughly overwhelmed by the flood of his divine influences, Matt. 3:11, and who "saved us through the washing of regeneration and renewing of the Holy Ghost." Titus 3:5. Through him they are born anew. John 3:5–8. It is he that "strives with man" (Gen. 6:3), and "convicts the world in respect of sin, and of righteousness, and of judgement" (John 16:8), and gives repentance (Acts 5:31, 32, cf. Acts 2:33), so warring against the lusts of the flesh, and bringing forth spiritual fruit in them, Gal. 5:16–25, that they "walk not after the flesh, but after the Spirit." Rom. 8:2–4. He also produces faith, Eph. 3:17, and "all joy and peace in believing, that" they "may abound in hope," Rom. 15:13, and knowledge of "the things which God hath prepared for them that love him." 1 Cor. 2:9, 10. "Through him we both have our access by one Spirit unto the Father," Eph. 2:18, "With all prayer and supplication praying at all seasons in the Spirit," Eph. 6:18, since we "have received the Spirit of adoption whereby we cry, Abba, Father," and "the Spirit himself beareth witness with our spirit, that we are children of God." Rom. 8:15, 16. Thus does he become to us the author of justification by the faith produced, and of sanctification, both cleansing and consecration, 1 Cor. 6:11, and of the spirit of adoption. Gal. 4:6. Likewise he reveals the glory of Christ to the believer, and changes him into the same image. 2 Cor. 3:18. This, as the context shows, is done through the word of God, which is the sword of the Spirit. Eph. 6:17. It is also effected through the ordinances of the gospel, so far as they are symbolical of his cleansing and nourishing work, as well as of the death and resurrection of Christ. Rom. 6:3, 4; Eph. 5:26; Titus 3:5, 6; 1 Cor. 11:26; John 6:48–63.

In all of these, and in his other work, the Spirit comes into the most intimate fellowship with the people of God. As the Father attains nearness by the endearing relation of the Fatherhood to sons who cry unto him with the spirit of adoption, and as the Son becomes an object of supreme affection because of his loving sacrifice and sufferings so the Spirit seeks the intimacy of an indweller in believers, that he may develop their graces and become to them a present witness and comforter in the bodily absence of their incarnate Lord. 1 Cor. 3:16, 17.

The subordination of the Spirit in this work is revealed, in general, in the statements that he is sent by the Father and the Son. John 14:16, 17; 15:26. But it is taught also, more particularly. It is Christ that is to baptize in the Spirit, Matt. 3:11, and thus through him to produce the results of his work. It is the Father unto whom men come through the Spirit in prayer. Eph. 6:18. It is the Father who justifies and adopts, though through the influences of the Spirit. It is the image of Christ, not of himself, into which he transforms believers. The ordinances also are of Christ's appointment, and are especially fitted to set forth his work, and only that of the Spirit in a secondary way. Even the indwelling is that believers may be "builded together for an habitation of God." Eph. 2:22.

We have thus seen that in the various outward works of the Trinity, the same subordination of office appears as is found in the mode of subsistence within. This subordination, in both respects, should be recognized because taught in God's Word. At the same time it must never be forgotten that the same Word declares as distinctly the perfect equality of the three persons in the divine nature, which allows no inferiority of any one of them as God.

CHAPTER 17

CREATION

IT is natural that the origin of the universe should have been one of the most prominent subjects of inquiry among men. Various theories have been presented, not only by those who have been guided by reason only, but even by others to whom revelation has been known but not accepted as authoritative. All theories, however, may be generally reduced to four.

1. That which asserts that matter is the one eternal, self-existent substance from which all else proceeds.

2. That which regards it as an emanation from God.

3. That which maintains that matter is itself eternal, but has been acted upon by God, who has used its substance in the construction of all things, thus giving to them form and life.

4. That which accords with the Scripture teaching, that the universe has been made absolutely out of nothing, by the active exercise of the will and power of God.

It is the duty of Theology to examine each of these theories, and to set forth the reasons for believing that matter is neither self-existent and independently eternal, nor an emanation from God, nor mere material used by him, but has been created out of nothing.

1. Matter is not the one eternal, self-existent substance from which all else proceeds.

(1.) If it is, then mind is the product of matter, and not matter that of mind.

The universe presents to us both mind and matter. Each of these must exist independently of the other, or the one must have been the production of the other. Which then has been the producing cause? Have the mental powers, which are exhibited by man, been the development of forces inherent in matter, which through various processes have finally attained to self-consciousness, and thought, and purpose, such as we find in man? Or is there some infinite mind which has originated all things, both mind and matter?

The greater reasonableness of the supposition that mind has originated matter is ably set forth by Dr. Hovey, in his Manual of Theology, pp. 28–39. He contends that it is more reasonable to suppose, (1.) that there is one original and self-existent force or being than more than one; (2.) that matter is a product of mind, rather than mind of matter; (3.) that the order of the universe is due to

149

a supreme mind, rather than to forces co-operating together without purpose; (4.) that the vegetable world is a product of mind organizing matter, rather than of matter organizing itself; (5.) that the animal world is a product of mind, imparting a higher organizing principle to vegetable elements, rather than of vegetable forces acting alone; (6.) that man, as a rational being, is a product of mind, giving a higher principle of life to animal being, rather than of mere vital forces acting without reason; (7.) that man, as a moral being, is a product of the supreme mind, itself moral, rather than of vital forces that have no moral insight; (8.) that man, as a religious being, is a product of the supreme mind, rather than of mere vital forces.

The above are simply condensed statements of the mere propositions laid down by Dr. Hovey. His full argument shows conclusively how utterly unreasonable is the idea that mind should have proceeded from matter, and not produced it. But, if so, it is equally unreasonable that matter should be the one originating cause of the universe.

(2.) The same fact appears from the existence of the laws which control matter. Matter has fixed limitations, within which alone it can act. Its movements, its changes of form, its developments, and indeed all things connected with it are governed by fixed, and, so far as we can see, unchangeable laws. These laws can be examined and known, and made the basis of the action of men. Now these laws can be accounted for only in one of three ways. Either they belong to matter as a necessity of its nature, or matter has the power to give to itself laws, or these laws have been imposed upon it by a superior intelligence. But if the first be true, then that necessity of nature would not only make these laws unchangeable, (for whatever exists of necessity, exists without possibility of change,) but would likewise make it impossible for men to conceive of any reasonable change in them in any respect. But the fact that there is such great diversity among the scientific theories which attempt to develop the laws controlling nature in many of its aspects, and that there seems no absurdity nor natural impossibility that the law should accord with any one of these theories, or be different from it—evinces that there is no absurdity nor unreasonableness in supposing that the material universe might have been placed under very different laws from those which exist.

But the second of these suppositions cannot he true, because matter must then, in some aspect, have had intelligence to understand, and establish law before the existence of mind in any form; for science teaches that created mind, (which, upon the supposition, is the only kind of existent mind,) comes forth in connection with the higher organisms of existence, and long after apparent operation of the laws which regulate matter.

It is certain, therefore, that the laws of matter have been imposed by a superior intelligence, and, consequently, that matter cannot be the eternal, self-existent substance, from which all else proceeds.

(3.) The incapacity of matter to create anything shows that it is not self-existent, and eternal. All that is claimed for matter is the power to develop one form into another. It is even denied that there has been any increase in its original materials since it first began to be. But it is evident that whatever cannot be the cause of existence to others, cannot be the cause of its own existence, or be self-existent. The latter is a far higher power than the former.

(4.) That matter is not eternally self-existent is also manifest from the fact that it exists in time. The laws of time require succession of moments and limits of duration. Matter could not he eternal in any other way than through the existence of an infinite series of finite periods, which is absurd.

2. Matter is not an emanation from God.

That which goes forth from God must either be from his nature, or from his mere will and power. But the latter would be a mere creation out of nothing, since it would not be something produced out of himself. An emanation from God must, therefore, proceed from his nature. But it cannot be of this character.

(a.) Because, if from his nature, it must possess the attributes of that nature, and must exist in the same mode of existence with it. But matter has none of the attributes which belong to God. Nor is the mode of its existence like his. It has neither self-existence, nor eternity of existence, nor even infinity of space or time, since it is composed of finite parts, and exists in successive moments which are finite and measurable. It has not intelligence, nor purposing power, nor can it have wisdom or goodness, neither can it exercise justice, nor experience love.

(b.) An emanation from the nature of God would be opposed to the doctrine of the unity of God. That which thus proceeds would be as truly God as that from which it comes forth. We should, therefore, have two Gods. Indeed, as matter itself is capable of indefinite division, there would be an indefinite number of Gods. The doctrine of the Trinity gives no support to such an emanation as matter would necessarily be. It does not teach an emanation from the nature of God, for the divine nature remains one only, and is not divided among the three persons, but is the common substance in which they subsist. In order that matter should subsist in God in like manner, it must itself have a conscious personal existence, and have all the attributes of God, and have the same mode of existence.

3. Neither is matter a substance upon which God has simply acted in the production of the Universe.

(a.) The evidence that it is not eternal shows that it was not thus present of itself with God furnishing material for his workmanship. If it existed at any time as purely inorganic, it must either have been first created in that condition, or permitted to lapse into it from its original form.

(b.) The power and right thus to act upon matter must either have been conferred upon God, as it is on us, or it must have arisen from his having created it. But as there was no one to confer this power upon God, the Universe must have been created by him.

4. The theory of a creation out of nothing, by the mere will and power of God, is then the only reasonable supposition upon which to account for the existence of the Universe. It is not an objection to this reasonableness, that it was first made known by Revelation. Being thus revealed, it appears to reason, not only to be fully accordant with all the facts and phenomena of matter, but to be the only theory which can account for them. That this theory has been suggested by the language of God's Word makes it no less reasonable than if suggested by some mere man. It is at once seen not to be an impossibility. It is not a creation out of nothing, in the sense that it has had no cause, or has been produced without the existence of forces adequate to the end. The cause and the forces are in God; in his will, and wisdom, and power, and goodness. It cannot be said to come from nothing, for it comes from God. The mind readily rests in such a theory. It fully answers all the demands of the problem to be solved. It is accompanied with none of the difficulties which press against the theories based upon the eternity of matter. The manner in which God works is indeed unknown to us; but that he may so work is highly accordant with reason.

The creation of the world out of nothing is the plain teaching of Scripture. It is true, that the phrase to "create from nothing" is not found, except in one of the apocryphal books of the Old Testament (2 Maccabees 7:28). But the fact itself is taught expressly in Heb. 11:3. "By faith we understand that the worlds have been framed by the word of God, so that what is seen hath not been made out of things which do appear." The account of the general creation in Genesis conveys the same idea, and a like impression is produced by the Scriptures generally. It has been argued from the verbs, used to declare the creation, both in Genesis and elsewhere; but the argument is doubtful, as these words are also applied to acts of creation out of pre-existent matter.

This creation out of nothing seems essential to the power of God over matter. If he did not create it, it exists independently of him; but if it is his creation, then he has absolute control, not only over the forms into which he has shaped it, and over the laws he has given it, but over matter itself in every respect, even over its longer existence for a moment of time.

A distinction is made between immediate or primary creation, which is that act by which God acts directly without the use of pre-existent materials, and mediate and secondary creations, which are those acts by which out of pre-existent materials he produces his creatures. The universe of matter was an immediate creation. The body of Adam was a mediate one, and so, also, are those of all his posterity.

Several objections have been presented against the full inspiration of the account of the Creation given in the first chapters of Genesis.

(1.) It is claimed that the general account which concludes with the third verse of the second chapter cannot be an inspired writing, because it was evidently taken from some other source, and incorporated in this book.

In reply It may be said:

(a.) That this has not been, and cannot be established.

(b.) That if it were, it would not affect its inspiration.

It is much more probable that the genealogies of Christ, given by Matthew and Luke, were from the records of the family of David. The inspiration of Matthew, and Luke, and Moses does not depend upon these having been made as direct revelations to them; but upon the fact that they were moved by the Holy Ghost to insert them in the books they were writing, such moving of the Spirit being, however, an evidence of the truthfulness of the records. If, therefore, it could be proved that the account of creation existed long before the days of Moses, this proof would, in no respect, militate against its inspiration.

(2.) Another objection is that Genesis represents the Creation as occurring in six literal days of twenty-four hours each, and that geological science has proved that the world was created in periods of time much longer.

But the account does not necessarily teach that this work was done in six such days.

(a.) Because the word "day" is sometimes an indefinite term, the true meaning of which must be ascertained by the context. It is applied to each of these periods in the first chapter, and also to all of them unitedly in Gen. 2:4. The Scriptures frequently use it very indefinitely, as the "day of trouble," "of wrath," "of temptation," "of vengeance," etc. It even embraces the whole period of a captivity as "the day of Jerusalem," Ps. 137:7; and "the day of Egypt," Ezek. 30:9. These, and many other applications, show that frequently it means merely a period, and the length of that period must be ascertained otherwise.

(b.) Because the Hebrew words translated "evening," and "morning," while almost always used for those portions of the day, do not necessarily indicate a day of twenty-four hours' duration, but may denote only the changes which occur periodically in any cyclical period. The root ideas of these words are "the mingling" (evening) and "the bursting forth" (morning). They are thus beautifully descriptive of a time of intermingling of the elements, leading to a period of darkness, and that again followed by the bursting forth of the appearance of a new creation, the whole forming one cyclical period. The length of the period is not necessarily indicated by them. The use, also, of these words before the appearance of the Sun and Moon on the fourth day, very decidedly confirms the idea that the periods need not be those of an ordinary day.

(c.) While it is admitted that the resting of God upon the seventh day, in connection with the language of the commandment respecting the observance of the Sabbath, favours the idea of days of twenty-four hours, even this does not make necessary such days. We know not what is exactly meant by God's resting on the seventh day. There is certainly something figurative, or anthropomorphic about it. The "rest" of this first chapter may represent the ceasing from creative work in this world, and the seventh day of rest, which man is commanded to observe, may be commemorative and typical of the former; this being brief and inferior, in comparison with that, as man is but an atom in the creation of the great God of this greater Sabbath.

From these facts it is manifest that we are not compelled to maintain that the creation was limited to six ordinary days. This is all that is necessary. If science can show the impossibility of such a six-day creation, we can reply that the Scriptures do not necessarily teach it. And the fact of this possibility of concurrence with possible scientific discoveries, heretofore so generally unlooked for, becomes strong evidence of the inspiration of this account of Creation.

(3.) Another objection is, that, according to any Scripture chronology which we have, man has been on the earth only six or eight thousand years, and yet that fossil remains of men have been found who must have existed fifty thousand years ago, or more.

(a.) But satisfactory proof of this has not yet been afforded. Scientific men themselves are not agreed about it.

(b.) But if true, the Scriptures are not necessarily wrong, nor uninspired. The chronology of the different forms in which the Old Testament has come down to us is known to vary. This is attributable to mistakes in copying, which can more easily occur in the representations of numbers, than of any other ideas. It may be that Adam was created more than eight thousand years ago, and that the original chronology of the Scriptures so taught. It may be that, in connection with that greater antiquity, if all were known about it, would appear explanations of the great age to which many of the patriarchs are said to have arrived. Nor is it impossible that other races of men existed before Adam, either endowed as he was, with both spiritual and animal life, or they with animal life only, and he with the specially added endowment of a spiritual nature. While it is granted that such has not probably been the fact, yet is it not impossible that it may have been.

While these various objections thus seem not to render impossible the absolute verity of this Genesis account of Creation, there are other facts which ought to be remembered which support the narrative.

1. That it is natural that the Scripture should use phenomenal language only as to scientific matters. We do this every time we speak of the sun rising and setting, and no one misunderstands, or is deceived. This is the only method in which a book for all ages could refer to scientific matters. Had the Bible used language exactly suited to the science of today, embracing all its best established theories, in less than fifty years it would have to be admitted that it could not be from God, because of its lack of truth. Had it been written in the language of true science originally, age after age would have rejected it as false. It could only treat science phenomenally.

2. But, while thus written, it often gives underlying evidence that God its author knew truths of science, that could not have been known to the science of that day. This is particularly shown in this account of Creation. Light here appears before the Sun and the Moon. The order of the creations accords generally with that taught by Geology from an examination of the stratifications of the rocks. Man is made after all other creations, and his body is made of the dust of the earth. Even the universe was not made as it now appears, for, while the first verse of the first chapter states the creation of both heavens and earth, the second teaches that, before the formative process began, the earth was in a chaotic condition. The truth is, that, so generally, and yet so accurately, are the statements made, that, even if it could be proved that the Universe is the production of original concurrent atoms, or of a universal fire mist, or the development of molecules, there is nothing in this Genesis account to commit it to the contrary. Even the creation of animal life, including that of man, is from the earth, which is directed to bring forth. The soul of man is the only living thing which is declared to have been a direct creation of God.

Several theories have been presented for the full reconciliation of Genesis and Geology. It is not necessary to state them here. It is enough that there are possible means of such reconciliation, and that any one, or more of them, may be true. The veracity of the Scriptures is otherwise abundantly proved. Here it is charged that they speak falsely. Were a man of well-known probity and honour thus assailed, and facts, however strong, or cumulative, presented against him, it would suffice to support his denial by showing that there are possible circumstances which may explain all seeming falsehood. So with the Scriptures. They are charged with error. It is enough to show one possible explanation. But, in this case, we can show several. This would suffice. But we are justified in challenging those who deny inspiration to account for the many coincidences with the scientific teaching found in this narrative.

CHAPTER 18

CREATION OF ANGELS

IN the last chapter reference was made only incidentally to the creation of intelligent, moral and spiritual beings. There are several matters connected with such creations which deserve special consideration. The creation of angels will be first treated because of their probable earlier existence, and superior nature, and position.

I. Some have denied the utility of this inquiry because men owe angels no duty of homage, or worship, and because their usual invisibility forbids that their presence for good, or evil, should be known. But it is surely important to know something of beings who have been so intimately associated with the past history of man, both for weal and woe. [See Article of Moses Stuart in Bib. Sacra, Vol. O, p. 88.]

II. It is said by some that reason decides against the existence of such beings, or at least against their appearance to man. But, on the contrary, nothing can be more rational than the belief that the God, whose animal creatures in this world are of so many kinds and gradations, should not stop with the first creation of moral and intellectual beings, but should extend upward his creative skill and power, throughout numerous classes of similar nature to man. Nor is there anything unreasonable in the supposition that, while ordinarily these may be confined to the exercise of influences under the laws of mind and spirit, at times, at God's will, they should appear in bodily forms recognizable by the senses. [Stuart in Bib. Sacra, Vol. O, pp. 90–93.]

III. But the Scriptures plainly teach that there are angels, and that they visit the inhabitants of this world.

Their general tenor teaches it. Even superficial readers of the Word of God must be convinced that it reveals the existence, and presence with man, of personal beings of another sphere, through whom God communicates to him, and aids, and protects him; as well as of other angels whose influence is for evil, and is destructive of happiness.

There are some, however, who declare that all such teachings are purely figurative, and that the good angels of the Word are "no more than the kindness and mercy of God, and the evil angels his afflictive, punishing or chastising acts."

Such interpretations deserve the charge of "handling the Word of God deceitfully." But even if these were admitted to be correct, as to much, or most of the language used, there are some instances of the appearance of angels which cannot thus be explained away. The interview between the angel and Hagar, Gen. 16:7–14, is one of these. That with the wife of Manoah is another, Judges 13:2–21. Signal instances also are those with Zacharias, Luke 1:5–20, and with Mary, Luke 1:26–38, and with Mary Magdalene, and the other women, Matt. 28:1–7. Those statements are especially conclusive which are made in Mark 12:25, and Luke 20:36, in which it is declared as to the saints, "after the resurrection that they neither marry nor are given in marriage; . . . for they are equal unto the angels." There is also no meaning in Hebrews 1:4 if there are no angels. [See Kitto's Ency., Art. Angels.]

IV. Various names are given to angels as expressive either of their nature or offices.

1. The chief of these is descriptive of their office. Angel means a messenger. It is a word not confined to them, nor to any other kind of messengers of God. (1.) It is used of ordinary messengers among men, 1 Sam. 11:3; Job 1:14; Luke 9:52; (2.) of prophets, Mal. 3:1; (3.) of priests, Mal. 2:7; (4.) of ministers of the gospel, Rev. 1:20; (5.) of impersonal agents, as of pestilence, 2 Sam. 24:16, 17. Plagues, likewise, are denominated "angels of evil," Ps. 78:49. Paul also calls his "thorn in the flesh" "an angel of Satan," 2 Cor. 12:7. (6.) It is also applied to the Second Person of the Trinity, as "the angel of his presence," Isa. 63:9, and "the messenger [angel] of the covenant," Mal. 3:1. (7.) The name, however, is generally applied to the angels of God as spiritual beings. See Kitto's Ency., Art. Angels.

2. The name Spirit is also given to them, Ps. 104:4; Mark 1:27; Heb. 1:7. This name is descriptive of their nature.

3. They are called "Sons of God," Job 1:6; 2:1; 38:7.

4. They are called "Gods." Compare Ps. 97:7 with Heb. 1:6.

5. They are called "servants of God," Job 4:18; Ps. 103:21.

6. They are called "Holy ones," Job 15:15; Dan. 4:13, 17.

7. They are called "Watchers," Dan. 4:13, 17.

8. They are called "Thrones, Dominions, Principalities, Powers, and Mights," Eph. 1:21; Col. 1:16.

9. There are other names which are probably applied to them, as "Cherubim," "Seraphim," and "Hosts," as when God is called the "Lord of Hosts." See Dr. J. Pye Smith, First Lines, p. 328. Also Kitto's Ency., Art. Angels.

V. We know very little of the nature of angels. They are spoken of; but not described in the Scriptures. Yet some facts plainly appear.

1. They are spiritual beings. This is indicated by the only name derived from their nature.

Dr. J. Pye Smith attributes to them corporeal powers analogous to the substance of light, or of the electric fluid, and claims that thus light is cast upon such Scripture passages as speak of their relations to space, and of their locomotion, as Luke 2:9; Matt. 28:2; Acts 1:10; 12:7. [First Lines, p. 329.]

Moses Stuart, on the contrary, maintains that "angels are incorruptible, immaterial, immortal, and, in their proper nature, impalpable to the senses." [Bib. Sac., Vol. O, p. 99.]

This seems to be the most correct and Scriptural view, as it is also the one most generally held. All the difficulties it encounters may he explained by the fact that we have to speak of angels as we do of God in the language of man, which cannot always convey exact and adequate ideas of them. [See Stuart in Bib. Sacra, Vol. O, pp. 94–98.]

The declarations that "a spirit hath not flesh and bones," Luke 24:39, that "God is a spirit," John 4:24, that the children of the resurrection will "neither marry nor are given in marriage, for neither can they die any more, for they are equal unto the angels," Luke 20:35, 36; Matt. 22:30, indicate that the nature of angels is truly spiritual. [Moses Stuart, Bib. Sac., Vol. O, p. 100.] The abode of the angels in heaven, and the offices they perform confirm this idea. After all, however, it is unimportant to decide whether they are simply spirits, or have some spiritual body, such as will belong to the saints after the resurrection. Either view maintains all that is essential to the spirituality of their nature.

2. They are intelligent beings. This seems to follow necessarily, from their being spirits. But it is plainly taught in the Scriptures. See Eph. 3:10; 1 Pet. 1:12; 2 Pet. 2:11. These passages imply that they are superior to men in this respect.

3. They possess moral natures. They are not only made capable of knowing God's excellence and of worshipping him, but are also spoken of as being under moral obligation, so that they are rewarded for obedience, and punished for disobedience. It may also be argued from the fact that their ministry in this life seems confined to moral and spiritual things. Heb. 1:14.

There are certain facts which result from the nature of angels.

1. As spiritual and intelligent beings, they must possess freedom of will.

2. They are not subject to the restrictions and conditions of the world of sense. They do not occupy space unless they have some bodily form. Nevertheless they are not omnipresent, as is God, but they have location. Neither do they attain knowledge through the senses, nor are they affected by bodily appetites or desires.

3. As long as they retain their original innocent condition they must be happy. It is believed from the general tenor of Scripture, that the angels that kept their first estate have been confirmed in their happiness. Such confirmation, however, results from the promises of God as a reward for their obedience, and is bestowed by him not as an act of justice, but in accordance with his veracity. No obedience can bring God under obligation to confirm.

4. They must also be possessed of great power.

Christ intimates that their power is greater than that of man, Matt. 26:53, and this fact is plainly taught in 2 Pet. 2:11. See also 2 Thess. 1:7, and Eph. 1:21. This power is seen also in their performance of supernatural works; as perhaps in the rolling away of the stone at the sepulchre of Christ, and in the opening of the prison-door of Peter. It was most wonderfully exhibited in the strengthening of the Saviour in Gethsemane by the angel which appeared. Luke 22:43.

Dr. A. D. C. Twesten makes the following five valuable suggestions as to the exercise by angels of power over man.

1. "Whatever may be the efficiency attributed to the angels, their relation to us can only be that of one finite to another finite cause; and is never to be imagined as similar to the relation which God, or Christ, or the Holy Ghost sustains to us."

2. "The efficiency of the angels is, therefore, always to be represented in accordance with the laws of reciprocal action established between finite beings; hence it never excludes our counter-action, or reaction, and can neither annul the power of nature, nor the freedom of the will."

3. "All action of angels upon the world of sense can take place only under the following conditions: that they enter into, or become one of the series of causes there at work; and that they themselves act by means of these causes, or in the same mode with them.". . .

4. "This entrance into the series of causes at work in the world of sense, may be looked upon as an original, a primitive, perhaps also a transient influence; but it can leave behind it effects which will propagate the primitive influence, and which may, therefore, be considered as parts of the angelic efficiency. Thus,

for example, the temptation of the first man by Satan continues to operate in the law of sin and death which was thus introduced into the world."

5. "The original entrance of angels into the world of sense seems not to depend upon their own good pleasure alone; but, if we may judge from its infrequency, to be limited to narrow bounds. In this respect, and in its very nature, it is analogous to miracles, and hence like these, appears to be specially attached to certain periods of divine revelation, or of the development of God's kingdom in this world." [See the translation in the Bib. Sacra., Vol. 1, pp. 774–775.]

VI. Our final inquiry will be into the offices discharged by these beings.

1. Their chief duty is to attend upon God, and perform his commands. This may be said indeed to include all that they do. They are God's messengers.

2. They are brought into contact with men by these commands. They are represented as present at the Creation, at the giving of the Law, at the birth of Christ, after the temptation in the wilderness, during the agony in Gethsemane, and at Christ's resurrection and ascension. They are deeply interested in the economy of Redemption and are constantly seeking to penetrate into its mysteries, and know its depths. They feel a deep interest in man, and become the medium of messages to him. They rejoice over his repentance, and are made the means of comfort, protection and guidance. "Are they not all ministering spirits, sent forth to do service for the sake of them who shall inherit salvation." Heb. 1:14. They are also made the messengers of God's vengeance to execute his wrath upon the sinful. 2 Sam. 24:16, 17; 2 Kings 19:35; 1 Chron. 21:15, 16; 2 Chron. 32:21; Acts 12:23. This punitive office belongs to good as well as bad angels.

3. From the intimate connection thus existing between angels and men, other offices have been assigned to them. Guided by Rabbinical fables, and led off by the peculiar views of Oriental philosophy, some have conceived that on each person in this life an angel attends to guard and protect him from evil.

This theory of a guardian angel has been held in various forms. Some have confined his presence to the good; some have extended it also to the wicked; some to the elect before or after conversion; some to all men alike; some have supposed two angels instead of one, the one good, the other bad. In like manner has the theory been held of guardian angels over nations; some confining that also to good nations, others extending it to all. That such views existed among the Jews, and that they were also prevalent among the earlier Christians may be admitted; but the scriptural authority for them is wanting.

The passages supposed to favour them may be readily explained otherwise. This idea of guardian angels is earnestly advocated by Prof. Stuart, in Vol. O, of the Bibliotheca Sacra. He claims that they attend the good only.

The strongest points that he makes are based upon the attendance of angels upon the footsteps of Christ. That attendance is readily granted; but they were attendants, not guardians. This is seen from the fact that, although they strengthened him while here on earth, as his agony seemed to require, that attendance is not confined to Christ in this life, but is spoken of as to be continued, even after the time of his ascension. Besides this, that which is fatal to the theory is, that it was not one special angel that was present, but several at one time, and probably different ones at different times. The sacred Scriptures never speak of any one of these as his angel, or as the angel, but only refer to an angel, or to angels. This, however, is but the general sense in which God is said to send his angels, that they may be ministering spirits. This sending is not questioned, but is very different from the supposition of the appointment to each man of one angel, who, from the beginning to the end of life, is to be ever present to watch over his welfare.

The Scripture references by which Prof. Stuart would prove this of individual men do not at all sustain him. They are Gen. 32:1, 2; 2 Kings 6:1–17; Ps. 34:7; Zech. 3:4–10; Matt. 18:10; Acts 12:7–15.

There are indeed but two passages which at all make likely the idea of guardian angels to individuals. One of these is Acts 12:7–15, in which we are told that when Peter, on his deliverance from prison, knocked at the door of the house in which were the disciples, they were led to say, "It is his angel."

Of this passage it may be said that it is doubtful whether reference was not made to the spirit of Peter; but even if not, the language is simply that of the disciples, expressing a sentiment that commonly prevailed, and one for which inspiration is not at all responsible, except as correctly reporting the language used.

The other passage is Matt. 18:10. This is well paraphrased by Knapp: "As we are careful not to offend the favourites of those who stand high in the favour of earthly kings, we should be still more careful not to offend the favourites of divine providence." "The humbly pious are those entrusted to the special care of those who stand high in the favour of God (who behold his face)." Knapp's Theology, p. 212.

The Scriptures that seem to sustain the notion of guardian angels over nations are Dan. 10:13–21; Dan. 12:1. But here "Cambyses and Alexander seem to be meant, and Michael is probably the Messiah." J. Pye Smith, First Lines, p. 331.

The following passages seem to be opposed to the idea of one angel to one man or nation: Gen. 28:12; 32:1, 2; 2 Kings 6:16, 17; Luke 16:22.

It is further to be objected:

1. That this notion seems unworthy of the rank and office of such beings. But it is replied that God watches over us. This, however, is very different from the constant daily attendance upon us of one being of such superior intelligence.

2. It is rendered needless by the watchful care of God.

3. It has led, and naturally so, to the worship of angels.

4. It is apt to derogate from the mediatorial glory of the Lord Jesus Christ. Dr. J. Pye Smith, p. 331.

VII. The number of the angels is unknown, but that it is very great is shown by the following passages: Dan. 7:10; Matt. 26:53; Heb. 12:22.

VIII. As to their dwelling-place nothing definite can be said. They dwell with God. But is this in one place or in many? We have no means of knowing.

CHAPTER 19

FALLEN ANGELS

SUPERIOR spiritual beings have heretofore been referred to, almost as though there are none except those who yet retain their position as sons of God. Only a hint or two has been given which would lead to the knowledge of the existence of others. But the important relations which angels bear to us, and the great power over us which they exercise, render useful the consideration whether evil angels actually exist, and in what position to us they may be supposed to stand.

The belief of evil spirits has been almost universal in the world. The exceptions may indeed be said to be only the few who, in more modern times, have supposed this universal opinion to be simply the result of superstition.

The Jews undoubtedly held this faith. It is not disputed that it is taught in their later books, and that in the time of Christ the belief in such spirits was universal. But it has been denied that such views can be traced prior to the time of the Babylonish Captivity. If by this is simply meant that prior to that time the Jews knew not of the fall of angels formerly pure, it is only equivalent to declaring that they knew not in what manner evil angels had come into existence. But if it is meant, as seems to be the ease, that they did not know of the existence of evil angels, the position may be easily refuted from the Scriptures. That this is the opinion of these objectors is plain from the fact that they suppose the origin of these ideas was the Persian belief of the two principles of good and evil which they had met with in Chaldea. That faith taught indeed the origin of evil in this world, but not among the spiritual intelligences above. Besides, it attributed the existence of evil to an antagonistic principle to the great good, perhaps equally powerful, yet constantly contending, perhaps finally to be vanquished.

The fact that the existence of these beings is taught at all, either in the Old or the New Testament, would be sufficient to make it an article of our faith. Yet, as this charge has been made, it is best to refer to it, and to show from the Scripture proofs that it is untenable. The truth is that with the exception of Zechariah 3:1, 2 (where the high priest Joshua is standing before the angel of the Lord, and Satan standing at his right hand to resist him), there is no passage in all the post-Babylonish Scriptures by which the doctrine of evil angels could be proved, while there are numerous such passages in the earlier books.

In the book of Job, supposed by some to be the oldest, and sometimes even ascribed to Moses, Satan is represented as presenting himself among the sons of God before the LORD. Job 1:6.

This may be said to be a merely dramatic work, yet scarcely can it be denied that the conception of such beings must have existed prior to a dramatic use of them.

In 1 Chron. 21:1, however, Satan is said to have provoked David to number Israel. In Ps. 109:6 the Psalmist says: "Set thou a wicked man over him, and let an adversary (Satan) stand at his right hand." The use of the word "devil" also teaches the existence of evil spirits. In Ps. 106:37 the Israelites are said to have sacrificed their sons and daughters unto devils (demons).

Evil angels are also spoken of by the name of "evil spirits." In Judges 9:23 God is said to have sent an evil spirit between Abimelech and the men of Shechem. In 1 Sam. 16:14 the Spirit of the Lord is said to have departed from Saul, and an evil spirit from the Lord to have troubled him; in ver. 15 Saul's servants recognize this fact in addressing Saul, and in verse 16 propose to send for a skillful player on the harp, through whom he should he made well, and in verse 23 this device is spoken of as successful.

When we turn now to the New Testament, we find the proofs even more abundant. No one questions that this is the apparent language of this part of Scripture, whatever explanations are resorted to for escaping its plain meaning. The passages are not here presented because they will be quoted in connection with other points, and enough of them will then be given to prove this a New Testament doctrine. Including both the singular and plural forms, the word "diabolos" is found in the New Testament about forty times, demon sixty times, Satan twenty-three times, evil spirit eight times, dumb spirit three times, and spirit of divination once.

The commonly received doctrine as to the original state of evil angels, is that they were once pure and holy, such as are now the angels of heaven, though not, as they, confirmed in holiness. This is founded upon the supposition that it is impossible for God to create beings otherwise than free from sin.

The only objection which can be made to this original innocence is suggested in such questions as these: How can a being perfectly holy be led to the commission of sin? How would a being realizing the character and power of the supreme being ever be so unwise as to revolt against it?

But these questions present only metaphysical difficulties which must vanish before actual facts. The existence of such beings is plainly taught; we are told in Scripture that they sinned, 2 Pet. 2:4, and all argument of this kind is merely an argument from our ignorance.

It might be supposed that appeal might he made to the case of Adam; but, while this is true to some extent, this difference must be observed, that there was present with our first parents an evil one to suggest the sin. Yet, even then, the suggestion might have arisen within the mind of either Adam or Eve as the result of desire in any way awakened, which, when fostered, may have become too strong. And, if this be psychologically possible with them, why may it not have been so with Satan and his angels?

It has been because of the difficulties which thus have seemed to perplex this question that on the one hand the very existence of such beings has been questioned; and, on the other, the theory has been advanced that Satan, either as created or uncreated, has always had a sinful nature, and been filled with enmity to God. Both theories are readily dispelled by the fact that the Scriptures speak of their having sinned with manifest allusion to some one particular act of sin.

Despite, however, this plain teaching of Scripture as to the existence of evil spirits, efforts have been made, even by Christian men, to explain away its plain language, and especially that of the New Testament. It has been claimed that all that Christ and his Apostles said upon this subject is to be accounted for upon the principle of accommodation. It is said that they knew the prejudices of the Jews, and that, not wishing upon an unimportant matter to excite these prejudices, they accommodated the language of their teachings to Jewish ideas, and used such words as seemed to imply belief in such beings.

(1.) But the principle here assumed is dangerous. How can we know that Christ taught anything, if we be allowed thus to strip his language of its natural force?

(2.) The object of Christ was not to accommodate himself to prejudices; but to remove them. What instance can be given of such conformity? None can be justly claimed. On the contrary, he said that he came not to send peace, but a sword, and to preach not a gospel of accommodation, but one of contention and exclusiveness. He drove out, with a whip of small cords, those who defiled the temple. He persisted in healing upon the Sabbath day. He inveighed against the traditions of the elders. He attacked the hypocrisy of the Scribes and Pharisees who were reputed most holy. Does any of this conduct look like that of one who would have shrunk from declaring the non-existence of Satan? Was not the doctrine of the resurrection as against the Sadducees, and of the salvation of publicans and sinners and the adoption of the Gentiles as against the Pharisees, even more unpalatable than would have been the denial of the existence of evil spirits?

(3.) The idea of mere accommodation to the Jews would not have involved the language upon this point used to his disciples in private. The time of the return of the seventy was peculiarly suitable to remove these prejudices from their minds. They came to Christ saying: "Lord, even the devils are subject unto us in thy name." Luke 10:17. And Christ only teaches more plainly the existence or such beings, declaring that he beheld Satan, as lightning, fall from heaven, at the same time assuring them that even the power to cast out devils was no subject of joy in comparison with the fact that their names were written in heaven.

(4.) A still stronger objection may be drawn from the circumstances of the temptation. There the devil is said to have tempted Christ. In cases of human temptation, it may be said that it is the principle of evil in the heart that moves the man to do wrong, and that thus he is tempted. But what principle like this was there in Christ? Upon what ground can he be said to have been tempted except by the personal solicitation of the evil one?

Another question of interest has been as to the cause of the sin of angels. Some, because of a misconception of the meaning of Gen. 6:2, have attributed it to lust. But this is not only contrary to the nature of angels, but also places the fall of man before that of the devil. Some have held that it consisted in the temptation of man. But he who tempted with evil intent and falsehood must himself have sinned beforehand. Besides, this tempter was one only, and the evil angels are many. Others think that it was envy of angels superior to them. This was the idea of the Jews, who, holding the theory of guardian angels over nations, supposed that some of them aspired to higher positions than were allotted to them. But the more common opinion is that it was a sin of pride. The apostle says of a bishop, that he must not be "a novice, lest being puffed up, he fall into the condemnation of the devil." 1 Tim. 3:6. From this it appears probable that pride was the sin of Satan, and that for this he was condemned. See Kitto's Cyc., Art. Satan. Dick's Theology, vol. 1, p. 377. Knapp, p. 218.

Their relation to each other in this sin has been still further a subject of inquiry. In the fall of man we recognize both a natural and federal head. Through these we see that all have been made sinners. But did the angels have a federal head, or did they sin individually each one for himself? There is a difficulty in either hypothesis. On the one hand, how could a federal head, when he had sinned, infuse, by that sin, an unholy nature into those whom he represented; on the other hand, as we recognize the first beginnings of sin to be in the desire, how could so many simultaneously have revolted against God?

In favour of the federal theory, may be stated the fact of the headship of one over the others, and the nature of the sin, pride, which may have arisen from the occupancy of a position of such power. Yet these do not necessarily imply it. Supreme position may have existed without federal relation.

In favour of the other theory may be adduced (1.) the co-existence at that time of all those angels that sinned; this was not true of all mankind, and is a reason why they needed to act differently. (2.) The immediate intercourse, because of their nature, which all others as well as their head may have had with God, to know his will and to perform it. In man this existed only in Eve, and may account for her personal sin before that of her representative. (3.) The greater lack of excuse that would exist in a fall as the result of individual probation. (4.) The fact that no provision of salvation has been made for them, either in the representative Saviour of man or in one for angels.

The main difficulty in the way of this theory may be removed by the natural supposition, that all the angels, or a portion of them to which all of these belonged, were put at one time upon probation, just as Adam was. In that probation some sinned, and some did not. The fall of all may, therefore, have been instantaneous. That one of them may have been the instantaneous instigator of this, is not improbable. That he may have held rank over them before, is in accordance with what is taught of the rank of all angels. That he might in this act have attained this position is also not improbable.

For the sin which they have thus committed, they are held accountable by God. They seem to have been already punished by being "kept in everlasting bonds under darkness, unto the judgement of the great day." Jude, verse 6. But on that day their punishment will be probably consummated.

In the meantime they are permitted access to this world. Satan is called the God of this world. 2 Cor. 4:4. This access is evident from the history of the fall, from that of the temptation of Christ, from the warnings given to believers against him as their adversary, and from the declarations made as to the power he exercises to blind the minds of them that believe not.

As a finite being, Satan must be limited in his approaches to man. The doctrine of Satan is often objected to, upon the ground that thus we make out a being of almost equal power with God, and everywhere present. But this power of constant approach arises, not probably from personal contact, but from the multitude of inferior agents which he thus controls. By these he is everywhere operating; perhaps not operating always thus directly upon each one; but always keeping in progress the influences which he puts in operation among men.

What then, we may inquire, is the extent of the power of evil spirits?

1. Undoubtedly they have great power over the minds of men. They may tempt, deceive, darken the minds of men, pervert the judgement of men, excite them to pride, anger and other evil passions. It was Satan that instigated the

Jews to put Christ to death. The old phraseology of the courts of justice in indictments for murder recognize his power. It is not confined to the subjects of his kingdom; but over the people of God also, even after they have been rescued from their slavery to Satan, does he maintain and exercise the power to tempt, though not to destroy.

2. Satan also possesses power over the bodies of men. In Job 2:7, it is said that he "smote Job with sore boils from the sole of his foot unto his crown." In Luke 13:16, a woman is spoken of who has been bound by Satan for eighteen years by disease. In Acts 10:38, one of the works of Christ is said to have been the healing of all who were oppressed with the Devil. In 1 Cor. 5:5, excommunication is spoken of as the delivering over of one to Satan for the destruction of the flesh. Satan is also said, in some sense, to have or to have had the power of death, Heb. 2:14.

It is here that naturally arises the question of demoniacal influence as proving, if true, the existence and number of such beings. Have Satan and his messengers the power thus to enter, and afflict the bodies of men?

The most serious objection to the idea of such possessions is that they have been confined to the age of Christ and the Apostles.

(1.) But this is not certain. We even have declarations to the contrary. The Jews of the second century professed that there were such in their day. This was true, also, of the Christians of the third century. But the evidence of such possessions at these periods is not conclusive. It is not probable that any existed at that time.

(2.) Dr. Macknight, quoted by Dr. Dick, Theol. vol. 1, p. 403, says "that the possessions mentioned may have been diseases carried to an uncommon height by the presence and agency of demons." And, if this is allowed, there have possibly been such in all ages.

(3.) But this difficulty must yield before the direct testimony of Scripture. A reason may be given for their especial prevalence in the time of Christ. The great struggle was about to take place between Christ and Satan, and uncommon freedom was doubtless granted to the Devil, and his assistants.

The following points show that the idea of demoniacal possessions is Scriptural.

(a.) The demons are expressly separated from the persons possessed. See Luke 6:17, 18; Matt. 12:43–45; Mark 1:32, 34; 9:18.

(b.) The actions and language show the personality of some evil being or beings within the sufferer. They beseech Christ not to torment them before their time; they answer his questions; they come out of the possessed and enter into the swine; they know Christ and call upon him as the Son of God.

(c.) The writers mention facts connected with them, needless to be mentioned, which favour this. The number of demons cast from Mary Magdalene is given. In Mark 9:29 Jesus says of a demon, "this kind can come out by nothing save by prayer."

(d.) Jesus addresses the demons, Matt. 8:32. He orders the demons to come out, and permits them to go into the swine. In Mark 9:25, Christ rebukes the foul spirit. See also Luke 4:35. In Mark 1:25, Christ orders the demon to hold his peace and come out.

These are sufficient to prove the Scripturalness of this doctrine, and to show that Christ did not speak and act merely from a spirit of accommodation.

3. As to their power over the laws of nature and natural causes.

They have no power to change the laws of nature. These are established by God, and are beyond the power of any of his creatures. He upholds and preserves with the same almighty power with which he created.

But, from Satan's superior wisdom, from his spiritual nature, and from his numerous emissaries, he has great power within the circle of those laws. It is thus that he performs the lying wonders by which, were it possible, he would deceive the very elect. It is thus that, in connection with his power over the mind, he has aided to establish false religions, to vitiate certain forms of the true religion, and to work as the great power of Antichrist in the world.

The connection held by him with the ancient heathen oracles is a subject worthy of study, and eminently suggestive of the extent of the power he exercises. Those oracles failed precisely where Satan's knowledge failed—the want of power to predict the future. Answers that affected present knowledge were abundant. Ambiguous replies that could hear various interpretations were frequent. "Undoubtedly," says Dr. J. Pye Smith, "fraud was practiced. . . . Still there appears satisfactory reason for believing that in some degree, and occasionally there was a real diabolical influence." [First Lines, p. 337.] The case of divination spoken of in Acts 16:16–18 seems conclusive upon this point; "a certain maid," says Luke, "having a spirit of divination met us, which brought her masters much gain by soothsaying. The same following after Paul and us cried out, saying, These men are servants of the Most High God, which proclaim unto you the way of salvation. And this she did many days. But Paul, being sore troubled, turned and said to the spirit, I charge thee in the name of Jesus Christ to come out of her. And it came out that very hour."

Dr. J. Pye Smith presents in his First Lines of Theology some valuable points in reply to the objections that may he made to the doctrine of wicked spirits, and also on the practical uses of the doctrine. [See pp. 337–340.]

CHAPTER 20

CREATION OF MAN

I. THE SCRIPTURE ACCOUNT

THE Scripture account of the creation of man is given in four places in Genesis. The first, in Gen. 1:26–28, is of both male and female. The second is of Adam only, in Gen. 2:7. The third is of the creation of the woman, whom Adam at that time called Isha (woman), because she was taken out of man (Ish). Gen. 2:18–23. Subsequently, ch. 3:20, he called her Eve because she was "the mother of all living." The fourth is found in Gen. 5:1, 2, and states that God called them Adam. There are allusions to the statements thus made in two other places in this book, namely, ch. 3:19, 23 and ch. 9:6, 7. The other Scriptures, both of the Old and New Testaments, endorse the correctness of all the facts stated in Genesis by frequent allusions to one or another of them as undoubted truths. See Ps. 100:3; 103:14; Ecc. 7:29; 12:7; Isa. 64:8; Mal. 2:10, 15; Matt. 19:4, 5; Mark 10:6, 7; Acts 17:25–29; Rom. 9:20; 1 Cor. 11:7–9; 15:45–47; Col. 3:10. The Scripture doctrine thus revealed is that man was created by God, being formed, as to his body, from earthy material, and as to his soul, by direct creation; that he was made male and female, one Adam, in the image after the likeness of God. The Adam thus made, the Scriptures also teach, was the progenitor of all the present race of men. Indeed they appear to allude to him as the embodiment of that race. Adam is not given as a proper name, as are Cain, and Abel, and Noah, but is used to express the creature God proposed to male, (Gen. 1:26), as both male and female. Gen. 5:2. "In all the other instances in the second and third chapters of Genesis, which are nineteen, it is put with the article, the man or the Adam. It is also to be observed that though it occurs very frequently in the Old Testament, and though there is no grammatical difficulty in the way of its being declined by the dual and plural terminations and the pronominal suffixes (as its derivative *dam* blood is), yet it never undergoes those changes; it is used abundantly to denote man in the general and collective sense, *mankind, the human race,* but it is never found in the plural number. When the sacred writers design to express *men* distributively, they use either the compound term sons of men (benei adam), or the plural of enosh, or ish." [Kitto's Cyc., Art. Adam, par. 3.] The importance of this fact will hereafter be seen. It is confirmed by the title of "the second Adam" given to Christ.

II. THE UNITY OF THE RACE

The expression above, "the present race of men," was not intended to intimate a belief that there have been more races of men than one. This, however,
has been contended for; but, while the possibility of other races before Adam or
contemporaneous with him may he admitted, the unity of the present race and
its common descent from Adam must be maintained.

The idea of a Praeadamite race "was first raised to notice by Isaac Peyrere,
who in 1655 published his book styled 'Praeadamitae.' He pretended to find
his Praeadamites in Rom. 5:12–14. The heathen, according to him, are the
Praeadamites, being, as he supposed, created on the same day with the beasts,
and those whose creation is mentioned in the first chapter of Genesis. Adam,
the father of the Jews, was not created until a century later, and is the one who is
mentioned in the second chapter. Since the time of Peyrere, this hypothesis has
been exhibited more connectedly; and has been asserted independently of the
authority of Moses; or in other words it has been asserted that the human race
is older than Moses represents it." [Knapp's Chris. Theol., p. 185.]

So far as this hypothesis is confined to the past existence of other races of men
who had passed away when Adam was created, or who were at least destroyed
before or at the flood, it may be admitted as a possibility. There is no direct
statement of Scripture to the contrary. Any proof which would make it certain,
or even probable, may be admitted. But while this is possibly, it is not probably
true. Nothing in Scripture, not even with great violence, can be wrested to its
support. The account of creation and the manner in which the Adam there created is spoken of is contrary to any idea that the creations in the first and second
chapters of Genesis are of any but the one race. The scientific evidence as to the
method of God's creations concurs with the biblical in furnishing no proof that
God has ever created the same animals at different periods, or from any other
than one original source of each species. While these facts, therefore, are not
conclusive against the possibility of more than one creation of human beings,
they render it highly improbable.

But so far as this is intended to deny the unity of the present race, and to
declare that any portion of it is not of Adamic origin, it is directly contrary to
the Word of God.

1. Because the Scriptures trace the race of men now existing back to Noah,
and through him to Adam.

2. Because they teach also that all others, except the eight saved in the Ark,
were destroyed by the flood. If any other races of men existed before that time,
which is not probable, they must then have been destroyed with the others of
the Adamic race.

3. They not only speak of all mankind in general as though of this one race, but declare expressly that God "made of one every nation of men for to dwell on all the face of the earth, having determined their appointed seasons, and the bounds of their habitation." Acts 17:26. The King James Version has "Made of one blood." This is especially emphatic because spoken to the Athenians, who claimed a special, separate origin from others.

4. The Scriptures account for the universal sinful condition of men, by not only a representative, but natural relation to Adam.

5. Salvation from sin is offered through Christ as the second Adam, whose fitness for his work was secured, not only by his representative relation, but also by his assumption of the same nature with man. Therefore his genealogy in Luke is traced back to Adam. It was also to "the whole creation," Mark 16:15, that Christ commanded his gospel to be preached, and "of all the nations," Matt. 28:19, that he ordered disciples to be made.

Science accords with Revelation in teaching the unity of the race.

1. It shows that among all men are the same essential characteristics which make a man. This is denied by none. There is the same outward form and inward structure, and also like mental and moral characteristics.

2. While variations in each of these respects unquestionably exist, they are all within the limits of a single species.

The science of Comparative Zoology shows:

(1.) That species are capable of great variations.

(2.) That the variations may become permanent.

(3.) That under favourable circumstances, with the lapse of time, this permanence becomes more and more fixed, and incapable of return to the original type.

(4.) That, however, there is after all a tendency to return, which develops itself under similar conditions with those of the original state.

(5.) That while offspring from parents of different species is possible, that offspring is itself either altogether unfruitful, or, as Dr. Cabell says, "the fertility is partial and temporary, rarely, if ever, extending through more than two generations." [Unity of Mankind, p. 77.]

(6.) That the variations in man are at least equalled by those in other species.

Dr. Bachman asserts that "every vertebrated animal, from the horse down to the canary bird and goldfish, is subject, in a state of domestication, to very great and striking varieties, and that in the majority of species these varieties are much greater than are exhibited in any of the numerous varieties of the human race." [Doctrine of the Unity of the Human Race, p. 181, quoted by Dr. Cabell in Unity of Mankind, p. 34.] "Blumenbach," says Cabell, p. 33, "long ago pointed out the great difference between the cranium of the domestic swine and that of the primitive wild boar, and remarked that this difference is quite equal to that which has been observed between the skull of the Negro and the European."

(7.) That the various races of men, when they intermarry, produce offspring which is itself continuously fruitful.

(8.) That while the Negro type of man, the most distinct, and the one showing the greatest variety from the Caucasian or white race, may be traced far back in the monumental history of Egypt, then is no delineation of it in the earliest records for nearly fifteen hundred years. This is admitted by Nott and Gliddon in their Types of Mankind, p. 259, though these writers speak of the Negro "as contemporary with the earliest Egyptians." [See Cabell, p. 91–92.]

3. The science of Comparative Philology also supports the doctrine of the unity of the human race. This science is as yet in its infancy, but has grown vigorously daring the short period of its existence. Already the languages of men have been reduced by some to four, by others to three, and yet by others to two different forms, and the tendency is to connect all language with some one common source. Whether this can be done or not is uncertain. The position is at least conceded that variety in language does not militate against the unity of mankind. It may be impossible to establish absolute unity of speech. The confusion at Babel renders this not improbable. But the investigations of this science show that the idea of several separate physical origins of the race is not true, because the grouping of men, as to physical race, does not correspond with the grouping rendered necessary by their different languages.

Prof. Whitney, who believes that the science of philology cannot now, or ever, decide either for or against this unity, says "it does not seem practicable to lay down any system of physical races which shall agree with any possible scheme of linguistic races. Indo-European, Semitic, Scythian and Caucasian tongues are spoken by men whom the naturalist would not separate from one another as of widely diverse stock; and on the other hand, Scythian dialects of close and indubitable relationship, are in the mouths of people who differ as widely in form and feature, as Hungarians and Lapps, while not less discordance of physical type is to be found among the speakers of various dialects belonging to more than one of the other great linguistic families." [Language and the Study of Language, p. 370.] The fact of this intermingling of dialects and races shows a common origin beyond the time of physical and linguistic changes. Thus do the two sciences, which were once so antagonistic to the doctrine of the unity of mankind, combine with each other to establish its truth.

III. THE NATURE OF MAN

The nature of man is composite. It is usually considered as a union of body and soul.

The body is material, and is the highest form in this world of material existence.

Matter is presented in creation in different forms. It is impossible to say whether it exists, or has ever existed, without special form and substance. Science only knows it as found in different materials, which are called primary, because we cannot reduce them to any more simple form common to more than one. Of these materials, all things that we know are composed. Matter is called inorganic in these simple forms, and yet there is a kind of organism even here. Some of this so-called inorganic matter attains to living organism in plants, which have what is called vegetable life. It exists in a still higher form in conscious, sentient being, known as animal life. The highest organism is in man as an animal. He partakes with other animals of bodily form, appetites, desires and passions. His bony structure is analogous to theirs, which approaches it closely, and yet with marked distinctions which manifest his yet higher life, with nobler capabilities. So, also, is it with his muscular covering or flesh, and his nervous system especially culminating in a brain of superior size and weight. Through the latter, man has capacity for superior intellectual powers over other animals, for the exercise of which his bodily shape is peculiarly fitted. In their mere animal life, the instincts of the lower animals are much stronger than in man, and more reliable. In man instinct is feeble because its place is more than supplied by his higher intellectual nature. It is only when his moral nature is involved, that instincts appear which approach in strength and unerring guidance those of the brute creation.

The personality of man, by which is meant his individual conscious existence, is distinctly associated with his higher nature, the intellectual and the moral. The brute evidently lives in itself and is what it is solely because of its animal life. It cannot go beyond it. There is no outward development in it of itself and even the utmost training by man can carry it no farther than to the development of memory, and obedience through fear, which belong to this animal existence. Even in these only such faint resemblances to man's higher faculties can be reached as man himself attains through self-training in the realm of animal instinct.

It is evident, therefore, that the higher nature of man, so far from being a part of his animal life, either accompanies it or takes its place, and dwells in the body, using it as a means of contact with the external world, in which man, as a spiritual being, is thus enabled to live, and exercise the faculties of his higher nature.

We have already learned the existence of spiritual beings, which, if they have, or can have, form and body at all, have only those of a spiritual nature. Man alone is possessed of both spirit and body. He is, therefore, the link which binds together the world of spirit and that of matter. His existence is not one only, but twofold. Nor is it made so by such a composition as confounds the two elements by mingling them into a third substance differing from each of these two. It is such as makes a union in one personality of both the natures, so that a man is as truly animal as though he were not spirit, and as truly spiritual as though he were not animal. Each nature retains in a mysterious union its own attributes, and properties, absolutely, so that one is merely animal, and the other purely spiritual, and the one personal conscious being is personal and conscious in each, in different or in the same moments, and is also conscious of being at the same time Man, or all that is involved in the united possession of both natures. The consequence of this also is a peculiar possession by Man of all the results of a communication of the properties of one nature to the other without any actual communication. Thus matter, which in itself is without self-motion, or feeling, and only becomes so in animal life, and in that life is without capacity for self-training and skillful manipulation through self-imposed habits, and which especially is not capable of sinful, or holy acts or habits, attains to each of these through the union with a spiritual person; and in a peculiar way, otherwise not possible, becomes receptive of punishment or reward for right or wrong doing. So also a personal spirit, which cannot through his spiritual nature be affected by matter, and cannot act upon it or use it, is through this union operative in it, and by means of the bodily powers is brought into contact with the world of material forces, and becomes a voluntary force in connection with the mechanical laws and forces of the universe. Thus is it, that through this union, man, probably alone, with the exception of God, introduces and accomplishes direct results of conscious purpose in the material universe. Good or evil angels, if they would there operate, must do it through the influences they can exert upon man.

The union of both body and soul is necessary to constitute man. Of necessity, his conscious individuality is inseparably associated with his spiritual nature, for in him there is no separate animal life in the body from that of the spirit which is united with it. Without that spirit, therefore, the body is but a form of clay. But the spirit alone is but a spirit. It has not all of human nature. It is not a man. To make man, the body is necessary, not necessarily the same body always, neither of the same size, nor with all its parts perfect, nor of the same ever continuing materials, nor without change, but such a body as belongs to human nature, and is fitted for the contact of the conscious personal spirit with the world of matter. If, at any time, therefore, the spirit and body shall be separated, the spirit will not properly be called man until a subsequent reunion. Until then it would be known and spoken of as the spirit of the man, or the soul of the man, but not as the man himself. Accordingly the Scriptures speak thus of all men during the period intervening between death and the resurrection of the judgement day. See Rev. 6:9; 20:4; Heb. 12:23, and, according to the interpretation which supposes Christ preached to departed spirits, 1 Pet. 3:19. It is thus also that the resurrection of the body, and its reunion with the soul become necessary to carry out the purposes of God, both as to the rewards and the punishments of the eternal future.

A question here naturally arises as to the nature of the contact between the personal spirit and the body. This we have no means of answering. It is a mystery which, as a fact, is both known and revealed, but of the manner of which we have no revelation, and no knowledge. All must be conjecture. Dr. J. Pye Smith gives in his "First Lines," p. 342, three theories: "(1.) That it is through physical influence materially of mental volitions, and cerebral and nervous action producing muscular motion; (2.) that it is due to occasional cause by which God's omnipotent and universal agency produces all the motions of the body to correspond with the volitions of the mind; and (3.) that it results from pre-established harmony by which it is arranged that they take place at the same time and space, without any influence upon each other." But these are all objectionable. The last makes the body and soul entirely without connection with each other. The second makes God, and not man, operate the body, and that too without the soul's agency in any respect, for that operation of God over the body only accompanies the action of the soul with which it has no connection except that of co-existence. The first is no explanation, for it accepts the physical connection, but does not state how it arises.

Both body and soul are by nature pure in their original condition, sin being found essentially neither in the one, nor in the other. There is nothing in matter that is corrupting, and nothing in the lower nature which of itself begets sin in an innocent soul. On the contrary, while temptation may present itself through the body, the actual sin is committed by the soul either separately or in union with the body. The sinlessness of the soul in its primeval state has been universally admitted.

Each of these constituents of man is a unit. The body is one, though composed of several members, and is affected through one sense only, namely, contact, though that one sense because of its different forms, is usually and conveniently divided into five. The soul also is one, and itself brings the man into contact with the world of mind and spirit. Its powers, likewise, though many, are not separate and independent faculties, but it is the soul that thinks, that feels, that purposes and that loves. For convenience these powers are in

Intellectual Philosophy divided into and discussed under the three heads of the Understanding, the Will and the Affections. These are exercised about all mental and moral truths. Even the knowledge of what is right and wrong is not attained by a different power from that by which we learn what is wise and great. What is called conscience, or the moral faculty, is concerned only with impressing upon us our duty to do the right, and not to do the wrong. But even this is simply the soul recognizing the nature of obligation to God.

Some have supposed that man has more than the twofold elements of body and soul. "Pythagoras, and after him, Plato, and subsequently the mass of Greek and Roman philosophers, maintained that man consists of three constituent elements, the rational spirit (νοῦς or πνεῦμα, *mens*), the animal soul (ψυχή, *anima*), and the body (σῶμα, *corpus*). Hence this usage of words became stamped upon the Greek popular speech. And consequently the apostle uses all three when intending to express exhaustively in popular language the totality of man and his belongings. "May your spirit and soul and body be preserved entire, without blame." 1 Thess. 5:23; Heb. 4:12; 1 Cor. 15:44. Hence some theologians conclude that it is a doctrine given by divine inspiration that human nature is constituted of three distinct elements.

"The use made of these terms by the apostles proves nothing more than that they used words in their current popular sense to express divine ideas. The word πνεῦμα designates the one soul emphasizing its quality as rational. The word ψυχή designates the same soul emphasizing its quality as the vital and animating principle of the body. The two are used together to express popularly the entire man.

"That the πνεῦμα and ψυχή are distinct entities cannot be the doctrine of the New Testament, because they are habitually used interchangeably and often indifferently. Thus ψυχή, as well as πνεῦμα, is used to designate the soul as the seat of the higher intellectual faculties. Matt. 16:26; 1 Pet. 1:22; Matt. 10:28. Thus also πνεῦμα, as well as ψυχή, is used to designate the soul as the animating principle of the body. James 2:26. Deceased persons are indifferently called ψυχαί, Acts 2:27, 31; Rev. 6:9; 20:4; and πνεύματα, Luke 24:37, 39; Heb. 12:23." [Hodge's Outlines, pp. 299, 300.]

Other passages, not mentioned above, upon which light is supposed to be thrown by this distinction, are 1 Cor. 2:14, 15; James 3:15; and Jude 19.

Others, which show a promiscuous use of these words, and thus that the distinction is incorrect, are Matt. 27:50; Mark 15:37; Luke 23:46; John 19:30; Acts 7:59.

This apparent teaching of the New Testament is also that of the Old. The account of man's coming into a living condition is given in Gen. 2:7; "And the Lord God formed man of the dust of the ground, and breathed into his nostrils the breath of life; and man became a living soul." The word נֶפֶשׁ here translated "living soul" means ordinarily mere animal life. It is the same word that occurs in Gen. 1:20, translated "creature that hath life," in 1:24 "living creature," in 1:30 "life," in 2:19 "living creature," in 9:12, 15, 16 "living creature." Gen. 2:7, therefore teaches that man attained his animal life by the inbreathing of God. But Deut. 4:29 uses this same word for the rational spiritual part of man. So also does Deut. 30:10. See also Job 16:4 and 1 Sam. 1:15. Gesenius Lexicon, Sec. 3, says: "To it are ascribed love, Isa. 42:1; Cant. 1:7; 3:1–4; Gen. 34:3; joy, Ps. 86:4; fear, Isa. 15:5; Ps. 6:4; piety towards God, Ps. 86:4; 104:1; 143:8, and confidence, Ps. 57:1. . . . The soul is said to weep, Ps. 119:28; to be poured out in tears, Job 30:16; to cry for vengeance, Job 24:12; and also to invoke blessings, Gen. 27:4, 25. More rarely things are attributed to the soul, mind, נֶפֶשׁ which belong, (a.) to the mode of feeling and acting, as pride, Prov. 28:25; patience and impatience, Job 6:11; (b.) to the will or purpose, Gen. 23:8; 2 Kings 9:15; 1 Chron. 28:9; (c.) to the understanding or faculty of thinking, Ps. 139:14; Prov. 19:2; 1 Sam. 20:4; Deut. 4:9; Lam. 3:20." Also, Sec. 5, he says: "with suffixes it is put very frequently for: I myself, thou thyself, etc." In Sec. 2, par. 3, he had already said as to the relation between this word and רוּחַ, that "they are sometimes opposed, so that נֶפֶשׁ is ascribed to brutes, and רוּחַ to men, Job 12:10; but רוּחַ is also ascribed to beasts in Ecc. 3:21." This word רוּחַ is that which is especially used of the spirit of God; but it is also "spoken both of man and beasts. Ecc. 3:19, 21; 8:8; 12:7; Job 12:10. . . ." Once the human spirit is called the רוּחַ of God, Job 27:3, as being breathed into man from God, and again returning to God. Gen. 2:7; Ecc. 12:7; Ps. 104:29. [Gesen. Lex. under רוּחַ See. 2.]

It is manifest from these facts that the two words are both used in the Old Testament to express both animal life and the higher spiritual nature, and, therefore, that no radical distinction exists between them. The same word which expresses the animal life of beasts is applied to man as a rational and moral being, as well as to his animal life. And the same which usually expresses the higher spiritual nature is also used even of brutes. It is also plain that the same act by which the spiritual nature was conferred upon man brought his animal life into being. In man, therefore, it would seem that the spirit becomes the actual living animating principle, and needs not to have superadded to it the mere animal life, but embraces it within the life which is that of the spirit. The doctrine of the Old Testament on this subject therefore corresponds with that of the New. The constituent parts of man are simply body and soul. When the animal life is the predominant idea, נֶפֶשׁ and ψυχή are most apt to be used, because the spiritual man is regarded especially in that aspect. When the idea of the higher nature is the main feature, רוּחַ and πνεῦμα are used, because reference to that peculiarity of it is most prominent. But the use of all of the words for either aspect shows that it is, after all, the one principle in man simply differently contemplated.

The powers of both soul and body are unlimited within their respective spheres; the word unlimited being taken not in the sense of infinite, but in the greatly more restricted one of indefinite. What man can physically accomplish, either as an individual over his own person or over others, or by combination with others over the world of matter, is so great that no one can ever say the limit has been reached. This is even more true of the soul in its intellectual and moral nature, in the exercise of thought and reason, and in the perception of moral truths and the attainment of holy perfection.

The soul of man, as a true spirit, possesses all the qualifications which belong to spirit. It has individual personality, consciousness, intellectual powers, free agency, capacity of moral action, is subject to law, is capable of voluntary sin, and is accountable to God for its actions, and for any self-caused spiritual condition of sin. It has natural ordained immortality, by which is meant not that God could not have deprived it of life had he chosen so to have ordained—for no created nature can have of itself any power, much less any right of continued immortality; but that God has conferred immortality upon the nature of spirits, and that they are thus immortal through his ordination.

IV. THE ORIGIN OF SOULS

As the soul of the first man was a direct creation of God, the inquiry naturally arises, are the souls of all his descendants thus created, or whence come they? This question becomes a difficult one because of the immateriality and unity and simplicity of the soul on the one hand, and on the other, because of the participation of the spirits of all men in sin.

1. To avoid these difficulties some have believed in the pre-existence of the souls of men, which, either voluntarily or as the punishment of previous sin, enter the bodies of men. In this manner their existence in a sinful condition may be accounted for without propagation of souls on the one hand, or the creation of the souls of sinful men on the other.

This theory of pre-existence has been held in three forms. The first supposes that all the souls of men were created at the same time with that of Adam, each for his respective body, with which it either voluntarily or necessarily unites itself at some fixed period in its earliest existence. Relations to Adam somewhat similar to those of the body, or rather relations which involve the whole man, both soul and body, may cause a sinful condition under which each man, both as to soul and body, is born sinful. The second form maintains that these souls or spirits are unfallen angels which, of their own accord, assume this union with the body, that through it they may attain to the higher relationships to God and the state of greater glory which belong to his redeemed. The third affirms that they are angels who had fallen in another sphere, unto whom God affords this additional probation, or upon whom he has imposed this position as a punishment of their sin.

The first of these forms, to be any explanation at all of the difficulties, must recognize an actual existence of the souls of all men at the same time with that of Adam. To say that the mere idea of these beings was present with the divine mind—in the sense in which Plato and his followers believed the whole creation to exist in the divine mind as a model in accordance with which all things have been made—or in the sense in which all things were present with God in the purpose which, according to the Scriptures, he eternally formed of their future existence, through which he knows them, and they are eternally co-existent with him—is to suppose an actual creation afterwards, and to leave unremoved every objection which may be pressed against the direct creation of each soul at the time of its entrance into the body, and to render useless any theory of pre-existence at all.

But if these souls actually existed, they must at their creation have had conscious life with intelligence and moral character.

The chief objections to the theory in this aspect are:

(1.) That no man has ever had consciousness of a pre-existent state, or memory of things which occurred therein. This fact ought to be conclusive against this theory, for that consciousness in the soul is not affected by its union with or separation from the body, is plain from our consciousness in our present existence, and from what the Scriptures teach of the condition of man between the hour of death and the resurrection.

(2.) The Scriptures give no hint of any creation or existence of the spirit of any man prior to its connection with the body.

(3.) No facts in the human life or in the constitution of man support the theory, nor does reason in any way suggest or sustain it. It has originated entirely in an attempt to escape difficulties.

(4.) It undertakes no explanation of the condition or position of these spirits, regarded either as innocent or guilty, while awaiting the period of their union with the body.

Against the second and third forms the same objection of lack of consciousness and memory exists. Against the second may be especially urged the impossibility for any purpose of a holy being voluntarily choosing a sinful condition, which the theory supposes permitted by God by granting to these spirits their sinful desire, for such choice would itself be sin. Against both the second and the third it may be said that the Scriptures nowhere ascribe the origin of sin in any of the human race to any other source than that of Adam, and that Heb. 2:16 expressly excludes angels from the benefits of Christ's redemption. The King James translation is, "For verily he took not on him the nature of angels, but he took on him the seed of Abraham." But the more correct translations of the Canterbury Revisers and of their American Committee are still stronger. The former is, "For verily not of angels doth he take hold, but he taketh hold of the seed of Abraham." The latter is, "For verily not to angels doth he give help, but he giveth help to the seed of Abraham."

2. Another theory as to the origin of souls which has very extensively prevailed, is that the souls of men, as well as their bodies, are derived from their parents. According to this, it is man as the whole man that begets and is begotten; and as body produces body, so it is thought that soul produces soul. It is commonly known as Traducianism from the Latin traducere, to lead or bring over, as the layer of a vine, for the purpose of propagation. This theory is based upon several grounds.

(1.) Its advocates claim that it is not wholly unsupported by the Scriptures. While Gen. 5:1, declares that God created man "in the likeness of God," in v. 3, it is said that "Adam begot a son in his own likeness after his image, and called him Seth." But this passage "only asserts that Seth was like his father. It sheds no light on the mysterious process of generation, and does not teach how the likeness of the child to the parent is secured by physical causes." [Hodge, Sys. Theol., vol. 2, p. 68.] The fact that God breathed into Adam the breath of life but did not into Eve, is also adduced as proof of the derivation of her soul from his, as well as of her body. But this is an argument from ignorance. We know not how Eve was animated into life, but surely in her case there was no begetting of any kind, and therefore from it, even allowing that her soul came from Adam, no light could be thrown upon that of others subsequent to it. The language of Christ to Nicodemus, (John 3:6), "that which is born of the flesh is flesh, and that which is born of the spirit is spirit," can have no application, because the spiritual birth, or soul-begetting, here spoken of is that of the new nature in man produced by the Holy Spirit of God. It would seem, therefore, that this theory has not any real support from any direct teaching of Scripture.

(2.) But, while this fact is admitted by many of its advocates, it is claimed that this theory accounts better than any other for the transmission of a sinful nature, and is thus especially supported by the Scripture doctrine of Original Sin. The Bible as well as experience teaches that men are born with a corrupt nature, and that the corruption is no less in the soul than in the body. This theory denies that God can directly create a sinful soul, and challenges a just explanation of the sinful state of man, even in infancy, unless it is due, as is the

sinful body, to its connection with that of the parent. It is unquestionably difficult, though not impossible, to give such an explanation as shall be satisfactory,
and hence this is a strong argument in favour of this theory. But, on the other
hand, it is improper and dangerous to say that the doctrine of original sin is not
true, if there be no propagation of souls. That doctrine is plainly revealed, and
is derived from unquestionable facts. Its correctness does not depend upon any
theory which may be presented for its explanation. All that is justifiable is to
show that this theory, if in no other respect objectionable, will account for it.
But the universal sinfulness of man may have otherwise arisen, and whether or
not we know the manner in which it has come to pass, we are not at liberty to
say that its truth depends upon the correctness of any theory which Scripture
has not distinctly connected with it.

(3.) It is also argued in favour of Traducianism that the account of Creation
in Genesis represents God as resting after the creation of man, both male and
female. It is said, that this rest is evidently one from direct creation, because God
is constantly creating mediately through the powers of reproduction conferred
on plants and animals; that, therefore, if the souls of men are produced from the
parent along with the body, there is only in each case an instance of this mediate
creation; but, that, if directly created by God, there appears to be no sense in
which he has ceased from creation, or can be said to have rested "from all His
work which He had made." But nothing can be argued conclusively from these
statements. We know not exactly what is meant by this Sabbath day rest of God.
But that it was not a perpetual rest in all direct and immediate acts, as well as
mediate is seen in various well known instances of God's direct action; as in the
conception of Christ by the Holy Ghost; in the working of miracles; and in the
work of the Holy Spirit in the regeneration of the souls of men.

(4.) Traducianism receives strong support from the transmission of the mental and moral characteristics of men from parent to child. These become equally
fixed and permanent with those of the body. They may be traced throughout
the various branches of any one race. They are found as national peculiarities
which distinguish one people from another. They appear in families, though
not so plainly manifested because of the many intermarriages with other families, and of the tendency to reproduce the spiritual as well as the bodily traits
of remote ancestors. They are often very strongly marked between parent and
child, and the transmission is so plain, that the general law has been laid down
that generally, though not universally, the sons follow the mental and moral
features of the mother, and the daughters those of the father. This argument
would be very decisive could we entirely separate the spiritual man from the
influence of the corporeal. "But," says Dr. Hodge, "this argument is not conclusive, because it is impossible for us to determine to what proximate cause these

peculiarities are due. They may all be referred, for what we know, to something peculiar in the physical constitution. That the mind is greatly influenced by the body cannot be denied. And a body having the physical peculiarities belonging to any race, nation, or family, may determine within certain limits the character of the soul." Sys. Theol., vol. 2, p. 70.

(5.) The advocates of this theory also urge that only thus can we account for such an incarnation of Christ as would make him truly of the race of man. His human soul must, like his human body, have proceeded from his mother. But the incarnation is a mystery as to the manner of which we cannot dogmatize, and from which especially we can draw no conclusions as to others of mankind. We know not even the connection with his mother of the human body of the Son whom she conceived. All that we know is that Jesus was truly her child, and that as such he was of our nature. How he became such is not fully revealed. But, if it be true of all others that their souls are direct creations of God, and yet that they are of the human race, then the fact that the soul of Christ was not derived from his mother would make him no less a man than all others. The incarnation of Christ indeed the rather favours the theory of Creationism; for if his soul and his body were both derived from his mother, it is impossible to see how sin was not transmitted to him as it is to others. On the theory of Creationism we can understand how he could be born sinless, as a pure soul might then have been united with the body miraculously prepared for him, which body itself, because produced by direct divine agency, would also be pure and sinless.

The chief, and almost the only objection to this theory of any weight, is that the idea of propagation of souls involves their materiality. If this be true the theory must be rejected, even if we are left without any satisfactory explanation. That we cannot solve the problem otherwise, does not show that it has no solution.

Any explanation of the transmission of souls must recognize in the soul something different from the body, and something that has all the elements necessary to a true spirit. To suppose, therefore, that the spirit in man is only a higher form of the animal life, to which have been added intelligence and moral capabilities, is to suppose the soul to be incapable of any separate existence from that animal life, and therefore, to be dispelled into non-entity with the death of the body. This is so contrary to what the Scriptures teach of its separate and continued existence after death as not to be admissible for a moment. It is because this has been believed to be necessarily true of it, if in any way material, and because propagation of souls has seemed to involve their materiality, that this theory has been so generally rejected.

But it may be questioned whether any such materialism is essential to a propagation of souls. It is claimed that extension belongs to matter alone, and that only through extension can there arise the capacity for increase in number. But this argues a knowledge of the nature of created spirits which we do not possess. The fact that the unity of nature and attributes in God as the Great Spirit, the Father of Spirits, involves actual simplicity in him, does not prove that the same is necessarily true of the spirits he has created. It is not certain that they may not have some kind of spiritual bodies. Is it not more than possible that he, who, though a simple spirit, can create spirit like himself, but not of his own substance, may be able to confer upon such spirits such a power of multiplication, that, what he does by direct agency in the first creation, he also may do through them in the mediate creations of other spirits? It is not affirmed that this is true, but is it possible to affirm that it cannot be true?

Besides, we should be careful how we dogmatize as to what can and cannot be true of spirits, when we now know so much to be true which *a priori* we should have judged to be impossible. Thus we now know through the creation of man that spirit can be so associated with matter as to give it a fixed location in space; as to bring it into such contact with matter as to be able to act through it, and upon it; and, more than this, that it is so affected by the condition of the material organism with which it is connected, that the outward manifestation and exercise of its powers is weakened or strengthened through that organism and its moral faculties influenced towards sin or holiness. These, and many similar facts, we now know to be true, which, without experience and Scripture teaching, we should have denied to be possible because of the substantial differences of spirit and matter. Even in the Divine Spirit we are taught that forms of plurality exist, which, without the instructions of the Word of God, we might have denied to be compatible with his spirituality and simplicity, yet, which, as now revealed, are seen to be in no respect inconsistent with these necessary peculiarities of the One God.

These facts are not sufficient to enable us to maintain this theory of Traducianism as true, but only as possible, but they at least suffice to keep us from asserting that descent of one spirit from another can only come through some material substance in the soul, and from accepting, as the only possible solution, any other theory which may be accompanied with objections equally insuperable.

3. The more prevalent theory as to the origin of souls is known as Creationism. It maintains that the soul of each man is directly created by God at the time of its union with its body.

The arguments in its favor are thus presented by Dr. Hodge.

(1.) "That it is more consistent with the prevailing representations of the Scriptures. In the original account of the creation there is a marked distinction made between the body and the soul. The one is from the earth, the other from God. This distinction is kept up throughout the Bible. Body and soul are not only represented as different substances, but also as having different origins. The body shall return to dust, says the wise man, and the spirit to God who gave it. Here the origin of the soul is represented as different from, and higher than that of the body. The former is from God in a sense in which the latter is not. In like manner God is said to form 'the spirit of man within him,' Zech. 12:1; to give 'breath unto the people upon it,' 'and spirit to them that walk therein,' Isa. 42:5. This language nearly agrees with the account of the original creation, in which God is said to have breathed into man the breath of life to indicate that the soul is not earthy or material, but had its origin immediately from God. Hence he is called 'God of the spirits of all flesh,' Num. 16:22. It could not well be said that he is God of the bodies of all men. The relation in which the soul stands to God, as its God and Creator, is very different from that in which the body stands to him. And hence in Heb. 12:9, it is said, 'We have had fathers of our flesh which corrected us and we gave them reverence: shall we not much rather be in subjection unto the Father of spirits, and live?' The obvious antithesis here presented is between those who are fathers of our bodies and him who is the Father of our spirits. Our bodies are derived from our earthly parents—our souls are derived from God. This is in accordance with the familiar use of the word flesh, where it is contrasted, either expressly or by implication, with the soul. Paul speaks of those who had not 'seen his face in the flesh,' of 'the life he now lived in the flesh.' He tells the Philippians that it was needful for them that he should remain 'in the flesh;' he speaks of his 'mortal flesh.' The Psalmist says of the Messiah, 'my flesh shall rest in hope,' which the apostle explains to mean that his flesh should not see corruption. In all these, and in a multitude of similar passages, flesh means the body, and 'fathers of our flesh' means fathers of our bodies. So far, therefore, as the Scriptures reveal anything on the subject, the authority is against Traducianism and in favor of Creationism.

(2.) "The latter doctrine, also, is clearly most consistent with the nature of the soul. The soul is admitted, among Christians, to be immaterial and spiritual. It is indivisible. The Traducian doctrine denies this universally acknowledged truth. It asserts that the soul admits of 'separation or division of essence.' On the same ground that the Church universally rejected the Gnostic doctrine of emanation as inconsistent with the nature of God as a Spirit, it has, with nearly the same unanimity, rejected the doctrine that the soul admits a division of substance. This is so serious a difficulty that some of the advocates of the ex-traduce doctrine endeavor to avoid it by denying that their theory assumes any such separation or division of the substance of the soul. But this denial avails little. They maintain that the same numerical essence which constituted the soul of Adam constitutes our souls. If this be so, then either humanity is a general essence of which individual men are the modes of existence, or what was wholly in Adam is distributively, partitively and by separation, in the multitudes of his descendants. Derivation of essence, therefore, does imply, and is generally admitted to imply, separation or division of essence. And this must be so if numerical identity of essence in all mankind is assumed to be secured by generation or propagation.

(3.) "A third argument in favor of Creationism, and against Traducianism, is derived from the Scriptural doctrine as to the person of Christ. He was very man; he had a true human nature; a true body and a rational soul. He was born of a woman. He was, as to his flesh, the Son of David. He was descended from the fathers. He was in all points made like as we are, yet without sin. This is admitted on both sides. But, as before remarked, in reference to realism, this, on the theory of Traducianism, necessitates the conclusion that Christ's human nature was guilty and sinful. We are partakers of Adam's sin, both as to guilt and pollution, because the same numerical essence which sinned in him is communicated to us. Sin, it is said, is an accident, and supposes a substance in which it inheres, or to which it pertains. Community in sin supposes, therefore, community of essence. If we were not in Adam as to essence, we did not sin in him, and do not derive a corrupt nature from him. But if we were in him as to essence, then his sin was our sin, both as to guilt and pollution. This is the argument of Traducianists repeated in every form. But they insist that Christ was in Adam, as to the substance of his human nature, as truly as we were. They say that if his body and soul were not derived from the body and the soul of his virgin mother he was no true man, and cannot be the redeemer of men. What is true of other men must, consequently, be true of him. He must, therefore, be as much involved in the guilt and corruption of the apostasy as other men. It will not do to affirm and deny the same thing. It is a contradiction to say that we are guilty of Adam's sin because we are partakers of his essence, and that Christ is not guilty of his sin nor involved in its pollution, although he is a partaker of his essence. If participation of essence involve community of guilt and depravity in the one ease, it must also in the other. As this seems a legitimate conclusion from the Traducian doctrine, and as the conclusion is anti-christian and false, the doctrine itself cannot be true." [Sys. Theol. vol. 2, pp. 70–72. See the whole discussion, pp. 65–76, especially the concluding remarks, pp. 72–76.]

There are chiefly two objections made to the theory of Creationism: (1.) that God is thus supposed by a direct originating act to create a pure soul to inhabit a sinful body, and thus to partake, necessarily, of its sin; or to create a soul for that purpose already sinful, and (2.) that direct creation is not accordant with his present relations to the world and manner of acting in it. To this latter it has already been replied, that we have instances of God's direct creations, which forbid the assertion that he acts only through secondary means. But it was not intended, then, to assert that God acts in the creation of souls, any more than in their regeneration, entirely apart from all connection with physical circumstances and causes. His action may occupy some relation to these circumstances and causes, though it may not be through them.

In the first section and first paragraph of this chapter in discussing the account of man's creation, attention was also called to the fact that the Scriptures appear to allude to Adam as the embodiment of the race of man, and it was added, "the importance of this fact will hereafter he seen." It would seem from that statement that in some form there is a certain unity in human nature. Those who hold the theory of Traducianism believe that "the souls of children, as well as their bodies, exist in their parents in Adam, either as *real beings,* like the seeds in plants, and so have been propagated from Adam through successive generations, which is the opinion of Leibnitz, in his "Theodicee," or they exist in their parents merely *potentially,* and come from them by propagation or transference." [Knapp's Christian Theol., p. 201.] Now, while the theory of propagation may he rejected, the fact of the unity of human nature still exists. The recognition of that existence will aid in solving many difficulties in theology, and, among others, may afford a probable solution of a direct creation of God, which does not involve responsibility on his part for the guilt of a newly-created soul. If it be true that human nature is one, and yet that men are many, it follows that a man is only "a manifestation of the general principle of humanity in connection with a given human body" [Hodge, vol. 2, p. 75], and that thus he becomes a conscious individual person of that humanity. This is analogous to, but yet quite different from, the threefold personal relations in the Trinity of the Godhead. The latter is a threefold, separate personal subsistence in one common, undivided and indivisible Divine nature or essence. The former embraces many separate individual personal manifestations of one human nature, his appropriate part of which is possessed by each person who thus becomes an embodiment in himself of the common humanity. If, then, it be accordant with God's general method of working, and with his purpose to produce this personal existence under proper conditions, new souls may be thus created whose connection with the common humanity may be as intimate as though they were originally contained in Adam for propagation, and who are therefore created sinful without any more relation of God to their creation than would have existed had they been propagated.

That the common method of God, in the production of life of any kind, may be of this nature is ably set forth by Dr. Hodge in answer to the declaration of Delitzsch that the continued creation of souls is inconsistent with God's present relation to the world, and that he now produces only mediately, i.e. through the operation of second causes.

"This," says Dr. Hodge, "is a near approach to the mechanical theory of the universe, which supposes that God, having created the world and endowed his creatures with certain faculties and properties, leaves it to the operation of these second causes. A continued superintendence of Providence may be admitted, but the direct exercise of the Divine efficiency is denied. What, then, becomes of the doctrine of regeneration? The new birth is not the effect of second causes. It is not a natural effect produced by the influence of the truth or the energy of the human will. It is due to the immediate exercise of the almighty power of God. God's relation to the world is not that of a mechanist to a machine, nor such as limits him to operating only through second causes. He is immanent in the world. He sustains and guides all causes. He works constantly through them, with them and without them. As in the operations of writing and speaking there is with us the union and combined action of mechanical, chemical and vital forces, controlled by the presiding power of mind; and as the mind, while thus guiding the operations of the body, constantly exercises its creative energy of thought, so God, as immanent in the world, constantly guides all the operation of second causes, and at the same time exercises uninterruptedly his creative energy. Life is not the product of physical causes. We know not that its origin is in any case due to any cause other than the immediate power of God. If life be the peculiar attribute of immaterial substance, it may be produced agreeably to a fixed plan by the creative energy of God whenever the conditions are present under which he has purposed it should begin to be. The organization of a seed or of the embryo of an animal, so far as it consists of matter, may be due to the operation of material causes guided by the providential agency of God, while the vital principle itself is due to his creative power. There is nothing in this derogatory to the divine character. There is nothing in it contrary to the Scriptures. There is nothing in it out of analogy with the works and working of God. It is far preferable to the theory which either entirely banishes God from the world, or restricts his operations to a *concursus* with second causes. The objection to Creationism that it does away with the doctrine of miracles, or that it supposes God to sanction every act with which his creative power is connected, does not seem to have even plausibility. A miracle is not simply an event due to the immediate agency of God, for then every act of conversion would be a miracle. But it is an event, occurring in the external world, which involves the suspension or counteracting of some natural law, and which can be referred to nothing, but the immediate power of God. The origination of life, therefore, is neither in nature nor design a miracle, in the proper sense of the word. This exercise of God's creative energy, in connection with the agency of second causes, no more implies approbation than the fact that he gives and sustains the energy of the murderer proves that he sanctions murder." [Sys. Theol., vol. 2, pp. 74, 75.]

The consideration of this question may be terminated by adopting the language with which Dr. Hodge closes his discussion.

"The object of this discussion is not to arrive at certainty as to what is not clearly revealed in Scripture, nor to explain what is, on all sides, admitted to be inscrutable, but to guard against the adoption of principles which are in opposition to plain and important doctrines of the word of God. If Traducianism teaches that the soul admits of abscission or division; or that the human race are constituted of numerically the same substance; or that the Son of God assumed into personal union with himself the same numerical substance which sinned and fell in Adam; then it is to be rejected as both false and dangerous. But if, without pretending to explain everything, it simply asserts that the human race is propagated in accordance with the general law which secures that life begets life; that the child derives its nature from its parents through the operation of physical laws, attended and controlled by the agency of God, whether directive or creative, as in all other cases of the propagation of living creatures, it may be regarded as an open question, or matter of indifference. Creationism does not necessarily suppose that there is any other exercise of the immediate power of God in the production of the human soul than such as takes place in the production of life in other cases. It only denies that the soul is capable of division, that all mankind are composed of numerically the same essence, and that Christ assumed numerically the same essence that sinned in Adam." [Sys. Theol., vol. 2, pp. 75, 76.]

V. THE IMAGE AND LIKENESS OF GOD

In the first account of creation God is represented as saying: "Let us make man in our image, after our likeness." Gen. 1:26. A natural question has arisen whether there is any difference between the words "image" and "likeness." It has been earnestly contended that there is some distinction to be made between them, and various conflicting opinions have been expressed as to what that distinction is. But it is not probable that any was meant or can be established. None is apparent between the original Hebrew words; and the Scriptural use of them elsewhere seems to imply that none exists. In Gen. 1:27, the first of these is used alone, and is twice used. In Gen. 9:6, we have the first word alone, while in Gen. 5:1, the second alone appears, although in Gen. 5:3, both are employed in stating the image and likeness of Adam in which Seth was begotten. The New Testament equally fails to make any distinction. In 1 Cor. 11:7 image (εἰκών) and glory (δόξα) are used; in Col. 3:10 image (εἰκών) alone and James 3:9 likeness (ὁμοίωσις). The assumption, therefore, that there is any distinction between the words is entirely gratuitous. The two are merely synonymous, and are used in accordance with a common Hebrew mode of speech.

A more important question is as to what is meant by that image or likeness.

1. There is certainly no reference to the bodily form of man. God, as pure spirit, has no body in the likeness or image of which man could be created. The body of man, although in many respects superior to that of the brutes, is in a great measure like theirs. The analogy between man and animals generally is very striking and especially that between him and those nearest to him in the stage of being. But there can be no analogy between him and God in this respect. In no way even could special honour be put on man in his physical nature, except as that nature gives evidence of the existence with it of those spiritual powers which elevate man above the brutes. It is as the dwelling-place of that spirit, and because of its intimate association with the life existent in that body, that any sacredness can be attached to the bodily form. It is this, therefore, that is doubtless meant by Gen. 9:6, where the shedding of the blood of man is made punishable on the ground that "in the image of God made he man."

2. That image and likeness consists in the possession of a spiritual nature. It is in this respect that man is like God, who is called "the God of the spirits of all flesh" (Num. 16:22; 27:16); and the Father of spirits (Heb. 12:9). The spirits of men are also spoken of as peculiarly the works of his hands (Ecc. 12:7; Isa. 57:16; Zech. 12:1), and it was to him that our dying Lord commended his spirit. (Luke 23:46.)

As thus spiritual, man has all the peculiarities of a true spirit.

(1.) He is a personal being with individual conscious existence and action.

(2.) He has the intellectual powers by which he knows all things within the sphere of his being.

(3.) He has that power of contrary choice which constitutes him a free agent, although controlled in that choice by the prevailing motive—by which is meant the motive which most pleases him, and which is, therefore, that to which his own nature gives prevalence.

(4.) He has a moral nature, or a nature with reference to which we can say "ought," and "ought not."

(5.) This moral nature as originally existent must have been (a.) not only without taint of sin, and (b.) without tendencies to sin, and (c.) not merely in a condition of such equipoise between sin and holiness as would make the soul indifferent to the one or the other, but (d.) must have been entirely inclined towards the right, with a holy taste for the holiness of God, having capacity to discern its beauty, and inclination to love him as its possessor, accompanied by readiness to obey the law of God, and perception of man's duty to serve him.

That such was the original condition of man's moral nature is evident from Eph. 4:24: "And put on the new man which after God hath been created in righteousness and holiness of truth." These elements, which belonged to the image of God in which man was created, have been lost. They are restored again in the renewing of man when created anew in Christ Jesus. That the whole image was not destroyed by the sin of Adam, appears from the fact that man is spoken of as in that image subsequent to the fall and before the renewal. See Gen. 9:6; James 3:9; 1 Cor. 11:7. But that there was a loss, not merely of innocence, but of original righteousness, is evidently to be inferred from the above mentioned passage in Ephesians.

(6.) Perpetuity of existence also belongs to the nature of created spirit, and is another point of similarity between all spirits and God. This is commonly called immortality. But created spirits have not an immortal spiritual life. The soul may die. The death of the soul, however, is not the cessation of conscious personal existence. It is simply the destruction of its spiritual life by its contamination by sin and its separation from the favour of God. What the Scriptures teach of the death of the soul shows, therefore, that natural immortality should not be affirmed of man's spiritual nature. But perpetual existence has been given by God to the nature of created spirits. He might have made that nature otherwise. But he has chosen that it shall be ever existent. This perpetuity of existence is, however, merely in his purpose. He could have willed otherwise. No creation of God could have such a nature as of itself to be imperishable. It has been argued from the simplicity of the soul that it cannot be destroyed by God. But evidently he who created without compounding could also destroy without dividing. But he has chosen to give such a nature to spirit that to that nature belongs perpetuity of existence. It is, however, not self-existent, as is God, for it has not in itself the power of self-existence. Without God it could no longer be. It must be preserved, in the conferred nature, by that same power which created it. But God has given this nature to spirits, which he purposes ever to preserve, and, through that gift and that preservation, they have an endless existence.

3. When God purposed to make man, he also said, "And let them have dominion over the fish of the sea, and over the fowl of the air, and over the

cattle, and over all the earth, and over every creeping thing that creepeth upon the earth." Gen. 1:26.

Because of this language some have supposed that this dominion was also a part of the image and likeness of God.

But, evidently, this was an office conferred upon the man made in God's image, and not a part of that image. The Scripture presents it as something that was to follow after the nature was conferred upon man. The resemblance between him and God, in this respect, is very striking. That becomes more so, when we recognize the fulfillment of this purpose in its highest sense in the mediatorial dominion of the God-man. But this position is one of office, and not of nature, and the image of God declared of man is manifestly an image of his nature.

VI. MAN PERFECT BUT NOT INFALLIBLE

It was after the creation of man that God saw, as to everything that he had made, that it was "very good," literally "exceedingly good." Gen. 1:31. On the previous days we are only told that he saw it was good. There seems here a special emphasis, therefore, as to the perfection of man's entire nature. The points of that perfection have been exhibited in showing that man was made in the image of God. But, that it did not include perpetual continuance in it, we know from the fact that man fell from it in sinning against God. His nature, therefore, was fallible. In this respect he was not peculiar, for, as we have heretofore seen, there have been angels also who kept not their first estate. Indeed fallibility belongs to the nature of created spirits. It is involved in their possession of the power of contrary choice, that whenever good and evil are presented, the latter may be chosen, and thus the spiritual creature may fall. Any idea of a probation implies the presentation of such choice. The fall of a spiritual king may be prevented, either by not appointing to it a probation, or presenting the trial under such circumstances as will leave no temptation to choose the wrong, or by God's so influencing the mind as to counteract all the power of such temptation. But, that God has a right to test his creature is unquestionable, as well as that he is not bound to surround him with such circumstances, or so to counteract the power of all temptation, as to make sinning impossible. But, if he should thus protect or decline to test, the natural fallibility of the creature would still be a fact. He is under these circumstances not liable to fall simply because God protects him from that liability. He has not an infallible nature. The holy angels are often spoken of as confirmed in holiness; but this is not due to any change of nature, but must either be known from a knowledge of God's purpose and perhaps of his promise, even if in part, or altogether to be accomplished by what they have seen of the fearful evil of sin in the other angels, or in man. Without such promise, or declared purpose of God, there is no assurance that they may not yet fall.

The perfection, therefore, of any created being does not consist in infallibility. The fact that man has fallen, argues nothing against his original perfection. For this, he needed only to have truly the nature which God gave him. God could not give him an infallible nature, though he could preserve him infallible in whatever nature he might choose to bestow. But he was under no obligation to do this; none to man; none to his own righteous nature. He had the right to test man at his will, and thus testing, to leave him to himself without constraint to the contrary, to choose as he might see fit. This he did, and man fell; but his fall was not due to the lack of any natural perfection.

CHAPTER 21

PROVIDENCE

INTIMATELY associated with the doctrine of Creation is that of Providence, which is, however, a distinct method of Divine activity. By acts of Creation, God brings into existence the things which he makes, and confers upon them their respective natures, qualities, properties, modes of existence, and laws of being, thought and action. By acts of Providence, he simply preserves these creations, or permits or causes decay or change in them, to such an extent, and within such limits as he has purposed; and, at the same time, in fulfillment of like purpose, he directs, controls and guides them in accordance with the natures he has given them, and the laws he has imposed upon them.

Providence is also closely allied to Predestination or Purpose; but the distinction between these two is also equally clear. The Purpose of God in his predetermined plan as to what shall be done in his creation by himself or by others. It fixes the events which shall happen, and the methods and agency by which they will take place. But Providence is the actual doing, or permitting the things purposed, and securing their ends thus designed. The purpose also is formed in eternity; the providential acts are performed in time.

But, despite these very obvious distinctions, Providence has been confounded both with the Purpose and Creation; some holding that there is no other Providence except what is involved in Purpose; and others going to the other extreme, and maintaining that Providence is after all only a continual creation, and that there is no other connection between antecedent and consequent events than exists in the Divine efficiency giving every moment renewed existence by acts of direct creative power. Each of these views is opposed to reason and Scripture, which teach that there is a divine efficiency operating in this world differing in many respects essentially from that exercised in creation. This efficiency is displayed both in the preservation and government of the universe, and of the things which are contained within it.

I. PROVIDENTIAL EFFICIENCY NOW OPERATING

1. In presenting the proof that providential efficiency is now operating in the world, it is natural that attention should be called to the almost universal belief in the providential action and care of God. This is based upon the same feeling

195

of self-dependence in man to which reference has been made in the proofs of
the existence of God. It is the witness to us which God gives, not only that he
exists, but that he supports and sustains us in every moment of being.

2. A second proof may be drawn from the world about us. Every argument
it has afforded for the being of a God becomes equally conclusive of his providential care. The argument from causation, in tracing back all causes to some
being who has the cause of his existence in himself, forces us to find in the present efficiency of such a being, the final ground for all things that now occur.
That from design leads us constantly to trace the purpose God has had in view
in each event of life, and thus proclaims the presence and efficiency of him
who is seen to be working out, even now, the purpose he has eternally formed.
Moreover, the evidence that the world now affords that it is not self-existent
and independent, proves the presence and efficient energy of one upon whom
it depends for the properties, qualities and life of its varied forms, and for their
continued existence.

3. The fact, which we have learned, of a creation out of nothing, shows that
the whole universe exists only through the will and power of God. Since it
could only thus come into being, so it could only remain in being. Any contrary doctrine could only be held by those who deny a creation out of nothing.
The history of philosophical opinions shows that this is true. The doctrine of
Providence has only been denied by those who have believed in the eternity of
matter. It is possible to conceive, in the absence of other proofs to the contrary,
that, as man constructed machines, and leave them to work through the laws
of nature, so, if nature were self-existent and eternal, and if it possessed of itself
all its attributes and qualities, the mere fact that God has given it form would
not necessitate his continued presence; he would be acting then, as man does,
in subordination to, and in the use of the properties and qualities of matter.
But, God may use these things in matter, he does not use them in personal subordination to their properties and qualities; but as himself the sovereign Lord.
He has given these qualities. He could take them away. He could counteract
them. He can destroy them. They exist only because he wills and causes. But
such "will" and "causes" is only his providential operation by which he preserves
them, and uses them, as their Lord, for his own purpose. His is the exercise of
present divine efficiency in them and through them.

4. The nature of God himself also furnishes indubitable testimony to his
providential operations. These arise in opposite directions; from the limitations
of his nature on the one hand, and its infinity on the other. As heretofore seen,
there are some things which God cannot do. He cannot do impossibilities. He
cannot confer his own incommunicable attributes upon another. This limitation arises from the fact that he is God, and beside him there can be none

else. It is this limitation which makes it possible to create a world which shall be self-existent and independent, and which, as being such, will not need his efficient action for its support and care. To do so would be to confer on it his own nature.

On the other hand, the illimitable nature of God's attributes makes it impossible that he should not be efficiently present always with his creation. His omnipresence does not simply make him capable of being everywhere. He cannot be absent from his creation. He cannot withdraw himself even if he will. His knowledge of all events within his creation is also necessity of his being. He cannot be ignorant of them if he would. The fact that he does not know of the existence of anything is of itself not only a proof that it does not exist, but that it cannot exist. Because of his goodness also he must wish the happiness of his creatures, and must make provision for that happiness. This arises not from any obligation to them, but from another necessity of his nature. He must be benevolently good. He must beneficently bestow wherever there are objects for such bestowal. The omnipresence, infinite knowledge and goodness of the Almighty God, therefore, render necessary his providential care over his creation. There can be but one thing that can hinder this benevolent care, and that is sin, which, by demanding the punitive exercise of God's justice, may change into punishment and misery that which otherwise would be happiness and joy. But this, so far from destroying providence, only introduces God as providentially acting in the form of government also, instead of preservation alone. He does not withdraw himself because of this sin. He is still present with the sinner. He continues to know his ways. He exercises providential care, and even sends blessings still upon him. He modifies his action only to correspond with the modified relation sin has introduced. Therefore, as the ruler and governor of the universe, he inflicts the punishment which sin has made necessary. Sin alone has brought into existence this restraining and punishing rule and government. But for it all would be merged into that fatherly care which seeks only to bless, and protect, and guide. The fact that there would be rewards does not prove any other kind of government; for the rewards of God are, after all, but gracious gifts, utterly undeserved, in no respect due except as sovereign bounties, and given under no obligation than arises from his own truth which binds him to his purposes and leads him to fulfill his promises.

5. The Scriptures abound in testimony to God's providential efficiency in the world. It is given in every imaginable form. General statements are made, as in Nehemiah 9:6, where the Lord is said to have made the heavens and their hosts, and the earth and seas and all that is therein, and to preserve them. Specific rule is declared over all the phenomena of nature, such as over clouds, wind, rain, hail, snow, ice, cold, frost, thunder, lightning, storm, earthquakes, and all other

natural events; many of which, formerly deemed accidental, are now seen to be governed by inexorable laws of God. The beasts of the field, and the birds of the air are said to be carefully watched over by him. It is even he that clothes the flowers with their beauty by encircling them with his own shining garment of light. But men are his especial care. He provides the food of their bodies, and in a peculiar way watches and rules over their souls and lives. This he does with respect to the wicked as well as the good. His care extends to individuals, to families, to nations, and throughout the world. It appears not in great events only, but in those exceeding small, even to the numbering of the hairs of each one's head. So minute is the supervision asserted, that some have even thought that the language of Scripture partakes of hyperbole. But the investigations of the microscope have shown that even to the insects the most minute and invisible to the human eye has God given most beauteous forms and perfect outward coverings. His creative care has therefore descended to the things most minute. Thus has the way been opened to the belief that the Scriptures even cannot tell us how minute is the providential care which God is now exercising over his whole creation.

II. PROVIDENCE IS NOT CONTINUOUS CREATION

The evidences of continuous divine action within the world have been so manifest that they may have been led to the opposite extreme of deeming them actually renewed at every moment.

So far as the intention has been to magnify the extent and individual number of the providential acts of God, there is no especial harm in thus loosely talking of them as continuous creations. It might be well said that the power necessary to continue all things in existence is as great as that which would bring them each moment out of nothingness into existent life; and that the particularity with which each of these innumerable existences is looked after and cared for is as minute as if each were at the moment endowed with existence, nature, qualities and powers. So long as we look at the mere glory to God's creative energy and power, there appears no other objection to the term continuous creation than its loose inaccuracy. But, viewed in other aspects, this doctrine is seen to be not only inaccurate and false, but extremely dangerous.

1. It takes away all the relation of cause and effect. No cause and its effects can have any relation to each other if both be separate creations of God. The former is not productive of the latter, nor the latter the result of the former. The one is not a cause, nor the other an effect. But if this be true, what confidence can we have in any of the phenomena of nature? I determine to accomplish some end. I put forth the energy I perceive necessary. The end is attained. I

believe it to be due to my action and purpose. But, according to this theory, the result is an act of God which occurs at the moment. It is not my action. It is not the result of my effort or power, but it is only something which God creates and which seems to have a connection with my purpose and effort, but has not. All reality is thus taken from life. If I find that I am mistaken here, I can have neither belief not confidence in anything. If there be no real cause here, then my mind deceives me when it urges me to seek a cause for all things, and not to rest, as to the universe, except in the belief of an uncaused First Cause. The tendency of such a theory is, therefore, to actual atheism. It seems to begin with a most credulous confidence in the Almighty, only to end in absolute disbelief of everything.

2. It leads to the acceptance of essential pantheism, if it does not drive to actual atheism. Every efficiency here is God himself acting. It is he that everywhere is alone the actor. The phenomena which accompany his actions are only phantoms, not realities. The acorn is not the fruit of the tree. It is his direct production. It is a new creation of his hands. When it is planted, it is neither the acorn, nor the soil, nor the seasons, nor the air, nor anything else which causes a tree to come forth and grow. It is God, who at each moment makes a new creation different from what has preceded, though apparently its successor. God thus becomes the animating soul of the universe, and acts in it as the souls of men do in their bodies.

3. It absolutely takes away all responsibility for sinful acts, and all virtue in those that are holy. These are no longer the acts of the individual. He is deceived when he thinks that he wills them or does them. There are no actions but those of God. Besides, there is no one to be responsible. If the creation is a new one at each moment, the creature who did the act is gone. There is no one to be punished. The curious phenomenon of multiplied contradictions is therefore presented here. There is no action of a man, for it is God that has acted. There is no man that has acted, because the one before us is another creation; and while we have been speaking, he too has disappeared, and another has taken his place. The deed has no character in its relation to man; for the man has not done it. God alone is responsible for it; for it is his act alone, into which has flowed neither the will, nor the power, nor the purpose, nor the activity of man, but only those of God.

4. It takes away all the evidences of outward creation, and introduces pure idealism. We believe in an outward creation because of the effects which, through the sense, it produces upon our minds. But, if everything is a direct creation, these impressions on our minds are themselves direct creations made by God, and not by the outward world. They give no evidence, therefore, of the existence of anything except of God and of the individual who is conscious of

receiving them. If they come from God alone, there is no necessity for something outwardly corresponding to them. God and each individual, therefore, may be all that exists. Certainly they are all of the existence of which any one can have any knowledge.

III. THE METHOD OF GOD'S PROVIDENCE

It is impossible for us to comprehend, much less to explain, the manner of God's providential action. We know no more of this than the manner in which he created. Ignorance of the method of either action is, however, no reason for believing that it does not exist. We, who cannot tell how our own spirits act upon and through our own bodies, may well accept the fact of the action of the universal Spirit, as everywhere operating, though much of the mysterious and incomprehensible is therein involved. A few statements may however be made, upon this subject, of facts which may be known.

1. That this action is universal. It is not limited to certain kinds of creation, but extends to all.

2. That it is not the same on each but accords with the nature of which is governed. The action upon the material universe is more purely mechanical, and governed by the operation of physical law. So far as life of any kind, whether vegetable, animal, or spiritual, is connected with. or composed of matter, these mechanical laws must also be actively enforced. But we know not how far even vegetable life is inseparable from mere mechanical law. Certainly not entirely so, since it is also dependent in some degrees upon the action of voluntary force and labor in man, who is an instrument under God of such life. In animal life we have the phenomena of instinct, as well as of self-acting and voluntary powers. The providence of God must here differ from its relation to mere material substances which are inert, and without senses, or volitions. But we can form no idea of the nature of the specific action thus rendered necessary. In man the providential action of God is further complicated by the extent of his reasoning powers, by the freedom of his will, by his self-control over his affections, by his original capacity to do right or wrong, and especially by his fallen condition. The most difficult problems as to God's providence naturally arise here. That we cannot solve them does not disprove providence. That the action of providence is in accord with the nature of man, and is consonant with the holiness, justice, and goodness of God, we feel assured. It is well for us to rest in such assurances in matters which we cannot penetrate. It is wise always to recognize that God acts according to his nature, in acting upon all things according to theirs. His own character, therefore, must characterize his actions, which must consequently be holy, just, wise, and good.

3. God's action must, therefore, accord with the free agency of man. Free agency belongs to the nature of an intelligent moral creature. He must have freedom of choice, or he would not be responsible for his action. The very essence of responsibility consists in the power of contrary action, had one so pleased. God's providential action cannot, therefore, be such as to destroy man's freedom of will, or the power of this contrary choice.

But this does not forbid the use of inducements to any specific action, nor the placing of man in circumstances which would influence, or control his acts. Were these influences compulsory, so as to force to action against his will, the freedom of man would be destroyed, and with it responsibility. But, wherever they are only persuasive, so as to lead him to delight in, or to choose a specific course of action, through his own good pleasure, liberty is preserved, and man is accountable for his choice. The providential influences of God are of this nature only. Experience so teaches, and the Scriptures so declare. Man is conscious, at every moment, that his act was the outcome of his own good pleasure. We could have no stronger proof that God has providentially acted in accordance only with our nature, except the word of God himself. This testimony is added, when he not only ascribes our sinful acts to our own will, but declares that he holds man responsible, and will punish him for them.

4. God may, however, originate action in man, by producing some such change as is the result of the exercise of direct power. The man may be conscious of this fact, and may feel assured that this change is not due to himself. In other ways, also, God may directly introduce controlling influences which forcibly originate new purposes in man, and so direct his will, that it finds that which is pleasing to itself far different from the past. But this action of God is of the nature of creative acts, and not of providential. The Scripture so speaks of them, and it may be doubted whether they belong to the realm of providence. Thus the words "creation," and "creature," are constantly applied to those who are vitally connected with Christ, because of the new heart which God has given, and of their renewal in the image of God.

But whether these acts are to be regarded as creative only, or as providential also, it is evident that in them the restrictions, arising from his nature, as to creative acts, appear. The compulsion is towards holiness, not towards sin. The new heart is one fitted for God's service, and it loves him, and desires to obey his statutes. He could not change a heart of holiness to one of sin, without its own voluntary action, any more than he could create a sinful being. He cannot directly tempt to sin, any more than he could make a man with original sin. His own righteous and holy nature is the guaranty of this, and forbids that he should act otherwise.

5. We are thus led to perceive what is the method of God's providential action as to the sins of men, and what are his relations to them.

One question as to his connection with sin no man can answer, namely, why he has allowed its existence at all. We can have no doubt that he could have prevented it. He can do anything not contrary to his own nature; and in that nature can be found no necessity for its existence. We can, however, see many ends which he has had in view in allowing it in his universe. But with all this, with our present knowledge of his will, we are compelled to confess that we cannot tell why he saw that it was better to admit than to exclude it.

On the other hand, however, no reason can be justly given why he should not have done so when he so purposed. There is nothing in its existence which makes him its author or shows any unholy action on his part in its introduction. Nor is there any evidence of any lack of power to prevent its origination, nor of any want of benevolent love to his creatures in permitting it.

Of the origin of sin in the universe our information is very meagre. We have already seen this as to the fall of angels. That of man, to be hereafter considered, gives us little information beyond as few facts. But, even in these brief statements, we are taught explicitly that sin is not due to any creative act of God, but that it came into existence entirely under his providential government. The dealings of God with it, at present under that providence, show the truth of the above statements. The Scriptures and our own experience are the sources of our information. From these we learn:

(1.) That sin exists only in accordance with the purpose of God. Had he not seen fit, it could never have appeared in the universe. Its presence proceeds from no necessity of his nature, nor from any antagonistic power which he could not resist.

(2.) It cannot occur at any time nor in any form without his permission. While he does not actively originate it, he holds such absolute control over it that no single event in connection with it can take place without his permission.

(3.) It cannot attain any end, however naturally operative towards it, which he has not designed shall be attained.

(4.) It cannot go any further than the limits he has assigned.

(5.) Through it he works out his own righteous purpose, and not the sinful designs of those who are committing the sin which he thus overrules.

(6.) In any one act the ends of himself and the sinner may greatly differ.

(7.) Likewise the same act may be sinful in the sinner, and not sinful in God. This is due to the difference of relations borne to persons and things by God and man. God has supreme control over life and property. Man has not. God may take away life or property by the hand of the assassin or the thief. He only does what it is his right to do. But it is sin in the man through whom he acts, because he has not the right to either of these things.

(8.) The sinful actions of men may be sinful, either from the motives which prompt them, the ends in view, or the means by which they are accomplished. God may concur in such acts, from motives, with ends, and in the use of means which are altogether most holy.

(9.) The concurrence of God with the sinner is limited to the support of the natural faculties, in which support there is neither sin nor innocence; sin consisting not in their use, but in the intention with which they are used, and the object sought by that use.

(10.) The concurrence of God according to the regularity of general laws seems eminently desirable. If, whenever man acted virtuously, his powers of action were sustained, but not so when acting otherwise, there would be really no free agency in man, for he would not have the power of contrary choice and action. On the other hand; there would no longer be such regular action of the universe as seems necessary for the happiness and comfort of mankind. The action of nature would every day be suspended in thousands of instances, and confusion would exist.

IV. DISTINCTION IN PROVIDENCE

There have been several distinctions made as to the providence of God.

1. The most common is that of General, or Universal Providence, and Special, Singular or Particular Providence. By general providence is meant the general care which God takes of the universe and all it contains, in preserving and upholding it under the general administration of the laws he has given it. By special providence is meant the minute care by which some events are supposed to take place immediately under his supervision or by his direct providential action.

It is unquestionably true that the acts of Providence extend to minute objects and specially marked events. But this is no reason for making this distinction which would seem to imply an indifferent, careless providence about all things else. The truth is that providence is of such a nature as to reach every natural event by the operation of general laws. It is a marked proof of the wisdom of God that he can so direct all the affairs of the universe as, without need of special action, to accomplish all the events he chooses. All providence, therefore, is general, because operated through general laws. It is also special, because every individual event comes to pass under God's own inspection, and through his own will and work.

"A general and special providence," says Dr. A. A. Hodge, "cannot be two different modes of divine operation. The same providential administration is necessarily at the same time general and special, for the same reason, because it reaches without exception equally to every event and creature in the world. A general providence is special because it secures general results by the control of every event, great and small, leading to that result. A special providence is general because it specially controls all individual beings and actions in the universe. All events are so related together as a concatenated system of causes, and effects, and conditions, that a general providence that is not at the same time special is as inconceivable as a whole which has no parts, or as a chain which has no links." [Outlines of Theology, p. 266.]

2. A second distinction is into ordinary and extraordinary providence. By the ordinary are meant those acts which, according to general law, commonly occur in everyday life, and which are supposed to display no extraordinary action or purpose. By the extraordinary are meant any acts, such as miracles or prophecies, which are not naturally to be expected, and are due to extraordinary divine intervention.

3. Another distinction is into mediate and immediate. This is similar to the last, except that this looks at providence from the agency of the divine act, whether done directly and without means, or mediately by means. The other views these acts according to their frequency and the impression thus produced by evident divine interposition.

4. A fourth distinction is into physical or real, and spiritual or moral. The former regards providence as exercised about natural objects or things, the latter about persons, especially in their moral and spiritual relations.

V. THE UNEQUAL DISTRIBUTION OF GOOD AND EVIL

The most serious objection to the doctrine of divine providence is deduced from the unequal distribution of good and evil in the world. Blessings are not apparently bestowed proportionately upon the good and afflictions upon the wicked. It has been claimed that this is an evidence that God does not watch over and govern the world. Dr. J. Pye Smith ably answers this objection. [See his First Lines, pp. 162–164.] The following is an abstract of his argument:

1. "A man who would reason fairly cannot but, on the very threshold of this argument, attend to the sinful condition of the whole human race. The *sin of man*,"

(1.) "*Merits* the experience of penal evils, in all their variety."

(2.) "This sin is the *cause* and *occasion,* sometimes directly, at other times more indirectly and remotely, of human sufferings."

2. "Upon the broad scale of observation and history many examples of retribution are to be observed."

3. "This distribution of good and evil is by no means so unequal as appears to superficial observation."

4. "Even good men are the chief occasions of their own sufferings."

5. "Their sufferings are made in the highest degree beneficial to them, as means of religious improvements." (Heb. 12:4–11.)

6. "The piety, virtue and good moral conduct of upright persons procure to them, in the ordinary course of affairs, a considerable measure of esteem, regard, kindness and service from their fellow-men; and consequently a much higher degree of personal and social enjoyment than they would have if they were not religious characters."

7. "The *objects* which men commonly regard as good in themselves and for their own sakes are in reality not so. They are good only as they are used; only when they are made the means of moral improvements."

8. "We are very far from being competent judges of the state of the heart, and the degree of real holiness possessed by the *subjective individuals:* but we know enough to by assured that *the reality* in these important matters is far from being in accordance with the obvious and superficial *appearance*. It cannot be doubted that in many instance men acquire credit with the public for great religious excellence which is by no means justly imputed, as to either the degree or sincerity of it; and that deep and humble piety exists in some instances where extraordinary and unfavorable circumstances surround its possessors as with a dark cloud."

9. "The afflictions of real Christians are instruments of the greatest internal blessings. They are also means of benefit to others by their exhibition of the most edifying examples, and by the weight which instruction and admonition thus receive."

10. "But we cannot judge of this question with any approach to completeness without bringing into the account the future state. The present state is but the imperfect and preparatory condition of our existence, the period during which all must be done that is to fit us for eternity. All temporal things are as nothing compared with this great issue of all our labours and trials."

CHAPTER 22

THE FALL OF MAN

THE chapter on the creation of man presented him in all the sinless perfection with which God can create an intellectual and moral spiritual being. It was there shown that this consisted, as the Scriptures declare, not merely in an innocent sinlessness, which left him without taint or tendency to sin, but in original righteousness, which comprised a love of holiness and natural choice of good rather than of evil.

The excellence of such a nature is seen in the difficulty which men have had in explaining the possibility of its fall. The value of this fact as testimony to the goodness of God is not to be overlooked. To escape this difficulty some have even maintained that there was originally in man a mere condition of equilibrium in which it was as easy to choose the wrong as the right. Nor can it be shown that, if this had been true, a trial upon probation, in which was given a choice of good and evil, with consequent reward and punishment, would have been unjust to man or derogatory to the character of God. But the plain teaching of Scripture is that man was not created in perfect equilibrium, but with a holy nature, the whole tendency of which was naturally towards the good and the holy. In thus fitting him for his trial, God is seen, by special endowment, to have given him most graciously all the powers possible to fit him for a wise choice in any instance in which he should be left to act according to his good pleasure.

I. HOW COULD MAN FALL?

In reply to the question how a being thus endowed could fall, the following suggestions may be made. While they may not be entirely satisfactory, they must be recognized as at least constituting a possible explanation of a subject so completely environed with difficulties.

1. The excellent nature thus bestowed was, after all, only that of a mere creature. The perfection, as such, could be only natural and bestowed, not essential and inalienable. Therefore, unless preserved by the purpose and acts of God, it might be lost.

2. It was that of a creature, the excellence of whose action consisted in always choosing the right and rejecting the wrong, but which had the power, should

206

the inclination arise, of making and pursuing a contrary choice. No natural or compulsory necessity existed to prevent such choice. The right would only be chosen so long as the motive to do so should be the prevailing one. While, therefore, the nature wholly inclined by its nature to the right would naturally and certainly act in that direction, yet if that nature could be so affected as to incline towards the wrong, there would be no hindrance to its sinful action.

3. Under such circumstances, against any gross violation of the law of God, or sinful rebellion against him, the heart would so naturally revolt that the beginning of sin in this direction would be almost impossible. But if any desire should be awakened in itself sinless when duly exercised, that desire might so increase as ultimately to acquire sufficient strength to overcome the right tendency of the nature, and to lead finally by undue exercise to wrong action for its gratification.

4. The foundation for such desire might be found in the wish to gratify the lower appetites, or to attain higher exercise of the intellectual faculties.

5. The cause of its springing up would naturally be the denial of some means by which it would appear that either or both of these wishes could be attained. This accords with the principle stated by the Apostle Paul. "I had not known coveting except the law had said, Thou shalt not covet." Rom. 7:7.

6. The natural result would be not immediately to determine to do the wrong, but to question the justice or intention with which the act was forbidden.

7. This doubt of God would so lead the nature towards sin that the act would then be done from the motive arising from the desire of gratifying either the sensual or the spiritual appetite.

II. HOW DID MAN FALL?

We have the account of the fall in Gen. 3:1–7. The statement is very brief yet complete. This is a proof of its inspiration, which also appears from its accurate agreement with the best thoughts men have been able to attain as to how such an event could take place.

The narrative shows that the attack upon man had to be made in a most subtle manner.

1. We have the occasion; in God's forbidding man to eat of the fruit of a certain tree, called "the tree of the knowledge of good and evil." Gen. 2:17.

2. We have that love of wisdom, natural and proper in an intelligent being, excited by the idea that through its increase would be given elevation in the scale of existence.

3. Led by this desire to think of its possible gratification, the very name of the tree whose fruit was forbidden seemed to confirm the language of the tempter.

4. The good thus attainable appeared to be one which God would so naturally wish to bestow, that it created doubt whether God could really have meant to forbid its use, and particularly whether he would fulfill his threats, or had even intended them to be effective to prevent the proposed action.

5. Then followed the result, the statement of which shows the processes through which the mind of the woman had gone; "when the woman saw that the tree was good for food, and that it was a delight to the eyes, and that the tree was to be desired to make one wise, she took of the fruit thereof, and did eat, and she gave also unto her husband with her, and he did eat." Gen. 3:6.

The Scriptures say but little of the difference between Adam and Eve in this transaction. The narrative of Genesis simply relates that the woman was the first tempted, and the first to sin, and that through her the fruit was given to the man. The only other allusion is that in which Paul states that "Adam was not beguiled, but the woman being beguiled hath fallen into transgression." 1 Tim. 2:14. This may mean only that the woman was tempted by Satan, while the man was not; or that Eve believed the tempter, and did not perceive the consequences of transgression, while Adam acted in full knowledge of them.

As to the reality of an external agent in the temptation, there has been no little dispute. Some have held that there was no actor, but that the temptation was the result merely of the emotions and desires of the woman. But the Scriptures say distinctly that there was a serpent, present and active. Temptation, through a serpent might have occurred in several ways.

1. A serpent might innocently and alone have been the occasion of the suggestion of the thoughts to Eve.

2. Some evil being might have accompanied the innocent acts of the serpent to suggest to her mind the thoughts by which he would tempt her to sin.

3. This evil spirit, in the form of a serpent, or taking possession of an actual serpent, might have used and uttered the language or suggested the thoughts attributed to him in the narrative.

4. A fourth explanation has been suggested, and is somewhat advocated by Turner in his Commentary on Genesis, p. 187. This supposes that the devil was the only agent, and that all reference to the serpent is allegorical.

The Scriptures seem to accord more nearly with the third of these theories. There appears to be no valid objection to the acceptance of this their most obvious import.

(1.) It is surely not inconsistent with the power ascribed to Satan that he should thus enter the form of a creature already existent, or even assume the appearance of such a creature. "For even Satan fashioned himself into an angel of light." 2 Cor. 11:14. The temptation of Jesus shows that Satan can assume bodily form. Mere mental suggestion cannot account for all that then occurred. It is necessary to believe that he appeared in bodily form to our Lord and addressed him in words uttered with the voice. This is involved in the offer recorded in Luke 4:7. "If thou therefore wilt worship before me it shall all be thine."

(2.) The force of the objection from the curse against the serpent, as against an innocent animal, vanishes with the light thrown by modern science upon creation. This shows that the serpent has always had its present form. The curse, therefore, so far as uttered against the animal is merely equivalent to an assertion of the continuance of what had always been, and only places before man a constant and dreaded memorial of the first sin. This is consistent with God's method of cursing and blessing as seen in the bow of Noah, Gen. 9:8–17, and Jacob's language as to Simeon and Levi in Gen. 49:5–7.

This third theory is favoured by the following facts:

1. The title serpent and dragon is given elsewhere in Scripture to Satan. See Rev. 12:3, 4, 7, 9, 12–17; Rev. 13:24, especially Rev. 12:9, "the old serpent, he that is called the Devil and Satan." See also Matt. 3:7, where John calls the Pharisees "an offspring of vipers," and compare it with John 8:44, our Lord's language: "Ye are of your father the devil."

2. The narrative in Genesis demands more than mental suggestion through a mere animal.

(a.) A characteristic special subtlety is ascribed to the serpent. If the temptation of Eve arose from mere mental suggestion to her by the purposeless acts of a purely irrational animal, the mention of this subtlety is unaccountable.

(b.) The thoughts suggested could not have arisen in the mind of the woman alone, nor in that of the woman through any mere act of the serpent. These are (aa.) That death would not ensue. (bb.) That the knowledge of good and evil would elevate them to be Gods (mighty ones).

3. The subsequent references in the Scriptures to this transaction show that this was the beginning of the great struggle of Satan for the ruin of man, which was to end in his destruction by the man Christ Jesus, the seed of the woman.

4. "In the New Testament it is both directly asserted, and in various forms assumed, that Satan seduced our first parents into sin. In Rev. 12:9, it is said, 'The great dragon was cast out, that old serpent, called the Devil, and Satan.' In 2 Cor. 11:3, Paul says, 'I fear lest . . . as the serpent beguiled Eve through his subtlety, so also your minds should be corrupted from the simplicity that is in Christ.' But that by the serpent he understood Satan is plain from ver. 14, where he speaks of Satan as the great deceiver; and what is said in Rom. 16:20, 'The God of peace shall bruise Satan under your feet,' is in obvious allusion to Gen. 3:15. In John 8:44, our Lord calls the Devil a 'murderer from the beginning, and the father of lies, because through him sin and death were introduced into the world.'" [Hodge, Syst. Theol., Vol. 2, p. 128.]

III. THIS, A FALL UNDER THE COVENANT OF WORKS

The fall of Man occurred when he was on probation under the covenant of works.

Theologians are accustomed to speak of two especial covenants, the one of works, the other of grace. These do not embrace all the covenants between God and man, which indeed have been very numerous. The others most prominently mentioned in the Scriptures are that with Noah, Gen. 9:11–17; with Abraham, Gen. 17:2–14; (repeated to Isaac, Gen. 26:2–5; and to Jacob, Gen. 28:13–15); with Israel in giving the law, Ex. 24:7; Deut. 5:2, 3; with Moses and Israel, Ex. 34:27; with David, 2 Sam. 7:12–16; with Solomon, 2 Chron. 7:12–22; and that of Nehemiah and the Israelites with God, Neh. 9:38 to 10:39. The two covenants of works and grace are spoken of in Gal. 4:22–31, and are called "the two covenants" in verse 24. That of grace is the covenant of redemption made by God with his elect, or more properly with Christ, the second Adam, as their representative. That of works, is the covenant of the law entered into between God and all mankind through the first Adam, their natural head and appropriate and appointed representative.

[Upon the Scripture use of the word covenant see Hodge's Outlines of Theology, pp. 309 and 367–369.]

A covenant is an agreement between two or more parties by which any one or more things are to be done under the sanction of rewards and penalties.

This is the ideal form of a covenant. Some parts of it may be wanting, and still it may be a covenant. Thus there may be penalties and no reward, or reward and no penalties. Also, the agreement may arise, not from mutual consultation, but from a command given and accepted. This may take place at the time it is given, and with the person to whom it is spoken, or the command may be given, or promise made, to be accepted and acted upon by any who may at any time choose. Thus, between a government and its responsible subjects, law becomes a covenant. Rewards also are promised, as for the killing of dangerous or destructive animals, or for the capture of criminals; or threats are uttered, for violation of the rights of others, either as to life, liberty, or property.

These preliminary statements may remove the difficulties sometimes felt as to the existence of a covenant of works. Law prescribed by God as lawgiver is admitted to exist together with its sanctions and penalties; and, as in human law, so here, no excuse can he made of want of formal agreement; because of the natural obligation to obey.

These facts are, however, more fully applicable to the covenant of works, regarded as the general law of obtaining and maintaining spiritual life, given to all mankind, and still held forth to them, than to the transactions under that covenant connected with Adam's fall.

In this latter the elements of a covenant more distinctly appear.

1. There are here the two parties to a covenant, God and man; the one prescribing what was to be done, or left undone; the other receiving the command to do or not to do it.

If it be objected to the parties, that God enjoined an act through his sovereign and supreme power and dominion, to which man dared not object; the sufficient reply is that God was no more sovereign lord than man was willing subject. The holy constitution of his nature, rendered his ready acceptance absolutely certain.

2. Here also we find the subject matter of a covenant, the forbidding under penalty the eating of a certain fruit. That which made this properly a part of the covenant, was that man knew that he was commanded not to eat; that he recognized God's right to command, and his duty to obey; that he had a natural inclination towards obedience; and that, accepting the command of God, he proceeded to submit himself to it.

Both the knowledge and assent of man, however, may be absent from the general covenant of works, where it appears under the especial form of law, or duty, whenever that absence is the result of man's sinfulness, and man still be held responsible. But in an innocent being this knowledge and assent are essential to responsibility. Yet that very innocence, because of the holiness of the creature's nature, secures such assent to God's law when known as completes the more formal covenant.

3. The third element of the covenant is the penalty, death, the meaning of which will be hereafter examined. The threat of God "thou shalt surely die" (Gen. 2:17), was known not only to Adam, but to the woman also, as appears from her conversation with the serpent. Gen. 3:1–3.

4. The promises made or implied constitute a fourth element. It is questioned whether promises were added to the covenant. None appear in the narrative. None were necessary to make this a covenant. None are necessarily involved except such as are implied as attendant upon the result of obedience. These, therefore, may be first stated as being thus implied, and such considerations may be added as, from our further information, suggest that others were actually expressed.

Those implied are:

1. Continuance of God's favour, which having been bestowed on them as innocent creatures, would continue to be shown if they should not disobey his commands.

2. Continuance of their happy, holy condition until by their own act they should forfeit it.

3. Continuance, therefore, unless in like manner forfeited, of the immortality natural to their souls; and as to their bodies, continuance of their then existent condition, or, if any change should occur, a change into higher forms, bestowed for their greater happiness.

4. To this may be added that their children, so long as this state of innocence should continue, would be born with like innocent and holy natures.

These results of obedience are implied.

(1.) In the benevolent holiness and justice of God's nature. Even if never stated to Adam as promises, they would be naturally inferred by him from his knowledge of God.

(2.) They are also implied in the very threat against disobedience, if, as we shall hereafter see, that threat involved not merely natural death, but also, and chiefly, that absence of God's favour and communion which is the death of the soul.

If death would follow disobedience, then life ought to follow obedience—life in all the opposites to death, and therefore life both of the body and the soul.

It would seem, therefore, that there ought to be no question that these blessings were believed by Adam to have been made dependent upon his obedience to God's commands.

But not only were these thus implied, but the fact that life was promised "is clearly taught in other passages of Scripture. Lev. 18:5; Neh. 9:29; Matt. 19:16, 17; Gal. 3:12; Rom. 10:5." [Hodge's Outlines, p. 311.]

There are three further points of inquiry as to the probation upon which Adam was thus placed.

1. How long was the probation to last if man continued innocent?

2. Was there to be but this one test of obedience?

3. Was confirmation in holiness and happiness promised our first parents in any way as a reward of obedience?

We may answer these by saying that, while we have no means of knowing how long man was to be tried under this particular form of covenant, it is more than probable that there was to be but the one form of test, and that, after a period which could not be very long, confirmation in spiritual life was to be attained if man continued obedient.

In favour of but one form of test is:

1. The fact that the simple purpose was to test man's confidence in God and obedience to his will. So long as a sufficient one was presented, no multiplication of tests was necessary.

2. God knew whether his purpose was to allow man to fall or not, and knowing this, knew what test would be sufficient. He needed to try man, not to show to himself but to others what man would do.

3. In a case like that of Job, when his purpose is to exhibit his grace in his creature, he may allow many tests, one after another, but when that purpose is to permit the fall of his creature, it is not probable that he would allow his hopes of success to be raised, after successive trials, to result only in final and more embittered disappointment.

With respect to confirmation in spiritual life as resulting from continuance in holy obedience, it may be remarked that:

1. The fact that God selected this one thing to forbid, while he granted indulgence in all others, indicates that it was for a special test. That test would naturally be accompanied by a promise as well as by a threat.

2. A further evidence of such a promise, as well as of its nature, is to be found in the statements about the tree of life. Its suggestive name, its prominent position "in the midst of the garden," (Gen. 2:9), its conspicuous character, such that it is one of the only two mentioned, its power of confirmation in life, which Gen. 3:22 shows to have been known to Adam—all of these indicate that the idea, not only of life, but of confirmation in life, had been conveyed to Adam.

3. The fall which resulted from the temptation shows that God's purpose in causing that tree to grow there was not to use it in the confirmation of Adam in holiness, for no such confirmation was to occur. We must find its use, therefore, in something prior to the fall. But in what, save to place constantly before Adam the promise of confirmed spiritual life, should the period of this probation be safely passed?

4. The necessity of his removal from the garden shows that some promise of confirmation in some existent condition thereafter unchangeable had been attached to this tree, to he fulfilled when man should be permitted to partake of it. Gen. 3:22.

Three objections have been made to this transaction.

1. That it made so much, even all, to depend upon a single act.

But this arises (1.) from the nature of sin; as guilt demanding punishment for any one transgression, even the least; and as corruption, rendering incapable of subsequent acts of holiness; and (2.) from the nature of God's justice, which cannot pardon sin unatoned for. Any one sin must therefore necessarily terminate probation.

2. That the test was in so unimportant a matter as the eating of a piece of fruit. But the more trifling the prohibition, the easier was the act of obedience, and the more flagrant that of disobedience.

3. That the precept was a positive and not a moral injunction.

But this very fact made it a better test of obedience, (a.) as testing the whole man; not his love of holiness only, nor his reverence for God, nor the tendencies of his holy nature, nor those of his will only, but all; (b.) as making a well and sharply defined test of his confidence and obedience towards God; and (c.) as plainly manifesting to the guilty the sin they had committed and the condition into which they had brought themselves.

CHAPTER 23

THE EFFECTS OF THE SIN OF ADAM

THE immediate effects of Adam's sin, as indicated in the narrative in Genesis, were (1.) shame, or fear of God's presence, and (2.) making excuse for his sin and casting the blame upon the woman and his maker. Gen. 3:7–13.

The immediate curse uttered against the woman was (1.) danger to her and her seed from the serpent and his seed, (2.) multiplied pain and sorrow in childbirth, and (3.) a condition of subservience to her husband. Gen. 3:15–16.

That against the man was (1.) that thorns and thistles should hinder the cultivation of the ground, (2.) that by hard labour in the sweat of his face should he eat his bread, and (3.) a positive declaration of the return of the man to the dust whence he had been taken. Gen. 3:17–19.

The evils thus threatened have not been confined to Adam and Eve, but have fallen also upon all their posterity. Whatever may be the connection between Adam and that posterity, it is generally admitted that the latter share with him all these evils.

In seeking then into the effects of Adam's sin we shall find them in connection with the evil condition of his posterity, as well as of himself.

The curses uttered in the garden are not to be taken as exhaustive of the curse threatened. They are such only as were immediately suggested by the peculiar attendant circumstances of Adam's sin, and are to be regarded merely as examples of its evil effects. Still even they have not been confined to Adam, but have come equally upon the race at large.

All the evil effects of Adam's sin are comprised under the one word "death." This was the threatened penalty. But what is meant by it?

I. Natural death is included. By this is meant the separation of the soul and the body, and the consequent decay of the body.

1. It has been objected that this is not a result of Adam's sin because the very nature of the body (dust) made it necessary that it should return to dust.

To this it may be replied:

(1.) That it is not certain that there were in man's body before his sin any elements of decay which would naturally lead to separation from the soul and to corruption.

(2.) But even if we admit that the body is naturally mortal and liable to corruption, it does not follow that had man not sinned, he would have died.

God might have continued forever to preserve his powers unimpaired, either by direct preservation or by some remedial means. Some think, not without reason that this would have been done through the tree of life.

(3.) The objection overlooks the fact that, from the nature of God's foreknowledge and purpose, things in themselves natural are made the punishments of others with which they are associated. In like manner also is it with his blessings. The whole narrative of the fall is full of examples of this principle. Of this kind is the serpent's curse, "upon thy belly shalt thou go, and dust shalt thou eat all the days of thy life," Gen. 3:14; of this also that connected with the natural injuries which men and serpents would inflict on each other, Gen. 3:15; that of the rule of the husband over the wife, Gen. 3:17; and that of the thorns and thistles in the ground and the sweat and the labour for the means of life, Gen. 3:18, 19.

2. A second objection against regarding natural death as part of the penalty is that the threatened penalty was a death which should occur on the very day the fruit should be eaten.

(1.) This might be an objection if it were claimed that the penalty of natural death was the only penalty, or if it could be shown that the death thus threatened was so exclusive as to forbid that natural death should be in any way associated with it.

(2.) It is even doubtful whether the corrupt tendency to death and its beginnings may not be ascribed to the very hour of Adam's sin. If that sin removed all hope of God's counteracting the natural mortality, this would be so; whether it was to be counteracted, as Lange quotes Knobel as supposing [Comm. on Genesis, p. 239], "through the tree of life," or by some other means. It would also be true if, as Lange thinks, the threatened penalty, "death, here corresponding to the biblical conception of death, must be taken primarily to mean moral death, which goes out of the soul or heart, and, through the soul-life, gradually fastens itself upon the physical organism." Comm. on Gen., p. 207. Under such circumstances the moral death would be the eventual cause of the physical death, and to the latter would be assigned the same time of beginning with the former. This might also be done, even if the gradual decay were a mere accompaniment of the moral death without being actually caused by it.

In favour of the idea that natural death is included in the penalty, there is:

1. The probability that while spiritual death does come upon man, the outward event, the name of which is used to express this evil result in the soul, would itself also constitute a part of that which is indicated by its name.

Hence it is that to one who does not carefully study the Scripture statements, the most obvious idea is that the death threatened was chiefly natural death.

2. This probability is rendered certain by the specific curse uttered in the garden after the transgression: "Dust thou art, and unto dust shalt thou return." Gen. 3:19.

3. It is confirmed by other passages of Scripture. Lange, Gen., p. 239, thinks that the teaching of the 90th Psalm is undoubtedly that death belongs solely to the punishment of sin. But whether so, or not, it is unquestionably the teaching of Romans 5:12–14; also of 1 Cor. 15:21, 22, 55, 56. [See some valuable remarks on this point in Edwards' Works, vol. 2, p. 373.]

II. Spiritual death was also an effect of Adam a sin. Our inquiry into natural death as a penalty leads us to look for some other and higher evil as resulting from sin. It must be something which occurred at the very time of eating, which affected that part of man that was naturally immortal, and which was also connected with that part with which conscious personality is inseparably associated.

1. It must therefore be the death of the soul.

The Scriptures present this in several aspects, showing it in each case not only by statements of what it is, but by contrasting it with the life of the soul. It is presented as (1.) Alienation from God. (2.) Loss of God's favour. (3.) Loss of acceptance with him.

It is contrasted with life in many passages, as Lev. 18:5; Deut. 8:3; 30:15–19; Ps. 119:17, 77, 116; Matt. 4:4; John 5:24.

That this death has come upon mankind is evident from the fact that the Scriptures speak of man in his fallen state as being "without God in the world," Eph. 2:12; as "alienated from the life of God," Eph. 4:18. It says that "all have sinned and fall short of the glory of God," Rom. 3:23. Also that "the wicked and him that loveth violence his soul hateth," Ps. 11:5. "For the wrath of God is revealed from heaven against all unrighteousness and ungodliness of men," Rom. 1:18. It is not only said that "he that believeth not hath been judged already," but that "the wrath of God abideth on him." John 3:18, 36.

It is also evident from the work of Christ, which was to reconcile man to God, and to propitiate his good will. Hence Christ speaks of himself as giving living water. We are said to live in Christ.

2. This spiritual death was not only the death of the soul—as seen in the various aspects of alienation, loss of God's favour and of acceptance with him, referred to above—but it also consisted in a corrupt nature. The Scripture statements as to this corruption show:

(1.) Its universal extent. It is found in every man. "There is no man that sinneth not," 1 Kings 8:46. "There is none that doeth good," Ps. 14:1; and this is emphasized in v. 3 by adding "no, not one." See also Rom. 3:10 and the argument of the context. Also Ps. 53:1–3; 130:3; Prov. 20:9; Ecc. 7:20; Isa. 53:6; 64:6; Rom. 3:23; 5:12, 14; Gal. 3:22; 1 John 1:8–10; 5:19.

To the above passages might be added arguments for the universal existence of sin from the declared necessity of regeneration in each man; from the direction to preach the gospel to every creature; and the assertion that there is no salvation for any man except in the name of Christ.

(2.) Its early appearance in man's life is another proof that corruption is the effect of Adam's sin. Certain passages of Scripture are supposed to refer to young children as though innocent of guilt. These are such as Matt. 19:13–15; Mark 10:13–16; and Luke 18:15–17, "Of such is the kingdom of God." Also Matt. 18:3: "Except ye turn and become as little children." Also 1 Cor. 14:20: "Be not children in mind: howbeit in malice be ye babes, but in mind be men." [See Gill's Body of Divinity, I., 474.]

But these passages do not teach freedom from corruption. On the other hand, corruption in early infancy is plainly taught. "The wicked are estranged from the womb: they go astray as soon as they be born, speaking lies," Ps. 58:3. "Behold I was shapen in iniquity, and in sin did my mother conceive me," Ps. 51:5. "Foolishness (wickedness) is bound up in the heart of a child," Prov. 22:15.

(3.) The fact of this corruption. Before the flood it is said: "And God saw that the wickedness of man was great in the earth, and that every imagination of the thoughts of his heart was only evil continually," Gen. 6:5. "Every one of them is gone back; they are altogether become filthy," Ps. 53:3; see also Ecc. 8:11; Matt. 15:19; Rom. 1st chapter at length, as to the heathen, in connection with Paul's question, Rom. 3:9. Similar descriptions appear in Isa. 59:3–14; in Gal. 5:19–21; Titus 3:3; 2 Pet. 2:13–18.

(4.) This corruption extends to every affection of the heart and mind. Mr. Goodwin, in the Lime Street Lectures, p. 128, says: "The soul is corrupted with all its faculties; the mind with darkness and ignorance, Eph. 5:3; being subject to the sensitive part, and strongly prejudiced against the things of God, 1 Cor. 4:24; the conscience with stupidity and insensibleness, Titus 1:15; the will with stubbornness and rebellion, Rom. 8:7; the affections are become carnal and placed either upon unlawful objects, or upon lawful in an unlawful manner or degree, Col. 3:2; the thoughts and imaginations are full of pride, and vanity, and disorder, Gen. 6:5. And as for the body, that is become a clog, instead of being serviceable to the soul, and all its members and senses instruments of unrighteousness to sin, Rom. 7:19. It is, I say, in general a universal depravation of every part in man since the fall; and more particularly it consists in a privation of all good, in an enmity to God and the things of God, and in a propensity to all evil." See also Hodge, vol. 2, p. 255, and Gill's Divinity, vol. 1, p. 474.

[Better proof texts than those referred to in the above quotation are Eph. 4:18 and Rom. 1:21 instead of Eph. 5:3; and Rom. 6:12; 7:24 and 8:5–7 instead of 1 Cor. 4:24.]

(5.) This corruption has not been equally developed in all. The doctrine of total depravity does not mean such equal development. The Scriptures recognize degrees of wickedness as well as of hardening of the heart, and even blinding of the minds of some. But they also represent that the lack of this development is due to differing circumstances and restraints by which some men are providentially surrounded.

(6.) This corruption does not destroy accountability or responsibility for present sins.

(a.) The Scriptures universally recognize man's liability to punishment for all the thoughts of his mind, and the desires of his heart or the emotions of his physical nature, as well as for his acts. These are characterized by more or less of heinousness according to their nature and the circumstances under which they are committed. The more intense the corruption, the more guilty is the man regarded.

(b.) The conscience of mankind approves these teachings of Scripture. We do not excuse men because of any state of moral corruption. The evidence of this is seen in the immediate difference which is made whenever physical compulsion or physical disease (insanity) leads to an act which otherwise would be regarded as sinful and blameworthy.

(7.) This corruption does not destroy the freedom of the will. This is the ground upon which men are held responsible by God and by human law and conscience. The condition of man is indeed such "that he cannot not sin," but this is due to his nature, which loves sin and hates holiness, and which prefers self to God. When man sins, he does so of his own choice, freely, without compulsion.

(8.) "The inability which is thus admitted," says Dr. Hodge, "is asserted only in reference to the things of the spirit. It is asserted in all the confession above quoted (he has been quoting various Protestant confessions) that man since the fall has not only the liberty of choice or power of self-determination, but also is able to perform moral acts, good as well as evil. He can be kind and just, and fulfil his social duties in a manner to secure the approbation of his fellow-men. It is not meant that the states of mind in which these acts are performed, or the motives by which they are determined, are such as to meet the approbation of an infinitely holy God, but simply that these acts, as to the matter of them, are prescribed by moral law.

"Theologians, as we have seen, designate the class of acts as to which fallen man retains his ability, as 'justitia civilis,' 'things external.' And the class as to which his inability is asserted is designated as 'the things of God,' 'the things of the Spirit,' 'things connected with salvation.' The difference between these two classes of acts, although it may not be easy to state it in words, is universally recognized. There is an obvious difference between morality and religion; and between those religious affections of reverence and gratitude which all men more or less experience, and true piety. The difference lies in the state of mind, the motives, and the apprehension of the objects of these affections. It is the difference between holiness and mere natural feeling. What the Bible and all the Confessions of the churches of the Reformation assert is, that man, since the fall, cannot change his own heart; he cannot regenerate his soul; he cannot repent with godly sorrow or exercise that faith which is unto salvation. He cannot, in short, put forth any holy exercise, or perform any act in such a way as to merit the approbation of God. Sin cleaves to all he does, and from this dominion of sin he cannot free himself." [Hodge's Syst. Theol., Vol. 2, pp. 263–4.]

(9.) This total corruption does not involve equality of sinfulness in all men. On the contrary, sin is increased by cherishing sinful thoughts; by indulgence in sinful habits; by throwing off the restraints of society; and is affected by circumstances of birth, education, etc. It is also true that by natural inheritance some are more prone to sin than others.

III. Eternal death is also the consequence of Adam's sin.

1. Without any actual sentence to eternal death, it would follow that the present alienated and corrupted condition of mankind would be forever.

(a.) Condemnation can only be removed by proof of innocence; by legal justification; or by voluntary pardon. But the justice of God forbids him to pardon sin without atonement. By the deeds of the law can no man be justified; and, above all, innocence can never be proved. Hence the Scriptures represent all men, not pardoned and justified through Christ, as condemned to everlasting death.

(b.) Corruption can only be removed by a cleansing of human nature sufficient to root out all taint of sin and to restore a holy disposition and habits. This is the work of the Holy Spirit in the people of Christ. All not thus sanctified by him are left forever corrupt. The Scriptures show such to be man's condition that he cannot cleanse himself.

Dr. Dagg says: "The Scripture representations of men's inability are exceedingly strong. They are said to be without strength, captives, in bondage, asleep, dead, etc. The act, by which they are delivered from their natural state, is called regeneration, quickening, or giving life, renewing, resurrection, translation, creation; and it is directly ascribed to the power of God, the power that called light out of darkness, and raised up Christ from the dead." [Dagg's Manual of Theology, p. 171.]

The following Scriptures distinctly assert this corruption and inability: "Can the Ethiopian change his skin or the leopard his spots? then may ye also do good that are accustomed to do evil." Jer. 13:23. So also John 1:13; 3:3; Rom. 5:6; 7:5, 21; 8:3; 9:16 and Eph. 2:1, 5. Such being the condition of man, it is seen to be impossible for him to be delivered by his own acts, even if he had the will to perform them. But for God's action there would be no deliverance, even if man had the will to deliver himself.

(c.) But men have not the will to be released. This is evidenced by the statements of Scripture about their love of sin, and the delight they take therein, as specially leading to the rejection of the gospel. John 3:19–21.

If, therefore, the doctrine of eternal death were no more than the natural continuance of the alienation and corruption of men, we see that in the absence of the means to remove these they must continue forever.

2. But this doctrine goes farther and teaches (a) the confirmation of men beyond future escape in this condition of sin and misery, and (b) its aggravation, or at least a farther development of it, which is restrained in this life, and only slightly and in a few instances indicated.

This is taught by showing: (1.) That the day of judgment has been postponed, and that men during the present life are in an intermediate state of probation. (2.) That at the appointed time the wicked shall be judged and their final doom assigned to them. (3.) That that doom shall be as eternal as the bliss of the righteous. The strongest words of the Greek language are used to express the eternity of that condition. (4.) That beyond that period there shall be no change of state nor opportunity of redemption. (5.) That the condition of punishment into which they will enter is that of the devil and his angels, which is an entirely depraved and corrupted state of bitter enmity to God, and to holy beings and things; a state without restraints, in which the soul is wholly given up to sin. The 1st chapter of Romans teaches us what the removal of such restraints will produce. (6.) Some intimation of what that state will be is given in the devil-blinded, self-hardened condition attained even in this life by the worst of men, who, in their wilful, blasphemous and high-handed opposition to God and holiness, show that they are spiritually possessed by the devil.

CHAPTER 24

THE HEADSHIP OF ADAM

THE Scriptures teach that the fall of Adam involved also that of his posterity. In the covenant, under which he sinned, he acted not merely as an individual man, the sole one of his kind, or one isolated from all others of his kind, but, as the head of the race, for his posterity as well as himself. The condition of mankind shows that they have all participated with him in the evils which resulted. The Scriptures teach that this is due, not merely to his natural headship, but to a representative or federal headship, because of which his act of sin may justly be considered as theirs, and they may be treated as though they had themselves done that act, each man for himself.

In order that a proper comparison may he made between the innocent and afterwards the sinful condition of Adam, and that which universally is found in his descendants, it will be well to recall the facts as to Adam in these respects, and those also which are seen to be true of mankind in general. The consideration of these will prepare the way for that of the relation between the parties to which the present condition of man is due.

I. THE FACTS AS TO ADAM

These may be briefly stated since they have already been set forth, and the present statement is only an epitome of that already given.

1. Adam was created perfect, because of which perfection he was not only without sin, but had a strong and controlling, though not invincible, inclination to holiness and obedience to God. Such must be the nature of every being that is innocent and uncorrupted.

2. This nature did not make him incapable of committing sin, but only made it very improbable that he would choose to do so. Such improbability naturally belongs to a nature whose whole inclinations are towards that which is good. But improbability is far from being impossibility.

3. The possibility of sinning necessarily inheres in every creature endowed with a moral nature and permitted freedom of choice between good and evil. This is no more than saying that a creature is fallible because he is not God, who alone is through his own nature infallible.

222

4. Adam, in the trial to which he was subjected, did fall, not accidentally nor ignorantly, but deliberately, knowingly, and of his own free will.

5. Prior to this fall there were exhibited in him the nature and condition which belong to an innocent and holy man, and which must be found in any of mankind who have not been affected by his sin. Subsequent to it he possessed the nature and condition of a corrupt and guilty man, which likewise must appear in all of those who have been affected by that sin.

6. The result of that sin was inability to continue in the state in which Adam was originally created, or to return to it.

7. This inability was not merely natural, but also penal. It was to the corruption of his nature through the defiling taint of sin, which was a part of that threatened death, which, not confined to nor chiefly consisting in the death of the body, included this corruption and consequent inability of the whole man, together with the loss of the complacent love of God, and of communion or fellowship with him.

II. FACTS AS TO ADAM'S DESCENDANTS

The facts as to the descendants of Adam show that they have universally partaken of his corrupted nature, and that, not even in their earliest years, have any had the innocent nature, with its strong proclivities to holiness, which constituted his original condition.

1. They are born with the corrupted nature which he acquired, together with all the other evils set forth as the penalties of his sin. This was true even of his first children, Cain and Abel, as it has been also equally true of all others even to the present time.

2. No one of these descendants has been able to recover the nature possessed by Adam before the fall. In each of them the same inability has existed which fell upon him.

3. No one has been able to escape the complete fulfillment of the penalty of death, in all its meanings, except through the work of Christ.

4. No other reason for this universal condition has been assigned than the one sin by which Adam fell, and it has, consequently, been generally recognized as, in some way, the result of that one transgression.

5. The conscience of mankind has universally taught that this condition of their natures is sinful, and is as fully worthy of punishment as the personal transgressions which proceed from it.

6. The Scriptures plainly assume and declare that God righteously punishes all men, not only for what they do, but for what they are. Men are indeed represented as more guilty and sinful than they know themselves to be, because,

through the restraints with which God surrounds them, their natures have not been fully developed into all the sin towards which they tend. This is the argument of the first part of the Epistle to the Romans, the turning point of which is Rom. 2:1. It is also illustrated in the case of Hazael. 2 Kings 8:12, 13.

7. It follows from the facts in these last two statements, that a corrupt nature makes a condition as truly sinful, and guilty, and liable to punishment, as actual transgressions. Consequently, at the very moment of birth, the presence and possession of such a nature shows that even the infant sons of Adam are born under all the penalties which befell their ancestor in the day of his sin. Actual transgression subsequently adds new guilt to guilt already existing, but does not substitute a state of guilt for one of innocence.

8. Not the judgement of God only, but that of man also, regards a sinful nature as deserving punishment equally with a sinful act. The law of man is necessarily confined to the punishment of the acts, because these alone give such testimony to the condition of the heart as man can correctly apprehend; but the character of any act is regarded as alleviated, or aggravated, by the character of the actor; and men are shunned or courted as they are deemed to be good or bad, without any other reference to their acts than as they testify to character.

From the above points it will be seen that men, as descendants of Adam, are invariably born, not with his original, but with his fallen nature, and, more than this, not only receive that corrupted nature which was a part of the penalty of his sin, but with it all the other penalties inflicted because of that sin. It is also plain, that a condition of sinfulness is regarded worthy of punishment, not only by the Scriptures, and by personal conviction of conscience, but by the universal sense of mankind; and consequently that men may be punished for the corrupt nature thus inherited, although they may not have been personally guilty of a single transgression. This naturally leads to the inquiry into the nature of the connection between Adam and his posterity through which such sad and serious results have occurred.

III. THE CONNECTION BETWEEN ADAM AND HIS POSTERITY

1. Manifestly the universal sinfulness of mankind is due to some kind of connection with Adam. Being thus universal, it cannot be accidental, nor without some controlling cause. Unless some change was made in human nature at large, or it became liable to new conditions, or there was a connection of the life and state of all with that of the one, no reason can be assigned for the fact that invariably the fallen condition, and not the original one is found in every man.

Yet it is manifest that while Adam's was the first sin, and while that was not committed according to the tendencies of his nature, all of his posterity have been born with the corrupt nature which thence ensued, with all its tendencies and its actual development in due time into personal transgressions.

2. This has not resulted from the mere imitation of an example; but is a deep rooted evil inherent in their natures. It is found there before they can perceive the example, much less imitate it.

3. Such is the natural relation borne by all men to Adam, as their common father, that nothing but his death before the birth of posterity, or some such miraculous influence as goes against nature, or at least acts apart from it, and is believed to have existed in the birth of Jesus, could have prevented all the evils which befell Adam from coming in like manner upon his posterity. By natural generation they must be born with sinful natures such as his, and must, therefore, be corrupt and guilty, eternally destitute of God's complacent love, and liable to natural death.

4. While the above would follow from mere natural law, the Scriptures teach us that Adam was not merely the natural, but also the federal head of the race. This is done not only in express language, but especially by teaching that the relation borne to Christ, our federal head in salvation, is similar to that borne to Adam in our sin.

5. This shows that the mass of mankind proceeding from Adam by natural generation sinned in him, not consciously, but representatively, and therefore are justly treated as though they had consciously sinned, because they are responsible for the act of their representative.

6. This adds nothing to the penalty which must have been suffered nor to the guilt which would have accrued from natural headship; for guilt is simply just liability to punishment.

7. In each case, whether of federal, or of natural headship, the same difficulties appear.

(1.) In each we are dealt with for an act with which we had no conscious connection.

(2.) In each we are made sinful, and therefore sinners, by that act; for the inherent corruption is spoken of and treated by God as sin in the highest degree to be reprobated and punished.

(3.) In each the consequences of sin are equally beyond escape.

If it he contended that under natural headship we could not be punished until we had actually sinned, it may be replied:

(1.) That this does not appear to be the fact, for at least some of the penalties, namely, corruption and natural death, and we believe all, are inflicted before actual sin.

(2.) That it would show no more equity or justice in God, nor any advantage to us, but rather disadvantage, that our probation, upon which the infliction of these penalties depends, should have taken place in the weakness of infancy, and under the disadvantages of an already corrupted nature, rather than in the personal and intelligent act of the one perfect man connected with us by natural generation.

8. But while, under the natural headship, every evil would befall which could arise under the representative, or federal headship; under the latter would come blessing, in the event that Adam should maintain his integrity, because, as represented in him, we should have been confirmed with him according to the gracious promises and power of God.

9. It would also appear that only through the representative headship could blessing come in the event of the fall. Had our fall been through merely natural headship we can see no way for recovery. But to the fall under the federal headship of Adam corresponds our salvation under the federal headship of Christ.

10. In support of the Scriptural theory, therefore, we can not only adduce the fact that the federal headship of Adam was just and right, because duly constituted by God, and that too in the fittest person of the whole race, but that it was an act of special mercy and grace, not only in itself, as involving the blessing of participation in the good as well as the evil, but as making a way for restoration in Christ the second Adam.

IV. THE SCRIPTURES TEACH A FEDERAL HEADSHIP

The Scriptures recognize both a natural and federal headship of Adam. The natural headship would have sufficed to account for all the effects of Adam's sin. The federal relationship becomes necessary, however, in connection with salvation through Christ. It is on this account that it is more prominently set forth in the New Testament as the common relationship of both the first and second Adam. The establishment of it as to the first Adam is, therefore, to be regarded as a special act of the grace of God, conferring the privileges of success where the evils of failure would not be increased, and preparing the way for future grace in the representation in Christ. The principle, however, upon which it is based, is a general one of nature, and one constantly recognized in the Scriptures.

1. It is natural and common for men to deal with each other on this principle of representation. Blessings are bestowed and injuries inflicted in accordance with it. Men become heirs to the noble or base characters of their ancestors as really as to their property. The friendship and affection entertained

for a father, and no less the dislike and aversion, are renewed as to the son. A similarity is presumed to exist between them, which is deemed a proper basis for such action, until the conduct of the child shows a difference of nature, and, by destroying this presumption, causes him to be differently treated. Nor is this confined to those who are connected, like father and son, in direct succession. The taint of a committed crime soils and stains a whole family, even in its collateral branches. A remote relationship with the guilty one is deemed a disgrace, and the one thus connected realizes himself to be shunned, even if pitied, by those free from such misfortune. On the other hand, the most distant connection with one distinguished for wisdom or virtue, for great deeds or for high position, is thought to be a matter of congratulation, not alone for any supposed substantial benefits that may accrue, but for the simple connection itself.

The same principle extends itself throughout all the circumstances and ramifications of the life of each man. Each takes pride or shame in the place of his birth, in his early or late companions, in the community, or state, or country in which he lives, in its progress or backwardness, in its good or bad character, in its power or weakness, in its knowledge or ignorance—in short, in any qualities of excellence or of inferiority which are attached to anything to which he belongs. Every man is in some measure represented, though not of his own choice, perhaps by bare accident, perhaps even against his own will, in all the circumstances and persons which surround him.

This principle only gains strength when connected with a duly appointed representative. The President or the King appoints an ambassador to a foreign court, and each citizen, though he had no hand in the appointment, is affected by the action of this, his representative. A representative to Congress is elected, against whom one has voted, and of the whole discharge of whose duties one approves, and yet such a one is bound by these very acts of the one whom he wished not as his representative.

2. The representative relation thus seen in mankind in general is recognized in the same forms in the Scriptures as existing in man's life with God.

(1.) It is distinctly declared in the aspect of love and hate towards the children of those who love and hate him in Ex. 20:5, and is even more prominently brought to view in Ex. 34:7. See also Deut. 4:40; 7:7–9; Lev. 20:5; 26:39; Num. 14:18, 33; Job 21:19; Ps. 89:29, 36; 109:12–16; Isa. 14:19–22; 65:6, 7; Jer. 32:18; Rom. 11:28.

(2.) For the fact that different conduct on the part of the children shall counteract the blessing or curse which comes because of the parent, see Lev. 26:40–42; Neh. 9:2, 3; Ezek. 18:10–23; Dan 9:4–27; 2 Cor. 3:16.

(3.) That all of a nation suffer and are punished for the sins of their rulers and representatives is taught throughout the whole history of God's dealings with Israel. A signal instance of this was the punishment of all Israel because of the sins of Eli and his sons. Compare 1 Sam. 3:11–14 with 1 Sam. 4:10–22. Another was in the pestilence sent because David numbered the people. 2 Sam. 24:2–17. The punishment of all who had killed the prophets is announced by Christ as concentrated on that one generation. Matt. 23:34–39. The death of Christ, which had been brought about by the rulers of the Jews, is charged upon the people themselves. Acts 2:23; 3:13–15. It is also charged elsewhere upon the rulers. Acts 5:30.

(4.) On the other hand, how often was the anger of God turned away or modified by the intercessory prayers of Moses, and for the sake of Moses; as in the battle with the Amalekites, Ex. 17:9–12; and when the golden calf had been made, Ex. 32:9–14; and in his covenant with Moses after the renewal of the tables of the law, Ex. 34:9–28; also after the report of the spies, Num. 14:15–21; and numerous other instances. The case of Elijah and the woman of Zarephath is another illustration. Favour is shown to her because of the prophet's sojourn with her. 1 Kings 17:20–22. It was because of the grace that Noah found with God that he and his family were saved in the ark. Gen. 7:1. Abraham's prayer secured from God the promise to save Sodom, if it contained ten righteous ones, Gen. 18:32. God promised to save Jerusalem, if one just man could be found, Jer. 5:1. These are but a few of the instances which show this to be a prevalent principle in the divine government.

3. The doctrine of representation was especially set forth in a religious aspect under the Old Testament economy in the sacrifices under the ceremonial law.

These sacrifices were anticipated under some more general law of sacrifice which was given to mankind in general. This was exemplified from the earliest times. This is supposed by some to have been the source of the coats of skins with which the Lord God clothed Adam and his wife immediately after the fall. Gen. 3:21. It is more plainly seen in the superiority of the sacrifice offered by Abel over that of Cain. Gen. 4:1–8. Noah also offered burnt offerings. Gen. 8:20, 21. Abraham also built altars to the Lord, calling upon his name. Gen. 12:7, 8; 13:3, 4, 18; 21:33. The idea of the burnt offering was familiar to Isaac, as appears from his question to his father, and the ram was actually there offered as a burnt offering in the place of Isaac. Gen. 22:7–9, 13. Isaac also built an altar at Beersheba and called upon the Lord. Gen. 26:23–25. Jacob did the same at Shechem, Gen. 33:18–20, and at El-bethel, Gen. 35:7, and at Beersheba, Gen. 46:1. Moses also offered sacrifices before the ceremonial law was given. Ex. 17:15, 16. We are told that this was even done by Jethro. Ex. 18:12. In Ex.

20:24–26 God prescribes to Moses that an altar to him must be of earth, or of unhewn stone, and without steps for its ascent.

It is almost certain that these more ancient sacrifices taught at least partially the same truths as those of the ceremonial law. But the ceremonies attached to the latter explicitly set forth the fact of representation, including the ideas of substitution, imputation and sacrifice. These are the constituent elements of any doctrine of representation which releases from sin. They are fully exhibited in the representation of men in Christ. In that in Adam the sacrifice does not appear, because his was a representation which involved guilt, and not atonement. While these sacrifices, therefore, illustrate all that is involved in the representation in Adam, they are properly types of that in Christ, by which guilt was removed and atonement made to God for sin.

(1.) In them we have the sinner and the victim substituted for that sinner. The offered animal becomes his representative. What is due to the man is inflicted upon that substitution. The act of the latter thus becomes that of the former, and, upon the supposition that the victim is authorized and adequate, there is a full discharge of further penalty or obligation.

(2.) There is not only a substitution of one for another, but an actual transfer to this one from that other of his sins, trespasses, uncleanness, or whatever else unfits him for acceptance with God. After this transfer the man is treated as though he had never been thus defiled, and the victim dealt with as though alone the offender. This transfer is what is commonly known as imputation. By it the sin of Adam is transferred to us, or in other words so reckoned to us or put to our account that we are treated as though it were ours. In like manner the sin of man was transferred to Christ, who bore it, though he knew no sin personally, and he was made sin (or a sin offering) for man, and was treated as though he were a sinner. On the same principle the righteousness of Christ is also imputed to man, who, though personally sinful, is treated as though he were righteous.

(3.) The third element is the sacrifice, by which satisfaction is rendered to the broken law, and God can be just and yet justify the ungodly. This was shown by the death of the victim whose life was thus given through its blood in behalf of those whom it represented, as was that of Christ upon the cross.

The whole attainment of salvation through Christ was thus symbolized through these Mosaic sacrifices. The antitype as well as the type depends upon the principle of representation. This forms the connecting link. The Mosaic sacrifices were not offered in general, but for specified persons. It was not sin in the abstract that was confessed, but the sins of special individuals. The fact of representation has thus been distinctly involved in the whole religious life set

forth in the Scriptures. It was only through the act of a duly appointed representative that guilt could be removed and salvation obtained.

4. The Scriptures represent this as the method by which guilt was incurred
through Adam. This is chiefly done in the well-known passage in the fifth chapter of Romans. The apostle is here arguing for the possibility of justification
through the act of Christ. He does this by drawing a parallel between Christ
and Adam, and the effects of Adam's sin and Christ's meritorious work. This
parallel could be drawn only on the ground of federal representation. Only thus
could it be in connection with Christ as it had been in connection with Adam.
Christ could in no sense be a natural head of man. He could only be a constituted or appointed representative head. He is thus everywhere set forth. So
the parallel made between him and Adam shows that the headship of the latter
was representative and not natural only. The same truth is also taught in 1 Cor.
15:45–49, not only in the names given of the first and second Adam, but by the
contrast between their natures and the effects produced by each. In these two
chapters from Romans and Corinthians we find ascribed to men, because of the
connection with Adam and as punishment of his sin, almost all the penalties
which were inflicted upon Adam in the threatened penalty of death. There is the
all-comprising word "death," declared to have come by sin, and that, the sin of
one man, Rom. 5:12; death, which came upon all, even over those who had not
sinned like Adam. In what respect "not sinned after the likeness of Adam's transgression" (v. 14) if reference be not made to the fact that there was no personal
sin, as there is none in infants? This seems clearly suggested by the interjected
expression "who is a figure of him that was to come;" (v. 14) for Adam was only
a figure of Christ by virtue of this representative headship. "Judgement unto
condemnation," another penalty of Adam's sin, is also declared to have come
through one, v. 16, 18. The death of the soul, as the opposite of its spiritual
life, is also asserted to have resulted from one man's offence, v. 17. The controlling power of this sin, which causes the inability to return to God and serve
him, is shown by the declaration that "sin reigned in death," (v. 21), which is a
result of the one man's disobedience mentioned in v. 19. If natural death is not
included in the word "death" in this chapter, and the denial that it is so included
is hardly possible, it is yet certainly connected with representation in Adam in
1 Cor. 15:22. These two chapters, therefore, show this representative relation of
Adam; and that because of it all men have sinned in him and are justly treated
as sinners.

The discussion of this representative relation of Adam has rendered necessary a reference to that of Christ. It will be appropriate, therefore, to present
in a tabular form the parallel between the consequences of these relations as a
further proof of the representative character of each of these persons:

THOSE REPRESENTED IN ADAM	THOSE REPRESENTED IN CHRIST
Sin is imputed.	Righteousness is imputed.
Treated as though sinners.	Treated as though righteous.
Not thus personally sinners.	Not thus personally righteous.
Not regarded as actually guilty of Adam's sin.	Not regarded as actually meritoriously possessed of Christ's righteousness.
But only sinners representatively.	But only righteous representatively.
Though not personally sinners in Adam, yet born sinful, and naturally becoming actual sinners.	Though not personally holy in Christ, yet born again unto holiness, and graciously becoming more and more holy until finally sanctified.
Condemned to all the penalties of death because of Adam's sin.	Released from penalty, and attaining to spiritual life and immortality, because of Christ's active and passive obedience.
Voluntarily accepting the relation to Adam, and persevering in the life of sin inaugurated by him.	Voluntarily, though by God's help and grace, accepting the relation to Christ, and persevering in the holy life into which he has brought them.

CHAPTER 25

CHRIST IN THE OLD TESTAMENT

THE history of the Jewish nation is peculiarly marked by its expectation of a Messiah. Christians believe that this was fulfilled in the birth of Jesus, the son of Mary. The object of this chapter is to show what testimony the Old Testament gave of the coming of such a personage, and what were its predictions about the nature of his person and work. This is preliminary to the more full information to be gathered from the Christian Scriptures. It is well to see that the true doctrine as to the Saviour of man is not that of the New Testament only, but of the whole Bible. The unity of divine revelation will thus appear. The testimony of prophecy will be added to that of the miracles which attended the life of Jesus and the ministry of his followers. The authority of the later revelation will be seen to rest, not upon these miracles alone but also upon the concurrence of its teachings with the inspired truth already accepted by the Jews. Our Lord himself and his apostles were constantly accustomed to appeal to these then existent Scriptures as testifying of him: Matt. 1:22, 23; 2:23; Mark 1:2; Luke 1:70; 4:21; 24:27, 44; John 1:45; 5:39, 46; Acts 2:25–31; 3:13, 22, 24; 7:52; 8:30–35; 10:43; 13:32–37, 47, 15:15–17; 24:14; 26:6, 22, 23; Rom. 1:2; 2 Tim. 3:15, 16, 2 Pet. 1:19–21. We may therefore profitably consider some of the more important predictions of the Messiah which appear in the Old Testament.

I. THE PROMISED SEED

The human character of the Messiah was foretold in the prediction that he should be of human seed. This was presented in three special forms: first, in the seed of the woman; second, in that of the patriarchs; and third, in that of the family of David.

1. *THE SEED OF THE WOMAN*

The earliest prediction of the coming Messiah took place in Eden. It is sometimes called the prot-evangelium or first gospel. Yet it should not be forgotten that, whatever of glad tidings it conveyed to man, it was uttered in the form of a curse upon the serpent. "And the LORD God said unto the serpent, Because thou hast done this, cursed art thou above all cattle, and above every beast of

232

the field; upon thy belly shalt thou go, and dust shalt thou eat all the days of thy life: and I will put enmity between thee and the woman, and between thy seed and her seed: it shall bruise thy head, and thou shalt bruise his heel." Gen. 3:14, 15. The whole tenor of subsequent Scripture, especially that of the New Testament, shows that this is not to be regarded as merely declarative of hostility between mankind and the serpent tribe, but more particularly of the future strife between Christ and Satan, and of the final triumph of the former over the latter. See especially John 8:44; 2 Cor. 11:3; Heb. 2:14; 1 John 3:8; and Rev. 12:9. To what extent our first parents comprehended the full blessedness of this promise cannot be ascertained. Much of the knowledge of the antediluvians, especially as to the gracious purposes of God in redemption, has been left unrecorded. But we have glimpses of their faith and knowledge which furnish reasons for believing that they were not left by God without sufficient information to lead them to expect a deliverer from their sinful and spiritually lost condition. The faith of Abel, by which he "offered unto God a more excellent sacrifice than Cain" (Heb. 11:4) and the "coats of skins" which "the LORD God made for Adam and for his wife" (Gen. 3:21), are strongly suggestive of bloody sacrifices, typical of Christ, commanded by God in the very beginning. The prophecy of the second coming of Christ which Jude (vers. 14, 15) tells us was made by "Enoch, the seventh from Adam," betokens a degree of knowledge to the very end of the world which, but for that record, would never have been imagined. We are therefore not to be hindered by any presumption that our first parents did not know what God was promising, from carefully scrutinizing the record left us, nor from giving to it all the fullness of meaning its literal interpretation may convey. Now that record taken in its strictest grammatical interpretation teaches not only that the promised seed had become a ground of hope to the woman, but that she had learned to associate with him who was to be the antagonist of the serpent the name of Jehovah himself.

The King James Version of the Scriptures translates her language upon the birth of Cain (Gen. 4:1): "I have gotten a man from the LORD." The Canterbury revision reads: "I have gotten a man with the help of the Lord." The literal rendering is: "I have gotten a man, the Jehovah himself." The Hebrew particle translated in the former of these versions "from" and in the latter "with the help of" is equivalent to the Greek "αὐτός" and the Latin "*ipse*." Dr. J. Pye Smith says: "The primary, proper, and usual force of the particle "אֶת" (eth) placed here before Jehovah is to designate an object in the most demonstrative and emphatical manner. In this use it occurs immediately before and after this clause, and forty times in the first four chapters of these primeval records, not including the instance before us. It is also prefixed to every proper name in the governed ease throughout the fifth chapter. This prodigious number of instances, all occurring in the same connection, in the same strain of topic and discourse, in the same most venerable documents (supposing them to have been pre-existing fragments, before the age of Moses), is surely sufficient to determine a grammatical question. It is true that, in subsequent periods of the language, this particle came to be used as a preposition to denote *with,* or *by the instrumentality of;* but this was only a secondary idiom, and many of ifs supposed instances, on a close consideration, fall into the ordinary construction. There seems, therefore, no option to an interpreter who is resolved to follow faithfully the fair and strict grammatical signification of the words before him but to translate the passage as given above" (I have obtained a man Jehovah). [Scripture Testimony to the Messiah, Book II., Chap. IV., Sec. 1.]

It is true that Eve was mistaken in supposing that the son thus born to her was the Messiah. The language of inspiration only asserts that she said this, without admitting that she was correct. Indeed, the record shows she was not. It is not here quoted, therefore, as proof of the divine character of the Redeemer, but only of the fact that she had believed the promise of God, was looking forward to its fulfillment, and had learned in some way to associate the name of Jehovah with the expected seed of the woman. It is also evident that not only did she believe that Jehovah was to be the Messiah, but that she expected his appearance in human form.

2. *THE PATRIARCHAL SEED*

A more definite and undoubted promise of the Messiah as "a seed" was made to Abraham and Isaac and Jacob. The apostle to the Galatians distinctly declares that "the Scripture, foreseeing that God would justify the Gentiles by faith, preached the gospel beforehand unto Abraham, saying, In thee shall all the nations be blessed." Gal. 3:8. He also says emphatically (Gal. 3:16) that this seed "is Christ." The predictions of this kind to Abraham are recorded in Gen. 12:3; 18:18; 22:17, 18. Each of these three passages refers in so many words to "the Seed," in connection with the spiritual blessing of the nations. Others, as indeed do the first two of these, contain also promises of the bestowal of the land of Canaan upon the natural descendants of Abraham. See Gen. 12:7; 13:14–17; 15:5–18; 17:8; 24:7. By this promise as to the nations the prediction in Eden, which had heretofore been general of the race, confined the birth of the Messiah to a descendant of Abraham. Both promises, that of the earthly Canaan and that of the spiritual seed, were repeated to Isaac (Gen. 26:2–5), (see also ver. 24); while to Jacob was given that of the earthly Canaan in the blessing by Isaac (Gen. 28:3, 4), and by God (Gen. 35:10–12) at Bethel, where the promise of both blessings had been previously made to him also by God, as recorded in Gen. 28:14.

These predictions constitute properly the patriarchal promise of "the Seed," which is more commonly spoken of as the promise to Abraham, because of his greater prominence, as well as because first announced to him. To what extent it was understood by them is also beyond our knowledge. But the language of Christ (John 8:56), "Your father Abraham rejoiced to see my day, and he saw it and was glad," shows a more full comprehension of the blessings promised than the recorded statements in Genesis would suggest. Perhaps to Abraham, "the father of all them that believe," was revealed somewhat clear ideas of the future person and work of his blessed Seed. It has been supposed, not without justification, that this occurred in connection with the commanded sacrifice of Isaac, related in the twenty-second chapter of Genesis. Certainly that occasion furnishes, if not a type, yet a very apt illustration of the offering up by the Divine Father of his only-begotten Son (cf. Heb. 11:17), whom he did not withhold from "the father of us all" (Rom. 4:16), nor from them which, being "of faith are blessed with the faithful Abraham" (Gal. 3:7). It is not, indeed, improbable that Abraham had before this been taught, or was so on this occasion, that by the sacrifice of "the seed," the blessing was to come which had been promised through him to mankind. Was not his reply to Isaac singularly prophetic when he said: "God will himself provide a lamb for the burnt-offering," Gen. 22:8? Especially may this be imagined when we find him calling the place of sacrifice "Jehovah Jireh;" so that it became a saying at least to the days of the record: "In the mount of the Lord it shall be provided." Gen. 22:14.

3. THE SEED OF THE FAMILY OF DAVID

This title is used in full recognition of the truth that Christ is almost constantly called the Seed or Son of David. It is intended only to recall the fact that Christ was also foretold as "a shoot out of the stock of Jesse, and a branch out of his roots" (Isa. 11:1), and that he is called "the Lion that is of the tribe of Judah, the root of David" (Rev. 5:5). Indeed, the prophecy, "until Shiloh come" (Gen. 49:10), which was made of Judah in the blessing of his sons by Jacob, has been largely regarded by Jewish as well as by Christian writers as a prophecy of Christ. This opinion is strengthened by the declaration that "Judah prevailed above his brethren, and of him came the prince." 1 Chron. 5:2.

The promise of the Seed of David was, like that to the Patriarchs, of a twofold nature: first, of the continuance of the kingly rule in Solomon, and, secondly, of the reign of Christ as the truly everlasting King.

The beginnings of both promises appear in the vision of Nathan, the prophet, which he made known to David when the latter was forbidden to build a house for God, and in the exultant and grateful prayer of David which followed (2 Sam. 7:4–29). David naturally regarded this as a promise of the continuance of his house "for a great while to come" (ver. 19). The words "for ever," as applied to any earthly kingdom, could only be thus relative. But this double prophecy included, as subsequently developed, another of a King truly everlasting, of whose kingdom there shall be no end, and with whom is really associated the "sure mercies of David."

This prophecy was uttered in the early part of the reign of David, and the understanding of it to which he attained may be traced through such of his Psalms as are of a Messianic nature. These, therefore, become exegetical of the original statements. The true key to the interpretation of these Psalms is to be found in David's comprehension of the theocratic nature of the government of Israel. The earthly was known to be only the vicegerent of the heavenly King. The glory of the royal office was to be exercised perpetually and everlastingly by Jehovah himself, and only temporarily by the one who from time to time might sit in God's place on the throne. Thus, in the conceptions and language of David, the two were mingled perpetually, and his thoughts and utterances passed instantaneously from the earthly monarch to the true King of Kings. Hence much of his language became prophetic, and led Israel onward to the idea of the Messiah as King of Israel. The following may be taken as some of the proofs of these facts and of the consequent characteristics of Messiah pointed out by him:

1. That Jehovah was theocratic King is distinctly asserted, Ps. 22:28; 24:1–10; 93:1.

2. Yet the king of whom he writes is also human; for he is a sufferer for others, whose prayers for deliverance show the intensity of his agony and despair. Ps. 22:1–22. These sufferings are the essential means by which those who fear the Lord will be called on to praise and glorify and fear God, and by which the meek shall eat and be satisfied, and hearts shall live forever and all the nations shall remember and turn to God and worship Him.

3. This was to be an exalted king. Ps. 2:6; 110:2, 5, 6.

4. To be a universal monarch. Ps. 2:10–12; 22:27; 110:5, 6.

5. His kingdom was to be everlasting. Ps. 145:13.

6. The king himself was to be glorious, reigning in truth, meekness and righteousness, and the sceptre of equity would be the sceptre of his kingdom. Ps. 45:4, 6.

7. He was to escape the corruption of the grave. Speaking in the person of the king, David said, "My flesh also shall dwell in safety, for thou wilt not leave

my soul to sheol; neither wilt thou suffer thy holy one to see corruption." Ps. 16:9, 10. (Cf. Acts 2:25–27; 13:35, 36.)

8. He is the begotten Son of Jehovah. Ps. 2:7.

9. David calls him his Lord. Ps. 16:2; 110:1 (Cf. Matt. 22:41–46; Mark 12:35–37; Luke 20:41–44; Acts 2:34–36).

10. He is also addressed as God. Ps. 45:6, 7.

11. He was to be a priest forever after the order of Melchizedek. Ps. 110:4. (Cf. 1 Sam. 2:34, 35, as a possible germ prophecy of this priesthood; but especially Hebrews, chapters 4–10.)

These references will suffice to show that David expected not only the perpetuity of the merely earthly kingdom, with its succession of monarchs of his family, but that he also looked in the same line of descent for a true appearance of Jehovah, whose reign in this human person would thus be universal, whose flesh would never see corruption, of whose kingdom there would be no end, whose power would be terrible and his wisdom and righteousness superhuman, to whom as his Lord, David would himself be subservient, who is already the begotten Son of God and can justly be called God, whose government would be especially spiritual, who, with the kingly, would combine a priestly office of peculiar character and origin, and yet whose sufferings would be intense, and these sufferings the foundation of the blessings of his people and of their devotion to God. Are not these the characteristics of the Christian idea of the Messiah as set forth in the New Testament? In whom, except in Jesus Christ, have these expectations been fulfilled? In what respect has he not met them fully?

II. CHRIST IN THE PROPHETICAL BOOKS

The Messiah, thus promised as the seed in the three forms we have considered, was the subject of frequent prophecy unto the days of Malachi. The predictions as to his birth became more distinct. The belief which separated him from all other kings of the nation and made him an especial object of hope and desire constantly increased. The association and identification of him with Jehovah appeared more clear. The application to him of the Divine names and attributes was made with less reserve. The nature and object of his sufferings and their saving efficacy were more plainly revealed, and the participation of the Gentiles in the blessings of his reign was more distinctly set forth.

1. *As to his birth.* Isaiah foretold the coming forth of "a shoot from the stock of Jesse and a branch out of his roots" (11:1), and of the birth from a virgin of a child who should be called Immanuel (7:14); and Jeremiah, the raising up unto David of a righteous Branch in whose days "Judah shall be saved and Israel dwell in peace," and whose name should he "THE LORD IS OUR

RIGHTEOUSNESS." Jer. 23:6. Gabriel announced that the Messiah would come and be cut off within seventy weeks from the time of the going forth of the commandment to restore and build Jerusalem. Dan. 9:24–27. Micah predicted the coming forth from Bethlehem Ephratah of the ruler of Israel "whose goings forth are from of old, from everlasting." Micah 5:2. Haggai declared that "the desirable things of all nations shall come" and fill the house then building with greater glory than that of Solomon. The Revisers, while so translating the word which, in the King James Version, is "desire," state in the margin that the Hebrew is "desire," which should suffice to retain the older translation regarded by many as a prophecy of Christ's appearance in that temple, especially when the extraordinary manifestations are considered as accompanying, viz., the shaking of "the heavens and the earth and the sea and the dry land." Haggai 2:6, 7. Finally, Malachi tells of a messenger who shall go before and prepare the way for the Lord, the angel of the covenant who will suddenly come to his temple.

2. *A special king.* The following passages will fully set this forth. Isa. 32:1; 33:17; 57:19; Jer. 8:19; 23:5; Ezek. 37:2; Dan. 2:44; Hosea 3:5; Micah 4:8, 9, and Zech. 9:9.

3. *The hope of Israel and Judah were as associated with Jehovah as king.* Isa. 6:5; 12:2, 6; 33:22; 43:3, 10, 11, 14, 15; 44:6, 23; 45:15, 21, 22, 25; 60:2, 9, 14, 16, 19, 20; Jer. 10:6–10; 23:5; 46:18; 48:15; 49:38; 51:57; Zech. 14:9, 16.

4. *The divine names and attributes are ascribed with less reserve to the predicted Messiah.* He is called "Immanuel." Isa. 7:14. His name was also to be "Wonderful, Counsellor, Mighty God, Everlasting Father, Prince of Peace." Isa. 9:6. Mention is made of one for whom the way in the wilderness should be prepared and a highway made straight after the manner of kings' journeying in ancient days. This one is called Jehovah, God; in him shall the glory of Jehovah be revealed, and he that tells good tidings to Zion is directed "Lift up thy voice with strength, lift it up, be not afraid; say unto the cities of Judah, Behold, your God! Behold, the LORD God will come as a mighty one, and his arm shall rule for him." Isa. 40:3, 5, 9, 10. The Branch of David foretold by Jeremiah was to be called "The LORD is our righteousness." Jer. 23:6. The ruler of Israel to come forth from Bethlehem Ephratah was one "whose goings forth are from of old, from everlasting." Micah 5:2.

5. *The nature and the object of his sufferings are more plainly revealed.* These are set forth with such marked distinctness in the 53rd chapter of Isaiah, that from it may be gathered all the main ideas which enter into the atoning work of Christ. We have there the substitution of a victim, himself innocent, in the place of the guilty; upon whom their sins are laid; who is wounded for their transgressions; with whose stripes they are healed; whose soul is made an offering for sin, and whose travail is rewarded with a satisfactory seed. The imputation of sin,

and its punishment and the reward are all from God. The lamb-like patience of the sufferer is no less descriptive of Jesus than are the sinlessness of his character, and the two-fold aspect of God exercising avenging justice and unceasing love. He is still God's righteous servant, whose work is worthy of great reward.

The angel Gabriel also said to Daniel: "After three-score and two weeks shall Messiah be cut off; but not for himself." Dan. 9:26. We have also that remarkable language of Zechariah applicable to Christ and to none other: "Awake, O sword, against my shepherd, and against the man that is my fellow, saith the LORD of hosts." Zech. 13:7.

6. *The participation of the Gentiles in the blessings was more distinctly enunciated.* The earlier prophecies to David had been simply; of conquered foes. In like manner also some of the later days spoke of triumphing Israel, or merely indicated the increase of the government without reference to special blessings. But the following refer to the Gentiles as blessed with the Jews, and even sometimes without them: Isa. 11:10; 42:1–17; 49:6–13; 62:2; Jer. 16:19–21; Hosea 2:23; Mal. 1:11.

Thus does it appear that the prophecies give still more complete development of the promises made in the seed of the woman and of the patriarchs and of the family of David, by which he who was the hope of Israel is made known also as the Saviour of mankind.

The discussions above will suffice to show how abundantly the Old Testament taught of the Messiah in the aspects referred to. But the doctrine of Christ in the Old Testament will not be completely shown without considering that manifestation in which he revealed himself as

III. THE ANGEL OF THE COVENANT

There were other manifestations of God to the senses of man. Such was that of the voice heard in Eden (Gen. 3:8), and by Moses from the burning bush (Ex. 3:2–5), and by the children of Israel out of the fire in Hebron, when they heard the voice of words and saw no form (Deut. 4:12), and by Moses at Sinai (Ex. 19:19), and by Samuel (1 Sam. 3:1–14), and by Elijah (1 Kings 19:9–20). But we have no reason to confine such a manifestation to the Son of God, especially as a like voice from the Father is recorded in the New Testament at the Baptism of Christ (Matt. 3:17), at the transfiguration (Matt. 17:5), and in answer to the prayer of Christ (John 12:28). By such a voice, or by dreams, or by other sensible means, must God also have forbidden the eating of the tree of knowledge, and commanded Noah to build the Ark, and communicated with Balaam (Numbers, chaps. 22 and 23), and with many of his true prophets to whom the "word of the Lord" came. But except in the interview with Balaam, when "the angel of the LORD" met him (Numbers 22:22–35), no reason presents itself why these communications should be ascribed to the second person of the Trinity alone. Whatever opinion one may have upon this point cannot be supported by any direct or positive language of Scripture.

But this is not true of the appearances of the angel of the covenant. The prophecy of Malachi should leave this question without doubt. "Behold," says Jehovah to Israel through that prophet, "I send my messenger, and he shall prepare the way before me: and the Lord, whom ye seek, shall suddenly come to his temple; and the messenger (angel) of the covenant, whom ye delight in, behold, he cometh, saith the LORD of hosts." Mal. 3:1. "Behold, I will send you Elijah the prophet before the great and terrible day of the LORD shall come." Mal. 4:5. We have here:

1. A distinct promise of the sending of the angel of the covenant, in whom Israel delights.

2. After the manner of Hebrew parallelisms he is identified with the Lord who shall come to his temple.

3. At first a mere messenger is announced as his forerunner, but afterwards it is declared that this shall be Elijah the prophet.

4. The office of the messenger or prophet is to prepare the way for the angel of the covenant.

Here is an undoubted reference to the coming Messiah. It could not otherwise be understood, even without the application made of it in the New Testament to Christ and his forerunner, John the Baptist. Matt. 11:10.

Having therefore identified the Messiah with the angel of the covenant, it only remains to show that this was a divine angel, having the names, attributes and authority of God, and receiving the worship peculiar to him alone.

1. *Divine names* are given to him and claimed by him.

(1.) That of JEHOVAH. By the inspired writers: Gen. 16:13; 18:1, 17, 20, 26, 33; Ex. 3:4, 7 (cf. ver. 2); 13:21 (cf. with Ex. 14:19); Joshua 5:13 (cf. with 6:2).

(2.) That of GOD. By Hagar, Gen. 16:13; by Jacob, Gen. 32:30; 48:15, 16; by the writer, Ex. 3:4, 6; by God himself, Gen. 31:13 (cf. ver. 11; also chap. 28:13–22 and 32:9); Ex. 3:6 (cf. ver. 2).

2. *The angel of the Lord is also identified with Jehovah and with God.*

(1.) *With Jehovah.* A signal instance of this is to be found in the events recorded in the 33d to the 40th chapters of Exodus. Because of the great sin of Israel in making and worshipping the golden calf recorded in the 32nd chapter, God was very angry with the people. He threatened them: "I will not go up in the midst of thee." Ex. 33:3. This filled Moses and the people with alarm, although God had promised to send an angel before them. Moses therefore went to the tent of meeting, and the pillar of cloud descended and stood at the door of the tent, and "The Lord spake with Moses." Ex. 33:8, 9. The reassuring promise was then given by Jehovah: "My presence shall go with thee, and I will give thee rest." Ex. 33:10.

This was followed by the hewing of the "two tables of stone like unto the first" (Ex. 34:2), and by the making of the tabernacle (chapters 35 to 40), upon the finishing of which "the cloud covered the tent of meeting, and the glory of the LORD filled the tabernacle. And when the cloud was taken up from over the tabernacle, the children of Israel went onward through all their journeys; but if the cloud were not taken up, then they journeyed not till the day that it was taken up. For the cloud of the LORD was upon the tabernacle by day, and there was fire therein by night, in the sight of all the house of Israel, throughout all their journeys." Ex. 40:33–38.

A comparison of the threat of Ex. 33:3 and of this record with the language of Ps. 99:7: "He spake unto them in the cloudy pillar," and Isaiah 63:9: "And the angel of his presence saved them," shows that the cloud was the visible manifestation of Jehovah to Israel, and that the angel of his presence embodied the glory of Jehovah. Its presence with Israel was the presence of Jehovah himself.

This identification of Jehovah with the angel is also exhibited with equal clearness by a comparison of Ex. 13:21 and 14:19. In the former it is said that "The LORD went before them by day in a pillar of cloud to lead them the way;" in the latter we read of "the angel of God which went before the camp of Israel."

(2.) *With God.* This identification of himself with God is made by the angel which appeared to Abraham, by saying: "Now I know that thou fearest God, seeing thou hast not withheld thy son, thine only son, from me." Gen. 22:12. (See also verses 15, 16.)

3. *Divine attributes* and authority are ascribed to the angel.

(1.) *Creative power.* He promised Hagar: "I will greatly multiply thy seed, that it shall not be numbered for multitude." Gen. 16:10. And in like manner said to Abraham: "I will certainly return unto thee when the season cometh round; and, lo, Sarah thy wife shall have a son." Gen. 18:10.

(2.) *Sovereignty* The power of absolute right over the cities of the plains is asserted in the foretold destruction of Sodom and Gomorrah, and his answers to the successive prayers of Abraham that upon certain conditions he would spare those cities. Gen. 18:18–33.

(3.) *The Judge of all the earth* is the efficacious title given by Abraham as he pleads with the Man before him, whom he recognizes as Jehovah, not "to slay the righteous with the wicked." Gen. 18:25. Two of the three men who appeared to Abraham are called angels (Gen. 19:1), and this third is manifestly "the angel of the Lord."

4. *Divine worship* is paid to and received by him. This worship was demanded of Moses at the Bush in which the angel of the Lord appeared (Ex. 3:2) when "God," by which name as well as that of Jehovah the angel is called, commanded him: "Draw not nigh hither: put off thy shoes from off thy feet, for the place whereon thou standest is holy ground." Ex. 3:5. A like command was given to Joshua (Joshua 5:15) by the man that appeared to him and claimed to be "the captain of the LORD's host," before whom "Joshua fell on his face to the earth and did worship." Ver. 14.

Thus does it appear that we have in the record abundant testimony to the identity with the Jehovah God of this angel of the covenant whom Malachi predicted as the coming hope of Israel. His appearance was not delayed until the time of his permanent incarnation. The seed of the woman appeared in human form and as angelic messenger and as glowing fire and cloud long before that "fulness of the time came" in which "God sent forth his Son, born of a woman" (Gal. 4:45), when the Word, which "was with God," "and was God" "in the beginning," "became flesh and dwelt among us." John 1:1, 2, 14. What relation these earlier manifestations had to the subsequent birth in the flesh or to the human nature then assumed is beyond our knowledge. Nor is it wise by conjectures induced by curiosity to prosecute inquiries which can accomplish no good and may be fraught only with evil. Speculation about the unknowable too often results in skepticism as to what is actually known, especially when such knowledge has come through revelation from God. It is sufficient to know that God added this outward "sign" to confirm faith in the promises he had given, and by it taught the future interposition of his own Son in human flesh for the deliverance of his true people, the spiritual Israel, from a severer bondage than that of Egypt, and the guidance of them by the Covenant Redeemer into the unspeakable blessings and glory of the Heavenly Canaan.

Thus did the Old Testament testify of Jesus the Christ, the Saviour of men. As the seed of the woman, he has utterly destroyed the power of the serpent, the great enemy of man. In him the day has come which Abraham foresaw and was glad. In him the Lion of Judah, the seed of David, appears as the King of Kings, the Lord of Lords, whose reign is universal, not over those living on earth only at any one time, but over all the living and the dead of this world, and indeed of the whole universe. His untold sufferings have secured the happiness of his people and their devotion to God. His kingdom is an everlasting kingdom. His priesthood has neither beginning nor end. He is the Lamb of God that taketh away the sin of the world. He ever liveth to make intercession for us. He hath made us kings and priests unto God. At his name every knee shall bow and every tongue confess that Jesus Christ is Lord to the glory of God the Father.

His flesh is indeed the tabernacle which is filled with the glory of Jehovah, in whom the ancient prophecy to Israel is fulfilled: "Behold your God!"

In the testimony thus given in the Old Testament as to Christ we perceive a portion of the evidence it also affords to that doctrine of the Trinity which was developed more clearly in the New Testament. Here is seen one not only identified with God and Jehovah, but also distinguished from him. Here also are other glimmerings of a tri-personality in God presented to a people unto whom God was especially revealed in his unity, and which had almost unconquerable tendencies to polytheism. What was thus revealed was understood very obscurely, if at all, in Old Testament days. For what purpose was it given except that in the later time might be apparent the unity of the doctrines of both Testaments, and the evidence of the inspiration of each in their testimony in common to this and to other doctrines which were divinely foreshadowed in the former, but have been distinctly declared in the latter revelation?

CHAPTER 26

THE PERSON OF CHRIST

I. THE doctrine of the Trinity lies at the foundation of that of Christ's Person.

That doctrine is that three persons subsist in one divine nature. It was one of these persons, and not the divine nature itself, that became incarnate.

1. It was not the Godhead that became incarnate, but one of the persons of the Godhead.

2. It was not the Father, and the Son, and the Spirit, but it was the Son alone.

3. It was not God abstractly and unitedly, but God personally, the Word that was with God, and that was God, that was made flesh.

4. It was not, therefore, that which was common to the three persons that assumed our nature; but it was that which, in the economy of the Trinity, is distinguished from the others.

5. It was, therefore, not the divine nature or essence, but a person who subsists in that divine nature equally with the others, yet who is distinguished, in his relation to that divine nature, from the other persons of the Trinity.

The doctrine of the Trinity is therefore essentially involved in that of the Person of Christ. It is because of the fact of individual personality in the divine Being, by virtue of which, though his nature and essence and being are so one that he is one God, he is yet three-fold, that personal distinctions also exist, and that one person, who is God, can become incarnate without involving the incarnation of the other persons.

Personal distinctions in the Trinity are not necessary to the incarnation of God, but are to that of a divine person.

They are also necessary to the work which Christ performed. Were God only one person, he could not manifest rule, and yet empty himself of it; could not send, and yet be sent; could not be lawgiver, and also voluntary subject; could not make atonement, and yet receive it; could not pour out wrath, and yet endure it.

The Scriptures, therefore, persistently teach, not that "God came," "was sent," "was made flesh," but that God "gave his only-begotten Son," "sent his Son not to condemn the world," "sent forth his Son made of a woman," "sent his only-begotten Son into the world," and that "the Father sent the Son to be the Saviour of the world." Indeed, the first chapter of John, which sets forth the doctrines of the Incarnation and Trinity, plainly declares (John 1:18): "No man hath seen God at any time; the only-begotten Son, which is in the bosom of the Father, he hath declared him."

II. This Person, in his incarnation, preserved unaltered his essential relations to the divine nature or essence.

1. The only Scripture passage which seems to oppose this is Phil. 2:5–8; but a proper consideration of this passage shows that it does not. The subordination, thus voluntarily assumed by the Son, was manifestly official, and that of one divine person to another. It could not have been a subordination of one divine nature to another, for there is but the one divine nature. It is, therefore, a subordination of one person to another, the Son to the Father. Neither, in that subordination, was there any separation of Christ from his divine nature. Such separation was not necessary to his incarnation. It was only necessary that he should appear to men as man, and not as God.

His divinity was, therefore, concealed in his human form. But he, being God equally with the Father and the Spirit, possessed, of right, rule and authority over all creatures and worlds. This he continued to possess essentially as God; but, as the Son, he yielded its exercise exclusively into the hands of the Father; so that during the period of his earthly residence, he consented to be as one that was sent, and thus as the servant of the Father, doing his will and obedient to his authority. The context shows this to be the only meaning. The object in introducing this statement is to induce the Philippians, in a like spirit of self submission, to esteem others better than themselves (a case, therefore, of subordination among equals). And after this statement about Christ, Paul enforces this obligation by showing how the Father had so rewarded this act of the Son, that the rightful dominion and power, which belong essentially to God, and to Christ therefore only in his divine nature, had been conferred upon him in his human nature, so that "every tongue should confess that Jesus Christ is Lord to the glory of God, the Father." Phil. 1:11.

It was this official position of rule and dominion which constituted the glory which he had with the Father, and which he prayed the Father to bestow upon him again. Such prayer was not necessary to secure it for himself as God, for, in his divine nature, be had continued to possess although not to exercise it; but it was necessary, since this was also to be conferred upon him as man, and in this respect it could only be conferred as a reward or gift, and by the consent of all the persons of the Trinity. (Compare the 2nd Psalm, especially verses 6–8, but the whole Psalm.)

The Scriptures go no further than this idea of official subordination. They say nothing of Christ leaving his divinity behind him, as though it had been cast off like a garment. They do not say that for his dwelling on earth his divinity had to cease or to be absorbed in that of the Father and the Spirit; nor that it had an indefinite existence in a transition state, awaiting a reunion after the incarnation work.

It is well to remember that they not only do not, but could not thus teach, for some men imagine this and overlook what may be next shown, namely:

2. That the Scriptures teach that while he was incarnate, he was truly God.

So fully is this taught, that we have no evidence at all of Christ's divinity which is not presented with equal force of him while on earth.

All the attributes of divinity are ascribed to him, eternity of existence, self-existence, omnipotence, omnipresence, omniscience, presence in heaven and on earth, the contemplation of and unity with the Father, and co-working with him. These are declared of him and manifested by him while he stood in the form of man in the midst of his disciples and the multitude.

It was while in the same form that he performed acts which none other than God can of himself do, declaring that these acts were done by his own power. He turned water into wine, not by the ordinary and slow process of nature, but instantly and without a word. He created bread and fish in the hands of his disciples. He controlled the winds and the waves. He forgave sin. He gave life to the dead. He made known events in distant places. He searched the hearts and revealed the secret thoughts of men. He laid down his own life and took it up again.

The constant workings of his divine power and energy, by which he is essentially, as God, always working with the Father, were indeed concealed; but thus, at times, before the people at large, and more frequently before his disciples, the divinity shone through the veil which ordinarily concealed it, and testified that he was as truly God as he was also man. See the remarkable statements of Christ himself as to his co-working with the Father in John 5:17–31.

3. He allowed himself to be treated as God during the incarnation.

How could he be called God during his days in the flesh, or receive worship as such? How could it be the will of the Father that men should honor the Son even as they honor the Father? How could Elizabeth call Mary the mother of my Lord? Or the angels announce to the shepherds that Christ the Lord was born? Or Peter declare to the Jews that they had crucified the Lord of glory? Or Paul describe the people of God to the Ephesian elders as the Church of God (or, according to another reading, "the Lord") which he had bought with his own blood? How can men be warned lest they crucify the Son of God afresh and tread him under foot? How could Thomas cry out to him, "my Lord and my God?" and how Peter confess, "Thou art the Christ, the Son of the living God"? It was because, though a servant, he was still the Lord, having his relations to his divine nature unimpaired, and entitled to the names, as he was also able to perform the acts and display the attributes of God.

The importance of this fact of the Scripture teaching cannot be over-estimated. In its appropriate relations to the other truths taught it becomes the foundation of every hope. It is not a mere speculation. It enters into the very life of the Christian, enabling him to say: "I know him whom I have believed, and I am persuaded that he is able to guard that which I have committed unto him against that day." 2 Tim. 1:12. It is not sufficient for us to know that the person who died for us was divine before he came into the world. The Scriptures assure us, and we need to comfort ourselves with the assurance, that he was equally divine when a babe in Bethlehem, when suffering upon the cross, when ascending from Olivet, and even now, while in human nature, he rules as Mediatorial King, or makes intercession with the Father as our great High Priest. We must even go beyond the idea of some kind of divinity, and recognize him as the unchangeable God, who was, and is, and ever shall be, the Almighty, the well-beloved Son of the Father, whom that Father always hears, and to whom all things have been entrusted, in order that the consummation of his glorious kingdom may be fully attained. The incarnation has been indeed, of only one person of the Godhead, but of a person truly and essentially divine, whose relations to the divine nature have remained unaltered during his incarnation on earth and in heaven.

III. That Christ became incarnate in such a sense that he became man.

The Scriptures tell us that "he was made flesh and dwelt among us;" that he was "made like unto his brethren;" that he was the "son of man;" that he was "man." The apostle says (Rom. 5:15): "one man Christ Jesus."

1. By this is not meant that this Divine person co-existed with a human person, so as to be, after all, two distinct existences or persons, the one receiving grace and favour from the other. In this sense God may be said to coexist with all men, especially with the righteous.

2. Nor is the idea only of such indwelling, that the glory of God is manifested as so specially present that the human person was the temple of the divine. In this sense God dwells even in material substances, as in the tabernacle and temple of God. In this sense the Holy Ghost dwells in the bodies of believers in a still more perfect union. And such indwelling will attain its highest form when God shall dwell in the temple to be composed of his redeemed saints.

3. But, though the body of Christ is the temple of God, it is such as the result of a union not less strict than one which makes the indwelling person actually and truly a man. While the relation to the divine nature remains unchanged, and Christ is still truly God, the relation to the human nature is so assumed that Christ also becomes truly man. He is born of a woman. He comes in the flesh. He assumes a human nature which becomes, as truly and really, though not as eternally and essentially his, as his divine nature.

The Scriptures reveal to us a proper humanity, consisting of a real body and a rational soul. Christ is represented as combining in his humanity all that is in ours, except that he, being without sin, exhibited that perfection of humanity which has appeared in no other of the race except in Adam before his fall.

1st. He had a human body. This is now no longer questioned. In early days heretical views existed on this point.

Because matter was deemed inherently evil, it was supposed Christ could have had no material body. His body was supposed, therefore, to have been merely a phantom, an appearance of a man. Probably to such a heresy the Apostle John refers. 1 John 4:3; 2 John 7. Those who in early times held this opinion were known as the Docetæ. But these heresies soon disappeared, and it is now no longer disputed that Christ had a true human body composed of bones, and flesh, and blood, as are the bodies of other men.

The Scripture statements as to this fact are unquestionable. Christ is spoken of as conceived in his mother's womb, as born, as drawing nourishment from her breast, as receiving circumcision, as growing in stature, as hungering, thirsting, wearied, as eating, drinking, sleeping. We are told of his bodily pain, of his bloody sweat, of his sinking under exhaustion, of his pierced body, of his bones that were not broken, of the wounds made in his hands by the nailing to the cross. The parts of his body are mentioned—his hands, his feet, his side, his head, his brow, his cheek and his breast on which the beloved disciple leaned. The entire representation presents him possessed of such outward form, influenced by such bodily feelings, and engaged in such bodily acts as assure us of the reality of his body. No other theory is possible except that of the Docetæ.

(1.) Against the Docetic theory it may be said that if the assumption of a real body were derogatory to Christ, the effort would not have been so persistently made to present that body as real and to induce the multitude and his disciples to believe it such.

(2.) Three passages in Scripture give direct testimony against it.

Heb. 2:14: "Since, then, the children are sharers in flesh and blood, he also himself in like manner partook of the same." While this refers, indeed, to human nature in general, it cannot be taken of that to the exclusion of the very characteristics by which that human nature is described.

The other two passages are stronger, for they directly bear upon phantom appearances, and Christ denied that such was his nature. One is the narrative of Christ walking on the sea to the boat which held the disciples, Matt. 14:22–33. In verse 26 they are said to cry out: "It is an apparition," and in verse 27 Christ to reply: "It is I."

The other is the account of that interview in which those who had walked with him to Emmaus report his presence with them to the Eleven, Luke

24:13–48. The language of verses 36–39 is: "And as they spake these things, he himself stood in the midst of them, and saith unto them, Peace be unto you. But they were terrified and affrighted, and supposed that they beheld a spirit. And he said unto them, Why are ye troubled? and wherefore do reasonings arise in your heart? See my hands and my feet, that it is I myself; handle me, and see; for a spirit hath not flesh and bones, as ye behold me having." He then showed his hands and feet, and still further called for meat, and ate "a piece of a broiled fish."

This action of Christ either meant nothing, or meant that he had, even then, a real body, with all its functions in due exercise.

The fact, therefore, that Christ in his incarnation possessed a real human body, subject to all the sinless infirmities of our bodies, is put beyond all question.

2nd. He had a human soul also. The evidence of this has been regarded almost equally conclusive. The only difficulty is that some suppose that if he had a human soul, he must have been two persons and not one only. Hence Apollinaris taught that he had no human soul, but that his divine nature took its place. His theory was rejected with almost singular unanimity, but it has been revived from time to time, gaining only brief and limited acceptance, only to be forgotten again when the true doctrine has been set forth.

The fact of such general acceptance of the existence of a human soul in Christ is strong evidence of its truth. It is not certain but strongly probable evidence. When the theory of the divine nature becoming the human soul has been known, such general faith in the other doctrine shows the impression naturally made by the Scripture; because there have been no reasons from prejudice, or passion, or self-interest, to mislead.

The objection that thus there must be two persons in Christ is an objection to the unity of his being; and this is all that leads to the acceptance of the doctrine of the divine nature as substituting the human soul. If, therefore, such be the union, that Christ can as one person subsist in two natures without involving that personal duality, the full objection to the human soul is removed. We shall see hereafter that this can be done. If it could not, then we should have two theories, each with difficulties: the one which arises only from our inability to comprehend what may after all be a psychological fact; the other, which involves such an explanation of the Scripture statements as to Christ as to deny that to be human action in him which would be so regarded in any other, and which also forces us to ascribe to divinity change, suffering, temptation, and death.

Let us examine these two theories first in the light of the Scriptures.

1. We most not forget what has been before stated as to the relations of the persons of the Godhead. Because of the unity of God the Son does not possess

a separate divine nature from that of the Father and the Spirit. When it is said, therefore, that Christ's divine nature took the place of his human soul, is it meant that the divine nature which he had in common with the Father and the Spirit assumed humanity? If so, the incarnation was of the whole Godhead, Father, Son, and Spirit.

Or is it meant that some kind or portion of divine nature which Christ had separately from the Father and the Spirit did that? If so, what was that divine nature? He had none except that which he had in common. To maintain otherwise is to assert, not a trinity of persons in the Godhead, but three Gods. The very unity of the divine nature forbids the doctrine of Christ's divine nature being the substitute of his human soul.

2. But compare the two theories as to Christ's intellectual and spiritual life here on earth.

Neither denies that there were intellectual and spiritual acts performed by Christ while in the flesh.

The common theory asserts that some were performed by Christ by virtue of his divine nature, and some by virtue of his human soul. The manifestly divine acts are ascribed to him as God, the manifestly human to him as man.

That there are divine acts is therefore held by those who hold this common theory, as well as by the others. They also admit that some acts are difficult so to classify as to determine whether they are divine or human.

The question between the theories, therefore, is whether there are any intellectual or spiritual acts or experiences of Christ here on earth which could not have resulted from a divine nature, but which are stamped with a distinctively human character? If there were any, Christ must have had a human soul.

The inquiry is limited to this, though we might press the arguments of the ancients against Apollinaris and his followers; as, how can the Scripture be justified in calling Christ a man and in representing his humanity as a qualification for his work of righteousness and atonement, if he had but a human body only? Does the body alone constitute humanity? If the body alone suffered, how then are the souls of men healed? If when he appeared upon earth as a man, he had only the body of a man, was he not, in the most important element of humanity, only an appearance or phantom of a man? Was it the body only of mankind that had sinned and was condemned, and did the soul need no redemption? Was the virtue secured by the divine nature in such incarnation human virtue? Was it indeed any virtue at all?

But these inquiries are not needed. The Scripture statements are themselves more than sufficient. What then do they say?

1. Of the theory of the substitution of the divine nature for the human soul not one hint is given throughout the entire Scripture. Not a syllable is

there which teaches anything more than that a divine person became incarnate. Nothing is said of the absence of a human soul; nothing of the incarnation being in only a partial human nature; nothing to show that the divine nature had any thing to do with the work, except that the divine nature was possessed by him who became incarnate, but possessed by him, not separately from, but unitedly with, the other persons of the Godhead. The Scriptures teach, not that the divine nature (God) became incarnate, but that he, who, as well as the Father and the Spirit, is God, became man.

2. But the instances of human emotion are abundant.

(a.) Notice first the experiences already mentioned in connection with the body; that it was not simply a temple in which Deity dwelt; but that Christ experienced in his body all those sinless passions and desires which arise from association of the body with a human soul. Whence come weariness, fatigue, thirst, etc.? Does the body experience them when separated from the soul? Did the body then affect the divine nature of Christ as it does a human soul? Is the divine nature capable of such affection from a mere material organization, a mere shell of a man? Would such an idea he admitted for a moment of the influence of our bodies on the Holy Ghost within? A more vital union must exist. That which thus affects must be personally united with the nature thus affected. Can the body of a man be thus personally united with the divine nature of Christ? Does the union with the nature occur in any other way than through union with the person in divine nature? If so, why may not the soul also be in like manner united? Is a twofold personality created in the one case any more than in the other? Yet the objection is made to the existence of a human soul that thus twofold personality must exist, and that as Christ is but one person, his divine nature must have been his human soul or must have been substituted for it.

But it may be said that the affections referred to are those of the body only, and that, even among men, they are not associated with the soul, and that the life indicated in them is only the physical life possessed by all animals, and that such life is not inconsistent with the absence of a rational soul. The position assumed is not correct; but, if granted, it gives no advantage to the theory we oppose. Is it not still the fact that the body exercises more or less influence on the mind, as well as the mind over the body? Bodily disease enfeebles the mind. The mind, by its will, sustains, and, by its mental trials, depresses the body. When, therefore, we see such results in Christ, we must attribute them to the same causes as among men. What then gave occasion and power to the tempter in the wilderness except the bodily desire arising from the previous forty day fast? To what was due Christ's inability to carry his cross to crucifixion, if not to the failure of his bodily powers, resulting from the mental agony endured in the garden and the judgement hall? In his temptation, too, what was tempted by his bodily hunger? Was it God? Was it the divine nature which had taken the place of a human soul? The apostle James declares (1:13, 14) "God cannot be tempted with evil." In the face of a declaration so positive, and so unqualified—written, too, after the temptation of Christ, and with a full knowledge of all its facts—we must believe that the intellectual and spiritual nature of Christ then tempted was not divine, and, therefore, must be human.

(b.) But the Scriptures not only show Christ liable to these mutual influences of body and mind, and to the resultant temptation by Satan; but they teach us that he also received the gracious influences of the Holy Ghost. That the body was thus affected is undoubted, for the body was conceived by the Holy Ghost. But the influence of the Spirit over the soul is also taught. At the baptism of Jesus we are told that "the Holy Ghost descended in a bodily form, as a dove, upon him." Luke 3:22. After the baptism Jesus, full of the holy Spirit, returned from the Jordan, and was led by the Spirit in the wilderness." Luke 4:1. After the temptation, "Jesus returned in the power of the Spirit into Galilee." Luke 4:14. At Nazareth, in his first recorded public discourse, "he found the place where it was written, the Spirit of the Lord is upon me, because he anointed me to preach good tidings to the poor." Luke 4:17, 18. "And he began to say unto them, Today hath this Scripture been fulfilled in your ears." Luke 4:21. These were certainly influences upon his soul. How could they have been exerted, and why so exerted, if that soul was the divine nature? What need could divinity have for consecration, for grace? What need to be led, or, as Mark (1:12) expresses it, to be driven into the wilderness? How could a divine being lack in that which was essentially divine? That the wants of the body might be supplied, is not strange. The body is human, but if he had no human soul, what was it that the Holy Ghost influenced?

(c.) The Scriptures, however, do not represent Christ as receiving aid from a divine person only. At the close of the temptation angels came and ministered to him. It may be said that this was only to the body; but it is doubtful if it were of the body only, for much of his temptation was mental. But, certainly, it was the agony of the spirit of Christ, and not of the body, which the angel in Gethsemane was sent to relieve.

(d.) We have also such action of Christ as is not consistent with the idea that he had no human soul. We find instances of such intellectual and spiritual restraint, limit and subjection as cannot be true of God.

The declaration that Christ marvelled at the unbelief of certain persons is perfectly intelligible, when spoken of a human soul; but not, when ascribed to the mind of Deity. So also Luke's statement that "Jesus advanced in wisdom and stature, and in favour with God and men." Luke 2:52. Also, that other assertion of Christ, so plainly and distinctly made, of his ignorance of the time of the final judgement, Matt. 24:36, can be comprehended as possible only of his human soul, to which had not been imparted the knowledge which he must have possessed as God.

What shall be said also of his subjection to his parents after the dispute with the doctors in the temple? Was it only bodily subjection? What does exclusively bodily subjection mean? Is it not the mind, and the heart, that yield obedience, and submit to authority? What, then, was it that was thus subject? Was it his divine nature? Was it God himself? Can God be thus subjected to a creature? Yet, if Christ had no human soul, there were then at Nazareth two human beings, to whom the infinite and omnipotent God, the Ruler of the universe, was subject in his real divine nature, giving them reverence and obedience, and recognizing in them an official superiority, and submitting to their will.

(e.) How account for Christ's prayers, if he had no human soul? Were they only prostrations of his body by the indwelling divine nature, or were they the utterances of a soul oppressed with heavy burdens, delighting in converse with God, and, knowing that there is a place for prayer, and seeking and rejoicing in the privilege of offering it? Is that soul, God? Or is it the man, Christ Jesus, lifting up the voice of supplication to his divine Father?

These prayers too, are for himself; not for others only; most frequently for himself. See a signal instance in Gethsemane. He proposes to withdraw for prayer with three of his disciples, telling them that his soul is exceeding sorrowful unto death. Mark (14:33) tells us that this was because "he began to be greatly amazed and sore troubled." "He went forward a little, and fell on the ground, and prayed that, if it were possible, the hour might pass away from him," v. 35. He returned "and again he went away, and prayed, saying the same words," v. 39. He did this three times. Is this not human action? What is there here befitting, or possible to a merely divine intelligence, or spirit? If his were a human soul, how otherwise would he have acted? But, if divine, what reality could there be in these emotions, what need could he have? What comfort, what strength could he gain in such an act? Upon the supposition of a human soul, the presence of that strengthening angel is accounted for, but, how explain the strength which any creature, however exalted, can give to the Almighty Creator?

(f.) The very language of Scripture as to the condition of his soul in that hour of trial, is conclusive. To the expression just quoted, may be added his prayer, that "if it were possible, the hour might pass away from him," Mark 14:35; also his petition, "remove this cup from me." Mark 14:36. "Now is my soul troubled," he exclaims, "and what shall I say? Father, save me from this hour, but, for this cause, came I unto this hour. Father, glorify thy name." John 12:27. "O, my Father, if it be possible, let this cup pass away from me." Matt.

26:39. What have we here but trouble, and anguish, and doubt, and fear, and trust, and desire of release, and yet full resignation? Are these characteristics of a divine mind? Or do we not see here the complete humanity of Christ revealed for our comfort and assurance? For what other purpose the record of these facts? Can God be honoured by showing his divine nature thus racked and agonized, in the performance of that great work which it is claimed must be done by God alone? Surely, it is the humanity of the Saviour that is thus revealed, even before the final agony and triumph. The proof that this same person is God, is not lacking. It is indeed the Son of God, who thus, in human soul, and body is doing the work. But it is his human soul, not his divine nature that thus pleads, and shrinks, and fears, and which still willingly submits, resolves to press on, is strengthened by God's messenger, and again, confident in God, goes forward with sublime self-devotion to the cross. The distance between this and God is infinite; this soul, the creature, the finite, the fearful, the mutable, the suffering, the trusting, the dying; and him, the creator, the infinite, the support of those who trust, the immutable, who cannot suffer, who cannot die. The acts due to the divine nature are marked, and characteristic, and so also are those of the human nature. While we look at the former, we must say, this is God; none but he can perform such acts, can possess such attributes, can be called such names. Equally, while we look at the latter, we must say, this is man. None but man can thus suffer, can thus be limited, can thus pray. The very nature of God forbids that he should change, that he should be limited, that he should be dependent, that he should be affected by anything outside of himself, that he should be ignorant of any future event.

Christ, therefore, had a human soul, as well as a human body. To deny this, and to assert that the divine nature became his soul, we must deny the unity of God, which establishes the undivided nature of his essence, and also the perfection of God, which makes him unchangeable, and omniscient, and independent, and impassible; and we must assert, when Scripture presents him amid intellectual and spiritual experiences, which are foreign to God, but are of the nature of the human soul, that those were not the experiences of a human soul, but of Divinity itself. If we thus deny that the names, attributes, acts, and experiences, natural to a human soul, are proof of complete humanity, we need not be surprised that others deny that he was God, however abundantly the Scriptures ascribe to him divine names, attributes and acts.

IV. There was but one person in the two natures.

We have not here a God and a man; but we have one who is God, and who also is man; and who, being thus one person, unites in himself through these two natures, the many exactly opposite characteristics needed for his work. Despite the contradictory character of his natures, the personality is but one.

That in him which we call "I," the myself which marks individuality, that in which he was not the Father in the Godhead, nor the Spirit, was common to both natures. With the divine nature, however, it is inseparably, necessarily, eternally and essentially united; for that nature cannot change, nor assume new relations; not even doing so when the divine person, which subsists in it, assumes humanity. But, with the human nature, the personality was associated voluntarily and separably, though permanently; the human nature having been created for that purpose, and assumed by the divine person of his own will, in the fullness of time. Hence our Lord invariably uses the word "I" whether in his human or divine nature or in both; whether speaking of himself as Son of God, or as Son of Man, or as the Messiah; and whether referring to his human actions and emotions, or to his divine works and attributes, or to his official work as Mediator.

But, as Christ assumed no additional personality to that which he had before the incarnation, and as personality in man is certainly essential, the question arises: Did he thus really become a man? Is this being made like unto his brethren?

1. To this it may be replied, that if the Scriptures represent this as all that was done, and yet teach that Christ became a man, that teaching is sufficient; we need no further testimony. God knows what is essential to the constitution of man.

2. But consider the difficulty thus presented. It is said that to be completely a man, Christ must also be a human person. Granted; but is his person not a human person so far as respects humanity alone, just as it is a divine person so far as respects divinity alone? Does individuality acquire character separated from the nature which belongs to it? Would Christ be any longer divine if separated from his divine nature? If he were to cease from his incarnation, would he be any longer a man? What is personality but individual existence, and what gives it character, as human, angelic, or divine, except the nature in which it inheres?

A person is simply an individual intellectual and spiritual existence in some nature. A divine person is one who is this in divine nature. An angel is one who is this in angelic nature. A man is such in human nature. Christ, therefore, was and is a man because of his individual intellectual and spiritual existence in human nature, and is God because of his individual intellectual and spiritual existence in divine nature. He is the God-man because as one being he is a person in both natures, having individual intellectual and spiritual existence in a human nature and also in the divine nature. He is, therefore, properly a human person and a divine person, but not two persons, for it is the subsistence of the one person in both of these natures that makes him one being only. He is as properly a human person, therefore, as he would be if not divine, just as he is as properly a divine person as he would be if not a man.

3. Within the same race, too, what constitutes personality? Is it the continued retention unchanged of the same identical portion of the common nature, the same body and soul? Science teaches constant change in the body, leaving not a particle now of what existed years ago. While the soul cannot thus be measured, experience teaches us that great changes occur even there; in its capacities, emotions, habits, tendencies, and in numerous other respects. Yet, amid all, the personality remains unchanged. Newton was the same person in maturity as when a babe.

4. Even the moral nature undergoes change without the change of personality, as shown in the difference in Adam before and after the fall, and in Paul at Stephen's martyrdom and when he exclaimed in contemplation of martyrdom, "I am already being offered." 2 Tim. 4:6.

5. Nor is it destroyed by actual separation from a part of the nature which belongs to it. The thief in Paradise was the same person to whom Christ spoke peace, though he had left his body hanging on the cross. The saints with Christ are the same persons who once dwelt on earth in bodies now mouldered into dust.

6. It is recognized as existing unimpaired even in a state of utterly unconscious connection, as in a senseless condition produced by outward pressure on the skull, or by the use of chloroform and other anesthetics; if this be not also the condition of healthy slumber.

If these are facts, why may not a person who possesses one nature assume another also, and yet he as truly a person in that nature as any others who possess it?

7. But someone may object that the difficulty arises, in the case of Christ, from the union in the one person of two natures essentially different, in one of which Christ had before existed, and with which he is essentially united, while the other is only assumed in time, and that, too, voluntarily.

But this finds sufficient analogy in the two-fold nature united in ordinary human persons. Personality here exists inseparably from the soul, separably from the body. This is evident when at death the personality is with the soul in the presence of God, not at all with the body in the corruption of the grave.

It is true that we cannot speak of these two elements of our nature as separated from each other as widely as humanity and divinity; yet how vast is the distance between matter and spirit! So vast, indeed, as to be only surpassed by that between the finite and the infinite.

It is also true that we cannot speak of such essential union between the human soul and its personality as we can between Christ and his divine nature.

Yet we have reason to believe the union so complete, that from the beginning of the soul's existence throughout all eternity, there shall be no separation.

Upon no grounds, then, can it be asserted that the absence of a separate personality for Christ's human nature made Jesus, in any respect, not like unto his brethren. Scripture affirms, and reason supports the idea, that the same person, existing and operating, we know not how, but according to the nature of God, was truly God; and, also, existing in human nature, and operating as we do through its conscious relations to the real body and human soul, of which that nature was composed, was truly man. In each nature he knew of his relation to the other; as God, knowing that he was man, and as man, knowing that he was God. Yet the divine nature did not partake of that human knowledge and experience which he had of affliction, suffering and temptation, any more than the human nature experienced the conscious relation of Christ to the Father in the divine nature, or possessed the attributes of omniscience or omnipresence. No limitations or changes which he experienced in his human nature could deprive him of complete divinity; nor could any influence nor any value, arising from the essential union of his person with his divine nature, take away from the absolute and real humanity assumed by Christ, and consciously realized by him, when he became man. However united, he was capable of separate experience, action, thought and knowledge, and, indeed, of separate conscious existence in the two natures. Thus is it at least with us. We have separate experiences of the sufferings and joys of our souls and our bodies, and this fact removes any difficulty in believing that it was so with Christ, as to his divine and human natures, when we find the Bible thus teaching.

It is here that we are to find the full explanation of the many seeming contradictions involved in what is taught us of the person and work of Christ. So intimate is the union of the one person with two such distinct natures, that we cannot always separate what Christ says of himself as God, from what is said of himself as man. This, however, may puzzle us in interpreting the Word of God, but not in harmonizing its statements. But, without this doctrine, the Word of God cannot be made to agree with itself. When, however, we remember that, though truly divine, he is human, and that because of the one person, all that he does in either nature may be as fully said to be done by him as though he had no other, we see the Scripture statements fall beautifully and regularly into their respective ranks, and, in that two-fold unity, each receives its full force. It is thus that he who is said to fill the universe was contained in the womb of Mary; that he whose are the cattle upon a thousand hills felt the pangs of famishing hunger; that he who made the world had not where to lay his head; that he who had given the fig-tree its fruit, and knew what it was bearing, came to it, if haply he might find anything thereon; that he to whom, as God, are known all things from the foundation of the world, yet offered up fervent prayers, with agony and strong supplication, not for others only, but chiefly for himself, and also declared that he knew not the judgement day; that he who, as God, had given salvation to men before his incarnation, because of the certainty of the work he would accomplish, yet, as man, approached with shrinking, and perhaps with fear of failure in his work, praying the Father that the cup might pass from him. And, hanging upon the cross, how amazing the mystery of contradiction! As God, he enjoys supreme felicity in the unchanged blessedness of his divine nature; as man, he is in vital agony both of body and soul. As God, the eternal outflowings of the mutual love of the Father, and of the Spirit, and of himself the Eternal Son, continue to bestow unabated mutual bliss. As man, he is the victim of the Father's wrath, which, because of the sin upon him, culminates in that Father's withdrawal amid the agonizing cry of the Son: "My God, my God, why hast thou forsaken me?" With a loud cry, the mortal man dies; but the eternal life of God remains unchanged.

The full statements of the Scriptures on this subject may be thus expressed.

1. There is one God, in three persons, distinct in personality but undividedly and unchangeably the same in essence and nature.

2. We may speak of a divine person, but not of a divine nature. We must say the divine nature.

3. A divine person, may, therefore, become incarnate, and yet the incarnation be not of the whole Godhead, for the persons are distinct; but the divine nature cannot, because, as common to all, its incarnation would be that of the whole Godhead.

4. It was a person of this Godhead, the Son, the Word, who so united to himself human nature, as to become a person in that nature, a man.

5. In this union he assumed all that constitutes a man. The fact that he had no other personality than such as had always subsisted in the divine nature, does not make him an impersonal man. It only forbids the idea of an additional personality exclusively in the human nature.

6. This human nature was assumed because necessary to the work of salvation, it being impossible that a being only divine could undergo the experience necessary to redeem man.

7. In its assumption the divine nature of Christ was wholly unchanged, and the human nature still remained purely human.

8. The characteristics of personality, however, allow a most vital union of the two natures in his one person.

9. Thus uniting in himself God and man, Christ suffered.

10. There was here, therefore, no participation of the divine nature in the suffering. Such participation would involve actual suffering of that nature.

11. But there was this connection of God, even of the undivided divine essence, that he who thus suffered subsists eternally and essentially in that essence, and is God.

12. Yet, intimate as is the connection of the two natures, they are not merged in each other, nor does the Son of God lose his separate conscious existence with either, nor the possession of those peculiarities which make the one divine and the other human. It is one person, truly God and truly man; as much God as though not man; as much man as though not God. The human can add nothing to the divine, except that it gives to the person that is divine the means of suffering for and sympathizing with us. The divine adds to the human, only that it gives to him that is thus man that dignity, and glory, and power, which enable him to perform the work of salvation, and to give to that work an inestimable value.

Another form of expression of the Scripture facts may also be given:

1. God is one in nature, essence and being; therefore there is but one God—one divine nature.

2. God is three in person—Father, Son and Spirit. Hence in the one undivided divine nature subsist three persons.

3. One of these persons (the Son), and one only (not the Father and Spirit also), became man. It was not the three persons that became man; therefore not the divine nature which is common to the three, but one person only. God, therefore, was manifested in the flesh, not because the Godhead or the divine nature became flesh, but because the Son or the Word, who is God because he subsists in the divine nature, became flesh.

4. In becoming man he still remained God, because he still continued to subsist in the divine nature.

5. In becoming man he became as truly man as he is truly God, because he assumed a true human nature in both its forms—body and soul—and subsisted in it as really as he did in the divine nature.

6. As it was the same person who became man as well as God, there were not two persons—one divine and one human—but one at the same time divine and human.

7. This one person, therefore, had, by virtue of his divine nature, all divine experience; and by virtue of his human nature, all human experience; thinking, willing and purposing as God, and exercising all the divine attributes of omniscience, omnipotence and omnipresence, etc., and thinking, willing and purposing as man, with limited powers and limited knowledge, subject to temptation, suffering, doubts and fears.

8. This one person was, therefore, able to suffer and bear the penalty of man's transgression, because, being of man's nature, he could become man's representative, and could also endure such suffering as could be inflicted upon man; yet, being God, he could give a value to such suffering, which would make it an equivalent, not to one man's penalty, but to that of the whole race.

9. All the difficulties in the way of believing these things to be true and possible are removed by the analogy which is seen in the union in man of two natures in one person. This shows, in a most remarkable way, an almost exact likeness in each man to that constitution and nature of the God-man which the Scriptures reveal in the doctrine of the person of Christ.

CHAPTER 27

THE OFFICES OF CHRIST

THREE offices are ascribed by the Scriptures to Christ—those of prophet, priest and king.

I. CHRIST AS PROPHET

This word is to be taken in its wider sense of inspired teacher.

It is frequently confined, in common language, to one who foretells future events. But it literally means one who speaks for his God, and denotes a divine teacher merely. Thus Moses is spoken of as a prophet, and Christ was foretold as a prophet who should be like unto Moses.

It is in connection with this that the term Logos, or Word, applied to Christ in the 1st chapter of John is appropriate.

With the office of teacher, Christ united, as was common with the prophets, the prediction of future events and the working of miracles. But the office of teacher was his special work as prophet.

This work is discharged in the following ways:

1. In the personal revelations which he made, before the days of his incarnation, to our first parents, to the patriarchs and to others of their day, to Moses and the people of God in the wilderness, and to various others, as Manoah, the children in the furnace, etc. These were made in appearances of human form, in the burning bush, in the pillar of cloud and fire, in the Shechinah, etc., etc.

2. In the inspired revelations which he made through holy men of old, who spake as they were moved by the Holy Ghost. The Old Testament Scriptures are composed of a portion of these.

3. While on earth in his incarnation.

(1.) Personally as, (a.) he set forth by his own acts the divine attributes, omnipotence, omniscience, omnipresence, eternity of existence, etc., and (b.) as he exhibited God's love for man, his hatred of sin, and his love of holiness and righteousness in the work of man's salvation.

(2.) By his instructions, as he taught (a.) in words to his disciples and others what he exhibited in his person as to the matters above stated, and (b.) the truths relative to the kingdom he was to establish, its nature, its subjects, the relations they should bear to each other, to him and the Father, and their future destiny and glory; as well as the condition and fate of those who should reject him.

4. By the instructions he gave through his apostles and other inspired men after his ascension.

5. By the revelation of himself in the lives and character of his true disciples in all ages.

6. By the instructions given through his preached word in all ages.

7. By the revelations of glory he shall make to the church of first-born ones in the world to come.

8. By the revelation which through these, he shall make of the glory of God to the universe of created intelligences.

II. CHRIST AS PRIEST

The office of "Priest" is one of divine appointment. That of Christ corresponds to that of the High Priest under the Mosaic economy, and is foreshadowed by it. The Epistle to the Hebrews sets this forth very plainly and explicitly. The priesthood of Christ, however, varies from that of the High Priest in several particulars. Christ's priesthood is perpetual, is in one person, without predecessor or successor, making one offering, once for all; an offering actually not symbolically effective, deriving value not from appointment alone, but from its nature also. In this case, also, the victim is the same person as the High Priest. Consequently Christ's office as priest is to be contemplated in the twofold aspect of priest and victim.

1. As Priest, he offers up the sacrifice, laying it upon the altar of oblation, and through it appeasing the wrath of God, making reconciliation between God and man, and securing, in its proper presentation, the removal of guilt and punishment from man.

As Priest he also intercedes with God for pardon or justification or other blessings for all for whom he died, in all the respects in which his death is available for each.

The first of these priestly offices was discharged upon earth, the second is discharging in heaven. It does not cease with his life on earth, but he is represented as continuing as an ever-living High Priest to make intercession for us, Heb. 7:23–25; sitting down at the right hand of God, Acts 2:33–36; Heb. 8:1; 9:12–21. (See the law as to the Jewish High Priest entering in once every year in Heb. 9:27; also in the law laid down in Ex. 30:10; Lev. 16:2, 11, 12, 15, 34; see also Heb. 7:27; 10:10. 1 Pet. 3:18, confines it to their sufferings and does not include the offering.) It is not for the purpose of offering the sacrifice that he is there, Heb. 9:24, 25; but to make intercession for those for whom the sacrifice has already been offered, Heb. 10:11, 12, 14–18. These passages show it was such an offering as actually sanctified (v. 10), and purified (v. 14) them that are sanctified.

While we are not to suppose that he is engaged in actual spoken prayer before God, we are also not to understand by this a mere influence of his sacrifice continued without further activity on his part, but some real activity corresponding fully to the essence of prayer and petition, to which is due all the blessings to which his people attain.

This intercession is made for his people, Luke 22:32, John 14:16; 17:9, 15, 20, 24; Eph. 2:18; Heb. 4:14–16. The passages in Isaiah 53:12 and Luke 23:34 have been adduced as indicating intercession which avails in some respect for all men. But such benefits are not the result of intercessory prayer, nor of Christ's atoning work conferring general benefits; but they come from the necessary co-existence of the persons thus benefited with those to whom the resulting benefits of the atoning work belong.

2. Christ as the victim.

(1.) His qualifications.

(a.) His sinlessness; for this position he needed to be pure, holy, harmless, undefiled, separate from sinners, and one in whom there was no sin. He must be a spotless Lamb.

(b.) His humanity; that he might be of common nature with those for whom he died, and that he might be capable of suffering, and of such suffering as man may endure.

(c.) His divinity; that his successful prosecution of the work might be assured, and that his offering might have merit sufficient to ransom those for whom he died.

(d.) His federal relation; that he might he a proper substitute for sinners, not any securing righteousness by obedience, but bearing and removing their guilt by making satisfaction for it.

(2.) The offering; thus qualified he was offered up as a victim; his body to the suffering which culminated in his death on the cross, and his soul to the anguish due to the realized presence of imputed sin, to the wrath endured from God, and to the separation from God's favor while bearing that wrath.

III. CHRIST AS KING

Christ announced to his disciples just before his ascension, "All authority hath been given unto me in heaven and on earth." Math 28:18. Peter at

Pentecost declared, "that God hath made him both Lord and Christ, this Jesus whom ye crucified;" Acts 2:36.

Constant references had been previously made to his kingdom. It was not simply spoken of as the kingdom of God, and kingdom of heaven, but as closely connected with Christ. Luke 22:29, 30; 23:42; John 18:37.

1. Christ as the God-man is Mediatorial king.

As Son of God he had the right of rule over the universe. Of this he emptied himself and became man, that he might become Mediator and do the work of salvation. Having become man he died on the cross. On this account he has been exalted, so "that in the name of Jesus every knee should bow, . . . and that every tongue should confess that Jesus Christ is Lord to the glory of God, the Father." Phil. 2:6–11. Compare Acts 2:22–36, especially verse 36. "God hath made him both Lord and Christ, this Jesus whom ye crucified." Also 1 Cor. 15:24–26.

2. Christ reigns over his spiritual kingdom, securing the final result of the establishment of that kingdom in the persons of all his people when he shall "present the church to himself, a glorious church." Eph. 5:27.

3. He reigns over his visible churches on earth through the laws he has given, through the Spirit by which he dwells in them, and by his providences, overruling, controlling, and accomplishing all his purposes.

4. The rules over this world as King of Kings, and Lord of Lords, causing all things to work together for his ends.

5. He rules over the universe. His sway is not limited to earth.

6. His Mediatorial reign is not confined to human subjects, but extends also to angelic. The angels of heaven are his attendants and his messengers.

7. He even rules over Satan and his evil angels. Their exercise of power for evil is permitted only for a time. Even during that time it is controlled by Christ; so that it is limited by his will, and is, therefore, truly subjected to him.

CHAPTER 28

THE ATONEMENT OF CHRIST

SEVERAL prominent theories have been presented, as to the atoning work of Christ, and the method by which God pardons sin.

1. The lowest of these is the Socinian. This proceeds on the principle that God is pure benevolence, that vindictive justice is incompatible with his character, and that upon mere repentance, God can and will forgive the sinner. The work of Christ, therefore, is regarded as one in which he simply reveals or makes known pardon to man. Nothing that he has done secures it, because he had nothing to do to this end. It was already prepared in the benevolence of God's nature, and is simply now made known. [Symington on the Atonement, pp. 2 and 3.]

The advocates of this theory explain away all that the Scriptures say on the subject of Christ's death for us, by maintaining that his life and death were mere examples to us of the manner in which we should live and submit to God. In their view, therefore, Christ is merely a great teacher and a bright example.

Some of these have even gone so far as to speak of the sacrifices of the ancient dispensation as things suitable only to a barbarous age, and so far from regarding them as types of Christ's sacrificial work, have looked on them as arrangements permitted only from sympathy for the weakness of the people, whom God ordered to offer them. [Nehemiah Adams, Evenings with the Doctrines, p. 197.]

The objections to this theory are:

(1.) It ill accords with the Scripture description of the nature of sin.

(2.) It is inconsistent with other attributes of God than mercy.

(3.) It is at variance with the letter and spirit of divine revelation.

(4.) It is irreconcilable with the exalted nature of the mediatorial reward conferred on Christ. [Symington, p. 3.]

2. A second theory of the Atonement is that which has commonly been called the Middle Theory. By this is not meant, that there are only these two and one orthodox theory; but, simply, that this stands between the theory of the Socinians and those theories held by persons, who, however, differing from each other, are regarded as Evangelical.

"This theory maintains that in consequence of what Christ did, a certain power to pardon sin was conferred upon him." [Symington p. 3.]

"This system supposes that God may pardon sin without punishment or satisfaction."

"But that a difference should be made between innocent persons who have never sinned, and those thus pardoned; that the latter may not boastingly suppose themselves on an equality with the former."

"This is done by the arrangement that, instead of a full pardon, they shall be pardoned on repentance, for the sake of something Christ was to do, because of which he is entitled to intercede for them."

(1.) "This scheme is only apparently superior to the former, in claiming that this is done, because of what Christ has done."

(2.) "It gives a defective view of the divine character."

(3.) "It does not explain the Scripture language as to Christ's work."

(4.) "It fails to account for the peculiarity and severity of his sufferings." [Symington, pp. 3 and 4.]

3. A third theory of the Atonement is that of moral influence. Its most noted advocates in this day have been Horace Bushnell and McLeod Campbell. It is difficult to say whether it, or the one last mentioned, approaches more nearly to that of the Socinians or is more remote from Evangelical ideas.

Like the so-called Middle Theory, it deems repentance alone to be essential for a sinner's acceptance with God. It maintains that there has never been any obstacle in the nature of God to the granting of full pardon upon mere repentance for sin. The necessity for Christ's life of suffering and death of agony is to be found only in the need of motives arising from the love thus exhibited to man to induce him to repent. It is for the sinner's sake that Christ has lived such a life of misery and woe as is incident to man. So far as this theory has been held by Socinians they have recognized the work of Christ simply as that of the exalted man, Christ Jesus. But as presented by Bushnell and Campbell, God in Christ has thus identified himself with man in his misery and sin. Campbell goes so far as to represent Christ as so fully thus made one with man as to have been the representative penitent and confessor of sin. It is the great love thus shown which exerts the strong moral influence which causes man to repent and to be reconciled unto God.

All the objections to the Middle Theory may with equal force he urged against this. To these may be added:

(1.) That, while that theory recognizes the power to forgive sin to have been bestowed upon Christ as the result of something Christ has done, this confines the effect of his work to the production of penitence in the sinner through the influence which the love he has thus displayed exerts in taking away the indifference and enmity of the human heart.

(2.) That, while this theory recognizes the great truth that the love of Christ exhibited in his sufferings and death, has a strong influence in leading men to reconciliation to God, it diminishes the extent to which this love has been manifested by denying that element in those sufferings which arose from their relation to the penalty endured for sin in the satisfaction of the justice of God.

(3.) That, as indeed is true of all schemes which depend entirely upon subjective influences in the sinner, it fails to present any method of salvation available for those who have had no knowledge of these sufferings. Thus are cut off from all the blessings of salvation, not only all infants and idiots, but also the many saints of God who died before the birth of Jesus.

4. A fourth theory of the Atonement is the Ethical one suggested by the Andover divines. It agrees substantially with the theory just considered, but because of the recent prominence of the "New Theology," of which Andover may be regarded as the most prominent exponent, it deserves especial consideration in the form set forth by that school. It has been most distinctly presented in a series of articles on "Progressive Orthodoxy," published editorially in the fourth volume (1885) of the *Andover Review.* The third of this series is on the Atonement. The quotations which follow are from that article.

The specific points of this theory are:

1. That Christ is universal mediator, and as such, must appear for the relief of any portion of the universe which needs his help.

"Christ mediates God to the entire universe. Through Christ the worlds were made, and through him they consist. In him were all things created, in the heavens and upon the earth, things visible and things invisible. To him ultimately not the earth only, but the whole universe is to be made subject, things in heaven and things in earth and things under the earth. . . . Not until he is known as Head of the universe do we perceive nor can we well understand, that he is the Life and Light of men. The whole truth, then, is that Christ is the revealing or manifesting principle; or, more exactly, that through the Logos, the Word, the Second Person of the Trinity, that which is absolute fullness and truth in God is communicated into finite existences; that through the Eternal Word the created universe is possible; that therefore the universe is Christ's, the revolving worlds, and they that dwell therein are his to the glory of God the Father. The created universe and all rational beings are through Christ and in Christ. Therefore he mediates or reveals God to any part of his universe according to the condition or need which may exist in that part. If at any point his world is sick, weary, guilty, hopeless, there Christ is touched and hurt, and

there he appears to restore and comfort. This earth is, it may be, the sheep lost
in the wilderness, while the ninety and nine are safe in the fold. Christ cannot
be indifferent to the least of his creatures in its pain and wickedness, for his universe is not attached to him externally, but vitally. He is not a governor set over
it, but is its life everywhere. He feels its every movement, most of all its spiritual
life and spiritual feebleness or disease, and appears in his glorious power even at
the remotest point. If there were but one sinner, Christ would seek him. If but
one planet were invaded by sin, Christ would come to its relief," p. 57.

2. His incarnation would probably have occurred if there had been no sin,
but the existence of sin changes its conditions, but not the power and reality of
Christ.

"The opinion has reason in it that there would have been the Incarnation
even if there had been no sin," p. 58. "It is, of course, true that in order to reveal
God in a world of sin and guilt the historical conditions, and especially the
suffering conditions, of our Lord's life must have been, in important respects,
what they would not otherwise have been. It is also probable that the profound-
est disclosure of the love of God in Christ has been made in the redemption of
sinful man. But only the conditions, not the power and reality of Christ, are
contingent on sin," p. 57.

3. The effect of Christ's work has been to change the relations of God to man
which secures a change in the relation of man to God. This is the reconciliation
effected.

"The very best word the gospel gives to express the complete result of Christ's
work is reconciliation, a word signifying that God is brought into a new relation
to man and that man is brought into a new relation with God. The ultimate fact,
however, is that God's relation to man is changed in Christ from what it otherwise could be, and that therefore man's relation to God is changed. Redemption
thus originates with God, who in Christ finds a way through obstacles to the
sinner, so that he can righteously forgive and bless. Because God is reconciled
in Jesus Christ man repents and begins a new life," p. 58.

4. In the work of Atonement there is no imputation or transfer of the sin of
man to Christ nor of Christ's righteousness to man.

"It is no longer believed that personal merit and demerit can be transferred
from one to another. . . . It is not believed that the consequences of sin can be

removed from the transgressor by passing them on to another. Conduct, character, and condition are inseparable. The results of sin are part of the ethical personality, and cannot be detached, nor borne by another," p. 60.

5. Yet in Christ as the substitute of man the race approaches God representatively suffering for sin and repenting of it.

"He is an individual, but an individual vitally related to every human being. He preferred to be called the Son of Man. Paul sees in him the Head of humanity, the second Adam. He is one who is not himself a sinner, yet is a man; who is not himself contending against sinful and corrupt tendencies, yet has so identified himself with humanity that its burden of suffering rested on him, and every man was within his reach of sympathy. . . .

"Humanity may thus be thought of as offering something to God of eminent value. When Christ suffers, the race suffers. When Christ is sorrowful, the race is sorrowful. Christ realizes what humanity could not realize for itself. The race may be conceived as approaching God, and signifying its penitence by pointing to Christ, and by giving expression in him to repentance which no words could utter. Thus we can regard him as our substitute, not because he stands apart, not because he is one and the race another, but because he is so intimately identified with us, and because in essential respects the life of every one is, or may be, locked in with his. . . . Here is the truth of McLeod Campbell's view of atonement. The entire race repents or is capable of repenting through Christ. It renders in him a complete repentance. . . ," pp. 61, 62.

6. This substitutionary suffering and penitence is not, however, available apart from the power of man to repent, and the attainment in the individual of repentance. It avails only because man, although a sinner, is still, under appropriate influences, capable of repenting, and the suffering of Christ for man, and his sympathy with him are able to awaken man to real repentance which is revolutionary and thorough.

"But Christ's power to represent or be substituted for man is always to be associated with man's power to repent. The possibility of redeeming man lies in the fact that although he is by act and inheritance a sinner, yet under the appropriate influence he is *capable* of repenting. The power of repentance remains, and to this power the gospel addresses itself. Christ suffering and sympathizing with men is able to awaken in them and express for them a real repentance. It is to this power that Christ, the holy and the merciful, attaches himself. Realizing it in some, and being able to realize it in all, he represents humanity before

God. Now the power of repentance, which, so far as it exists, is the power of recuperation, is superior to the necessities of past wrong-doing and of present habit. It is the one fact which can never be estimated for what it may do, which baffles the calculation of the wisest observers. The penitent man, so far as he really repents, is in the exercise of a freedom which resists and almost subjugates the forces of evil. In union with Christ, who brings spiritual truth and power to man, repentance is radical. Man left to himself cannot have a repentance which sets him free from sin and death. But in Christ he is moved to repentance which is revolutionary. . . . It is not true, we admit and insist, that repentance without Christ is availing for redemption, for man of himself cannot repent; but, on the other hand, it is not true that Christ's atonement has value without repentance. Christ's sacrifice avails with God because it is adapted to bring man to repentance. This gives it ethical meaning and value," pp. 62, 63.

7. The sufferings and death of Christ can be substituted for the punishment of man, not because the guilt of man was borne by him and was atoned for in the way maintained by the older Calvinistic divines, but because:

(1.) By them, as truly and fully as by such punishment, was expressed the abhorrence of God for sin, and the righteousness of the law.

(2.) Because in this way is revealed the love of God, who so seeks the sinner as to manifest that even his wrath is but his love which cannot allow the sinner to be blessed in his sin.

(3.) Because thus is an end put to separation from God, which is the first and greatest punishment of sin; and in view of Christ's death it would be puerile to exact literal punishment of those who are thereby made sorry for sin and brought in penitence to God.

(4.) Because by his knowledge of them man is brought to repentance.

"The punishment and consequences of sin make real God's abhorrence of sin, and the righteousness of law. The sufferings and death of his only Son also realize God's hatred of sin, and the righteous authority of law; therefore punishment need not be exacted."

*   *   *   *   *   *   *   *   *

"It must be confessed, however, that it is not clear how the sufferings and death of Christ can be substituted for the punishment of sin; how, because Christ made vivid the wickedness of sin and the righteousness of God, man is therefore any the less exposed to the consequences of sin. We must go on to the fact that Christ makes real very much more than God's righteous indignation against sin. The punishment of sin does not save men. It only vindicates God and his law. Christ, while declaring God's righteousness, reveals God seeking men, and at the cost of sacrifice. He shows that God loves men, and energizes in Christ to bring them to himself; that really the wrath of God is only a manifestation of the love of God, since God cannot allow the sinner to be blessed in his sin. The very fact, that God's Son cannot be among men for their redemption except at the cost of suffering from the sin of man and of dying at their hands, shows both the intrinsic badness of sin and the undiscouraged love of God to sinners. What really occurs is the approach of God to men in Christ, who shows by his words and life the Father unto them; who draws them back to God in recoil from sin, and whose sufferings, by reason of sin, condemned sin more unmistakably than the punishment of it could have done.

"Sin is to be looked on not only as an obstacle which keeps man from coming to God, but also as an obstacle which keeps God from coming to man. God loves man, and would bless him. But sin impedes God's love, sets it back, awakens God's disapproval, so that instead of blessing he must condemn and punish. The ideal relation of God is love, but the actual relation is wrath. The sin of man prevents God's love from flowing forth, so that the God of love is in reality hostile to man. In Christ God can come to man in another relation, because Christ is a new divine power in the race to turn it away from sin unto God.

"God does not become propitious because man repents and amends, for that is beyond man's power. He becomes propitious because Christ, laying down his life, makes the race to its worst individual *capable* of repenting, obeying, trusting; and he does this in such a way that God's abhorrence to sin is realized, the majesty of law honored, the sinner and the universe convinced of the righteousness of the divine judgments.

"The first and the greatest punishment of sin is separation from God, the withdrawal of those influences from God by which man is blessed. The consequences of sin in body and character are secondary, are only results of separation from God. It is because God is far away that such consequences follow. In Christ, the lowly, the suffering, the triumphant, God can come near to man to bless him. Christ brings God the Person to man the person, and in such manner that God is known as the God of holy love, the loving and holy Father. The goodness of God leads man to repentance. Man is at peace with God, and the worst punishment of sin is righteously removed.

"It is true, then, that Christ suffered for our sins, and that because he suffered our sins are forgiven. But the suffering was borne because it lay in the path to redemption. The realization of God's love in Christ was possible only through the suffering and death of Christ; and because he suffered and died in bringing the knowledge and love of God to men it is no longer necessary that men should suffer all the consequences of sin. The ethical ends of punishment are more than realized in the pain and death of the Redeemer, through whom man is brought to repentance. His death is a new fact, an astonishing, revealing, persuasive, melting fact, in view of which it would be puerile to exact literal punishment of those who are thereby made sorry for sin and brought in penitence to God. But it is all inseparable from repentance or appropriation. There is thus a limit to the vicarious principle. It is limited in its application by the personal relation of every man to Christ. He who is not moved to penitence and faith by Christ is under a greater condemnation. If he is incorrigible the condemnation is final and irreversible," pp. 63–65.

8. The application of the gospel is made by the Spirit who regenerates no one except through that one's personal knowledge and experience of it.

"It is the function of the Holy Spirit to take the things of Christ, and show them unto men. So far as we know the Holy Spirit does not regenerate men except through the knowledge, motive, and power of the gospel," p. 67.

9. Justice to God's own love requires that this revelation of himself be made known to every sinner.

"Justice is concerned that every attribute of God should be displayed; is as jealous for the rights of love as for those of holiness. If it is God's very nature to love, if it is a desire of his to save men from sin, justice sees to it that love is not deprived of its rights, and is not hindered in any of its impulses. We may go so far as to say that it would not be just for God to condemn men hopelessly when they have not known him as he really is, when they have not known him in Jesus Christ. And it is evidently the intent of God that all men should know him through Christ. The judgment does not come till the gospel has been preached to all nations. The gospel is preached to a nation, not when within certain geographical boundaries it has been proclaimed at scattered points, but only when in reality all individuals of all the nations have known it," pp. 66, 67.

Various objections may be made to the theory thus presented, which are common to it and the theory of Moral Influence.

The following, however, are some of those which are suggested by its distinctive features:

1. Against the idea of universal mediation by Christ.

(1.) That its plausibility arises from an indefinite and mixed idea of mediation, because of which a relation of actual mediation is based upon facts which do not involve such a relation. A mediator is not an agent by which an act is done by one person for another, as would have been the creation of the world had Christ alone accomplished it for God. A mediator is not a medium of communication by which one person conveys information to another. Yet the writer so claims when he says: "Therefore he mediates or reveals God to any part of his universe." p. 57. A mediator is one who intervenes between two persons to bring them into agreement or accord with each other. It is in this sense only that it is applicable to the position occupied by Christ between God and sinful man. It is not allowable, therefore, to base a theory of the position thus occupied and the work accomplished in it upon any relation occupied by Christ as the agent through whom the worlds were made, or the revealer through whom God makes himself known.

(2.) But Christ is not even a universal medium.

(a.) He is not so in creation, for creation is not his work alone, but is the work of God, in which each of the Persons of the Trinity co-operated (see chapter xvi on the Outward Relations of the Trinity, pp. 140–42). His work, therefore, could not have been so exclusive as to make allowable the idea that the Father and the Spirit so stood apart from creation, or have, subsequently, been so isolated from the universe as to make Christ the sole medium between God, or between the other Persons of the Trinity, and that creation. Yet such is manifestly the idea upon which is based the universal unity of Christ with creation and his mediation for it with God.

(b.) He is not a universal medium in revealing the nature and glory of God to the whole universe, for the Scripture no where teaches that he has thus revealed God, except in connection with the work of Incarnation and Redemption. But the revelation made in this is only stated to be to men and to heavenly inhabitants. Nowhere is taught either the fact or the possibility that such a revelation is made by him to the Devil and his hosts. It may be that the corruption and blindness caused by their sin denies to them, as these do to unregenerate man, the capacity to receive such truth. But, upon whatever ground we may account for it, or although no reason can be assigned for it, the fact remains that the Scriptures give no hint that devils participate in that knowledge of God's wondrous excellence which the gospel teaches is made known by Christ to men and angels.

(3.) Neither is any foundation given in Scripture or reason for belief that any intermediary is necessary between God and his innocent creatures. The position he occupies towards sinless beings is unquestionably set forth in the language of Gen. 1:31, "And God saw everything that he had made, and, behold, it was very good." The Scriptures in general represent God's pure and holy angels as in his presence, as receiving communications from him, and as messengers sent forth by him to minister to the heirs of salvation. The only intermediary between God and an innocent being which the Scriptures mention was between God and Christ himself, when, after his temptation "angels came and ministered unto him," Matt. 4:11, and, when, after his prayer in Gethsemane for the removal of the cup "there appeared unto him an angel from heaven, strengthening him." Luke 22:43.

(4.) But all foundation for a theory of universal mediation is destroyed by the fact that no such mediation has occurred in connection with sinful beings other than man. Especially here has it not been true that "if at any point his world is sick, weary, guilty, hopeless, there Christ is touched and hurt, and there he appears to restore and comfort," p. 57. Who in all creation have been more guilty, or who more hopeless than the "angels which kept not their own principality, but left their proper habitation," and whom it is said "he hath kept in everlasting bonds under darkness unto the judgement of the great day?" Jude 6. Neither in times before nor in the work of his incarnation has Christ provided redemption for these as universal Mediator. In the redemptive work of his incarnation we are expressly told that he did this not, for it is said that "verily not of angels did he take hold, but he taketh hold of the seed of Abraham." Heb. 2:16. Indeed Paul seems to teach that no mediation could have been for any other race than man, when in the context he says, "since then the children are sharers in flesh and blood, he also himself in like manner partook of the same" (v. 14), and when he elsewhere asserts that the "one mediator between God and man" is "himself man, Christ Jesus."

It seems, therefore, that so far as the idea of universal mediatorship by Christ is essential to it, this theory cannot be accepted. Yet the writer in the review puts it forth as the true starting-point of the inquiry for "a doctrinal statement which shall be comprehensive, satisfactory, and, at the same time, free from ethical objections and inconsistencies," p. 56.

The further objections suggested to the theory itself will test its freedom from these objections and inconsistencies.

2. This theory cannot be an adequate expression of the Scripture teachings about Christ's sufferings and death, because it sets forth nothing in them, because of which God can justly pardon and accept the sinner. The sinner is recognized as deserving punishment. But that punishment is not borne by Christ. All that Christ does is to suffer, but the sufferings and death are not recognized as punishment endured in the place of the sinner. Neither is there any transfer to Christ of the guilt or of the sin of man. Christ is not a substitute to bear the penalty of sin, but only a substitute who represents the race in its approach to God in the confession of sin and repentance for it. This explanation of his sufferings and death does not, therefore, remove the sin of man, nor make atonement for it.

It is said, however, that thus is taken away the greatest punishment of sin, the separation from God. But no reason is assigned why approach between God and man is thus obtained, except that in the death and sufferings of Christ God expresses his abhorrence of sin and manifests the righteousness of the law. But what is there in these sufferings and that death as expounded by this theory which exhibits God's feelings in these directions? It is said, because, rather than save man in his sin or leave him to its just punishment, God sent his Son, although he must suffer and die at the hands of men. But this is the rather an exhibition of God's mercy toward man desiring to avert the sufferings man must endure. There is no evidence of his abhorrence of sin, though he is unwilling that man should continue a sinner. Sin may be looked upon only as great calamity, not as heinous evil. It may be considered only as would be poverty in one of the sons of a rich man, in the deprivations of which the father is unwilling that the son he would restore, should remain in that restoration to his family.

Neither does it appear why these sufferings and death are necessary, because of Christ's life with man on this earth. It is affirmed that this is so, but no reason is given for such necessity. Christ in his union with the race is said to be the great confessor and penitent. But why also the great sufferer and martyr? Why could he not have appeared among men without suffering at their hands, or being put to death by them? The theory does not represent him as receiving suffering and death from God, except in this providential way. Is it not plain that no explanation of his sufferings and death can be given which does not recognize these as inflicted by God, and however wickedly by man, only by man as the instrument of the suffering, the cause of which is the sin which he bore for man and the ultimate source of which is God, not in his mere providential action, but as the avenger of sin and of the violations of his righteous law? But this theory recognizes no such explanation and so far at least fails to show how, because of Christ's work, God can "himself be just, and the justifier of him that hath faith in Jesus." Rom. 3:26.

3. Neither can this theory find anything in its explanation of the sufferings and death of Christ which enables him to make such a revelation of God as could not have been made without them. When the death of Christ is viewed on the one hand as the result of the inexorable demands of justice, which can only thus be satisfied for sins committed and guilt incurred in the violation of moral law, and, on the other hand, of those of mercy which will offer up all rather than not rescue those whom it would pardon, and additionally of those of truth which cannot swerve from an adequate fulfillment of all that it has threatened, and of those of love which clings with inseparable affection to those whom it deems its own; then is made such an exhibition of the attributes of God as no thought can fathom and no words express. Hence in his incarnation and sacrifice Christ has made such a revelation of God as could not otherwise

have been attained. But what revelation of what attribute of God is expressed in the sufferings of Christ according to this theory which cannot be uttered in words and taught without those attendant sufferings and death? Yet, if the subjective salvation which this theory presents as wrought out in the sinner could have been accomplished without these sufferings and that death, as it thus appears it could have been if dependent only on the revelation thus pointed out as made, then is it certain that Christ would not have died. It is precisely similar to the supposed case of the possibility of righteousness by law as to which Paul declared that if true then "Christ died for nought" Gal. 2:21.

4. The plan of salvation is represented in Scripture as one of grace without the works of law, but this theory makes it one partly by Christ's work and partly by that of the sinner. Repentance on the part of the sinner is so absolutely necessary, not as a consequence, but as an effective cause that it is even said that "it is not true that Christ's atonement has value without repentance," p. 63.

5. The act of the sinner by which his justification is attained is stated in Scripture to be faith; and as to that justification or righteousness it is said, "For this cause it is of faith, that it may be according to grace; to the end that the promise may be sure to all the seed." Rom. 4:16. But this theory makes repentance the sole requisite in the sinner, it being left us to infer that faith is not excluded wherever it is necessary to repentance as a subordinate concomitant. This theory would make necessary such a revision of the word of God as would substitute repentance for faith in hundreds of places. It is a singular fact that in this article of about five hundred and fifty lines of a broad octavo page the word "faith" occurs but once, and that in this sentence, "He who is not moved to penitence and faith by Christ is under a greater condemnation," p. 65. How different from the doctrinal expositions of the work of Christ contained in the word of God. It would have been impossible for Paul to write one-tenth as much on this subject without using the word "faith." It would have been equally impossible for the Andover editor to have done so had he held the view of Christ's work taught by the inspired apostle.

6. Another objection to this theory is its teaching about regeneration. If this never occurs, "except through the knowledge, motive and power of the gospel," in what way can infants be saved? And if by the gospel is meant not merely a promise of salvation, without definite knowledge of the revelations made in the work during the incarnation, how have the saints of old attained salvation? Yet, evidently, such must be the meaning, as this theory declares repentance to be necessary in every sinner, and that "it is only in Christ that he has such knowledge of God and of himself as is necessary to a repentance which is revolutionary," p. 62. Hence there can be no salvation for any man who has not personally known the gospel as revealed in connection with Christ's work on earth.

7. Still another objectionable feature appears in the necessity asserted for the preaching of the gospel to each individual man before justice pronounces its final word.

(a.) This idea is based upon a strained interpretation of Mark 13:10. "The gospel must first be preached unto all the nations."

(b.) It is inconsistent with the statements as to the difference of knowledge possessed by men before the judgement-day and the different action towards them by the judge on that account. Christ spoke of those in that day who shall have known and of those who shall not have known the will of the Lord, and declares that the punishments of these will differ. But according to this theory all men will have known of the gospel. Luke 12:47–48. Paul also taught differences in the judgement of men when he wrote, "For as many as have sinned without law shall also perish without law: and as many as have sinned under law shall be judged by law." Rom. 2:12.

(c.) The idea is baseless that God is under any obligation to man or to himself to secure this universal announcement.

To man God can be under no obligation. He owes nothing except to himself. Therefore the idea of obligation is most adroitly put by the writer, as one to God himself. "If it is God's very nature to love, if it is a desire of his to save men from sin, justice sees to it that love is not deprived of its rights, and is not hindered in any of its impulses," pp. 66, 67. That the language is fallacious may be shown by presenting another proposition, at the basis of which the same necessity in God exists; thus if it is God's very nature to be just, if it is a desire of his to punish men for their sin, justice sees to it that justice is not deprived of its rights, and is not hindered in any of its impulses. The questions in both cases are what are those rights and what are those desires?

Besides this the language used would be equally appropriate after man has rejected the gospel. It would thus furnish an argument for a constant repetition of the gospel offer to each one that has rejected it, and that indefinitely. Indeed if the benevolent wish of God not to punish offenders is a sure hindrance to that punishment, then could they never be punished, for the benevolent love of God flows forth to all his creatures, even in their sins. He has no delight in the death of the wicked. But with God desire is not purpose any more truly than with man. The purposes of God will certainly be accomplished. They will always be in accordance with his nature. But the Scripture teaches no such purpose as that the gospel will be preached to each individual.

5. A fifth theory is what is commonly called the Governmental Theory of the Atonement.

Those who hold this theory maintain that God cannot consistently forgive sin upon mere repentance and faith; but that the necessity for its punishment does not arise from the nature of God, and his abhorrence of sin; wherefore there is no principle in him which requires all sin to be punished for itself alone; but from the necessity which exists for maintaining his moral government in the universe. "They therefore regard the sufferings of Christ as intended to make a moral impression upon the universe by their display of God's determination to punish sin, and thus to make the forgiveness of sin consistent with the good government of the universe." [Hodge's Outlines, p. 301, 1st Edition.]

The objections to this theory are:

1. The nature which it ascribes to sin. It does not regard it essential that all sin should be punished. Therefore sin does not in itself intrinsically deserve punishment.

2. It places the punishment of sin on a wrong basis, namely, the good of the universe as involved in the moral government God; and not because it deserves punishment as sin.

3. God is here beheld, not as a righteous judge taking vengeance on the violators of his law, nor as a rightful king punishing those who have rejected his authority, but simply as a benevolent being entirely regardless of his own nature, or of the difference between right and wrong, punishing some men for the good of others.

4. According to this theory the necessity for punishing sin rests, not in its own nature, but because there are more created beings in the universe than those who have sinned. Had God created one man, or one angel only, and had that angel sinned, there could have been no reason, either in the broken law, or in the dishonour to God, for his punishment, unless other beings were also to be created.

5. This theory claims no support from Scripture; but is presented simply as a philosophical explanation, to avoid the difficulties supposed to exist in the ordinarily received doctrine of the necessity of punishment by God.

6. It is opposed by Scripture in every particular involved in it; the nature of sin; the desert of punishment; the vengeance of God against the violator of his law; the fact that God acts of his own will, and does not draw the reasons of his action from without; the teaching of Scripture about the priestly office of Christ, the work he has done, the position he bore to us as being made sin for us; the ground of our redemption; the causes of condemnation and a hundred other particulars, which show that the Scriptures are not merely not silent on this subject but that the contrary doctrine lies at the very basis of all its instructions.

6. A sixth theory of the Atonement is that of the Arminians, who hold that Christ died, and that for sin; but only in the sense that makes it consistent for God to offer salvation to men on the ground of evangelical obedience, and not of perfect legal obedience.

This theory teaches a general atonement without any application of it on the part of God. Connected with the doctrine of sufficient grace to each man, it supposes that the individual does, or does not exercise faith, and obedience, and thus secures eternal life or loses it.

The objections to this theory are:

1. "That it gives an indefinite conception of what Christ did. Either it involves no satisfaction to divine justice and to the law, or it implies universal satisfaction. In the first case it dishonours God, in the second it forces us to hold the doctrine of universal salvation." What is meant by the expression, that "he is faithful and just to forgive us our sins, and to cleanse us from all unrigh-teousness," if God is not justly under obligations, for what Christ did, to give salvation to all for whom he died?

2. If it be said that the object was simply to make salvation possible for all, the reply is that this is not what the Scriptures represent. They speak positively of salvation as procured, not the means of salvation; and of certain salvation, not possible salvation. "The effects of Christ's death are spoken of in Scripture as reconciliation and justification, Rom. 5:10; Eph. 2:16; remission of sins, Eph. 1:7; peace, Eph. 2:14; deliverance from wrath, 1 Thess. 1:10; from death, Heb. 2:14; from the curse of the law, Gal. 3:13; from sin," 1 Pet. 1:18. [Hodge's Outlines, p. 314, 1st Edition.] We are spoken of as justified when ungodly.

3. This view of the atonement is utterly incompatible with the Scripture doctrines of Innate Corruption, Regeneration, Election, Justification, Adoption, and Sanctification. Every proof of the true doctrine on these points is an argument against it.

4. This theory makes it possible that Christ should have died in vain.

5. This theory makes salvation partly of God and partly of man, in the most objectionable form. It represents God as permitting Christ to die that the demands of the law may be lowered.

7. A seventh theory is the Lutheran, which teaches that Christ's death was intended to make such a satisfaction to the justice of God that he could offer salvation to all that believe in him.

The objection to this theory is that by rejecting the doctrine of Election it omits a part of the truth. The statement, as made, is not opposed to the views usually held by the orthodox. Salvation is thus offered to all, and offered because satisfaction for sin has been made to the justice of God. But for whom is this salvation? They say, as we do, for those that shall believe. And hence the question between us is, Who will believe, and how will this faith be effected? The doctrine of Election teaches that they shall believe whom God hath chosen, for whom he sent Christ, for whom Christ died; and shall believe as the result of the gracious influences of the Spirit purchased by Christ's work.

8. The eighth theory of the Atonement is that which declares it to be general, but asserts that it is limited in its application. According to this theory, the work of atonement was not wrought out by Christ for the elect as such, nor for the church, either as foreseen, or designed to be composed of those to be saved; but for sinners, as sinners. The work of atonement had nothing to do with the persons to whom it was to be applied considered as an atonement, but only had respect to men as guilty sinners in God's sight. The work to be accomplished was precisely what would have been, had there been no election, no church to be established, no work of grace to be wrought on the heart, but each person left to act in its reception, or rejection, as he should choose.

It is in its application only that it has respect to Election, and thus is it made particular, not because in time it is applied to certain persons, but because it was designed in eternity to be thus applied. The application itself, however, involves the design of the atonement; but, simply, that which is made in respect to each individual, when, by regeneration and faith, he is vitally made partaker of Christ. It does not include the sovereign pleasure of God in the purpose to apply. This is involved in election.

The most distinguished advocate of this theory is Andrew Fuller, a man of the clearest perceptions, and of remarkable power of precise statement. His views on the subject appear in the Conversation on Particular Redemption, Andrew Fuller's Works, Vol. II, p. 692 to 698. He has here sought to establish a theory not substantially different from that of the older Calvinists, but after all, one which has merely at first sight the appearance of being better. The distinction on which he attempts to establish it, however, appears not to be correct. The following extracts from his discussion will show his position. The disputants are Peter and James; the latter presents the views of Fuller. Peter gives the theory as he understands it thus:

"The particularity of the Atonement consists in the sovereign pleasure of God with regard to its application."

James replies: I should rather say "the particularity of Redemption consists in the sovereign pleasure of God with regard to the application of the Atonement, that is with regard to the persons to whom it shall be applied."

Again says James: "You say the position in question places the particularity of Redemption in its application. Whence, if you will recollect yourself, you will find that it places it in the Sovereign pleasure of God with regard to application."

Again Peter: "But, have you ever made use of the term application so as not to include the divine intention?"

James: "I am not aware of having done so."

Again: He sums up by saying that his "object in the distinction has been merely to distinguish what the death of Christ is sufficient for, from what it was the design of the Father and Son to effect through it."

Again: "I do not consider particular redemption as being so much a doctrine of itself as a branch of the great doctrine of Election."

"Atonement and Redemption are both effects of Christ's death, but in such order as that one is the consequence of the other."

Again: In the previous conversation on substitution he says, p. 690: "Concerning the death of Christ, if I speak of it irrespective of the purpose of the Father and the Son, as to the objects who should be saved by it, referring merely to what it is in itself sufficient for, and declared in the gospel to be adapted to, I should think I answered the question in the Scriptural way by saying, it was for sinners as sinners. But if I have respect to the purpose of the Father in giving his Son to die and to the design of Christ in laying down his life, I should answer, it was for the elect only."

This theory agrees with the ordinary theory in:

1. Regarding satisfaction for sin necessary.
2. Recognizing that this has been made by Christ.
3. Claiming that the value of Christ's death is sufficient for the world.
4. Declaring that its benefits accrue to some only.
5. Maintaining that this limitation is because of God's purpose, and not because of action on the part of man.

It differs from it in that it makes Redemption and Atonement two different works, instead of the same work viewed in two different aspects. The older doctrine regards the atonement as a reconciliation of sinners to God, but of sinners, who are thus redeemed from the condition of bondage and misery in which they had been. Atonement, therefore, is reconciliation, Redemption is deliverance; but of the same persons by the same work, and at the same time, each being involved in the same decree. The new theory makes atonement an act of reconciliation by Christ's death, not of the persons redeemed alone, but of the whole world, and this, as the result of a general decree to send Christ to reconcile the world to God. Redemption comes under the decree of Election which has nothing to do with reconciliation; and, by it, only certain persons have the benefit of the reconciliation thus effected, not because of their own acceptance or faith, but because God gives to them all the advantages of the work of atonement and withholds them from all others.

The objections to this view are:

1. That it represents the whole world as actually reconciled to God by Christ's death. If so, on what ground is this reconciliation destroyed? The doctrine of universal salvation is therefore involved.

2. If this is not the view, then, when the Scriptures speak of our reconciliation to God, nothing more is meant than that a mere mode of reconciliation has been arranged, so that the divine justice has been simply so satisfied that a medium of acceptance with God has been provided. But, if there is merely a medium of acceptance provided, how can men be spoken of as actually reconciled to God? In what proper sense can Christ be said to have borne our sins, and to have been wounded for our transgressions, if his act was merely the arrangement of a medium for salvation? Christ, to make atonement, must have been substituted in our place, borne our sins, had imputed to him our trespasses, and the chastisement of our peace must have been upon him. But, if so, a true atonement must have been made. It could not have been the mere arrangement of a medium of salvation. It must have been salvation itself. And, if for all, all must be saved.

3. This theory is inconsistent with one of the facts admitted by its advocates; that the death of Christ was a penal sacrifice. Penalty and guilt have no respect to sin in the abstract, but only to it as associated with sinners. If the work of atonement simply wrought out a medium of access, then it was a mere general exhibition of God's hatred of sin, having no respect to particular persons. On the governmental theory that such an arrangement was necessary simply to display before the universe the evil of sin, this idea of atonement might be allowed. But on the theory of satisfaction to justice, the atonement must be made by a penal sacrifice.

4. This only apparently has any advantage over the usual older Calvinistic theory.

(1.) It confines salvation to the elect.

(2.) It gives salvation as the result of God's action.

(3.) It ascribes no greater value to Christ's death. The older theory, except as held by those who gave it a commercial character, taught that what Christ needed to do for one man, would have been sufficient for all.

(4.) It, with that theory, ascribes the limitation to God's purpose; the one holding the purpose in actual salvation; the other the purpose in the application of salvation.

(5.) God can under either, with equal sincerity, make the gospel offer to all.

(a.) Each holds that a sufficient basis for salvation exists if God had chosen to extend it.

(b.) Each holds that God knows that only those chosen by him will accept.

(c.) Each teaches that this acceptance is due to special grace.

(d.) Each maintains that it was God's purpose to withhold that special grace from some; a purpose formed in eternity and recognized as existing when the sacrifice was offered, and when the offer of salvation is made.

(6.) This seems at first more in accordance with the expressions of general atonement made in the Scriptures; but it appears on examination that the act there spoken of cannot be limited to the meaning here given, and that either these passages teach universal salvation, or they have a meaning, as used by Christ and his Apostles, which does not involve the idea of such equal universality as includes in the same respect in every way every one of the posterity of Adam.

(7.) This theory, like all others of a general atonement, lies under the difficulty that it extends reconciliation, or a medium of reconciliation, to persons, who by death have been confirmed in destruction, or it shuts off from its benefits all who have died before Christ. The theory of limited atonement recognizes all who are included in it as saved by virtue of it. The virtue secured, therefore, is applied to all to whom it belongs. The fact that the Lamb was slain before the foundation of the world, or, in other words, the certainty of Christ's death, makes salvation beforehand possible, and permits God to bestow it. The death of Christ only fulfills what has thus been relied on. But in the case of a general atonement made for the whole race, we have Christ dying, not simply for those who shall not be saved, but for those who are already damned.

(8.) This theory is incompatible with those expressions of Scripture which speak of Christ's death as though it were confined to the elect.

John 10:11, 15, 26–28. "I am the good shepherd; the good shepherd layeth down his life for the sheep, . . . and I lay down my life for the sheep, . . . but ye believe not because ye are not of my sheep. . . . My sheep hear my voice, and I know them, and they follow me: and I give unto them eternal life; and they shall never perish, and no one shall snatch them out of my hand."

(a.) The sheep here are those to whom he will give eternal life.

(b.) They are those for whom he lays down his life.

(c.) They are not all, because he tells those who were rejecting him that they were not his sheep.

(d.) The whole language used implies that the salvation of the sheep alone is the object for which his life is laid down.

John 17:9, 19. "I pray not for the world, but for those which thou hast given me. . . . For their sakes I sanctify myself, that they themselves also may be sanctified in the truth."

Rom. 5:8, 9. "But God commendeth his own love toward us, in that, while we were yet sinners, Christ died for us. Much more then, being now justified by his blood, shall we be saved from the wrath of God through him."

Here those for whom Christ died are plainly declared to be thus justified by his blood, and the certainty of salvation from wrath is maintained.

See also the passage in Rom. 8th chapter, where the Apostle uses the language of exultation. In verse 32. "He that spared not his own Son, but delivered him up for us all, how shall he not also with him, freely give us all things?"

(a.) For us all: here is the true extent of the atonement. The all, are those who are truly saved.

(b.) Those for whom he has thus been delivered, feel assured that he will give also all grace, so that their salvation is secure. But this is true only of the elect; therefore, for them alone and not for others, was Christ "not spared."

Verse 34. "Who is he that shall condemn? It is Christ Jesus that died." This is the sufficient answer as the apostle teaches; but according to the theory of Fuller it is the application of Christ's death, and not the death itself, that removes condemnation.

Eph. 5:25. "Husbands, love your wives, even as Christ also loved the church, and gave himself up for it."

Titus 2:14. "Who gave himself for us, that he might redeem us from all iniquity, and purify unto himself a people for his own possession, zealous of good works." It is for the "us" who compose this people, that Christ has given "himself."

1 Peter 1:20. The very manifestation of Christ in the world is said to have taken place for those "who through him are believers in God."

The arguments in favor of this later theory are (1.) that the Scriptures use expressions, which favor a general atonement, at the same time that they speak of a specific object in Christ's death. It is claimed that both, the general atonement, and the particular application are thus taught.

(2.) The second argument is that this will make the specific offer of the gospel to all appear more sincere than the other form.

These arguments will be considered in connection with the last theory of atonement, commonly called the Calvinistic theory. It is that of Calvin and the churches which he established. It is the theory of the Regular Baptists of the past. No other prevailed among those who have held distinctively Calvinistic Baptist sentiments until the days of Andrew Fuller. He, because of his great ability, contributed greatly to the acceptance of the modification which we have just been considering. After stating the older Calvinistic theory it will be shown that it is the Scriptural doctrine of the atonement in each of its particulars. It has been assumed heretofore that the nature of the Atonement is such as is taught by this theory. After this proof inquiry will be made into its extent, whether it is general or particular. In that place will naturally come up the questions as to the true explanation of the passages which have been thought to teach a general atonement.

7. The Calvinistic theory of the atonement is, that in the sufferings and death of Christ, he incurred the penalty of the sins of those whose substitute he was, so that he made a real satisfaction to the justice of God for the law which they had broken. On this account, God now pardons all their sins, and being fully reconciled to them, his electing love flows out freely towards them.

The doctrine as thus taught involves the following points:

I. That the sufferings and death of Christ were a real atonement.

II. That in making it Christ became the substitute of those whom he came to save.

III. That as such he bore the penalty of their transgressions.

IV. That in so doing he made ample satisfaction to the demands of the law, and to the justice of God.

V. That thus an actual reconciliation has been made between them and God.

Each of these will need explanation and amplification, as well as proof, that its precise meaning may be clearly ascertained.

I. The first point to be proved is that the death of Christ was a real atonement.

By this is meant that the death of Christ was not merely a moral example, as say the Socinians; that it was not a mere exhibition of God's determination to maintain his government for the benefit of his creatures, according to the governmental hypothesis; that it has not only a manifestation of God's abhorrence of sin by which man could be led to penitence, as held by the New Theology; that it was not merely an arrangement set forth in the universe as the means of lowering the demands of the law, as say the Arminians; but that it was a sacrifice for sin, the great antitype of the Mosaic sacrifices, by which, guilt and condemnation is taken away from those for whom he made it, and they are made at-one with God. The proof that this was the nature of Christ's act, is:

1. That this is the generally received notion of sacrifice in all nations.

2. That the earliest record of sacrifice, in the history of Cain and Abel, points to the idea that God had appointed a mode of expiation for guilt. The sacrifice of Abel was in one sense no better than that of Cain. Each was a gift; but that of Abel was a sacrifice of blood, in testimony of acknowledged guilt; that of Cain merely a thank offering. The Lord had respect to the offering of Abel, and when Cain was angry, the Lord remonstrated with him, and said: "If thou doest

well, shalt thou not be accepted? and if thou doest not well, sin coucheth at the door." Gen. 4:7. This account establishes the fact that the idea of sacrifice, which thus has prevailed among all men, originated in early instruction by God, beginning from the time of our first parents.

3. When we come, however, to look at the sacrifices of the Mosaic economy, we find still the same idea taught, and even more fully; since the type was now confined to the nation through which the antitype was to appear. That economy shows that the blood of animals was constantly offered to God; that this was done by his command as making reconciliation and atonement; that in these offerings was always involved the idea of sin committed by the people, or the individual, or the priests, or a ceremonial defilement of the nature of sin, which made essential the cleansing of the altar itself or the persons officiating; that, in the act of sacrifice, the hand of the individual, or of the elders, or of the priests was laid upon the head of the animal for the confession of sin upon it, that it might be made a proper sacrifice; that the animal was then slain or sent away; and that, as the result of all these arrangements, the forgiveness of sin followed.

This latter idea may appear too strongly put, but it is owing to our overlooking the fact that the sins thus atoned for were not all the sins of the Israelites, but only the sins which took place in their civil relations as individuals, or as a nation to God. The forgiveness of them involved, therefore, only the temporal blessings thus associated. As they were typical of Christ and of a heavenly Canaan, so those who looked through the type to the antitype received full pardon for all sins, because of the offering that God was to make, and in which they trusted. In either case, however, there was actual remission of sins. For the national or individual sins, for which God had appointed this method of pardon, there was actual remission because of the sacrifice, and, in those who looked forward to Christ, and for whom, therefore, his sacrifice was made, there was also actual remission of the sins thus laid upon him.

Another caution is also suggested here. We speak of the sacrifices of old as the means God appointed for the pardon of sin. And in like manner we speak of God's method of salvation being by the death of Christ. But, in either case, we do not mean by the expression that the means of salvation alone was in the sacrifice, but salvation itself. The law of sacrifice was the method of God for the remission of sin, but the sacrifice itself secured the actual remission: so, the death of Christ may be contemplated as God's method of saving sinners so long as we are speaking of it as the arrangement or scheme devised by God to accomplish a certain work; but, as itself a sacrifice, the death of Christ secured salvation, and not the mere means of salvation.

4. Such, now, being the usage of the word sacrifices among all men, and especially in the Jewish nation, did we find merely the word sacrifice used in

reference to Christ, we should be justified in believing that there was made by him a real sacrifice or atonement. If the New Testament or the other Scriptures said nothing of the nature of his work or of its effects, we should be fully warranted in saying that, because it was a sacrifice, it secured an actual remission of sins by the shedding of his blood. Were we confined to this argument, therefore, we might simply show that the New Testament does speak of him as the Lamb of God, as our Passover, and as having died for us, and thence we might argue that he has made a real atonement for us. But we may go much farther and show that it actually teaches this fact.

5. It is clearly taught that by Christ's sacrificial death was made an offering for sin which actually secured the pardon of the sinner.

The prophets of old spake of it in this wise.

Thus in Isaiah 53:6, 10, 11. "All we like sheep have gone astray, . . . and the Lord hath laid on him the iniquity of us all. . . . Yet it pleased the Lord to bruise him; he hath put him to grief: when thou shalt make his soul an offering for sin, he shall see his seed, he shall prolong his days, . . . He shall see of the travail of his soul, and shall be satisfied: by his knowledge shall my righteous servant justify many: and he shall bear their iniquities."

The points here are: (1.) Our sins are laid on him. (2.) He is afflicted. (3.) He is made an offering for sin. (4.) Thus he justifies many (not all—and why these?), because "he shall bear their iniquities."

Daniel 9:24, 26. "Seventy weeks are decreed upon thy people and upon thy holy city, to finish transgression, and to make an end of sin, and to make reconciliation for iniquity, and to bring in everlasting righteousness, . . . And after the threescore and two weeks shall the anointed one be cut off, and shall have nothing."

The New Testament teaching corresponds with that of the Old.

John 1:29. The announcement of the Messiah by John shows that the sacrifice of Christ was the prominent work of his life. "Behold, the Lamb of God which taketh away the sin of the world." The same announcement was made again the next day.

John 6:51. The Saviour says, "the bread which I will give is my flesh, for the life of the world."

The above are positive declarations. We must take them in the fullness of the declaration made. It may be necessary to show how these expressions are applicable only to some and not to every individual in the world, to avoid the error of Universalism, but they distinctly declare of all to whom they may be applied that sin was taken away and life given by the atonement.

Matt. 20:28. "The Son of man came not to be ministered unto, but to minister, and to give his life a ransom for many.

Matt. 26:28. "This is my blood of the Covenant which is shed for many unto remission of sins."

Acts 20:28. "The church of God which he purchased with his own blood."

Romans 5:10. "We were reconciled to God through the death of his Son."

2 Cor. 5:18, 19. "But all things are of God, who reconciled us to himself through Christ, and gave unto us the ministry of reconciliation; To-wit, that God was in Christ reconciling the world unto himself, not reckoning unto them their trespasses, and having committed unto us the word of reconciliation."

Eph. 5:2. "Christ . . . gave himself up for us, an offering and a sacrifice to God for an odour of a sweet smell."

Col. 1:14, 19, 22. "In whom we have our redemption, the forgiveness of sins. . . . For it was the good pleasure of the Father that in him should all the fulness dwell; And, through him to reconcile all things unto himself, having made peace through the blood of his cross; through him I say, whether things upon the earth, or things in the heavens. And you being in time past alienated and enemies in your mind in your evil works, yet now hath he reconciled in the body of his flesh through death, to present you holy and without blemish and unreprovable before him." This passage includes all the points under the head we are now discussing. We have here a sacrifice by Christ in his death; through his blood peace is effected, and forgiveness of sins; not the means, but the things themselves; actual forgiveness, actual peace.

The whole Epistle to the Hebrews is proof upon this point.

1 Peter 1:18–20. "Knowing that ye were redeemed, not, etc., but with precious blood, as of a lamb without blemish and without spot, even the blood of Christ."

1 John 2:2. "He is the propitiation for our sins; and not for ours only, but also for the whole world."

1 John 4:10. "God sent his Son to be the propitiation for our sins.

The passages adduced will suffice to show that Christ's work was a real sacrifice; that by his blood he procured pardon, peace, redemption and remission of sins for those whom he represented. How many or how few these are does not here affect the question. The work here done was a sacrifice and was completely accomplished.

The proof to be given of the other points will add materially to the evidence of the nature of the work of Christ in this respect.

II. In order to make this atonement Christ became the substitute of those whom he came to save.

Here, also, we may refer to the position in this respect occupied by the offering under the Mosaic laws, as well as to the general notion of sacrifice.

The language of Job 1:1–5 indicates that he recognized the fact that substitutes might be put, and would be accepted in the place of those who were guilty of offences to God. And this may be taken as evidence of the usually received opinion before the segregation of Israel, as well as of that among the Gentiles subsequent to that event.

But the declarations of God as to the Levitical sacrifices and the method of their observance exhibit this more clearly.

In the first chapter of Leviticus God gives to Moses directions, as to the offering of sacrifices by the people: among other things he says, verse 4, of the individual making the offering, "He shall lay his hand upon the head of the burnt offering; and it shall be accepted for him to make atonement for him."

This is the substitution of the victim. We have in Leviticus 10:17, where Moses blames Eleazar and Ithamar, the sons of Aaron, for neglecting to eat the sin offering, the declaration of the substitution which took place in the priest. Christ bore both offices.

"Wherefore have ye not eaten the sin offering in the place of the sanctuary, seeing it is most holy, and He hath given it you to bear the iniquity of the congregation, to make atonement for them before the Lord?"

Both these cases are mentioned to show that there was a substitution of the priest, and one of the victim. It was in the latter sense that Christ bore the sins of the people and made atonement.

The account of the scapegoat, in Leviticus 16:20–22, furnishes another instance of substitution, which, as another use will be made of it, is not referred to here at length. It is, however, a signal example of such a substitution, as put an animal in the place of Israel, and made him, as their substitute, to bear their iniquities.

These declarations of the substitution of the victim are numerous in Exodus and Leviticus, and are referred to in all the Mosaic books. They, therefore, made familiar to the Jewish people the notion of substitution, and impressed upon them the need of a victim, for the making of atonement, who should actually stand in the place of those who were to be atoned for. The language of the Scriptures as to Christ, therefore, could not have been otherwise understood. As used by the Prophets, by John the Baptist, and by the inspired writers of the New Testament it must have been intended to make this impression, which must inevitably have been produced. So much is this so, that the prophetic language of Isaiah, relative to Christ's sufferings, was felt to be so completely fulfilled in them, that almost all the language in the New Testament, which speaks of his atonement, is tinged by the expressions there used.

Let us look at the 53rd chapter of Isaiah, then, as indicative of the teachings of the sacrifices, and of the work foretold to be accomplished.

The whole chapter speaks of substitution and inflicted penalty. The following passages refer to substitution:

Verses 4 and 5. "Surely he hath borne our griefs, and carried our sorrows: yet we did esteem him stricken, smitten of God, and afflicted. But he was wounded for our transgressions, he was bruised for our iniquities: the chastisement of our peace was upon him; and with his stripes we are healed."

Verse 6. "The Lord hath laid on him the iniquity of us all."

Verse 11. "By his knowledge shall my righteous servant justify many: and he shall bear their iniquities."

Verse 12. "He bare the sin of many, and made intercession for the transgressors."

The following passages show that the New Testament recognized the fulfilment of these prophecies, and that in Christ was found the antitype of the sacrifices of old in this respect.

Matt. 20:28. "The Son of man came . . . to give his life a ransom for many."

Matt. 26:28. "This is my blood of the covenant, which is shed for many unto remission of sins."

John 11:47–52 gives an account of a council among the Jews, in which a certain remark was made by Caiaphas, which the Evangelist claims as a prophecy and applies to Jesus.

See verses 49–52. "But a certain one of them, Calaphas, being high priest that year, said unto them, Ye know nothing at all, nor do ye take account that it is expedient for you that one man should die for the people, and that the whole nation perish not. Now this he said not of himself: but being high priest that year he prophesied that Jesus should die for the nation; and not for the nation only, but that he might also gather into one the children of God that were scattered abroad."

Rom. 5:8. "While we were yet sinners Christ died for us."

Rom. 8:32. "He that spared not his own Son, but delivered him up for us all."

2 Cor. 5:21. "Him who knew no sin he made to be sin on our own behalf."

Gal. 1:3, 4. "Our Lord Jesus Christ, who gave himself for our sins.

Gal. 3:13. "Having become a curse for us."

Eph. 5:2. "Christ also loved you, and gave himself up for us, an offering and a sacrifice to God, for an odour of a sweet smell."

1 Thess. 5:9, 10. "For God appointed us not unto wrath, but unto the obtaining of salvation through our Lord Jesus Christ, who died for us, that, whether we wake or sleep, we should live together with him."

1 Tim. 2:5, 6. "For there is one God, one mediator also between God and men, himself man, Christ Jesus, who gave himself a ransom for all; the testimony to be borne in its own times."

There are several questions which arise in consequence of this substitution on the part of Christ.

One as to the qualifications essential to it which he possessed.

Another as to the manner in which substitution can be effected.

Another as to the justice with which an innocent person can be put in the place of a guilty one.

And yet another, whether Christ, being thus substituted, became personally a sinner.

These questions belong the rather, however, to a discussion of imputation and are only relevant here, because that doctrine is implied in this doctrine of atonement. The only exception is the first. The second and third have already been discussed in treating of the representative relation of Adam and the principle of substitution involved in it, and in the law of sacrifices.

As to the fourth point it may be said that Christ is not represented in Scripture as made personally a sinner by substitution; neither were the sacrifices of old regarded as personally obnoxious to God. But they were so officially; that is, in their positions as substitutes; and Christ became so, being made a curse for us. But this official substitution did not make him a sinner, but only caused him to be treated as such.

The first question may be answered thus:

1. That the possession of a human nature, such as ours, is represented in Scripture as essential to his position as substitute.

2. The possession of a divine nature, in consequence of which he was a divine person, was also requisite to give an infinite value to his work.

3. It seems also essential that he should not have been two persons, a divine person, and a human person; else could not the value of the acts performed in his human nature have been greater than those of any other innocent man. It was, therefore, not the human nature of Christ that was substituted for us, but Christ himself; yet it was not Christ in his divine nature that suffered, but value was given to the suffering from its being the suffering of one who also essentially possessed the divine nature.

The doctrine of the Trinity lies, therefore, at the basis of that of the atonement, and hence the denial of the latter by all those who reject the former.

4. A holy nature; a lamb without spot or blemish.

5. As consequent upon the possession of such a union of natures in himself Christ could make a voluntary offering of himself, by which merit could be procured and penalty endured for others.

6. That he should be designated by the Father to this position, that he might be the legal representative of his people and their covenant head.

III. In so offering himself, Christ actually bore the penalty of the transgressions of those for whom he was substituted.

1. This point is involved in the two that have preceded it, and consequently may be argued from the evidence afforded by them. These points mutually confirm each other. Thus, in bearing the penalty, he appears to have been substituted for us and to have been made a sacrifice. In being made a sacrifice, he has been substituted and has borne the penalty. We may, therefore, present all the proofs that Christ was a sacrifice, and was the substitute for our sins, as so much in favor of the fact that he bore the penalty of transgression.

But we may otherwise learn from the Scriptures themselves that this penalty was actually borne by Christ. It is taught:

2. In those passages in which Christ is represented as having home our iniquities. The meaning of this clause is definitely fixed by the Scripture usage. In the following passages this phrase is applied to Christ:

Isaiah 53:6. "The Lord hath laid on him the iniquity of us all."

Isaiah 53:11. "By his knowledge shall my righteous servant justify many, and he shall bear their iniquities."

Isaiah 53:12. "He was numbered with the transgressors; yet he bare the sin of many."

Heb. 9:28. "Having been once offered to bear the sins of many, shall appear a second time apart from sin, to them that wait for him unto salvation."

1 Peter 2:24. "Who his own self bare our sins in his body upon the tree."

The following passages show that the phrase "to bear iniquity" means to bear the penalty of iniquity.

Lev. 5:1. "And if any one sin in that he heareth the voice of adjuration, he being a witness, whether he hath seen or known, if he do not utter it, then he shall bear his iniquity."

Lev. 5:17. "And if any one sin and do any of the things which the Lord hath commanded not to be done; though he know it not, yet is he guilty and shall bear his iniquity."

Lev. 7:18. "If any of the flesh of the sacrifice of his peace offerings be eaten on the third day, it shall not be accepted, neither shall it be imputed unto him that offereth it: it shall be an abomination, and the soul that eateth of it shall bear his iniquity."

Lev. 19:8. "But every one that eateth it shall bear his iniquity, because he hath profaned the holy thing of the Lord: and that soul shall be cut off from his people."

Lev. 24:15. "And thou shalt speak unto the children of Israel, saying, Whosoever curseth his God shall bear his sin."

Numbers 14:34. "After the number of the days in which ye spied out the land, even forty days for every day a year, shall ye bear your iniquities, even forty years, and ye shall know my alienation."

Ezekiel 18:20. "The soul that sinneth, it shall die. The son shall not bear the iniquity of the father, neither shall the father bear the iniquity of the son."

Ezekiel 44:10, 12. "But the Levites that went far from me, when Israel went astray, which went astray from me after their idols; they shall bear their iniquity." "Because they ministered unto them before their idols, and became a stumbling block of iniquity unto the house of Israel; therefore have I lifted up mine hand against them, saith the Lord God, and they shall hear their iniquity." [See Magee on the Atonement, vol. 1, pp. 200–220, for an able and learned discussion of the meaning of the phrase "bear iniquity."]

3. Another class of passages shows that Christ bore the penalty of sin by representing him as suffering because of it, and as bearing the penalty attached to it. Such passages used as to an innocent person show that he bore the penalty for others, but in most it is distinctly declared that it was for his people.

Suffering is of three kinds: (1.) Calamity or misfortune, which has no reference to sin. (2.) Chastisement, which is designed for the improvement of the sufferer. (3.) Punishment or penalty, which is designed for satisfaction to justice. The language of Scripture shows that the sufferings of Christ were of the last class.

(1.) That class of passages which represents Christ as suffering because of our sin, or that his sufferings were connected with our sins.

The passage in Isaiah 53:4, 5 is a signal example. "Surely he hath borne our griefs, and carried our sorrows: yet we did esteem him stricken, smitten of God, and afflicted. But he was wounded for our transgressions, he was bruised for our iniquities: the chastisement of our peace was upon him; and with his stripes we are healed."

In accordance with this vision of the prophet we have the accounts given in the New Testament.

Rom. 4:25. "Who was delivered up for our trespasses."

Heb. 13:12. "Wherefore Jesus also, that he might sanctify the people through his own blood, suffered without the gate."

1 Pet. 2:24. "Who his own self bare our sins in his body upon the tree."

1 Pet. 3:18. "Because Christ also suffered for sins once, the righteous for the unrighteous, that he might bring us to God."

More passages might he given were it not that the Scriptures more frequently state the nature of this connection, and they will be quoted in the succeeding class under this head.

(2.) The second class of passages which treats of the connection of Christ's sufferings with our sins is that which represents those sufferings as the penalty of our sins, or which declares that Christ bore that penalty.

The penalty which Christ bore for us, includes all the suffering which he endured on our behalf. It is not confined to any one act of his life, but, as those sufferings culminated in the agony of the cross, the penalty is spoken of chiefly as borne there. His previous sufferings, the miseries to which he was subjected, and the evils he endured, were but as the beginning, and a small beginning of the penalty which he there completed.

The penalty due for our transgressions was death, the full meaning of which is only foreshadowed to us by the death of the body. Added to this is the separation from God, by reason of the moral death which ensued from sin, and the condition of condemnation for sin. The former must be eternal, unless restoration to God is effected. The latter involves eternal death in its mere execution.

Christ bore the guilt of those for whom he died, and thus it became fit that upon him God should inflict the penalty.

The result has been the removal of condemnation and the reconciliation effected between us and God. In the removal of these evils eternal death is taken away.

As to the death of the body, according to God's wisdom, and in a manner similar to his course in many other cases, the curse is made no longer a curse, because the sting is removed, and the death of the body, otherwise so intimately connected with eternal death, now introduces the Christian into eternal life.

The death of Christ included the penalty in all its fullness. In it he offered up his body and was laid in the grave. In it the separation from God took place by which he was led to feel himself forsaken. "My God, my God, why hast thou forsaken me," was his cry of agony. That his death was not eternal, as would ours have been, arose from the fact that in the execution of the sentence of condemnation, God found in him not such a victim as mere man would have been, unable to atone, or render full satisfaction; but one whose glorious nature gave infinite value to suffering, and who could feel most keenly, yet could bear without destruction, the wrath of God.

The Scriptures represent just such a penalty to have been endured by Christ, accompanied by just such agonies. No one can read the accounts given by the evangelists without being impressed by the fact that they ascribe just such a character to his sufferings on Calvary.

But, independently of their general statements, we have the class of passages just referred to, that in which Christ's suffering is represented as the penalty of our transgressions.

In Zechariah 13:7 we have that remarkable prophecy which can be applied to Christ as it has never been applied to any save Christ. "Awake, O sword, against my shepherd, and against the man that is my fellow, saith the Lord of hosts." The context speaks of a purging of Jerusalem, out of the trial of which a third part shall be brought, and the means by which this is done is the smiting of the shepherd, and the scattering of the sheep, through which action they are refined, and he says, "they shall call on my name, and I will hear them: I will say, It is my people; and they shall say, The Lord is my God." Zech. 13:9.

Isaiah 53:5. "The chastisement of our peace was upon him; and with his stripes we are healed." The latter part of this verse is quoted in 1 Peter 2:24.

Isaiah 53:8. "For the transgression of my people was he stricken."

Verse 9. Declares his perfect innocence and then

Verse 10 says: "Yet it pleased the Lord to bruise him; he hath put him to grief: when thou shalt make his soul an offering for sin, he shall see his seed, etc."

Matt. 20:28. "Even as the Son of man came, . . . to give his life, a ransom for many."

Rom. 5:10. "For if, while we were enemies, we were reconciled to God by the death of his Son, much more, being reconciled, shall we be saved by his life."

Rom. 6:10. "For the death that he died, he died unto sin once."

1 Cor. 15:3. "For I delivered unto you first of all that which also I received, how that Christ died for our sins according to the Scriptures."

2 Cor. 5:14, 15. "For the love of Christ constraineth us; because we thus judge, that one died for all, therefore all died; And he died for all, etc."

2 Cor. 5:21. "Him who knew no sin he made to be sin on our behalf."

Gal. 3:13. "Christ redeemed us from the curse of the law, having become a curse for us."

Col. 1:21, 22. "And you, being in time past alienated . . . yet now hath he reconciled in the body of his flesh through death."

Heb. 9:26. "But now once, at the end of the ages, hath he been manifested to put away sin by the sacrifice of himself."

IV. We have thus seen (1.) that the sufferings and death of Christ were a real atonement; (2.) that in making it Christ became the substitute of those whom he came to save; (3.) that as such he bore the penalty of their transgressions. From these the fourth point follows, that in so doing, he made ample satisfaction to the demands of the law, and to the justice of God.

1. The very fact that he was the substitute of the sinner, and that he bore his penalty shows that the satisfaction he made was ample; Christ could have made none that was not. Anything he could do must be acceptable to God; for God delighteth in him. Any act of his must be of infinite value to accomplish any

end for which he designed it. Any penalty borne by him must have found a victim fully sufficient to fulfill every demand. The very fact that he has been substituted and has borne the penalty, shows that he has made ample satisfaction.

2. But this is also seen in the fact that the declaration is made that thus the demands of the law are fulfilled and not lowered. The language of Christ on this point is explicit.

Matt. 5:17. "Think not that I came to destroy the law or the prophets: I came not to destroy, but to fulfil."

Rom. 7:1–6. The apostle argues that we are no longer bound to the law, but bound to Christ; that our obligations have been annulled, and that, henceforth, "we have been discharged from the law, having died to that wherein we were holden; so that we serve in newness of the spirit, and not in oldness of the letter." This whole argument implies and is based upon the idea that the law has been fulfilled for us by Christ, who has thus delivered us from the bondage of obligation, that we might serve with the spirit of love.

Freedom from the law on our part, accompanied by the declaration that Christ came not to lower it, but to fulfill it, shows that in the atonement for us, he has made ample satisfaction for all our sins and failures, as well as secured for us complete righteousness by his perfect obedience.

We may here add also the prophecy of Isaiah 42:21, "It pleased the Lord, for his righteousness sake, to magnify the law and make it honourable," and the fact that Christ is called "The Lord is our Righteousness," in Jeremiah 23:6, and also that the Apostle Paul in Philippians 3:7–11, renounces his own righteousness of the law that he might have that "which is through faith in Christ, the righteousness which is of God by faith." This fact implies a conviction of the ample extent of the righteousness which is by Christ.

3. That an ample satisfaction is made to justice is seen also in the fact that mercy and justice are said to be reconciled in Christ. These are represented as antagonistic; mercy pleading for the sinner, and justice demanding his punishment; truth requiring the fulfillment of the threatened penalty, which is consistent with peace, only by the death of Christ.

Psalm 85:10. "Mercy and truth are met together; righteousness and peace have kissed each other."

Isaiah 45:21. "There is no God else beside me, a just God and a Saviour."

Isaiah 32:17. "And the work of righteousness shall be peace, and the effect of righteousness quietness and confidence forever." This is a wonder.

The same fact seems to be declared in the song of the angels, on the plain of Bethlehem, Luke 2:14. "Glory to God in the highest, and on earth peace among men in whom he is well pleased."

4. This is also seen in the approval which God gave to the work of Christ. Had that work not been satisfactory, we should not have expected the actual declarations of approval of it. That approval is evidenced.

(1.) By Christ's testimony to it. He tells us that he came to do the will of his Father; that his Father sent him not to condemn the world; but gave him, that whosoever believeth, might not perish but have everlasting life.

(2.) In the manifested expressions of approbation by God in the miracles by which Christ attested his mission, as well as by the witness of John.

(3.) In God's own words of approval, at his Baptism, at the Transfiguration on the Mount, and at other times.

(4.) In the angelic messengers sent to strengthen him in his work, and to minister to him after the temptation in the wilderness, and in the garden.

(5.) That most signal evidence, afforded, as is constantly declared, as a seal of approval, which is seen in the resurrection of Jesus from the dead.

5. The ample character of this satisfaction is further seen in the declarations by the sacred writers of the certainty of the salvation that is based upon it. Every offer of salvation made is a passage in proof of this point. The words of the Commission, "He that believeth, and is baptized, shall be saved" (Mark 16:16), and the offer of the apostle, "Believe on the Lord Jesus, and thou shalt be saved, thou and thy house" (Acts 16:31), are positive affirmations.

6. But it may be said that all of these points only prove God's approval of whatever was done by Christ, without showing that in that work satisfaction has been made. While this is not admitted, we find further proof in the sixth place in such passages as show that so ample has been the work of Christ that even a sinner is warranted to approach and claim salvation in Christ's name, and that God gives it as due to the merits and work of Christ.

Heb. 4:16. "Let us therefore draw near with boldness unto the throne of grace, that we may receive mercy, and may find grace to help us in time of need."

Heb. 10:19, 22. "having therefore, brethren, boldness to enter into the holy place by the blood of Jesus, . . . let us draw near with a true heart in fulness of faith."

Eph. 3:12. "In whom we have boldness and access, in confidence, through our faith in him."

1 John 1:9. "If we confess our sins, he is faithful and righteous to forgive us our sins, and cleanse us from all unrighteousness."

7. The ample satisfaction of the atonement made is also seen in the fact that it is declared perfect for its end in the language of the Apostle in Heb. 9:25–28, where he argues the incompleteness of the Mosaic sacrifices, because they had to be offered more than once, and the perfection of Christ's, because "now once

at the end of the ages, hath he been manifested to put away sin by the sacrifice of himself."

And again in chap. 10:10. "We have been sanctified through the offering of the body of Jesus Christ once for all."

1 John 1:7. "The blood of Jesus his Son cleanseth us from all sin.

A question arises in view of this ample satisfaction, in what way may it be regarded as gratuitous when it is thus a full recompense for all. This is well answered in Hodge's Outlines of Theology, p. 308, 1st Edition. The answer includes five points.

(1.) Christ did not die to make the Father love the Elect, but was given to die because of that love.

John 3:16. "God so loved the world, that he gave his only begotten Son, that whosoever believeth on him might not perish, but have eternal life."

1 John 4:9, 10. "Herein was the love of God manifested in us, that God hath sent his only begotten Son into the world, that we might live through him. Herein is love, not that we loved God, but that he loved us and sent his Son to be the propitiation for our sins."

(2.) Christ made full satisfaction to divine justice in order to render the exercise of love consistent with justice.

Rom. 3:26. "For the showing, I say, of his righteousness at this present season: that he might himself be just, and the justifier of him that hath faith in Jesus."

Psalm 85:10. "Mercy and truth are met together; righteousness and peace have kissed each other." The greater the obstacle and the more costly the price demanded of love by justice, the greater the love and the more free.

On this ground God commendeth his love.

Rom. 5:8. "But God commendeth his own love towards us, in that, while we were yet sinners, Christ died for us."

(3.) God the Father and God the Son are one God, identical in nature, moved by the same love, and exacting the same satisfaction.

(4.) Penal satisfaction differs from pecuniary. If a Sovereign appoints or accepts a substitute, it is all of grace.

(5.) To Christ as Mediator, the purchased salvation of his people belongs of right from the terms of the eternal covenant, but to us, that salvation is given in all its elements, stages and instrumentalities, only as a free and sovereign favour. The gift is gratuitous, if the beneficiary has no shadow of claim to it, and if no conditions are exacted of him. The less worthy the beneficiary is, and the more difficult the conditions which justice exacts of the giver, the more eminently gratuitous the gift is.

V. The fifth point to be shown, is that by this work an actual reconciliation has been effected.

1. The points already proved show this. If an atonement has been made by one who was actually substituted in the place of the guilty; who, as so substituted, paid the penalty and rendered full satisfaction to the law, so that the law has no longer any claims; then there has been undoubtedly an actual reconciliation. Peace has been made by the cross between God and man.

2. The plain declarations of Scripture are, that God has been reconciled to us by Christ.

Rom. 5:10. "For, if while we were enemies, we were reconciled to God through the death of his Son, much more, being reconciled, shall we be saved by his life." Similar declarations are found in 2 Cor. 5:19; Eph. 2:13, 16, 17; Col. 1:20–22. They are not given at length, because they will have to be presented immediately for another purpose.

It may be said that reconciliation is admitted, but that this means only a method of reconciliation.

3. Therefore it must be shown that actual reconciliation has been made, from what the Scriptures say of the purpose had in view in reconciliation, which was actually to save, not to make salvation possible.

Luke 19:10. "For the Son of man came to seek and to save that which was lost."

2 Cor. 5:21. "Him who knew no sin he made to be sin on our behalf; that we might become the righteousness of God in him."

Gal. 1:4. "Who gave himself for our sins, that he might deliver us out of this present evil world, according to the will of our God and Father."

Gal. 4:4, 5. "God sent forth his Son, born of a woman, born under the law, that he might redeem them which were under the law, that we might receive the adoption of sons."

1 Tim. 1:15. "Faithful is the saying, and worthy of all acceptation, that Christ Jesus came into the world to save sinners; of whom I am the chief."

The purpose of God is thus seen, not to make salvation possible, but actually to save, to redeem, to make righteous, etc.

Still it may be said, that this purpose might be effected by a method of reconciliation.

4. But the Scriptures, in speaking of what is actually effected by Christ's work for those who are reconciled by it, show that the reconciliation was actually made in that work itself. The time at which it was done, and what was done at that time show this.

Rom. 5:10. "For if while we were enemies, we were reconciled to God through the death of his Son, much more, being reconciled shall we be saved by his life." The time was, "while we were enemies," at the time of Christ's death. The application of salvation follows this reconciliation.

Gal. 3:13. "Christ hath redeemed us from the curse of the law, having become a curse for us."

Eph. 1:7. "In whom we have our redemption through his blood, the forgiveness of our trespasses according to the riches of his grace."

Eph. 2:14–16. "For he is our peace, who made both one, and brake down the middle wall of partition, having abolished in his flesh the enmity, even the law of commandments contained in ordinances; that he might create in himself of the twain one new man, so making peace; and might reconcile them both in one body unto God through the cross, having slain the enmity thereby."

Col. 1:20. "And through him to reconcile all things unto himself; having made peace through the blood of his cross.

1 Thess. 1:10. "Even Jesus, which delivereth us from the wrath to come."

1 Peter 1:18, 19. "Knowing that ye were redeemed, not with corruptible things . . . but with precious blood, as of a lamb without blemish and without spot."

All these passages speak of these effects, as actually accomplished by Christ, in his death upon the cross. [See Hodge's Outlines, p. 314, 1st Edition.]

5. The connection between the gift of the Spirit and the work of Christ shows, that there has been actual reconciliation. The promise of the Spirit to us is made, and that Spirit is given, as a reward of Christ's death. That death is declared to have this gift as one of the purposes to be effected by it.

Acts 2:33. "Being therefore by the right hand of God exalted, and having received of the Father the promise of the Holy Ghost, he hath poured forth this, which ye see and hear." This shows that the gift of the Spirit is the result of Christ's exaltation, which was also taught by Christ, when he said that, unless he went away, the Spirit could not come.

Gal. 3:13, 14. "Christ redeemed us from the curse of the law, . . . that we might receive the promise of the Spirit through faith."

Titus 3:5, 6. "He saved us, through the washing of regeneration and renewing of the Holy Ghost, which he poured out upon us richly through Jesus Christ our Saviour."

These passages show that,

(1.) The gift of the Spirit was purchased by Christ's death.

(2.) That that gift secures actual salvation.

(3.) That it must be given to all for whom he has died.

(4.) That in that death actual reconciliation is consequently secured.

The discussion of the nature of the sacrificial work of Christ has in great part prepared the way for that of the EXTENT OF THE ATONEMENT. But while the previous inquiry has necessarily included some statements as to the limitation which the Scriptures put upon this work, and presented some facts which establish such limitation, a special treatment of this branch of the subject is nevertheless necessary.

Here also we have several theories.

I. The first is that of the Universalist, who connecting the nature which the Scriptures assign to the atonement with some expressions which seem to assert its universal extent, hold the notion of such a universal atonement, as actually secures the salvation of all men.

The objections to this view are:

1. That salvation is confined in the Scriptures to those that believe, and all men are not believers.

2. That the gospel is spoken of as the only means of salvation, and the gospel is not even preached to all.

3. That express threats are uttered in the word of God against those who die in their sins.

4. That at least one sin is expressly mentioned, that shall not be pardoned.

5. That the arrangement of God's plan of salvation is such as shows that the people of God are saved from their sins, not in them; consequently the unholy are not saved.

6. The descriptions of the judgement day deny universal salvation.

7. The Scripture doctrine of the Hell prepared for the punishment of the wicked shows it to be untrue.

These and many other facts show that the atonement is limited in some way. The question arises in what way.

II. A second theory makes the atonement itself general, but limits its benefits to those who exercise faith.

It is claimed that thus only can be interpreted the passages which speak of a work for the world, consistently with any limitation; that thus only can God justly offer salvation to all; and that this theory fully meets all the conditions on which salvation is offered.

It cannot be denied that salvation is offered and will be given on the condition of faith and repentance; nor that there are general expressions which assert that Christ's work of atonement has efficacy beyond the limits of the Elect; but these facts must be so explained as to harmonize with the nature of the atonement and its relation to those for whom it was specially made. The follow-ing objections, therefore, may be made to this theory:

1. Any atonement, general in any such sense as not to be limited in God's purpose, is inconsistent with what we have seen to be the nature of the atonement.

2. It does not accord with justice that any should suffer for whom a substi-tute has actually borne the penalty and made full satisfaction.

3. It makes salvation the result in part of faith; but faith is the result of rec-onciliation, not its cause; it is the gift of God.

4. It is inconsistent with the many passages which teach the doctrine of an Election of man to salvation not because of foreseen faith.

5. It is inconsistent with those passages which point out the connection of the purpose of God with the salvation of those who are saved.

III. A third theory is that this limitation is one of purpose; that God designed only the actual salvation of some; and that, whatever provision has been made for others, he made this positive arrangement by which the salvation of certain ones is secured. In favor of this theory it may be said:

1. That this is in accordance with the doctrine of Election.

2. That it explains how it is that such a salvation as the Scriptures represent to have been wrought out by Christ is attained by some, and by some only.

3. It alone agrees with the language of limitation used in some Scriptures, as to Christ's death; either in those passages in which it is specially appropriated to Christians; or those in which he is spoken of as a ransom "for many." This class of passages is numerous.

The difficulties against this theory are:

1. That the offer of salvation is made to all men.

2. That the Scriptures speak of Christ's death as for the world, and in such a way as to contrast the world at large with those who believe.

An explanation of these passages must therefore be given, which, while it retains the full force intended in Scripture of these general expressions, and maintains the sincerity of God's offer of the gospel to all, shows at the same time its harmony with the doctrine of a definite purpose of God.

1. It was with the intention of doing this that Andrew Fuller suggested his theory of the atonement. But, as has been shown, that theory accomplishes the desired end only by ascribing such a nature to the atonement, as makes it only a method of reconciliation for the people of God, and not actual reconciliation.

2. A far better explanation is given by Dr. A. A. Hodge in the following ques-tion and answer:

"Ques. 17. State first negatively, and then positively, the true doctrine as to the design of the Father and the Son in providing satisfaction."

"I. Negatively—1st. There is no debate among Christians as to the *sufficiency* of that satisfaction to accomplish the salvation of all men, however vast the number. This is absolutely limitless. 2nd. Nor as to its *applicability* to the case of any and every possible human sinner who will ever exist. The relations of all to the demands of the law are identical. What would save one would save another. 3rd. Nor to the *bona fide* character of the offer which God has made to 'whomsoever wills' in the gospel. It is applicable to every one, it will infallibly be applied to every believer. 4th. Nor as to its *actual application.* Arminians agree with Calvinists that of adults only those who believe are saved, while Calvinists agree with Arminians that all dying in infancy are redeemed and saved. 5th. Nor is there any debate as to the universal reference of *some* of the benefits purchased by Christ. Calvinists believe that the entire dispensation of forbearance under which the human family rests since the fall, including for the unjust as well as the just temporal mercies and means of grace, is part of the purchase of Christ's blood. They admit also that Christ did in such a sense die for all men, that he thereby removed all legal obstacles from the salvation of any and every man, and that his satisfaction may be applied to one man as well as to another *'if God so wills it.'*"

"II. But *positively* the question is what was the design of the Father and Son in the vicarious death of Christ. Did they purpose to make the salvation of the elect certain, or merely to make the salvation of all men possible? Did his satisfaction have reference indifferently as much to one man as to another? Did the satisfaction purchase and secure its own application, and all the means thereof, to all for whom it was specifically rendered? Has the impetration and the application of this atonement the same range of objects? Was it, in the order of the divine purpose, a means to accomplish the purpose of election, or is the election of individuals a means to carry into effect the satisfaction of Christ otherwise inoperative?"

Our Confession (The Westminster) answers:

Ch. viii, § 5. "The Lord Jesus, by his perfect obedience and sacrifice of himself, . . . purchased not only reconciliation, but an everlasting inheritance in the kingdom of heaven for all those whom the Father hath given unto him."—Ch. iii, § 6. "As God hath appointed the elect unto glory, so hath he, by the eternal and most free purpose of his will, foreordained all the means thereunto. Wherefore they that are elected, being fallen in Adam, are redeemed in Christ. . . . Neither are any other redeemed by Christ . . . but the elect only."

Ch. viii, § 8. "To ALL those for whom Christ hath purchased redemption, he doth certainly and effectually apply and communicate the same."—"Articles of Synod of Dort," Ch. ii, § 1, 2, 8.

"The design of Christ in dying was to effect what he actually does effect in the result. 1st. *Incidentally* to remove the legal pediments out of the way of all men, and render the salvation of every hearer of the gospel objectively possible, so that each one has a right to appropriate it at will, to impetrate temporal blessings for all, and the means of grace for all to whom they are providentially supplied. But, 2nd, *Specifically* his design was to impetrate the actual salvation of his own people, in all the means, conditions, and stages of it, and render it infallibly certain. This last, from the nature of the case, must have been his real motive. After the manner of the Augustinian Schoolmen, Calvin, on 1 John 2:2, says, 'Christ died sufficiently for all, but efficiently only for the elect.'" [Outlines of Theology, pp. 416 and 417 of the second edition.]

3. Another statement upon this subject may prove more satisfactory, although it embraces no more than is actually implied in the above extract from Dr. Hodge. It has only the advantage of recognizing more explicitly the relation of the atoning work of Christ both to the world and to the elect; a relation clearly indicated to be such that he can be called, in some general sense, the Saviour of all men, though he bears this relation more especially to those who believe. 1 Tim. 4:10. The statement suggested is, that while, for the Elect, he made an actual atonement, by which they were actually reconciled to God, and, because of which, are made the subjects of the special divine grace by which they become believers in Christ and are justified through him; Christ, at the same time, and in the same work, wrought out a means of reconciliation for all men, which removed every legal obstacle to their salvation, upon their acceptance of the same conditions upon which the salvation is given to the Elect. According to this statement:

(1.) Christ did actually die for the salvation of all, so that he might be called the Saviour of all; because his work is abundantly sufficient to secure the salvation of all who will put their faith in him.

(2.) Christ died, however, in an especial sense for the Elect; because he procured for them not a possible, but an actual salvation.

(3.) The death of Christ opens the way for a sincere offer of salvation by God to all who will accept the conditions he has laid down.

(4.) That same death, however, secures salvation to the Elect, because by it Christ also obtained for them those gracious influences, by which they will be led to comply with those conditions.

(5.) The work of Christ, contemplated as securing the means of reconciliation, is a full equivalent to all that the advocates of a general atonement claim; for they do not suppose that more than this was done for mankind in general, while Calvinists readily recognize that this much has been done for all.

(6.) But, while the making of an actual atonement for the Elect is not inconsistent with the securing of a method of atonement for all, the assertion that such was the special work done for them complies with the nature of the atonement as heretofore seen and shows how Christ could be especially their Saviour, and also the Saviour of all.

CHAPTER 29

ELECTION

THE words Elect, Election, Foreordination, Chosen, Foreknow, and Foreknowledge occur so frequently in Scripture, that it is allowed by all that the Scriptures teach a doctrine of Election of some kind. The chief controversy is as to what that doctrine is.

Several theories have been presented as descriptive of the instructions of the Scriptures.

I. First there is the theory set forth by the celebrated John Locke in his Commentary and Paraphrase of the Epistles of Paul. It has been called the theory of Nationalism. According to this, Election consists "in the choice of certain whole nations into the pale of the visible Church Catholic, which choice, however, relates purely to their privileged condition in this world extending not to their collective eternal state in another world." The cause of this election is: "That same absolute good pleasure of God, which, through the exercise of his sovereign power, led him to choose the posterity of Jacob, rather than that of Esau, that, upon earth, they should become his peculiar people and be made the depositaries and preservers of the true religion." ["Faber's Primitive Election," p. 22.]

The objections to this theory are evident, and may be briefly stated.

1. That the election spoken of in the New Testament is all election of persons within a nation, and not of the nation itself. A distinction is made between the Jewish nation, and the remnant of them according to the election of grace. Rom. 11:5. It is also said in verse 7: "That which Israel seeketh for that he obtained not; but the election obtained it, and the rest were hardened."

Mr. Locke attempts to remove this difficulty by supposing that the Israel here spoken of is the whole nation before the loss of the ten tribes, and that the remnant is all of the rest that remained Jews at the time Paul wrote. But, that the present nation was the Israel referred to Paul himself shows by applying to it, in Romans 10:21, the title of Israel. "But as to Israel," he saith, "All the day long did I spread out my hands unto a disobedient and gainsaying people." The Israel to whom Isaiah, who is here referred to, went, was Judah; his prophecies were but seldom made to the Ten Tribes.

2. A distinction is also made between persons in the same nation; the elect being separated from others, as in Matt. 24:22–24, where fearful calamities are

306

foretold, and it is said, that prophets shall arise, etc., and that if it were possible they shall deceive the very elect.

The parallel passage is in Mark 13:20–22.

3. Against this theory may also be quoted such passages as show that the called, and the elect are not identical, as:

Matt. 22:14. "Many are called, but few chosen."

II. A modification of this theory has been made or rather another one has been suggested so similar that the idea has evidently been caught from that of Locke. It is given by George Stanley Faber in his work on "The Primitive Doctrine of Election." It may be called the theory of Church Election, or of External Church privileges. Mr. Faber states it as follows: "The idea is that of an Election of individuals into the pale of the visible church, with God's moral purpose that through faith and holiness they should attain everlasting life; but yet with a moral possibility of their abusing their privileges even to their own final destruction."

1. It is argued in favor of this, that "we never find one particular set of Christians addressed as being especially elect to the exclusion of all other Christians, who, together with the unconverted world at large, are thence exhibited as reprobates. But we constantly find that all the members of the local church addressed are collectively saluted as being in God's purpose and design elected through holiness to glory."

In reply it may be remarked:

(1.) That this argument proceeds upon the erroneous supposition that there were persons called Christians in Apostolic times who did not actually profess to be converted persons, and therefore were not properly to be regarded as such.

Every argument in favor of a converted church membership is an argument against this supposition, and, therefore, against this theory.

(2.) Or it proceeds upon a second erroneous supposition, namely, that the Apostles undertook to pronounce infallibly upon the spiritual condition of those to whom they wrote. On the contrary, proceeding upon the rule, "By their fruits ye shall know them," they, in the judgement of charity, spoke of those to whom they wrote as though they were actually Christians, because professedly such, and maintaining outwardly the life of such. Thus they are called "holy," in like manner as they are called "elect," and are said to be "holy and without blemish before him in love" (Eph. 1:4), and to have redemption, and the forgiveness of trespasses, v. 7, and to have obtained an inheritance, of which the sealing of the Spirit was an earnest.

2. In favor of this view, it is asserted that the Apostle teaches us in Rom. 9:6–26, that the terms election and elect are used in the same sense in which they are used in the Old Testament.

To this it may be replied:

(1.) That if true it favors the theory of Nationalism rather than this.

(2.) That the Apostle himself distinguishes between the extent of the election, which had before existed, and that which was now manifested. "They are not all Israel who are of Israel." "Neither because they are Abraham's seed are they all children," (Rom. 9:7); thus indicating that the limitation had been formerly made according to the national extent, but that now a segregation is made from this. The two elections, therefore, differ in extent.

(3.) But the difference is also in kind. This is what affects this theory most closely. Even under the old election, not all the children, but simply the one of the promise is the one in whom the election exists. Under the new, the same thing is true, the election is not of all to whom the external privileges connected with it belong, but of those only who are partakers of the promise. In this respect they are similar, and so Paul indicates: "The children of the promise are reckoned for a seed." Rom. 9:8. But formerly the promise was of Isaac, wherefore it was said, "In Isaac shall thy seed be called." Rom. 9:7. And that promise was of the land of Canaan, which was granted actually to all of his descendants as a class. So also now, the children of the promise are the elect; but they are not all to whom the external privileges of hearing the gospel, or even of entering the church of Christ, are given, for unto these as a class this promise is not fulfilled; but, simply, to those who truly embrace the gospel, and by faith in Jesus are vitally united to him. It is to this class only that the election refers. There is, therefore, a difference in kind indicated by the Apostle.

3. It is said that the addresses to the churches contained in the letters of the Apostles, indicate the election of the whole churches, and that, consequently, election must be merely to external church privileges. Dr. Faber does not cite the passages at length, because he thinks that any attentive reader, by attending to them, will readily perceive their palpably universalizing tendency. But he adduces as proof the beginnings of Romans, 1 Corinthians, Ephesians, Colossians, 1st and 2nd Thessalonians and 1 Peter.

(1.) Of these, singular to say, none speak of election in the addresses to the churches, except Ephesians, the two Thessalonians and 1 Peter. But the others all speak of the saints and of a calling to sanctification. The truth is, that, as they professed to be God's children, the Apostle, in the judgement of charity, speaks of them as such, and this is shown by the language of all the salutations as well as of the epistles at large.

(2.) The language in Ephesians is used as inclusive, not only of those to whom he wrote, but of himself also. It evidently is intended to refer to him and them, as having like hopes, and being partakers of like promises. That, at least, it is not intended to refer to the mere privilege of church membership, is evident from the fact that the apostle speaks of these persons as "sealed with the Holy Spirit of promise," ch. 1:13. They are spoken of as having been "quickened," (ch. 2:1), as having been "dead through your trespasses and sins," (ch. 2:1), and as having been the "children of wrath even as the rest," ch. 2:3. Such language scarcely comports with an address to those whom the Apostle had not reason to believe to be converted persons.

The epistles to the Thessalonians, to which Faber also refers, are even more distinctly against him. For, here, we have not simply to infer what were the feelings which led to the expressions used by the Apostle; but he himself tells us of the fact that he knew their election, and assigns the reasons of his belief. These are not because they enjoyed the outward privileges of the church; but because of their work of faith and labors of love, and patience of hope, and because the gospel came not to them in word only, but also in power, and in the Holy Ghost, and in much assurance.

As to the first Epistle of Peter it may be said.

(a.) That the elect spoken of are "sojourners of the dispersion in Pontus, Galatia, Cappadocia, Asia and Bithynia." This at least creates the presumption that they had no especial opportunities of church privileges. This, however, is doubtful.

(b.) They are, however, spoken of in chapter 1, verses 3, 4 and 5, as begotten . . . "unto a living hope, . . . unto an inheritance . . . reserved in heaven for you, who, by the power of God, are guarded through faith unto a salvation." Again, they are spoken of, verses 7 and 8, as loving Christ, as believing in him and rejoicing with joy unspeakable.

4. Yet, again, three passages are adduced in which a whole church as such is styled elect, and it is argued thence that this is the Scriptural meaning of election. These passages are, 1 Pet. 5:13, "She that is in Babylon elect together with you saluteth you." 2 John, 1st verse, "The elder unto the elect lady and her children," and verse 13, "The children of thine elect sister salute thee."

(1.) Of these passages it may be said that the application of any of them to a church is doubtful. This is evident from any English version of all but the first, and the literal rendering of that is, "The, from or in Babylon, that is elected with you, saluteth you." It would be bad to form a theory upon such doubtful passages.

(2.) Admitting these, however, to have the meaning asserted, and that an elect church would be spoken of as such only with reference to the privileges thus conferred upon its members; it does not follow that this is the only sense which election can have. It must be shown not only that there is such an election, but that nothing else is spoken of under that name before this theory can be established as the only election taught. The truth is, that the general nature of the terms, elect, choose, etc., makes it practicable to have several kinds of election, and the nature of the election has to be decided by those declarations of its character and purpose which accompany it.

(3.) Under any view of Election, save that of Nationalism, it would be perfectly appropriate to apply the word elect to the body as such which is supposed to be composed only of elect members. Thus we often speak of Congress, or of a State Legislature as the assembled wisdom of the State or Country, because such is hypothetically its character; it being supposed to be composed of men who represent by their wisdom that of their constituents. So the church may be spoken of as elect, because composed of those supposed from the best sources of knowledge to be the elect of God.

5. The fifth argument is from the parables of the labourers in the vineyard, Matt. 20:1–16, and the marriage of the King's son, Matt. 22:2–14.

"These," says Faber, "contain the passages where the term Elect or Chosen first occurs and in these parables the Chosen or the Elect are all those who so far obey the call of the gospel as to enter the pale of the visible Christian Church." And in order to show that they are not secure there from destruction, the case of the man without the wedding garment is mentioned.

It may be replied, as to the first of these parables, that Faber does not point out any indication of such loss of any persons in the churches, as is implied in this parable. The parable is merely instructive as to the fact of God's sovereignty, and as to his bestowment of blessings on whom he will. The phrase is added, "many be called but few chosen," which is the key to the parable, and yet in no wise bears upon the subject under discussion, save to show that there are two classes, the called and the elect, and that the first comprises many, the latter few; facts which oppose the theory of the author, who claims that the elect are not the few that are saved, but are the same as the many who are called to the external privileges of God's truth.

The second parable is even more distinctly against him. In it there are three classes: the first, those who are called, and pay no attention to the invitation to the feast; the second, those who enter to partake of it, who may be regarded as the ones gathered here on earth into earthly churches; the third, the class marked by the separation from among them of the one who had not on a wedding garment, which represents the self-deceived in Christ's earthly churches. Immediately after the order for his destruction is given by the king, it is added, "For many are called, but few chosen." Does not the word chosen here evidently point out those who are the saved, as distinguished from those who are outwardly privileged, either as the outwardly called who refuse, or the called who enter the church and enjoy its privileges? If so, the author's view of Election is false.

These are the only arguments, that can properly be so called, that are advanced in favor of this theory, and the above statements fully show that the Scriptures nowhere teach the doctrine of Election as thus set forth. The theory has been examined more at length than its own merits deserve, partly, because it is not so generally known, but more especially, because it has the sanction of a man of known ability and scholarship though of admitted fanciful and unsound judgement.

III. Finding now that election is in no respect one to external privileges, we pass to the third theory which has been suggested; that of perseverance in foreseen faith, set forth by Arminians of all classes.

In connection with this idea of election is also taught a universal atonement, offered upon condition of faith to all persons, to each of whom is given sufficient grace to accept or reject it. Upon this acceptance or rejection, salvation depends.

This theory of election, therefore, asserts that:

(1.) The salvation of individuals is the result of their own choice and perseverance.

(2.) The election made by God is simply an election of a class.

(3.) So far as the election of individuals took place in eternity, it was only as God foresaw what would be the result of the election of a class.

(4.) That it is an election made upon condition that they would accept the offer of the gospel.

IV. As this theory is just the opposite in every respect of the Calvinistic theory of personal, unconditional, and eternal Election, it is better to put the two in direct contrast, and to proceed to the proof that the Scriptures teach the latter, and not the former.

The latter theory is that God (who and not man is the one who chooses or elects), of his own purpose (in accordance with his will, and not from any obligation to man, nor because of any will of man), has from Eternity (the period of God's action, not in time in which man acts), determined to save (not has actually saved, but simply determined so to do), [and to save (not to confer gospel or church privileges upon)], a definite number of mankind (not the whole race, nor indefinitely merely some of them, nor indefinitely a certain proportionate part; but a definite number), as individuals (not the whole or a part of the race, nor of a nation, nor of a church, nor of a class, as of believers or the pious; but individuals), not for or because of any merit or work of theirs, nor of any value to him of them (not for their good works, nor their holiness, nor excellence, nor their faith, nor their spiritual sanctification, although the choice is to a salvation attained through faith and sanctification; nor their value to him, though their salvation tends greatly to the manifested glory of his grace); but of his own good pleasure (simply because he was pleased so to choose).

This theory, therefore, teaches that election is:

(1.) An act of God, and not the result of the choice of the elect.

(2.) That this choice is one of individuals, and not of classes.

(3.) That it was made without respect to the action of the persons elected.

(4.) By the good pleasure of God.

(5.) According to an eternal purpose.

(6.) That it is an election to salvation and not to outward privileges.

To the Scriptures alone must we look for the truth upon this subject.

Upon opening them we find that the words Election and Elect are used in various senses.

1. They signify a choice to office whether by man or God.

Luke 6:13. Christ's choice of the twelve Apostles.

Acts 1:21–26. The selection of an Apostle in the place of Judas.

Acts 9:15. Saul is called a chosen vessel.

1 Pet. 2:6–8. Christ is spoken of as the corner-stone, elect, precious that is laid in Zion.

2. The choice of Israel to their peculiar national privilege of being the chosen or separated people of God; as in Acts 13:17. "The God of this people Israel chose our fathers."

3. It is once used for a choice made of salvation by an individual.

Luke 10:42. "Mary hath chosen the good part which shall not be taken away from her."

4. In a large majority of cases it has reference to the choice to salvation, either in the purpose or act of choice by God.

It is to the doctrine taught in this last class of passages that our inquiries are to be turned.

(1.) Election is an act of God, and not the result of the choice of the Elect.

This is not now an inquiry into the reason of Election; but simply into the agent. Does God choose the elect, whether by his own purpose, or because he foresees that they will believe, or for any other reason? Is election an act of God?

The fact on this point would appear more clearly if we were to exchange the common word choice or chosen with the equivalent word elect.

The following passages are sufficient, though the examples are far more numerous.

John 13:18. "I know whom I have chosen."

John 15:16. "Ye did not choose me, but I chose you" (not to their offices as apostle, but), "that ye should go and hear fruit."

Rom. 8:33. "Who shall lay anything to the charge of God's chosen ones?"

Rom. 9:15. "I will have mercy on whom I have mercy."

Eph. 1:4. "Even as he chose us in him."

Eph. 1:11. "Having been foreordained according to the purpose of him who worketh all things after the counsel of his will."

2 Thess. 2:13. "God chose you from the beginning unto salvation."

(2.) This choice is one of individuals and not of classes.

This position needs to be explained. It is not denied that the Elect are to be true believers, and that true believers are the Elect. The character of the Elect does not, therefore, enter into this question. The issue is simply, does God choose all who shall believe, and are they, as such, his elect? or, does he choose his elect, and will they, as such, believe? Is belief the result of God's election, or is God's election the result of man's faith?

Acts 13:48. "As many as were ordained to eternal life believed." This is a historical statement made subsequent to the event, not by man's knowledge but by inspiration.

Eph. 1:4, 5. "Even as he chose us in him, . . . having foreordained us unto adoption as sons."

2 Thess. 2:13. "But we are bound to give thanks to God alway for you, brethren, beloved of the Lord, for that God chose you from the beginning unto salvation in sanctification of the Spirit and belief of the truth." Here the choice is made to salvation, and the means to salvation, sanctification and faith, are indicated; no prerequisite or means being stated as to Election. It is not as believers that they are elected; but as elected, that they are saved.

Rom. 8:29. "Whom he foreknew he also foreordained to be conformed to the image of his Son." The foreknowledge here is of persons, not of personal acts, not of those whose faith he foreknew, nor, as would be essential to their theory, is it of the class of believers as such. The Arminian theory would require the substitution of the words "as believers" or "you as believers" instead of those which are used.

It is not, therefore, to the class of believers, but to individuals that election refers. But, it may be asked, does it not refer to them in that character? Did not God choose those whose faith he foresaw?

(3.) The third point then to be proved is, that it was not because of any act or merit of theirs, but irrespective of anything but his own good pleasure, that this Election was made.

This is merely a negative form of the same fact stated by the next point affirmatively. It is better, therefore, to unite this with the succeeding one, which is,

(4.) That the election is made through the mere good pleasure of God.

Some of the passages simply affirm a choice by God's Sovereign will; others, while asserting this, also deny merit in those elected; and still others represent the fact of sovereignty by asserting a choice of such persons as would not ordinarily be chosen. The following are some of the passages which prove these points.

(a.) Such as simply assert sovereign will. Such are Matt. 24:40–41 and Luke 17:33–36. These declare the sovereign choice of God by showing such choice exercised as to persons in the same situation, so that the one shall be taken and the other left; "two men on one bed;" "two women grinding at the mill;" "two men shall be in the field;" one of each shall be taken and the other left.

John 3:3–8. Regeneration is here spoken of as essential to entrance into the kingdom of God. This precedes any act on which election is said by any to depend. Yet the sovereignty of God in this is declared in verse 8. "The wind bloweth where it listeth, and thou hearest the voice thereof, but knoweth not whence it cometh, and whither it goeth; so is every one that is born of the Spirit."

John 6:37, 39, 44, 64, 65. "All that which the Father giveth me shall come unto me. . . . This is the will of him that sent me, that of all that which he hath given me I should lose nothing. . . . No man can come to me except the Father which sent me draw him. . . . Jesus knew from the beginning who they were that believed not, and who it was that should betray him. And he said, for this cause have I said unto you, that no man can come unto me, except it be given unto him of the Father."

John 15:16. "Ye did not choose me, but I chose you, and appointed you, that ye should go and bear fruit." The object to be attained cannot be the cause.

John 17:2. "As thou gavest him authority over all flesh, that whatsoever thou hast given him to them he should give eternal life." See also verses 6–12.

Acts 22:14. Ananias says to Paul, "The God of our fathers hath appointed thee to know his will."

Eph. 1:5. In the fourth verse having referred to God's choice of us before the foundation of the world, he says in this fifth, "Having foreordained us unto adoption as sons through Jesus Christ unto himself, according to the good pleasure of his will, to the praise of the glory of his grace." In verse 11 we are said to be predestinated to our inheritance "according to the purpose of him who worketh all things after the counsel of his will."

James 1:18. "Of his own will he brought us forth by the word of truth."

(b.) Such as deny merit in the persons elected as well as assert the sovereign choice of God.

Ezek. 36:32. In this passage, after describing the blessings connected with the new dispensation, and the gift of the Spirit and the new heart which he would give them—gifts which the Calvinistic theory regards as the result of election; but which the Arminian maintains to be its cause—God adds, "Not for your sakes do I this, saith the LORD GOD, be it known unto you; be ashamed and confounded for your ways, O house of Israel."

John 1:11–13. "He came unto his own, and they that were his own received him not. But, as many as received him, to them gave he the right to become children of God, even to them that believe on his name; which were born not of blood, nor of the will of the flesh, nor of the will of man, but of God."

In Rom. 9:11–16. Election is illustrated by the case of the twins; "the children being not yet born, neither having done anything, good or bad, that the purpose of God according to election might stand, not of works, but of him that calleth. . . . So then it is not of him that willeth, nor of him that runneth, but of God that showeth mercy."

Rom. 11:5–6. "Even so then at this present time also there is a remnant according to the election of grace. But if it is by grace, it is no more of works; otherwise grace is no more grace."

(c.) Such as so describe the persons chosen as to imply this.

Matt. 11:25, 26. "At that season Jesus answered and said, I thank thee, O Father, Lord of heaven and earth, that thou didst hide these things from the wise and understanding and didst reveal them unto babes; yea Father, for so it was well pleasing in thy sight."

Luke 4:25–27. Christ illustrates this sovereignty of God by mentioning that many widows had been in Israel, yet had only a heathen widow been blessed; and again many lepers, and yet only a heathen leper cured. "Of a truth I say unto you, there were many widows in Israel in the days of Elijah . . . and unto none of them was Elijah sent, but only to Sarephath in the land of Sidon, unto a woman that was a widow. And there were many lepers in Israel in the time of Elisha the prophet; and none of them was cleansed, but only Naaman the Syrian."

Acts 26:12–23. Paul's description of his personal condition at his conversion shows that God chose him not for his merits but from his own good pleasure.

1 Cor. 1:26–30. "For behold your calling, brethren, how that not many wise after the flesh, not many mighty, not many noble, are called; but God chose the foolish things of the world that he might put to shame them that are wise; and God chose the weak things of the world, that he might put to shame the things that are strong; and the base things of the world, and the things that are despised, did God choose, yea, and the things that are not, that he might bring to nought the things that are, that no flesh should glory before God. But of him are ye in Christ Jesus, etc."

Gal. 1:15, 16. Paul says, "When it was the good pleasure of God, who separated me even from my mother's womb, and called me through his grace, to reveal his Son in me, that I might preach, etc."

Ephesians 2:1–13. The description of the condition of those who were dead in trespasses and sins, and in that state were quickened, proves that the quickening and salvation was due to no merit of their own.

The texts thus exhibited under these three classes prove conclusively that not on account of their own merits, but because of the good pleasure of God, does he choose men. They have been presented at some length, because this is after all the point upon which all that is important in this controversy turns. For, although other matters are equally essential to the doctrine, the whole opposition arises from an unwillingness on the part of man to recognize the sovereignty of God, and to ascribe salvation entirely to grace. This proof, however, has been by no means exhausted, the attempt having been to select some only of the numerous passages, and mainly such as from their conciseness allow of presentation in full. Let the Scriptures be read with reference to this doctrine and every passage marked which indicates God's dealing with men as an absolute sovereign, and also every declaration which ascribes Election or the fruits of it to his choice and not to the will or acts of men, and every illustration afforded that this is God's usual method, and it will appear that scarcely any book of Scripture will fail to furnish testimony to the fact that in the acts of grace, no less than those of providence, God "doeth according to his will in the army of heaven and among the inhabitants of the earth." Dan. 4:3–5.

(5.) Another important fact to be shown is the eternity of Election in opposition to the idea that it was in time. The proof on this point is two-fold. There are (a.) those passages which show that the Election took place before existence in this world or before the world began, and (b.) those which actually declare that it was eternal. Between the two classes of passages there is really, however, very little difference, as, from the nature of the case, what took place before time must have been in Eternity, and besides, the object of proof of an eternal Election is simply to show that it was not dependent on human action, but simply on the will of God.

(a.) Those which show that the election took place before man's existence, or before the world began.

Jer. 1:5. "Before I formed thee in the belly, I knew thee, and before thou camest forth out of the womb, I sanctified thee."

Matt. 25:34. "Then shall the King say unto them on his right hand, Come, ye blessed of my Father, inherit the kingdom prepared for you from the foundation of the world."

Eph. 1:4. "Even as he chose us in him before the foundation of the world."

2 Thess. 2:13. "But we are bound to give thanks to God alway for you, brethren, beloved of the Lord, for that God chose you from the beginning unto salvation in sanctification of the Spirit and belief of the truth."

2 Tim. 1:9. "Who saved us, and called us with a holy calling, not according to our works, but according to his own purpose and grace, which was given us in Christ Jesus before times eternal."

Compare also the language used as to the names written in the Lamb's book of life.

Rev. 13:8. "And all that dwell on the earth shall worship him (that is the beast), every one whose name hath not been written in the book of life of the Lamb that hath been slain from the foundation of the world."

Rev. 17:8. "And they that dwell on the earth shall wonder, they whose name hath not been written in the book of life from the foundation of the world, when they behold the beast how that he was, and is not, and shall come."

Referring to the adherents of the Lamb as persons "with him," it is said in verse 14, "They . . . that are with him called and chosen and faithful."

Rev. 21:27. "And there shall in no wise enter into it any thing unclean, or he that maketh an abomination and a lie: but only they which are written in the Lamb's book of life."

(b.) The passages which distinctly declare that this, which may be thus inferred to have been an eternal Election, is really such.

1 Cor. 2:7. "Even the wisdom that hath been hidden, which God foreordained before the worlds unto our glory."

Eph. 3:11. "According to the eternal purpose which he purposed in Christ Jesus our Lord."

(6.) It remains to be proved that this Election is one to salvation, and not to mere external privileges.

Jeremiah 31:31–34:

Verse 31. Tells of a day when a new covenant shall be made.

Verse 32. Says that this shall not be like that made with their fathers (not one of external privileges).

Verse 33. But of this sort, "I will put my law in their inward parts, and in their hearts will I write it; and I will be their God, and they shall be my people."

Verse 34. "And they shall teach no more every man his neighbour, and every man his brother, saying, Know the Lord: for they shall all know me, from the least of them unto the greatest of them, saith the Lord: for I will forgive their iniquity, and their sin will I remember no more."

Speaking again of the restoration of Israel, the same prophet adds a like passage in chap. 32:37–40. A similar passage is to be found in Ezekiel 36:24–27.

John 10:16. "Other sheep I have which are not of this fold; them also I must bring, and they shall hear my voice; and they shall become one flock, one shepherd."

John 10:26. "Ye believe not, because ye are not of my sheep."

Verse 27. "My sheep hear my voice, and I know them, and they follow me."

Rom. 8:28–30. "We know that to them that love God all things work together for good, even to them that are called according to his purpose." Paul now proceeds to tell who these are. "For whom he foreknew, he also foreordained to be conformed to the image of his Son, that he might be the first-born among many brethren: and whom he foreordained, them he also called: and whom he called, them he also justified: and whom he justified, them he also glorified." This passage shows that foreknowledge, foreordination to holiness, calling, justification, and a state of glory are inseparably connected, and hence that the election, from which they proceed, is to salvation.

Eph. 1:4–9. This passage speaks of our being chosen before the foundation of the world, "that we should be holy and without blemish before him in love: having foreordained us unto adoption as sons through Jesus Christ unto himself, according to the good pleasure of his will, to the praise of the glory of his grace, which he freely bestowed on us in the Beloved: in whom we have our redemption through his blood, the forgiveness of our trespasses, according to the riches of his grace, which he made to abound toward us in all wisdom and prudence, having made known unto us the mystery of his will, according to his good pleasure which he purposed in him."

2 Thess. 2:13. After referring to others who were to have the same outward privileges, but upon whom God would send strong delusion, the Apostle says in this verse, "For we are bound to give thanks to God alway for you, brethren, beloved of the Lord, for that God chose you from the beginning unto salvation," etc.

1 Peter 5:10. "The God of all grace who called you unto his eternal glory in Christ," etc. Here the Apostle is speaking of that effectual calling, which is the result of Election, and tells us that it is a call unto eternal glory.

CHAPTER 30

REPROBATION

THE doctrine of Election is intimately associated with and involves that of Reprobation. The latter has met with even greater opposition, and misconstructions of what the orthodox teach on this subject have been even more numerous.

The Scriptural statements as to Reprobation are that God, in eternity, when he elected some, did likewise not elect others; that as resulting from this non-election, but not as efficiently caused by it, he passes by these in the bestowment of the special favours shown to the Elect, and, as in like manner yet further resulting, condemns men because of sin to everlasting destruction, and while they are in the state of sin and condemnation, he effects or permits the hardening of their heart, so that his truth is not appreciated, but actually rejected.

According to this statement there are four points involved in the decrees as to Reprobation:

1. The decree not to elect.
2. The decree to pass by in bestowing divine grace.
3. To condemn for sins committed.
4. To harden against the truth all or some persons, already sinners, and to confirm them in sin.

In considering this doctrine we are met by the difficulty arising from the want of knowledge of God's purpose in action. It may be questioned whether we can arrive at this at all; yet to understand this subject fully, we must know that purpose. If, therefore, we cannot learn it, we see with what propriety we must submit simply to accept what God says.

A careful examination of the four points indicated will show that the third and fourth of them have necessary reference to sinners, and that the other two have not. These are only thus connected, because God, in carrying out his purpose, has chosen to do it by the creation of man, and by permitting him to fall. This may be shown by supposing God to have some great object in view to be accomplished by beings selected from those to remain holy, as through a part of the angelic hosts. He selects some as the ones through whom he will accomplish his purpose; he rejects the others as not choosing so to use them. He gives to the former special grace to fit them for their work or to remove from them any imperfection for it. His plan not having required that they be permitted to

319

fall, the act of rejection and refusal to add the special grace given to others constitutes in this case all of Reprobation. The purpose of God as to man, on the other hand, affected a fallen race, and hence the other two points, in accordance with his determination to permit man to fall, are associated with and made a part of the decree of Reprobation, with which otherwise they would have no necessary connection.

The fact that God has permitted man to fall is undoubted. It is beyond our power to show how it is consistent with his justice and mercy. That it is so should be acknowledged by all, because God has done it.

In like manner must we deal with any result that flows from any doctrine in connection with that purpose. If it was right for God to permit man to fall, in order to carry out his purpose, it is right to condemn him for his sin. But the connection of condemnation for sin thus permitted with rejection from the number of those through whom that purpose is effected, extends no farther than that, from the circumstances of the case, the rejected in one part of the decree become the condemned in another.

The relation borne by these two parts of the decree will be better seen by the following table showing what is done on the one side for the Elect, and on the other for the rejected.

1. Election from good pleasure.	1. Rejection from good pleasure.
Sin having been committed.	
2. To recover by the gospel and special grace.	2. Not to recover, but to leave sinners.
3. As thus recovered, to glorify.	3. As left sinners, to condemn for sin, and to harden some of those thus left.

In thus arranging this table no reference has been had to the views of either Sublapsarians or Supralapsarians. The doctrine of Reprobation is not affected by the scheme of either. This may be shown by presenting the order of the decrees as taught by each.

The Supralapsarians teach that there was:

1. God's decree to glorify himself in the raising up of the church in which his grace should be peculiarly manifested.

2. To create the men whom he had selected and rejected for its composition.

3. To permit to fall.

4. To send Christ to redeem.

The Sublapsarian view is:

1. A decree to create.

2. To permit to fall.

3. To elect some to everlasting life.

4. To send Christ for their redemption and salvation.

The only difference in the decree of Reprobation as held by either of these views is that the Sublapsarians suppose man to have been decreed as fallen, before decreed as elected, or rejected; yet they deny that the rejection was because of the sin of the non-elect, for if so, they say, the others would have been rejected, being equally in sin. The Supralapsarian view supposes that the election to a certain purpose and the rejection took place before the decree to permit to fall had been entertained. According to each theory, therefore, the last two points of the decree have only what has been called an accidental connection with it.

This preliminary statement will prepare the way for the Scriptural proof of the points indicated.

I. The decree to reject some.

1. This is involved in the doctrine of Election. The choice of some and not of the whole, involves the non-election and thus the rejection of others.

2. But it is plainly taught in Scripture:

(1.) In such passages as declare salvation not to be attained because God has not given the means. These will be presented under the next general head.

(2.) In such as declare salvation not to be attained because men are not of the Elect, as

John 6:65. "No man can come unto me, except it be given unto him of the Father."

John 10:26. "Ye believe not, because ye are not of my sheep."

1 Cor. 1:26. "For behold your calling, brethren, how that not many wise after the flesh, not many mighty, not many noble, are called: but God chose, etc."

(3.) In all such passages as declare the preordination, or appointment by God of these persons either to condemnation or destruction. Though not the direct result of this decree so as to be efficiently caused by it, these things yet prove the rejection of some who, under the circumstances thus accidentally arising, are thus preordained.

1 Peter 2:8. "A stone of stumbling, and a rock of offence; for they stumble at the word, being disobedient; whereunto also they were appointed."

Jude 4. "There are certain men crept in privily, even they who were of old set forth unto this condemnation."

1 Thess. 5:9. In this chapter, the Apostle tells of the evil that in the last day shall come upon certain ones, and then says: "For God appointed us not unto wrath but unto the obtaining of salvation through our Lord Jesus Christ."

(4.) In the illustrations from the twins, the potter, and the clay in the 9th chapter of Romans.

(5.) In the same chapter the words used are expressive directly of the truth involved.

Rom. 9:18. "So then he hath mercy on whom he will, and whom he will he hardeneth."

(6.) The Apostle was teaching this doctrine in the ninth chapter of Romans and in verses 20 and 21 anticipated and answered the objection of one inquiring, why God should punish those who are thus fulfilling his will, by saying: "Nay, but, O man, who art thou that repliest against God? Shall the thing formed say to him that formed it, why didst thou make me thus? Or hath not the potter a right over the clay, from the same lump to make one part a vessel unto honour, and another unto dishonour."

II. The second point of proof is that God passes by some in the bestowment of his special grace.

That God does bestow many of the means of grace on many not to be saved is admitted; but what needs to be shown is that there are special effective means which distinguish the Elect, and which are not bestowed on others.

The language of Scripture on this point is twofold. There are passages which simply speak of the withholding of privileges, and others which seem to go beyond this and assert a positive influence exerted to keep men from the truth. The meaning of this latter class of passages will be examined when we come to speak of the fourth point. At present they are presented as though they meant no more than the mere neglect to bestow these spiritual advantages.

Deut. 29:4. "The Lord hath not given you an heart to know, and eyes to see, and ears to hear, unto this day."

Job. 17:4. "For thou hast hid their heart from understanding, therefore shalt thou not exalt them."

1 Sam. 2:25. After Eli had exhorted his sons to refrain from making the people of the Lord transgress, it is said, "Notwithstanding they hearkened not unto the voice of their father, because the Lord would slay them."

Isaiah 6:9. "Go, and tell this people, Hear ye indeed, but understand not; and see ye indeed, but perceive not."

Rom. 11:7, 8. "That which Israel seeketh for that he obtained not, but the election obtained it, and the rest were hardened according as it is written, God gave them a spirit of stupor, eyes that they should not see, and ears that they should not hear unto this very day."

Matt. 13:11–15. "Unto you it is given to know the mysteries of the kingdom of heaven, but to them it is not given. For whosoever hath, to him shall be given, and he shall have abundance; but whosoever hath not, from him shall be taken away even that which he hath. Therefore speak I to them in parables, because seeing they see not, and hearing they hear not, neither do they understand. And unto them is fulfilled the prophecy of Isaiah, which saith, by hearing ye shall hear, and shall in nowise understand; and seeing ye shall see, and shall in nowise perceive. For this people's heart is waxed gross, and their ears are dull of hearing, and their eyes they have closed; lest haply they should perceive with their eyes, and hear with their ears, and understand with their heart, and should turn again, and I should heal them." The parallel to the first part is Luke 8:10, and to the last Mark 4:12. Similar passages also are in John 12:39, 40 and Acts 28:25–27.

2 Cor. 3:15. "But unto this day, whensoever Moses is read, a veil lieth upon their heart."

These texts will suffice when it is remembered that to the plain declarations here made, may be added the proof afforded by all those passages which, teaching that God bestows on the elect alone salvation, with such attendant blessings as without fail lead to it, show that these blessings are also withheld from the non-elect.

At present it is assumed that this is done simply as an act of withholding. What is meant by this will be shown hereafter.

The question has been raised as to the two points considered above, whether the decree which has respect to them is positive or negative. By a positive decree is meant one which involves an actual direct exercise of the will of God. A negative decree is one in which the effect purposed flows as the result of the actual exercise of the will on something else.

The answer to this question depends upon the nature of the union of the different parts of the decree of reprobation. By some theologians all four of the points involved in the decree are included in one and by Reprobation they mean the actual preordination to damnation of certain persons, just as effectively as the preordination of others to salvation by Election. Others conceiving this to be a false statement have separated the first and second point from the third and fourth, uniting them together, however, as one, and giving to it the name of Preterition. The great difficulty which these had to encounter, arose from the fact that while it is true that the mere neglect to bestow certain blessings on some, may take place without their being conceived of as in the mind, and may, therefore, be a mere negative act, the choice of some so necessarily involves the rejection of others as to require that rejection to accompany the act of choice. Rejection must, therefore, have accompanied Election. In the very fact that some were chosen, was involved the rejection of others. [But even here it is not to be overlooked that rejection was not from God's favour, not from salvation, not from hope of mercy. Rejection has nothing to do with any of these. The loss of these results from sin]. But the intimate connection between chosen and not chosen does not exist in the bestowment of gifts and graces. These were conferred on those chosen, and not conferred on those not chosen. Hence no positive act of God occurs as to those not chosen. Consequently it is better to divide this part of the decree and regard Rejection as a positive act, and Preterition in bestowing grace as a negative one.

From the first and second, the third and fourth points result consequentially but not effectively. This has been before shown. They do not result from these, so as to be their consequences, but they are actually caused only by the sin of man and are causally related only to it. It is neither as an effect of Election or Rejection or of Preterition that man has fallen, or sins, or is condemned, or will be destroyed. The simple effect is that he is not rescued, and consequently is left where he would have been without these acts. They do not lead to destruction. They simply do not rescue from it.

III. The third point needs no proof at present. The condemnation for the sins man commits is too plainly taught in the Word of God. From this condemnation the Elect are rescued by special grace, the Rejected are left liable to it and consequently suffer from it.

This decree of God is positive, involving especially an act of God's will in reference to the sin that is to be punished.

IV. The fourth point of Reprobation is the hardening some or all of the Rejected against the truth, and the confirmation of them in their sin.

Some or all sinners are spoken of as hardened, because according to the definition given to this hardening process must it be limited or not. If the hardening of God means no more than the mere permission of those influences by which this is accomplished, then it is universal, because the evil influences of the heart and of Satan undoubtedly lead to a constant increase of indisposition for God's service. But if that process is to be regarded as a special act of God, it must be confined to those persons whom God by special acts of goodness or justice hardens so that they, in an extraordinary sense, are set against the truth and are led to reject it.

The language used in Scripture upon this point is very decided. The only question is about the meaning to be put on it as to a single point. It is best to state the two positions recognized as true and then add the other about which the discussion arises.

1. God is represented as hardening the heart.

2. This is admitted by all to be done so far as permitting it to work out its own destruction or not interfering to prevent the evil influences which would have that tendency.

It is not necessary to present the Scripture proof of these points which is abundant, because it will plainly appear in connection with the third which is that

3. God does himself operate upon and affect the heart and faculties of the individual so that he is hardened against the acceptance of the truth of the Gospel. This point is supported by many passages of Scripture and should be, at least briefly, considered.

(1.) It may here again be suggested that it, upon an examination of the Scriptures, this is seen to be God's teaching, we are bound, in the simplicity of faith, not only to receive it, but also to continue with firm confidence to believe and maintain that it is perfectly consistent with the character of God. The fact that we cannot show it to be so, ought not to make us hesitate a moment after we are convinced that God has taught it.

(2.) But if so taught, it may be made to appear perfectly consistent with God's righteous action and should be recognized as such.

The contrary has been argued from the alleged fact that thus the sinner is prevented from accepting the gospel plan of salvation. But this is not true. His previous condition has already caused this. It is not any action of God withholding grace or conferring further disability that leads any man to reject the gospel. All are already in such a state of depravity that they will certainly refuse it. This is proved from the fact that those who reject the gospel are not only not confined to the hardened, but comprise all sinners, and that nothing can prevent this result but a positive act of God by which he rescues man from his evil nature as well as from its effects.

The only evil then that arises to the sinner is that, under these influences, he sins more freely or more flagrantly than he would otherwise have done, or that his sinful nature more rapidly develops itself. But if it be wrong in God to do anything by which this shall be accomplished, it will be wrong to cast man into hell; for the change of state from this life to that has this tendency.

This illustration suggests indeed what God under these circumstances is doing, which is nothing more than inflicting punishment on the individual because of his sin. He is a sinner in God's sight. His sin deserves punishment, and God punishes him by making his increased power to do wrong the punishment of the wrong already done.

In this view of the doctrine it is nothing worse than one very commonly taught by Arminians as well as by Calvinists of all kinds—that of the closing of a day of grace, when the time comes at which the line is passed beyond which God no longer shows favour. That doctrine which asserts an eternal shutting out of light as the penalty of resistance to truth is of precisely the same nature as this the most objectionable form in which this point of Reprobation can he presented.

(3.) But, again, whence are the influences which thus tend to salvation? Do they arise from the rights of man, or from the claims which he as man may be said to have upon his Creator? Not at all. They are involved, not in Creation, but in Redemption. They are influences, therefore, which belong, in the purpose of God, to the elect only. This is true, whether we regard the atonement as particular, or as general with a particular application.

These influences, therefore, come to man simply as the chosen of God. God may withhold them from all others. He does withhold them from the heathen. He might withhold them from those to whom they are thus given. But if God may justly withhold them from any, he may, with equal justice, stay the hand that would be stretched out to take what he has intended shall not be given. So long as the things which he withholds or prevents man from taking are not things on which man has any claim, God cannot be charged with injustice in thus acting. Admitting this doctrine, therefore, in its worst form it may be defended.

(4.) But fourthly, we are liable to hold this form of the doctrine simply from want of consideration as to the method of God's action, as well as from overlooking the language of Scripture elsewhere. Let these be regarded, and it will appear that God does not teach us that he directly hardens the heart of any. We must remember

(a.) That there is a sense in which God is said to do everything that is done. Whatever happens must either be done by him, or permitted by him; and must be done or permitted directly or indirectly, according as his action is immediate or through secondary means. Now it is the custom of the Scriptures to speak of God as doing whatever is done in any of these ways. If, therefore, we have no indications of the mode of his action, we cannot, from the mere declaration that the Lord did it, decide that he did it directly, or indirectly, efficiently, or permissively. Thus Joseph said to his brethren, "It was not you that sent me hither, but God" (Gen. 45:8), and yet we know that these men were willing instruments of God. The Scripture declarations as to reprobation, or hardening, are not stronger than these which are thus used relative to other matters where we know that God only acted indirectly and permissively.

(b.) There are causes at work fully sufficient to accomplish all that God would thus purpose without requiring efficient and causal action. These are the sinful depravity of the heart and the wiles of Satan. It can hardly be supposed that, when the work to be done could thus be effected, God would not leave it to be thus done.

(c.) In James 1:13, 14, the apostle uses language inconsistent with the idea that God efficiently leads to sin. "Let no man say when he is tempted, I am tempted of God: for God cannot be tempted with evil, and he himself tempteth no man: but each man is tempted, when he is drawn away by his own lust and enticed."

(d.) Whenever the heart is hardened as the result of any action of God, it is always as the result of merciful action, which should have had an opposite tendency. Thus was it with Pharaoh, and thus was it with the Jews in the time of Christ.

(5.) An examination of the passages which refer to the hardening of the heart will show that (a.) some expressly declare this hardening to have been by means, or by the individuals themselves; (b.) that others are explained by parallel or allied passages to have this meaning; and (c.) that there is nothing inconsistent with this view.

1. Passages which affirm this hardening to be the work of the individuals themselves.

2 Kings 17:14. The people of Israel carried away by the Assyrians are said to have hardened their necks like their fathers. See also Neh. 9:16–29 and Jer. 7:26.

2. Passages which furnish explanations. To these belong the famous passages concerning Pharaoh. There could be no stronger expressions than those there used.

(1.) God foretells that he will harden Pharaoh's heart. Ex. 7:3.

(2.) It is expressly said that Pharaoh's heart was hardened. Ex. 7:13.

(3.) God declares that for this very purpose did he raise up Pharaoh that he might show his glory. Ex. 10:1, 2.

(4.) And yet Pharaoh is expressly declared to have hardened his own heart. Ex. 8:15, 32. Notice in this case the way of hardening; whenever the curse was sent, Pharaoh yielded; whenever it was removed, his heart was hardened. And, that this was not an accidental connection, is seen by the fact that in Ex. 9:34, it is said of Pharaoh that, "when Pharaoh saw that the rain and hail and the thunders were ceased, he sinned yet more, and hardened his heart."

Another passage, which has often been commented on, is that in 1 Kings, 22nd chapter, where Ahab calls on his prophets and receives assurance of success (verse 6). He sends for a prophet of God (verses 7–9) who gives him the same answer (verse 15), probably ironically, as Ahab immediately turns and says to him, "How many times shall I adjure thee that thou speak unto me nothing but the truth in the name of the Lord" (verse 16). The prophet then proceeds to tell of the scattered house of Israel, as sheep that have no shepherd, thus foretelling evil. The king says to Jehoshaphat, "did I not tell thee that he would not prophesy good concerning me, but evil" (verse 18). Then the prophet proceeds to tell a vision wherein God is represented as wishing to destroy Ahab and asking of all his hosts, who will persuade Ahab that he may go and fall at Ramoth Gilead. And after various replies one Spirit came and said, that he would persuade him by being a lying spirit in the mouth of all his prophets. And the prophet adds, "Now therefore, behold, the Lord hath put a lying spirit in the mouth of all these thy prophets; and the Lord hath spoken evil concerning thee." This 1 Kings 22:21–23, is the place that is frequently referred to as a case of God's misleading Ahab. Independently of the fact that the prophet uses drapery for what he says, he tells the King distinctly God's will, and, as his prophet who ought to be heard, declares the truth. This passage ought not to weigh for a moment in favor of the idea that God seeks effectively to harden, and thus to destroy.

Again, we have a class of passages, for they are many, such as the one before referred to as showing Reprobation, Matt. 13:11–15. This passage follows the Septuagint translation. The corresponding passages (Mark 4:11, 12, and Luke 8:10) follow the Hebrew of Isaiah 6:9, 10, and are still stronger than Matthew. But Matthew may be taken as explanatory of the parallel and other like passages. The doctrine meant was so plainly understood that the language is not always guarded. It may not have been by Christ in its utterance. But we have here the intended meaning manifested in a single phrase, "and their eyes they have closed lest haply they should perceive," "and should turn again and I should heal them."

The passage in Isaiah 63:17, is easily explained in like manner: "O Lord, why dost thou make us to err from thy ways, and hardenest our heart from thy fear?"

3. Passages not inconsistent with this interpretation.

On the contrary, in view of what has been said, this interpretation seems most natural. These are fair examples.

Deut. 2:30. "But Sihon, king of Heshbon, would not let us pass by him: for the Lord thy God hardened his spirit, and made his heart obstinate, that he might deliver him into thy hand, as at this day."

Acts 19:9. "But when some were hardened, and disobedient, etc., . . . he (Paul) departed from them."

Rom. 9:18. "So then he hath mercy on whom he will, and whom he will he hardeneth." The example referred to here is that of Pharaoh which, as we have seen, is a case of self-hardening under mercies.

CHAPTER 31

OUTWARD AND EFFECTUAL CALLING

THE atoning work of Christ was not sufficient for the salvation of man.

That work was only Godward, and removed only all the obstacles in the way of God's pardon of the sinner.

But the sinner is also at enmity with God, and must be brought to accept salvation, and must learn to love and serve God.

The first step here is to make known to man the gospel, which contains the glad tidings of this salvation, under such influences as ought to lead to its acceptance.

The Gospel is, therefore, commanded to be proclaimed to every creature, inasmuch as there is in the work of Christ a means of redemption for every one. This is the external call of the Gospel.

This proclamation, however, meets with no success because of the willful sinfulness of man, although, in itself, it has all the elements which should secure its acceptance.

God knowing that this is true, not only of all mankind in general, but even of the elect whom he purposes to save in Christ, gives to these such influences of the Spirit as will lead to their acceptance of the call. This is called Effectual Calling.

1. The Gospel is commanded to be preached to all. This is proved

(1.) By such passages as show that the outward privileges of God's word are no longer to be confined to Israel, but are to be extended to the Gentiles also. This had been foretold in prophecy.

Gen. 18:18; 26:4; Psalm 2:8; Isa. 42:1–4; 49:6, 7, 8; 55:5; 60:3; 65:1–12; Jer. 16:19; Mal. 1:11.

It is also taught in the New Testament in various ways.

Matt. 8:11–13; 12:18–21; 21:33–41; 22:1; 28:19; Mark 12:1–9; Luke 4:20–27; 14:16–24; 20:9–16; John 3:16; 4:20, 21, 39.

(2.) By the history of the extension of this gospel to the Gentiles by the Apostles and their contemporaries, who so preached it, as to show that the Gentiles were not first to become Jews in order to be made partakers of that gospel.

Acts 10th Chapter. Peter sent to Cornelius.

Acts 11:1–18. Peter's report of that visit.

Acts 11:19–30. The gospel sent to Phoenicia, Cyprus and Antioch.

Acts 13th Chapter. The labors of Paul and his companions.

Acts 15th Chapter. The conference at Jerusalem.

Rom. 1:13–16, and generally the whole of the epistle and of Paul's other epistles to the churches, especially Galatians.

The above two classes of passages serve to show how the universal preaching of the gospel was impressed upon the early Christians, and consequently that they would be led to give full meaning to other unlimited expressions.

(3.) By such passages as directed the gospel to be preached to all. Mark 16:15; Acts 2:21; Rom. 10:13.

(4.) By such as show the freeness with which salvation was offered to all as individuals. Acts 2:39; 11:14; 16:31; 2 Cor. 5:19–21; 1 Tim. 1:15; Tit. 2:11; Rev. 22:17.

(5.) The restrictions which separated the Jews and the Gentiles being removed, the universal offers of salvation made previously to the Jews, may now be applied to all men in general. Isaiah 1:18; 55:1–7; Ezek. 18:21, 32; 33:11.

(6.) The language of Christ to those to whom he spake may also be thus applied. Matt. 11:28; John 7:37.

The above classes of passages show that this call of the gospel is made indiscriminately to all men. No differences of nation, or class, or condition; no question as to election, or non-election, nor as to the purpose to make it effectual, enters into this call. It is made to everyone. Nothing is known to those who are to proclaim the gospel which can make its offer to one any more sincere than to another. Whatever differences men may make from personal feeling, or national sympathy, or local attachment, are not only not commanded by it, but are often inconsistent with it.

2. This offer of the gospel meets of itself with no success.

(1.) The testimony of all who have preached it has been that, without special influence of grace from God, the preaching has been in vain. The prayers made to God constantly for such aid furnish universal evidence of such convictions.

(2.) The same testimony is as universally given by those who have received the gospel. Each one ascribes his salvation to the special influences of God.

(3.) This also is the teaching of the Scriptures which declare this fact. Eph. 2:8, is only a specimen of the universal teaching, which will appear more fully elsewhere.

3. This failure is not due to any deficiency in the gospel.

(1.) None can doubt the fullness of the scheme of redemption contained.

(2.) None can question the facts as to personal sin and need of Christ which are made known.

(3.) None can deny the freeness with which it is offered.

(4.) No one can deny that he is one of those to whom it is offered.

(5.) All persons admit that God will give it to any who will forsake sin and strive to lead a new life trusting him for help.

(6.) Every one is convinced that he can turn away from all acts of sin and live the contrary life of holiness and obedience, if he will.

(7.) It is universally acknowledged that God is worthy to be believed in every statement he makes.

It is because of the above and kindred facts that our Lord says: John 12:48. "The word that I spake, the same shall judge him in the last day."

4. The Scriptures teach us why this word is rejected. It is not from want of evidence, nor from intellectual doubt, but always because of something sinful, either in the heart or will.

Some of the reasons which the Scriptures thus give are presented in Hill's Bible Readings, p. 99, as follows:

(1.) Pride, which may be national, Matt. 3:9; John 8:33; Acts 13:45; 17:5; 22:21, 22; intellectual, Matt. 11:25; John 9:39–41; Rom. 1:21, 22; 1 Cor. 1:19–21; or social, John 7:48.

(2.) Self-righteousness. Mark 2:16; Luke 7:39; 18:10–14; Rom. 10:3.

(3.) Love of praise. John 5:44; 12:43.

(4.) Love of the world. 2 Tim. 4:10; James 4:4; 1 John 2:15.

(5.) Love of money. Mark 10:17–24; Luke 16:13, 14; 1 Tim. 6:9, 10.

(6.) Cares of the world. Matt. 13:7–22; Luke 10:40.

(7.) Fear of man. John 7:13; 9:22; 12:42.

(8.) Worldly self-interest. Mark 5:16, 17; John 11:48.

(9.) Unwillingness to separate from impenitent friends. Luke 9:59–62.

(10.) Unwillingness to believe what they cannot understand. John 3:9; 6:52–60; Acts 17:32; 1 Cor. 2:14.

(11.) Unwillingness to have their sins exposed. John 3:19–20.

(12.) Unwillingness to submit to God's authority. Luke 19:14; 20:9–18.

(13.) Prejudice against the messenger. Matt. 12:24; 13:57; John 1:46; 6:42; 7:52; 9:29.

(14.) Spiritual blindness. Matt. 13:15; 1 Cor. 2:14.

(15.) Unfaithfulness to the light which they had. John 12:36.

(16.) Waiting for a convenient season. Acts 24:25.

(17.) Frivolous excuses. Luke 14:18.

(18.) Lack of deep convictions. Matt. 13:5; 22:5.

(19.) Lack of earnestness. Luke 13:24.

(20.) Neglect of the Bible. Luke 24:25; John 5:39; 7:27; Acts 17:11–12.

(21.) Neglect of religious meetings. John 20:24.

(22.) Blindness to special opportunities. Luke 19:44.

(23.) Desire for special signs. Matt. 12:38, 39; 16:1–4; John 6:30; 1 Cor. 1:22.

(24.) Regard for human traditions. Matt. 15:9; Mark 2:23–28.

(25.) Insincerity. Matt. 15:7–8; 21:25–31; Acts 24:26.

(26.) A controversial spirit. Matt. 22:15–40.

(27.) A murmuring spirit. Matt. 25:24.

(28.) Having no desire for God. John 5:42; Rom. 1:28.

(29.) Hatred of God and of Christ. John 15:22–25.

(30.) Hatred of the truth. Acts 7:51–54; 2 Thess. 2:10–12; 2 Tim. 4:3.

(31.) The power of the devil. Matt. 13:4–19; John 8:44; 2 Cor. 4:3, 4.

5. The offer of the gospel thus referred to is denominated the External Call.

It is made to man through the senses, and consists in a declaration of the nature of salvation and an offer of it upon the conditions of faith and repentance. It is enforced by statements as to the sinful condition of man and his need of a Saviour; by the command of God to repent and believe; and by exhortations and threats, as inducements to the acceptance of salvation through it. It is spoken of in the Scriptures, as a call, in passages which have no reference to its becoming effectual, and in some which contrast it with the effectual calling of others. Prov. 1:24; Isa. 65:12; Matt. 9:13.

6. But, in contrast with this usage, is the more common one, by which the called in the Scriptures are those who are actually brought to the reception of the truth and participation in salvation.

(1.) In those passages which speak to church members of their calling as something different from the mere outward call. Rom. 8:30; 9:11–24; 1 Cor. 1:9–26; Gal. 1:6–15; 1 Thess. 2:12; 5:24; 2 Thess. 2:14; Eph. 1:18; 4:1–4, 5; 2 Tim. 1:9; Heb. 3:1; 1 Pet. 2:9; 5:10; 2 Pet. 1:3–10.

(2.) Christian believers are spoken of as the called. Rom. 1:6; 8:28; 1 Cor. 1:24; Heb. 9:15; Rev. 17:14.

7. The effectual call of these is due to the purpose and act of God. Matt. 11:25; Rom. 8:29, 30; Rom. 9:15, 16; 1 Cor. 1:26–31.

8. The agent by which this is accomplished is the Holy Spirit by whose influences the saved are led to the exercise of repentance and faith. John 6:44, 46; 1 Thess. 1:5, 6.

9. Such an agency is necessary to overcome the moral condition of man as "blind" and "dead in trespasses and sins." 1 Cor. 2:14; 2 Cor. 4:4; Eph. 2:1, 5.

10. In connection with this doctrine of the Effectual Calling of some, has arisen a question as to the sincerity of God in making the outward call to those who do not accept. It is said that the fact that it is made by him, knowing that men will not accept it without his efficient grace, and yet not purposing to give that grace, argues insincerity in the offer.

To this the following replies may be made:

(1.) If it be true that he does make the outward call, and does not give to all, but to some only, the efficient grace, the very character of God is an assurance of his sincerity. The real question here, then, is an inquiry into these two facts. If they be taught in the Scriptures, it is impious and blasphemous to doubt God's sincerity.

(2.) This inquiry would never have arisen, had God only made the general offer and left all men to perish in its rejection. But, if so, his additional grace to some does not in any respect argue his insincerity in the partial grace thus shown to others.

(3.) The very nature of the gospel offer, as before stated, shows God's sincerity. It is one which has all the inducements for its acceptance which one can imagine, and that acceptance depends simply upon the willingness of each man to take it.

(4.) Lest any should doubt the sincerity of God, he assures us of that fact in his Word. Paul describes him, 1 Tim. 2:4, as one "who willeth that all men should be saved." God himself says, Ezek. 33:10, 11: "And thou, son of man, say unto the house of Israel: Thus ye speak, saying, Our transgressions and our sins are upon us, and we pine away in them; how then should we live? Say unto them, As I live, saith the Lord God, I have no pleasure in the death of the wicked; but that the wicked turn from his way and live; turn ye, turn ye from your evil ways; for why will ye die, O house of Israel?"

Compare this with Heb. 6:13–18: "For when God made promise to Abraham, because he could swear by none greater, he sware by himself, saying, Surely blessing I will bless thee, and multiplying I will multiply thee. And thus, having patiently endured, he obtained the promise. For men swear by the greater; and in every dispute of theirs the oath is final for confirmation. Wherein God, being minded to show more abundantly unto the heirs of promise the immutability of his counsel, interposed with an oath: that by two immutable things, in which it was impossible for God to lie, we may have a strong encouragement, who have fled for refuge to lay hold of the hope set before us."

11. The attempt has been made by Lutheran theologians, and adopted by some others, to harmonize the sincerity of God's External Call with the salvation of some only, by supposing that God gives equally to all his Spirit, which makes salvation effectual in some, but that those who reject the gospel resist the Spirit given to them, and thus refuse, while the others yield to it, and thus are saved. They say, therefore, that it is thus true that all have the Spirit equally, and yet that the salvation of the saved may be said to be by the grace of God.

The natural objection to this explanation is that not only is the salvation of men ascribed to grace, but to grace alone, to the exclusion of all merit and work.

See Rom. 3:27 to 4:25; 9:11 and Gal. 2:16. But if some do not resist and others do, however much of grace there is, there is certainly some merit in those not resisting by which they can boast over others who resisted. Notice especially Rom. 4:16: "For this cause it is of faith, that it may be according to grace; to the end that the promise may be sure to all the seed."

Another objection is that the salvation of the saved is distinctly based in the Word of God on the Election of some: "Even as he chose us in him before the foundation of the world, that we should be holy and without blemish before him in love: having foreordained us unto adoption as sons through Jesus Christ unto himself, according to the good pleasure of his will, to the praise of the glory of his grace, which he freely bestowed on us in the Beloved." Eph. 1:4, 5, 6.

CHAPTER 32

REGENERATION AND CONVERSION

AT the outset of a discussion of these two subjects we are met by the question, whether they are not one and the same thing. They are unquestionably so intimately associated that it is difficult to separate them and point out the distinctions between them. The Scriptures connect the two under the one idea of the new birth, and teach that not only is regeneration an absolute essential in each conversion, but that in every intelligent responsible soul conversion invariably accompanies regeneration. It is not strange, therefore, that they are often confounded. Yet, after all, the Scriptures also teach that regeneration is the work of God, changing the heart of man by his sovereign will, while conversion is the act of man turning towards God with the new inclination thus given to his heart.

REGENERATION

I. It is best first to collect together the various terms and expressions in which this whole matter is taught.

1. Forms of the verb γεννάω *(gennao)*, which means "to beget."

John 1:13; 3:3, 4 (two places), 5, 6, 7, 8; 1 Cor. 4:15; Philemon 10; 1 John 2:29; 3:9 (two places); 4:7; 5:1 (three places); 5:4, 18 (two places).

2. Compound forms of γεννάω *(gennao)*.

1 Pet. 1:23. "Having been begotten again, not of corruptible seed, but of incorruptible, through the word of God, which liveth and abideth."

Titus 3:5. "He saved us through the washing of regeneration and renewing of the Holy Ghost."

3. The word ἀπεκύησεν *(apekuesen)* is used in James 1:18, and means to bring forth or bear young, and there evidently means to bring to the condition of sonship.

4. Κτίσις *(ktisis)* and κτίζω *(ktizo)*, which mean creation and create, are found in 2 Cor. 5:17; Gal. 6:15; Eph. 2:10, 15; 4:24.

5. Συνεζωοποίησιν *(sunezoopoiesen)*, he quickened together with (Christ). Eph. 2:5; Col. 2:13.

In addition to the above uses of single words are the following passages which speak of the word of God as an effective instrument, but not as a creative power. These, however, do not connect this instrument with either regeneration or conversion necessarily; but speaks of it (a.) as a means of partaking of the divine nature, 2 Pet. 1:4; (b.) as a means of purifying, John 15:3; (c.) as a means of Christian defense, Eph. 6:17; and (d.) as an instrument of powerful conviction and destruction of the wicked, Heb. 4:12.

II. From the Scriptural teaching we see that the whole work of Regeneration and Conversion is included under the one term regeneration.

It is true that but few of the passages refer to anything save the work of God; yet these few sufficiently teach the use of the word in regeneration to lead us not to reject, as a part of it, that result of God's act which, in connection with the word, leads to the full union of its subject with Christ through repentance and faith.

The passages in connection with Paul as God's instrument, 1 Cor. 4:15, and Philemon 10, would not be conclusive, but they are made so by others.

However much James 1:18 suggests a different aspect of the work, namely, the bringing forth that which has been begotten, still it so nearly connects that idea with the begetting as to create doubt if the whole work may not be virtually involved.

But 1 Pet. 1:23, by the use of the compound of γεννάω *(gennao)*, shows that all the work of the Spirit, including both the new heart and the leading of it to conscious faith, is properly to be spoken of by the same term as a mere change of heart.

The whole work is thus spoken of, however, because God is operative from the beginning to the end, but this does not prove that he does not operate differently in one part from what he does in the other.

III. The Scripture teaching is that God operates immediately upon the heart to produce the required change, by which it is fitted to receive the truth, and mediately through the word in its reception of that truth.

1. He operates immediately upon the heart to prepare the way for the truth. This is evident

(1.) From the description given of man's spiritual condition.

(a.) As spiritually dead. Eph. 2:1.

(b.) As blind. Eph. 4:18.

(c.) As slaves to sin. John 8:34; Rom. 6:17, 19.

(d.) As needing deliverance from the powers of darkness. Col. 1:13.

(e.) As incapable of knowing or discerning the things of the Spirit. 1 Cor. 2:14; Eph. 4:18.

(f.) As incapable of changing himself. Jer. 13:23.

(g.) As defiled in conscience. Tit. 1:15.

These passages show man in a condition from which he must be rescued even to understand and appreciate the truth of God.

(2.) The Scripture attributes the birth to the will of God exclusively, thus showing that in some aspect it is not to be regarded as due to the reception of the truth. John 1:13.

[For sections (3.), (4.), (5.) and (6.), see Hodge's Outlines, p. 451.]

(3.) The influence of the Spirit is distinguished from that of the Word. John 6:45, 64, 65; 1 Cor. 2:12–15; 1 Thess. 1:5, 6.

(4.) A divine influence is declared to be necessary for the reception of the truth. Ps. 119:18; Acts 16:14; Eph. 1:17–20.

(5.) Such an internal operation on the heart is attributed to God. Matt. 11:25; Luke 10:21; Phil. 2:13; 2 Thess. 1:11; Heb. 13:21.

(6.) The nature of this influence is evidently different from that effected by the truth. Eph. 1:19; 3:7; 2 Tim. 2:25.

(7.) This influence is spoken of as a preparation of the heart for the truth; which, therefore, must be distinct from the truth or its reception. Luke 8:8, 15; Acts 16:14.

This preparation of the heart comes from God. 1 Chron. 29:18, 19; Ps. 119:18; Prov. 16:1; Acts 16:14; Rom. 9:23.

2. The Spirit acts mediately through the Word.

(1.) He inspired that Word and sends it forth for the accomplishment of the ends designed. John 14:16; 2 Tim. 3:16.

(2.) He aids the ministry and others in making it known. 1 Cor. 4:7; 2 Thess. 3:1.

To the extent that these are his agents he uses the Word.

(3.) The instrument thus used is in itself effective as truth. Heb. 4:12. Therefore, Christians are commanded in their spiritual warfare to take the Word of God as the sword of the Spirit. Eph. 6:17. It is, however, made especially so to the heart prepared for it by his illuminating influences, which reveal its beauties and its suitableness, and by the aid of the memory which recalls, and the conscience which applies, and the affections which lay hold upon it. 2 Tim. 3:15, 16, 17.

(4.) Christians are, therefore, said to be "brought forth, (James 1:18), by the word of truth," because that is the seed sown in the prepared ground through which they are led by repentance and faith to union with Christ and sonship of God.

(5.) Since this use of the Scriptures is due to their own fitness to present motives to action, the Spirit of God is not limited to this Word alone but uses such other truth, and such events of life as may be effective towards the contemplated end. Thus any events in God's providence, as afflictions, or dangers, or personal sins, or the conversion of others, or aught else that may lead to seeking God, are used as a means of awakening, or of giving deeper conviction, or of enforcing the Scripture truths which lead to conversion.

(6.) This is especially true of the ordinances of Baptism and the Lord's Supper duly set forth before mankind. So far as these ordinances are fitted to convey truth, or to impress duty, they are instrumental in regeneration.

(7.) But neither of them regenerates or confers regeneration.

(a.) This is not done by the Lord's Supper. It has been argued from John 6:51–58, where Christ promises eternal life to those who shall eat his flesh and drink his blood, and denies it to all who shall not. The language used refers to spiritual participation in his salvation. It is similar to the promise to the woman at Sychar that "Whosoever drinketh of the water that I shall give him shall never thirst; but the water that I shall give him shall become in him a well of water springing up into everlasting life." John 4:14. It is argued that Christ must have meant partaking of his real body, because he did not correct the Jews who, because they so understood him, rejected him. But, John 8:51–53, he did not correct a similar mistake which led to a similar result when he said in verse 51, "If a man keep my word he shall never see death."

(b.) Even more distinctly is this true of Baptism. Spiritual effects are spoken of in connection with this ordinance. Thus we have "the washing of regeneration and renewing of the Holy Ghost." Titus 3:5. We have Paul exhorted by Ananias, Acts 22:16, "arise and be baptized and wash away thy sins," and the language of Christ, John 3:5, "Except a man be born of water and the Spirit, he cannot enter into the kingdom of God." The first of these has reference to the cleansing influence of regeneration by the Spirit in like manner as his renewing, which is spoken of in the immediate context and has no reference to baptism. That the last refers to baptism is at least doubtful; but admitting that it does, which is doubtless true of the second, we have here outward baptism, only as symbolizing an inward change and not producing it. The following reasons plainly show that neither of these ordinances has regenerating power.

(1.) That ordinances can only be signs of grace and cannot confer it.

(2.) They may convey truth symbolically, and only such truth is fitted to affect the mind. But nothing symbolized by these two can confer regeneration upon those receiving them.

(3.) They are appointed to be used only by those who have been regenerated. Baptism is an act of obedience, symbolizing the death of believers to sin, and resurrection to new life, and setting forth their union with Christ in his death and burial. The Lord's Supper is to be partaken of by those already, as Christian believers, united together in church fellowship.

(4.) That this was the use of Baptism is evident from the practice of the Apostolic Christians. Acts 2:41. The baptized had received his word. This followed repentance and preceded baptism. The addition to the text in Acts 8:37 could not have taken place had it not been for the universal prevalence of the idea that faith necessarily precedes baptism. Paul before his baptism had received the Lord Jesus and his eyes had been opened and the Holy Ghost given. Acts 9:18. Cornelius and his house also received the Holy Ghost and spake with tongues before their baptism. Acts 10:44–48. The Jailer at Philippi manifestly believed before he was baptized. Baptism without antecedent faith was treated as invalid in certain disciples at Ephesus. Acts 19:1–5.

(5.) That this was also true of the Lord's Supper is shown by the fact that it was partaken of only by churches, and the members of churches are everywhere spoken of and treated as converted persons; also by the further fact that it was a memorial service ("in remembrance of me") and a memorial implies previous knowledge of the persons and facts remembered. But only such a knowledge and remembrance could be blessed, as involved faith in Jesus. 1 Cor. 11:28, 29.

(6.) The Spirit does not make truth effective by giving it additional force to that which it has naturally, but by so affecting the mind that the man is prepared to receive it with its own due force. Thus he changes the mind, illuminates the mind, helps it appreciate and lay hold of truth. Only thus does he make truth effectual. Therefore, the outward washing or partaking can have no effect to renew, or regenerate the heart, which must itself have been prepared, before it can even appropriate the truths conveyed by these ordinances.

The above statements are only intended to meet the views of Romanists and such others as claim regenerating influence of sacraments, and not those of such as make Baptism only a condition of pardon. The latter claim that regeneration is through the word only and are met by the proofs that the Spirit acts independently of the word.

CONVERSION

I. This is the result of regeneration. The new heart is prepared to turn to God and does actually so turn. Without regeneration, the sinfulness of man keeps him away from God, causes him to set his affections upon self and his own pleasure, and to find gratification in things which are opposed to God and holiness. The regenerated heart has new affections and desires and is, therefore, fitted to seek after God and holiness.

II. It is both the act of God and of man co-operating with him.

1. It is the act of God. It is thus described in the Scriptures.

1 Kings 18:37. "Thou hast turned their heart back again."

Ps. 80:3. "Turn us again, O God; and cause thy face to shine, and we shall be saved."

Ps. 85:4. "Turn us, O God of our salvation."

Song of Sol. 1:4. "Draw me; we will run after thee."

Jer. 30:21. "I will cause him to draw near, and he shall approach unto me."

Jer. 31:18. "Turn thou me, and I shall be turned."

Ezek. 36:27. "And I will put my Spirit within you, and cause you to walk in my statutes, and ye shall keep my judgments, and do them."

John 6:44. "No man can come to me, except the Father which sent me draw him."

2. It is the act of the regenerated heart actively co-operating in thus turning.

Deut. 4:30. "Thou shalt return to the Lord thy God."

Prov. 1:23. "Turn you at my reproof."

Hosea 12:6. "Therefore turn thou to thy God."

Isaiah 55:7. "Let him return unto the Lord."

Joel 2:13. "Rend your heart, and not your garments, and turn unto the Lord your God."

Acts 11:21. "A great number that believed turned unto the Lord."

III. The question naturally arises what is the nature of conversion. In reply it may be said that it consists:

1. Not in mere outward reformation.

2. Not in return from backsliding.

3. But in the turning of the heart to God and holiness. It is a turning of the thoughts, desires and affections of the heart from sinful and carnal lusts and pleasures toward holy things, and God, and Christ, and salvation. It is a turning from darkness to light, from the power of Satan to God. [See Gill's Divinity 2:132–4.] It consists "in a man's turning actively to God under the influence of divine grace." [Gill 2:135]

IV. This conversion comprises:

1. A knowledge of the true God, and acceptance of him as such.

2. Knowledge of personal sin, guilt and condemnation.

3. Sorrow for sin and desire to escape condemnation.

4. Determination to turn away from sin and seek God.

5. Conviction of personal need of help in so doing.

6. Knowledge of Christ as a Saviour from sin.

7. Personal trust in Christ and his salvation.

NOTE. A man in one sense maybe called converted as soon as he has truly turned to God and is also seeking to know and do his will. This is that amount of conversion which is so nearly contemporaneous with regeneration as to be liable to be supposed to exist at the same moment with it, and which indeed in a being capable of thought on such subjects must be its immediate effect.

But what the Scriptures and common language comprise in this word is repentance and trust in God's saving power, and, in connection with Christian knowledge, trust in Jesus Christ as a Saviour. The attainment of the fullness of such conversion is by the gradual appreciation of truth, resulting not only from regeneration, and knowledge, but from spiritual illumination of the mind.

V. The relation of regeneration to conversion will, therefore, appear to be one of invariable antecedence.

Wherever the appropriate truth is at the time present its relation is almost that of producing cause, for the prepared heart at once receives the truth. Hence, as this is so generally the case, they have been usually regarded as contemporaneous and by some even as identical. But that regeneration is the invariable antecedent is seen,

1. From the fact that the heart is the soil in which the seed, the Word of God, is sown, and that seed only brings forth fruit in the good soil. The heart is made good soil by regeneration.

2. Regeneration (as in infants) may exist without faith and repentance, but the latter cannot exist without the former. Therefore, regeneration precedes.

3. Logically the enabling act of God must, in a creature, precede the act of the creature thus enabled. But this logical antecedence involves actual antecedence, or the best conceptions of our mind deceive us and are not reliable. For this logical antecedence exists only because the mind observes plainly a perceived dependence of the existence of the one on the other. But such dependence demands, if not causal, at least antecedent existence. Here it is only antecedent.

VI. There is not only antecedence, but in some cases an appreciable interval.

1. This is true even of conversion regarded as a mere turning to God. Between it and regeneration must intervene in some cases some period of time until the knowledge of God's existence and nature is given, before the heart turns, or even is turned towards that God.

(1.) This must be true of all infants and of all persons otherwise incapable of responsibility, as for example idiots.

(2.) There is no reason why it should not be true of some heathen. The missionaries of the cross have been sought by men, who knew nothing of

Christianity, but whose hearts, unsatisfied with the religion of their fathers, were restlessly seeking for what their soul was crying out.

2. It is still more manifestly true of full Christian conversion.

(1.) The Scriptures teach this in many examples of persons pious, holy, and fearing God, yet unacquainted with the full truth which secures union with Christ.

Ethiopian Eunuch: Acts 8:26–40.

Paul: Acts, chapter 9, 22 and 26. Galatians, chapters 1st and 2nd.

Cornelius the Centurion: Acts 10:2.

Lydia: Acts 16:14.

(2.) The experience of ministers in all ages with persons seeking and attaining salvation confirms this idea. The attainment of conversion may be marked by stages. The sinner is at first totally indifferent. The Word produces on him no effect. Then (1.) there is an evident willingness to give serious attention to the truth of God. God has opened the heart as he did that of Lydia. (2.) There is conviction of sin, sense of its vileness, and of its dangerous effects. (3.) The soul, oppressed by these, strives to do something by which to attain salvation, but finds all in vain. (4.) At last accepting the truth of God's Word it rests in trust of a personal Saviour.

VII. The term conversion is not technically applied to any change, except that which follows upon regeneration, and consists in the Godward turning of one heretofore turned entirely away from God. The return of men who have backslidden, or fallen into grievous sin, is also called "a return to God," and such a return is possibly what is called "conversion" in Peter's case. Luke 22:32. But conversion is theologically used exclusively of the first act.

CHAPTER 33

REPENTANCE

THE Scripture doctrine of Repentance is to be learned in part from the meaning of the original Greek word used to express it, and in part from its application to a matter which is within the sphere of morals.

I. There are two forms of words used in the New Testament which are translated repent and repentance.

Only one of these is used of the repentance associated with salvation from sin. This is the verb μετανοέω *(metanoeo)*, and the corresponding noun μετάνοια *(metanoia)*. The other verb is μεταμέλομαι *(metamelomai)*, the noun of which does not appear in the New Testament, but occurs in the Septuagint in Hosea 11:8. The verb is used in the Septuagint in Psalm 110:4; and Jer. 20:16. It is also the word used in the New Testament in Matt. 21:29, which says of the son who had refused to obey his father's command to work in the vineyard, "afterward he repented himself and went." It likewise is found in Matt. 21:32 and 27:3, this latter being the case of Judas. Paul uses it in Rom. 11:29; and 2 Cor. 7:8, 10. It is also the word used in Heb. 7:21. In all other places, translated repent and repentance in the New Testament, the original is *metanoeo* or *metanoia*. This word means to reconsider, to perceive afterwards, and hence to change one's view, mind, or purpose, or even judgement, implying disapproval and abandonment of past opinions and purposes, and the adoption of others which are different. In all cases of inward change there is not necessarily a change of outward conduct, nor is such inward change accompanied by regret. These results would flow from the nature of that about which that change has arisen.

We arrive, therefore, at the meaning of Christian repentance partly through the meaning of these Greek words, but also partly because it is exercised about a question of morals. It is seen that it involves a change in the outward life because such change is a result of the change of inward opinions. It also includes sorrow for sin because a change of view as to the nature of sin and of holiness must be accompanied by regret and sorrow as to the past acts of sin.

The word μεταμέλομαι *(metamelomai)* means to change one's care, to regret; the idea of sorrow always accompanying it.

The two words are nearly synonymous in their secondary meaning, and each is used in this secondary meaning in the New Testament. Μετανοέω *(metanoeo)*, however, traces the feeling of sorrow and the change of life back to an inward change of opinion and judgement as to the nature of sin and holiness, and of the relations of man and God. It is perhaps on this account that it is exclusively used for true repentance in the New Testament. This is not simply sorrow, or remorse, which may pass away, or lead in despair to other sins, or fill the soul with anxiety; but a heartfelt change in the inward soul towards God and holiness, which is lasting and effective, and which may be associated with peace and joy in believing.

II. To set forth explicitly what Christian Repentance is, it may be stated that it includes

1. An intellectual and spiritual perception of the opposition between holiness in God and sin in man. It does not look at sin as the cause of punishment but abhors it because it is vile in the sight of God and involves in heinous guilt all who are sinners.

2. It consequently includes sorrow and self-loathing, and earnest desire to escape the evil of sin. The penitent soul does not so much feel the greatness of its danger as the greatness of its sinfulness.

3. It also includes an earnest turning to God for help and deliverance from sin, seeking pardon for guilt and aid to escape its presence.

It is also accompanied by deep regret because of the sins committed in the past, and by determination with God's help to avoid sin and live in holiness hereafter. The heart heretofore against God and for sin is now against sin and for God.

From these facts it will be seen that

(1.) The seat of true repentance is in the soul. It is not of itself the mere intellectual knowledge of sin, nor the sorrow that accompanies it, nor the changed life which flows from it; but it is the soul's apprehension of its heinous character, which begets the horror and self-loathing which accompany it, and the determination to forsake sin which flows from it.

(2.) That true repentance is inconsistent with the continuance in sin because of abounding grace.

(3.) That true repentance consists of mental and spiritual emotion, and not of outward self-imposed chastisements. Even the pious life and devotion to God which follow are described not as repentance, but as fruits meet for repentance.

III. The Scriptures teach that the author of true repentance is God operating by truth upon the renewed heart.

Acts 5:31. Christ is said to have been exalted "to give repentance to Israel, and remission of sins."

Acts 11:18. "Then to the Gentiles also hath God granted repentance unto life."

The means used is the preaching and other exhibition of the truth. Repentance like faith comes through the hearing of the word. By this men are exhorted to that duty, and gain the knowledge of the truths taught by God, through spiritual apprehension of which men are led to the truth.

CHAPTER 34

FAITH

I. ITS important position.

As disbelief was so prominent in the sin of the first Adam so faith is most prominent in the redemption through the second Adam.

It holds an important connection with every act and condition of salvation. It is by faith that men come into vital union with Christ, through faith that they are justified, through faith that they can acceptably worship, through faith that the Christian lives, through faith that his sanctification progresses, it being the means of his conquering the world, of his exercising hope in his future, and becoming more and more identified with Christ in his spiritual reign here and hereafter. These facts evince its importance and the necessity of fully understanding what is meant by it.

II. Its meaning.

It corresponds with our words, belief and trust—with belief so far as it refers to the acceptance of facts and statements, or of the veracity of a person—with trust so far as a person or object is made the foundation of reliance. We believe a fact, a statement, a person; we trust or rely upon that fact, statement or person as something upon which we build. In the one case we have faith in, in the other we put faith in.

The noun πίστις *(pistis)* and the verb πιστεύω *(pisteuo)* are used in each of these senses in the Scripture, and also in the two unitedly; (1.) as to mere belief of the truth either savingly or otherwise. 2 Thess. 2:13; Heb. 10:39; John 2:22; John 5:46; Acts 26:27; Jas. 2:19.

(2.) In the sense of reliance.

John 2:24. "Jesus did not trust himself unto them."

John 7:5. "For even his brethren did not believe in him."

2 Tim. 1:12. "I know him whom I have believed."

1 John 4:1. "Beloved, believe not every spirit."

(3.) But the almost invariable usage of the New Testament includes both elements, the belief of a person and of the facts about him, and reliance upon them and him for salvation.

The difference between these three forms of belief is apparent.

1. Mere belief may be weak and motiveless, and thus it may result in indifference as to action; or it may be a mere opinion, the holding or not holding of which is not felt to be a matter of consequence; or it may be a mere notion taken up without sufficient evidence.

2. Mere trust in a person or thing, may result from confidence in the word of another, or in the actions of others, or from something in our experience teaching us that we may venture, though we know no reason why we should thus trust. Thus someone tells us that this is the train we wish to take—or we go over a bridge over which others have gone—or we ford a stream through which we see by tracks that others have driven. Here our trust is much more, if not altogether, in the testimony of others than in any knowledge of, or confidence in that to which we commit ourselves.

It is only through the combination of the two that we have faith, which must be an intelligent trust. By it we believe not only in him upon whom we trust, but we do so because we believe the facts which make him trustworthy.

Hence it is that the Scriptures use it in the twofold sense, uniting the two ideas in the case of believers in Christ, because not only do they rely upon Jesus, but, from the belief of the facts concerning him taught in God's Word; they know whom they have believed, and why they should believe him.

Christian faith, therefore, is personal reliance upon Christ for salvation because of belief of God's testimony as to our sinful and ruined condition, and as to what Christ has assuredly done to save us.

It is based, therefore, upon the knowledge of this testimony as given by our own consciences and the Word of God. It is consequently an act of the mind. As the truth thus apprehended is spiritual, so it is apprehended spiritually by the heart. As it occurs in the heart of a sinner, so it must be the act of a regenerated heart which alone is inclined to such belief as constitutes trust. And it is attained by this heart through the illuminating influences of the Spirit of God.

III. The nature of saving faith will further appear by noticing its objects.

These objects are not mere abstract truths, nor opinions, nor facts, but only such as are connected with a person.

1. One object of faith is God the Father, not considered alone as the Father, but both as Father, and as representing the Godhead.

(1.) As representing the Godhead. As such, it has him also for its object, not in all the aspects he bears to man, for it does not apprehend him as Creator, Preserver, Ruler, or Benefactor. These are aspects believed in, but they are not the basis of saving faith.

This has respect to him only in those relations in which he is viewed in special connection with salvation.

(a.) As a God of holiness, hating sin, himself infinite in purity, before whom even the angels are chargeable with folly.

(b.) As a God of justice, who will certainly punish every sin, even the least.

(c.) As the righteous judge, who will show no favor, and who has appointed a day wherein he will judge the world.

(d.) As the omniscient searcher of hearts, who knoweth even the most secret thoughts and intents of the heart.

(e.) As the almighty and living God, into whose hands it is a fearful thing to fall.

(f.) As the God who delights not in the death, but rather in the salvation of the wicked.

(g.) As the God, whose love for the world has sent his own Son for its salvation.

(h.) As a God, merciful and gracious, and long suffering, etc. Ex. 34:6, 7.

(i.) As a God, forgiving iniquity, transgression, and sin.

(j.) As a God, promising and giving the aid of his Spirit to such as seek him.

(k.) As a God, that justifies those who trust in him for pardon through Christ.

(l.) As a God, that can and will secure the final salvation of his people. John 10:28, 29; Rom. 11:29; Phil. 1:6; 1 Pet. 1:5.

(2.) In God the Father as Father.

(a.) Who hath, from the beginning, chosen us in Christ. 2 Thess. 2:13; Eph. 1:4.

(b.) Who hath loved us. 2 Thess. 2:16; 1 John 4:19.

(c.) Who hath adopted us as sons, 1 John 3:1, 2, and consequently as joint heirs with Christ, Rom. 8:17.

(d.) As the unchangeable bestower of grace. James 1:17; Rom. 11:29.

(e.) As the author of exceeding great and precious promises. 2 Pet. 1:4; 2 Cor. 1:20.

2. Another object of faith is Christ.

(1.) In his person and work.

(a.) As Son of God, giving dignity and value to the work of atonement.

(b.) As man; as duly representing us, as having properly suffered for us, and as fully sympathizing with us.

(c.) As the God-man, so uniting the divine and human natures in one person, that we can say that he that is the Son of God, the Lord of glory, bore our sins and died for our salvation.

(2.) In his testimony, as to himself as sent by God, and as to his work as approved of God.

(3.) In his abounding love and grace, as seen in his humiliation, and the greatness of his personal sacrifice for us.

(4.) In his earnest desire that sinners should come to God through him.

(5.) In his assurances of the answers of our prayers.

(6.) In his promises of grace unto the end.

(7.) In his constant presence with us, sympathizing, aiding, pleading for us, and securing our acceptance with God.

(8.) In all his offices, Prophet, Priest, and King.

3. The Holy Spirit is also an object of faith.

(1.) As to his promised presence.

(2.) As to the work within the heart, being his work.

(3.) As to his power to accomplish it unto the end.

REMARK. It is thus seen that not only the Godhead as such, but the separate persons in it, are objects of saving faith. Hence the union of them all in Baptism. Even if it be true that "baptized in the name of the Lord Jesus" means that a different formula was used, still this baptism involved a knowledge of the Trinity, and would have been virtually a baptism with respect to that Trinity.

IV. The nature of saving faith may be still further seen by noticing other words by which it is expressed. [See Gill's Divinity, 2:395–400 for full statement of following points taken, except the fourth, from him.]

1. As looking to Christ. Isa. 45:22; Micah 7:7. Illustrated by the uplifted serpent. John 3:14, 15.

2. As coming to him. Isa. 55:1; Matt. 11:28; John 6:37, 44, 45, 65.

3. As fleeing to him and laying hold upon him. Heb. 6:18.

4. As eating and drinking him. John 6:51–58.

5. As receiving him. Col. 2:6.

V. That the above is the nature of saving faith will still further appear by contrasting with it other kinds of faith which have been attempted to be substituted for it.

1. Implicit faith. Romanists claim that faith must be in the church—simply in it; in its doctrines so far as known; but in them as believed upon the church's authority and not upon any other apprehension of their truth.

This is really to make the church a fetish, a mere charm which gives salvation simply to one who trusts salvation in its hands.

It is as though, with our belief implicitly in the Bible, we should say that one who believes the Bible is saved, whether he knows its contents or not.

Our trust, neither in Christ, nor in the Bible, is of this kind. It is based upon an intelligent, not a blind confidence of the truths taught. We simply put blind faith in anything we do not comprehend, because God has taught it. But the whole hope of salvation and faith, in every other respect which is effective and operative, is in what we believe, not in the fact that it is true, but in the knowledge which the fact that it is true conveys to us. Our salvation does not rest in the belief that the books of the Bible teach the truth, but in belief of the things which they teach.

2. Historical faith. This is a mere intellectual belief of the truths taught in the Scriptures as historical facts; as that there was such a person as Jesus, who, being the Son of God, wrought out salvation and has now commanded all men to repent and be baptized for the remission of sins.

One fact that favours the substitution of this for the faith which trusts in Christ with the heart, is that in the apostolic days, such was the danger of professing Christ that none would be apt to do so, who did not heartily believe in him. Another is that as the new religion presented itself in salient points in opposition to the old, the acceptance of these points could be due only to a heartfelt belief in Jesus. Hence the language of 1 John 4:15, "Whosoever shall confess that Jesus is the Son of God, God abideth in him, and he in God," and other similar passages.

Fortunately, however, we have sufficient teaching to show what is the true faith.

There is the case of Simon Magus, Acts 8:13–24. Manifestly he had historical faith, and yet the Apostle is led to say of him, verse 21, "Thou hast neither part nor lot in this matter: for thy heart is not right in the sight of God." The case of Judas also is one of bare historical faith.

That faith, however, is a work of the heart, is manifest from the following passages:

Acts 2:37. "They were pricked in their heart."

Rom. 10:8–10. "Shalt believe in thy heart that God raised him from the dead, . . . with the heart man believeth unto righteousness."

See an illustration of the difference between historical faith and hearty acceptance of the truth in John 12:42, 43 and Rom. 10:16–21.

2 Cor. 3:3. "In tables that are hearts of flesh," also verse 6, "the letter killeth, but the Spirit giveth life."

Heb. 10:22. "Let us draw near with a true heart."

2 Tim. 2:22. Christians are described as those who "call on the Lord out of a pure heart."

It is also proved by all we have seen of the necessity and nature of Regeneration, Conversion and Repentance.

Hodge, [Outlines, p. 473], gives this further proof from the effects of faith. "The Scriptures declare that by faith the Christian 'embraces the promises,' 'is persuaded of the promises,' 'out of weakness is made strong,' 'waxes valiant in fight,' 'confesses himself a stranger and pilgrim seeking a better country.'" As faith in a threatening necessarily involves fear, so faith in a promise necessarily involves trust. "Besides, faith rests upon the trustworthiness of God and, therefore, necessarily involves trust. Heb. 10:23 and the whole 11th chapter."

3. Assurance of personal interest in Christ's salvation; so that one may say, I know that Christ died for me, that I am one of his elect, that my sins were removed by him, and I have been reconciled to God by him.

Such cannot be the nature of saving faith, because

(1.) This is not the experience of an early, but of an advanced stage of Christian life.

(2.) Because this is not the object of Christian faith. That object is Christ, and the statements of God's truth concerning him and salvation. Those statements are general so far as the revelation is made. They are made personal by our acceptance. But our faith enters into that condition. If we can satisfy ourselves that our faith is undoubtedly genuine, not merely temporary, but actually one rooted in Christ, we may gain this assurance, but that assurance would rest not on God's Word, nor on Christ's salvation, but on the evidence afforded by the Spirit's work in our hearts. [See Hodge's Outlines, p. 478.]

(3.) The Scriptures give an example in Paul of a true Christian who could say "I buffet my body and bring it into bondage: lest by any means, after that I have preached to others, I myself should be rejected." 1 Cor. 9:27. See also Phil. 3:12–14.

(4.) "From the exhortations addressed to those who were already believers to attain to assurance as a degree of faith beyond that which they already enjoyed." [Hodge's Outlines, p. 478.]

(5.) "From the experience of God's people in all ages." [Hodge's Outlines, p. 478.]

Rem. 1st. The assurance, however, which is not thus a part of saving faith, is one which can be attained, and doubtless frequently has been attained.

(a.) This is directly asserted. Rom. 8:16; 2 Pet. 1:10; 1 John 2:3; 3:14; 5:13.

(b.) Scriptural examples are given of its attainment, as Paul. 2 Tim. 1:12; 4:7, 8.

(c.) "Many eminent Christians have enjoyed an abiding assurance, of the genuineness of which their holy walk and conversation was an indubitable seal." [Hodge's Outlines, p. 478.]

Rem. 2nd. The grounds upon which a man can be assured of salvation are

(a.) The divine truth of the promises of salvation.

(b.) The inward evidence of those graces unto which those promises are made.

(c.) The testimony of the Spirit of adoption, Rom. 8:15, 16, witnessing with our spirits that we are the children of God, which Spirit, Eph. 1:13, 14; 2 Cor. 1:21, 22, is the earnest of our inheritance, whereby we are sealed to the day of redemption. [West. Conf., chap 18, quoted in Hodge's Outlines, p. 479.]

"This genuine assurance," says Hodge (Outlines p. 479), "may be distinguished from that presumptuous confidence which is a delusion of Satan, chiefly by these marks. True assurance, 1st, begets unfeigned humility, 1 Cor. 15:10; Gal. 6:14; 2d, leads to ever increasing diligence in practical religion, Ps. 51:12, 13, 19; 3d, to candid self-examination and a desire to be searched and corrected by God, Ps. 139:23, 24; 4th, to constant aspirations after nearer conformity and more intimate communion with God, 1 John 3:2, 3."

4. Temporary or delusive faith. This has many marks of a true faith. Hence it is not only the intellectual reception of historical facts, but a joyful acceptance of them. This is the case of the seed in the stony places which represents the man that heareth the word and anon with joy receiveth it. But the parable teaches us that the soil was not prepared. It is, therefore, not in the regenerated heart that it arises. The evidence of its temporary character, therefore, will soon appear. It lacks the following characteristics of saving faith and may thus be distinguished from it:

(1.) Continuance in trusting Christ, and in devotion to him and his service.

(2.) Desire to be useful in the work of Christ.

(3.) Attendance to Christian duty.

(4.) Love of prayer and the Word of God, and of the meetings with his people for worship.

(5.) Devoted love to the children of God as such.

(6.) Progress in knowledge of self and sin, and of Christ as a Saviour.

(7.) Progress in loving holiness and hating sin, with increased conviction of, and humility concerning sinfulness.

VI. It is through this saving faith that we attain vital union with Christ. It is, however, not a meritorious ground, nor a procuring cause of such union, but simply the mere act of clinging to him and trusting in him which becomes the instrumental cause of such union. Rom. 4:16.

1. There are several senses in which Christians are spoken of as in Christ.

(1.) By election; "Chosen in him."

(2.) By federal representation in his atoning work.

(3.) From the union of believers with him by faith.

Rom. 16:7. "Who also were in Christ before me."

2 Cor. 5:17. "Therefore, if any man is in Christ, he is a new creature."

2. This union is represented in the Scriptures by the figure of a vine and its branches in John 15:1–6, by that of a living stone unto which as lively stones Christians are built up a spiritual house (1 Pet. 2:4–6), by Christ, as the head, of whom Christians are the members (Eph. 4:16), and as husband and bride (the church), Eph. 5:25–32. [Hodge's Outlines, p. 483.]

3. On the one hand this union does not involve any mysterious confusion of the person of Christ with the persons of his people; and on the other hand it is not such a mere association of separate persons as exists in human societies. But it is a union which (1.) determines our legal status on the same basis with his,

(2.), which revives and sustains, by the influence of his indwelling Spirit, our spiritual life from the fountain of his life, and which transforms our bodies and souls into the likeness of his glorified humanity.

It is therefore

(1.) "A spiritual union. Its actuating source and bond is the spirit of the head, who dwells and works in the members." 1 Cor. 6:17; 12;13; 1 John 3:24; 4:13.

(2.) "A vital union, i.e. our spiritual life is sustained and determined in its nature and movement by the life of Christ through the indwelling of the Spirit." John 14:19; Gal. 2:20.

(3.) "It embraces our entire persons, our bodies through our spirits." 1 Cor. 6:15, 19.

(4.) "It is a legal or federal union, so that all of our legal or covenant responsibilities rest upon Christ, and all his legal or covenant merits accrue to us."

(5.) "It is an indissoluble union." John 10:38; Rom. 8:35, 37; 1 Thess. 4:14, 17.

(6.) "This union is between the believer and the person of the God-man in his office as Mediator. Its immediate instrument is the Holy Spirit, who dwells in us, and through him we are vitally united to and commune with the whole Godhead since he is the Spirit of the Father, as well as of the Son." John 14:23; 17:21, 23. [Hodge's Outlines, pp. 483 and 484.]

VII. The difference between faith and hope.

That they are not the same is evident from 1 Cor. 13:13, where they are plainly distinguished from each other; also in Rom. 5:2–5; 1 Pet. 1:21; Heb. 11:1. Illustrated by Rom. 4:18.

It is objected that the view taken, that saving faith involves trust, makes it the same as hope, and, therefore, faith must be of such a nature, as not to include trust.

But Christian faith and hope differ,

1. In their nature. (a.) Faith is a reliance upon something now present as known or believed. Hope is looking forward to something in the future, with more or less expectation of receiving it. Faith may become the assurance of things hoped for but not the hope that looks forward to them.

Faith is belief, Hope is expectation. Each involves the idea of trust, but with the use of different prepositions. Faith is trust in or reliance upon any person or thing. Hope is trust of some person or thing, or expectation of the happening of something desirable.

See every passage in Cruden's Concordance where "hope" is, of which the following are specimens: Acts 23:6; 24:15; 26:6; 28:20; Rom. 8:24; 15:4; 1 Cor. 15:19; 2 Cor. 3:12; Col. 1:5, 23, 27; 1 Thess. 5:8.

(b.) Joyful expectation enters into the nature of hope, but not into that of faith. It is only because the things believed beget a joyful hope, that the Christian's trust can be mistaken for hope.

2. Hope is the result or effect of faith and, therefore, not faith itself. Rom. 5:2–5; Rom. 15:4, 13; Gal. 5:5; Heb. 11:1.

3. They differ in their objects. Faith rests upon Christ and his work for our salvation and upon the promises made of blessings. Hope rests in the blessings resultant from that work and those promises. Its object is salvation, freedom from sin, heaven, glory hereafter. We cannot say we have faith in salvation, but in the Saviour and his work; we have not faith in future freedom from sin; but we have it in the promised deliverance. Likewise we have not faith in heaven or glory; but in these as promised to us.

CHAPTER 35

JUSTIFICATION

NO doctrine of Scripture is more important than that of justification. It involves the whole method of the salvation of sinners. It is vitally connected with all other fundamental doctrines. A correct conception of it cannot exist when other truths are ignored, or only partially received. The opinions held upon this point control in great part the theological views in general of all Christian individuals and parties. The importance of a correct knowledge of what God has taught on this subject cannot therefore be exaggerated.

The discussion of this doctrine will be best presented by a definition of the word Justification, accompanied by proof of the several statements involved in that definition.

Justification is a judicial act of God, by which, on account of the meritorious work of Christ, imputed to a sinner and received by him through that faith which vitally unites him to his substitute and Saviour, God declares that sinner to be free from the demands of the law, and entitled to the rewards due to the obedience of that substitute.

I. IT IS A JUDICIAL ACT OF GOD

That God is its author is emphatically declared by Paul in Rom. 8:33; "It is God that justifieth." As he is the lawgiver and judge so must he also be the justifier.

The act is not one of sovereignty, as is election, because he does not justify merely of good pleasure, but because the demands of the law have been met. Yet his act is free, and of grace, because it is of his own choice that he accepts a substitute, and because Christ and his meritorious work have been graciously secured and given by God himself. See Rom. 3:24.

The virtue of the act consists in its being his judicial act. Any one might perceive or declare the demands of the law to be satisfied upon knowledge of that fact. Any one might proclaim that the rewards of Christ's merit have been secured. But, whether declared of the value and efficacy of Christ's work in itself or of its application to an individual, such a declaration would not be justification. It only becomes so when uttered by God in his capacity as Judge. All others could only recognize or declare the fact. The declaration of the judge sets the sinner free from all demands of the law, and confers upon him all the blessings appertaining to this new condition.

This judicial act of justification is made necessary because the law has been broken. One who has completely fulfilled the law needs not to be justified. His position before the law is that of one personally just or righteous; not of one that is justified, or declared righteous, or treated as such, though not personally so. He may be said to be justified, because recognized or treated as such, though the ground of such action is that he is personally just. Thus the term "justified" is properly applied to the doers of the law, and that of "just" denied to the mere hearers of the law in Rom. 2:13. But while the terms may thus be used of one personally just, he, nevertheless, needs no such justification, because his righteousness is not questionable. His position, like that of those who fully obey human laws, is recognized without any special act affirming it.

Hence it is that the Scriptures so commonly use the word "just," δίκαιος (dikaios), of one who is, in some one or in all respects, perfectly conformed to the law by his own acts, and who is, to that extent, therefore, personally holy, applying the term not to men only or even to Christ, who was made under the law, but also to God himself. See Matt. 1:19; 5:45; 9:13; Luke 23:50; Acts 3:14; 7:52; 22:14; Rom. 3:26. This usage has given rise to the opinion of some that justification is not simply a judicial act, but that it involves holiness in the one justified, and in the case of justified sinners an infusion of holiness in the act of justification.

But that this is an error is obvious—

1. From the fact that justification is presented as the opposite of condemnation (Rom. 8:33, 34), and not of sinfulness. Condemnation is never spoken of as the infusion of a corrupted nature, and consequently justification would not involve that of a holy nature.

2. That the justified are not declared in Scripture to be free from sin or possessed of holy natures, but are represented as still struggling against sin, and not only sin which arises from outward temptations, but that proceeding from the motions of sin within.

3. The change of nature which causes that of character is called in the Scriptures "regeneration," and differs essentially from justification. The former is the special work of the Holy Spirit. The latter is the act of God the Father. That is an effect wrought inwardly, which develops itself in a continuous and progressive process which the Scriptures call sanctification. If justification includes an infused righteousness as the opposite of sinfulness, then it includes sanctification, and there is no ground for the scriptural distinction between them.

4. The usage of other words in connection with justification shows it to be a forensic act. The term "righteousness," δικαιοσύνη (dikaiosune), which, like "righteous," δίκαιος (dikaios), is used in connection with personal righteousness,

as of God in Acts 17:31, and of Christ "the Faithful and True," Rev. 19:11, and of the martyrs in Heb. 11:33, and of human obedience to the law in Rom. 10:3, 5; Phil. 3:6, 9, is, in connection with God's justification of sinners, applied, though chiefly by the Apostle Paul, to "the righteousness which God bestows or accepts," and which is imputed to the sinner or reckoned to his account.

Another term, δικαίωσις (dikaiosis), signifies "the act or process of declaring righteous," viz., justification.

The word δικαίωμα (dikaioma), which means "that which is declared righteous," and hence a statute or command, as something which the law of God declares to be a righteous requirement, is used in connection with justification for "the deed by which one declares another righteous, and is partially equivalent to dikaiosis."

The principal word which is used for expressing the nature of God's action in justification is δικαιόω (dikaioo), "to justify," which means everywhere "to declare righteous," "to regard and represent as righteous," and not "to make righteous" in the sense of conferring personal righteousness.

This usage of terms shows plainly that justification is a judicial act of God, in which he does not confer holiness, but only declares the relation occupied to the law by the one who is in Christ.

II. THE GROUND OF THIS JUSTIFICATION

It is manifest from what has already been said that the justification of the sinner must depend on something not personally his own. The Scriptures teach that it is due not to his own good works but to the meritorious work of Christ which is imputed to him, or put to his account.

1. They teach us negatively that it is not due to his own good works.

(1.) They expressly deny that justification can be by the works of the law. Rom. 3:20; Gal. 3:11; Eph. 2:9.

(2.) They assert that, could it thus have been attained, Christ's death has been useless. Gal. 2:21; 5:4.

(3.) Sinfulness is declared to be the condition of every man, which excludes the possibility of works untainted by sin. Rom. 3:10.

(4.) The law is said to demand such complete obedience that "whosoever shall keep the whole law and stumble in one point, he is become guilty of all." James 2:10.

(5.) We are told that "if there had been a law given which could make alive, verily, righteousness would have been of the law." Gal. 3:21.

(6.) It is likewise stated as necessary to the certainty of attaining salvation that "it is of faith that it may be according to grace." Rom. 4:16.

These statements show that, not only are men not saved by works alone, but not even by works combined with grace. Justification cannot arise, therefore, from the good works of men. Not even has its condition been so modified that a partial obedience can be accepted, whether this stands alone or is supplemented by, or is supplementary to the merits of Christ. Something entirely outside of man must constitute the basis of justification.

2. The Word of God declares this outside something to be the meritorious work of Christ.

(1.) In general

(a.) By declaring that the righteousness of God is connected with our relations to, or belief in Christ. Rom. 3:22, 26; 5:1; 10:4; 1 Cor. 1:30.

(b.) By stating that redemption is in Christ Jesus. Rom. 3:24.

(c.) By setting him forth as the only foundation of salvation.

(d.) By asserting salvation to be found only in Christ. Acts 4:12.

(e.) By asserting a definite relation between our sin and Christ, and his righteousness and ourselves. 2 Cor. 5:21.

3. More specifically by connecting the salvation and justification of man with Christ's merits.

This may be shown.

(a.) In connection with his sufferings, or what is usually called his passive obedience.

1. Christ is presented as "the Lamb of God," John 1:29, in evident allusion to the sacrificial offerings of the olden days, and Paul speaks of him as one "whom God set forth to be a propitiation, through faith, by his blood." Rom. 3:25.

2. He is presented as one who has died for us. Rom. 5:6, 8; 8:34; 14:15; 1 Cor. 8:11; 2 Cor. 5:14, 15; 1 Thess. 5:10; and specifically as having died for our sins. 1 Cor. 15:3.

3. We are said to be justified by his blood (Rom. 5:9), and reconciled by his death (Rom. 5:10), and by his cross (Eph. 2:16).

(b.) Our justification is due also to the active obedience of Christ, and not to passive obedience only.

1. Righteousness involves character, conduct and action, even more than suffering endured as penalty. The sinlessness of Christ is therefore plainly taught, and especially in connection with imputation. 2 Cor. 5:21.

2. The gracious salvation he brings is said to establish the law.

3. He assures us, that he came to fulfill the law. Matt. 5:17.

4. The obedience of Christ is not only contrasted with the disobedience of Adam, but is declared to be the means by which many shall be made righteous. Rom. 5:19.

It thus appears, that the ground of justification is the whole meritorious work of Christ. Not his sufferings and death only, but his obedience to, and conformity with the divine law are involved in the justification, which is attained by the believer. The question is here sometimes asked, how the active obedience of Christ can avail to us, when he was himself a man and under the law, and owed obedience personally on his own behalf. The answer to this is twofold, in each case depending upon the doctrine of the incarnation of the Son of God. On the one hand, the position was one voluntarily assumed by the Son of God. He was under no obligation to become man. He was not, and could not be made man without his own consent. In thus voluntarily coming under the law, his obedience would have merit to secure all the blessings connected with the covenant, under which he assumed such relations. But besides this, the fulfillment of the law would not simply be that fulfillment due by a mere man, which is all the law could demand of him on his own behalf, so that the merit secured is that due to the Son of God, thus as man rendering obedience to the law. That merit is immeasurable and is available for all for whom he was the substitute.

III. THE IMPUTATION

This meritorious work of Christ, called in the Scriptures "the righteousness of God," is imputed by God to those whom he justifies, as the ground or cause of their justification. It is reckoned to their account. They are treated as though they had themselves done that which Christ has done for them.

This imputation is in accordance with the action of God throughout the economy of human affairs. Adam as the representative of man sinned, and his sin has been imputed to all of his descendants, and they are treated as though personally sinners. Christ stood also as the representative of his people and their sins were imputed to him and he was treated as though personally a sinner. Likewise his righteousness is imputed to them, and they are treated as though personally righteous.

In each of these cases there is, however, no such transfer as makes one personally what he is representatively. It is not the imputed sin of Adam which makes men personally sinners. The corrupted nature is one of the natural consequences of that sin, and is a punishment of it. So the imputation of our sin to Christ did not make him personally a sinner. He was still of himself "the holy and righteous one." In like manner, the imputation of Christ's righteousness does not make man holy and righteous personally. In each of these cases it is only relation to the law which is expressed.

IV. THE RELATION OF FAITH TO JUSTIFICATION

It is not every sinner that is justified. It is the believer in Jesus. An important inquiry, therefore, is as to the relation of faith to justification. The Scriptures teach that faith is reckoned for righteousness. Rom. 4:5, 9.

By this is not meant, that faith is accepted in the place of righteousness as the cause of justification, for, as we have seen, that place is occupied by the meritorious work of Christ. Nor is it meant, that the righteousness of God has so lowered the law, that something less than obedience can be accepted by him as a full satisfaction of that law; because the demands of the law have not been lowered but have been completely fulfilled by Christ. Besides this would be to make of faith a work, by which salvation is secured, and the Scriptures deny that it has this character. Rom. 4:16. "We are never said to be justified, διὰ πίστιν (dia pistin), on account of faith, but only διὰ πίστεως (dia pisteos), through faith, or ἐκ πίστεως (ek pisteos), of faith, εἰς πίστιν (eis pistin), unto faith, and ἐπι τῇ πίστει (epi te pistei), by faith. The fact that faith is counted for righteousness shows, that in itself it is not righteousness and has no merit, but it only so "reckoned on the ground of something outside of itself, viz.: the saving work of Christ."

It is evidently so reckoned, because by faith the sinner appropriates to himself the work of Christ, and becomes vitally united with him. Faith may, therefore, be regarded as the condition upon which justification is bestowed upon those to whom Christ is presented as a Saviour, to be received and rested upon for salvation. "Faith," says Dr. Charles Hodge, "is the condition of justification. That is, so far as adults are concerned, God does not impute the righteousness of Christ to the sinner, until and unless he (through grace) receives and rests on Christ alone for salvation." Sys. Theol. Vol. 3, p. 118. It is a condition which has in it no merit in itself, but which only seizes upon merit in another. It is also an act of the sinner, to which he is graciously disposed and led by God himself through the power of the Holy Spirit.

V. THE RELATION OF WORKS TO JUSTIFICATION

We have already seen that works cannot enter meritoriously into justification as its procuring cause. But the Scriptures evidently associate works in some manner with justification. Paul himself says that "love is the fulfillment of the law," Rom. 13:10, and declares that that which avails in Christ Jesus is "faith working through love," and that "the whole law is fulfilled in one word, even in this, thou shalt love thy neighbor as thyself." Gal. 5:6, 14. There is here an evident correspondence with, if not allusion to, the frequent teachings of our

Lord, and especially to his answer to the Pharisee about the great commandment of the law. Matt. 22:34–40.

The teaching of the apostle James, is not, therefore, to be held to be opposed to the other Scriptures when he speaks of a justification by works. His language is very strong. He says that "faith apart from works is dead." He asks, "was not Abraham, our father, justified by works, in that he offered up Isaac, his son, upon the altar?" He inquires, "thou seest that faith wrought with his works, and by works was faith made perfect," and especially declares, "ye see how that by works a man is justified and not by faith only." James 2:20, 21, 22, 24.

What then is the relation of works to justification?

1. Certainly not as a procuring cause, or a meritorious ground. The faith with which James associates works, and upon a level with which he seems to place them, does not itself occupy this position.

2. The works are not such as precede justification or are contemporaneous with it, and hence cannot be a cause, nor even a condition such as we have seen faith to be. Even in the case of Abraham the justifying work referred to occurred long after the justification which he attained by faith. Compare Rom. 4:9–11; Heb. 11:8; Gen. 15:6; 17:1–27; 22:1–19.

3. The works are referred to as means of manifesting as well the faith as the justification claimed to be by faith. James 2:18.

4. The apostle's object is to deny the living character of any faith which has not wrought with works and has not been perfected through works.

It is thus evident that works occupy the position of subsequent, not antecedent, accompaniments of justification. They manifest that justification has taken place, because they are invariable consequence. They do this, however, not before man only, but God also, and consequently he, as well as man, perceives them, and because of them the believer performing these good works is justified before God. But such justification is not that actual justification which takes place in connection with faith, which is the judicial act of God declaring the relation of the believer to the law, but that declarative or manifesting justification, which cannot exist except as the result of the actual justification, but which is so inseparably connected with the latter that by its presence, or absence, the existence or non-existence of justification is distinctly established.

VI. THE BENEFITS INCLUDED IN JUSTIFICATION

The benefits conferred by justification are many.

1. Freedom from the condemnation of the law. This includes:

(1.) Forgiveness of all sin. Not for the past only, but throughout the Christian's life.

(2.) Discharge from his relation to the law as a rule of bondage, for which is now exchanged his service to it in the newness of the spirit. Rom. 7:6.

(3.) Peace with God—assured peace—because dependent on the merits of Christ and not those of himself.

These and all other blessings which may be included under the general idea of pardon are necessary results of justification.

2. But justification confers righteousness as well as pardon. Not only are sins remitted but men are made partakers of the righteousness procured by Christ which is imputed to them. They are thus recognized before the law as righteous persons, not simply as persons pardoned for breaking the law, but as those who are rewarded for having fulfilled all its demands.

3. But there are other blessings which arise from the relation to Christ of those whom God justifies. That relation was shown in the chapter on Faith (pp. 352–53). It is a vital and spiritual as well as a legal and federal union between Christ and his people. By virtue of this they are identified with him in his relation to God as their Representative and Covenant Head, and are made partakers of all the blessings which he has obtained as an inheritance. It is thus that they are adopted into the family of God and become his sons and daughters; thus are they sanctified by the Holy Spirit partly in this life, and progressively advance until complete holiness shall be theirs in Heaven. Thus also do they persevere in the divine life, being preserved or kept by God through faith unto complete salvation. By the same act of faith which is the condition of justification is secured by those united to Christ, the privilege of complete participation in the rewards of their federal head. They shall be heirs with him, shall reign with him, shall be partakers of his glory. No imagination can compass the reward which shall be theirs together with Christ. The Scriptures seem to teach that whatever Christ shall be or possess in his human nature they also shall be and possess.

VII. THE TIME OF JUSTIFICATION

We may finally inquire into the time at which justification occurs.

1. It does not occur periodically but is a single act, and not one repeated with reference to new sins. This arises from its nature as an act of God declaring the relation of the believer to the law and from the ground of that act, the never failing merits of Christ. The pardon which the Christian seeks of God is that of a child for offences against a father's love, and not of a culprit before an avenging judge. The sufferings which Christians endure are not avenging punishments for sin, but chastisements from a Father who chastises those whom he loves and scourges those whom he receives.

2. It is an instantaneous and not a continuing work as is sanctification. It is God's act declaring the sinner's relation to the law. That sinner is under condemnation until justified. As soon as justified his condemnation ceases. He cannot be partly condemned and partly justified. He is under condemnation until brought into that condition which secures his justification. When that moment comes God must justify.

3. But when is that moment? The Scriptures teach that it is when man believes. It is in the moment of trust in a personal Saviour.

It was not at the time that Christ finished his work and laid the foundation of justification in his merits and satisfaction. By these justification was secured but not bestowed. It was not in Eternity as is Election by which the subjects of the future justification were chosen. It is at the moment of belief when faith, which is its condition, is experienced. Then is consummated that which was purposed in eternity and which was made possible and certain by the work of Christ. The hour of faith was even the period of justification before the incarnation of Christ because of the faith which rested personally upon him through the promises of God, and the acceptance by God of the meritorious work of Christ as though already existing because of the absolute certainty that it would be performed.

CHAPTER 36

ADOPTION

ADOPTION is that privilege, bestowed upon those who are united with Christ, and justified by faith, by which they are admitted into the family of God, adopted as his children, and made joint heirs with his own Son.

In the strict sense of the word "Son," this title can be given only to the Eternal Son of God, who is the only begotten of the Father (John 1:14), and is exclusively "the effulgence of his glory, and the very image of his substance." (Heb. 1:3).

But others are called participatively sons of God, as probably the angels (Job 1:6; 38:7), as Adam (Luke 3:38), and as Israel (Ex. 4:22; Hosea 11:1; cf. Rom. 9:4). The sonship of angels and of Adam, manifestly proceeds from their creation by God in his image, and likeness. That of Israel, however, is to be ascribed to the typical relation which that nation occupied to the true people of God. The application to Christ in Matt. 2:15, of the sonship declared of Israel in Ex. 4:22, and Hosea 11:1, together with the adoption to which Paul refers, Rom. 9:4, shows, that Israel's sonship, like Israel's election, was but a type, the fulfillment and reality of which were to be found only in the antitype. So far as Israel itself was concerned, the title could mean no more, than that that nation had been chosen by God to be outwardly his people, the depository of his holy oracles, and the means through which his salvation would come to man. John 4:22.

The sonship ascribed to the believer in Christ, will be best understood by considering its gracious origin, its peculiar nature, and the wondrous blessing which it confers.

I. ITS GRACIOUS ORIGIN

1. It is not due to any natural relation, either originally possessed, or restored through justification.

2. Nor does it arise from any new image or likeness of God, which has come through regeneration.

3. It is the simple gift of God's love to those who by faith are brought into union with his proper Son.

4. It is an act originating entirely in the good pleasure of God. Eph. 1:5.

5. It is due, meritoriously, only to the work of Christ. It could be founded thus upon nothing else.

6. It is conferred like justification upon all who by faith receive Christ. John 1:12.

7. It is bestowed at the beginning of the Christian career, when there could be no ground for supposing it due to the character or acts of the recipient.

II. ITS PECULIAR NATURE

If what has been said shows that the gift of sonship to the believer is a gracious act of God, that fact will appear more plain as we study the peculiar nature of that sonship.

1. It is an act by which God chooses to take those who are not his children, and to make them such by adopting them into his family. Because of this they "are no more strangers and sojourners, but ye are fellow citizens with the saints, and of the household of God." Eph. 2:19.

2. As they are united in this sonship with his own Son, who "is the image of the invisible God, the first born of all creation," (Col. 1:15), "the beginning of the creation of God," (Rev. 3:14), so does their sonship partake of the nature of his not in its divine relations, but in those by which he is also, even in that human nature, the Son of God. Luke 1:35.

3. It is an everlasting sonship; because its continuance depends not upon what they do, and are, but upon what he has done, and is.

4. It is one in which Christ Jesus "is made unto us wisdom from God and righteousness, and sanctification, and redemption." 1 Cor. 1:30. Thus are all their deficiencies removed and exchanged for the glory of his abundant fullness.

5. It is one in connection with which is fulfilled the prayer of Christ, "that they may all be one; even as Thou, Father, art in me, and I in Thee, that they also may be in us; . . . . that they may be one, even as we are one; I in them, and Thou in me, that they may be perfected into one." John 17:21–23.

6. To such a perfection of sonship do they consequently attain, that not of, nor through themselves, but solely through Christ Jesus, do they thus become "partakers of the divine nature," (2 Pet. 1:4), attaining as near as creatures may, to the position and character of proper sonship to God.

III. ITS WONDROUS BLESSINGS

The blessings connected with this sonship are scarcely less wonderful than is its nature.

1. Intimate fellowship with Christ and God. "Wherefore," says the apostle, "thou art no longer a bond servant, but a son." Gal. 4:7. "No longer," said Jesus, "do I call you servants; . . . but I have called you friends." John 15:15.

2. The guidance of the Holy Spirit; "as many as are led by the Spirit of God, these are the sons of God." Rom. 8:14.

3. The witnessing presence of the Holy Spirit: "the Spirit himself beareth witness with our spirit, that we are children of God." Rom. 8:16.

4. The conscious recognition in our hearts of God's relation to us as Father. "God sent forth the Spirit of his Son into our hearts, crying, Abba, Father." Gal. 4:6; also Rom. 8:15.

5. "If children, then heirs; heirs of God, and joint heirs with Christ." Rom. 8:17.

6. Unknown glory in future likeness to Christ: "it is not yet made manifest what we shall be. We know that, if he shall be manifested, we shall be like him." 1 John 3:2.

7. The inheritance includes all things: "he that overcometh shall inherit these things; and I will be his God, and he shall be my son." Rev. 21:7; cf. 1 Cor. 3:21–23.

IV. IT DIFFERS FROM JUSTIFICATION

It has been contended that "adoption cannot be said to be a different act or grace from justification." [Dabney's Theology, p. 627.] "It appears to me," says Dr. Dick, [Lect. 73, Theol., vol. 2, p. 224,] "to be virtually the same with justification, and to differ from it merely in the new view which it gives of the relations of believers to God, and in the peculiar form in which it exhibits the blessing to which they are entitled." Turretine says also, "that adoption is included in justification as a part which, with the remission of sins, constitutes this whole blessing; nor can justification be distinguished from adoption, unless so far as it is taken strictly for the remission of sins; whilst in its own formal conception it includes also acceptance unto life which flows from the imputation of the righteousness of Christ." Turretine's Theol., B. 16, c. 6, sec. 7.

The position taken by these writers is a contrary extreme to that which some have held, viz.: that justification consists only of pardon. It is not to be doubted that justification is more than this, and includes restoration to the favor of God, and to eternal life. But these might have been bestowed without conferring upon the justified the peculiar blessings contained in Adoption. "Adoption," says Buchanan [on Justification, p. 262], "is distinct in some respects from justification. For although both denote a change in relation, it may be affirmed that, according to Scriptures, pardon, acceptance, and adoption, are distinct privileges, the one rising above the other in the order in which they have been stated;—that if it be conceivable that a sinner might have been pardoned, without being accepted to eternal life, it is equally conceivable that he might have been both pardoned and accepted, without being adopted as a son;—and that, while the first two first properly belong to his justification, as being both founded in the same relation—that of a Ruler and Subject—the third is radically distinct from them, as being founded on a nearer, more tender, and more endearing relation—that between a Father and his Son."

Dabney argues that there is no difference between the two because the "instrument is the same—faith—and because the meritorious ground of adoption is the same with that of justification, viz.: the righteousness of Christ."

But these facts, which are admitted, are due to another, which is that the faith by which we are justified is one which secures to us union with Christ. It would not necessarily follow that this union confers upon us only a single blessing or a number of blessings which may be combined together under one name. We can only learn this by examination. If, therefore, it shall appear that there are distinctions between the accompanying blessings, to the extent that these exist must those blessings be regarded as different.

That there are distinctions appears to be plain from the following considerations:

1. The Scriptures speak separately of justification and adoption, and do not state that the latter is, in whole, or in part, the same as the former.

2. Justification is ascribed to the righteous character of God as it formal ground. In it he is only gracious in accepting and providing a substitute. Adoption is expressly referred to the love of God. 1 John 3:1. The fact that these cannot be interchanged, and justification referred to love, or adoption to justice, shows a decided distinction between them.

3. While there is a change of relation in each of them, in justification it is a change of relation to the law, and only through that to the lawgiver and judge; in adoption it is a change of relation to the family of God and thus to God as the Father.

4. While faith is that through which each is attained, in justification it is a condition precedent to a forensic act which we are assured that God will do because of righteousness as well as faithfulness (1 John 1:9); while in adoption it is merely receptive of Christ, securing that union through which the paternal love of God flows freely on no other ground than faithfulness to his promises.

5. The act of justification is never ascribed to the Son, and is seen to be plainly a prerogative of the Father as God; but it is said of the Son that "as many as received him, to them gave he the right to become children of God, even to them that believe on his name." John 1:12. In some sense, therefore, which is not true of justification, adoption is connected as a gift with the Son as well as the Father.

The above considerations are sufficient to show that there is a real basis of distinction between Justification and Adoption, and that the latter is not included in the former. They are separate effects which flow from the union with Christ attained through faith; because of which we are made partakers of all the benefits of his meritorious work. Justification is one of these; and by it we obtain pardon, and favour with God, which is eternal life. Adoption is yet another which confers upon us the especial privilege of children and heirs of God. It is no more to be confounded with justification than is sanctification, which is also an effect of the same union with Christ, for, although its distinctions are not so many, nor so broad, yet to the extent that they exist, they are as real.

"This closer and more endearing relation to God, which is constituted by Adoption, is necessary, in addition to that which is included in our Justification, to complete the view of our Christian privileges, and to enhance our enjoyment of them, by raising us above the spirit of bondage which is unto fear; and cherishing the spirit of adoption whereby we cry, Abba, Father. It is necessary, also, to explain how the sins of believers are not visited with penal inflictions, properly so called, but are nevertheless treated in the way of fatherly chastisement; and, still further, to show that the kingdom of heaven hereafter will not be bestowed as wages for work done, but as an 'inheritance,' freely bestowed, on those, and those only, who are 'joint heirs with Christ.'" Buchanan on Justification, pp. 263, 264.

CHAPTER 37

SANCTIFICATION

THE correctness of the statements, as to the forensic nature of justification, and its being an act of God which declares simply the relation of the justified to the law, will more plainly appear from what we shall learn of the nature of Sanctification, which is another of the privileges bestowed upon the people of God, as the result of their union with Christ.

I. MEANING OF THE TERMS USED

While justify, as has been seen, means simply to declare just, or to treat as just; sanctify means to make holy. The usage of Scripture is as clear in this case as in that. The word "holy" in Scripture has, however, various meanings. It is sometimes applied to things, and not to persons only. (1.) It is used in the sense of that which is set apart or dedicated to an especial use. Thus, God threatens that instruments of vengeance will be "prepared" (sanctified) against "the king's house of Judah," Jer. 22:7. But the dedication is most frequently for some holy use. Thus, "holy" is applied to the Sabbath day (Ex. 31:14); and to the house of God (Lev. 16:33); and to the water (Num. 5:17); and to the vessels of the young men (1 Sam. 21:5). (2.) Things are also called holy from their connection with holy persons. Thus, the "place" on which Moses stood was proclaimed "holy" on account of its connection with Jehovah (Ex. 3:5); likewise the Mount of Transfiguration (2 Pet. 1:18). (3.) As descriptive of an act free from sin, and performed with holy motives. Thus, the kiss of Christian salutation, called in 1 Pet. 5:14 a kiss of charity, is in several other places called a "holy kiss." 1 Cor. 16:20; 2 Cor. 13:12; 1 Thess. 5:26. (4.) "Holy," as tending to produce holiness; as "most holy faith" (Jude 20). (5.) It is most generally used as descriptive of personal character, whether the holiness be perfect, as in God, or angels, or glorified saints; or partial, as seen in his people on earth. A few of the many instances of its application to this last class are 1 Sam. 2:9; Acts 9:13; Rom. 15:25, 26; Phil. 4:21; Eph. 1:1; Col. 1:2; Rev. 18:24.

The doctrine of sanctification has reference to the first and last of these usages of "holy;" to the last more especially, as including the character of holiness produced by the continuous working of the Holy Ghost through the word of truth; but also to the first, as involving that dedication of person and life to God, which constitutes that "living sacrifice, holy, acceptable unto God," which is the believer's "reasonable service." Rom. 12:1. Christian holiness includes both character and life. "Sanctification" is the process by which these are accomplished. The "sanctified" are those who are thus made holy. To "sanctify" is to make them thus holy.

II. WHO ARE SANCTIFIED

The sanctified are those only who are in Christ Jesus, who have been regenerated, and have been justified through faith.

1. No man can cleanse or purify his heart or life. He lacks especially the will to do so. If he should determine to attempt it, the temptations, which will assail him, will soon overcome that will.

2. The law cannot furnish controlling power to this result; not because of its own deficiencies, but because of its weakness through the flesh. Rom. 8:3.

3. The difficulty of the work to be done consists in its not being a mere reformation of a bad life and habits, which is measurably within the power of man, and is sometimes accomplished so far as the mere outward life among men demands; but in its including the destruction and removal of man's sinful condition, and habits, and action, which he by nature ardently loves, and the substitution for them of their very opposites in every respect.

4. Regeneration, therefore, is necessary, as antecedent to the work of sanctification. A new nature must be attained which will love and seek after holiness, and struggle forward, dissatisfied until it shall be perfected. The Scriptures, therefore, represent sanctification as occurring only in those who have been regenerated, and to whom a new heart and a new spirit have been given.

5. But, not only regeneration, but justification also, must precede sanctification. Yet certainly not for the same reasons; for regeneration is, like sanctification, a change in nature, and character; and justification a change only in relation to the law. There is, therefore, no such natural connection of sanctification with justification as there is with regeneration. Nor is there anything meritorious in the position of the justified person. For the meritorious ground of all blessings can be found only in the person and work of Christ. But, as the merit of Christ becomes that of the believer only in justification, and, as the faith by which we are united with him is also the condition of justification, so must justification precede the blessings which flow from that union, and from justification itself. The same necessity for precedence arises because in justification are furnished the motives by which the Christian is led through the Spirit. The Psalmist of old sang "There is forgiveness with thee, that thou mayest be feared," Ps. 130:4, and the Apostle John declares "Every one that hath this hope

[of sonship and likeness to Christ] set on him purifieth himself, even as he is pure." 1 John 3:3. Paul, also, teaches that the condition of obedience with the newness of the spirit, is that we have been discharged from the law. Rom. 7:6. The believer must co-operate in the work of sanctification. His reception of the Word of God, his reliance upon its promises, his struggles against sin, and his earnest longings for holiness are important elements in his sanctification. But the existence of these depends upon the belief that God has pardoned his sins, and will accept and bless him, which is the consequence of the personal trust in Christ which constitutes justifying faith.

This precedence of justification to sanctification is distinctly set forth by the Apostle in the order in which the parts of salvation are arranged in Rom. 8:29, 30 and Phil. 3:9–12.

III. THE NATURE OF SANCTIFICATION

What now, we may inquire, is the nature of the sanctification which is wrought out in the believer?

1. It is a personal sanctification. It is accomplished in each individual personally, and not in that of a common representative as is the righteousness which justifies.

2. It is a real sanctification, not merely one that is imputed, as is righteousness. Holiness is not merely "accounted to men," so that they are treated as though holy, but they are made holy. Holiness becomes the characteristic of their natures. It is habitually exercised in their lives. It will eventually be possessed in perfection. It is real and in no sense only virtual.

3. It is of the whole nature. The renewed nature, given in regeneration, shows that sanctification includes the whole spiritual part of man. It is not to be confined to mere outward actions. God's spiritual nature demands not only spiritual worship, but holy spiritual emotions and affections; and these belong to the heart. Hence the need of inward conformity to his will and commands is so especially set forth in the New Testament, as to mark its teachings as essentially spiritual. We are also plainly taught that between the outward fruit, and the inward condition, is such a connection that the latter is the actual producing power of the former, and is manifested by it. Matt. 12:33–35; Luke 6:43–45.

But sanctification is to be extended to the body likewise. Its appetites and passions are to be controlled, wicked actions are to cease, and unholy habits to be put away, the members of the body are to be mortified, all filthiness of the flesh to be cleansed, good works are to be exhibited to mankind, and such high moral duties to be performed as are imposed upon Christians as obligatory towards each other and the world.

The Scriptures exhort to sanctification of the whole nature, both body and soul. See 2 Cor. 7:1; Eph. 4:17–24; Col. 3:5–10; 1 Thess. 5:23. That of the body alone is urged. Rom. 6:12, 13: 1 Cor. 6:20; 1 Thess. 4:3–7. The apostle tells the Ephesians about his prayers for their spiritual sanctification. Eph. 1:17–19.

4. It is not a sanctification to be completed in this life.

It is not, like justification, a single act, but is a continuous process. The work goes on throughout the lifetime of the believer, nor is it completed before death.

(1.) This is manifest from the frequent exhortations to sanctification addressed to those who are already believers in Christ, and who are actually called saints. Many of the passages containing these have been given in the preceding section.

(2.) It is also shown by the warnings, about the danger of backsliding, addressed to Christian believers. Such was that to Peter by our Lord, the reality of the danger of which was shown by his subsequent grievous fall. Luke 22:31, 32. See examples of other such warnings in 1 Cor. 10:12; Col. 1:23; Heb. 3:12, 13; 12:15.

(3.) The fearful condition of actual apostasy is presented for the purpose of teaching the true people of God the extent to which knowledge of his grace may be possessed without the attainment of actual and final salvation. Heb. 6:4–6; 10:26–29; 2 Pet. 2:20. The object of this instruction is to warn against committing sins, and indulging habits to which they are still prone.

(4.) Christians are not presented in the New Testament as completely pure and holy, but, on the contrary, the very best of them acknowledge the existence of sinful tendencies, and pronounce any idea of freedom from the presence of sin to be a delusion. The faults of good men, such as Peter, James and John, and Thomas, and Paul and Barnabas (Acts 15:37–40) are especially mentioned, and John who declares that "whosoever is begotten of God sinneth not" (1 John 5:18) is the very apostle who, in a previous part of that very same epistle, teaches that "if we say we have no sin, we deceive ourselves, and the truth is not in us." 1 John 1:8. Paul constantly speaks of himself as still struggling against the power of sin, as not counting himself to have attained, as buffeting his body and bringing it into bondage lest he should be rejected, and thus he gives us, in his descriptions of his own experience, a pattern of what has been almost universally acknowledged as that of every other Christian.

5. But sanctification will not always be incomplete. In heaven perfect purity and holiness will be the portion of the believer.

(1.) The purpose of God, in the foreordination of those whom he foreknew, is that they shall "be conformed to the image of his Son." Rom. 8:29. This conformity shall be attained in heaven, for "if he shall be manifested, we shall be like him; for we shall see him even as he is." 1 John 3:2. Such likeness involves personal sinless purity.

(2.) Paul's triumphant language as to the resurrection shows that this will be true of the body no less than of the soul. 1 Cor. 15:50–57.

(3.) The Scriptures declare as to the New Jerusalem that "there shall in no wise enter into it anything unclean, or he that maketh an abomination and a lie: but only they which are written in the Lamb's book of life." Rev. 21:27. Peter says that the inheritance reserved in heaven for the saints is incorruptible and undefiled. 1 Pet. 1:4.

6. The partial sanctification of this life is also progressive. It is not a certain degree of attainment, possessed by all alike, and remaining always in this life the same; it is a growth from the seed planted in regeneration, which is constantly bringing forth new leaves, and new fruit; it grows with increased intellectual knowledge of God's truth, with a clearer perception of human sinfulness and corruption, with stronger faith and brighter hope, and more confident assurance of personal acceptance with God, with a more heartfelt conception of the sacrificing love of Christ, and with a more realizing belief in his constant presence and knowledge of what we do. It even increases from its own acquired strength and through the suffering and doing in which it is developed. In these and many other ways do Christians grow in grace and in the knowledge of Christ, and in conformity to his image, "cleansing themselves from all defilement of flesh and spirit, perfecting holiness in the fear of God." 2 Cor. 7:1.

When, however, this sanctification is said to be progressive, it is not meant to deny the imperfections before referred to, nor to assert that there is a constant rise upward to God and toward his holy perfection. The Christian life on earth is a warfare with sin, and the believer is not always without failure. He often yields to temptation, sometimes falls even into most grievous sin. The personal experience, presented by Paul, in the seventh chapter of Romans, is so strong a statement of such struggles that some have been inclined to confine its application to a time prior to acceptance of the gospel. But there can be no question of the applicability to Christians of the declaration made to the Galatians, "The flesh lusteth against the spirit, and the spirit against the flesh; for these are contrary the one to the other; that ye may not do the things that ye would." Gal. 5:17.

But the progress of sanctification is nevertheless continuous. These temptations and struggles enter into that progress, and not only they, but even the sins and falls which mar the Christian life. The process of sanctification is like the ascent of a mountain. One is always going forward, though not always upward, yet the final end of the progressive movement of every kind is the attainment of the summit. Sometimes, because of difficulties, the road itself descends, only more easily to ascend again. Sometimes certain attractions by the way cause a deviation from the route most suitable for ascent. Often it is feared that there has been no higher attainment, often that it has been but a continual descent, until, perchance, some point of view is gained from which to look down upon the plain whence the journey was begun and behold the height which has already been overcome. Often, with wearied feet, and desponding heart, the traveller is ready to despair, because of his own feebleness, and the difficulties which surround. But he earnestly presses forward and the journey is completed, the ascent is made, the end is attained.

IV. THE AUTHOR OF SANCTIFICATION

1. From what we have learned of the persons who are sanctified, and of the nature of the work performed, it is evident that the author of it must be more than man. The Scriptures teach that it is God.

The work is attributed to God without reference to any distinction of persons. 1 Thess. 4:3; 5:23. It is also ascribed to the Father, John 17:17; Heb. 13:21; and to Christ, Eph. 5:26; Tit. 2:14.

But it is the especial work of the Holy Spirit, who is the author of the process of Sanctification, as he is also the act of Regeneration. 1 Cor. 6:11; 2 Cor. 3:18; 2 Thess. 2:13; 1 Pet. 1:2.

(1.) He enlightens the mind. John 14:26; 1 Cor. 2:9–16; Eph. 1:18; 3:18, 19; 1 John 2:20, 27. On this account he is called "the Spirit of truth," John 14:17; 15:26; 16:13; and the "Spirit of wisdom." Eph. 1:17.

(2.) He gives spiritual strength (Eph. 3:16), lusting against the flesh (Gal. 5:17), enabling the believer to mortify the deeds of the body (Rom. 8:13), leading the sons of God (Rom. 8:14), and enabling them to purify their souls in obeying the truth. 1 Pet. 1:22.

(3.) Inasmuch as he dwells within them (Rom. 8:9), so that they are his temple (1 Cor. 3:16), with whom they are sealed as the earnest of their inheritance (Eph. 1:13, 14), so, also, does he bear witness with their spirits that they are the children of God, and, removing the spirit of bondage to fear, bestows on them the spirit of adoption, whereby they cry "Abba, Father." Rom. 8:15, 16.

(4.) The fruit of this indwelling Spirit is declared to be "in all goodness and righteousness and truth." Eph. 5:9. It is specifically stated to be "love, joy, peace, long-suffering, kindness, goodness, faith, meekness, temperance." Gal. 5:22.

2. But, while there is such need of a divine author of sanctification, it is a work in which the believer is passively a recipient, but one in which he actively co-operates. This is exhibited in various ways in the Word of God.

(1.) Christians are called upon to recognize this presence of the Spirit. 1 Cor. 3:16, 17. They are exhorted to "walk by the Spirit," and assured that, in so doing, they "shall not fulfill the lust of the flesh." Gal. 5:16. They are taught that "they that are after the flesh do mind the things of the flesh, but they that are after the Spirit the things of the Spirit." Rom. 8:5. They are told that, because of the indwelling Spirit, "we are debtors, not to the flesh to live after the flesh," and thus, by implication that we are debtors to live after the Spirit. Rom. 8:12. They are charged to "grieve not the Holy Spirit of God, in whom ye are sealed unto the day of redemption." Eph. 4:30. In these, and in other ways, their co-operation with the Spirit in the work is implied quite plainly.

(2.) They are exhorted to engage in the work of self-purification. The apostle exhorts the Ephesians not to "walk as the Gentiles also walk, in the vanity of their mind, . . . to put away . . . the old man, which waxeth corrupt after the lusts of deceit; and be renewed in the spirit of their mind, . . . and to put on the new man, which after God, hath been created in righteousness and holiness of truth." Eph. 4:17–24.

(3.) This self-purification is declared to be the work of every one that has the hope of likeness to Christ. 1 John 3:3.

(4.) Direct promises and commands, and exhortations to perfection and holiness, imply co-operative action in those who are in the process of attaining sanctification. Matt. 5:48; 2 Cor. 7:1.

(5.) All warnings against the power of temptation, the lust of the flesh, the subtlety of Satan, the influence of the world, the grievous character of sin; all exhortations to lead a virtuous and godly life, to set the affections on heavenly and divine things, to consecrate the soul and body to God; all motives to these ends drawn from the work of Christ, as an exhibition of divine love and mercy, as an example of purity of life, and of patient suffering, or as personally connected with the believer because of his union with the Lord—in short, all that the Scriptures contain fitted to lead the Christian to a higher spiritual life, is evidence of his co-operation with the Holy Spirit in the work of sanctification.

The author of sanctification is indeed the Divine Spirit, but the Christian actively unites with that Spirit, "working out his own salvation with fear and trembling," being exhorted and encouraged to do so, because "it is God which worketh in him, both to will, and to do, for his good pleasure." Phil. 2:12, 13.

V. THE MEANS OF SANCTIFICATION

The manner in which the Spirit operates in sanctification is beyond our knowledge. In none of the acts of God can we tell how he exerts his power, not even in creation. "As thou knowest not," says the preacher, "what is the way of the wind, nor how the bones do grow in the womb of her that is with child; even so thou knowest not the work of God who doeth all." Ecc. 11:5. In sanctification the Spirit moves as mysteriously as we are taught that he does in regeneration. John 3:8. In general, undoubtedly, it is in accordance with the laws of mind and of spiritual life. Yet we know no reason why there is not a place for supernatural action in sanctification, as well as in regeneration. We can only know the effects produced, and the means which are revealed in the Word of God, and in Christian experience.

1. The primary means which the Spirit uses for our sanctification, as both of these sources of information teach, is the truth of God. "Sanctify them in the truth; thy word is truth" (John 17:17), was the prayer of the Lord, in which the whole work, both of consecration and cleansing, is set forth as thus to be accomplished. (See also John 17:19). "Growth in the grace" is inseparably connected with growth "in the knowledge of our Lord and Saviour Jesus Christ." 2 Pet. 3:18.

This is further taught in Scripture by

(1.) Such passages as connect spiritual life with truth; as John 6:63; 8:32.

(2.) Such as ascribe quickening power to the word of God; as Ps. 119:50, 93.

(3.) Such as teach the that truth is promotive of obedience; as Ps. 119:34, 43, 44.

(4.) Such as declare its usefulness in preventing sin; as Ps. 119:11.

(5.) Such as associate it with cleansing from sin; as Ps. 119:9; 1 Pet. 1:22.

(6.) Such as state that it produces hatred of sin; as Ps. 119:104.

(7.) Such as assert its power to lead to salvation; 2 Tim. 3:15–17.

(8.) Such as say that "all things that pertain unto life and godliness" have been given through the knowledge of God, and Christ; as 2 Pet. 1:2, 3.

(9.) Such as imply that growth in grace is due to greater knowledge; as Heb. 5:12–14.

(10.) Such as account for inability to accept higher doctrinal truth, by such weakness as should be characteristic only of those who are babes in Christ; as 1 Cor. 3:1–3.

(11.) Such as set forth the Word of God as "the sword of the Spirit;" as Eph. 6:17.

(12.) Such as announce that all the ministerial gifts bestowed by Christ are "for the perfecting of the saints, unto the work of ministering, unto the building up of the body of Christ; till we all attain unto the unity of the faith, and of the knowledge of the Son of God, unto a full grown man, unto the measure of the stature of the fulness of Christ." Eph. 4:11–16.

2. In connection with this primary means of divine truth others are presented. But they are not only secondary, but actually subordinate means to the Word of God. They rather furnish occasions for the exercise of the means of sanctification contained in the truth of God than are proper means of themselves to that end. In themselves they have no efficacy, and only accomplish the

end of sanctification by bringing the believer into connection with the truth of God.

(1.) Such are the providences of God, which tend in various ways to arouse and move his children, and avail unto sanctification so far only as they recall, and lead to the apprehension of divine instructions. They are frequent and effective means of such apprehension, and, through this, of the believer's growth in holiness. Such especially are the afflictions, sent as chastisements by the Heavenly Father upon his children. Such, also, are the temptations and trials to which they are subjected. Such, likewise, are the infirmities of the flesh, and perplexities of the spirit which God permits to remain, or causes to arise in his own elect. In these, and in numerous other ways, as well as what is called good, as of what is called evil, does God surround his people with the acts of his providence. But these acts themselves avail not unto their sanctification but are only made effective through the truth of God apprehended amid such events, and received as spiritual food for the growth of the believer.

(2.) The good works of the Christian, furnish another secondary means for his sanctification. By these are not meant works that are good in a legal sense, for such goodness would require a perfection and freedom from taint which no work of fallen man can possess; but it is the privilege of the Christian to live unto the Lord, and the name of good works is given in Scripture to such outward actions as are the results of his life through the Spirit.

These good works are the result of sanctification; but, in their performance, they naturally become the means of further sanctification. John 14:23; Eph. 3:16–20. Yet, is this accomplished, not apart from, but in connection with, the truth of God. The new development will always be in the direction of the particular truths, contemplated in their performance. These will furnish the motives to further action, the strength for additional duty, the earnest purpose of deeper consecration, or whatever else the Spirit may graciously use for a more complete sanctification of the believer.

(3.) Prayer is still a further means to the same end; which, from its nature, can be effective only through the believer's apprehension of divine truth.

Hence the worthlessness of mere lip service (Isa. 29:13; Ezek. 33:31; Matt. 15:8), or vain repetitions, Matt. 6:7. Not only are they offensive to God, but without value to the soul. Hence also the necessary spirituality of divine worship, because that only is true worship which is the service of the soul. John 4:23, 24. Prayer, which is a mere formal or mechanical utterance of words, can have no value; because the one that offers it, does so in ignorance, or forgetfulness of the truth of God appropriate to accompany it.

(4.) The Lord's Day is another secondary means of sanctification, which manifestly becomes such only in the Christian's use of divine truth; either such as is suggested by God's appointment of such a day, or such as is attained through the opportunity for such purpose which it affords.

(5.) The association of believers in church relations, is another means ordained by God for the increase of individual spiritual life and consequently of sanctification. This is attained not only through social prayer, and the preaching of the Word, but also by Christian watchcare and discipline, and by the mutual sympathy and aid of believers in matters both temporal and spiritual. Whatever in these pertains to sanctification, must be connected with the recognition of divine truth in the moving influences which bestow, or the accepting thankfulness which receives.

(6.) The ministry given by Christ, is also a means for the sanctification of his people, in the preaching of his truth, in the spiritual guidance and rule of the flock, and in the sympathizing bestowment of the consolations of his grace. But, even these, though officially appointed, cannot either of themselves, or by virtue of their office, confer or increase spiritual grace. Their ministry is one only of the Word of God, and it is only through his inspired truth "that the man of God may be complete, furnished completely unto every good work." 2 Tim. 3:17. What these works are, is shown by verse 16, viz.: "for teaching, for reproof, for correction, for instruction which is in righteousness." Ministers are in no other sense vehicles of grace. They are not appointed as personal channels of access to God, or of the bestowment of blessings by him, except so far as he has made it their duty to make known his truth. In connection with that truth they are means of sanctification to his people, and only thus are to be regarded as occupying relations between their fellow-men and God.

(7.) The ordinances of baptism and the Lord's Supper are also means of sanctification. It is especially important to understand in what respects they are so. Upon this subject there are several opinions.

By the Papal Church these, with five others (confirmation, penance, matrimony, extreme unction and orders), are regarded as the Sacraments of the New Law. As to their efficacy as means of grace

1. This Church maintains that the Sacraments are, in and of themselves— wherever conferred with the intention of the church, and where the recipient does not put obstacles in the way—active causes to produce the grace which they signify, by virtue of the sacramental action itself, instituted by God for this end. The sufferings of Christ concur as the meritorious, but not as the efficient cause, which also depends neither upon the merit of the agent, nor upon that of the receiver.

They make distinctions, however, as to the necessity of these two Sacraments; regarding baptism as absolutely necessary to justification, in which they include sanctification; but the Lord's Supper as only necessary because commanded and eminently useful.

The efficacy which is thus ascribed to the Sacraments is that of what is called an *opus operatum*, in which grace is conferred *ex opere operato*, viz: from the mere act done. It denies that faith alone in the divine promise suffices to obtain the grace. Will, faith, and repentance, in the adult, are necessarily required as dispositions on the part of the subject, but only to remove obstacles, for, as fire burns wood, not because the wood is dry, nor because the fire is applied to it, but because of the power in the fire to consume, so, they maintain that a sacrament, by its own inherent power, confers the grace when no obstacle prevents, such as would be dampness in wood to the power of fire to burn.

[See statements and extracts from the Canons of the Council of Trent, and from Bellarmine, contained in Hodge's Outlines, pp. 597–600].

The objections to this explanation of the use of the Sacrament as means are,

(1.) That the ordinance is thus regarded as effective in itself, disconnected from any divine truth which may be symbolized in it, or taught in its objective presentation, or suggested through the Christian experience which accompanies its reception. The Scriptures nowhere teach such efficacy apart from the truth of God.

(2.) To no immediate connection of God with these, is ascribed their effective power. They are held to be mere appointments of God to be applied through man, and grace is taught to be as inherent in them as is, in any merely physical substance, any natural quality which God has bestowed upon it.

(3.) The faith which is declared requisite to remove obstacles is "mere assent" to receive, and not the appropriating faith of personal trust in Christ which alone is the saving faith of the Bible. Hodge's Sys. Theol., vol. 3, p. 512.

(4.) This doctrine of the Sacraments places the salvation of every one entirely in the power of others. Whatever his own faith, unless someone else will baptize him, he cannot attain justification and sanctification.

(5.) Inasmuch as the sacraments are valid to convey grace only when performed with "the intention of doing what the Church does," no one can know that the grace has been conferred, since he cannot know the mind of the administrator.

2. A second opinion, different in many respects as to the efficacy of the Sacraments, has been held by almost all Protestants.

(1.) In opposition to the doctrine of Rome, they teach that the Sacraments, which are but two, Baptism and the Lord's Supper, are not in themselves means of grace, and have no separate inherent power to convey it.

(2.) They say, however, that these are "real means of grace," that "they are not, as Romanists teach, the exclusive channels; but they are not channels." Hodge's Sys. Theol., vol. 3, p. 499.

(3.) They also assert that they are "sacred signs and seals of the covenant of grace." Westminster Confess., ch. 27, sec. 1.

(4.) They hold that the efficacy of the Sacraments depends "upon the work of the Spirit, and the word of institution, which contains, together with a precept authorizing the use thereof, a promise of benefit to worthy receivers." West. Conf., ch. 27, sec. III.

This position is preferable to that of the Romanists inasmuch as:

1. It recognized the necessary presence of the Spirit in connection with the grace bestowed, and thus denies that this proceeds exclusively from any natural inherent power.

2. The benefits are said to be conferred only upon those "who worthily receive the Sacraments." By this possibly meant persons receiving them through the exercise of true faith in Christ. Such is generally the position assumed by the various theologians of these churches as to the adult recipients of the Sacraments. But it should have been more clearly stated in their creeds. The language used could mean this in adult receivers only. Yet it is almost certain that the intention was to include infants among those who "worthily receive." He, however, who "worthily receives" through faith must be capable of personal faith. If the receiver is not himself a believer, he does not receive "through faith." He may receive *because* of the faith of another, but it is *through* the personal exercise of faith, and not on account of its exercise by others, that the Scriptures teach that the Christian is blessed in connection with the ordinances.

The objections to this form of the doctrine are:

1. The continued use of the word sacrament. It has no Scripture authority. It has led many to attach a superstitious sacredness to these ordinances.

2. The use of the word "seal" is also objectionable. A seal is a visible stamp, or impression which is made upon a paper or some other substance for the purpose of certifying to the truth of some fact thus implied. It may either be attached personally by the one whom it represents, or by some person authorized by him; but its presence by his authority is his testimony to the genuineness or correctness of what is witnessed.

Now either of the ordinances makes a visible mark upon their recipients. They are thus without an important characteristic of the seal. Neither of them is affixed to a designated individual by divine authority. The authority to administer is only a general one. No man can put marks upon the elect of God which shall authoritatively certify that they are his. Neither Baptism, nor the Lord's Supper, becomes such an authentication either to the recipient or to others. This is found in the conscious possession of true faith, or in the manifestation of that faith by the good works of his life.

This common usage of the word "seal" in connection with the ordinances has no other Scriptural support than the reference to Abraham in Rom. 4:11. "He received the sign of circumcision, a seal of the righteousness of the faith which he had while he was in uncircumcision." Cf. Gen. 17:11. But the rite then performed had the characteristics of a seal which have been denied of Baptism and the Lord's Supper. It was a visible mark and not only so, but it was applied to the individual man Abraham by direct divine authority.

3. Objection may also be made to the word "sign" in the sense in which it is used. These two ordinances are indeed "signs;" but signs of what Christ did and suffered, and not of what is done to is people. Yet it is in the latter sense that the word "sign" is exclusively used by those holding this opinion.

4. The use of these two words has let to the mistake about the manner in which these two ordinances are means of grace, which constitutes the fatal error of this opinion. They are means of grace as they set forth truth, as they teach something, and only in this way do they convey grace. In the act of receiving, that grace may be conferred either from the consciousness of an act of obedience or through the apprehension and comprehension of the truth symbolized. It can come in no other way. The strongest expression in Scripture in favour of the grace-conveying power of an ordinance—that in 1 Pet. 3:21, in which the apostle speaks of "water: which also after a true likeness (in the antitype) doth now save you, even baptism,"—is at once explained by him to be not the ordinance, but the spiritual condition in which it is received, viz. "not the putting away of the filth of the flesh, but the interrogation (inquiry, appeal) of a good conscience toward God through the resurrection of Jesus Christ."

Serious has been the error which has resulted from these expressions and the doctine taught in connection with them. It has led men actually to teach that the grace of God has been really conferred upon or pledged to a recipient by the agency of the administrator. In the Anglican Catechism the question is put to the child: "Who gave you this name?" to which it is taught to reply: "My God-father and God-mother, in my baptism, wherein I was made a member of Christ, the child of God, and an inheritor of the kingdom of heaven." Here the ordinance performed upon an unconscious subject is taught to have produced regenerating power. This doctrine of baptismal regeneration has been commonly regarded as unscriptural and false by evangelical Christians. But is the effect declared of this baptismal act any more a matter of the mere human choice and will and action of some one who is not the recipient, than is the result ascribed by an eminent Presbyterian theologian to the baptism of the child of a believer? He says: "And so when a believer adopts the covenant of grace, he brings his children within that covenant in the sense that God promises to give them, in his own good time, all the benefits of redemption, provided they do not willingly renounce their baptismal engagements." Hodge's "Syst. Theology," vol. 3, p. 555.

3. The true statement of the sanctifying power of these ordinances seems the rather to be—

(1.) A denial of all inherent power in them as means of grace.

(2.) Recognition of them as conveying truth by symbolical instruction.

(3.) The fact that they are partaken of because of the command of Christ also makes the act of obedience to him a means of grace to the recipient.

(4.) Only as truth is, in some way or other, brought by them to the acceptance of the heart and mind, can they have sanctifying power.

It is thus seen that all the means of sanctification are connected with the truth, and are secondary to it. They only become such, as they convey truth, or as they suggest truth, or as they are employed in the recognition of some truth.

CHAPTER 38

FINAL PERSEVERANCE OF THE SAINTS

THE doctrine of the final perseverance of the saints teaches that those who are effectually called of God to the exercise of genuine faith in Christ will certainly persevere unto final salvation. This is not taught of a class of mankind in general, as something that will usually be true of the persons composing that class, but of each individual in it—so that not one will finally apostatize or be lost; but each will assuredly persevere and be saved.

This fact is taught explicitly in the Word of God, which sets it forth as due to the purpose and power of God and the grace which he bestows, and not to any excellence or power in the believer. Indeed, such is stated to be the weakness of man that, if left to himself, he would assuredly fall, against the danger of which he is constantly warned; a danger to which even the best instructed and most sanctified are liable, and which is evidenced by the sins which are committed, which are often of a most heinous character, sometimes extending to actual denial of the faith, and backsliding from God; showing that but for God's mercy and grace, final apostacy would occur. But, from the danger thus due to himself, he is rescued by the power and grace of God, who, by his watchful preservation, keeps guard over his unworthy children, preventing their total estrangement from him, and bringing them finally unto the salvation he has designed for them. In so doing, however, he does not act independently of their co-operation, but leads them unto salvation through their own perseverance in faith and holiness.

1. The Scriptures teach the final salvation of all believers.

(1.) The Psalmist sang, "Though he fall, he shall not utterly be cast down: for the Lord upholdeth him with his hand. . . The Lord loveth judgement, and forsaketh not his saints; they are preserved forever." Ps. 37:24–28. The wise man said: "The path of the righteous is as the shining light, that shineth more and more unto the perfect day." Prov. 4:18. Isaiah, referring to the true Israel of God, said "Fear not, for I have redeemed thee; I have called thee by thy name, thou art mine. When thou passest through the waters, I will be with thee; and through the rivers, they shall not overflow thee: when thou walkest through the fire, thou shall not be burned; neither shall the flame kindle upon thee. For I am the Lord thy God, the Holy One of Israel, thy Saviour. . . Every one that is called by my name, and whom I have created for my glory; I have formed him; yea, I have made him." Isa. 43:1, 2–7. "Israel shall be saved by the Lord with an everlasting salvation; ye shall not be ashamed nor confounded world without end." Isa. 45:17. "The heavens shall vanish away like smoke, and the earth shall wax old like a garment, and they that dwell therein shall die in like manner: but my salvation shall be forever, and my righteousness shall not be abolished." Isa. 51:6. "Incline your ear, and come unto me; hear, and your soul shall live; and I will make an everlasting covenant with you, even the sure mercies of David." Isa. 55:3. "I will make an everlasting covenant with them, that I will not turn away from them, to do them good; and I will put my fear in their hearts, that they shall not depart from me." Jer. 32:40.

Christ himself, referring to the "false Christs and false prophets," who shall rise professedly in his name, teaches the impossibility of deceiving the elect of God by saying "So as to lead astray if possible even the elect." Matt. 24:24. He likewise declared "He that heareth my word, and believeth him that sent me, hath eternal life, and cometh not into judgement, but hath passed out of death into life." John 5:24. To the Samaritan woman he said, "Whosoever drinketh of the water that I shall give him, shall never thirst; but the water that I shall give him shall become in him a well of water springing up unto eternal life." John 4:14. He also affirmed even more expressly the final salvation of each of his people by declaring: "My sheep hear my voice, and I know them, and they follow me: and I give unto them eternal life; and they shall never perish, and no one shall snatch them out of my hand. My Father which hath given them unto me, is greater that all; and no one is able to snatch them out of the Father's hand. I and the Father are one." John 10:27–29.

The apostle Paul presents the effectual calling of those whom God had foreordained to be conformed to the image of his Son, as connected absolutely with their being glorified by him. Rom. 8:30. In the same chapter, vv. 35–39, he declares their separation from the love of Christ impossible. Writing to the Corinthians, he assures them that Christ will "confirm" them "unto the end," so that they shall be "unreprovable in the day of our Lord Jesus Christ," adding "God is faithful, through whom ye were called into the fellowship of his Son Jesus Christ our Lord." 1 Cor. 1:8, 9. To the Philippians he also declares himself "Confident of this very thing that he which hath begun a good work in you will perfect it until the day of Jesus Christ." Phil. 1:6. In like manner he says to the Thessalonians "The Lord is faithful, who shall stablish you and guard you from the evil one." 2 Thess. 3:3. Peter also writes to the "sojourners of the dispersion" as unto the persons who had been begotten unto a living hope by the resurrection of Jesus Christ from the dead, unto an inheritance incorruptible, and undefiled, and that fadeth not away, reserved in heaven for you, who by the power of God are guarded, through faith unto a salvation ready to be revealed in the last time." 1 Pet. 1:3–5.

(2.) This doctrine is inseparably associated with the other doctrines of grace which we have found taught in God's Word. So true is this, that they are universally accepted, or rejected together. The perseverance of the saints is a part of every Calvinistic confession. It is rejected by Romanists, Lutherans, and Arminians. All the evidence, therefore, of the truth of the doctrines already examined, may be presented in favour of this which is a necessary inference from them. In like manner, all the independent proof of this doctrine confirms the separate doctrines, and the system of doctrine, with which it is associated.

2. The Scriptures declare that the sure salvation of each believer is due to the purpose of God. This would be naturally inferred from some of the doctrines to which reference has just been made. But it is distinctly asserted. Those who believe are said to have been "ordained to eternal life." Acts 13:48. Those finally glorified are said to have been foreordained to be conformed to the image of his Son, and, therefore, called. Rom. 8:29. Referring to the falling away of some, the apostle writes to Timothy declaring that nevertheless the "Firm foundation of God standeth, having this seal, "The Lord knoweth them that are his" (2 Tim. 2:19), thus establishing the identity of those that are thus known with those who shall remain steadfast. Our Lord himself declared this final salvation to be the will of God. "This is the will of him that sent me, that of all that which he hath given me I should lose nothing, but should raise it up at the last day." John 6:39.

3. The final salvation of the believer is ascribed to the power of God.

It is the power of Christ, and of God, which makes it impossible that the sheep shall be snatched from their hands. John 10:27–29. It is God that will perform the good work which he had begun. Phil. 1:6. "It is God which worketh in you," says the apostle to the Philippians, "both to will and to work for his good pleasure." Phil. 2:13. Peter addresses his readers as those "Who by the power of God are guarded through faith unto salvation ready to be revealed in the last time." 1 Pet. 1:5. He likewise invokes that "Grace . . . and peace be multiplied" to those who "have obtained a like precious faith," . . . "seeing that his divine power hath granted unto us all things that pertain unto life and godliness." 2 Pet. 1:1–3. The Apostle Paul declares that it is God that is to be thanked because of the growth of faith. 2 Thess. 1:3. In the same chapter he says, "We also pray for you, that our God may count you worthy of your calling, and fulfill every desire of goodness, and every work of faith, with power." 2 Thess 1:11. It is in reliance, upon this power, that Paul triumphantly wrote to Timothy, "I know him whom I have believed and am persuaded that he is able to guard that which I have committed unto him against that day." 2 Tim. 1:12.

4. The final salvation is also ascribed to the grace of God. Not only is the power of God exercised; but it is graciously exercised. His aid is a gift of unmerited favour. The apostle to the Romans asserts that salvation must needs be of faith, that it might be of grace, "to the end that the promise may be sure to all seed." Rom. 4:16. It is only "as many as are led by the Spirit of God" that "are the sons of God." Rom. 8:14. "It is not of him that willeth, nor of him that runneth, but of God that hath mercy." Rom. 9:16. This gracious character, which is ascribed to the whole work of salvation, is not less true of it in the end, than in the beginning. Hence, when the apostle prays for his brethren at Thessalonica, "may your spirit and soul and body be preserved entire without blame at the coming of our Lord Jesus Christ," he immediately adds "faithful is he that calleth you, who will also do it." 1 Thess. 5:23, 24. That faithfulness consists in the fulfillment of gracious promises, and not of matters of obligation and duty.

5. That the perseverance of believers depends necessarily upon the purpose and power and grace of God, will still further appear from the natural weakness of the Christian and his liability to fall. Even an innocent and pure human being must be fallible, because he is a mere creature, and may therefore choose evil instead of good. We have a sad illustration of this in the fall of our first parents. It may be doubted whether the confirmation of holy angels, or saints, is due to anything in themselves, or in their condition, or state. It is most probable that their only ground of confidence is in the purpose and promise of God. But the Christian is not free from sin. He does not in this life attain perfect sanctification. Hence the constant tendencies to sin, the liability to temptation from within, and from without, and the utter dependence upon the grace of God for his progress in the divine life. These have been pointed out in the discussion about his sanctification. The Scripture teaches the fact expressly in such passages as 1 John 1:8–10, and 2:1. It is also to be inferred from the frequent warnings against the power of temptation, and the necessity of resisting it from whatever source it may arise. We are taught not only the liability to sin from our own corrupted natures, and from the influences of the world around; but also that we have a spiritual enemy to contend with in Satan who zealously, and with much craft and subtilty, seeks the destruction of the children of God.

Nor does the Bible alone give warnings of what may possibly happen, but the religious experience also of the Christian which is one of constant struggles against the evil of sin. These struggles the Word of God teaches not only to be consistent with a state of gracious acceptance with God, but to be an evidence of such a state; inasmuch as they show the believer is no longer "dead in trespasses and sins," but is engaged in a conflict to destroy, and escape them. In this warfare the strange condition is presented of divine strength perfected in human weakness. While the Scriptures command watchfulness and prayer against temptations (Mark 14:38), and enforce the command by the fearful conflict of our Lord in Gethsemane, they also encourage believers by the assurance that "God is faithful, who will not suffer you to be tempted above that ye are able; but will with the temptation make also the way of escape, that ye may be able to endure it." 1 Cor. 10:13. "Wherefore," said the apostle, "I take pleasure in weaknesses, in injuries, in necessities, in persecutions, in distresses, for Christ's sake: for when I am weak then am I strong." 2 Cor. 12:10. In the preceding verse he gives the reason why he thus rejoices, viz.: He said unto me, my grace is sufficient for thee: for my power is made perfect in weakness."

6. The weakness thus taught of the Christian is not confined to those who have just begun their career of faith, or who are babes in Christ, but is found also in the best instructed, and most sanctified, to such an extent as to make necessary their continued watchfulness and prayer. It was to those whom the apostle wrote, "in every thing ye were enriched in him, in all utterance and all knowledge . . . so that ye come behind in no gift," 1 Cor. 1:4–7, that he found it necessary to say "let him that thinketh he standeth, take heed lest he fall," 1 Cor. 10:12. They also whose "faith" was "proclaimed throughout the whole world," Rom. 1:8, needed the warning "Well; by their unbelief they were broken off, and thou standest by the faith. Be not high-minded, but fear: for if God spared not the natural branches, neither will he spare thee." Rom. 11:20, 21. They were our Lord's chosen companions whom he taught to pray, "Bring us not into temptation, but deliver us from the evil one." Matt. 6:13. These also were the ones to whom primarily the warning of Christ was given with the accompanying scene at Gethsemane. Even Paul at the very moment in which he declared, "I therefore so run, as not uncertainly; so fight I, as not beating the air," added, "but I buffet my body, and bring it into bondage: lest by any means, after that I have preached to others, I myself should be rejected." 1 Cor. 9:26, 27.

7. Nor are examples wanting, not merely of faults and errors committed by Christian men, but of grievous sins; and these in men of the highest religious privileges and attainments. Such was the desertion of Christ by all the apostles, when he was betrayed into the hands of his enemies (Mark 14:50), the thrice denial of his Lord by Peter (Mark 14:66–72), the sharp contention between Paul and Barnabas (Acts 15:39) and the blameworthy conduct of Peter and of the other Jews who dissembled with him, and of Barnabas at Antioch. Gal. 2:11–13. All of these are instances of grievous falls in those who were true believers in Jesus. They can also be paralleled in the lives of God's true servants in the Old Testament times, in the sin of Abraham, Gen. 20:5–13; of Moses, Num. 20:7–13; of Eli, 1 Sam. 2:22–36; of David, 2 Sam. 12:1–14; and of Hezekiah, 2 Kings 20:12–21.

The extent to which this weakness of man is seen to exhibit itself is evidence not only of what, but for the intervention of God, might occur in each case, but, also, that, so far as man is concerned, the final apostasy of each one is not only possible but probable, nay certain. We thus have additional proof that the final salvation is due to the purpose, power and grace of God.

8. This salvation, is, however, secured only through the co-operation of the believer. It is not one bestowed on him in his sins; but through deliverance from his sins. It is not merely preservation by God, but also perseverance of the believer, in faith and holiness, unto the end. It is the good work begun in the Christian which is performed until the day of Jesus Christ. Phil. 1:6. The confirmation to the end secures that they shall be "unreprovable in the day of our Lord Jesus Christ." I Cor. 1:8. The preordination is unto conformity to the image of his Son. Rom. 8:29. This is secured by various means:

(a.) Faith is one of these.

Christians "by the power of God are guarded through faith unto a salvation." 1 Pet. 1:5. "Whatsoever is begotten of God overcometh the world: and this is the victory that hath overcome the world, even our faith." 1 John 5:4. "As many as received him, to them gave he the right to become children of God, even to them that believe on his name." John 1:12. "These are written, that ye may believe that Jesus is the Christ, the Son of God; and that believing ye may have life in his name." John 20:31.

(b.) It is also accomplished by consecration to God.

This is earnestly enjoined upon the people of God because of the great privileges bestowed upon them. Paul besought the Romans by the mercies of God to present their bodies a living sacrifice unto God. Rom. 12:1. He urged the Ephesians to be followers of God, as dear children, and walk in love, not allowing certain sins which he mentioned to be once named among them as they were unbecoming to saints. Eph. 5:1–4. The writer to the Hebrews, also, surrounding himself and his brethren with a cloud of martyrs, exhorts "lay aside every weight, and the sin which doth so easily beset us, looking unto Jesus the author and perfecter of our faith." Heb. 12:1.

(c.) Self-purification from sin is another of the means.

We find Paul urging upon his brethren at Rome "Neither present your members unto sin as instruments of unrighteousness; but present yourselves unto God, as alive from the dead, and your members as instruments of righteousness unto God," Rom. 6:13. So, also, in view of their adoption by God, he exhorts the Corinthians, "Let us cleanse ourselves from all defilement of flesh and spirit, perfecting holiness in the fear of God," 2 Cor. 7:1. "They that are of Christ" are said to "have crucified the flesh with the passions and the lusts thereof," Gal. 5:24. The Apostle John declares that "every one that hath this hope set on him purifieth himself, even as he (Christ) is pure," 1 John 3:3.

(d.) The warnings of God's Word are also means to the same end. They imply the importance of Christian exertion, and the value of effort as well as the possibility of danger. The Hebrews were warned that they should fear lest, a promise being left of rest, any of them should seem to come short of it. Heb. 4:1. They are especially warned to go on unto perfection, upon the statement that "As touching those who were once enlightened, and tasted of the heavenly gift, and were made partakers of the Holy Ghost, and tasted the word of God, and the powers of the age to come, and then fall away, it is impossible to renew them again unto repentance; seeing they crucify to themselves the Son of God afresh, and put him to an open shame," Heb. 6:4–6. This was a description of such persons as they themselves were; of real Christians. They were, in themselves, in real danger of such a fall. They were only secure from it through the purpose and power and grace of God. This danger was therefore a fit cause for exhortation to them to push forward unto perfection. There were doubtless many around them who had appeared, or had professed to have the privileges here referred to, who, by their desertion of Christianity, were inflicting grievous evil upon the cause of Christ. These Christians were tempted to commit the same sin. Should they do this, they could not be renewed again unto repentance; and this warning was given as the means under God of restraining them from sin. It is thought by some that this passage shows the possibility of a fall from grace, and therefore is contrary to the doctrine of the perseverance of the saints. It is admitted that, regarded in their own strength only, there was this possibility of fall in the persons addressed. But the doctrine we are considering does not regard the believer as preserved and as persevering only through himself. He is thus kept by God; not by his own power. One of the means by which this is done, is that he is warned of the danger in which he is of himself, that he may co-operate with God, so as not only to be preserved, but also to persevere in the divine life. Of like purpose, and to the same effect, are the other warnings found in the tenth chapter of this epistle in verses 26–29, 38, and those in 2 Pet. 2:20, 22, and elsewhere in the Scriptures.

The means mentioned are only some of the numerous ways in which the Christian is led to persevere in the divine life, actively co-operating with the grace of God. It is because God bestows, and man attains, as the apostle Peter so completely sets forth in his preceding remarks, that he exhorts his brethren, "give the more diligence to make your calling and election sure," adding, "for if ye do these things, ye shall never stumble: for thus shall be richly supplied unto you the entrance into the eternal kingdom of our Lord and Saviour Jesus Christ." 2 Pet. 1:10, 11. It is because of the divine help afforded through the incarnation, and humiliation, and consequent exaltation of Christ Jesus, that the apostle could urge the Philippians, "work out your own salvation with fear and trembling; for it is God which worketh in you both to will and to work for his good pleasure." Phil. 2:12, 13.

It will be seen, from the preceding statements, that the doctrine of the perseverance of the saints does not deny that Christians are liable to sin, not that they do sin, nor that they do turn away from God, and backslide from their Christian profession, and even fall into grievous wrong, by which they displease God, and lose confidence and hope in him, and become barren and unfruitful in good works; nor does it deny that final apostasy would be possible to the Christian if he were left to the exercise of his own will, subject, as he would be, not only to the natural fallibility of a creature, but to the still continuing lusts of his flesh, and tempted not only by these, but by the attractions of the world, and the malice of Satan. But it asserts, that it is the purpose of God that none shall finally be lost who have been given to Christ by the Father, and have been by faith vitally united with him, and justified through him; and that, for the fulfillment of this purpose, the power of God is sufficient to keep them unto final salvation, and the love of Christ is so invincible, in his forbearance, mercy, and grace, that nothing can separate them from it. It also teaches, that they are not saved while indulging in sin, and walking after their own lusts; but that they are sanctified through the work of the Holy Spirit, which enables them to persevere in the divine life in co-operation with his influences, that their life and salvation is not a mere gift without effort on their part, but a growth through perseverance unto the end in the use of the appointed means.

It is well to notice briefly some of the objections presented to this doctrine.

1. One of the most plausible of these is based upon the apostasy of the nation of Israel despite the many promises with which it was blessed.

But the analogy of God's dealings with his ancient people, favours, rather than opposes, the doctrine of final perseverance. Their history presents to us just such cases of backsliding and recovery, as have been pointed out as true of Christian believers. The backsliding was through their sin, the recovery through the power and grace of God. The one followed the other, at greater, or less intervals, but always followed it. Is it said, however, that Israel is now entirely cast away? But such is not the teaching of the Word of God. Paul expressly denies this, and teaches their restoration to God when the fullness of the Gentiles has come in. Rom. 11:26. It is to be remembered also that the calling of Israel was that of the nation, and not of the individual within it. That fact that many Israelites have been lost eternally and beyond rescue, does not affect the fulfillment of any gracious purpose of God towards the nation as such.

There are many, however, who interpret all the promises for the future as made simply of the gathering of the spiritual Israel. Even were this position incorrect there has been no failure in God's covenant relation to the natural

Israel, for the promises to it were all based upon the condition of their faithfulness to God. God, therefore, has not failed, even if he has cast them off forever.

It is especially to be noticed, also, that the new covenant made in Christ, is one which includes not only the promise of the blessings, but of the establishment in his people of the conditions upon which these blessings depend. The nature of the new covenant is set forth in the prophecy of Jeremiah, and, with its statements, many other Scripture passages concur. From its very nature, it is impossible that the blessings promised in it should not be given to all the people of God. "Behold, the days come, saith the Lord, that I will make a new covenant with the house of Israel, and with the house of Judah: not according to the covenant I made with their fathers in the day that I took them by the hand to bring them out of the land of Egypt; which my covenant they brake, although I was an husband unto them, saith the Lord. But this is the covenant that I will make with the house of Israel after those days: saith the Lord; I will put my law in their inward parts, and in their hearts will I write it, and I will be their God, and they shall be my people: and they shall teach no more every man his neighbor, and every man his brother, saying, know the Lord: for I will forgive their iniquity, and their sin I will remember no more." Jer. 31:31–34. See also Jer. 32:38–40.

2. It is again objected that the warnings against apostasy, and exhortations to perseverance, imply the impossibility and danger of fall on the part of those to whom they were addressed. Even if this were absolutely true, it would not be proof that any have fallen away, or shall fall away. These very warnings might become effective to guard against the danger, as the signs set up in hazardous places, are the means by which the danger is avoided. But, as has been already explained, this danger arises solely from the believer if left to himself; the certainty that he will not finally fall away depends upon God's purpose to preserve him, and to enable him to persevere. These warnings and exhortations are, therefore, perfectly consistent with his safety, and are the signs of danger which God sets up to prevent the fall of his servants.

3. It is objected, however, that, while we have instances of some who are rescued from their grievous sins and backslidings, the Scripture also gives examples of others who are left to perish. But the doctrine of God's Word is that of the perseverance of believers; of the elect of God; of those called to be saints. An examination of the cases mentioned will show no reason for believing those who thus fell away to have been of this class. Indeed, in most cases the contrary is taught. The case of Judas is the most prominent. It would seem more nearly to correspond, than any other, with the privileges referred to in Heb. 6:4, 5, and yet Christ proclaimed his condition, as not that of a Christian, about a year before his betrayal. "Did I not choose you the twelve, and one of you is a devil? Now he spake of Judas, the son of Simon Iscariot." John 6:70, 71. We need no

better proof that this man, in the betraying of our Lord, did not fall from a state of grace and salvation into the perdition to which he was doomed.

So also as to Simon Magus, Peter expressly declared, "Thou hast neither part nor lot in this matter: for thy heart is not right before God. . . I see that thou art in the gall of bitterness and in the bond of iniquity." Acts 8:21, 23. The apostle John seems, in general terms, to state the truth as to all those who finally depart from the faith. "They went out from us, but they were not of us; for if they had been of us, they would have continued with us: but they went out, that they might be made manifest how that they all are not of us." John 2:19.

CHAPTER 39

DEATH AND THE SOUL'S IMMORTALITY

WE proceed next to the consideration of the death of man, and other topics which are intimately connected with it. In the present chapter will be discussed death; the immortality of the soul; and the condition of the latter between the hour of death, and that of reunion with the body.

I. DEATH

The term death is most commonly applied to that separation of soul and body which is the most manifest form in which the penalty of sin is seen among men. That there is a death of the soul also, and that it is something far more terrible than the death of the body, has been shown in the chapter on the "Effects of Adam's sin," pp. 215–21. But, this death of the soul is spiritual in its nature, and does not forbid the continued existence of the soul; and its dread realities will be more plainly evinced in the unseen hereafter. Consequently the separation of body and soul makes a more profound impression among living men, and to it the term death is almost exclusively appropriated.

It is sometimes called "natural," or "physical" death, to distinguish it from that which is "spiritual;" the death "of the body," as opposed to that "of the soul;" and "temporal" death, in contrast with that which is everlasting.

This separation of body and soul is the almost universal destiny of men. The Scriptures, however, teach that Enoch did not die but "God took him," Gen. 5:24, and that he "was translated that he should not see death," Heb. 11:5; also that Elijah "went up by a whirlwind into heaven," 2 Kings 2:11. Some have supposed that, in like manner Moses escaped death, but it is expressly stated that he died, and was buried in the land of Moab. Deut. 34:5, 6. But Paul declared that at the second coming of the Lord, "we that are alive, that are left, shall together with them be caught up in the clouds, to meet the Lord in the air: and so shall we ever be with the Lord." 1 Thess. 4:17. Even more explicitly he said "we shall not all sleep, but we shall all be changed, in a moment, in the twinkling of an eye, at the last trump: for the trumpet shall sound, and the dead shall be raised incorruptible, and we shall be changed." 1 Cor. 15:51, 52. This is the fashioning anew of "the body of our humiliation that it may be conformed to the body of his glory" foretold in Phil. 3:21.

But, while death comes thus almost universally to all, there is a marked difference between its connection with the righteous, and with the wicked.

The death of the wicked is easily accounted for. It constitutes a part of the penalty of sin, to which, the Scriptures teach, all men are liable (Rom. 5:12, 14; 1 Cor. 15:21, 22, 53–56), but from which, as such, the people of God are exempted because Christ has redeemed then from the curse of the law. The "death of the saint" instead of being accursed, is "precious in the sight of the Lord," (Ps. 116:15), and this because he has redeemed them. Ps. 72:14. His death is a death "unto the Lord." Rom. 14:8. Death is his. 1 Cor. 3:22. Its sting has been removed. 1 Cor. 15:56. But no one of these things is true of the wicked. He has neglected, or rejected the offer of salvation through Christ Jesus. There is no other method of escape from the penalty; and it rests upon him in all its fullness.

It is not so easy to account for the death of the righteous. As he is no longer liable to the penalty of sin, there is no legal ground upon which he must endure death, and, because of which, he cannot be released. This is confirmed by the fact that some righteous have not died, and others will only be changed. But, while death may not thus be legally necessary, it may subserve many purposes in the gracious providence of God, and is, ordinarily, the best way for the Christian to attain the "change" for which he is destined. This should be believed even if it could in no respect be explained.

It ought not to be forgotten that this is not the only dealing of God with his people, which evidently arises from some wise purpose which he has not fully revealed. They might have been taken out of the world as soon as they were justified. Yet, that this is graciously and wisely prevented, is evident from Christ's declining to pray for it. John 17:15. They might have been preserved from affliction, and persecution, and similar inflictions from God or man. That these are blessed to them, is no proof that they would not have been more blessed without them, for they are taught to look forward to greater bliss in their exemption from them in heaven. Our Lord prayed that they might be kept from the Evil One, and they are doubtless protected from his power in answer to this prayer, but they are still left subject to his influences, and temptations, and are very far from escaping the presence and pollution of sin. In all of these things, we see some reasons for the action of God, though our knowledge is imperfect and incomplete. It ought not to be thought strange if, in like manner, we can only account partially for the death of true believers.

1. Some have thought that, for the attainment of perfect sanctification, it is necessary that the soul and body be separated, and the body reduced to its original elements. That this is not necessary is manifest from the examples of exemption from death already stated. But it may be admitted to be the ordinary

method which God has ordained for such sanctification. For the desired perfection, there must be removal of the passions and appetites of the flesh by which man is tempted not only from himself, but through himself. The "change" at the last day accomplishes this in an extraordinary manner. The more ordinary method of God seems to be through death, in which, by its separation from the sinful body, the soul is freed from these temptations, and enabled to live perfectly the life of holiness for which it longs.

2. Another opinion which has been expressed, is, that death is natural to man, and that it, from its nature, becomes the means of his passing from a lower to a higher condition; in which through a more advanced organism the soul may live a more exalted life.

This opinion may be held either about the original, or the fallen condition of man. If about the original condition, it involves the position that the body of man was created mortal, and that its death, as a penalty, was not something superadded when man sinned; but is simply the natural condition of man's life used by God as penalty, and so made known to man.

If held, however, only as to man's present natural condition, it would not necessarily involve an original mortality.

As to this opinion, in either form, as well as to the former, it is necessary that it recognize death simply as the ordinary method of man's passing into another life; for in respect to each of them the exemption of some shows that the end may be by other means accomplished. It derives some support from the analogy of the necessity of death in the seed for its change to a higher form presented in 1 Cor. 15:36–38.

3. Death is supposed by some to be necessary for a life of faith, rather than of sight, in the Christian. It is thought, that, on this account, it would be injurious to make so marked a distinction between the righteous, and the wicked, as would exist in the death of the latter and the change of the former in some other way. But the reason for this opinion is not apparent. It might be true, were the Christian personally changed in body as soon as he believes. But it would not be, if the change should occur only at the time when, otherwise, his death would take place. Doubtless the translation of Enoch was one fitted to produce a profound impression on his contemporaries. It certainly had had no evil influence on his own life. So, if the Christian should have no other certainty of exemption from death, than he now has of salvation, he could derive no motives from that exemption which would militate against his life of faith. It is much more probably because God does not choose to continue the miraculous testimony to the truth of Christianity throughout all time. But had he done this, the lives of Christians in the later ages would have been no less lives of faith than were those of Apostolic times.

4. It has been more generally stated that death is a means of chastisement. It has been shown that, while suffering is common to both, it is inflicted in punishment, by an angry God, in the way of penalty and in chastisement, but by a loving Father, only for correction and discipline; and thus, that the same event, death, may be a curse to the wicked, and a blessing to the righteous. It has been argued that this is the reason why even a Christian man must die. This is true so far as the death of a Christian is a cause of suffering and pain, either in death itself, or in his contemplation of it. It is undoubtedly often a cause of this kind. Even to the Christian it assumes not always an aspect altogether pleasant. He naturally shrinks from its loathsome embrace. It is an enemy, even if it is "the last enemy," and one over which he is "more than conqueror." But death is not always regarded with dread. The Christian's thoughts sometimes leap forward to it with exultant joy. Especially is it true, that seldom, if ever, in the hour of death is the true Christian filled with apprehension and gloom. His own death becomes no chastisement in the event itself. God in that hour gives such sustaining grace that each of his servants is hopeful, peaceful, joyful, even sometimes triumphant.

5. Whether able or not definitely to state on what grounds the Christian is subjected to death, we know that it is a blessing to him. The inquiry into its cause and the various reasons suggested proceed apparently on the supposition that it is an evil which it would be desirable had he been spared. But the Scriptures speak of death as among the "all things" which belong to the Christian. 1 Cor. 3:22. This does not deny its possibly painful character, but asserts that, however painful, it is made his possession, and therefore is used for his benefit. This is in accordance with the universal law of blessing to him which the apostle announces in Rom. 8:28: "We know that to them that love God all things work together for good, to them that are called according to his purpose." The principle of this law, however, admits either blessing or suffering. The suffering in connection with death was pointed out under the previous division. It will suffice briefly to indicate here some of the blessings also associated with it.

(1.) Death is a blessing to the Christian because, through its contemplation, his sanctification and purification in this life is carried forward. This contemplation of it includes all aspects in which it presents itself, whether painful or otherwise.

(2.) It is a blessing because in it he looks forward to the attainment of final freedom from sin and to perfect sanctification.

(3.) It is a blessing because he recognizes it as the portal to the possession of eternal life.

(4.) Death is a blessing because it gives him an opportunity of giving strong testimony in favor of Christ and his religion.

(5.) It is felt to be a blessing because it opens the doors to immediate conscious personal presence with his Saviour.

These points are obvious and need not be elaborated.

II. IMMORTALITY

When the immortality of the soul is spoken of, its unending future life is usually meant. This is the immortality which is common to the righteous, and the wicked. The righteous, however, possess, also, that true immortality which the Scriptures teach to be that of the true life of the soul.

1. The unending life of the soul has been argued upon various grounds.

(1.) Reason alone has been supposed by many to furnish adequate arguments in proof of its truth.

(a.) The longing of the soul for immortal existence has been deemed to be an instinct implanted within, which gives assurance of its gratification. But, while, with a few, there may have been aspirations after a nobler and better life than that of earth, it may be questioned whether, in the vast multitude of men, there is more than a shrinking from the loss of such life as is possessed in the present stage of existence. The instinct seems, therefore, to be rather that dread of death which is not unknown to the mere animal, and which is given for the protection of the life that now is, and not as a basis of hope of that which may be hereafter.

(b.) The inequality, which is so manifest in the apportionment of good and evil to the characters and conduct of men on earth, has, almost universally, led to the belief of a future life, in which these will be duly adjusted. But, by these facts, is taught merely a future life, and not one necessarily of an unending duration; but only of sufficient length for such adjustment. It is the Word of God alone that teaches that the bliss or woe, which is the portion of man at death, will continue forever. It must be acknowledged, however, that, as universal as has been the belief in a state of future rewards and punishments, equally so has been the opinion that it shall never end.

(c.) This general belief in an unending life, has also been accounted for on the supposition that it is an intuitive perception of the mind. But it does not appear that such knowledge as reason can give of what the soul is, and of what endless existence means, awakens at once the conviction that the soul must exist forever. The most thoughtful men, who have been guided by nature only, have been afflicted with doubts, and alternate hopes, and fears, without attaining more than earnest, or, at most, confident expectations, much less such knowledge of a continuous future, as would result from the existence of an intuitive conception.

(d.) The capacity of indefinite progress in the mental and moral powers of men, has seemed, to many, to indicate a stage of being in which it may be developed. But no one will assert that there is here more than an indication, which is opposed by the evidence of the great waste in the productions of nature, and which, therefore, needs confirmation from some more decisive source to become other than a mere expectation.

(e.) Some metaphysicians have argued the indestructible nature of the soul from its pure simplicity. They have believed it to be uncompounded, and, therefore, incapable of dissolution, and consequent destruction. This is based upon the belief that it is purely spiritual, and that simplicity is a necessary attribute of spirit. But these facts are difficult to prove. They are by no means undisputed among those who rely on reason alone. It is from the Scriptures that we learn the different origin of body and soul, and that the latter came not from matter. Philosophy has not always regarded that soul as a unit. The terms "soul", "mind", and "spirit," indicate a tendency to recognize, at least, some threefold aspects in the human spirit, in accordance with which, even while asserting the absolute unity of the soul, Mental Philosophy has recognized the threefold division of the will, the understanding, and the affections. It is well known that the most of the Grecian philosophers, following Plato, held to a distinction between ψυχή (*psuche,* the animal life or soul), and νοῦς *(nous)* and πνεῦμα (*pneuma,* the rational spirit). Even some Christian writers of our own day have maintained the same views. In this state of uncertainty, therefore, reason cannot speak convincingly of an ever continuing life of man, on the ground of the simplicity, and consequent indestructibility, of his spiritual nature.

It appears, therefore, that, from reason alone, all that can be attained, even as to a merely future state, is expectation; or at most belief upon uncertain grounds. It is true that, if it could be established, that the soul dies with the body, certain hopes, and fears would remain unaccounted for, and certain problems of divine government would be unexplained; but these could, at most, only produce conviction of some future state; and would prove nothing as to its unending or even indefinite duration.

(2.) The Scriptures, however, teach plainly the continued existence of all men after death.

(a.) It is everywhere assumed as a fact, neither to be doubted, nor proved; but that will be at once received without question.

(b.) The cases of Enoch and Elijah gave signal proof of another world than this into which even men might enter. But they furnished no evidence that any other than these two would go thither. They simply showed that the possible existence of men, otherwise than on this earth, has been actually realized in these servants of God. But, so far from thus furnishing conclusive proof of the future life of other men, the fact that these were not removed through death, but by extraordinary means, naturally suggested the possibility that exemption from death is necessary to that life, and that all those who go down to the grave perish together. It was only to those otherwise taught of the continued existence of the soul, that their removal gave confirmatory proof of such immortality. In like manner, we are taught the same truths by the presence of Moses, and Elijah, at the scene of the Transfiguration. The appearance at various times of angels to men furnishes additional proof of another world. The resurrection and ascension of Jesus Christ confirm most conclusively the doctrine of a future life.

(c.) The Scriptures teach, in the account of the creation of man, that his soul did not originate from the dust; but was a direct spiritual creation of God. Gen. 2:7. They make further statements about the difference between soul, and body, confirmatory of the distinction made in their creation. Gen. 25:8; 35:29; Ecc. 12:7; Matt. 10:28; Acts 7:59.

(d.) They make express reference to the existence of the soul after death. 2 Sam. 12:23; Job 19:25–27. [Conant translates this passage. "But I, I know my Redeemer lives, and in aftertime will stand upon the earth; and after this my skin is destroyed, and without my flesh, I shall see God. Whom I, for myself, shall see, and my eyes behold, and not another, when my reins are consumed within me"]. Matt. 22:32; 25:46; Luke 16:19–31; John 11:25; 2 Cor. 5:1–4.

(e.) They make known that this future life is the lot of the wicked, as well as of the righteous; teaching that it is one of happiness to the latter, and of condemnation and misery to the former. Matt. 25:46; John 6:47; 12:25; 1 Cor. 15:17–20.

(f.) They declare the continuance of this, at least until the day of the Resurrection and Final Judgement. Job 21:30; Ecc. 3:17; Luke 14:14; John 5:28, 29; Acts 24:15; Rom. 14:10; 1 Cor. 15:51, 52; 2 Cor. 5:10; 1 Thess. 4:13–17.

(g.) They represent the decisions of the judgement day as fixing the destinies of men, for an unending existence. The evidence of this teaching will be given in the discussion of "The Judgement Day."

The Scriptures are thus seen to teach conclusively the doctrine of an unending future life of all men. This, as has been stated, is what is commonly referred to as the immortality of the soul.

Before passing from this part of the discussion, special attention is called to the following statements of what is included in this kind of immortality.

1. Unending existence essentially belongs to spiritual natures. When, therefore, the Scriptures have taught that the soul is a spirit, the way is prepared for the metaphysical argument based upon the simplicity of the soul, and its consequent indestructibility. It is common, therefore, to speak of the natural immortality of the soul. By this is meant, that, because of its nature, it has an unending life. It has no elements of dissolution in it. Life belongs to it, because

it is spirit. Just as God has made extension, and divisibility, properties of matter, so, has he made unending life a natural property of the spirit.

2. But this essential property of spirit must ever be recognized as one conferred upon it. It is because God has so made spirit, that it has unending life. It is not a property that belongs to it from any necessity in God, or out of God. It is the result of his purpose, or will, and of his power. He has made spirit to be thus, Because he has so willed. Doubtless, had he otherwise chosen, the result would have been different. To believe otherwise is to put an unjustifiable limit upon his power, and upon his absolute freedom of will, as to all outward matters. It thus appears that they speak falsely, even blasphemously, who say that God could not destroy, or annihilate spirit, if he should choose. That which prevents annihilation, is that he has not so chosen, and will not so choose.

The impossibility is not in the lack of power, but in the unchangeableness of his will. This is no imperfection of inability, but the highest perfection of immutability.

The immortality, which has been thus far discussed, is that which is common to both the righteous and the wicked. In the beginning of this part of this chapter, it was stated that the righteous possess also that immortality which is the true life of the soul. The death of the soul, and its life, are set forth in the Word of God as something distinct, not only from that of the body, but even from the unending natural life of the soul. The spiritual death of the soul has been described in the chapter on the Effects of Adam's Sin, pp. 215–21, as something different from natural death, and as constituting the most fearful of the penalties inflicted because of sin. It was there shown that the Scriptures describe it in the various aspects of alienation from God, loss of God's favour, and corruption of the moral nature. The true immortality of the Christian consists in the removal of all these evils, and the bestowment upon him of their corresponding blessings. That this is done, and that this is the condition into which he is thus brought will abundantly appear from the following passages of Scripture. Matt. 10:39; 16:25 (cf. Mark 8:35); 18:9; (parallel passages, Mark 9:45; Luke 9:24; 17:33; John 12:25); 19:17; John 3:36; 5:24, 40; 6:33, 35, 50–58, 63; 20:31; Rom. 6:4; 8:6, 13; 2 Cor. 3:6; Eph. 4:18; 1 John 3:14; 5:12.

The contrast in immortality, between the righteous and the wicked, is very marked. "The wicked is thrust down in his evil doing: but the righteous hath hope in his death." Prov. 14:32. "When a wicked man dieth, his expectation shall perish." Prov. 11:7. But "blessed are the dead which die in the Lord;" . . . . "for their works follow with them." Rev. 14:13.

The happiness of this immortality of the Christian is the greater because it is a state in which he is confirmed forever. The law of this condition, both of the righteous, and the wicked, is laid down in Rev. 22:11. "He that is unrighteous, let him do unrighteousness still: and he that is filthy, let him be made filthy still: and he that is righteous, let him do righteousness still: and he that is holy, let him be made holy still." As the wicked shall not change his state, so shall not the righteous, his. The day of his trial and probation is over, and he stands secure of the bliss of heaven, confirmed by the unfailing promises of God. The scenes, through which he has passed on earth, fill him with no apprehensions that his weakness and insufficiency, will disable him from performing the perfect service of heaven. The recollection of Adam's trial will suggest to him no possibility that he will be subjected to a test which will dissolve forever the bonds which unite him to God. Even the sin of the angels will not alarm him. For he is now assured of that "eternal life which God, who cannot lie, promised before times eternal." Tit. 1:2. This is immortality indeed. This, and not mere continued life, is the life and immortality which he confers, "who abolished death, and brought life and incorruption to light through the gospel." 2 Tim. 1:10.

III. THE INTERMEDIATE STATE

The Scriptures teach that the soul and body that have been separated in death, will be reunited at the Judgement Day. Meantime, the body crumbles into dust, and appears to be totally destroyed. The spirit has returned unto God who gave it. Ecc. 12:7. Hence, at his martyrdom, we hear the first dying Christian "calling upon the Lord, and saying, Lord Jesus, receive my spirit." Acts 7:59.

It is not in accordance with the methods of God in his revelations to man to answer the many inquiries which curiosity might suggest as to this intermediate state of the soul. But much more is taught about it than would at first be imagined. Such facts as are given are valuable to confirm and strengthen faith, and to give consolation. Those may first be mentioned which are common to the righteous and the wicked, and these may be followed by separate statements of the things wherein they differ.

1. As to those respects in which the condition of the righteous and the wicked is the same.

(1.) The soul exists without a body. Unquestionably it has not the body which it had on earth. But some have thought that it has some kind of a body, some spiritual body, which merely corresponds to, and is only thus identified with that of this life. But Paul's discussion of the resurrection shows, that the "spiritual" body is one that is to be raised out of the grave in which the natural body was buried, and that it is "at the last trump" that "the dead shall be raised," 1 Cor. 15:44, 52–54.

Some have argued, that body of some kind is necessary to give location to these spirits. But a spirit may have location without occupying space as a body does. Here may be recalled the quotation made by Hodge from Turretine as to the different relations that bodies, created spirits, and God, sustain to space; given on page 64 of this volume.

(2.) The condition is consequently one of an imperfect life. It is the life of the spirit only, and not that of the man. Human nature is composed of both body and spirit; and his body is as truly a part of a man as is his soul. The condition, therefore, in which disembodied spirits exist, is not that of perfect men, but only of human spirits. This, which is an inference which may be drawn from the two-fold nature of man, is supported by the manner in which the Scriptures refer to the persons in this intermediate state. They are not spoken of as "men," but as "souls," and "spirits." Heb. 12:23; Rev. 6:9; 20:4.

Another proof of this want of perfection of this condition is seen in the fact that the saints attain full entrance into their joy, and the wicked full infliction of their woe, only after the resurrection. Matt. 13:40–43, 49, 50; 25:34, 41, 46; 1 Cor. 15:44–54.

(3.) Both righteous and wicked have conscious life. This might have been inferred from the nature of spirit, which must always be in a state of conscious existence. But it is a plain teaching of the Bible. Luke 16:22–31. The word "Hades" here means the place of departed spirits, and, as the scene occurs after the death of Lazarus, and before the final judgement, so must it be assigned to the intermediate state. In this the rich man is represented as in conscious torment.

The conscious condition of the righteous is taught in 2 Cor. 5:1–8; Phil. 1:21–24; and also in the passages connected with Paradise. Luke 23:42, 43; 2 Cor. 12:4; Rev. 2:7; 22:2.

(4.) Neither the righteous nor the wicked are under probation in this intermediate state. Luke 16:22–31; 2 Cor. 5:10; Rev. 22:11. Even if the language in 1 Pet. 3:19, 20 and 4:6 teaches, as some have taught, that our Lord went to the place of departed spirits, and preached to them; so that to those who had died up to the time of his death was given a probation in the gospel preached to them by him; that would be but a single instance of a favour shown to those who had died before his crucifixion; and, so far from proving a probation beyond the grave, would, from its exceptional character, imply the contrary.

2. The aspects of the intermediate state peculiar to the righteous.

(1.) It is a condition of happiness. Paul declared that "to die is gain," and to depart this life far better than to remain in it. Phil. 1:21–24. He wrote to Timothy, looking forward exultingly to the hour of his death. 2 Tim. 4:6–8. He also referred to his longing for this future, as possessed by him in common with his brethren. 2 Cor. 5:1–8. In the parable of the rich man and Lazarus, the happiness of the latter is described by his being in Abraham's bosom. Luke 16:23.

(2.) It is a condition in which the believer is present with Christ. This is also taught in all the passages referred to in the previous paragraph, except the last; and constitutes in each of them the ground of the happiness which they declare.

(3.) The believer is also said to be in Paradise. Whatever this may mean, whether only a condition or a place, it is unquestionably true that it is intended to convey the idea of the enjoyment of very great happiness. The passages in which Paradise is mentioned are, Luke 23:43; 2 Cor. 12:4; Rev. 2:7. That these teach that it is a place can only be denied on the ground that very highly figurative language is used. Only the first of these, however, refers to the presence of Christ with anyone, and this contains only his promise to the thief on the cross, "To-day shalt thou be with me in Paradise." But the location of Paradise, as made known by the Apostle Paul, 2 Cor. 12:1–4, taken in connection with this first passage, makes it more than probable that it is the place where the saints are with Christ. The Scriptures teach that "Christ was received up into heaven, and sat down at the right hand of God." Mark 16:19; Luke 24:51; Acts 1:11; Acts 2:33, 34; Acts 7:55, 56; Eph. 1:20; Heb. 10:12; 1 Pet. 3:22. We are also taught that he must there remain "until the times of restoration of all things." Acts 3:21. Now, in the account Paul gives of his ecstatic vision in 2 Cor. 12:1–4, he tells us that he was "caught up even to the third heaven," and "caught up into Paradise," which locates Paradise either in or above the third heaven, or makes the two identical. So also Rev. 2:7, taken in connection with Rev. 22:2 and 21:10–27, states that the tree of life, "which is in the Paradise of God," is "in the midst of the street" of "that great city, the holy Jerusalem, descending out of heaven from God, having the glory of God," in which was no temple, "for the Lord God the Almighty and the Lamb are the temple thereof," and is "on either side of the river," which is described as "a river of water of life, bright as crystal, proceeding out of the throne of God, and of the Lamb." The place of the abode of the saints is with Christ, who is in the heavens with God. It is to that place that most probably the name Paradise is given in the Scriptures.

(4.) In that abode the saints are not probably inactive. Some have thought this because their condition is spoken of as one of "rest" and "sleep." But evidently the former of these terms is used simply to declare the end of the toils and labours of this life, and the enjoyment of exemption from their present spiritual as well as temporal trials. This does not imply that there are not intellectual and spiritual duties and meditations suitable to that abode, such as may give due scope to that activity, which seems essential to personal conscious spirits. The "sleep" more probably refers to the appearance of the body in death, and is beautifully expressive of the calm repose with which the Christian sinks into final dissolution.

(5.) Neither is the intermediate state a place of cleansing from sin. That it is so is held by the Church of Rome. That church teaches that at death all unbaptized adults, and all who have fallen into and continued in mortal sin after Baptism, go immediately to hell. All who have been baptized, and remain in union with that Church, and have attained a life of Christian perfection, go immediately to heaven. Unbaptized infants occupy what is called "the Limbus infantum," a place in the higher part of hell, which the flames do not reach, and suffer only a "paenam damni" (penalty of loss), and have no share in the "paenam sensus" (penalty of actual suffering), which afflicts adult sinners. But "the great mass of partially sanctified Christians, dying in fellowship with the church, yet still encumbered with imperfections, go to purgatory, where they suffer, more or less intensely, for a longer or shorter period, until their sins are both atoned for and purged out, when they are translated to heaven, during which intermediate period they may be efficiently assisted by the prayers and labours of their friends on earth."

"They confess that this doctrine is not taught distinctly in Scripture, but maintain, 1st, that it follows necessarily from their general doctrine of the satisfaction for sins; 2nd, that Christ and the Apostles taught it incidentally. . . . They refer to Matt. 12:32; 1 Cor. 3:15." Hodge's Outlines of Theology, pp. 556, 557.

But the first of these passages is manifestly but a strong way of declaring that the sin referred to shall never be pardoned, without authorizing the inference that there are other sins which will be pardoned in the world to come. The second passage, by the various things which are built upon the true foundation, which, if false or insufficient, shall be burned, refers not to personal character, but to teachings.

This doctrine of purgatory is based upon the very unscriptural theory of salvation through personal works and sufferings, which the Church of Rome holds, in connection with sacramental grace, to be supplementary to the meritorious work of Christ. While it has no support from Scripture, it is opposed to all that the Scriptures teach about the intermediate state of the righteous.

3. The aspects of the intermediate state peculiar to the wicked.

The Scripture teaching here is much more meagre. The four statements already mentioned, in which their condition and that of the righteous are similar, comprise almost all that is said. As peculiar to them, however, may be added,

(1.) That Christ, in the parable of the rich man and Lazarus, speaks of their condition as (a.) one of torment Luke 16:23–25, 28, (b.) from which there is no escape to the condition of bliss of the righteous, verse 26, and (c.) as endured in a place of torment, vs. 23, 28.

(2.) Those who interpret 1 Pet. 3:19, 20 as referring to a personal preaching by Christ to the dead in Hades, necessarily hold that the wicked are "in prison." But, otherwise, we have no other proof than seems to be conveyed in the "impassable gulf" mentioned in Luke 16:26.

(3.) It is a place in which they are reserved for punishment in the day of judgement. 2 Pet. 2:9.

(4.) The only place spoken of in connection with the wicked during the intermediate state is Hades, or the place of departed spirits, which is always translated Hell in the King James Version, but is transferred in the Canterbury Revision. The passages in which Hades is used are Matt. 11:23; 16:18; Luke 10:15; 16:23; Acts 2:27, 31; Rev. 1:18; 6:8; 20:13, 14.

CHAPTER 40

CHRIST'S SECOND COMING, AND THE RESURRECTION

THE incarnation of the Son of God is not his last manifestation in the flesh to men on earth. The Scriptures speak of another appearing, in connection with which is taught the resurrection of the dead, and the final judgement. Each of these subjects demands special discussion. In some works on theology, the doctrine of the Resurrection is first treated because of its intimate connection with death and immortality; and because it terminates the intermediate state. But, inasmuch as the coming of Christ will precede the resurrection of the dead, it seems best that it be first considered.

I. THE SECOND COMING OF CHRIST

1. The fact is distinctly revealed.

Whatever doubts any may have about the passages sometimes quoted as teaching it in the Old Testament, there can be none that it is clearly made known in the New.

(1.) It was taught by our Lord. Matt. 16:28; 24:36–40; 26:64; Mark 13:26; 14:62; Luke 21:27.

(2.) It is the teaching of the Apostles and other inspired writers. 1 Cor. 1:7; 15:23; 1 Thess. 2:19; 3:13; 4:15; 5:23; 2 Thess. 2:1, 8; Heb. 9:28; James 5:7, 8; 2 Pet. 3:4; 1 John 2:28.

2. The manner of it is distinctly set forth.

(1.) It will be a personal appearance. It is not questioned that Christ may be said to come in other ways than personally. The hour of death is admitted to be the way in which he comes at present to his saints, at what is to them the end of time. But the Scriptures teach such an especial personal final coming as can only be fulfilled in the bodily appearance of Christ to men. Mark 8:38; Acts 1:11; Heb. 9:26–28; 1 Thess. 4:16.

(2.) His coming will be "apart from sin, to them that wait for him, unto salvation," as contrasted with that time in which "he hath been manifested to put away sin by the sacrifice of himself," and was "offered to bear the sins of many." Heb. 9:26–28.

(3.) It will be an appearance with power and glory; "for the Lord himself shall descend from heaven, with a shout, with the voice of the archangel, and with the trump of God," (1 Thess. 4:16); "in the glory of his Father," (Matt. 16:27); and "in his glory, and all the angels with him," (Matt. 25:31); fulfilling to believers their expectation of "the appearing of the glory of our great God and Saviour Jesus Christ." Tit. 2:13.

(4.) It will be instantaneous and unexpected. It is indeed to be preceded by signs both spiritual and physical. But, as with those in the days of Noah and Lot, few will recognize these signs. Matt. 24:37–39; Luke 17:28. Even to these the coming will be instantaneous; as a flash of lightning, Matt. 24:27; as a thief in the night, 1 Thess. 5:2; Rev. 16:15.

3. The time of Christ's coming. This is represented as peculiarly unknown. Christ declared that even the Son knew not when it would be. It is hidden from all men. Matt. 24:36; Mark 13:32. Our Lord rebuked the disciples, just before his ascension, for questioning him again upon this subject. Acts 1:7. The apostle Paul indeed wrote to the Philippians, "The Lord is at hand," (Phil. 4:5), and Jesus Christ announced, "The time is at hand," (Rev. 1:3), and to the church at Philadelphia sent the message: "I come quickly," Rev. 3:11. This is again repeated unto his servants in Rev. 22:7, 12, 20. But that these expressions, if they refer, as they apparently do, to his second coming, were not intended to teach what man would call an early coming, is evident from the fact that this second coming has been delayed over eighteen hundred years. The apostle Peter gave those in his day who were troubled about this delay the true solution, writing them: "But forget not this one thing, beloved, that one day is with the Lord as a thousand years, and a thousand years as one day." 2 Pet. 3:8.

4. The aspects in which he will come.

(1.) Christ always spake of his coming as that of the Son of Man. By this he himself taught the same truth with which afterward the angel at the ascension reassured the disciples who stood "gazing up into heaven," namely, that he that shall come then shall be the "same Jesus" which was taken up. It will then be in human form that he will appear, and with the same sympathizing human as well as divine love towards his own which he so wonderfully displayed while on earth.

(2.) But the apostle Peter, at Pentecost, said, "Let all the house of Israel therefore know assuredly that God hath made him both Lord and Christ, this Jesus whom you crucified." Acts 2:36. Hence the apostles, almost exclusively, speak of Christ as Lord in connection with his second coming. This was their common name for Christ, and thus they recognized the glorious reward bestowed upon him for the salvation wrought for them, and the "all power" given unto him in heaven and earth.

(3.) It is as Judge of the whole earth that he shall appear, both as Son of Man and as Lord; thus giving confidence to those who know him and have believed in him, and striking with terror those who have rejected his love.

(4.) He also comes as King to take final possession of his kingdom, to share its blessings and glory with all his willing subjects, and to inflict punishment upon all who have refused to have him reign over them.

5. The signal events which that coming will introduce.

These are the resurrection of the bodies of the dead, and the change of those of the saints who are still alive; the judgement of all men; and the bestowment, according to the highest equity, of his due reward or punishment upon every one of mankind.

II. THE RESURRECTION OF THE BODY

The first in point of time of the events which accompany the second coming is the resurrection of the bodies of the dead.

1. This fact is the teaching both of the Old and the New Testaments.

It is admitted that some places in which resurrection is mentioned may speak only of a reappearance upon the stage of being of those who have died, and do not necessarily assert the final resurrection of the body. Thus our Lord's reply to the Saduccees, Luke 20:37, only involves the idea of continued life. So also his language in Luke 14:14; John 6:39; and that to Martha, and her reply, John 11:23, 24.

It may also be acknowledged that, sometimes, the life and death, in connection with which resurrection is taught, is only spiritual, and that of the soul only. This seems to be the case in John 5:24–26, although the resurrection of the body is not unnaturally spoken of in the verses immediately succeeding.

There are also places in which the resurrection of the body is spoken of, but not the general, or final resurrection. These may be quoted only as showing that such a resurrection is not impossible. Thus, the writer to the Hebrews refers to the faith of Abraham in the power of God "to raise" Isaac "up even from the dead." Heb. 11:19. We are also told that, after the death of Christ, "the tombs were opened; many bodies of the saints that had fallen asleep were raised; and coming forth out of the tombs after his resurrection they entered into the holy city and appeared unto many." Matt. 27:52, 53. The resurrection of Christ himself is taught to be a fulfillment of prophecy, Acts 2:24–31; 13:34–37, and a proof, not only of the possibility of a resurrection from the dead, 1 Cor. 15:12–18, but even an assurance, and earnest of the resurrection of the bodies of his people. 1 Cor. 15:20–23, 35–45, 48–54.

But there are enough passages, of no doubtful import, both in the Old and New Testaments, which establish a general resurrection of the bodies of all men, as Isa. 26:19; Dan. 12:2–13; Hos. 13:14; and John 5:28, 29; Rom. 8:11–22, 23; 1 Cor. 15:20–23, 42–45, 48–54; Phil. 3:21; 1 Thess. 4:13–17. The last two passages refer, indeed, to the change in the body only; the last one also to the change in those who shall not die, but remain at the coming of Christ; their appositeness is readily recognized.

2. The resurrection will not be confined to the righteous only; but will include the wicked also.

The New Testament treats sometimes exclusively of the resurrection of the righteous. This is not unnatural; for all hope connected with it is confined to them. So blessed is that hope, that it was fit that it should be frequently held out for their encouragement and comfort. Especially the connection between their resurrection and that of Christ, as the first fruits of them that sleep, tended to lead them into the joys produced by the consciousness of union with him, and their triumph with, and through him. This was not to be confined to their spiritual resurrection with him in newness of spiritual life; and this fact needed to be enforced, lest that of the body should be forgotten in their experience of that of the soul. The objections to it also arose in connection with Christian hope. It is not strange that some should have denied it, even among the people of God, as the Apostle wrote to the Corinthians was true of some of them. 1 Cor. 15:12. The doctrine was too wonderful to believe. Perhaps they had specific objections to it in that day, as there have been in other ages of Christianity, even down to our own times. We are not to be surprised, that others also should have declared that it was passed already, and should have thus overthrown the faith of some. 2 Tim. 2:18. It became necessary, therefore, that it should be especially emphasized to the Christian believers of that day. With the single exception of "those that remain," who were to be "changed," it is expressly announced as the joyful destiny of all believers. Thus, Paul wrote to the Corinthians that "as in Adam all die, even so in Christ shall all be made alive." 1 Cor. 15:22. That this assertion related only to believers is evident, not only from the natural construction of the original Greek, but from the fact that his language is limited in the context to them "that are Christ's at his coming." 1 Cor. 15:23. In like manner, also, comforting the Thessalonians as to the Christian dead, he assigns as a reason why they should "sorrow not, even as the rest which have no hope," (1 Thess. 4:13), that "if we believe that Jesus died and rose again, even so them also that are fallen asleep in Jesus will God bring with him;" asserting the change in those that shall remain on earth, and stating that "the dead in Christ shall rise first." 1 Thess. 4:14–18.

But, that this teaching about the righteous, was not intended to exclude the resurrection of the wicked, is plain enough from other places. Thus, our Lord said "all that are in the tombs shall hear his voice, and shall come forth; they that have done good, unto the resurrection of life; and they that have done ill, unto the resurrection of judgement." John 5:28, 29. What is also especially significant, in view of his teachings exclusively elsewhere as to the resurrection of the just, is that Paul, in his address before Felix, confessed that he had "hope toward God, . . . that there shall be a resurrection both of the just and the unjust." Acts 24:15. In the vision of John of the day of judgement he saw that "the sea gave up the dead which were in it; and death and Hades gave up the dead which were in them, . . . and if any one was not found written in the book of life, he was cast into the lake of fire." Rev. 20:13–15. These passages show distinctly a resurrection of the wicked also from the grave, and, therefore, a resurrection of their bodies.

3. The nature of the resurrection body.

We are told nothing as to the nature of the resurrection bodies of the wicked. But enough is said as to those of the saints to show that their change will be most blessed.

The all embracing fact is distinctly declared that they shall be like unto that of their Lord. If we knew the precise nature of his body we should know the nature of those of all his saints. But it is enough to know that he will "fashion anew the body of our humiliation, that it may be conformed to the body of his glory." Phil. 3:21. We are taught many things, however, about the resurrection body; the chief source of information being the fifteenth chapter of 1st Corinthians, where Paul states,

(a.) That it will be incorruptible,

(b.) That it will be immortal,

(c.) That it will be a glorified body,

(d.) That it will be raised in power,

(e.) That it will be identical with the present body. That which is raised is the "it" which is sown. It is "this corruptible" that "puts on incorruption," this "mortal" that "puts on immortality."

(f.) Yet is the identity one which exists not without a great change, v. 51.

(g.) Yet with no greater change than occurred in the body of Christ. It is his image which is to be borne instead of that of Adam, v. 49.

(h.) When Paul asserts that "flesh and blood cannot inherit the kingdom of God," v. 50, he means only to deny that a corrupt and mortal body can thus inherit, and not to assert that such inheritance is not true of a glorified body of material substance, from which all corruption and mortal elements have been removed.

(i.) We consequently see what he means by the spiritual body in vv. 44–46, where he contrasts it with the "natural," and declares the resurrection body to be "spiritual." It is not spiritual in the sense that it is not material; for it is composed of matter. But, it is spiritual, as being fitted for the spiritual life hereafter, as it had previously been natural, as fitted for the animal life of this world. This is the pneumatic body as opposed to the physical. As the first body had been suited to the present life, and could not be used in the life to come without change; so the resurrection body is suited to the life to come, and not to the present stage of being. Hence it is that the change, with or without death, does not take place until the time of reunion in which the pneumatic life is to begin.

4. There shall be a general resurrection of the bodies of the righteous, and of the wicked at the coming of Christ to judgement.

(1.) The rewards of the righteous are especially associated with Christ's coming in the great day. Matt. 16:27; Luke 12:37; 1 Cor. 1:7, 8; 1 Thess. 3:13; 2 Thess. 1:7, 10; 1 Pet. 5:4; 1 John 2:28; 4:17.

(2.) The suffering and punishment of the wicked are also intimately connected with the day of Christ's coming to judgement. John 12:48; 2 Pet. 2:9; Rev. 1:7.

(3.) There are passages also in which both the reward of the righteous, and the punishment of the wicked are set forth unitedly in connection with the second coming of Christ. Matt. 16:24–27; 24:36–51; Mark 13:24–27; Rom. 2:1–16; 1 Cor. 4:5; 2 Pet. 2:9; 2 Pet. 3:7–9.

(4.) The righteous and the wicked are judged together. Ecc. 3:17; Dan. 12:2; Matt. 16:27; Acts 17:31; Rom. 2:16; 2 Cor. 5:10; Heb. 9:27.

(5.) The resurrection of the dead occurs at the same time with the judgement. Dan. 12:2; Rev. 20:12, 13.

(6.) The resurrection and the change that occurs in it are also associated with the coming of Christ. 1 Cor. 15:52; Phil. 3:21; 1 Thess. 4:16.

(7.) The judgement and the coming of Christ, take place in immediate conjunction. Matt 16:27; 25:31–46; 2 Pet. 3:7–10.

(8.) The resurrection of both just, and unjust, shall occur at the same time. Dan. 12:2; John 5:28, 29; Acts 24:15.

(9.) The unrighteous are kept unto the day of judgement. 2 Pet. 2:9.

(10.) At the time of Christ's coming, the world is to be destroyed, and the promise fulfilled of "new heavens and a new earth wherein dwelleth righteousness." 2 Pet. 3:8–13. But, that day is also the day of "judgement and destruction of ungodly men;" for which "the heavens that now are and the earth by the same word have been stored up for fire," v. 7.

These statements show that the general teaching of the Word of God is that the Lord will come; that at his coming there shall be a general resurrection of the just and unjust, who shall be judged according to the deeds done in the body. Not only is it not taught that there are two resurrections of the body, the one of the righteous at the second coming of the Lord, and the other of the wicked at the general judgement after an interval of one thousand years; but the judgement and the coming of the Lord are recognized as contemporaneous. The day of both events is called by various names, some of which are repeated more than once: as "the day," (1 Cor. 3:13); "that day," (Matt 7:22); "the day of judgement," (2 Pet. 2:9); "the day of God," (2 Pet. 3:12); "the day of the Lord," (1 Thess. 5:2); "the day of our Lord Jesus Christ," (1 Cor. 1:8); "the day of Jesus Christ," (Phil. 1:6); "the day of Christ," (Phil. 2:16); "the day of the Lord Jesus," (1 Cor. 5:5); "the last day," (John 6:39); "the great day," (Jude 6); "the great day of their wrath," (Rev. 6:17); "the day of wrath and revelation of the righteous judgement of God," (Rom. 2:5); "that great and notable day of the Lord," (Acts 2:20); "the day when God shall judge the secrets of men . . . by Jesus Christ," (Rom 2:16); "the day that the Son of Man is revealed," (Luke 17:30); "the coming of our Lord Jesus," (1 Thess. 3:13); "the appearing of our Lord Jesus Christ," (1 Tim. 6:14); "the revelation of Jesus Christ," (1 Pet. 1:13); the "appearing of glory of our Great God and Saviour Jesus Christ," (Tit. 2:13), etc.

There is, however, one passage of Scripture which some claim teaches one resurrection of the bodies of the just, and another of those of the unjust; and places them at a wide interval apart, with numerous intervening parts. Those who maintain this view hold that the thousand years of the Millenium succeed the second coming of Christ, and the resurrection of the righteous. This passage constitutes the twentieth chapter of the book of Revelation. It is the record of that vision, in which John saw the angel bind Satan, in the bottomless pit, for a thousand years; during which the souls of the saints lived, and reigned with Christ. "This," says John, "is the first resurrection." v. 5. On those having part in it, "the second death hath no power." v. 6. When the thousand years have expired, Satan shall be loosed out of his prison, and go out to deceive the nations. When the number of the forces which he gathers, which are like the sands of the sea, surround the camp of the saints, these forces will be devoured by fire from Heaven, and the devil cast into the lake of fire and brimstone. Then appears the great white throne, and the judgement of the dead, both small and great, and the judgement of the dead out of the books. And then death and Hades are cast into the lake of fire. "This," says John, "is the second death." v. 14.

It is readily admitted as to this passage that whatever is truly taught in it must be accepted as the word of God. But,

(1.) We must be careful how we receive any interpretation which does not accord with the rest of Scripture. Before doing so, we should examine thoroughly both the interpretation we wish to accept, and the views attained from other parts of the Word of God. We know that Scripture cannot contradict itself, when rightly interpreted. All its parts must, therefore, be carefully compared to see in what interpretation they agree.

(2.) If, after the best efforts to harmonize this with the other portions of God's Word, it should seem to be irreconcilable with them, the apparent interpretation of this passage should yield to that of others; not so much because it is one only, as compared with a great number; but because it is found in a book of highly figurative prophecy, in which the literal interpretation is not so justly to be pressed, as in others, which are not of this character, and in which the literal meaning is more apt to be the mind of the Spirit.

(3.) The language of this passage, however, is, at least, in some respects, opposed to the idea of two resurrections of the body; the first, that of the saints to reign with Christ for a thousand years, and the second, that of the wicked to judgement.

(a.) Because those who are represented as belonging to the first resurrection, are not spoken of as clothed in resurrection bodies; but, on the contrary, John declares simply that he saw "the souls of them that had been beheaded for the testimony of Jesus, etc." v. 4.

(b.) It is not only not said that those who partake of the first resurrection are not among the dead, who are subsequently delivered up by death and Hades to be judged, v. 13, but it is implied that they are among these by the universal terms used when John says that he "saw the dead, the great and small, stand before God," v. 12. But, if this be true, then there must be either two resurrections of the bodies of the saints, or one of the resurrections at least cannot be of the body.

(c.) Especially is it not taught that the resurrection to judgement is confined to the wicked, nor that the first resurrection is of the bodies of all the saints; because along with the books "which were opened," "another book was opened, which is the book of life: and the dead were judged out of the things which were written in the books, according to their works," v. 12; "and if any was not found written in the book of life, he was cast into the lake of fire," v. 15. This language implies that, among those then raised and judged, there were some whose names were written in the book of life. Consequently, reference must here be made to the general resurrection and judgement, taught elsewhere as contemporaneous, and the first resurrection cannot be that of the body; or only some of the saints partake of the first resurrection; or there must be two resurrections of the bodies of the saints. The first of these is the only interpretation that accords with what is elsewhere taught.

(4.) The interpretation of this passage which makes it harmonious with all other Scripture is, (a.) That the resurrection is a spiritual resurrection of the soul from the death of sin, of which Scriptures elsewhere speak so plainly as being a passage from death unto life. See John 5:24–26; Rom. 6:2–7; Eph. 2:1, 5; 5:14; Phil. 3:10, 11; Col. 2:12, 13; 1 John 3:14; 5:11, 12.

(b.) That the second death, which has no power over those which have part in the first resurrection, constitutes the punishment of those condemned at the judgement day, which consists in their being cast, both body and soul, into a lake of fire.

(c.) The thousand years of the binding of Satan is a period of time, of unknown, perhaps of indefinite length, possibly from the time of Christ's conquest of Satan, in his death, resurrection, and ascension, or possibly from some other period, even perhaps of a later epoch in the history of Christianity, during which Satan is restrained from the exercise of the power he might otherwise put forth against man; the thousand years terminating at some time prior to the day of Christ's second coming; at which time Satan shall be loosed to consummate his evil deeds by such assaults upon the saints as shall bring down the final vengeance of God at the appearing of Christ in glory.

(d.) The judgement and the resurrection, in Rev. 20:12, 13, are general, and are those of the last day which immediately follow the coming of Christ.

CHAPTER 41

THE FINAL JUDGEMENT

THE partial processes of God's judgements are not only constantly occurring, but are often distinctly manifested. Hence many expressions of Scripture, in which his judgements are spoken of, have no certain reference, and others, no reference at all, to the final judgement of all men. But, in numerous other places, such a judgement is made known. We are taught the appointment of a time when there will be a public, general judgement of all the righteous, and the wicked.

I. A SPECIAL TIME APPOINTED FOR IT

It is expressly declared that "He hath appointed a day, in the which he will judge the world in righteousness." Acts 17:31. The numerous designations of the day of the coming of Christ, and of his judgement of men, were pointed out in the preceding chapter. Among those peculiar to the judgement are "the day of judgement," (2 Pet. 2:9); "the great day," (Jude 6); "the great day of their wrath," (Rev. 6:17); "the day of wrath and revelation of the righteous judgement of God," (Rom. 2:5); and "the day when God shall judge the secrets of men by Jesus Christ." Rom 2:16.

The duration of the time thus appointed cannot be determined. The indefinite meaning of the word "day" forbids any statement of even its probable length. It has been argued that, from the vast numbers to be judged, and the many events connected with the life of every man, it will comprise a long period of time. But the rapidity with which, in some conditions, the mind will run over the course of a long life, in a moment of time, shows that a period of even exceeding brevity may suffice for a full revelation and judgement of all persons and events. The indefiniteness of the word should, however, caution us against the assumption that the day must be of only a few hours duration.

II. THE JUDGEMENT WILL BE PUBLIC AND GENERAL

This has been denied by some who think that the judgement of each man occurs at death. These hold that to confine the judgement to that at death only, is not contrary to the real meaning of Scripture, which they suppose is not to be

415

found in the literal language used, but in such an interpretation as will accord with the fact that the destiny of each man is fixed, and that consciously to himself, at death. They think that the indefiniteness of the word "day" permits a continuous process of judgement extending over the whole period connected with the deaths of men.

The chief basis of this theory is that the certainty attained at the death of each man, as to his position towards God, makes unnecessary any further judgement, because his case has thus been already judged. But we have very little knowledge of the amount of that certainty, especially in the case of the wicked. The righteous man, because of his presence with Christ, doubtless knows that his salvation is secure; but who can tell what alternate hopes and fears may constitute a part of the torture of the wicked in the intermediate state? But, even if he is also certain of his fate, there may be weighty reasons for a public manifestation of his position. Even "the angels, when they sinned," whose condition in this respect is certainly equally ascertained, are said to be "reserved unto judgement," as well as unjust men whom the Lord keeps "under punishment unto the day of judgement." 2 Pet. 2:4, 9. It may be that the day of judgement is appointed, in order that the full sentence, as to the reward or punishment of each man, may be uttered, when he stands clothed in the resurrection body, in which these are to be suffered, or enjoyed during all the future. Other purposes will be subsequently suggested in connection with the vindication of God, and the manifestation of the causes and circumstances of his action, which, independently of any relation of the judgement to any individual man, make a public judgement day not unsuitable. The certainty of that publicity will appear from the person of the Judge. But, in addition to all other considerations, the Scriptures use language about the judgement day, and its events, which cannot be justly interpreted otherwise than as teaching it to be public in the sight of all, and general to all, not particular to each man. The declarations of its universally sudden appearance, of the angels and the glory which shall attend the descending Judge, of the convulsions of nature, of the burning up of the world, of such a gathering of all nations as permits a separation before all into two distinct classes, and the fact that some will rise up in special condemnation of others; these, and other statements, are utterly inconsistent with only a particular judgement of each at death. Especially is it impossible to reconcile the statement, that the resurrection of men will precede the final judgement, with any theory which makes this occur at death. All of this is independent of the further reply which may be urged, that no indefiniteness of the word "day" would permit the idea that a time, appointed within the life of mankind, should extend throughout the whole period of that life. It ought at least, to be a somewhat limited portion of the time which contains it.

It is scarcely necessary to add that this judgement will be so general as to include all mankind. Whatever different opinions may be held as to its being at death to each one, or at one special time to all, or that the time is longer, or shorter, or long enough to include the thousand years which the Millenarians suppose to intervene between the judgement of the righteous and the end of judgement in that of the wicked, it is admitted by all that the judgement will be universal. The Scripture asserts this very plainly. Before the Judge "shall be gathered all the nations." Matt. 25:32. "Each one of us shall give account of himself to God." Rom. 14:12. It states that it shall even be so universal as to embrace the angels who kept not their first estate. 2 Pet. 2:4; Jude 6.

III. THE PERSON OF THE JUDGE

God alone is competent to perform this office of Judge in the great day. He alone has the right to Judge. He alone has the necessary qualifications. Chief among these is that perfect rectitude of character by which only can justice be exercised with due regard to the law and those under it, according to strict principles of equity. Equally important, however, is that complete knowledge of the law which leaves unknown neither its requirements, nor its penalties, nor its rewards, nor its possible relaxations. He also has that omniscience by which all things are known to him, even the innermost secrets of men; not their actions only, but their inward thoughts and hidden motives, even their natures and the possibilities of those natures. This, which is essential to due judgement, can be found only in him who searcheth the reins and hearts, and thus knows what is in men. His, too, is the infinite wisdom which can make due application of the law, in all its aspects, to the whole conduct and character of those to be judged; and his the infinite power to execute that law, as well in the bestowment of its rewards, as in the infliction of its punishments.

Hence the Scriptures speak of God as "the judge of all," (Heb. 12:23); and of his judgement according to truth and righteousness, which cannot be escaped, Rom. 2:2, 3, 5. In the Apocalyptic vision, John "saw the dead, the great and the small, standing before the throne" when the books were opened for judgement. Rev. 20:12, 13.

But this judgement is not by God, as God. Jesus told the Jews that "neither doth the Father judge any man, but he hath given all judgement unto the Son." John 5:22. The cause of this is that the Son is not only divine, but human, and that his relation to humanity endows him with peculiar qualifications for this office, which, like those for the salvation of man, could not be possessed by one only divine. Christ, therefore, taught his disciples that the judge would be the "Son of Man," (Matt. 16:27, 28; 25:31–34), and declared to the Jews, that the Father "gave him [his Son] authority to execute judgement, because he is the Son of Man." John 5:27. Indeed, it would seem that the judgement is to be exercised peculiarly by Christ as man; for it is at least especially announced of him in his nature. Peter preached to Cornelius, concerning Jesus of Naz-ereth, "that this is he which is ordained of God to be the judge of quick and dead." Acts 10:42. Paul wrote of "the day when God shall judge the secrets of men according to my gospel by Jesus Christ," (Rom. 2:16); and encouraged the Corinthians by declaring that "we must all be made manifest before the judge-ment seat of Christ," (2 Cor. 5:10) and, on Mars' Hill, announced that God had "appointed a day in the which he will judge the world in righteousness by the man whom he hath ordained." Acts 17:31.

We cannot hope to understand all the reasons for this appointment of Christ, as Son of Man, to the judgement of all. They are connected, in part, with the position of King and Lord, to which he has been assigned for the complete triumph of his kingdom, and the manifestation of God's power and grace. They are also doubtless associated with the relation which, as man, he occupies to mankind, and especially to the church of "first-born ones." But it is certain that, by the connection of the office of judge with Christ as man, is removed every obstacle in the way of a public, visible judgement. Since it is the Son of God who is the Son of Man, all that makes it necessary that God be the judge is found in him. But as man, the judge is no longer the invisible God, who can only be seen in the works of his Creation, and Providence; but God in Christ, the God-man, in his visible material form, who, therefore, can be manifested before the eyes of all, in a judgement which is, not simply general, as inclusive of all, but public, as openly manifested before all. It appears, therefore, that the person of the judge adds another reason to those heretofore mentioned why any judgement which occurs at death will be supplemented by, and consummated in, the final judgement of the last day.

IV. THE PURPOSES OF THIS PUBLIC JUDGEMENT

Still further proof of the same fact will appear from some, at least, of the purposes of this public judgement.

1. In the purpose fulfilled by the revelation of it to men in this life. The conviction of such a judgement to come produces a decided influence for good upon the conduct of men in this life. Doubtless is it on this account that it is taught so plainly, and so frequently, and in so many ways, that none should fail to be impressed with the certainty of its occurrence. This would, indeed, in no small degree, be accomplished by the knowledge of a private and individual

judgement at the hour of death. But it is manifest that this effect is greatly enhanced by the terrors and solemnities with which the Bible clothes the scenes of that day. That its publicity is in itself fearful is evident from the extent with which even those shrink from a revelation of their sins, who as believers in Jesus, confidently hope for a favourable sentence from God. The question so frequently asked whether the sins, as well as the good works, of God's people will then be revealed, is the fruit of this apprehension.

It is probable, however, that the influence of the expectation of this judgement is unimportant, as compared with the purposes connected with it actual occurrence. These are to be found in the manifestations of God, and Christ, and of men in that great day.

2. The purposes that appear in connection with the day itself.

(1.) As to God.

(a.) It will furnish a worthy arena for the display of the attributes of God. A continuous purpose of God, in connection with his intelligent creatures, has been to make known to them the glory of his character. This is assigned as a reason even of his spiritual quickening of his people together with Christ. Eph. 2:4–7. Now, no mention can be made of any one of his attributes, which he has thus far revealed, which will not, at the judgement day, be signally displayed. This will be especially true of his vindicatory justice, the perfection of which has been, in some degree, dimmed, while, because of his forbearance and grace, he has delayed the due punishment of sin. Hence, this day is called "the great day of their wrath," (Rev. 6:17), and "the day of wrath and revelation of the righteous judgement of God." Rom. 2:5. Yet, how signally will then, also, appear the wisdom of his purpose, the truth and faithfulness of his promises, his power to accomplish his will, his universal benevolence, his sacrificing love, his unbounded mercy, his delivering power, his conquering grace, and, not to attempt to enumerate further, everything that can be imagined as constituting that holiness which, in one word, embraces all moral perfection.

(b.) The wisdom and equity of God, in his providential and gracious dealings with men, will then, also, be apparent. These often give rise to perplexity, even in those who most firmly believe in God as one who does all things justly, and well. In this life men are called to exercise faith in God in all these matters. That faith will be vindicated by the manifestations at that time both of his character and acts. The inequalities of this life, and the prosperity of the wicked, and the adversity of the righteous, will then be not only equalized, but all will clearly see the wisdom, justice, and goodness of God, in giving them a place here in his providential government. It is more than probable that, in the full exhibition of all his purposes in Creation and Grace, that insoluble problem of this life—the presence of sin in a world created, and governed by an Almighty, and

Holy God—will become a manifestation of unspeakable glory in God. Then, too, will appear, even more plainly than now, the righteousness of his choice of some to salvation, and condemnation of others for sin; and, also, the full responsibility of men for every sin, even when their circumstances and previous action have rendered certain things which they will do. Then, too, will be seen such sufficiency, in each man, of the light possessed, if he had walked therein, and of his power for good, if he had exercised it, as makes him guilty in the sight of God, and worthy of the punishment which he will inflict.

(2.) As to Christ.

But it is not simply the revelation of God; but of God in Christ.

(a.) In that wonderful combination by which the created spirit, and even created matter of human nature were, through the making flesh of the divine Word, (John 1:14), enabled to do that work which neither man nor God could separately do. Where, but on the throne of judgement, could this personage be seen by any except those who are made partakers of his glory? How fit is his appearance to fill with anguish those who have rejected him, and with exultation and praise all those who have trusted him. He appears not only as Judge, but as King and Lord, whose dominion as Lord is now shown to be universal, and whose kingship, in the hearts of his people, he now rewards by welcoming them to entrance into his joy, and participation in his glory.

(b.) The glory of Christ's work will also then appear.

In its displays of the divine attributes; of truth, in the fulfillment in him of the threatened curse of sin for all those saved by him; of inexorable justice, which requires that honouring of the law, not only in obedience, but also in penalty, exacted even from the Son of God, from him that is the fellow of Jehovah; and of love and mercy, which demand to be exercised even at the cost of the most fearful sacrifice. Pre-eminently will the glory of that work be seen in the harmony displayed in the exercise of these attributes; of justice in a way of mercy and love; of each of these in a way of justice, and of all of them in a way of holiness and truth. The judgement day will clearly exhibit these perfections, and their harmony, to all the intelligences of God.

The glory of that work will also be seen in the manifested conquest of Satan. For the accomplishment of the purpose of God, he has long been permitted to exercise power and malignity. It will, at the judgement day, appear that it was always done by the sufferance of God, who chose not to conquer, and punish him and his angels, except through the Son of Man. The fact that this victory over Satan has not been one of divine power, but has been wrought out by the Son of God in his human nature, renders his defeat more signal and humiliating to him. It is a complete avengement of the temptation of the first Adam.

The delivering power from sin shown in the work of Christ will also exhibit its glory in a peculiar manner.

We can imagine an angel willing to undertake the conquest of Satan at the command of God. But, here was the work which no angel would have attempted, nor even had any hope of accomplishing. There were many problems, in connection with it, which could not be solved. How is the penalty which has been incurred to be endured, or to be escaped? How is the righteousness demanded, to be fulfilled, now that man has become a sinner? How can sin be eradicated, and an unholy nature be restored to its purity and original righteousness? How is another to secure these things in men? And, if not secured in them, how can the sin of a sinner, both in action and condition, be hidden from God? How can God be just and yet justify the ungodly?

Christ has solved all these problems, and more than done all the work which was needed. The sinner, united by faith to Christ, has now an assured safety, an unfailing righteousness, a more than sufficient satisfaction, a covert utterly impenetrable by the wrath or justice of God; and he will stand before the judgement seat of Christ, in the presence of men and angels, to manifest his Saviour's power in eradicating sin, by the good works wrought out by that Saviour's disciple in mortal flesh, even under the higher law of Christian duty.

(3.) As to man.

With respect to man especially, the purposes of the judgement day make it fit that it should be general, and public.

(a.) Because then will be revealed the character and acts of men.

It is set forth as a day when "each one of us shall give account of himself to God," (Rom. 14:12), which account shall comprise "every idle word that men shall speak." Matt. 12:36. This is to be at that time "when God shall judge the secrets of men." Rom. 2:16. The object of this trial is not to ascertain what men have done, but to make manifest to those who are judged, as well as to all others, the things which are already known to God. To this end, even the sins unknown to the offenders, and good deeds forgotten by the righteous, will be brought to light. Matt 25:31–46. We are told that the Lord "will both bring to light the hidden things of darkness, and make manifest the counsels of the hearts: and then shall each man have his praise from God." 1 Cor. 4:5.

(b.) Because then will judgement be made as to each individual.

For this cause is it that "we must all be made manifest before the judgement seat of Christ; that each one may receive the things done in the body according to what he hath done, whether it be good or bad." 2 Cor. 5:10; Rom. 14:12. The very name of the day shows the object of its appointment, and the nature of the transactions in this direction, which will then occur. The descriptions of the judgement day, however figurative they may be supposed to be, mark this as an undoubted teaching of God's Word. The wicked are condemned, because both of character and conduct. How this may be, can easily be understood. But the righteous are accepted, and rewarded, upon the same grounds. The reason of this is not so apparent. It doubtless is based upon the meritorious work of Christ, through which, by faith, they have been justified by God even in this life. But the references to their own personal acts show, also, a personal justification in that great day. This is the justification by works, seen in them even while on earth. It is the manifestation of the life-giving principle imparted to them on earth in regeneration, and exhibited by them during the processes of sanctification. The good works are the fruits of that vital union with Christ, by which "the life also of Jesus" is "manifested in our body." 2 Cor. 4:10; (cf. Gal. 2:20, and Rom. 8:1–4).

In the judgement, unto which men will thus be brought in the last day, there will be account taken of the light and knowledge which they have possessed. The heathen will be judged by a different law from that which will be applied to those who have had the light of revelation. Paul plainly teaches that the former have a law under which they live, (Rom. 2:14, 15), in want of conformity to, and violation of which they are "worthy of death," (Rom. 1:32); and that they are judged only by the law which they have. Rom. 2:12. Christ taught the same truth, generally, as applied to all the various degrees of knowledge, when he spoke of the servants, to be beaten with few or many stripes, according to their knowledge of their Lord's will. Luke 12:47, 48. He also taught it especially in comparing the degrees of guilt and condemnation of those who enjoy the knowledge of the gospel and those who lived before its proclamation. Matt. 12:41, 42; Luke 11:29–32; (cf. John 12:47, 48).

(c.) That the judgement is public and general is seen in what is said of the public bestowment of rewards and punishments.

The language here may perhaps be figurative, but must mean something, and can mean no less than the publicity of the awards Christ will give. No private judgement at death would account for the statements that all are to be gathered before Christ, and are to be separated by him into those on the right hand and those on the left, (Matt. 25:32, 33); nor for the declaration that, "in the end of this world, the Son of Man shall send forth his angels, and they shall gather out of his kingdom all things that cause stumbling, and them that do iniquity," Matt 13:41; nor for that further teaching in v. 49, that "the angels shall come forth and sever the wicked from among the righteous."

V. THE PLACE OF THE FINAL JUDGEMENT

It is evident, from what we have already seen, that the judgement scenes will occupy some place in the universe of God. Christ is to appear as the Son of

Man, and, therefore, clothed in the body of his human nature, although that body will then have been glorified. The bodies of men, both righteous and the wicked, will have been previously raised, so that they shall be judged in the body for the deeds done in the body. The bodies, then, both of the Lord and of all men, will not only occupy space, but will so occupy it as to be mutually recognized as being in space.

The place may also be believed to be in some connection with our present earth. It is fit that this, which has been the scene of all the events which will culminate in the judgement day, shall also be the place of that final trial. It is natural to suppose that, as the first coming of the Lord was to this earth, to bear sin for the redemption of man, so his second coming in triumph, without sin unto salvation, will be to that part of the universe which has been thus signally distinguished as the theatre of God's most gracious work. The statements of Scripture are indeed meagre, but they say nothing which may not be interpreted in perfect consistency with this opinion. Yet, after all, the conclusion that the trial will be in connection with this earth, is so much a matter of inference only, as not to forbid that it may be at some other point in the universe. All that we are definitely told is that "we that are alive, that are left, shall together with them be caught up in the clouds to meet the Lord," (1 Thess. 4:17), and that "the heavens shall pass away with a great noise, and the elements shall be dissolved with fervent heat, and the earth and the works that are therein shall be burned up." 2 Pet. 3:10. But, while this does not deny, it does not necessarily teach, the destruction of the whole universe. The catastrophe may be limited to this earth and its atmosphere, and yet all the phenomena mentioned may occur. We also know that combustion of matter is not its destruction, but only a change in its form. This accords with the prediction of a new heavens and a new earth, (2 Pet. 3:13), and with those expressions which refer to it as a "restoration of all things" (Acts 3:21), and teach "that the creation itself also shall be delivered from the bondage of corruption into the liberty of the glory of the children of God." Rom. 8:21. But, whether the earth alone is to be purified by fire, or, as seems not so probable, the whole universe; or whether the judgement scene is to be connected with earth, or with some other point in the present, or in the renewed universe, it seems certain that it must be in some place. The place which is most probable is in connection with the point of space now occupied by this earth, and either in the atmosphere above it, during or after the configuration, or on the earth itself before it shall be burned.

Chapter 42

THE FINAL STATES OF THE RIGHTEOUS AND THE WICKED

IN the last chapter, nothing was said specifically of the awards of the judgement day. Yet is the public bestowal of these the culminating point of interest in that occasion. Judgement, without the expression of its results, in rewards and punishment, would be empty and vain. Hence the Scriptures do not leave us ignorant of what sentences will be pronounced upon the righteous, and wicked, and of what will be the final state of each. Of necessity, these must, in some respects, resemble those of the intermediate state; of which the condition of the righteous and wicked after judgement will be an enlargement and a culmination. It is not strange, therefore, that the Scriptures teach more fully, and emphatically upon these subjects.

I. THE FINAL STATE OF THE RIGHTEOUS

There is upon this point little dispute as to the meaning of the Scripture statements. As they are numerous, they will best be presented under several classes of description.

1. The sentence of the judgement day may be stated.

Our Lord declared that "then shall the king say unto them on his right hand, Come, ye blessed of my Father, inherit the kingdom prepared for you from the foundation of the world." Matt. 25:34. This is called "eternal life" in v. 46. As this is, probably, a description of the nature of the blessings to be attained, rather than a declaration of the literal language that will then be used, other statements may here be added which are of the same nature. One that is given in the parable of the talents, in which his lord said to him of the five talents, "Well done, good and faithful servant: thou hast been faithful over a few things, I will set thee over many things: enter thou into the joy of thy Lord." Matt. 25:21, (cf. Matt. 24:27). The righteous are spoken of as "wheat," and it is said that the householder at the harvest time will say to the reapers, "gather the wheat into my barn," Matt. 13:30. Our Lord, in his explanation of this parable, says of those thus represented by the wheat, "then shall the righteous shine forth as the sun in the kingdom of their Father," v. 43. Corresponding to this language, is the declaration of Peter, that, "when the chief shepherd shall be manifested, ye shall receive the crown of glory that fadeth not away." 1 Pet. 5:4. There may be added, also, the promises made in Revelation to "him that overcometh," viz.: to eat of the tree of life which is in the paradise of God," (chap. 2:7); "that he shall not be hurt of the second death," (2:11); "That he shall be given of the hidden manna," and "a white stone, and upon the stone a new name written," (2:17), and given authority over the nations, (2:27), to "rule them with a rod of iron," (2:27); to "be arrayed in white garments," (3:5), and "walk with me (Christ) in white," (3:4), to be made "a pillar in the temple of my God, the new Jerusalem, and the new name of Christ, written upon him," (3:12); to sit down with Christ in his throne, 3:21; "to inherit these things," with the promise, "I will be his God, and he shall be my son." 21:7. These declarations, however figurative, are descriptive of the condition of the saints in glory, and may, therefore, be appropriately added to the sentence of their Lord.

2. The future state of the righteous, is also stated, with reference to his past condition on earth, as "salvation," (Mark 16:16; 1 Thess. 5:9; 2 Tim. 2:10); deliverance from every evil work," (2 Tim. 4:18); "redemption," (Rom. 8:23; Eph. 4:30); "liberty," (John 8:36; Rom. 8:21); "rest," (Heb. 4:10; Rev. 14:13); deliverance from earthly sufferings, such as hunger, thirst, tears, etc., (Rev. 7:16, 17); "no night," (Rev. 21:25; 22:5); "no uncleanness," Rev. 21:27.

3. It is also described, in contrast with present possessions, as blessedness, (Matt. 25:34); perfect knowledge, (1 Cor. 13:12); holiness, (1 Thess. 3:13; Rev. 21:27); glory, (Rom. 8:18; 2 Cor. 4:17; 2 Tim. 2:10; 1 Pet. 5:4); life, (Mark 8:35; 9:43, 45, 47; John 5:29; Rom. 8:13); crown of life, (James 1:12); eternal life, Matt. 19:29; 25:46; John 6:27, 47, 54; Rom 2:7.

4. Declarations are made which connect the believer with Christ, viz.: as of his being with Christ, (1 Thess. 4:17); in the presence of his glory, (Jude 24); holding his glory, (John 17:24); conformed to the body of Christ in his glory, (Phil. 3:21); Christ showing him the riches of his grace, (Eph. 2:7); Christ glorified in them, (2 Thess. 1:10); entering into the joy of their Lord, (Matt. 25:21, 23); reigning with Christ, 2 Tim. 2:12, etc.

5. Statements are made about their activity in the heavenly life. The rest of heaven is not a state of inactivity. This is pointed out in the very passage which speaks of this rest as a particular blessedness: "Blessed are the dead which die in the Lord from henceforth: yea, saith the Spirit, that they may rest from their labours (toil, trouble, suffering, pain, weariness); for their works (deeds, works, especially those of necessity or duty,) [see Lexicon of Liddell-Scott,] follow with them." Rev. 14:13. Here we are taught that, while they rest from onerous and painful toil, they continue to be actively employed. We may not know what all of these employments shall be. They will be such as will be suited to their

intellectual and moral nature and position. The statements of the book of Revelation give us an insight into what some of them may be. The servants of God are there depicted as serving God, Rev. 7:15; 22:3; as giving praises in song, Rev. 14:2, 3; 15:3, 4; 19:5, 6; as engaged in prayers of adoration, Rev. 6:9–13; 7:11, 12; of thanksgiving, Rev. 11:17; and in acts of humiliation, Rev. 4:10.

6. The blessedness of the future state of the righteous, is also set forth in connection with the place of their abode.

This is usually called heaven. It is readily admitted that the word "heaven" is used otherwise than for the abode of God, and Christ, and angels, and the future dwelling-place of the saints. But in numerous places it has only this special signification. The following selection of passages will suffice. Matt. 5:12, 45; 6:20; Luke 6:23; 15:7; 22:43; John 3:13; 6:38; Rom. 1:18; 1 Cor. 15:47; 2 Cor. 5:1; Eph. 1:10; 3:15; Phil. 3:20; 1 Thess. 1:10; 4:16; 2 Thess. 1:7; Heb. 9:24; 1 Pet. 1:4; 3:22.

The plain teaching of these passages, and of others that might be mentioned, is that heaven is a place, and not merely a condition of happiness.

The same fact is justly argued from its being the abiding place of Christ. His human body must occupy a specified place in space. It has been replied to this argument that, "since deity and humanity are indissolubly united in Christ's single person, it is difficult to consider Christ's body as limited to place, without vacating his person of its divinity." But this objection is made in forgetfulness of the fact that Christ, in his divine relation, is not limited by his human nature, much less by his human body. This was shown by him, while on earth, when, in conversation with Nicodemus, he spake of himself as being in heaven, (John 3:13), although his body was manifestly on earth. Was his ubiquity as God interfered with by his location then in space as man? It was in like manner that Christ saw Nathanael under the fig tree, when he was not bodily present. John 1:48.

The idea of ubiquity of the body of Christ has been abandoned, however, while still it is denied that his human soul is limited to space. Thus it is said that "since deity and humanity are dissolubly united in Christ's single person, we cannot regard Christ's human soul as limited to place without vacating his person of its divinity."

But this is equally erroneous. Divine attributes are not conferred on Christ's soul because of its union with a divine person. But ubiquity, or omnipresence is a divine attribute. It is much more difficult for us to understand how the unity of Christ's person did not convey to the human soul all knowledge belonging to Christ as God. Yet we are distinctly told (Matt. 24:36; Mark 13:32), that there was such a limitation of knowledge as to the time of Christ's second coming, as could only be true of Christ in his human nature, and not of him as God. The perfect humanity of Christ, which is his as truly as his perfect divinity, makes necessary such location in space as is suitable to a human soul. Whatever superiority may accrue to either the human body or soul of Christ can never place either of these beyond the excellence of created existence, or confer upon either the nature or attributes of God.

No similar objection, however, can be made to an argument to the same effect, drawn from the bodies of the saints. Heaven cannot be regarded as only a state in which they have communion with God, but must be accepted as the place of their abode in their glorified bodies, in which they dwell with each other, and rejoice in the state of happiness and glory which is also theirs.

We have no means of ascertaining the location of heaven. That this earth, in its renewed condition, may be the future heaven is favoured by Rom. 8:19–23; 2 Pet. 3:5–13, and Rev. 21:1–3. But these passages are entirely too indefinite and doubtful to give any certainty, or even very strong probability, on this point.

Heaven is spoken of in certain descriptive terms. It is called "a better country, that is a heavenly." Heb. 11:16. It is the place which we shall have a "a building from God, an house not made with hands, eternal in the heavens," (2 Cor. 5:1, 2); and "a place" among the "many mansions" in the "Father's house;" John 14:2. It is called "the kingdom," Matt. 13:43; 25:34. It is possible that heaven is also meant by the "Jerusalem that is above," (Gal. 4:26), and "the new Jerusalem which cometh down out of heaven," (Rev. 3:12), and "the holy city Jerusalem," (Rev. 21:10); as well as by Paradise, Luke 23:43; 2 Cor. 12:4; Rev. 2:7, (cf. Rev. 21:10–27).

7. The blessedness of this state of the righteous is made supreme by the fact that it will last forever. It will never end; it will never be diminished. If there be any change, it will be from its increase; because of better intellectual perception and knowledge of God, and of divine things; because of a constantly and increasingly endearing communion with God in Christ; because of an increased capacity to behold the glory of Christ; and because of a greater exaltation of the spiritual nature in the worship and service of the Lord. There is no reason why there may not be such increase in beings whose natures can never attain the infinity of excellence and the complete fullness which belong only to God.

This perpetuity of the happiness of the saints is stated in various ways.

(1.) It is called "eternal life," and "everlasting life" in the King James Version, which are translations of the same Greek words. They are translated "eternal life," or "life eternal" in Matt. 25:26; Mark 10:30; John 3:15; 10:28; 12:25; 17:2; Acts 13:48; Rom. 2:7; 5:21; 6:23; 1 Tim. 6:12, 19; Tit. 1:2; 3:7; 1 John 1:2; 2:25; 5:11–13; Jude 21. They are translated "everlasting life," or "life everlasting" in Matt. 19:29; Luke 18:30; John 3:16, 36; 4:14; 5:24; 6:27, 40, 47; Rom. 6:22; Gal. 6:8; 1 Tim. 1:16. The Greek should have been translated in all these places by the same word; and the better word would have been everlasting, because only a relative eternity, or what is called eternity *a parte post,* belongs to created things. God alone has true eternity. [See pages 68–70.]

(2.) It is declared to be "for ever," John 6:51, 58; and "for ever and ever," Rev. 22:5.

(3.) Similar expressions are also used, as "everlasting tabernacles," Luke 16:9; "eternal weight of glory," (2 Cor. 4:17); "glory in the church and in Christ Jesus unto all generations for ever and ever," (Eph. 3:21); "eternal comfort," (2 Thess. 2:16); "Salvation which is in Christ Jesus with eternal glory," (2 Tim. 2:10); "eternal salvation," (Heb. 5:9); "eternal redemption," (Heb. 9:12); eternal inheritance," (Heb. 9:15); "eternal glory," (1 Pet. 5:10); "eternal kingdom of our Lord, and Saviour Jesus Christ," 2 Pet. 1:11.

(4.) In John 4:14; 8:51, 52, and 10:28, it is declared of believers that "they shall never thirst;" "never taste of death;" "and never perish;" by which is taught the same everlasting condition expressed in the three preceding classes. Reference is made in these passages to the spiritual life of the soul.

The numerous declarations of everlasting life and happiness, thus classified above, make certain what might have been inferred from the scriptural statements of the natural immortality conferred upon spirit, which forbids its annihilation; and from security, against the spiritual death of the soul, arising from the gracious work of Christ wrought out, for, and in the believer, through which he is forever delivered from the condemnation, and presence of sin, and clothed in the unfailing righteousness of God. The same blessing is unquestionably attained through the relation borne to Christ by the saints, as constituting the church of first born ones, which is his bride, Eph. 5:23–33, and also that body, of which he is the head, which is declared to be "the fulness of him that filleth all in all." Eph. 1:23. The vital connection between Christ and his people has no elements of dissolution, and, therefore, everlasting must be that cause of their existence announced by him when he said, "because I live, ye shall live also." John 14:19.

II. THE FINAL STATE OF THE WICKED

The judgement day is no less signally to be marked by the punishment decreed against the wicked, than by the blessings conferred upon the righteous. These, also, are set forth in the Bible, and in fearful words of warning; and should be effective for driving men to Christ for salvation, while the day of probation continues.

1. We have here the sentence to be uttered against those who are still in sin. It occurs in the same chapter with that of the righteous. Christ tells us that "Then

shall he (the King) say also unto them on the left hand, Depart from me, ye cursed, into the eternal fire, which is prepared for the devil and his angels, . . . and these shall go away into eternal punishment." Matt. 25:41, 46. A similar sentence occurs in Luke 13:27, "I tell you, I know not whence ye are; depart from me, all ye workers of iniquity."

The different elements, included in this sentence, are also taught of the wicked elsewhere in the Scriptures; some examples of which may be here added.

(1.) Punishment: "He that disbelieveth shall be condemned," Mark 16:16; "the resurrection of judgement," John 5:29; "rendering vengeance to them that know not God . . . who shall suffer punishment," 2 Thess. 1:8, 9; "keep the unrighteous under the punishment unto the day of judgement," 2 Pet. 2:9.

(2.) Pain: (a.) as expressed by fire. (Matt. 13:42, 50; 18:8, 9; Mark 9:43–48; 2 Thess. 1:8; 2 Pet. 3:7); (b.) fire and brimstone, (Rev. 14:10; 19:20; 20:10; 21:8); (c.) flame, (Luke 16:24); (d.) "the unquenchable fire," (Mark 9:44, 48; cf. Luke 3:17); (e.) "tribulation," Matt. 24:21, 29; Rom. 2:8, 9.

(3.) Deprivation: severed from among the righteous. Matt 13:49; "outer darkness," Matt. 25:30; "cast forth without," Luke 13:28; "shall not inherit the kingdom of God," 1 Cor. 6:9; "no rest," Rev. 14:11; "blackness of darkness hath been reserved forever," Jude 13.

(4.) The punishment and suffering are recognized by those punished and that recognition is shown by their "weeping and wailing, and gnashing of teeth." Matt 8:12; 13:50; 25:30; Luke 13:28. The Rich Man is represented as acknowledging his torments. Luke 16:24.

2. The nature of this punishment.

(1.) It is unwarrantable to take for granted that it will not be in part physical. The wicked will go from the judgement seat with the bodies which belong to them in their resurrection state. We know not what will be the nature of these bodies, and, therefore, have no right to affirm that they may not be capable of physical pain. That the language of Scripture, as to fire and brimstone, is figurative, is true. But men are not authorized, on that account, to deny that some physical pain, and, that of a most excruciating and agonizing character, will form a part of the agony and woe of the hereafter of the sinner. So far from men drawing comfort from any conviction they may have that there will not be literal fire, they should only the more be filled with dread and apprehension of some fearful condition, which the Scriptures here attempt to describe by terms which express the severest anguish men can endure in the body; the statements made evidently falling far short of telling the nature of a punishment which our present condition forbids that we should understand. In the range of animal life here on earth, we know that the higher the organism the more keenly is it alive to suffering as well as enjoyment. This teaches us to expect that the bodily enjoyments of the saints will far surpass anything ever experienced on earth. If the resurrection bodies of the wicked are, in any degree, higher than those of this world, the only result will be to make them capable of anguish utterly inconceivable by men in their present state.

(2.) The spiritual agony, then to be endured, is equally beyond the possibility of present expression. We may say that it will necessarily consist in certain evils; but who can tell how great those evils will then be realized to be. Some of them may be suggested: as, consciousness of an unclean and unholy nature; when there is no way to cleanse or escape it; conviction of the nature and ill desert of sin; when sinful habits have such prevalence and control that sin must still be committed willingly, yet with horror of what is done, indications of which are seen in men in this life, who, by debauchery, or drunkenness, are driven forward to evil even against their will; remorse for past indulgences, for neglected opportunities, for rejections of Christ, especially as then will be seen how nigh unto each one had come the kingdom and grace of God; knowledge of banishment perpetually from the presence of Christ, and deprivation of the favour and love of God—these, and evils like unto them, with the mutual reproaches of the damned, for the influences of each other by which such evil has come, will make a Hell compared with which all the torture men have ever known in this life will be looked back to as though it were heaven itself.

3. The place of this punishment.

There are three words used in Scripture which are translated "Hell" in the King James Version, viz.: Hades, Tartarus and Gehenna. Hades is simply transferred in the Canterbury Revision. It is used for the general place of departed spirits, both righteous and wicked. In no place is punishment, or torment, associated with it, except in Luke 16:23, in the parable of the Rich Man and Lazarus. This is to be explained, in accordance with the use of the word in all other passages, by the fact that, as Hades contains the wicked, as well as the righteous, and as the wicked there are in a state of sin and suffering, so the rich man in Hades was tormented, while Lazarus who was in the same general abode, was enjoying the blessed state expressed by his being in Abraham's bosom.

The word Tartarus appears only as a participle ταρταρώσας (tartarosas) of the verb ταρταρόω (tartaroo), which means to cast down to Tartarus. The place in which it is found is 2 Pet. 2:4, which is translated "For if God spared not angels when they sinned, but cast them down to hell, and committed them to pits of darkness, to be reserved unto judgement." The Revisers point out in the margin that the word Hell is expressed in the Greek by Tartarus. This passage evidently has respect to the condition of these angels before the judgement day.

The places in which Gehenna occurs are Matt. 5:22, 29, 30; 10:28; 18:9; 23:15, 33; Mark 9:43, 45, 47; Luke 12:5, and James 3:6. All of them refer to torture and punishment hereafter. This is distinctly associated with the punishment of the judgement day, in Matt. 18:9, by the preceding verse where "eternal fire" is used as the equivalent term to Gehenna; in Matt. 23:33, where Christ asks the Scribes and Pharisees, "How shall ye escape the judgement of Hell (Gehenna)"; in Mark 9:43, where the language is "to go into Hell (Gehenna), into the unquenchable fire," and in Luke 12:5, in which Christ says, "Fear him which, after he hath killed, hath power to cast into Hell (Gehenna)."

It has not been inaptly remarked that Gehenna is used by Christ himself in all of the twelve passages in which it occurs in the New Testament, except James 3:6.

4. The duration of this punishment.

The New Testament teaching upon this subject is that it will endure throughout all the infinite future. This is expressed in various ways.

(1.) By the term εἰς τὸν αἰῶνα (eis ton aiona), "forever."

This occurs about thirty times in the New Testament. An earnest and learned opponent of the doctrine of Eternal punishment, (Oxenham in "What is Truth as to Everlasting Punishment?" p. 101), has been able to point out only one place in the New Testament where he thinks the meaning of "forever" cannot be applicable to this form of words. It is the language of Paul in 1 Cor. 8:13, translated "I will eat no flesh forevermore." For any other use, Oxenham is obliged to refer to the Septuagint, where he claims that it is used of "duration, throughout the age of the Mosaic dispensation," "of the world," "of a family," and "of the political condition of slavery." But this application accords with that very derivation, made by the best lexicographers, that makes αἰών (aion), equivalent to the Latin aevum, which word, however is the basis of the very idea of eternity which is the sole meaning of εἰς τὸν αἰῶνα (eis ton aiona), in the latter Hellenistic Greek of the New Testament.

This term is applied to the punishment of the wicked, in Jude 13.

(2.) Other similar expressions to the first are used where plural forms of αἰών (aion) appear, as εἰς τοὺς αἰῶνας τῶν αἰώνων (eis tous aionas ton aionon), "forever and ever," in Rev. 19:3, and 20:10, and εἰς αἰῶνας αἰώνων, (eis aionas aionon). Rev. 14:11. The plural forms only intensify, and certainly do not diminish the duration.

(3.) The word αἰώνιος, (aionios). This word occurs about seventy times in the New Testament, and invariably in the sense of eternal or everlasting duration. Just as the English word "eternal" refers to the true eternity which is in God alone, so is this word applied to God in Rom. 16:26; and to the Holy Spirit or to the divine nature of Christ, in Heb. 9:14. In like manner, as we inadequately divide eternity into eternity a parte post, and eternity a parte ante, meaning by each indefinite, unlimited and illimitable duration in the past or in the future, from the present, or some fixed period of time; as from the time of Christ's appearance on earth; so this word is used for each of these two kinds of eternity. It has no other application in the New Testament than to one or other of these three forms of eternity. As applied to the endless life of the righteous or wicked, it signifies the future eternity, or eternity *a parte post*.

Those who oppose the doctrine of eternal punishment suppose that there are many ages, or periods of the existence of man, and they attempt to explain the language used accordingly. But while the phrases upon which this opinion is based, might as a matter of language mean this, there is no evidence from Scripture of the existence of any such several periods. The only distinction clearly made is between the dispensation prior to the time of Christ, and that since his day; the Scriptures evidently regarding that as the central point, unto which all things tended in the past, and from which all things proceed in the future.

It is not to be overlooked that these words, which express the eternity of the punishment of the wicked, are those by which the eternal life of the righteous is also made known. As that is unending in its happiness, so this is in its punishment and suffering. These words express as strongly as the Greek language can, the everlasting duration of the destiny assigned to each at the judgement day.

This is questioned by Oxenham, who says, p. 114, "There are several ways in which Almighty God could have expressed this endlessness of future punishment, if he desired to tell us that it would be endless; ways, about the meaning of which there could be no mistake; ways, in which, in Holy Scripture, he has expressed the endlessness of things which will be endless: e.g., of his own dominion God declared by the prophet Daniel that it was 'an everlasting dominion, *which shall not pass away*, and his Kingdom that which shall not be destroyed,' Dan. 7:14. Of the endless life of the blessed, our Lord declared, Luke 20:36, neither *can they die anymore*. By the angel Gabriel, Luke 1:33, God announced that of the Kingdom of Jesus Christ *there shall be no end*. Where is any language used of the Kingdom of Darkness, or of future punishment, or of the wicked? Where is it said of the lost that they can live no more? Whereof future punishment, that of it there shall be no end?"

To this it may be replied,

(a.) That, if no similar instances can be given relative to future punishment, and the wicked, yet so far as any of these expressions are used of the righteous, they are explanatory of the kind of eternity ascribed to their happiness; and, as this is described by the same words as that of the misery of the wicked in all other cases, these instances teach us the meaning of these common words, when applied to the wicked, by thus explaining them when applied to the righteous.

(b.) That the same ingenuity, and quibbling, which attempts to deprive the expressions used of their true meaning, would be applied in like manner to such terms as these.

If a similar passage to that from Daniel could be presented, we should immediately have pointed out to us that it was to the Son of Man that the kingdom was given, and that, of this very kingdom which "shall not pass away," we are told that "then cometh the end when he shall deliver up the kingdom to God, even the Father; when he shall have abolished all rule, and all authority and power." 1 Cor. 15:24.

(c.) But there are like instances which may be adduced. In Luke 20:36, "neither can they die any more," the impossibility of dying is expressed by οὐδὲ δύνανται (oude dunantai.) Corresponding to this is the language used by our Lord to the Pharisees in John 9:21, "Ye shall seek me and shall die in your sin: whither I go *ye cannot come*," οὐ δύνασθε ἐλθεῖν (ou dunasthe elthein).

Parallel to the expression in Luke 1:33, "there shall be no end," οὐκ ἔσται τέλος (ouk estai telos), is "the endless genealogies," γενεαλογίαις ἀπεράντοις (genealogiais aperantois), in 1 Tim. 1:4; for, although different words are used to express endlessness in the Greek, they are of substantially equal force. Oxenham is himself authority for the strong meaning of ἀπεράντοις (aperantois), for he refers to ἀπείρον (apeiron), α and πέρας, from which ἀπέραντος (aperantos) is likewise formed, as meaning "without a limit," and says of it and others "by these and by several other words and expressions of unmistakable meaning, Almighty God could have expressed the endlessness of future punishment if he had desired to do so," p. 115. Yet, had he used this word, or others of the same form, how quickly should we have been referred to the endless genealogies as exegetical of them.

With respect to the two final questions of Mr. Oxenham, the passage in 1 Cor. 6:9, may be suggested as one that fully meets them. "Know ye not that the unrighteous *shall not inherit* the Kingdom of God," (see also verse 10). The same expression occurs in Gal. 5:21. The insincerity with which such questions are asked is seen in the fact that, when these and similar passages are presented, these opponents resort to the assumption that the unrighteous will not always be unrighteous, and that only so long as unrighteous shall they not inherit; but that they may do so after their unrighteousness has passed away. They will attempt to maintain the possibility of this in the face of such a passage as Rev. 22:11, "He that is unrighteous, let him do unrighteousness still: and he that is filthy, let him be made filthy still."

(4.) Here may properly be added three other expressions as to the unending nature of the punishment of the wicked.

(a.) Ἀΐδιος *(aidios)*, which appears in the "eternal Godhead" of Rom. 1:20, and in the everlasting chains of the angels which kept not their first estate in Jude 6. As the wicked are to be sentenced to the "eternal fire which is prepared for the devil and his angels" (Matt. 25:41), this passage has probable reference to the duration of the punishment of both devils and wicked men.

(b.) Ἀσβέστος *(asbestos)*, unquenchable fire. Oxenham claims that all that is involved in this word is that the fire "is unquenched," and that the language does not forbid a time when it may be quenched. This word occurs in three undisputed places in Scripture, Matt. 3:12; Mark 9:43, and Luke 3:17, and in three others, Mark 9:44, 45, 46, which Westcott and Hort omit from their text, and which are also omitted in the Canterbury Revision. Mark 9:48 has a different form of the same word. Oxenham objects to the translation "unquenchable," and insists upon the meaning, "is unquenched;" but the duration of the punishment and the propriety of the translation "unquenchable" is shown by the words, "where their worm dieth not," used in connection with the expression in verse 48.

(c.) Οὐ τελευτᾷ *(ou teleuta)*, "does not end," "ceases not," is declared of the worm in Mark 9:48. Τελευτᾷ *(teleuta)* corresponds exactly in meaning, as well as in root, with the τέλος *(telos)* in the οὐκ ἔσται τέλος *(ouk estai telos)*, in Luke 1:33, which Oxenham regarded as so strongly expressive of endlessness as to challenge the finding of such a term applied to the future punishment of the wicked.

5. Objections and opposing theories.

The objections to this doctrine of eternal punishment, and the opposing theories, may be briefly stated and replied to.

First, the objections.

(1.) It is objected, that the punishment is disproportioned to the sin. But,

(a.) No one but God can know what is the real desert of sin, and if he has plainly taught us that it deserves eternal punishment, we may be sure that the infliction of such punishment must be right, and in accordance with what it merits. The question is simply, What does God say? and upon this point he has taught us plainly.

(b.) The objection is based upon the idea that all the sin that will be punished is that committed in this life. It is true that men will be only judged for the deeds done in the body. But these will not constitute all the sins which will be punished hereafter. A part of the penalty of the sins of this life is such a corrupted nature as will make men sin in the life to come. The Scriptures teach that there will be sinful acts and habits after death. Rev. 22:11. Ever-continuing sin will deserve ever-continuing punishment. If sin is worthy of any punishment at all, and if, at every moment sin is committed, punishment may be forever, without assuming that any one or more sins will cause everlasting infliction.

(c.) Mark 3:29 tells of "an eternal sin." [See Greek text of Westcott and Hort.]

(d.) The objection supposes that the punishment of the damned is something actively inflicted by God, and not the working out and result of the natures of men. It will doubtless consist, in great part, in their sinful and corrupt natures, which will still work out sin, and thus continue to separate from the favour and complacent love of God. The only probable exception will be "remorse," arising from the memory of past sins and neglected opportunities; and these are not active inflictions of God, but the results of former sin.

(2.) It is said that God is too merciful to inflict everlasting punishment. But,

(a.) God, in declaring that he will inflict it, thus declares that he is not too merciful to do so.

(b.) God teaches us that, while he takes no delight in such punishment, it is demanded by justice, which is as unabounded an attribute of his nature as mercy.

(c.) God has given signal exhibitions in his providential government that he can and will punish severely. As a moral Governor, his punishment must be proportioned to the offense. His merciful disposition cannot interfere with his righteous action. Even in the salvation of those saved through Christ, it is necessary that he should be just in justifying the believer in Jesus.

(3.) It is claimed that provision has been made in Christ for the certain salvation of all men.

If this be so, there is no difficulty in God's justice in the bestowment of salvation upon all. But that such is not the case is manifested,

(a.) By the fact that salvation is offered only on the condition of repentance and faith. None, therefore, can have part in that salvation except those who fulfill this condition.

(b.) Regeneration is declared to be essential to entrance into the kingdom of Christ. Those who are not thus born again can, therefore, have no part in his salvation.

(c.) Not only is holiness declared to be essential to admission to heaven, but it is foretold, expressly, that certain classes of unholy men shall have their part in the lake which burneth with fire and brimstone; and at the head of the list given are "the fearful and unbelieving." Rev. 21:8.

(d.) While the value of Christ's work is indeed ample for all, we are taught that its benefits are not bestowed upon all. There are special sins mentioned which will exclude those who commit them from all hope of salvation. Matt. 12:31; Luke 12:10; Heb. 6:4–6, (cf. verse 9); 10:26, 27, (cf. verses 28–31). But the assertions made about the certain punishment of those who commit these particular sins are not stronger than the declarations of the certain damnation of all the finally impenitent and unbelieving.

(4.) Inasmuch as it is asserted in 1 Tim. 2:3, 4, that "God our Saviour . . . willeth that all men should be saved, and come to the knowledge of the truth," it is even claimed that it is the purpose of God to save all.

That the word θέλει *(thelei)*, translated "willeth," often involves purpose or determination on the part of God is readily admitted, as well as that, if it mean this here, all men will be saved according to that purpose. But such purpose cannot be concluded from this passage alone, unless it accords with what is elsewhere taught; much less when it is in direct opposition to the general tenor of the Bible, as well as to distinct statements to the contrary. The reason for this is that this word does not always mean "will," in the sense of purpose, but is sometimes used in that of a mere "wish." There are many cases in Scripture in which God is said to wish what not only he does not purpose to accomplish, but what actually fails to take place.

There are numerous examples in which this word has only this meaning of "wish": thus as used in general of men only, Matt. 7:12; 12:38; 15:28; of Christ, Matt. 23:37; Mark 14:36; Luke 13:34; John 17:24; and of God, 1 Cor. 15:38; Heb. 10:5, 8. Θέλημα *(thelema)*, the corresponding noun, is used as expressive simply of this "wish" of God in Mark 3:35; Rom. 2:18; Eph. 6:6; and in other places.

(5.) It is further objected that God must forgive those who are truly penitent, and that the wicked, in the full knowledge of God and sin afforded by the next world, must certainly repent.

(a.) This objection arises from a misconception of the nature of the repentance acceptable to God. It is not mere sorrow for sin, especially for its effects, of which probably hell will be full; it is reformation of character, turning away from sin and seeking holiness. Sorrow accompanies it, but does not constitute it. It is not awakened by the painful effects of sin, but by conviction of its evil nature. How can such sorrow arise in those who have learned to love sin? Or such reformation in those who are confirmed in habits of sin? Remorse for the past, loathings of their then condition, even desires to overcome the power which enchains them, may abundantly exist, but, as often occurs in this life, where passion and appetite get the mastery of men, pleasure will be taken in sin, and evil appetites indulged, even when it is hated with all the bitterness of a despairing soul.

On the other hand, what is the teaching of Scripture as to God's readiness to accept the penitent after the day of opportunity has passed away? What does the case of Esau teach, Heb. 12:16, 17? What is meant to be taught by the language of Wisdom, Prov. 1:24–28? Did Christ accept, did God forgive the wretched, sorrowing, remorseful Judas? Or was his penitence permitted to plunge him into the further sin of suicide? Even here on earth, where the day of probation ordinarily ends only in death, such rejection of such sorrow for sin is possible. Who shall dare to say that it is impossible in the hereafter? "For if they do these things in the green tree, what shall be done in the dry?" Luke 23:31.

(b.) "Punishment appears to have very little, if any, tendency to work reformation in offenders. It often deters from crime, but it rarely brings one to genuine repentance.

(c.) "During the middle state, if at any time after this life, a return to God might be expected; yet the language of Scripture does not permit us to expect it then." Hovey's Manual of Sys. Theol., p. 362.

(d.) The experience of this life shows that, for any violation, even of physical law, the penalty attached to it must be endured, and that no sorrow for what has been done, nor determination to avoid such action in the future, will release from the evil which follows. Why should it be supposed that, after the judgement, law will be less inexorable than now, or that penitence and reformation will then, of themselves, avail any more than they do now? Even in this life, repentance and faith have no value nor power in themselves, but are only effective as conditions upon which the salvation in Christ is offered. But the Bible carefully warns men that this offer, on these conditions, is only made in this life. To suppose it is possible in the hereafter requires not only the possibility of repentance and faith then but also that salvation through Christ will then be still attainable. This can only be upon the supposition that men will have a future probation, and the same or other means of grace than those here afforded.

(6.) In further objection, therefore, it is assumed that another probation will then be enjoyed. The strongest form in which this objection is urged, is that, inasmuch as despite the positive threatenings of God to our first parents that they should die, he had purposed to provide redemption for at least a part of mankind; therefore, despite the positive statements as to the future condemnation and punishment of the wicked, there may still be mercy in store, and final deliverance from the presence and taint of sin, as well as its punishment.

The replies afforded to this are obvious.

(a.) The case quoted affords a warning to those who teach contrary to what God teaches. Our first parents were even then, before their sin, assured that the threatened sentence would not be executed. But this came from Satan, who is declared by Christ to be "a liar and the father thereof." John 8:44. Those who, upon any other authority than God, call in question any statement which he makes, should feel that they do it at the peril of their own souls and that of those whom they teach. Matt. 15:8, 9, 13, 14; 23:13, 15, 16; Luke 6:39. Those who deny a doctrine which they know is taught in God's Word, or attempt by any subterfuge or mere supposition to induce others to reject it, act precisely the part of Satan in the transaction of the fall.

(b.) The penalty which God threatened has actually been inflicted upon all mankind. Even the death of the body has only thus far been escaped by two of the race. But spiritual death, the death of the soul, manifestly the especial death of the curse, for this alone was inflicted upon the day of transgression, has, in the corrupted and sinful nature, become the so-called "natural" state of mankind. The objection evidently supposes that eternal death was also threatened against Adam. But this is not true. It becomes part of the penalty only because it is the consequence of moral corruption and depravity, which must continue to deserve punishment, and also to work out sin deserving of still further punishment, unless some means of deliverance from this corruption shall arise. Eternal death, therefore, was not a penalty threatened against Adam, but only a consequential penalty, resulting from what was threatened, and which, therefore, may be escaped through the deliverance in Christ.

But eternal death is threatened against the finally impenitent of the present probation. The case of Adam, therefore, teaches us that it will assuredly be inflicted upon them. As God did not withhold the flood of corruption and misery, which the corrupted nature has brought upon mankind—the deliverance of any from which demanded the gift and the sufferings of his own Son—we may be assured that, in like manner, he will inflexibly allow eternal punishment to come upon all against whom he has threatened it.

(c.) When all suspicion that God may intend something different from what he says in his threats to prevent sin, has been removed by perceiving that he has, to the letter, fulfilled his threat against Adam; we are prepared to give due weight to what he teaches about the possibility of future probation.

To the question of one asking, "Lord, are there few that be saved?" Christ replied, "Strive to enter in by the narrow door, for many, I say unto you, shall seek to enter in and shall not be able." Luke 13:24. [See the context, which shows reference to entrance into the kingdom in the future world]. The exhortation of Isaiah 55:6, "Seek ye the Lord while he may be found" implies a time when he may not be found. This exhortation has reference to the new and everlasting covenant of the sure mercies of David. [See verse 3]. How distinctly does the hortatory question of Heb. 2:1–3 apply here; when we see, not merely how steadfast has been the word spoken by angels, but how literally fulfilled has been that uttered by God. Well may all ask, "How shall we escape if we neglect so great salvation?" The intimate connection between this passage and the exhortation against the hardening of the heart in the present moment in Hebrews 3:7–11, are worthy of especial note, as well as the warning of verse 12, and the continued exhortations and warnings, as far as and beyond chapter 4:7, which declares of the present period of probation, "He again defineth a certain day, saying in David, after so long a time To-day, as it hath been before said, To-day, if ye shall hear his voice, harden not your hearts." The declaration, "Behold now is the accepted time; behold now is the day of salvation," 2 Cor. 6:2, with the context, in like manner teaches that the present is the only period of probation.

(d.) It may be questioned whether very many persons who die impenitent do not come under some one of the forms of sin which are specifically declared unpardonable, viz.: willful sins, (Heb. 10:26); falling away, (Heb. 6:46); and the blasphemy against the Holy Ghost, Matt. 12:32. Certainly they all come under the declaration of Christ of everlasting punishment.

(e.) Nor should such passages be forgotten here as Luke 16:26, which teaches that, even in Hades, there is an impassable gulf between the righteous and the wicked; as John 8:21, in which Christ told the Pharisees that they could not come to him in the future world; and Rev. 22:10, 11, which teaches the continued unrighteous and unholy condition and conduct of the finally impenitent. The language of Christ about Judas, (Matt. 26:24), is not quoted against all, because spoken of one man only, though none can tell how many others it may be true. But there are doubtless very many liable to the similar woe denounced by Christ; that "it is profitable for him that a great millstone should be hanged about his neck and that he should be sunk in the depth of the sea." Matt. 6:6; Mark 9:42; Luke 17:2.

Second, the opposing theories.

There are different forms in which the objections to the eternal punishment of the wicked take the shape of doctrinal theories.

(1.) The theory of annihilation. This does not deny that the punishment will be eternal; but only that there will be eternal conscious pain. It supposes, however, that the death of the sinner is absolute annihilation of being, and that in this sense only is it an eternal punishment. This theory admits that the soul may suffer hereafter, for a longer or shorter time, according to its deserts, but that there will be a time when existence will absolutely cease. The object of those who hold this theory, is not opposition to everlasting punishment, on the ground that God cannot justly punish so severely, or is too merciful to do so, but to escape the idea that sin and misery will always exist under the government of God.

This theory claims Scriptural support from the use of such words as speak of the condition of the wicked hereafter. One of these is ἀπώλεια *(apoleia)*, translated sometimes "perdition," and sometimes "destruction," in both the King James Version and the Canterbury Revision. It appears, in reference to the future punishment of the wicked, among other places, in John 17:12; Rom. 9:22; Phil. 3:19; Heb. 10:39; 2 Pet. 3:7.

But this word is very far from having the idea of annihilation. It is simply an equivalent to our English words destruction, loss, ruin, misfortune. In Matt. 26:8; and Mark 14:4, it is used of the ointment poured upon Christ's head, and translated "waste." In all other passages it apparently refers to the future condition of the wicked. But these two show that it does not mean annihilation, as indeed it does not elsewhere, either in the Classic or Hellenistic Greek. The verb ἀπόλλυμι *(apollumi)* signifies no more than to destroy utterly, and is chiefly used in Homer for death inflicted in battle. [See Liddell and Scott's Lexicon].

Another word is ὄλεθρος *(olethros)*. This occurs in connection with the punishment of the wicked, in three or four places in the New Testament, viz.: in 1 Thess. 5:3; 2 Thess. 1:9; and 1 Tim. 6:9. In none of these does it mean more than destruction, by which word it is translated, not only in these places, but also in 1 Cor. 5:5. This last place is that in which Paul directs the Corinthians to "deliver" the incestuous man "unto Satan for the destruction of the flesh, that the spirit may be saved in the day of the Lord Jesus." Surely, no one imagines that the annihilation of the flesh is meant.

Neither does this word mean any greater destruction than is involved in death.

Another expression is "the second death;" "And death and Hades were cast into the lake of fire. This is the second death, even the lake of fire." Rev. 20:14.

The lake of fire, the casting into which is here said to be the "second death," is expressly set forth as the place in which "the beast and the false prophet" are, and in which "they shall be tormented day and night for ever and ever," verse 10. There is certainly no annihilation here, for annihilation is inconsistent with torment continued forever.

It may be stated in general, as to all the places which speak of the destruction and death of the soul, that reference is made to its spiritual loss of God's favour and of holiness, and not to the extinction of its being. This extinction would be contrary to the natural immortality conferred on spirit. It is not even true, so far as we can know, that even matter will ever be annihilated. What is called its destruction is simply such change of form as makes it unfit for the uses for which it had been so formed. Thus we speak of the utter destruction of a house, of machinery, of an animal, not being the annihilation of the matter which composed it; but the destruction of the form in which that matter appeared, and which was essential for its use. In like manner, the death of the soul means its becoming unfit for the uses for which it was made; viz.: for happiness, for holiness, for the service of God, for the complacent love of God and for the reflection of his image. Such an utter deprivation of all the faculties for which the moral nature of man was made, may well be called its death, even its utter destruction.

(2.) Restorationism.

This is based upon three different grounds, each of which may be held separately, or any two, or all of them together. Two of these have been sufficiently considered in the replies already made to the objections against Scriptural doctrine.

One of these is that reformation of life will hereafter take place among some, at least, of the condemned, through natural ability and sufficient grace and the influences of the Spirit; and that thus these will be made holy, and therefore acceptable to God.

The other is that the benefits of the work of Christ, will, after this life, also be for the first time imparted to many men, and if this is done salvation must ensue.

It is to be noticed, however, that when the objections, previously answered, are put in the form of a theory, the idea that there can be no everlasting punishment, is modified so as to assert only that all but a few will be saved. This is done to escape the cases of Judas and others already mentioned. But in so doing, all the principles, upon which the possibility of such future salvation is based, have to be abandoned, and the theory becomes a mere supposition, without any support, presented in the face of positive declarations of the Word of God to the contrary.

The third ground upon which Restorationism is imagined, is that the Scriptures speak of such restoration. The chief passage supposed to teach this is Acts 3:20, 21, "that he may send the Christ who hath been appointed for you, even Jesus: whom the heaven must receive until the times of restoration of all things." The passage itself fixes the period of the time of the restoration, which is at the second coming of the Lord. This precedes the judgement, and thus necessarily that of the restoration supposed by these parties.

Another passage is Eph.. 1:9, 10, which speaks of God "having made known unto us the mystery of his will, according to his good pleasure which he purposed in him unto a dispensation of the fulness of the times to sum up all things in Christ, the things in the heavens and the things upon the earth." The fullness of the times here is probably the present dispensation, and has nothing to do with some new period. See Gal. 4:4, "When the fulness of the time came, God sent forth his Son, etc." cf. Heb. 1:2; 9:10; 1 Pet. 1:20. So, again, in Col. 1:19, 20, it is said to have been the good pleasure of the Father, "through him (Christ) to reconcile all things unto himself, having made peace through the blood of his cross; through him I say, whether things upon the earth or things in the heavens." This place is also quoted to show that all will be finally saved.

This use made of these two passages, Eph. 1:9, 10, and Col. 1:19, 20, to build up a doctrine, without other support from the Word of God, and so contrary to so much that is therein taught, is a warning against the pernicious manner in which isolated passages of the Word of God are separated from their contexts, and used to establish preconceived theories. Both of them occur in epistles written exclusively to professed Christians. The subject of both of them is the Church of Christ. The all things in heaven, or earth, mentioned in each of these epistles, are those only which are connected with the church. So far as persons are referred to, they are those who constitute "every family in heaven and on earth," Eph. 3:15, called also "the general assembly and church of the first born who are enrolled in heaven," Heb 12:23. They have, therefore, not the remotest reference to any future restoration to holiness, and happiness, and God, of those condemned at the judgement.

Name Index

Scripture Index

Justification is God's
quittal of sinners, who
all sin, through the s
made; not for any thin
done by them; but on
and satisfaction of Ch
resting on Him and his
            12. Sanctifi

Those who have been
tified, by God's word a
This sanctification is pr
of Divine strength, whic
pressing after a heavenly
to all Christ's comman
            13. Perseverance

Those whom God hath
and sanctified by His
nor finally fall away f